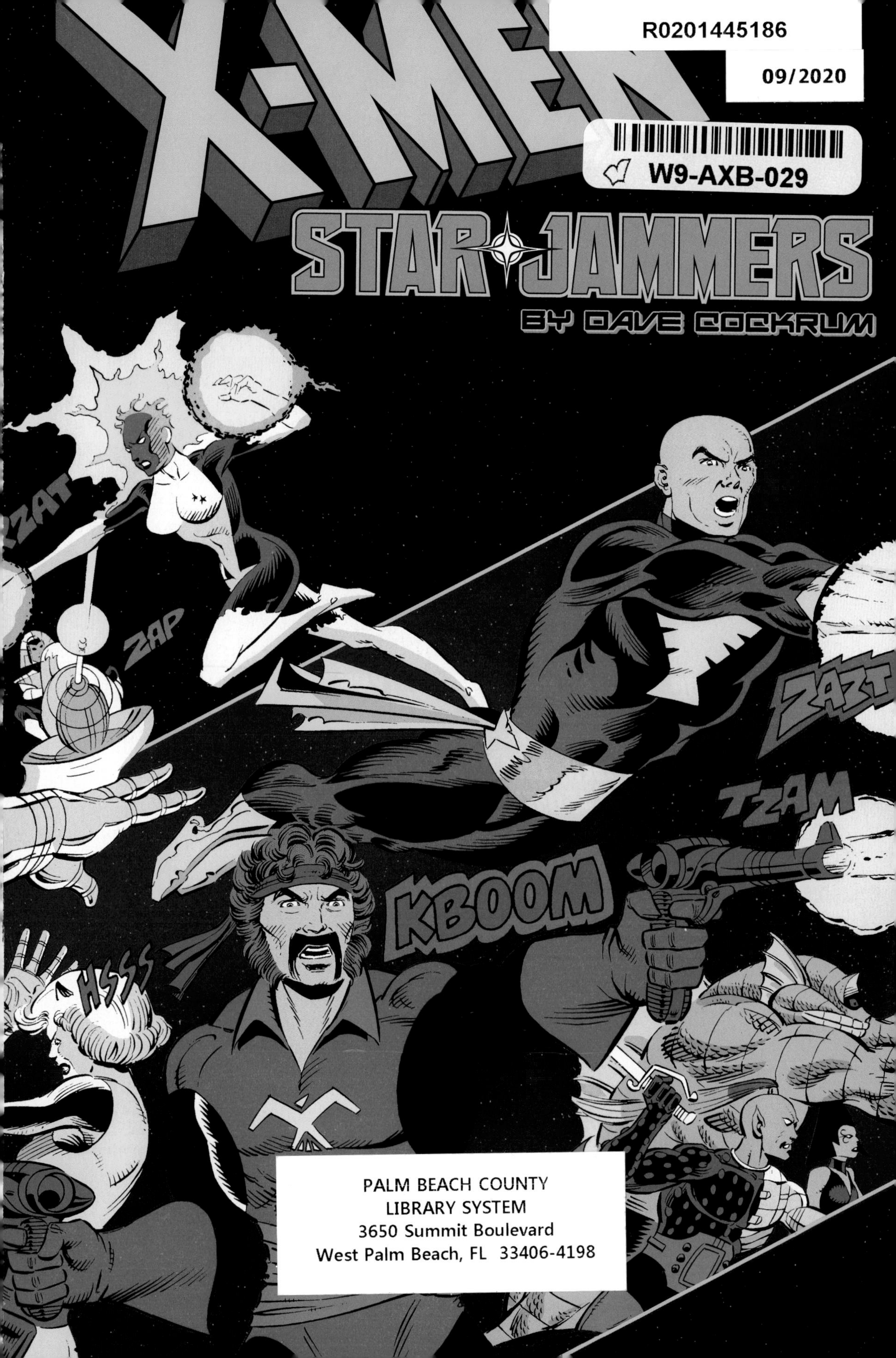
X-MEN
STAR JAMMERS
BY DAVE COCKRUM
ZZAT
ZAP
ZAZT
TZAM
KBOOM
HSSS

CHRIS CLAREMONT & TERRY KAVANAGH
WRITERS

DAVE COCKRUM, JOHN BYRNE & PAUL SMITH
PENCILERS

DAN GREEN, TERRY AUSTIN, BOB WIACEK & JEFF ALBRECHT WITH **JOSEF RUBINSTEIN**
INKERS

ANDY YANCHUS, DON WARFIELD, GLYNIS WEIN, BOB SHAREN, JANINE CASEY, LYNN VARLEY & JOHN WILCOX
COLORISTS

JOE ROSEN, TOM ORZECHOWSKI, JANICE CHIANG & AGUSTIN MAS WITH **DENISE WOHL**
LETTERERS

DANNY FINGEROTH & KELLY CORVESE
ASSISTANT EDITORS

ARCHIE GOODWIN, LOUISE JONES & MARK GRUENWALD
EDITORS

DAVE COCKRUM, BOB WIACEK & VERONICA GANDINI
FRONT COVER ARTISTS

DAVE COCKRUM & BOB WIACEK
BACK COVER ARTISTS

X-MEN CREATED BY **STAN LEE & JACK KIRBY**

COLLECTION EDITOR **MARK D. BEAZLEY** ▪ ASSISTANT EDITOR **CAITLIN O'CONNELL** ▪ ASSOCIATE MANAGING EDITOR **KATERI WOODY**
ASSOCIATE MANAGER, DIGITAL ASSETS **JOE HOCHSTEIN** ▪ MASTERWORKS EDITOR **CORY SEDLMEIER** ▪ SENIOR EDITOR, SPECIAL PROJECTS **JENNIFER GRÜNWALD**
VP PRODUCTION & SPECIAL PROJECTS **JEFF YOUNGQUIST** ▪ RESEARCH & LAYOUT **JEPH YORK** ▪ PRODUCTION **JOE FRONTIRRE** ▪ BOOK DESIGNER **STACIE ZUCKER**

SVP PRINT, SALES & MARKETING **DAVID GABRIEL** ▪ DIRECTOR, LICENSED PUBLISHING **SVEN LARSEN**
EDITOR IN CHIEF **C.B. CEBULSKI** ▪ CHIEF CREATIVE OFFICER **JOE QUESADA** ▪ PRESIDENT **DAN BUCKLEY** ▪ EXECUTIVE PRODUCER **ALAN FINE**

X-MEN: STARJAMMERS BY DAVE COCKRUM. Contains material originally published in magazine form as X-MEN #107-108, UNCANNY X-MEN #154-158 and #161-167, and X-MEN: SPOTLIGHT ON STARJAMMERS #1-2. First printing 2019. ISBN 978-1-302-92046-3. Published by MARVEL WORLDWIDE, INC., a subsidiary of MARVEL ENTERTAINMENT, LLC. OFFICE OF PUBLICATION: 135 West 50th Street, New York, NY 10020. **Printed in the U.S.A.** DAN BUCKLEY, President, Marvel Entertainment; JOHN NEE, Publisher; JOE QUESADA, Chief Creative Officer; TOM BREVOORT, SVP of Publishing; DAVID BOGART, Associate Publisher & SVP of Talent Affairs; DAVID GABRIEL, SVP of Sales & Marketing, Publishing; JEFF YOUNGQUIST, VP of Production & Special Projects; DAN CARR, Executive Director of Publishing Technology; ALEX MORALES, Director of Publishing Operations; DAN EDINGTON, Managing Editor; SUSAN CRESPI, Production Manager; STAN LEE, Chairman Emeritus. For information regarding advertising in Marvel Comics or on Marvel.com, please contact Vit DeBellis, Custom Solutions & Integrated Advertising Manager, at vdebellis@marvel.com. For Marvel subscription inquiries, please call 888-511-5480. **Manufactured between 9/6/2019 and 10/8/2019 by LSC COMMUNICATIONS INC., KENDALLVILLE, IN, USA.**

10 9 8 7 6 5 4 3 2 1

In 1977, the X-Men were embroiled in the middle of "The Phoenix Saga," a long-running storyline that took the mutant team into outer space for the very first time.

Professor X had begun having nightmares — the same recurring dream over and over of an alien in a spaceship fleeing an armada of pursuers. Every night the dream grew more vivid and intense until he could almost see the alien's face.

Meanwhile, the X-Men were attacked and captured by a new generation of Sentinels and brought to their base on an orbital platform above Earth. The X-Men eventually broke free and defeated the Sentinels, but the only way to return home was in a space shuttle with damaged shielding — and a dangerous solar flare was fast approaching.

Marvel Girl, gambling that her telekinesis could hold back the flare's effects, piloted the shuttle back to Earth, but she was soon overwhelmed and bombarded with radiation. The shuttle crashed in Jamaica Bay, New York — and Marvel Girl burst from the water with incredibly heightened powers, proclaiming that she had become the Phoenix!

Over the next few weeks, the X-Men were beset by several foes including the Juggernaut, Black Tom Cassidy, Magneto and the cosmic Firelord, all of whom had been manipulated into attacking the team by a mysterious figure called Eric the Red.

Suddenly, the alien figure from Professor X's dreams materialized in real life — revealing herself as Shi'ar princess Lilandra Neramani, a fugitive from her people who had forged a mind link with Professor X as she fled to Earth. Lilandra's brother, Shi'ar Emperor D'ken, had ordered her capture and execution — and Eric the Red, a Shi'ar agent on Earth, had been trying to eliminate the X-Men to prevent Lilandra from allying with them.

Eric the Red captured Lilandra and fled through a teleport stargate back to the Shi'ar Empire. However, Phoenix — displaying power levels that surprised even her — easily reactivated the stargate. As Professor X remained behind, the X-Men pursued Lilandra through the stargate...and suddenly found themselves very far from home...

And now, in the middle of all this cosmic chaos, a team of interstellar pirates is about to make their first appearance — a swashbuckling, adventure-seeking rebel group known as the Starjammers!

The heroic Starjammers, co-created by the *X-Men* creative team of Chris Claremont and Dave Cockrum, would soon forge close ties with the X-Men and would reappear many times over the coming decades. But before their official debut in *X-Men #107*, three of their number — Corsair, Ch'od and Cr'reee — made a brief cameo appearance at the end of *X-Men #104*...

WRITER **CHRIS CLAREMONT** • PENCILER **DAVE COCKRUM** • INKER **SAM GRAINGER**
COLORIST **ANDY YANCHUS** • LETTERER **BRUCE PATTERSON** • EDITOR **ARCHIE GOODWIN**

X MEN
MARVEL® COMICS GROUP
APPROVED BY THE COMICS CODE AUTHORITY
30¢
107 OCT 02461
THE ALL-NEW, ALL-DIFFERENT
X-MEN
©1977 MARVEL COMICS GROUP
COCKRUM
BEGINNING! THE INCREDIBLE SAGA OF--
THE STARJAMMERS!
WILL IT BE THE END OF THE X-MEN?!

Cyclops. Storm. Banshee. Nightcrawler. Wolverine. Colossus. Children of the atom, students of Charles Xavier, MUTANTS––feared and hated by the world they have sworn to protect. These are the STRANGEST heroes of all!

Stan Lee PRESENTS: THE UNCANNY X-MEN!™

CHRIS CLAREMONT, AUTHOR * DAVE COCKRUM, ARTIST * DAN GREEN, INKER * JOE ROSEN, LETTERER; ANDY YANCHUS, COLORIST * ARCHIE GOODWIN, EDITOR

A MOMENT AGO, THEY'D BEEN ON EARTH. *
WHERE THE BLAZES ARE WE?!?
*A MOMENT FOR OUR MERRY MUTANTS, TRUE, BUT SINCE X-MEN #105 FOR THE REST OF US--ARCHIVIST ARCHIE.

WHERE NO X-M
THE WORLD IS AS OLD AS TIME, AND ITS CITIES HAVE STOOD SILENT AND EMPTY SINCE BEFORE MANKIND WAS BORN.
CYCLOPS...?
I... DON'T KNOW, STORM.
OUR COMING HERE WAS PHOENIX' DOING, AND I'VE A FEELING EVEN SHE DOESN'T KNOW THE WHY OR WHEREFORE.
ALIENS!
JUDGING FROM THE LOOKS OF OUR RECEPTION COMMITTEE, MY FRIENDS--
--I WONDER IF WE'LL LIVE TO LEARN THE ANSWERS.

N HAS GONE BEFORE!
FOR YEARS BEYOND NUMBER, THE WORLD HAS REMAINED UNTOUCHED BY ANY LIVING BEING, ITS SANCTITY INVIOLATE. NOW, THAT HAS CHANGED. AND FOR THE FIRST TIME SINCE CREATION THE WORLD WILL KNOW WAR.
AND THE WINNER OF THIS WAR WILL HOLD THE FATE OF THE UNIVERSE IN HIS HANDS.
GLADIATOR-- COMRADES! WHO ARE THESE PEOPLE?!
THEY MATERIALIZED OUT OF THE STARGATE RIGHT AFTER PRINCESS LILANDRA-- BUT ARE THEY FRIENDS? OR FOES?

CYCLOPS, IT'S... INCREDIBLE! I CAN UNDERSTAND THEIR LANGUAGE.
COUNT YOUR BLESSINGS, STORM. LET'S SEE IF THEY'D RATHER TALK THAN FIGHT.
YOU... BEINGS! WE ARE THE X-MEN, FROM THE PLANET EARTH!
WE'VE COME FOR THE WOMAN, LILANDRA, AND ERIC THE RED!
ALIENS, I AM GLADIATOR, PRAETOR OF THE IMPERIAL GUARD. YOU ARE SURROUNDED BY THAT GUARD AND OUTNUMBERED.
THE PRINCESS YOU SEEK IS A TRAITOR TO THE EMPIRE AND OUR PRISONER. WE WILL NOT GIVE HER UP.

THEN WE'LL TAKE HER!
ORACLE, LOOK OUT!
THE MAN CALLED CYCLOPS-- HIS ENERGY BEAM HAS FELLED MENTOR!
HE'LL PAY FOR THAT, ORACLE-- I SWEAR IT! BY CHIDA, I'LL CRUSH THE LIFE FROM HIS BODY WITH MY BARE HANDS!
SHZAK!
IMPERIALS-- ATTACK!!

IT BEGINS.
AND, IN MOMENTS. A ONCE-TRANQUIL PLAIN...
...IS TURNED INTO A SCENE OUT OF HELL.
BOM!
BANSHEE, FOLLOW MY LEAD! WE'LL HAVE A BETTER CHANCE IN THE AIR!

SCATTER THEM, SEAN CASSIDY! KEEP THEM OFF BALANCE!
BUT THEN WHAT, WIND-RIDER? THINGS HAVE BEEN HAPPENING SO FAST SINCE MAGNETO AMBUSHED US-- *
--WE'VE SCARCE TIME TO CATCH OUR BREATH. WE FIGHT-- WE MAY DIE-- AND FOR WHAT?!
* X-MEN #104. BUT FOR THE X-MEN, NOT EVEN A DAY AGO-- ARCHIE.

WELL, SUMMERS, HERE'S ANOTHER FINE MESS YOU'VE GOTTEN US INTO. WHAT'S WITH JEANNIE?!

WHAT D'YOU EXPECT?! HER POWER JUST SHOT US ACROSS THE UNIVERSE! SHE'S OUT ON HER FEET!

BACK OFF, WOLVERINE! OR, SO HELP ME, I'LL--

WHOEVER THEY ARE, THESE ALIENS FIGHT WELL. THE SHEER FEROCITY OF THEIR ATTACK HAS GIVEN THEM THE EDGE THUS FAR.

HOBGOBLIN, CAN YOUR SHAPE-CHANGING POWERS COME UP WITH SOMETHING TO BLUNT THAT EDGE?

YIKES.

I THINK I HAVE JUST THE THING, TEMPEST.

A BARRACH'AN SHOVEL-BEAST!

ANYONE GOT A SHADOW I COULD HIDE IN?

FIND COVER, NIGHTCRAWLER. I WILL TRY TO HOLD THIS HORROR AS LONG AS I CAN!

PETER--NO! SOMEHOW--BY THOUGHT ALONE--THAT HOBGOBLIN CHARACTER CAN CHANGE HIS SHAPE INTO ANY FORM HE PLEASES! YOU CAN'T STAND AGAINST--
SNEP
WAIT A MINUTE! WITH MY IMAGE INDUCER, SO CAN I.

IT'S A LONG SHOT--AND MY BEAST WILL ONLY BE A VISUAL TRICK, WHERE HOBGOBLIN'S IS REAL--BUT I'M COLOSSUS' ONLY HOPE.
FUNNY. I'D BEEN PLANNING TO THROW THE IMAGE INDUCER AWAY...
RRRAURK!

NOW, IF ONLY HOBGOBLIN DOESN'T CALL MY BLUFF--BUT BECOMES SO STARTLED BY THE APPEARANCE OF A CREATURE BIGGER AND MEANER-LOOKING THAN HIMSELF...
...THAT HE LETS HIS CONCEN-TRATION SLIP...
LENIN'S GHOST! TWO OF THEM!
GRAURRL?

...AND REVERTS TO HIS NORMAL FORM!
PERFEKT!

PLEASANT DREAMS, MEIN HERR.
HE CAN ACTUALLY CHANGE HIS PHYSICAL SHAPE--THAT'S PHANTASTISCH! WUNDERBAR!
ZAK!
I WISH I COULD DO THAT. IT'S TOO BAD WE'LL NEVER GET TO MEET AS FRIENDS.

GOBLIN'S DOWN, TOO! AND THAT CLAWED ALIEN--WOLVERINE--IS GOING FOR ORACLE!
MY MENTAL POWERS AREN'T STOPPING HIM!
BEHIND HIM! IT'S STAR-BOLT!

ASSASSIN! YOU DARE THREATEN THE WOMAN I LOVE?!
AARRRGH!
BRZZK!
FALL, WOLVERINE, BEFORE THE UNFETTERED FURY OF THE SOLAR FIRE-STORM!

WELL DONE, 'BOLT. I THINK YOU'VE SINGED HIS WHISKERS, AND TAUGHT HIM A WELL-DESERVED LESSON.

WHA--?!?
LADY, IF ANYONE'S LEARNIN' ANY LESSONS, IT'S YOU AN' YER FLAME-FACED BUDDY!
WHAM!
SHORT-AN'-SWEET, HONEY-BUNCH--
--NOBODY LAUGHS AT WOLVERINE!!

HURTIN' FROM THAT FLAME BLAST, BUT I CAN'T LET IT BOTHER ME. I GOTTA KEEP TRIMMIN' THE ODDS.
AN' WHAT THE HEY, THIS FIGHT'S TOO GOOD T' MISS!
YOU! FUR-FACE! YEAH, I'M TALKIN' T' YOU, BUB!

WOLVERINE NEEDS A TARGET, FELLA-- AN' IT LOOKS LIKE YOU'RE ELECTED!
BROWW

MAGNIFICENT! YOU'VE CHOSEN WORTHY CHAMPIONS, LITTLE SISTER.
SUCH A PITY YOUR CAUSE IS DOOMED. AS ARE YOU.
D'KEN! SHAKARI--PLEASE! STOP THIS MADNESS BEFORE IT'S TOO LATE!
SILENT-BE, WOMAN! FOR YOU COMES DEATH, AND WORSE-THAN-DEATH.
MADNESS?! WITHIN THIS CRYSTAL LIES ULTIMATE POWER, A FORCE NOTHING IN THE UNIVERSE CAN WITHSTAND!
AND IT WILL BE MINE!

WHAT DO YOU...? OH, NO. LORD OF LIGHT, NO.
D'KEN, I AM YOUR SISTER! YOU WOULD NOT DARE!

FOOLISH WOMAN, IT IS ALREADY DARED. AND DONE!
LADY SHARRA PRESERVE ME! IT'S... THE SOUL-DRINKER!

THAT SCREAM--LILANDRA! THERE'S. SOMETHING MATERIALIZING NEXT TO HER ON THE DAIS.
CAN'T GET TO HER ON FOOT--

--AND I DON'T HAVE A CLEAR SHOT FOR MY OPTIC BEAMS! JEAN--?!
I'M TRYING, SCOTT. BUT STILL FEEL... SO WEAK. I NEED TIME TO... BUILD MY STRENGTH...
I'M... SORRY.
NEVER FEAR, MY FRIENDS. I'LL RESCUE YON DAMSEL FAIR.

WITH THAT, THERE'S A CRACK OF **FLAME**, THE STENCH OF **BRIMSTONE**, AND NIGHTCRAWLER IS STANDING **NEXT** TO THE PRINCESS...

...SUDDENLY WISHING HE'D TELEPORTED **SOMEWHERE ELSE**.

MEIN GOTT. WHAT ***IS*** THAT THING?

NIGHTCRAWLER?! **FLEE**, MY FRIEND! I AM **LOST**-- SAVE YOURSELF WHILE YOU **CAN**!

I'M A MAN OF MY **WORD** PRINCESS.

LEAVE ME, I **BEG** YOU!

I TOLD CYCLOPS I'D **RESCUE** YOU, AND RESCUE YOU I **SHALL**...

...ASSUMING THIS VERDAMMT **CHAIN** EVER--

SNAP!

--BREAKS!

LILANDRA'S FREE!!
CURSE THAT TWO-TOED ALIEN! I SUMMONED THE SOUL-DRINKER TO TAKE ONLY ONE, SPECIFIC SOUL-- LILANDRA'S!

GET OVER THERE, FOOLS! MAKE SURE THAT THE DEMON TAKES MY SISTER'S SOUL-- AND NONE OTHER!
LET'S GO, PRINCESS! I THINK WE'VE JUST ABOUT WORN OUT OUR WELCOME UP HERE.
PRINCESS?! WHAT'S THE MATTER WITH YOU, WOMAN?!?
NIGHTCRAWLER, I-- I--
--I... CAN'T!!
HUH?! SHE'S PETRIFIED WITH FRIGHT! THAT SOUL-THINGIE MUST HAVE HER IN SOME KIND OF MIND-LOCK.

SO HORRIBLE... NO. PLEASE, NO...
BLAST! DEMON BEHIND ME, BUG-EYED TYPES CHARGING IN FRONT-- WE'VE NO WAY OUT...

BAMF
...SAVE ONE.

SHRRIEEEEEEKK!

NIGHT-CRAWLER! YOU MADE IT!
B-BARELY.
NEVER... TELE-PORTED WITH 'NOTHER PERSON... BEFORE. DIDN'T REALIZE STRAIN 'D BE SO... GREAT. ANYONE LARGER THAN... PRINCESS, I THINK WOULD'VE KILLED US BOTH.
AS IT IS, CAN'T EVEN... STAND.

ALL RIGHT, PRINCESS, TALK! YOU ASKED OUR HELP, AND THE X-MEN CAME, BUT WE HAVEN'T A CHANCE UNLESS WE KNOW WHAT WE'RE HERE FOR AND WHAT WE'RE SUPPOSED TO DO!
AND MAKE IT FAST. WE'RE RUNNING OUT OF TIME!
YOU SPEAK TRUER THAN YOU KNOW, CYCLOPS.

"THE HORROR BEGAN WHEN MY IMPERIAL BROTHER DISCOVERED THE EXISTENCE AND LOCATION OF AN ANCIENT... FORCE. THE DEADLIEST WEAPON IN HISTORY, D'KEN THOUGHT, AND HE WANTED IT FOR HIMSELF.
"I OPPOSED HIS PLAN IN COUNCIL, AND HE HAD ME ARRESTED.

"WORD WAS LEAKED THAT I'D TRIED TO KILL MY BROTHER AND USURP THE THRONE. THE IMPERIAL FLEET--OF WHICH I WAS GRAND ADMIRAL--SPLIT DOWN THE MIDDLE.
"AND THERE WAS CIVIL WAR. THE FINAL BATTLE WAS FOUGHT ABOVE THIS VERY WORLD.

"I WAS BEING HELD ABOARD THE IMPERIAL FLAGSHIP, EN ROUTE FOR MY CEREMONIAL EXECUTION.
"D'KEN WANTED THE LAST SIGHT I SAW TO BE HIS TRIUMPH.

"INSTEAD, I ESCAPED. I STOLE A SCOUTBUG AND SABOTAGED THE FLAGSHIP--TOO LATE TO DO ANY GOOD.
"MY SHIPS WERE BEATEN, MY CAUSE LOST.

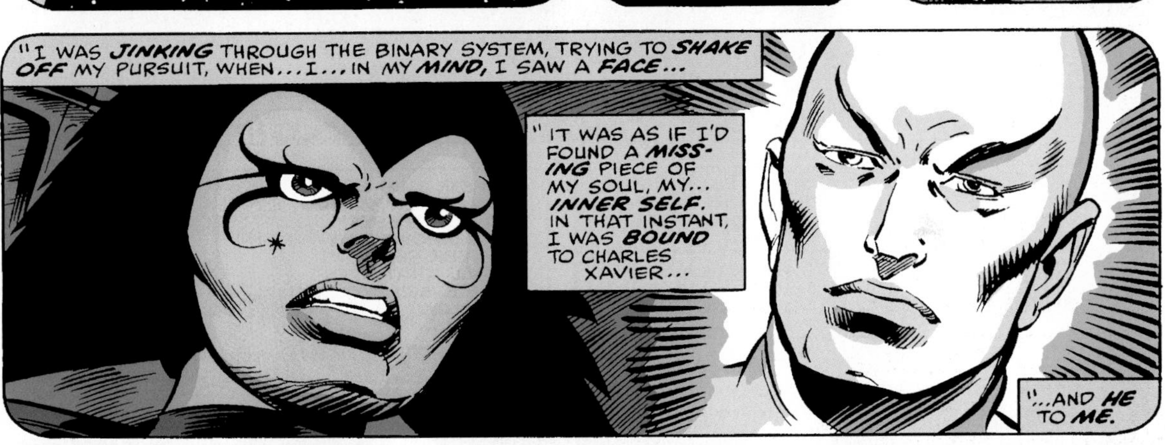
"I WAS JINKING THROUGH THE BINARY SYSTEM, TRYING TO SHAKE OFF MY PURSUIT, WHEN... I... IN MY MIND, I SAW A FACE...
"IT WAS AS IF I'D FOUND A MISSING PIECE OF MY SOUL, MY... INNER SELF. IN THAT INSTANT, I WAS BOUND TO CHARLES XAVIER...
"...AND HE TO ME.

"THERE WERE OTHER IMAGES AS WELL: XAVIER MARSHALING THE COLLECTIVE WILL OF HUMANKIND TO FIGHT OFF A MINOR, FREE-BOOTING RACE, THE Z'NOX.*
*X-MEN #65 --A.G.

"IT WAS THAT BURST OF POWER WHICH HAD BRIDGED THE AWE-SOME DISTANCE BETWEEN US. UNFORTUNATELY, IT HAD ALSO ALERTED D'KEN'S TELEPATHIC SPIES.

"THEY SENSED THAT MY RAP-PORT WITH XAVIER WOULD DRAW ME TO EARTH. INDEED, THAT IT WOULD ALLOW ME NO OTHER CHOICE.

"WE'VE KNOWN OF EARTH FOR MANY YEARS, MY FRIENDS, HAD OBSERVERS THERE EVER SINCE IT BECAME A CROSS-ROADS PLANET FOR HALF THE STARFARING RACES IN THE MILKY WAY.
"D'KEN CONTACTED OUR AGENT ON EARTH, DAVAN SHAKARI, THE MAN YOU KNOW AS ERIC THE RED.

"HIS ORDERS WERE SIMPLE: KILL XAVIER OR, FAILING THAT, PREVENT ME FROM CONTACTING HIM-- WHATEVER THE COST. WHICH MEANT, FIRST OF ALL, THE X-MEN HAD TO BE ELIMINATED.

"SHAKARI TOLD ME HE LEARNED OF YOU FROM LORNA DANE-- POLARIS-- THOUGH HE REFUSED TO SAY HOW HE LEARNED OF HER.

"HE TRIED TIME AND AGAIN TO DESTROY YOU -- USING POLARIS AND HAVOK, AND THEN YOUR OLDEST, DEADLIEST FOES -- YET EACH TIME HE FAILED.*

*X-MEN'S #'S 97,101-105--AG.

"WITH FIRELORD'S UNWITTING AID, HE FINALLY SUCCEEDED IN CAPTURING ME. HE THOUGHT HE'D WON-- UNTIL PHOENIX' POWER SENT YOU THROUGH THE STARGATE AFTER ME."
FINE, LILANDRA, BUT WHAT'S THIS ALL BEEN FOR?!?
THE OLDEST OF ALL REASONS, CYCLOPS.

POWER. THIS GREAT M'KRAAN CRYSTAL IS A... GATEWAY TO THE POWER MY BROTHER SEEKS, A GATE THAT OPENS ONCE EVERY MILLION YEARS...
...WHEN THOSE NINE DEATH-STARS ENTER A CERTAIN ALIGNMENT.
AND WITHIN THE CRYSTAL, SO THE LEGEND SAYS, CAN BE FOUND POWER ABSOLUTE.

AYE, PRINCESS! AND WHAT RIGHT HAVE YOU TO DENY IT TO YOUR EMPEROR?! YOU SWORE AN OATH TO SERVE D'KEN!
THIS TRANSCENDS AN OATH SWORN TO A MADMAN!
OPEN YOUR EYES, GLADIATOR, BEFORE MY BROTHER'S DREAMS OF IMPERIAL GLORY CLOSE THEM FOREVER!

"I DO NOT CARE," GLADIATOR SNARLS. "OURS IS NOT TO QUESTION, OURS IS TO OBEY! OUR EMPEROR HAS SAID THAT YOU AND YOUR COMPANIONS MUST DIE!"
FROM THE WAY THINGS HAVE BEEN GOING THE PAST FEW MINUTES ACROSS THE FACE OF THIS IMPROMPTU ARMAGEDDON...
...THE EMPEROR'S JUST ABOUT GOTTEN HIS WISH.
NUMBERS ARE BEGINNIN' T' TELL, BOYO. I'M THINKIN' I'LL NEVER GET A CHANCE T' TELL MOIRA MACTAGGERT HOW MUCH I...

MAN, OL' FUZZ-FACE SURE DIDN'T WANNA PART WITH HIS THREADS, BUT I GUESS I CONVINCED HIM.
THEY FEEL KIND'A FUNNY, BUT THEY BEAT FIGHTIN' IN THE ALL-TOGETHER.
SOMETHIN' TELLS ME I GOT BACK JUST IN TIME, TOO.

HEADS UP, TROOPS! WOLVERINE'S COMIN' AT'CHA!
FANG, THIS IS NO TIME FOR YOUR JOKES!
WAIT! YOU'RE NOT FANG!
DON'T WORRY LITTLE ASTRA. I'LL MAKE SURE THOSE CLAWS...

POOM!
...NEVER COME NEAR YOU!!

WE'VE GOT THEM ON THE RUN!
UNDERSTOOD, TEMPEST! WE'LL KEEP HAMMER-ING THEM UNTIL THEY DROP!
KEEP UP THE PRESSURE, 'BOLT!

GLADI-ATOR--!
NO, LILANDRA! I'LL NOT LISTEN!
PREPARE TO MEET YOUR GODS, OUTWORLDER.
NOT IF I CAN HELP IT, PAL. I'VE GOT A HANDLE ON THINGS-- I HOPE--BUT IT ISN'T GONNA DO US ANY GOOD UNLESS I CAN PULL THE X-MEN TOGETHER.
AND DO IT NOW! THE TEAM'S GETTING PULVERIZED! THEY NEED MY...

ZAP!

HE WAS GOING TO SAY, "HELP."

--AND TO THINK, ONCE, I COULD HAVE CARED FOR SUCH AS YOU!
GLADI-ATOR, I SEEK TO SAVE THE EMPIRE!
D'KEN WILL DESTROY IT!

HOW DO YOU KNOW?!
I DON'T KNOW-- I FEAR! FROM THE LITTLE I KNOW OF THE FORE-RUNNERS WHO CREATED THIS "FORCE" HE SEEKS, AND FROM THE NAME THEY GAVE IT:
"THE END OF ALL THAT IS!"

YOU'RE WASTING YOUR BREATH, PRINCESS. GLADIATOR WON'T BELIEVE YOU.
BE THANK-FUL THAT OTHERS AREN'T SO PIG-HEADED.
SHZAK!
WHO--?!

ENTER: A LEGEND...
CORSAIR, DO MINE EYES DECEIVE ME?
SOMEONE'S STARTED THE FIGHT WITHOUT US?
AYE, LEADER. WHO IS'T WOULD DARE CHEAT RAZA OF HIS BLOOD-RIGHT?!
I DON'T KNOW, AND I DON'T CARE. THIS TRIP, THE STAKES ARE HIGHER THAN PERSONAL VENGEANCE.
'SIDES, RAZA, THERE ARE IMPERIAL GUARDS ENOUGH FOR EVERY-BODY.
SHARRA AND K'YTHRI-- THE STARJAMMERS!!
FIND COVER, FEATHER-HEAD! STARJAMMERS ON YOUR SIDE, TRUE-- BUT YOU STILL IMPIE ROYALTY.
NONE OF US'D WEEP IF BLASTER BEAM CUT YOU IN TWO.

BE GENTLE, HEPZIBAH-- AS YOU SAID, PET, LILANDRA'S ON OUR SIDE.
NOT YOUR PET, CORSAIR--
--AND NAME NOT HEP-ZI-BAH. REMEMBER THAT!
I CAN'T PRONOUNCE YOUR NAME, M'LOVE-- REMEMBER THAT?

I DON'T UNDERSTAND ANY O' THIS. ARE WE BEIN'... RESCUED?
THAT YOU ARE, SMALL HUMAN!
BANSHEE, THE MONSTER SPEAKS... ENGLISH!

I AM COLOSSUS, CH'OD. MY COMPANIONS AND I ARE X-MEN. I AM... PLEASED TO KNOW YOU...
...I THINK.
DOESN'T EVERYBODY?
BY-THE-BY, MY NAME IS CH'OD. MY COMPANIONS AND I ARE STARJAMMERS. WE ARE HEROES.
FUNNY HOW QUICKLY THINGS CAN CHANGE.

ONE MOMENT, THE IMPERIAL GUARD IS ON TOP. AND THE NEXT-- SURPRISED AND SLAMMED OFF-BALANCE BY THE STARJAMMERS' SUDDEN ATTACK--THEY'RE NOT.
KOW!
BEFORE THEY KNOW IT, THE FIGHT'S ALL OVER.

NOT BAD, FOLKS. I'VE SEEN SOME HEAVY STOMPIN' IN MY TIME...
...BUT THIS TAKES THE CAKE.
HEY, ONE-EYE, WE GOT WHAT WE CAME FOR, RIGHT? THAT PRINCESS CHICK? HOW 'BOUT WE HEAD ON HOME WHILE WE GOT THE CHANCE?
NICE IDEA, WOLVERINE, BUT IT ISN'T THAT EASY.
I MUS' BE GETTIN' OLD, Y'KNOW? FIGHTS LIKE THIS USED T' BE A LOT MORE FUN.

YOUR... PET, CH'OD, IT IS... VERY NEAT.
I KNOW. YOU'RE NOT SO BAD YOURSELF, HUMAN.
CEASE THY PLEASANTRIES, LUMMOX. THIS BATTLE BE FAR FROM WON. IT'LL TAKE MORE'N ONE SALVO TO FINISH YON IMPERIAL GUARD.
WE'VE EARNED A RESPITE, NOTHING MORE.

RAZA'S RIGHT, I'M AFRAID. AND AS I SUSPECT WE'RE ALL HERE FOR THE SAME REASON-- TO STOP THE EMPEROR-- WE'D BEST GET DOWN TO BUSINESS.
FINE. AND, CORSAIR... THANK YOU.
NO SWEAT, PAL. WE'D HAVE BEEN HERE SOONER IF WE HADN'T HAD TO SNEAK OUR WAY IN.

AMERICAN SLANG AND ACCENTS THIS FAR FROM HOME? I'VE HEARD OF COINCIDENCE, BUT THIS IS RIDICULOUS.
I'D BETTER DO A FAST MIND-SCAN, JUST TO MAKE SURE WE'RE IN FOR NO SURPRISES.
NO! IT CAN'T BE. BUT-- OK. SCOTT NO! IT IS! HIM!

DO YOUR WORST, FOOLS, IT WILL MAKE NO DIFFERENCE!
MY PEOPLE ARE FELINE, D'KEN--
--AND CATS EAT BIRDS.

YOU FORGET, BARBARIAN, THAT MY AVIAN RACE CONQUERED YOURS AND MADE YOU SLAVES!
AND I SHALL CONQUER YOU! LOOK TO THE SKY, CRETINS-- YOU'RE TOO LATE! THE DEATHSTARS ARE ALIGNED.
IN ANOTHER MOMENT, THE GATEWAY WILL OPEN--

--AND POWER ABSOLUTE WILL BE MINE!!
AS IF ON CUE, BLINDING BLUE-WHITE LIGHT SPEARS OUT OF THE EVENING SKY...
...POURING INTO THE M'KRAAN CRYSTAL LIKE SOME GIGANTIC WATERFALL OF ENERGY.

SLOWLY, THE ANCIENT GEM BEGINS TO PULSE, THE POWER WITHIN BUILDING GEOMETRICALLY, THE CRYSTAL GLOWING EVER-BRIGHTER UNTIL IT SEEMS ALMOST LIKE A STAR ITSELF.
AND THEN, WHEN THE GEM CAN TAKE NO MORE, THIS NEW-BORN "STAR" EXPLODES!

IN THAT INSTANT, ALL EXISTENCE GOES...

BLINK.

WHICH BRINGS US TO STARCORE AND ITS CREATOR-- A SUDDENLY VERY FRIGHTENED MAN-- PETER CORBEAU.
IT HIT US TOO, DR. RICHARDS. A TOTAL DISRUPTION OF OUR PHYSICAL REALITY.
FOR A FRACTION OF A SECOND, WE CEASED TO EXIST.
I KNOW. THE EFFECT WAS FELT ON EARTH.
BUT WHAT COULD HAVE CAUSED IT, MAN?!

I'VE NO IDEA, THOUGH WE'VE SOME POSSIBILITIES.
BUT I CAN TELL YOU WHAT WILL HAPPEN IF THESE COSMIC "BLINKS" KEEP UP OR GET WORSE. THE FABRIC OF TIME AND SPACE WILL TEAR ITSELF APART.
THE UNIVERSE-- AS WE KNOW IT-- WILL DIE.

NEXT: AND NOW-- ARMAGEDDON!

X-MEN TM
MARVEL® COMICS GROUP
APPROVED BY THE COMICS CODE AUTHORITY
35¢
108 DEC 02461
THE ALL-NEW, ALL-DIFFERENT
X-MEN TM
©1977 MARVEL COMICS GROUP
TM
COCKRUM
ARMAGEDDON NOW!

Cyclops. Storm. Banshee. Nightcrawler. Wolverine. Colossus. Children of the atom, students of Charles Xavier, MUTANTS——feared and hated by the world they have sworn to protect. These are the STRANGEST heroes of all!

Stan Lee PRESENTS: THE UNCANNY X-MEN!™

CHRIS CLAREMONT AUTHOR * JOHN BYRNE ARTIST * TERRY AUSTIN INKER * WOHL & ORZ, LETTERERS * A. YANCHUS, COLORIST * ARCHIE GOODWIN EDITOR

ARMAGEDDON NOW!

THE WORLD HAS NO NAME. IT IS SIMPLY... THE WORLD, AND IT IS AS OLD AS TIME. FOR UNCOUNTED EONS, NO LIVING BEING HAS WALKED ITS SURFACE.

THAT HAS CHANGED.

LORD IN HEAVEN-- THE SKY!

WHAT'S HAPPENIN' T' THE SKY?!?

FOR THE FIRST TIME SINCE CREATION, THE WORLD HAS KNOWN WAR-- A WAR THAT, FOR THE BRIEFEST OF MOMENTS, THE X-MEN AND THEIR NEW-FOUND ALLIES, THE STARJAMMERS, THOUGHT THEY'D WON.

NOW, THEY'RE NOT SO SURE.

CH'OD, CALL "WALDO" IN THE 'JAMMER. I WANT A FULL-RANGE SENSOR SCAN OF THAT CRYSTAL. WE'VE GOT TO KNOW WHAT THAT EFFECT MEANS.
UNDERSTOOD, FRIEND CORSAIR.
JEAN, ARE YOU--?
WE'RE ALL FINE, BUB. HOW'S ABOUT WE GET OUTTA HERE WHILE THE GOIN'S GOOD? THIS PLACE GIVES ME THE CREEPS.

AND WHERE WOULD YOU HIDE, WOLVERINE, FROM A FORCE THAT'S CALLED, "THE END OF ALL THAT IS"?
GIVING UP, FEATHER-HEAD? THOUGHT BETTER OF YOU.
WE YET LIVE, LILANDRA. WHILE WE LIVE-- WE FIGHT!

FIGHT WHAT?! A UNIVERSE GONE MAD AROUND US?
AYE, CYCLOPS. WE'VE BEEN KEPT IN THE DARK LONG ENOUGH.
THAT PRINCESS LILANDRA TOLD YE AN' JEAN WHAT THIS IS ABOUT. NOW TELL US!

AND SO, HE DOES-- BEGINNING WITH THE X-MEN'S HEADLONG FLIGHT THROUGH AN ALIEN STARGATE.
PROFESSOR XAVIER HAD SENT THEM TO RESCUE LILANDRA, BUT THERE TURNED OUT TO BE MORE TO IT THAN THAT. LILANDRA'S BROTHER, EMPEROR D'KEN, HAD COME HERE SEEKING POWER ABSOLUTE...

... POWER HE PLANNED TO USE...
...UNLESS HE WAS STOPPED.
THE X-MEN DID THEIR BEST AGAINST THE IMPERIAL GUARD--

-- BUT ALL SEEMED LOST UNTIL THE ARRIVAL OF THE STARJAMMERS...
...SWUNG THE FINAL TIDE OF BATTLE IN THEIR FAVOR.

THAT WAS WHEN THE ROOF FELL IN, AS LIGHT FROM NINE MYSTIC DEATHSTARS STRUCK THE GREAT M'KRANN CRYSTAL-- AND ALL EXISTANCE WENT... *
BLINK
*FOR COMPLETE DETAILS SEE LAST ISH --Archie.

WHICH BRINGS US TO STARCORE -- A UNITED NATIONS SUNWATCH STATION, THE MOST ADVANCED SPACELAB EVER BUILT...
... AND RIGHT NOW, THE HOME OF SOME VERY FRIGHTENED PEOPLE.

AMONG THEM, STARCORE'S NOBEL PRIZE-WINNING CREATOR, PETER CORBEAU...
MR. PRESIDENT, I DON'T KNOW! ALL I CAN TELL YOU IS WHAT HAPPENED!
FOR AN INSTANT, EVERYTHING WITHIN RANGE OF STARCORE'S SENSORS SIMPLY, LITERALLY CEASED TO EXIST.
ROG 2000

AH FIND THAT A LITTLE HAHD TO BELIEVE, DR. COAHBEAU. MY SCIENCE ADVISORS DISPUTE THE ACCURACY OF YOUH DATA.
THAT'S RIGHT, PETER. OUR STUDY GROUP FEELS THAT YOU'VE --
YOU CAN FEEL WHAT YOU LIKE, JOEL. THAT WON'T CHANGE A BLESSED THING.
STARK INT.

THIS IS NO TIME FOR FLIPPANCY, CORBEAU.
I'M BEYOND FLIPPANCY, RICHARDS. I THINK I'M EVEN BEYOND AWE.
GOOD GOD, DON'T ANY OF YOU UNDERSTAND?!?

WE REGISTERED A TOTAL DISRUPTION OF THE NUCLEAR AND GRAVIMETRIC LINES OF FORCE THAT BIND ALL MATTER TOGETHER. AND IF THIS DISRUPTION SHOULD OCCUR AGAIN, LADIES AND GENTS...
...WE COULD VERY WELL BE WITNESSING THE END OF OUR UNIVERSE AS WE KNOW AND LIVE IN IT.
OH, MY STARS AND GARTERS.

THANK YOU, DOCTOR. WE'LL KEEP IN TOUCH.
IS THAT IT, T'CHALLA?! CORBEAU TELLS US THE UNIVERSE IS GOING TO DIE-- AND ALL YOU CAN SAY IS, "WE'LL KEEP IN TOUCH"!
WE'RE THE AVENGERS, BLAST IT! WE'VE GOT TO BE ABLE TO DO SOMETHING!

NOT THIS TIME, MY LOVE. IT'S TOO BIG AND TOO FAR AWAY. LIKE IT OR NOT, THIS ONE IS OUT OF OUR HANDS.
OH, HANK! HOLD ME CLOSE. I-- I'M SCARED.
I KNOW, BABY. SO AM I.

MEANWHILE, ON A WORLD WITH NO NAME, CYCLOPS IS JUST FINISHING HIS STORY, WHEN...
HAIL AND FAREWELL, X-MEN AND STARJAMMERS!
WHAT THE--?!
THERE'S SOMEONE UP ON THE CRYSTAL'S DAIS!
CORSAIR AND CYCLOPS, THEY'RE SO ALIKE, IT HURTS. LORD, I WISH I'D NEVER MINDSCANNED THE STARJAMMERS.
HOW CAN I TELL SCOTT WHO CORSAIR TRULY IS?

I AM JAHF, ALIENS, AND I AM A GUARDIAN OF THIS GATE INTO ETERNITY.
MY CHARGE IS A SIMPLE ONE, AND FINAL -- SO LONG AS THE GATE IS OPEN, NO ONE MAY APPROACH THE CRYSTAL...
...AND LIVE.

YOU'RE GONNA STOMP US, PIP-SQUEAK?
WOLVERINE, BE CAREFUL.
WE DON'T KNOW WHAT WE'RE UP AGAINST.

YOU BE CAREFUL, BUB. THAT'S YOUR BAG, AIN'T IT? 'SIDES, I AIN'T GONNA HURT THE LI'L FELLA-- MUCH.
THAT'S FOR SURE.

BOW

UH... 'JAMMER TO CORSAIR, I MARK A SMALL, ORGANIC, HUMANOID FORM, APPROXIMATELY A METER-SIX LONG... 70 KILOS MASS...
HE'S ONE OF OURS, "WALDO". HOW'S HE DOIN'?
WOULD YOU BELIEVE ESCAPE VELOCITY? AND, BLESS MY CIRCUITS, HE'S STILL ALIVE.
GO GET HIM -- AND WHATEVER IT TAKES, KEEP HIM ALIVE.
I COPY. HOW'RE THINGS DIRTSIDE?
DON'T ASK.

UNGLAUBLICH!
FZAK!
MY OPTIC BLASTS ARE HITTING HIM FULL FORCE, AND ALL THE IMP DOES IS LAUGH!
THIS MIDGET JUGGERNAUT IS TOSSING US AROUND AS IF WE WERE CHILDREN!
BOM

NO FAIR, ARMORED ONE-- SNEAKING UP ON TINY JAHF FROM BEHIND.
WOULD YOU CARE TO JOIN YOUR COMPANION, WOLVERINE, IN ORBIT?

DO NOT FEAR, COLOSSUS-- I HAVE YOU!
GUARDIAN, HEAR ME! WE MEAN YOU NO HARM. GIVE US LEAVE--
--AND WE WILL DEPART YOUR WORLD AS QUICKLY AS WE CAME.

I SENSE TRUTH IN YOUR WORDS, INTRUDER, BUT THAT WILL NOT SAVE YOU.
MY PROGRAMMING ALLOWS NO EXCEPTIONS. YOU ARE HERE-- AND YOU MUST PAY THE FINAL PRICE.

PERHAPS PHOENIX CAN MAKE YOU CHANGE YOUR MIND, GUARDIAN.
JEAN--!
STRAIN... INCREDIBLE! STILL... WEAK FROM TRANSPORTING THRU STARGATE... BUT... CAN'T LET THAT STOP ME!

A THOUSAND KILOMETERS ABOVE THE PLANET, PHOENIX SNARES A SMALL, WANDERING METEOR...

... AND A SECOND OR TWO LATER, SHE BRINGS IT DOWN ON TOP OF JAHF.
THAM

FOR LONG, SILENT MOMENTS, SHE STANDS LIKE A STATUE, AS SHE FEELS POWER--HER POWER--THRILL THROUGH HER SOUL...
...PART OF HER GLORYING IN IT. PART OF HER TERRIFIED.

AND THEN...
MOST IMPRESSIVE, PHOENIX.
A PITY ALL THAT EFFORT WENT FOR NOTHING.

DON'T TELL ME, LITTLE BROTHER. I ALREADY KNOW WE'RE IN TROUBL--
UNNNFF!
STORM!
USE YOUR WIND POWERS, WOMAN! WE NEED A CYCLONE!
AS GOOD AS DONE, CYCLOPS. BUT HOW WILL THAT HELP US?

IT'LL COVER US WHILE WE PULL BACK AND REGROUP. WE'RE JUST WASTING OUR TIME TACKLING THE IMP HEAD-ON. WE NEED A PLAN--
EH?!?
SORRY, CYKE--BUT I'VE ALREADY GOT A PLAN.
BANSHEE! WHERE ARE YOU GOING?!

SOMETHIN' THAT IMP SAID ABOUT PROGRAMMIN'--IF HE'S SOME KIND O' ROBOT, I'M BETTIN' MY SONIC SCREAM'LL SCRAMBLE HIS CIRCUITS SOME.
I'M BETTIN' ME LIFE.
THERE HE IS! USIN' ME SCREAM AS AN AIRBORNE SONAR LED ME RIGHT TO HIM!

GLORY! HE TURNED SO FAST, CAUGHT ME BEFORE I WAS SET!
CAN'T LET HIM GRAB ME THROAT!

LORD, THE PAIN--FEELS LIKE HE'S GRINDIN' ME RIBS T' POWDER!
GOTTA... KEEP... FIGHTIN'! ONLY NEED ONE... BREATH.

EEEEEEEEEEEE
ARRRGH!

I AM MODT-- THE SECOND GUARDIAN!

MY POWER IS A THOUSAND TIMES GREATER THAN JAHF'S! AND SHOULD I FALL, YOU WILL FACE A GUARDIAN WHOSE POWER IS A THOU-SAND TIMES MINE.

SO IT WILL GO, UNTIL YOU ARE DESTROYED.

FRAK!

ZORP!

WORDS HAVE NEVER BEATEN THE X-MEN, MONSTER!

VERY WELL, CYCLOPS. MY DEEDS WILL SPEAK FOR ME!
RAZA, LOOK OUT!
WORRY NOT FOR ME, COLOSSUS. RAZA HAS FACED WORSE DEATHS IN HIS TIME...
WHOM!
...AND SURVIVED THEM ALL.

NOT THIS TIME, YOU SEMBLANCE OF A MAN!
THIS DAY, I'LL SEE A DOUBLE TRIUMPH-- THE DEATH OF THE STARJAMMERS--
--AND THE ACQUISITION OF POWER ABSOLUTE!

IS YOUR EMPEROR MAD? DOES HE NOT REALIZE THE GUARDIAN WILL SLAY HIM, TOO?
HE IS NOT MY EMPEROR...
...AND YES, HE IS MAD. HOLD, EARTHER! THE STARJAMMER CALLS US!

RAZA, THIS IS "WALDO"! WHEN THAT SECOND GUARDIAN APPEARED, THERE WAS ANOTHER "COSMIC BLINK"--!
WHATEVER THE EMPEROR'S UNLEASHED, IT'S DISRUPTING THE BASIC FABRIC OF THE UNIVERSE!

THOU--!
THOU WOULDST NOT BE CONTENT WITH THE RAVAGING OF WORLDS--

-- THOU MUST NEEDS DESTROY ALL THAT EXISTS TO SATISFY THY INSANE LUST FOR POWER?!
UNHAND ME, LOUT! I AM THE EMPEROR!
THOU ART A MURDERER!

AND THOU WILT DIE A MURDERER'S DEATH!
THE EMPEROR SCREAMS AS HIS BODY HITS THE FACE OF THE CRYSTAL, BUT HE DOES NOT DIE.
INSTEAD, THERE'S A BLINDING FLARE OF LIGHT, A GHOST-IMAGE OF TIME SPINNING TO A HALT...
...AND, SUDDENLY, ALL PRESENT...

...ARE SOMEWHERE ELSE.

AT FIRST GLANCE, IT'S A CITY, MUCH LIKE ANY OTHER CITY: BUILDINGS, STREETS, PLAZAS, ALL DESIGNED BY BEINGS WHO WERE BOTH ARCHITECTS AND ARTISTS. A SILENT CITY, WHERE NOTHING MOVES, NOTHING LIVES, AND THE AIR IS STALE WITH THE DUST OF MORE YEARS THAN A MAN CAN COUNT.

ALMOST WITHOUT REALIZING IT, THE X-MEN AND STARJAMMERS BUNCH CLOSER TOGETHER AND FIND THEMSELVES TALKING IN WHISPERS.

I'VE NEVER SEEN SUCH SPACE, SUCH EMPTINESS --YET I FEEL CLOSED IN. TRAPPED. CAGED.

I'LL DRINK TO THAT, STORM. BUT WHAT IS THIS PLACE?

I DO NOT LIKE THIS PLACE.

ONE MOMENT WE'RE GETTING CLOBBERED BY THAT GIANT-ECONOMY-SIZED ROBBIE THE ROBOT. THE NEXT, WE'RE ZAPPED HERE--AND HE'S NOT.

HUSH, SCOTT. DON'T YOU SEE, MY LOVE? WE'RE INSIDE THE CRYSTAL.

THE GUARDIAN WAS CHARGED WITH KEEPING US OUT. HE HAS NO PLACE HERE--NO POWER OVER THOSE WHO PASS HIM.
WE'RE... INSIDE THE CRYSTAL? HOW--?
REALITY AS WE KNOW IT HAS NO MEANING HERE.

AND WITHIN THIS SPHERE IS THE... HEART OF IT ALL. I CAN FEEL... LIFE, SCOTT. AND PAIN. SOMETHING IS CALLING TO ME.
SCOTT, I SENSE SUCH... BEAUTY.

JEAN, WHAT ARE YOU TALKING ABOUT?
PHOENIX-- YOUR HAND!
SHE WOULD SAY SOMETHING, SCREAM SOMETHING--
--BUT SHE NEVER GETS THE CHANCE, AS BEAMS OF BLOOD-HUED LIGHT LASH OUT FROM THE SHIMMERING SPHERE, ONE TO EACH LIVING BEING AROUND IT...
...PLUNGING PAST THEIR MENTAL DEFENSES AS IF THEY DON'T EXIST...
...TURNING MINDS AND SOULS INSIDE OUT...
...BEFORE DROPPING THEM INTO-- NIGHTMARE!
FOR NIGHTCRAWLER, IT'S A MOB SCENE IN A REMOTE, BAVARIAN VILLAGE. HE'S BEING HUNTED, CAUGHT, KILLED--
--BY HIS FRIENDS, THE PEOPLE HE TRUSTS, CARES FOR, LOVES MOST OF ALL IN THE WORLD--THE X-MEN.
FOR CORSAIR, IT'S A MEMORY. TWO MEN FACING EACH OTHER OVER THE BODY OF A MURDERED WOMAN.
KATE! OH, MY GOD-- KATE!!
CORSAIR'S WIFE.
FOR THE EMPEROR, IT'S FACING THE SOUL-DRINKER-- HIS PET, DAEMONIC EXECUTIONER-- KNOWING THAT THIS TIME, IT'S COME FOR HIM.

AND SO IT GOES, EACH INTRUDER FINDING HIMSELF SNARED IN HIS OWN PERSONAL, PRIVATE HELL. FOR JEAN GREY, THAT HELL IS DEATH.
BUT THERE IS SOMETHING DIFFERENT ABOUT HER NIGHTMARE. THERE IS TERROR, AND YET THERE IS ALSO A POWERFUL SENSE OF DÉJÀ VU.
FOR, MONTHS AGO, WHEN SHE PILOTED A CRIPPLED SPACE SHUTTLE THROUGH THE WORST SOLAR STORM IN LIVING MEMORY-- *
*X-MEN #100--ARCH.
--SHE DIED, HER BODY CONSUMED BY SOLAR RADIATION.
AND SHE WAS REBORN.
THE NIGHTMARE... IT'S NOT AFFECTING ME ANYMORE!
I THINK I UNDERSTAND. WHEN I DIED, MY FEAR OF DEATH DIED WITH ME...

...AND NOTHING I'LL EVER FACE WILL BE EVEN HALF AS TERRIBLE.
THAT SCREAM-- CYCLOPS!
HIS OPTIC BLASTS ARE OUT OF CONTROL!

THE SPHERE'S FINAL DEFENSE--IT'S BACKFIRING! THE NIGHTMARE FIELD WORKS FINE AGAINST BEINGS WHOSE POWERS REQUIRE ANY KIND OF CONSCIOUS THOUGHT. BUT CYCLOPS IS JUST THE OPPOSITE.
HIS EYE-BEAMS ARE ON ALL THE TIME. AND WITH HIS MIND TRAPPED IN A NIGHTMARE-- HE'S MORE DEADLY --NOT LESS!
SCOTT-- DON'T!!

THE BEAM-- IT SHOULD HAVE CUT ME IN TWO!
OH, MY GOD.

MY ENTIRE BODY'S BECOME EPHEMERAL --LIKE I'M SOME SORT OF LIVING GHOST!
ALL RIGHT! SO I'LL WORRY ABOUT THAT LATER-- FIRST I'VE GOT TO STOP SCOTT BEFORE HE DOES ANY MORE DAMAGE.
UNNNGNH!

TOO LATE, PHOENIX!
THAT SOUND--?! OH, NO! THE SPHERE!!
AS SCOTT FELL, HIS EYE BEAMS HIT IT HEAD ON--AND NOW IT'S SHATTERING! WHATEVER'S LOCKED INSIDE IS BREAKING FREE!
WHAT DO I DO NOW?! I DON'T KNOW WHAT'S IN THERE, AND EVEN IF I DID, HOW AM I SUPPOSED TO STOP IT? I--I'M ALL ALONE!
SKA-RAKK!

THE FIRST THING... IS NOT TO PANIC. I AM AN X-MAN. I'VE BEEN IN TOUGH SPOTS BEFORE, AND I'VE ALWAYS COME THROUGH WITH FLYING COLORS.
SOMEHOW, I SENSE THAT SPHERE AND I ARE BOUND TOGETHER--AS IT LOSES IT'S HOLD ON REALITY, I LOSE MINE.
THE ANSWER --THE REASON WHY--MUST BE INSIDE.

AND, AS SHE ENTERS...
MY MIND! THE IMAGES --THE NIGHTMARE--IT'S GONE!
AS IF... IT HAD NEVER BEEN.

I MANAGED TO CANCEL THE NIGHTMARE FIELD AS I SHIFTED INTO THE SPHERE. BUT--WHAT'S HAPPENED TO ME...?
I'M... BEAUTIFUL. I'M JEAN--YET I'M PHOENIX. AND I FEEL ...AS IF, FOR THE FIRST TIME IN MY LIFE, I'M... TRULY ALIVE!

HER JOY SUSTAINS HER AS SHE SOARS DEEP INTO THE SPHERE--AND THEN, WITHOUT WARNING, SHE'S AT ITS HEART. AND WORDS, THOUGHTS, FEELINGS--ALL FAIL HER. BECAUSE NO HUMAN MIND--NOT EVEN HERS--CAN BEGIN TO COMPREHEND THE DARKSOME MAJESTY THAT IS A NEUTRON GALAXY.

THERE'S SUCH... POWER HERE.
BOUND WITHIN THIS... GEODESIC LATTICEWORK OF... ANTI-ENERGY? I DON'T HAVE THE WORDS--THE CONCEPTS--TO DESCRIBE IT, BUT THIS LATTICE... IT'S ALIVE!
AND IT'S... DYING.

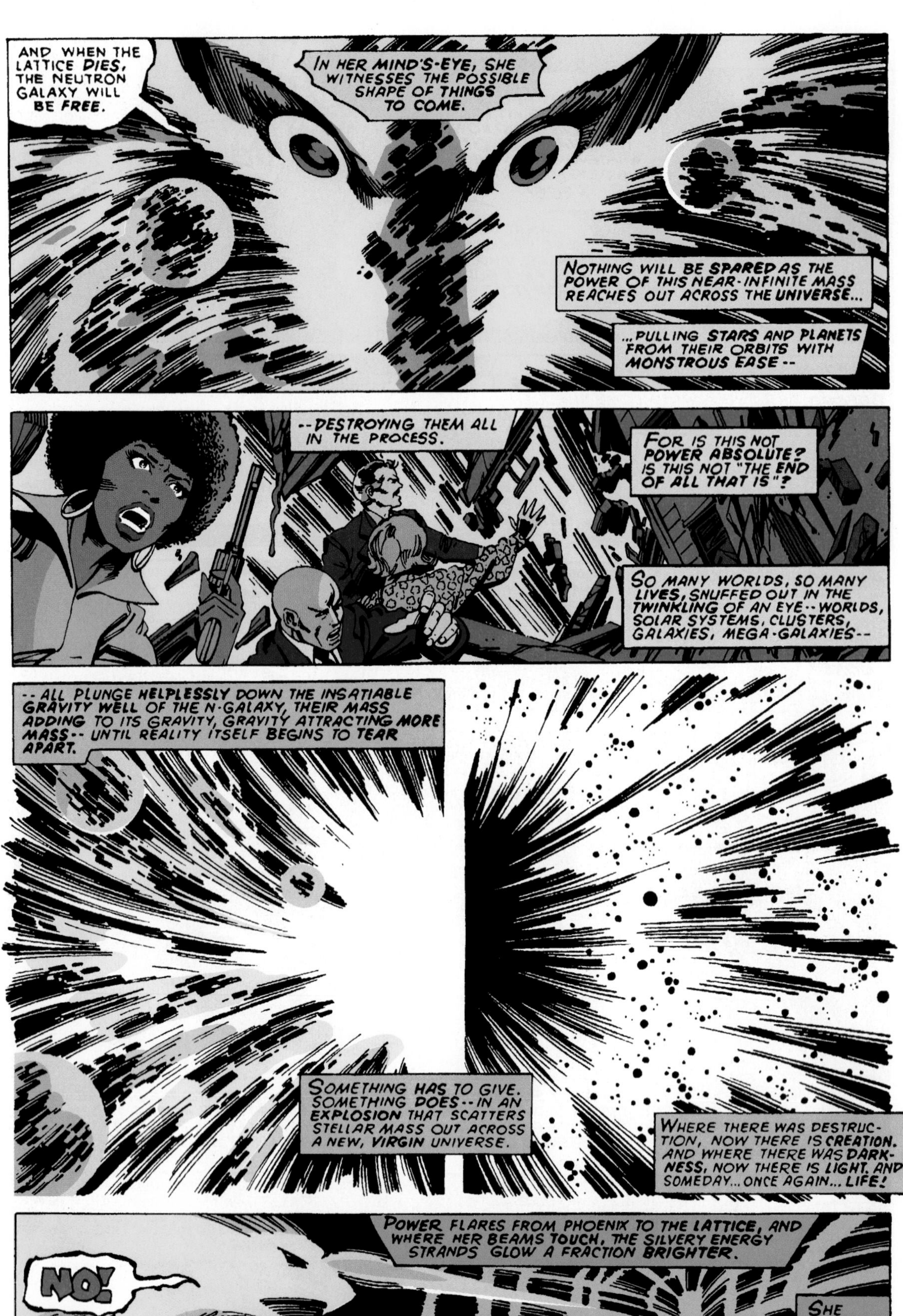
AND WHEN THE LATTICE DIES, THE NEUTRON GALAXY WILL BE FREE.
IN HER MIND'S-EYE, SHE WITNESSES THE POSSIBLE SHAPE OF THINGS TO COME.
NOTHING WILL BE SPARED AS THE POWER OF THIS NEAR-INFINITE MASS REACHES OUT ACROSS THE UNIVERSE...
...PULLING STARS AND PLANETS FROM THEIR ORBITS WITH MONSTROUS EASE--
--DESTROYING THEM ALL IN THE PROCESS.
FOR IS THIS NOT POWER ABSOLUTE? IS THIS NOT "THE END OF ALL THAT IS"?
SO MANY WORLDS, SO MANY LIVES, SNUFFED OUT IN THE TWINKLING OF AN EYE--WORLDS, SOLAR SYSTEMS, CLUSTERS, GALAXIES, MEGA-GALAXIES--
--ALL PLUNGE HELPLESSLY DOWN THE INSATIABLE GRAVITY WELL OF THE N-GALAXY, THEIR MASS ADDING TO ITS GRAVITY, GRAVITY ATTRACTING MORE MASS-- UNTIL REALITY ITSELF BEGINS TO TEAR APART.
SOMETHING HAS TO GIVE. SOMETHING DOES--IN AN EXPLOSION THAT SCATTERS STELLAR MASS OUT ACROSS A NEW, VIRGIN UNIVERSE.
WHERE THERE WAS DESTRUCTION, NOW THERE IS CREATION. AND WHERE THERE WAS DARKNESS, NOW THERE IS LIGHT. AND SOMEDAY... ONCE AGAIN... LIFE!
POWER FLARES FROM PHOENIX TO THE LATTICE, AND WHERE HER BEAMS TOUCH, THE SILVERY ENERGY STRANDS GLOW A FRACTION BRIGHTER.
NO!
SHE DOES HER BEST...

...BUT IT'S NOWHERE NEAR GOOD ENOUGH.
I CAN SEE THE TRUE PATTERN OF THE LATTICE IN MY MIND-- A NETWORK OF INTERLOCKING STASIS FIELDS NEUTRALIZING THE POWER OF THE N-GALAXY.
OUR ONLY HOPE IS TO KNIT THE LATTICE BACK TOGETHER AGAIN BEFORE ITS DETERIORATION PASSES THE POINT OF NO RETURN. I THINK I KNOW HOW TO DO IT--

--BUT I DON'T HAVE THE STRENGTH!!
THE PHOENIX IS A BEING OF ENERGY, AND THE N-GALAXY ABSORBS ENERGY. IT'S ABSORBING ME! IT'S PULLED ME SO FAR AWAY FROM THE HUMAN PLANE OF REALITY--
--THAT IT'S AS IF I NO LONGER EXIST!

BUT YOU DO EXIST!
YOU NEED AN ANCHOR IN THIS COSMIC MAELSTORM, JEAN. I WILL BE THAT ANCHOR.
AAHHHH... YESSS...
NO! STORM-- ORORO, YOU DON'T KNOW WHAT YOU'RE SAYING!
THE "ANCHOR" YOU OFFER IS YOUR LIFE-FORCE!

IT IS MY LIFE TO GIVE, MY FRIEND.

EVEN IF I TOOK IT ALL, ORORO, IT STILL WOULDN'T BE ENOUGH.
BUT YOU'VE GIVEN ME AN IDEA. WHERE ONE WON'T SERVE, TWO WILL GIVE ME WHAT I NEED, AND ...PERHAPS... LEAVE BOTH DONORS ALIVE!
CORSAIR --HELP ME!
WHY... SHOULD I?

MAJOR SUMMERS --PLEASE! THERE'S NO MORE TIME!
TAKE MY HAND!!

YOU KNOW MY NAME? HOW?!
I'LL EXPLAIN LATER!
IT TAKES HER BUT A MOMENT--

--AND WHEN THAT MOMENT'S DONE...
SEE YA, FOLKS-- THAT IS, IF THIS STUNT OF MINE WORKS. IF IT DOESN'T--
--LOOK AFTER CYCLOPS FOR ME, CORSAIR. HE'S THE MAN I LOVE...
...BUT HE'S ALSO YOUR FIRST-BORN SON.

MY-- OH, LORD, SCOTT?!
SCOTT!

IT BEGINS.
SHE RETURNS TO THE HEART OF THE SPHERE, TO THE NEUTRON GALAXY. AND THERE, SHE... CHANGES--
--WOMAN TO BIRD-FORM, FLESH TO LIVING ENERGY, JEAN GREY TO PHOENIX-- POWER FLARING STAR-BRIGHT AROUND HER IN THE ABSOLUTE DARKNESS.

SHE REACHES OUT, IMAGES CASCADING THROUGH HER MIND, THOUGHTS AND FEELINGS BECOMING TANGIBLE--SHE TOUCHING THEM, THEY HER-- THE PATTERNS OF HER LIFE, OF THE X-MEN'S LIVES, BECOMING ONE WITH THE LATTICE PATTERN SURROUNDING THE N-GALAXY.

REALITY TWISTS, COLLAPSES, REFORMS--THE STRAIN MORE THAN MIND OR BODY CAN BEAR --AND SHE NO LONGER KNOWS WHETHER SHE'S BIRD-FORM OR HUMAN, WHETHER SHE'S TRAPPED WITHIN THE SPHERE...

...OR GROWN SO LARGE SHE DWARFS THE ENTIRE SOLAR SYSTEM.

SHE FALTERS--PANIC SEIZING HER AS SHE REALIZES THAT FOR ALL HER AWESOME POWER, SHE STILL CAN'T DO IT ALONE. AND THEN, SUDDENLY, SHE ISN'T ALONE. THE SPIRITS OF THE X-MEN ARE WITH HER, GIVING OF THEMSELVES AS STORM AND CORSAIR GAVE.

IN THAT INSTANT--AS SHE FEELS HER POWER, THE POWER OF HER FRIENDS, SING WITHIN HER; AS SHE REENERGIZES THE ENERGY LATTICE --IT'S AS IF A DOOR HAS OPENED BEFORE HER EYES.

A NEW PATTERN FORMS--SHAPED LIKE THE MYSTIC TREE OF LIFE--WITH XAVIER ITS LOFTY CROWN AND COLOSSUS ITS BASE. EACH X-MAN HAS A PLACE, EACH A PURPOSE GREATER THAN HIMSELF OR HERSELF.

AND THE HEART OF THE TREE, THE CATALYST THAT BINDS THESE WAYWARD SOULS TOGETHER, IS PHOENIX. TIPHARETH. CHILD OF THE SUN, CHILD OF LIFE, THE VISION OF THE HARMONY OF THINGS.

IT'S THE LAST THING SHE SEES AS SHE COMPLETES THE LATTICE, EXHAUSTION TOPPLING HER INTO UNCONSCIOUSNESS. IT'S AN IMAGE SHE'LL CARRY WITH HER TILL SHE DIES.
WHICH MAY TURN OUT TO BE SOONER THAN SHE THINKS...

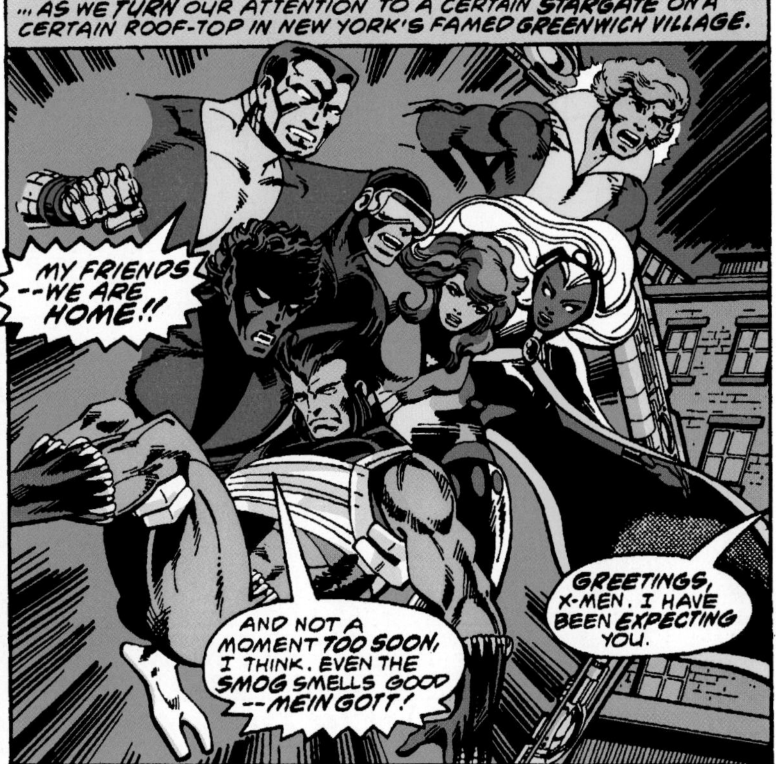

...AS WE TURN OUR ATTENTION TO A CERTAIN STARGATE ON A CERTAIN ROOF-TOP IN NEW YORK'S FAMED GREENWICH VILLAGE.
MY FRIENDS --WE ARE HOME!!
AND NOT A MOMENT TOO SOON, I THINK. EVEN THE SMOG SMELLS GOOD --MEIN GOTT!
GREETINGS, X-MEN. I HAVE BEEN EXPECTING YOU.

NEXT ISSUE: THERE SHALL COME A HERO!

hough the X-Men had saved the universe, Phoenix's increased power levels eventually corrupted her
nd she committed suicide rather than succumb to her evil impulses. Lilandra returned to the Shi'a
mpire and took the throne, and the X-Men soon gained a new member in Kitty Pryde, a teenager with
he ability to phase through solid matter...

STAN LEE PRESENTS: THE UNCANNY X-MEN!™
CHRIS CLAREMONT * WRITER
DAVE COCKRUM, BOB WIACEK AND JOSEF RUBINSTEIN ARTISTS
JOE ROSEN LETTERER * D. WARFIELD COLORIST
LOUISE JONES * EDITOR
JIM SHOOTER EDITOR-IN-CHIEF
REUNION
FOR OVER AN HOUR, CYCLOPS AND STORM-- PAST AND PRESENT LEADERS OF THE UNCANNY X-MEN, THAT OUTLAW TEAM OF MUTANT SUPER HEROES-- HAVE BEEN PLAYING THEIR OWN UNIQUE VERSION OF HANDBALL IN THE GYMNASIUM OF THE VENERABLE SUBURBAN NEW YORK MANSION THAT ONCE SERVED AS THE X-MEN'S SECRET HEADQUARTERS.
MY POINT!
TO THEM, THIS IS A QUIET ENDING TO A QUIET DAY-- A RARE, WELCOME CHANGE OF PACE IN THEIR HECTIC, HELTER-SKELTER LIVES.
BOTH ARE BLISSFULLY UNAWARE THAT THIS IS MERELY THE CALM BEFORE THE TEMPEST.

MY ADVANTAGE, SCOTT. ONE MORE POINT AND I WIN THE GAME.
ORORO
SCOTT
15
14

I'LL BELIEVE THAT WHEN I SEE IT, ORORO. SO FAR, NEITHER OF US HAS EVER BEEN MORE THAN A POINT AHEAD OF THE OTHER.
OHHHHH, BROTHER...
TIRED?

EXHAUSTED. YOU LOOK PRETTY BUSHED YOURSELF.
PLAYING IS HARD WORK, BUT I'VE STILL STRENGTH ENOUGH TO BEAT YOU.
ENOUGH TO TRY, AT ANY RATE.
YOU SERVE, SCOTT.

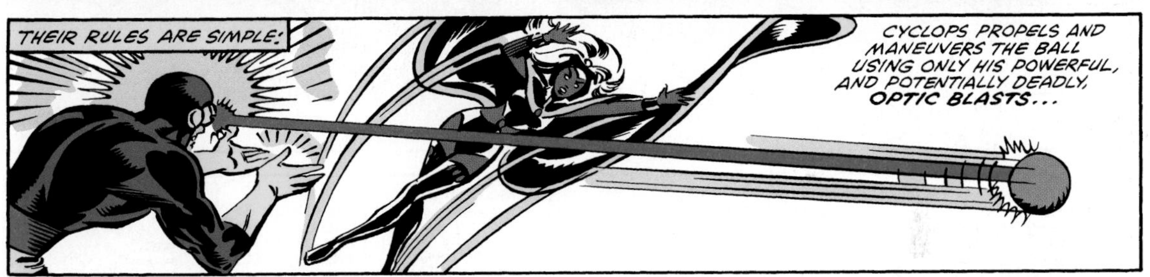
THEIR RULES ARE SIMPLE:
CYCLOPS PROPELS AND MANEUVERS THE BALL USING ONLY HIS POWERFUL, AND POTENTIALLY DEADLY, OPTIC BLASTS...

...WHILE STORM--WHO MUST REMAIN AIRBORNE DURING THE GAME--MANIPULATES IT WITH THE WINDS SHE CONTROLS. BEYOND THAT, ANYTHING GOES.
YOU KNOW, SCOTT, THIS METHOD OF HONING OUR POWERS MAY BE CRUDER THAN THE DANGER ROOM...

...BUT IT IS ALSO MUCH MORE FUN.

THANK WOLVERINE FOR THE IDEA.
I THINK, AT LAST COUNT, NIGHTCRAWLER OWED HIM A TRUCKLOAD.
THOUGH HE AND NIGHTCRAWLER USUALLY PLAY FOR BEER.
AHA! THIS LAST VOLLEY THREW STORM A FRACTION OFF-BALANCE.
SHE'S GIVEN ME THE OPENING I WAS LOOKING FOR.

A SPLIT-SECOND APART, CYCLOPS FIRES A PAIR OF OPTIC BLASTS...
...IN SEEMINGLY RANDOM PATTERNS AROUND THE ROOM. ONE FLASHES RIGHT IN FRONT OF STORM, EASILY MISSING THE BALL, MOMENTARILY DISORIENTING HER. BEFORE SHE CAN RECOVER, THE SECOND BEAM RICOCHETS OFF A WALL BEHIND HER TO DEFLECT THE BALL ONTO THE FLOOR.

YOUR POINT. WE'RE TIED ONCE MORE.
THAT WAS A VERY NICE--AND NASTY--MOVE, SCOTT.
WOLVERINE WOULD HAVE BEEN PROUD OF YOU.

CONSIDER IT MY SWANSONG. I'M BEAT.
I, TOO. SHALL WE CALL THIS A DRAW?
THE LATEST IN A SERIES. THE GAMES I WIN WITH EXPERIENCE...

...ARE BALANCED BY THE ONES YOU WIN WITH SKILL. AND VICE VERSA. YOU'RE VERY GOOD.
YOU SOUND SURPRISED.
I LIKE BEING THE BEST. IT'S NOT EASY GETTING USED TO HAVING A RIVAL, MUCH LESS AN EQUAL. C'MON, LET'S HIT THE SHOWERS.

INTERLUDE:
A BILLION AND A HALF KILOMETERS OUT-SYSTEM FROM EARTH...
...A TINY, TOUGH, MAGNIFICENT SPACECRAFT RUSHES TOWARDS INTERSTELLAR SPACE.

THIS IS VOYAGER 2, AN UNMANNED NASA PROBE THAT--TOGETHER WITH ITS COMPANION CRAFT VOYAGER 1--HAS ASTOUNDED SCIENTIST AND LAYMAN ALIKE...
...WITH ITS BREATH-TAKING VIEWS OF THE OUTER PLANETS.

ITS ON-BOARD SYSTEMS HAVE BEEN QUIESCENT SINCE VOYAGER DEPARTED SATURN ORBIT, TO CONSERVE POWER FOR THE URANUS FLYBY IN JANUARY, 1986.
HAD ITS SCANNERS BEEN ACTIVE THIS DAY, VOYAGER'S CREATORS--BACK AT PASADENA'S JET PROPULSION LABORATORY--
--WOULD HAVE LEARNED FAR MORE ABOUT THE UNIVERSE HUMANITY INHABITS THAN THEY EVER BARGAINED FOR.

THE STARSHIP IS INDISPUTABLY ALIEN. ITS PILOT IS NOT.
AFTER TWENTY YEARS, MAJOR CHRISTOPHER SUMMERS, UNITED STATES AIR FORCE, IS RETURNING HOME...

...TO A PLANET--AND A SON--HE BARELY REMEMBERS.
I'M ALMOST AT THE END OF A JOURNEY I NEVER THOUGHT I'D MAKE. I WISH THE CIRCUMSTANCES WERE DIFFERENT.
BUT IF THEY WERE, I PROBABLY WOULDN'T BE HERE.

FUNNY. AS A KID, I ALWAYS DREAMED OF EXPLORING SPACE. MY DREAM CAME TRUE--AT THE COST OF EVERYTHING I HELD DEAR. AND IF I HAD IT ALL TO DO OVER AGAIN, I-- EH?! THE SCANNERS!
A SHI'AR DREADNOUGHT!
BREEEP!
THEY'VE FOUND ME!!

INTERLUDE: IN THE HEART OF THE LEGENDARY BERMUDA TRIANGLE LIES AN ISLAND RAISED FROM THE OCEAN FLOOR BY MAGNETO, MUTANT MASTER OF MAGNETISM, FOR USE AS HIS BASE.
RECENTLY, IT WAS THE SITE OF AN EPIC CONFRONTATION BETWEEN HIM AND THE X-MEN.* AFTER HIS DEFEAT...
*X-MEN #150--LOUISE.

...THEY APPROPRIATED THE ISLAND FOR THEIR OWN USE.
YOU NEED A HAND WITH THOSE CRATES, COLOSSUS?
NYET, DR. CORBEAU. WHEN I AM IN MY ARMORED FORM...
...MY STRENGTH IS QUITE CONSIDERABLE. I CAN EASILY HANDLE THIS LOAD. BUT YOUR OFFER IS APPRECIATED.
THOSE COMPUTER ELEMENTS GO TO THE LABORATORY, PETER.

<I KNOW WHERE THAT IS, PIOTR NIKOLIEVITCH. I WILL SHOW YOU THE WAY.>
THIS SIDE UP
THIS SIDE UP
<LEAD ON, LITTLE SISTER.>
AS THEY LEAVE THE WHARF, NIGHTCRAWLER MATERIALIZES IN A CHARACTERISTIC BURST OF SMOKE AND FLAME.

ACH! THIS ISLAND IS SO ANCIENT, SO... ALIEN. WE KNOW VIRTUALLY NOTHING ABOUT IT.
I WONDER IF IT IS A SAFE HAVEN FOR ILLYANA--OR THE X-MEN?
CONSIDERING HOW OFTEN THE SECURITY OF OUR MANSION HAS BEEN BREACHED OF LATE, NIGHTCRAWLER, WOULD IT HAVE BEEN ANY SAFER TO REMAIN AT HOME? I DOUBT IT.
PROFESSOR, YOU READ MY THOUGHTS!

I APOLOGIZE, KURT. BUT THEY WERE SO OBVIOUS, AND SO STRONG, I COULDN'T HELP IT. YOU KNOW THERE'S A GROWING ANTI-MUTANT SENTIMENT IN THE STATES.
I FEAR-- FROM WHAT I'VE LEARNED RECENTLY-- THAT IT MAY HAVE OFFICIAL SANCTION. FOR THE MOMENT IT IS SIMPLY TOO DANGEROUS TO REMAIN IN WESTCHESTER.

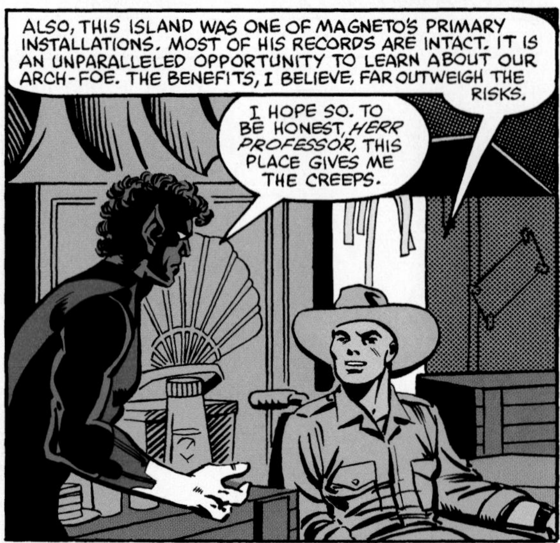
ALSO, THIS ISLAND WAS ONE OF MAGNETO'S PRIMARY INSTALLATIONS. MOST OF HIS RECORDS ARE INTACT. IT IS AN UNPARALLELED OPPORTUNITY TO LEARN ABOUT OUR ARCH-FOE. THE BENEFITS, I BELIEVE, FAR OUTWEIGH THE RISKS.
I HOPE SO. TO BE HONEST, HERR PROFESSOR, THIS PLACE GIVES ME THE CREEPS.

ELSEWHERE, ATOP THE TOWER THAT SERVES AS THE X-MEN'S LIVING QUARTERS...
...STANDS A WOMAN NAMED CAROL DANVERS.
AS MS. MARVEL, SHE WAS A MAINSTAY OF THE AVENGERS-- THE WORLD'S MIGHTIEST SUPER HERO TEAM--

--BUT THAT WAS BEFORE SHE LOST HER POWERS, HER MEMORY, AND VERY NEARLY HER LIFE AT THE HANDS OF ROGUE AND THE BROTHERHOOD OF EVIL MUTANTS.*
PERHAPS IT WOULD HAVE BEEN BETTER IF I HAD DIED. I FEEL SO CUT OFF FROM EVERYTHING, EVERYONE. THE MORE I LEARN AND REMEMBER...
*IN AVENGERS ANNUAL #10 --LOUISE.
...THE MORE I REALIZE HOW MUCH I'VE TRULY LOST, THAT CAN NEVER BE REGAINED.
MAJOR?
WHO?! WOLVERINE!

YOU STARTLED ME. I DIDN'T HEAR YOU APPROACH.
NO ONE EVER DOES.
PARDON MY ASKING, BUT DIDN'T WE MEET A FEW YEARS AGO?
YEAH--WHEN YOU WERE AIR FORCE INTELLIGENCE AND I WAS CANADIAN SECRET SERVICE. YOU AN' YOUR PARTNER, COLONEL MIKE ROSSI AN' ME RAN SOME PRETTY HAIRY CAPERS TOGETHER.
THOSE WERE GOOD TIMES.

I DON'T REMEMBER. NOT YOU, NOT THE MISSIONS, NOT EVEN ROSSI.
I LOVED HIM, WOLVERINE, YET I CAN'T PICTURE HIS FACE, HEAR HIS VOICE, AND WHEN I THINK OF HIM--
--I FEEL NOTHING!

S-SORRY. I... I DIDN'T MEAN TO COME APART LIKE THAT.
'S'ALRIGHT. BLAST! WHAT IS IT, KITTY? THAT WAS THE WRONG WALL TA PHASE THROUGH AN' THE WRONG TIME TA DO IT.
OH. YEAH. I SEE THAT. THE PROFESSOR SENT ME TO FIND YOU.
YOU'VE DONE THAT. NOW SCRAM, I'M BUSY.
GO, WOLVERINE. I'LL BE FINE. REALLY.

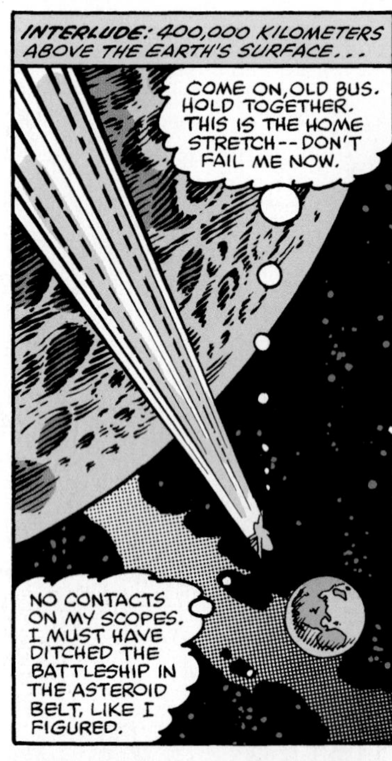

INTERLUDE: 400,000 KILOMETERS ABOVE THE EARTH'S SURFACE...
COME ON, OLD BUS. HOLD TOGETHER. THIS IS THE HOME STRETCH--DON'T FAIL ME NOW.
NO CONTACTS ON MY SCOPES. I MUST HAVE DITCHED THE BATTLESHIP IN THE ASTEROID BELT, LIKE I FIGURED.

PLASMA TORPEDOS--COMING FROM AHEAD OF ME! THE SHI'AR!
I UNDERESTIMATED THEM. THE MOMENT THEY LOST ME THEY MUST HAVE COME STRAIGHT HERE.

THEY'RE USING THEIR MAIN BATTERIES. MY SHIELDS WON'T HOLD AGAINST THAT KIND OF FIREPOWER.
CORSAIR, M'LAD, YOU'RE REPUTED TO BE THE BEST PILOT IN SPACE. HERE'S YOUR CHANCE TO PROVE IT.

WHILE CORSAIR--LEADER OF THE STARJAMMERS, A DEVIL-MAY-CARE BAND OF INTERSTELLAR FREEBOOTERS--RUNS A VIRTUALLY IMPASSABLE GAUNTLET OF NUCLEAR MISSILES AND ENERGY BEAMS...

...WE RETURN ONCE MORE TO PROFESSOR XAVIER'S SCHOOL FOR GIFTED YOUNGSTERS.

I MUST SAY I'VE OUTDONE MYSELF.

THOUGH, WHEN IT COMES TO COOKING, MY STANDARDS ARE PRETTY LOW.

DINNER'S READY, ORORO.

I HAVE THE MAIL, SCOTT.

ANYTHING INTERESTING?

BILLS, MAGAZINES, CIRCULARS--THE USUAL, OH, HERE'S A POST CARD FROM KITTY!

"HAVING A WONDERFUL TIME. WISH YOU WERE HERE." HOW ELOQUENT.
AH, KITTEN. SHE TRIED FOR A CARIBBEAN TAN AND GOT SUNBURNED INSTEAD. SHE'S PRACTICING HER DANCING. SHE'S DETERMINED TO BE IN THE PIECE HER TEACHER, STEVIE HUNTER, IS CHOREOGRAPHING. I MUST TELL STEVIE THAT.
EVERYONE IS WELL, THOUGH CAROL SEEMS QUITE DEPRESSED.
THAT'S SOME POST-CARD.

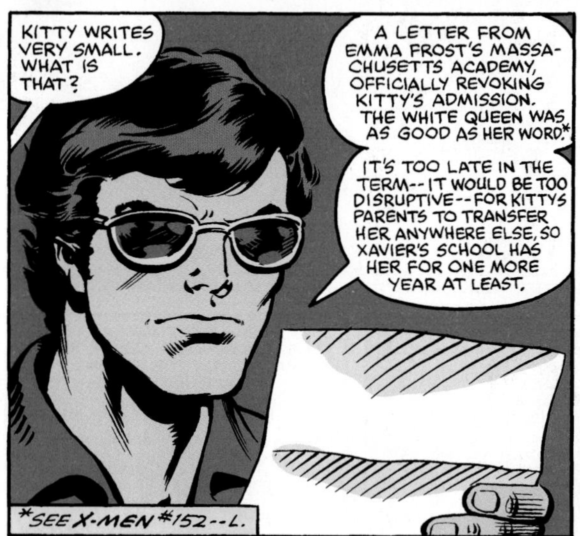
KITTY WRITES VERY SMALL. WHAT IS THAT?
A LETTER FROM EMMA FROST'S MASSACHUSETTS ACADEMY, OFFICIALLY REVOKING KITTY'S ADMISSION. THE WHITE QUEEN WAS AS GOOD AS HER WORD.*
IT'S TOO LATE IN THE TERM-- IT WOULD BE TOO DISRUPTIVE--FOR KITTY'S PARENTS TO TRANSFER HER ANYWHERE ELSE, SO XAVIER'S SCHOOL HAS HER FOR ONE MORE YEAR AT LEAST.
*SEE X-MEN #152--L.

YOU UNDER-RATE YOURSELF. THIS IS ALL QUITE DELICIOUS.
THANKS.
SCOTT, YOU CALLED ME YOUR "RIVAL" EARLIER. AM I? DO YOU WISH TO RECLAIM YOUR OLD POSITION AS TEAM LEADER?
DO YOU WISH TO GIVE IT UP?

I... AM NOT CERTAIN. I TOOK IT RELUCTANTLY. THE RESPONSIBILITY... FRIGHTENED ME.
BUT OVER THE MONTHS...

...I HAVE GROWN TO ACCEPT IT. I AM GOOD AT IT-- THOUGH I CONCEDE YOU ARE THE BEST.
AGAIN, THANKS. BUT TO BE HONEST, I'M NOT SURE I WANT THE JOB BACK.

SO MUCH HAS CHANGED, IS CHANGING, IN MY LIFE. I FEEL LIKE I'M AT A CROSSROADS--
GOOD LORD!
THAT ROARING SOUND--!
WHAT THE BLAZES IS HAPPENING?!?

A -- SPACECRAFT!?!
CAREFUL! IT'S SCATTERING DEBRIS ALL OVER THE LAWN!
IT'S HEADING FOR THE LAKE!

CRASH!
IN A MATTER OF SECONDS, BOTH X-MEN ARE IN THE WATER, SEARCHING FOR SURVIVORS.

SOMEONE MUST HAVE SEEN OR HEARD ITS APPROACH.
HOWEVER WILL WE EXPLAIN THIS?

YOU'RE THE BOSS, ORORO. I'M SURE YOU'LL THINK OF SOMETHING.
WONDERFUL.
THERE'S THE PILOT!

HE'S STILL ALIVE!
SCOTT, I RECOGNIZE--!
ME, TOO. IT'S CORSAIR.
HE IS FAR MORE THAN THAT, MY FRIEND.

AND I FEAR THE TIME HAS COME TO BREAK MY OATH NEVER TO REVEAL TO YOU THE TRUTH ABOUT HIM.
LORDS OF THE EARTH AND AIR!
ORORO, I THINK WE CAN FORGET ABOUT EXPLANATIONS.

CORSAIR DREAMS-- AND THE IMAGES ARE AS VIVID AS LIFE, THE PAIN AS REAL, THE GRIEF AS SHARP.
HIS PLANE WAS BURNING. ANNE GAVE SCOTT THE ONLY PARACHUTE, WRAPPED ALEX IN HIS BIG BROTHER'S ARMS, AND SHOVED THE TWO BOYS OUT THE ESCAPE HATCH.
THEN, SHE RETURNED TO HER HUSBAND'S SIDE, AND BOTH OF THEM WERE SWEPT ACROSS THE UNIVERSE...
MORE RECENT MEMORIES SCATTERSHOT ACROSS HIS MIND'S EYE:
...WHERE SHE PAID FOR HER LOVE AND LOYALTY...
...WITH HER LIFE.
...AN AMBUSH, DAYS AGO-- FOUR STARJAMMERS VERSUS A BATTALION OF IMPERIAL COMBAT TROOPERS.
THE ODDS WERE HOPELESS. REGARDLESS, ONE OF THEM HAD TO GET AWAY, TO REACH EARTH, TO ALERT THE X-MEN. CORSAIR WAS THE OBVIOUS CHOICE.
SO, WHILE CH'OD, RAZA AND MS. HEPZIBAH HELD OFF THE IMPERIALS, CHRISTOPHER SUMMERS FLED INTO THE NIGHT.
AND, FOR THE SECOND TIME IN HIS LIFE, FEELS HIS HEART BREAK.
GOOD EVENING, CYCLOPS. PARDON MY DROPPING IN UNANNOUNCED...
CAN THE SNAPPY PATTER, CORSAIR. EXPLAIN THIS LOCKET AND THESE AIR FORCE DOGTAGS.
THE WOMAN'S FACE IS... FAMILIAR. AND THE TWO BOYS ARE ME AND MY BROTHER, ALEX.
THE TAGS ARE MINE, SCOTT. THE WOMAN IS MY WIFE, THE CHILDREN MY SONS.
YOU'RE LYING!
SCOTT-- FORGIVE ME, BUT HE IS NOT.

HOW THE BLAZES DO YOU KNOW, STORM?
LOOK OUT!
SIDRIAN HUNTERS!
IT'S ME THEY'RE AFTER!
SHREEEEEE

THEY'LL HAVE TO WAIT THEIR TURN.
UNTIL I GET SOME ANSWERS, CORSAIR, YOU'RE MINE!

SUITS ME. BUT WE CAN'T STAY HERE.
WE NEED ROOM TO MANEUVER!
FOLLOW ME DOWNSTAIRS!

MORE OF THEM, CYCLOPS!
THEY'RE POURING THROUGH EVERY WINDOW IN THE HOUSE. YOU SEEM TO KNOW THESE HORRORS, CORSAIR -- HOW DO WE FIGHT THEM?

THEIR PRIMARY WEAKNESS IS INTENSE HEAT. MY BLASTER SLOWS 'EM DOWN. A GOOD-SIZED FUSION BOMB WOULD RUPTURE THE ENTIRE MATRIX.
YOU WOULDN'T HAPPEN TO HAVE ONE HANDY, WOULD YOU?

ON THE SURFACE, CORSAIR JESTS, YET HIS UNDERTONE IS DEADLY SERIOUS. IF HE POSSESSED SUCH A WEAPON, HE WOULD USE IT -- REGARDLESS OF THE COST TO THE SURROUNDING COMMUNITY.
WHAT SORT OF MAN IS HE?
WE NEED TIME TO REGAIN OUR BALANCE, TO THINK AND PLAN. IT IS UP TO ME TO PROVIDE IT.

SHE SUMMONS THE WIND THAT IS HER NAMESAKE AND SETS IT SPINNING IN THE PARLOR. IN SECONDS, STORM GENERATES AN INCREDIBLE, IRRESISTIBLE VORTEX THAT REACHES THROUGH THE HOUSE, GATHERING IN EVERYTHING THAT ISN'T FASTENED DOWN.

THE FURNITURE DOES NOT SURVIVE. OUR HEROES, PROTECTED BY STORM FROM HER CREATION, DO.
REGRETTABLY, SO ALSO DO THEIR FOES.

THE SIDRI ARE FREE-LANCERS, WORKING FOR BOUNTY.
THE IMPERIAL SHI'AR WOULD NEVER USE THEM, SO IT'S UNLIKELY THEY CAME FROM THE DREAD-NOUGHT.
THAT LEAVES THE OPPOSITION... THE TRAITORS WHO KIDNAPPED LILANDRA.

MY FATHER--ALIVE! AS A KID, I DREAMED OF THIS MEETING. I PRAYED FOR IT.
NOW THAT IT'S HAPPENED, I FEEL...HAPPY, ANGRY--MOSTLY NUMB.
I DON'T KNOW WHAT TO DO, OR SAY.

SCOTT IS TRYING TO HIDE IT BUT HIS EMOTIONS ARE TEARING HIM APART INSIDE. AND IT IS PARTLY MY FAULT. BLESSED GODDESS I KEPT SILENT ABOUT CORSAIR TO SPARE HIM PAIN...
...ONLY TO CAUSE HIM EVEN GREATER PAIN.
WHAT NEXT?
YOU TELL ME, FIGHT OR RUN?
RUN.

WE NEED THE OTHER X-MEN AND WE MUST DRAW THESE MONSTERS AWAY BEFORE INNOCENT CIVILIANS BECOME INVOLVED.
WE'LL USE THE *BLACKBIRD.* I'LL CALL YOU OVER OUR MICRO-TRANSCEIVERS WHEN WE'RE READY TO LIFT-OFF.
AND I SHALL COME.
IF I AM ABLE.
WHAT'S SHE TALKING ABOUT?!

STORM'S ACTING AS OUR REARGUARD, TO BUY US THE TIME WE NEED TO REACH THE PLANE.
ONE WOMAN AGAINST THE SIDRI?!
IT'S THE ONLY WAY.
COME ON!

YOU CAN'T LEAVE HER!
THE HANGAR'S A MILE DOWN THIS TUNNEL, HIDDEN BENEATH A COPSE ON THE ESTATE. SECURITY SENSORS INDICATE NEITHER HANGAR NOR TUNNEL HAVE BEEN BREACHED. THIS MONOCAR WILL HAVE US THERE IN A COUPLE OF MINUTES.

YOU COLD-BLOODED--!
THEY'LL TEAR HER APART! WE HAVE TO HELP HER!
SHE'S YOUR *FRIEND*, SCOTT! DON'T YOU *CARE*--?!
STORM... *ORORO!*

YES!!
BUT I'LL LEAVE HER JUST THE SAME...
...AS I'D EXPECT HER TO LEAVE ME.

THE SIDRI ARE GENERATING ADDITIONAL ARMOR, MAKING THEMSELVES MORE RESISTANT TO MY LIGHTNING BOLTS.
AND THE STRAIN IS BEGINNING TO WEAR ME DOWN.
I CANNOT MAINTAIN THIS EFFORT MUCH LONGER.

MEANWHILE, ABOARD THE X-MEN'S CUSTOM-DESIGNED, SPECIALLY MODIFIED VERSION OF THE FAMED SR-71 BLACKBIRD...
STORM, THIS IS CYCLOPS. TIME TO GO.
SCANNERS READ ALL CLEAR TOPSIDE. ALL I HAVE TO DO IS POP THE SURFACE HATCH, FIREWALL THE THROTTLES AND WE'RE ON OUR WAY.
Kitty's Dragon

AND NOT A MOMENT TOO SOON.
I HAVEN'T TRIED THIS MANEUVER IN AGES. I HOPE IT WORKS.

THE PHYSICAL COST TO HER IS SHATTERING...
...AS SHE USES HER ELEMENTAL POWERS TO CONJURE A MONSOON, CREATING A FLASH FLOOD IN THE NARROW TUNNEL WHICH SHE HURLS AT THE ALIENS...

...YET SHE STILL FINDS STRENGTH ENOUGH TO STREAK DOWN THE TRANSIT TUNNEL TO THE HANGAR AT FULL SPEED.
THIS IS WHY BOTH SCOTT AND I KNEW I HAD TO STAY-- BECAUSE WHEREVER THE BLACKBIRD WENT, I COULD FOLLOW. ONCE SHE WAS AIRBORNE, SCOTT COULD NOT.

SECONDS LATER, THUNDER RIPPLES ACROSS THE TOWN OF SALEM CENTER-- SCARING EVERYONE AWAKENED BY THE CRASH OF CORSAIR'S STARSHIP--
--AS TWO ULTRA-HIGH-PERFORMANCE JET ENGINES PUNCH 77,000 KILOGRAMS OF SLEEK, EBONY AIRCRAFT STRAIGHT UP INTO THE SKY.

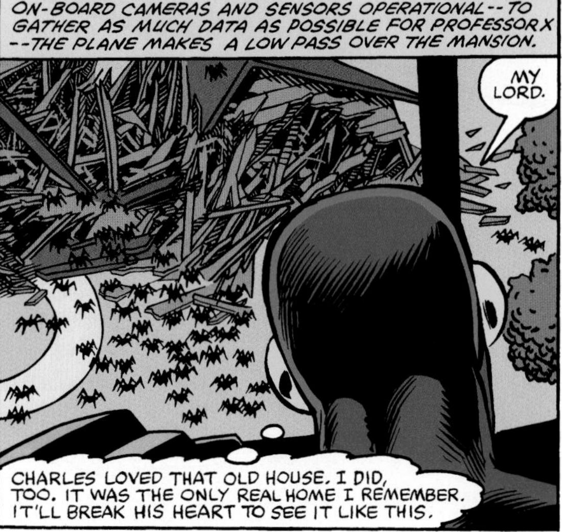
ON-BOARD CAMERAS AND SENSORS OPERATIONAL--TO GATHER AS MUCH DATA AS POSSIBLE FOR PROFESSOR X--THE PLANE MAKES A LOW PASS OVER THE MANSION.
MY LORD.
CHARLES LOVED THAT OLD HOUSE. I DID, TOO. IT WAS THE ONLY REAL HOME I REMEMBER. IT'LL BREAK HIS HEART TO SEE IT LIKE THIS.

"KEEP YOUR EYES PEELED," HE TELLS THE OTHERS. "THEIR SHIP SHOULD BE SOMEWHERE NEARBY. MAYBE WE CAN PUT IT OUT OF COMMISSION."

"TAKE ANOTHER LOOK, LAD," CORSAIR REPLIES GRIMLY. "THE SIDRI DON'T NEED A SHIP.

"THEY *ARE* A SHIP!"

ON THAT NOTE, LET'S SHIFT OUR SCENE BRIEFLY TO THE F.A.A. REGIONAL AIR TRAFFIC CONTROL CENTRE ON LONG ISLAND, RESPONSIBLE FOR ROUTING AND DIRECTING ALL AIRCRAFT IN THE NEW YORK AREA.

TROUBLE, PHIL?

UNIDENTIFIED CONTACT, ROY.

POPPED UP OUTTA NOWHERE IN WESTCHESTER. VECTOR IS DUE SOUTH TOWARDS THE CITY AT LOW ALTITUDE. IT WON'T ACKNOWLEDGE MY TRANSMISSIONS.

I'LL ALERT THE AIR FORCE-- ***GOOD GRIEF!*** WHAT THE HECK IS ***THAT?!?***

I-- I DON'T KNOW. BUT IT'S AS BIG AS A SKYSCRAPER--

"--AND IT'S BARRELING FULL-TILT INTO THE MOST CROWDED AIR-SPACE ON EARTH!"

YOW!!

CYCLOPS TRIES TO CLIMB AWAY FROM THE CITY...
...BUT THE SIDRI CUT HIM OFF, FORCING HIM INTO A LOW-LEVEL GAME OF CAT AND MOUSE THAT BEGINS AT MANHATTAN'S TRIBOROUGH BRIDGE...

...AND CONTINUES DOWN THE EAST RIVER.
I MAY BE STATING THE OBVIOUS, LAD, BUT THIS IS HARDLY THE WAY TO SAFE-GUARD INNOCENT LIVES.
THANKS, "POP." I NEEDED THAT.
WE CAN'T USE CONVENTIONAL WEAPONS.
THEY'RE TOO DANGEROUS TO OTHERS, TOO DIFFICULT TO CONTROL.
BUT THAT DOESN'T MEAN WE'RE HELPLESS. FAR FROM IT.
I'VE BEEN WAITING FOR A CHANCE TO FIELD TEST THIS EXPERIMENTAL WINDSHIELD. LOOKS LIKE THIS IS IT.
HE FIRES A FULL-POWER OPTIC BLAST.
AS THE BEAM HITS THE CANOPY-- ITSELF COMPOSED OF A SYNTHESIS OF PLASTIGLASS AND RUBY QUARTZ-- SPECIAL POLARIZING ELEMENTS FOCUS AND AMPLIFY ITS ENERGY...
...AS A RUBY DOES WITH COHERENT LIGHT IN A LASER.
ZAP!
THE EFFECT IS MOST IMPRESSIVE.

AND, INSOFAR AS THEIR FOE IS CONCERNED, TOTALLY SEQUENTIAL.
A NICE TRY, SCOTT, BUT WHEN THE SINDRI MERGE INTO THEIR SHIP MATRIX, THE BOND THAT LINKS THEM IS ALMOST IMPOSSIBLE TO BREAK.
SUPPOSE WE DISRUPT THAT MATRIX, WHAT GOOD WILL THAT DO US?

A VIOLENT DISSOLUTION WILL ACT LIKE A GIGANTIC SHORT CIRCUIT. IT'LL STUN THEM-- LONG ENOUGH FOR US TO ESCAPE, OR PERHAPS EVEN DESTROY THEM.
BUT SHATTERING THE MATRIX REQUIRES A PHENOMENAL AMOUNT OF ENERGY. I DOUBT YOU CAN HACK IT ALONE.

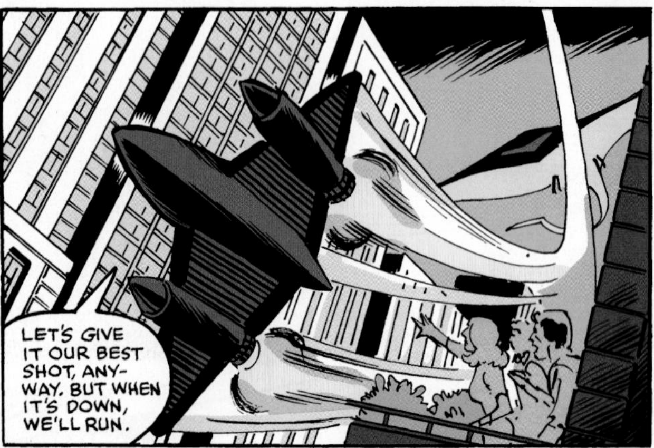
LET'S GIVE IT OUR BEST SHOT, ANYWAY. BUT WHEN IT'S DOWN, WE'LL RUN.

NEVILLE, THAT'S AN AEROPLANE!
SO IT IS, M'DEAR.

VERY NICE FLYING, SON. I COULDN'T HAVE DONE BETTER MYSELF.
THE NAME IS CYCLOPS, MISTER. YOU HAVEN'T THE RIGHT TO CALL ME ANYTHING ELSE.
SCOTT, THE FORCES OF NATURE ARE OFTEN FAR GREATER THAN THE WOMAN WHO SUMMONS THEM.

IF YOU KEEP HAMMERING AWAY AT THE SINDRI, WHILE I CREATE A GALE...
IT'S WORTH A TRY, ORORO, BUT WE'RE BOTH PRETTY TIRED. CAN YOU MAINTAIN TOTAL CONTROL OVER YOUR STORM?
I SHALL HAVE TO, SHAN'T I?
GOOD LUCK.

TO DO WHAT IS NECESSARY, I MUST WARP WEATHER PATTERNS THROUGHOUT THE NEW YORK METROPLEX. THE EFFECTS OF SUCH AN ATMOSPHERIC TRAUMA WILL BE FELT FOR DAYS, PERHAPS LONGER. AND THEY MAY BE SEVERE.
YET IF I DO NOTHING, WE THREE ARE SURELY DOOMED.
ARE OUR LIVES WORTH ENDANGERING THE CITY?

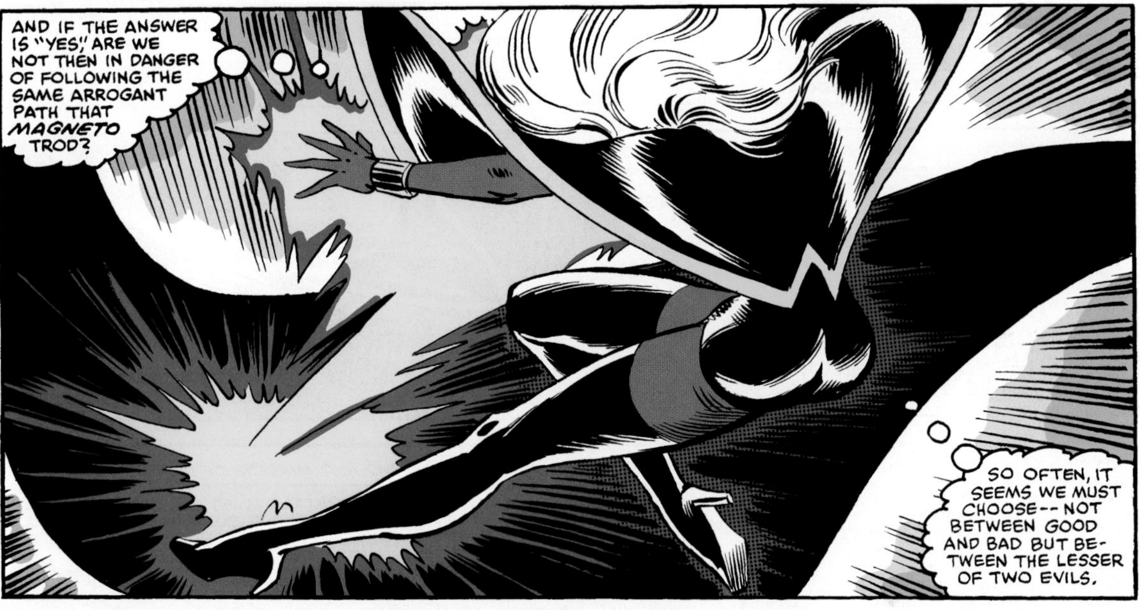
AND IF THE ANSWER IS "YES," ARE WE NOT THEN IN DANGER OF FOLLOWING THE SAME ARROGANT PATH THAT MAGNETO TROD?
SO OFTEN, IT SEEMS WE MUST CHOOSE-- NOT BETWEEN GOOD AND BAD BUT BE-TWEEN THE LESSER OF TWO EVILS.

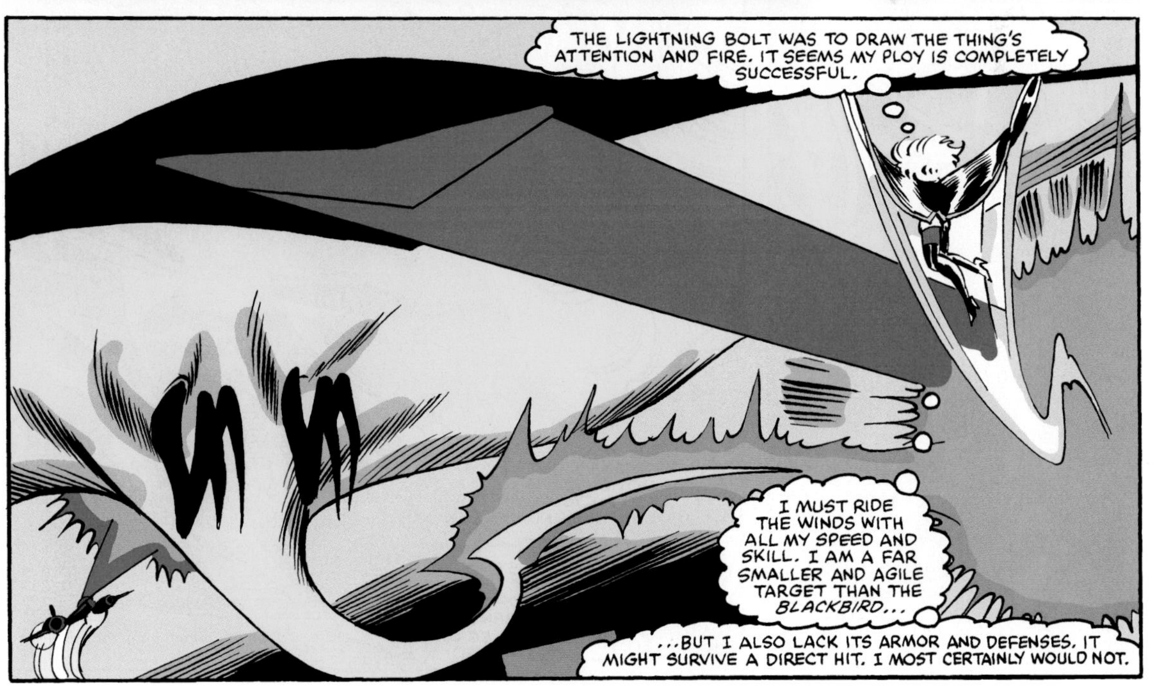
THE LIGHTNING BOLT WAS TO DRAW THE THING'S ATTENTION AND FIRE. IT SEEMS MY PLOY IS COMPLETELY SUCCESSFUL.
I MUST RIDE THE WINDS WITH ALL MY SPEED AND SKILL. I AM A FAR SMALLER AND AGILE TARGET THAN THE BLACKBIRD...
...BUT I ALSO LACK ITS ARMOR AND DEFENSES. IT MIGHT SURVIVE A DIRECT HIT. I MOST CERTAINLY WOULD NOT.

HOWEVER, AS THE AERIAL DOGFIGHT RAGES ACROSS THE UPPER NEW YORK BAY, WHAT BOTH X-MEN FEARED FINALLY COMES TO PASS. AN NYPD HELICOPTER, ON ROUTINE HARBOR PATROL...
POLICE
NYPD
...STRAYS TOO CLOSE TO THE ACTION...

...AND IS MISTAKEN BY THE SINDRI FOR ONE OF THE COMBATANTS.
STORM, CAN YOU HELP THEM?

EASILY, CYCLOPS, PROVIDED YOU KEEP OUR FOE OCCUPIED.
WE'RE DEAD, RIGHT, GINO? THAT'S AN ANGEL, COME TO TAKE US TO HEAVEN.
LOU, I DON'T BELIEVE WHAT I'M SEEIN'!

RELAX YOUR BODIES, OFFICERS. I WILL NOT LET YOU FALL. I WILL HAVE YOU SAFELY ON THE GROUND IN A MATTER OF MOMENTS.
WHO--WHAT--*ARE* YOU, LADY?!?
I AM STORM. AN X-MAN --AND A FRIEND.

SECONDS LATER, AFTER COMPLETING HER MISSION OF MERCY...
THIS BATTLE MUST BE ENDED--QUICKLY! THE LONGER IT CONTINUES--ESPECIALLY HERE--THE GREATER THE PROBABILITY OF INNOCENTS BEING HARMED.
THE WIND PATTERNS I SET IN MOTION HAVE FORMED A CYCLONE AROUND THE SINDRI--EXCELLENT.
NOW I MUST INTENSIFY IT. UNLESS THE FABRIC OF THE MATRIX-CRAFT IS IMMENSELY STRONG, THEY MUST FLEE OR BE DESTROYED.

I WONDER: DO MY QUESTIONS, MY DOUBTS, MAKE ME THE WRONG PERSON TO LEAD THE X-MEN?
I WONDER IF SCOTT IS FREE OF THEM?
SUDDENLY, IT'S THE SINDRI MATRIX WHICH IS ON THE DEFENSIVE...
...AS STORM'S CYCLONE FOLLOWS IT WHEREVER IT GOES, WHILE CYCLOPS BLASTS IT AGAIN AND AGAIN WITH HIS ENHANCED EYE BEAMS.

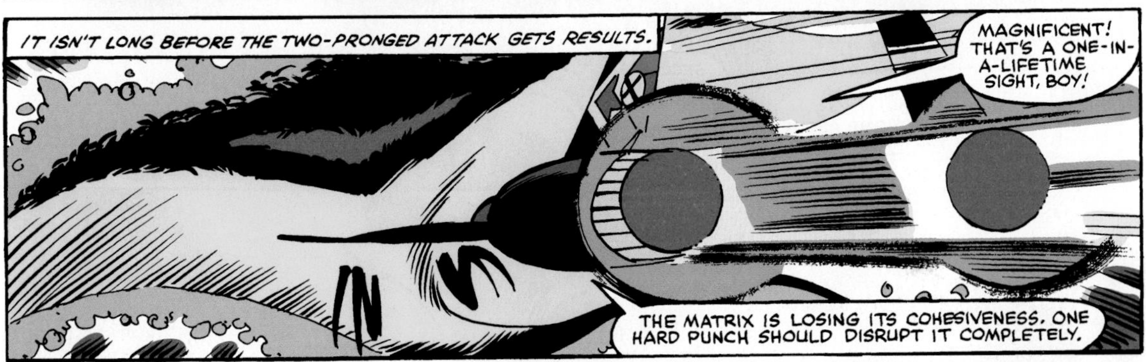
IT ISN'T LONG BEFORE THE TWO-PRONGED ATTACK GETS RESULTS.
MAGNIFICENT! THAT'S A ONE-IN-A-LIFETIME SIGHT, BOY!
THE MATRIX IS LOSING ITS COHESIVENESS. ONE HARD PUNCH SHOULD DISRUPT IT COMPLETELY.

USING HIS OPTIC BLASTS LIKE A BATTERING RAM, CYCLOPS SMASHES THE BLACKBIRD AT FULL THROTTLE THROUGH THE HEART OF THE ALIEN.
WITH AN EERIE, ALMOST HUMAN SHRIEK OF AGONY, IT SHATTERS...

...ITS THOUSANDS OF LESSER SELVES TOPPLING TO THE GROUND LIKE LIVING SNOW.
SOUND THE EMERGENCY HORN!
EVACUATE THE AREA --ON THE DOUBLE!

A PETROLEUM STORAGE FACILITY! PERFECT, CYCLOPS. YOU COULDN'T HAVE CHOSEN A MORE IDEAL SITE IF YOU'D TRIED.
THE MATRIX IS IN SHOCK NOW. IT'S VULNERABLE. AND THE MOST EFFECTIVE WEAPON AGAINST IT IS HEAT.
BLAST THAT TANK FARM--SET THE OIL AFIRE--AND THE EXPLOSION IS SURE TO KILL IT.

"KILL IT?!" YOU MEAN, THAT THING'S ALIVE? I...I THOUGHT IT WAS A CONSTRUCT, A MECHANISM.
IT'S A COLONY CREATURE, LIVING AND SENTIENT. SO WHAT?
I CAN'T-- I WON'T-- KILL, CORSAIR.
THIS IS NO TIME FOR SCRUPLES, BOY. IT HAS NO COMPUNCTIONS ABOUT KILLING YOU-- OR ANYONE ELSE WHO GETS IN ITS WAY.
YOU SANCTIMONIOUS FOOL, WE CAN'T LET IT REINTEGRATE! WE'VE ONLY SECONDS TO ACT.
SECONDS BEFORE WHAT?
STORM, STOP HIM!
WHY? CORSAIR-- DON'T!
I'M SORRY, BUT I'VE NO ALTERNATIVE. I'VE FOUGHT THESE THINGS, YOU HAVEN'T. THIS IS THE ONLY WAY, BELIEVE ME.
NOW, WE CAN GO.
WHAROOM!!

"LILANDRA WAS KIDNAPPED, MY STARJAMMERS AND I WERE IMPLICATED AND THE TRAIL LEFT BY THE TERRORISTS LED STRAIGHT TO EARTH.

"A FAST BATTLE FORCE--LED BY CHANCELLOR ARAKI AND ADMIRAL OF THE FLEET LORD SAMÉDÀR--SET OUT IMMEDIATELY TO RESCUE HER. LEAD ELEMENTS OF THE FORCE HAVE ALREADY ARRIVED IN LOCAL EARTH SPACE.

THEY'RE PREPARED TO GO TO ANY LENGTHS TO LIBERATE THEIR EMPRESS, OR AVENGE HER. AND IF, IN THE PROCESS, THEY HAVE TO REDUCE THE EARTH TO A LIFELESS, BURNED-OUT CINDER--

--SO BE IT!

NEXT ISSUE: DEATH-BIRD!

60¢
155
MAR
02461
©1981 MARVEL COMICS GROUP
MARVEL® COMICS GROUP
APPROVED BY THE COMICS CODE AUTHORITY
THE UNCANNY
X-MEN™
TM

Stan Lee PRESENTS: THE UNCANNY X-MEN!™

CHRIS CLAREMONT * DAVE COCKRUM & BOB WIACEK * JOE ROSEN * GLYNIS WEIN * LOUISE JONES * JIM SHOOTER
WRITER — ARTISTS — LETTERER — COLORIST — EDITOR — EDITOR-IN-CHIEF

FIRST BLOOD
IT'S A TERRIBLE THING TO HAVE YOUR LIFE SUDDENLY TURNED UPSIDE-DOWN, TO SEE ALL THE PRECEPTS AND BELIEFS UPON WHICH YOU'VE BASED THAT LIFE TRASHED AND THROWN AWAY IN A MOMENT OF TIME, A FEW SHORT WORDS.
FOR TWENTY YEARS, SCOTT SUMMERS-- MEMBER OF A TEAM OF MUTANT SUPER HEROES KNOWN AS THE X-MEN-- HAS BELIEVED HIMSELF TO BE AN ORPHAN, WITHOUT FAMILY-- SAVE HIS YOUNGER BROTHER, ALEX-- WITHOUT ROOTS, WITHOUT A PAST. HE LONG AGO RESIGNED HIMSELF TO THAT GRIM, LONELY REALITY.
NOW, THAT REALITY HAS BEEN DESTROYED BY A SIMPLE, DEVASTATING REVELATION: SCOTT'S FATHER LIVES! HE IS CORSAIR, LEADER OF THE STARJAMMERS (A BAND OF INTER-STELLAR FREEBOOTERS) AND HE HAS RETURNED TO EARTH TO SEEK HIS SON'S HELP.
THE REUNION HAS NOT THUS FAR BEEN PLEASANT.

SCOTT, I KNOW SOMETHING OF HOW YOU FEEL...
DO YOU, STORM?
I, TOO, AM AN ORPHAN, REMEMBER?
I THOUGHT YOU WERE MY FRIEND.

I AM.
A FRIEND DOESN'T BETRAY A TRUST, OR LIE. YOU KNEW CORSAIR WAS MY FATHER-- YOU'VE KNOWN FOR MONTHS, EVER SINCE THE X-MEN FIRST MET HIM*--YET YOU NEVER TOLD ME.
AS YOU SAID, A FRIEND DOES NOT BETRAY HER TRUST.
*ISSUE # 107 --L.

I PROMISED JEAN I WOULD NOT REVEAL THE TRUTH TO YOU.
WHY DIDN'T SHE TELL ME?! WE LOVED EACH OTHER--OR SO I THOUGHT--YET SHE KEPT THAT SECRET...
...EVEN WHEN OUR MINDS WERE LINKED EN RAPPORT. WHY?!

BECAUSE I ASKED HER TO.
I'D BEEN AWAY FROM EARTH TOO LONG. I HAD NO INTENTION OF GOING BACK, AND SINCE YOU'D OBVIOUSLY FORGOTTEN ME, SCOTT, I THOUGHT IT BETTER NOT TO REVEAL MYSELF AS A FATHER YOU'D SEE ONCE, BRIEFLY, AND PROBABLY NEVER AGAIN.

I THOUGHT ONLY TO SPARE YOU PAIN.
DID YOU?!!
ARE YOU SURE YOU WEREN'T MOTIVATED BY GUILT, AND SHAME AT COMING FACE-TO-FACE WITH THE CHILDREN YOU'D DESERTED?!
THAT'S UNFAIR, SCOTT. YOUR MOTHER AND I DIDN'T LEAVE YOU BY CHOICE. WE WERE KIDNAPPED BY THE SHI'AR.
TWENTY YEARS AGO!
AND IN THOSE TWO DECADES, DID YOU EVER EVEN TRY TO LEARN WHAT HAPPENED TO ALEX AND ME?!

WE THOUGHT WE KNEW. WHEN OUR PLANE WAS ATTACKED, ANNE STRAPPED YOU TWO INTO A PARACHUTE AND SHOVED YOU OUT THE ESCAPE HATCH. WE SAW THE CANOPY CATCH FIRE. WE THOUGHT YOU WERE BOTH KILLED IN THE FALL.
LATER, ANNE--YOUR MOTHER--WAS EXECUTED BEFORE MY EYES AND I WAS SOLD INTO SLAVERY. I DIDN'T COME HOME BECAUSE I FELT I HAD NOTHING TO COME HOME TO.
IS GRIEF A CRIME, SCOTT? IS IGNORANCE? IF SO, I STAND CONVICTED. DOES THAT SATISFY YOU?

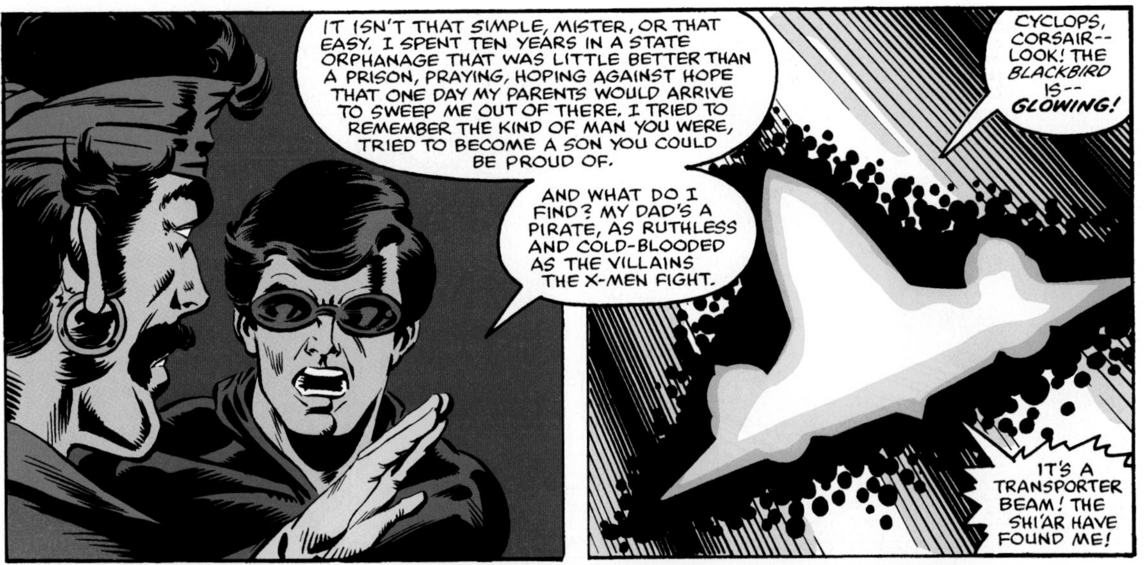
IT ISN'T THAT SIMPLE, MISTER, OR THAT EASY. I SPENT TEN YEARS IN A STATE ORPHANAGE THAT WAS LITTLE BETTER THAN A PRISON, PRAYING, HOPING AGAINST HOPE THAT ONE DAY MY PARENTS WOULD ARRIVE TO SWEEP ME OUT OF THERE. I TRIED TO REMEMBER THE KIND OF MAN YOU WERE, TRIED TO BECOME A SON YOU COULD BE PROUD OF.
AND WHAT DO I FIND? MY DAD'S A PIRATE, AS RUTHLESS AND COLD-BLOODED AS THE VILLAINS THE X-MEN FIGHT.
CYCLOPS, CORSAIR-- LOOK! THE BLACKBIRD IS-- GLOWING!
IT'S A TRANSPORTER BEAM! THE SHI'AR HAVE FOUND ME!
AN INSTANT LATER, FORTY THOUSAND KILOMETERS ABOVE THE EARTH, ON THE TRANSPORTER DECK OF A SHI'AR DREADNOUGHT...
I'M FLATTERED. OUR RECEPTION COMMITTEE CONSISTS OF ARMORED COMBAT TROOPERS AND MEMBERS OF THE IMPERIAL GUARD. THEY'RE TAKING NO CHANCES.

SUDDENLY...
BY THE WHITE WOLF!
WHAT THE FLAMIN'--?!
...BACKSTROKE-- HEY! WHERE'S THE OCEAN?! WHERE AM I?!?
PROFESSOR XAVIER AND THE REST OF THE X-MEN-- INCLUDING KITTY!-- THEY'VE BEEN TAKEN, TOO!
COLOSSUS TRANSFORMS HIS BODY FROM FLESH AND BLOOD TO ORGANIC STEEL...

...WHILE WOLVERINE EXTENDS RAZOR-KEEN ADAMANTIUM CLAWS FROM HOUSINGS BUILT INTO HIS FOREARMS...
COLOSSUS, NIGHTCRAWLER--COVER CHARLEY AND THE KID!
NO, WOLVERINE. SHEATHE YOUR CLAWS. MY TELEPATHIC ABILITIES REVEAL THAT WE ARE IN NO IMMEDIATE DANGER.
HERR PROFESSOR, SEE WHO'S WITH CYCLOPS AND STORM!
I'VE NEVER SENSED SUCH TURMOIL IN SCOTT'S THOUGHTS--AND NO WONDER! CORSAIR IS HIS FATHER?!?
I'M GLAD TO SEE YOU, PROFESSOR, ALTHOUGH I COULD WISH FOR BETTER CIRCUMSTANCES.

GREETINGS, X-MEN. IN THE NAME OF THE SHI'AR, I, GLADIATOR, PRAETOR OF THE IMPERIAL GUARD, BID YOU WELCOME.
LORD CHANCELLOR ARAKI, WHO ARE THESE BARBARIANS THAT GLADIATOR ADDRESSES WITH SUCH RESPECT?
HAD YOU SCANNED THE BRIEFING TAPES I PROVIDED, ADMIRAL, YOU WOULD KNOW. THESE X-MEN ARE A BAND OF MUTANTS--HUMANS BORN WITH ENHANCED PHYSICAL AND/OR MENTAL ABILITIES--GATHERED TOGETHER BY THEIR TEACHER, PROFESSOR CHARLES XAVIER.

"THOUGH FEARED AND HATED BY MANY OF THEIR FELLOW TERRANS, THEY ARE A FORCE FOR JUSTICE ON THEIR WORLD."
REMAIN CALM, X-MEN. I KNOW THERE IS NO LOVE LOST BETWEEN US AND THE SHI'AR, BUT WE WILL NOT FIGHT UNLESS PROVOKED.
RIGHT NOW, CHARLEY, I'M FEELIN' REAL PROVOKED.

CONTROL YOURSELF, WOLVERINE. THAT IS AN ORDER.
ARAKI, WHAT IS THE MEANING OF THIS?! WHY ARE WE HERE? I DEMAND AN IMMEDIATE AUDIENCE WITH EMPRESS LILANDRA.
THAT IS NOT POSSIBLE, XAVIER. IF YOU WOULD LEARN THE REASON WHY-- FOLLOW ME.

SHORTLY, IN A NEARBY BRIEFING ROOM...
THE IMAGES IN THIS HOLOGRAM FIELD CONFIRM THE STORY CORSAIR TOLD ME AND SCOTT.*
AT THE LAST MEETING OF HER GRAND COUNCIL, LILANDRA WAS ABDUCTED BY TERRORISTS AND MANY OF HER MINISTERS WERE SLAUGHTERED.
LILANDRA-- MY BELOVED!
WOW!
* SEE LAST ISH--LOUISE.

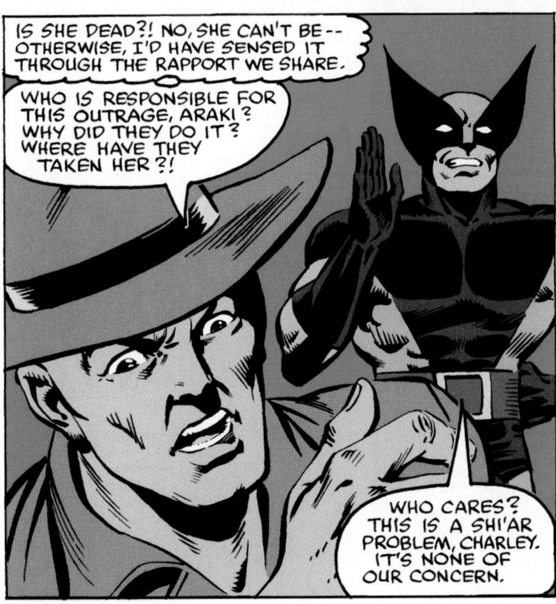
IS SHE DEAD?! NO, SHE CAN'T BE-- OTHERWISE, I'D HAVE SENSED IT THROUGH THE RAPPORT WE SHARE.
WHO IS RESPONSIBLE FOR THIS OUTRAGE, ARAKI? WHY DID THEY DO IT? WHERE HAVE THEY TAKEN HER?!
WHO CARES? THIS IS A SHI'AR PROBLEM, CHARLEY. IT'S NONE OF OUR CONCERN.

WRONG, WOLVERINE. IT IS VERY MUCH YOUR CONCERN.
THE TRAIL LEADS TO EARTH. THE EVIDENCE IMPLICATES INHABITANTS ON YOUR WORLD.
ARE YOU SERIOUS?! WE CAN BARELY FLY TO THE FLAMIN' MOON, BUB. YOU CLOWNS LIVE IN ANOTHER GALAXY!

SUPPOSE LILANDRA IS HERE, WHAT DO YOU PROPOSE TO DO ABOUT IT?
LIBERATE HER IF SHE IS ALIVE. AVENGE HER IF SHE IS NOT. CORSAIR IS ONE OF THE CONSPIRATORS. HE WILL BE PUNISHED FOR HIS TREASON. WE WILL USE XAVIER'S PSYCHIC BOND WITH THE EMPRESS TO ENABLE US TO LOCATE HER.
THEN WE WILL SEND A FORCE OF IMPERIAL GUARD AND COMBAT TROOPERS TO EFFECT HER RELEASE.

NO! I AM SHIVARN'N HALANAU--THE IMPERIAL CONSORT. I FORBID THAT COURSE OF ACTION. IT WOULD CERTAINLY RESULT IN LILANDRA'S DEATH AND THE DESTRUCTION OF LIVES AND PROPERTY ON EARTH AS WELL.
YOU ARE BARBARIANS, LACKING EVEN A RUDIMENTARY WORLD GOVERNMENT. YOUR LIVES, YOUR PUNY PLANET, MEAN NOTHING TO THE SHI'AR.
DO YOU DEFY MY LAWFUL COMMAND, ADMIRAL?

YOU ARE CONSORT, XAVIER, LILANDRA'S CHOSEN LIFEMATE. YOUR ORDER WILL BE OBEYED-- TO A POINT.
I WILL WITHHOLD IMPERIAL ACTION FOR ONE ROTATION OF YOUR WORLD ABOUT ITS PLANETARY AXIS...
...TO ALLOW YOUR X-MEN AN OPPORTUNITY TO RESCUE THE EMPRESS. AFTER THAT, HOWEVER, I SHALL TAKE WHATEVER ACTION I AND ADMIRAL LORD SAMEDAR DEEM APPROPRIATE.

AS A GUARANTEE OF YOUR GOOD FAITH, I REQUIRE TWO OF YOUR STUDENTS TO REMAIN HERE AS HOSTAGES.
DO YOU DOUBT MY WORD, ARAKI, OR MY LOVE FOR LILANDRA?!
THESE ARE DANGEROUS TIMES, XAVIER. I DOUBT EVERYTHING AND EVERYONE.

CYCLOPS, I'D APPRECIATE YOUR SUGGESTIONS IN THIS MATTER. AND YOURS ALSO, STORM, OF COURSE.
I AM TEAM LEADER, NOW, YET THE PROFESSOR ASKS SCOTT FIRST. AS SCOTT SAID, OLD HABITS DO DIE HARD.

THE CONFERENCE IS BRIEF, THE DECISION RELUCTANTLY UNANIMOUS.
I'M SCARED, PROFESSOR.
BUCK UP, KATZCHEN. I'LL PROTECT YOU.
THERE'S NO NEED TO WORRY, KITTY.
I MUST ACT QUICKLY-- UNDER COVER OF OUR FAREWELL EMBRACE-- TO FORGE A MIND-LINK WITH KITTY...

OH!
KATYA!
...AND FILL HER BRAIN WITH ALL MY KNOWLEDGE OF THE SHI'AR. FORGIVE ME, CHILD. I KNOW THIS SUDDEN, UNEXPECTED INFLUX OF DATA SEEMS OVERWHELMING, BUT IT MAY SAVE OUR LIVES, AND OUR WORLD.
SHE IS ALL RIGHT, X-MEN. SHE MERELY FAINTED.

I HAVE SET YOU AND KITTY AN IMPOSSIBLE TASK, NIGHTCRAWLER. SO MUCH DEPENDS ON YOUR SKILL, YOUR INTELLIGENCE, YOUR COURAGE.
YOU MAY COUNT ON US, PROFESSOR.
AUF WEIDERSEHN, MEINE FREUNDE, LORD GRANT WE MEET AGAIN.

THE TRANSPORTER DEPOSITS THE X-MEN AMIDST THE RUINS OF XAVIER'S SCHOOL,* AND THOUGH HE HIDES HIS FEELINGS WELL, THE SIGHT DOES INDEED BREAK XAVIER'S HEART.
FROM THERE, IT'S A RELATIVELY QUICK DRIVE TO A MANSION-- ON NEW YORK CITY'S ULTRA-CHIC FIFTH AVENUE-- KNOWN AND FAMED THROUGHOUT THE WORLD...
...AS HEADQUARTERS OF EARTH'S MIGHTIEST TEAM OF SUPER-HEROES, THE AVENGERS. THE THREAT FACING HUMANITY IS TOO GRAVE, AND TIME TOO SHORT, FOR THE X-MEN TO HANDLE IT BY THEMSELVES. THEY NEED ALL THE HELP THEY CAN GET.
*DESTROYED LAST ISH--L.

REGRETTABLY, ONLY ONE AVENGER-- THEIR NEWEST MEMBER, TIGRA, THE WERE-WOMAN--
--AND THEIR BUTLER, JARVIS, ARE IN RESIDENCE. THE REST OF THE TEAM IS AWAY ON VARIOUS MISSIONS.
A TELEPHONE CALL TO THE BAXTER BUILDING GETS A RECORDED MESSAGE THAT THE FANTASTIC FOUR ARE LIKE-WISE UNAVAILABLE.
WE'RE ON OUR OWN-- SO WHAT ELSE IS NEW.
WE BEEN IN THIS DUMP FOR FLAMIN' HOURS-- WAITIN', SITTIN' ON OUR DUFFS, DOIN' NOTHIN'! WHAT THE BLAZES IS CHARLEY PLAYIN' AT?! WE AIN'T GOT TIME TO WASTE.
AT LEAST WE ARE ON EARTH, TOVARISCH, AND AMONG FRIENDS. THINK OF KATYA AND NIGHTCRAWLER, TRAPPED ABOARD AN ALIEN SPACESHIP.

CHEER UP, BUNKIES! NO SENSE LETTING DOOM-AN'-GLOOM RULE THE DAY--
YRRROWL?!?
BACK OFF, LADY CAT.
I AIN'T IN THE MOOD.
SNIKT

AND I DON'T SCARE EASY! YOU WANT TO MATCH YOUR CLAWS AGAINST MINE, PIPSQUEAK?!
HEY!
YOU EAGER TO LOSE ALL YOUR NINE LIVES AT ONCE, SWEET-HEART?!
WOLVERINE, TIGRA-- STOP THIS!

I DON'T BELIEVE THIS. KITTY BEHAVES MORE LIKE AN ADULT THAN THE LOT OF YOU PUT TOGETHER!
TEA AND SANDWICHES, SIR? ARE YOU CERTAIN YOU WON'T REST, PROFESSOR? IF YOU'LL PARDON MY SAYING SO, YOU DON'T LOOK WELL.
I WOULD LOVE A REST, JARVIS AND, TO BE HONEST, I FEEL WRETCHED.
BUT I'LL SURVIVE, THANK YOU.
WHAT HAPPENED, CHARLEY?

WOLVERINE, I REALLY DO HATE THAT NAME. IF YOU MUST BE FAMILIAR, PLEASE CALL ME "CHARLES!" OR BETTER YET, "PROFESSOR."
I TRIED TO ESTABLISH TELEPATHIC CONTACT WITH LILANDRA. I WAS ANTICIPATED. OUR FOES RIGGED A PSIONIC AMBUSH. I BARELY MANAGED TO ESCAPE.
BUT I ESTABLISHED A ROUGH FIX ON LILANDRA'S LOCATION. SHE IS VERY CLOSE-- SOMEWHERE IN NEW YORK, PERHAPS EVEN MANHATTAN.
WHEN I AM RESTED, I SHALL MAKE ANOTHER ATTEMPT TO REACH HER. BY THE WAY, WHERE IS CORSAIR? I HAVE SOME QUESTIONS FOR HIM.
I MARK HIS SCENT, CHARLEY, BUT IT'S REAL FAINT. HE ISN'T IN THE HOUSE.
NEITHER IS STORM. THEY'RE BOTH GONE. BUT IF IT'S THAT URGENT, I CAN TRACK 'EM, NO SWEAT.

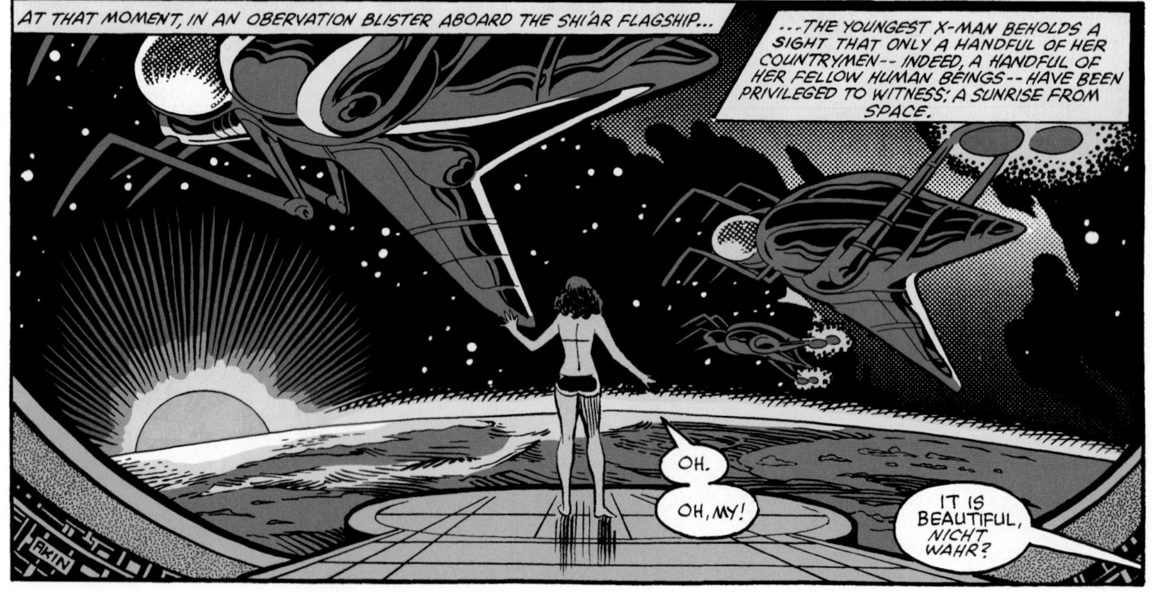

AT THAT MOMENT, IN AN OBERVATION BLISTER ABOARD THE SHI'AR FLAGSHIP...
...THE YOUNGEST X-MAN BEHOLDS A SIGHT THAT ONLY A HANDFUL OF HER COUNTRYMEN-- INDEED, A HANDFUL OF HER FELLOW HUMAN BEINGS-- HAVE BEEN PRIVILEGED TO WITNESS: A SUNRISE FROM SPACE.
OH.
OH, MY!
IT IS BEAUTIFUL, NICHT WAHR?
AKIN

I'VE SEEN PICTURES--IN BOOKS, ON TV, IN MOVIES--BUT THE REALITY IS SO... MAJESTIC. SO BEAUTIFUL, IT TAKES MY BREATH AWAY, KURT, AND LEAVES ME AS TONGUE-TIED AS PETER.
WE CAN'T LET THE SHI'AR--WE CAN'T LET ANYONE--DESTROY THE EARTH. WE CAN'T!
WE WON'T, KITTY. YOU HAVE MY WORD.

ACH! YOU'RE SHIVERING, CHILD! WHY ARE YOU STILL WEARING YOUR BATHING SUIT?! EVEN IN THE CONTROLLED ENVIRONMENT OF THIS STARSHIP, YOU MUST BE CHILLY.
I AM, A BIT--BUT I'VE BEEN TOO EXCITED, AN' SCARED, UP 'TIL NOW, TO NOTICE.

DIDN'T ANYONE PROVIDE A CHANGE OF CLOTHES?
THEY DID BETTER THAN THAT. GET A LOAD OF THIS GIZMO I DISCOVERED.
WHAT DOES IT DO?

IT MAKES CLOTHES.
HMMMN...
ANY STYLE I PROGRAM, IN A PERFECT FIT.
MOST IMPRESSIVE.
COMPLETE WITH MAKE-UP AND HAIRSTYLE FROM THE RIDICULOUS...
FASCINATING.

...TO THE SUBLIME.
KITTY!?!

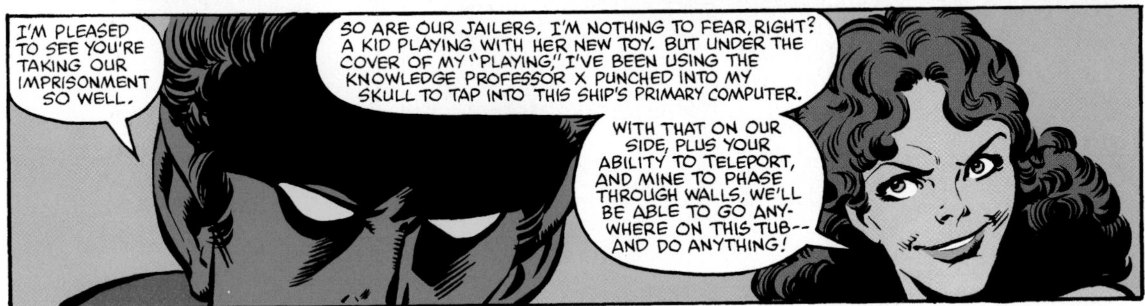

I'M PLEASED TO SEE YOU'RE TAKING OUR IMPRISONMENT SO WELL.
SO ARE OUR JAILERS. I'M NOTHING TO FEAR, RIGHT? A KID PLAYING WITH HER NEW TOY. BUT UNDER THE COVER OF MY "PLAYING," I'VE BEEN USING THE KNOWLEDGE PROFESSOR X PUNCHED INTO MY SKULL TO TAP INTO THIS SHIP'S PRIMARY COMPUTER.
WITH THAT ON OUR SIDE, PLUS YOUR ABILITY TO TELEPORT, AND MINE TO PHASE THROUGH WALLS, WE'LL BE ABLE TO GO ANYWHERE ON THIS TUB--AND DO ANYTHING!

IT'S SO DIFFERENT, ORORO, SO MUCH BIGGER, MORE CROWDED. THE LAST TIME I VISITED NEW YORK, NONE OF THESE BUILDINGS EXISTED. THE ENTIRE FACE OF THE CITY--OF THE COUNTRY, OF THE WORLD--HAS CHANGED, ALMOST BEYOND BELIEF.
AND YET, IT ALL SEEMS SO PRIMITIVE TO ME.
I'VE BEEN SO FAR, SEEN SO MUCH. MY WORLD ISN'T... MINE ANYMORE.
I'VE HEARD SIMILAR SENTIMENTS FROM COLOSSUS.
E 57 ST
DON'T WALK

BECAUSE OF HIS EXPERIENCES AS AN X-MAN, PETER FEARS HE HAS LOST FOREVER THE SIMPLE FARMER'S LIFE HE ONCE ENJOYED. IN HIS HEART, HE KNOWS HE CAN NEVER TRULY RETURN TO THAT. HE WILL NOT--CANNOT--EXCHANGE WHAT HE HAS, WHAT HE IS, FOR WHAT HE ONCE WAS.
NONE OF US CAN.

SCOTT WAS RIGHT. I SHOULD HAVE TRIED TO COME BACK. BUT WHEN ANNE DIED--I DIED. HOW DO I EXPLAIN A LOSS LIKE THAT, AND WHAT IT DOES TO A MAN?
HE WOULD UNDERSTAND.
NO. TO UNDERSTAND, YOU HAVE TO LIVE THROUGH IT.
PRECISELY.

HE WAS IN LOVE WITH JEAN GREY--PHOENIX. I DIDN'T SEE HER AMONG THE OTHER X-MEN.
SHE IS DEAD, CHRISTOPHER.
OH, MY POOR BOY. THEY WERE SO HAPPY, SO... RIGHT TOGETHER. HOW DID IT HAPPEN?
575

MEANWHILE, IN A CONSTRUCTION SITE ACROSS MADISON AVENUE...
TARGET IN SIGHT, MILADY.
AND SO, ONCE MORE THE STORY OF DARK PHOENIX IS TOLD.

AT YOUR COMMAND, CORSAIR DIES--
--AND THE TERRAN WIND-RIDER WITH HIM!

THEY APPEAR TO BE PRIME SPECIMENS, FIT PERHAPS FOR THE *MOTHER-OF-US-ALL* HERSELF.
DESTROYING THEM SEEMS SUCH A WASTE.
THEY ARE DANGEROUS, SKUR'KLL. GIVEN HALF A CHANCE, THEY MAY WELL DESTROY US ALL.
THEY MIGHT EVEN PROVE A MATCH FOR YOUR PRECIOUS "MOTHER."

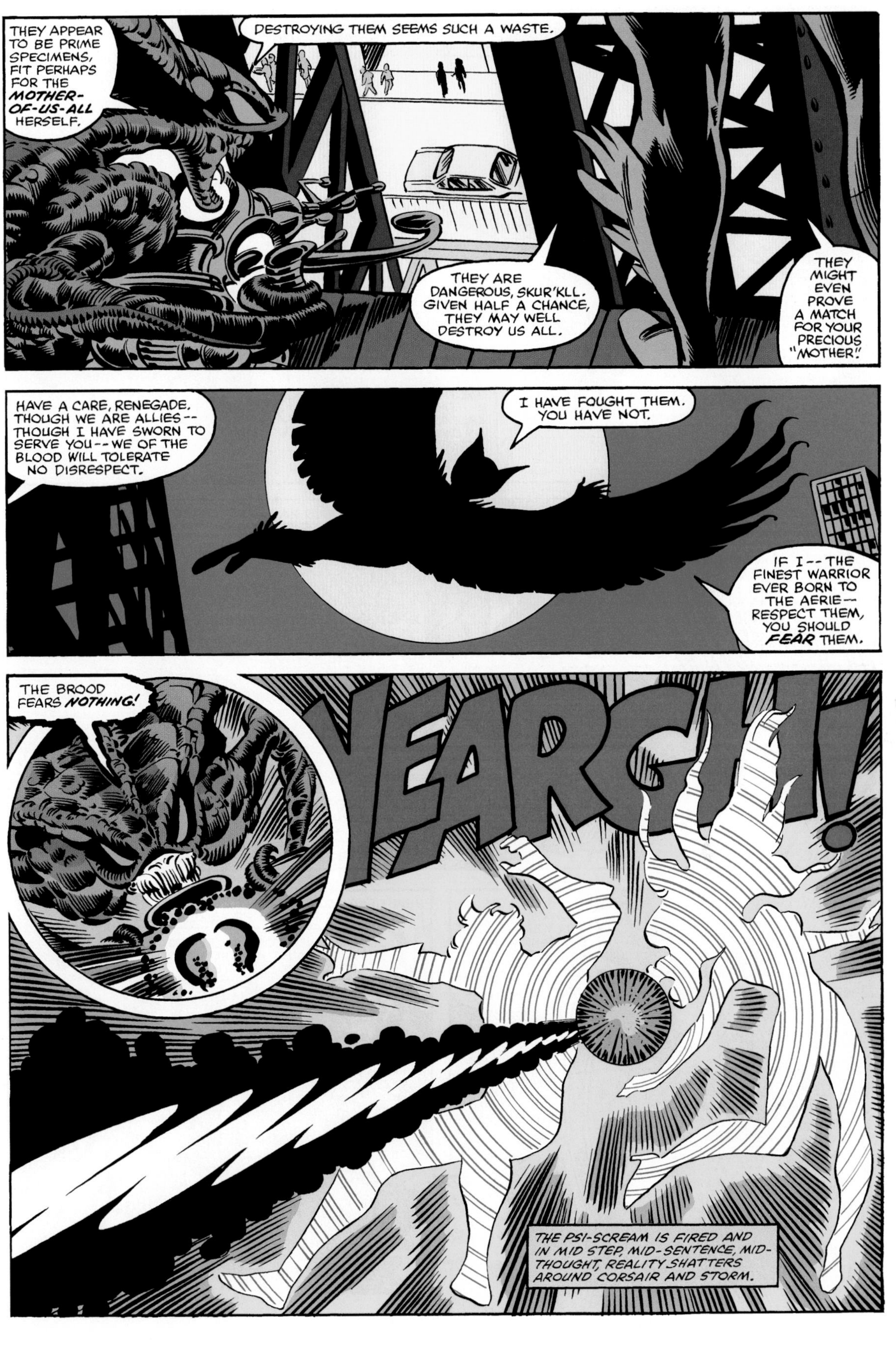

HAVE A CARE, RENEGADE. THOUGH WE ARE ALLIES -- THOUGH I HAVE SWORN TO SERVE YOU -- WE OF THE BLOOD WILL TOLERATE NO DISRESPECT.
I HAVE FOUGHT THEM. YOU HAVE NOT.
IF I -- THE FINEST WARRIOR EVER BORN TO THE AERIE -- RESPECT THEM, YOU SHOULD *FEAR* THEM.

THE BROOD FEARS *NOTHING!*

YEARGH!

THE PSI-SCREAM IS FIRED AND IN MID STEP, MID-SENTENCE, MID-THOUGHT, REALITY SHATTERS AROUND CORSAIR AND STORM.

IMAGES OF THEIR MOST PRIMAL FEARS AND HATREDS ARE RIPPED FROM FROM THEIR DEEPEST SUBCONSCIOUS...
...TO BE TWISTED AND RESHAPED--TO MAKE THEM EVEN MORE HIDEOUS--BEFORE FINALLY BEING UNLEASHED. UNDER SUCH AN ONSLAUGHT, EVEN THE STRONGEST OF MINDS WOULD QUICKLY GO INSANE.

THE PSI-SCREAM WORKED PERFECTLY. THE TWO OF THEM ARE HELPLESS.
I WOULD HAVE PREFERRED A TRUE TEST OF MY ABILITIES. BUT I HAVE WORKED TOO LONG, TOO HARD. THERE IS MUCH AT STAKE--TO RISK A FAIR FIGHT.

I DO YOU HONOR, CORSAIR, FOR YOU AND YOUR COMPANION ARE AMONG THE FIRST TO FALL BEFORE THE NEW EMPRESS OF THE SHI'AR--
--DEATH-BIRD!
UNNNGNH!
BEAUTIFUL, SCOTTY! RIGHT ON TARGET! YOU KNOCKED HER FOR THE PROVERBIAL LOOP!
CORSAIR AND STORM ARE IN DEADLY PERIL. WE MUST AID THEM, CYCLOPS, BEFORE IT IS TOO LATE.

FORCE BOLT-- FIRED FROM THE YOUTH'S EYES--
--STUNNED ME! I'M FALLING!
LEAVE THE LADYBIRD TO ME, GUYS. I COULD USE THE WORKOUT.
DON'T LET THE SNAPPY PATTER--OR YOUR EXALTED STATUS AS AN AVENGER-- GO TO YOUR HEAD, GREER.* YOU READ ABOUT DEATHBIRD IN THE AVENGERS FILES. SHE'S A VERY TOUGH COOKIE. WHEN SHE BUSTED OUT OF JAIL, NOT LONG AGO,** SHE NEARLY TORE THE PLACE APART.
*GREER GRANT NELSON, TIGRA'S REAL NAME. ** AFTER BEING CAPTURED BY HAWKEYE IN AVENGERS #189--LOUISE.

HOWDY-DOODY, FLYGAL. I'M TIGRA, NEW HERO ON THE BLOCK!
I'M YOUR BASIC CAT BY NATURE-- AND YOU'LL NEVER GUESS WHAT WE DO TO CANARIES.
I NEITHER KNOW NOR CARE, HATCHLING. BUT IF THAT IS A THREAT--
--IT IS A HOLLOW ONE!

YIKES! SHE'S FAST AND STRONG...
...AND EACH TIME I CONNECT, I FEEL LIKE I'M SLUGGING GRANITE!
YOU HAVE COURAGE, TIGRA, BUT YOU ARE A FOOL TO CONFRONT ME IN MY ELEMENT...

...SO FAR, FAR AWAY FROM YOUR OWN.
WHOOPS!

NICE TRY, LADYBIRD. BUT SPEAKING AS ONE OF THE WORLD'S PREMIER GYMNASTS...
...I DON'T SNUFF THAT EASILY!

MOST IMPRESSIVE. FOR A FINAL PERFORMANCE.
WITH PRACTICED EASE, DEATHBIRD UNCLIPS A PAIR OF JAVELINS FROM HER GAUNTLETS...
...AND EXTENDS THEM TO FULL SIZE.
MY ENERGY JAVELINS WILL LEAVE NOTHING LEFT OF THE LOT OF YOU--

--SAVE ASHES!

PROFESSOR--LOOK OUT!
WHUNFFF!!
COLOSSUS!
SKANG

YOW! THAT'LL TEACH SOMEONE WHERE NOT TO PARK.
KRAKOW!
THAT "SOMEONE" IS ME, LADY! AN' THOSE FREAKS ARE GONNA PAY FOR WHAT THEY DID!
I'M CALLIN' THE COPS!

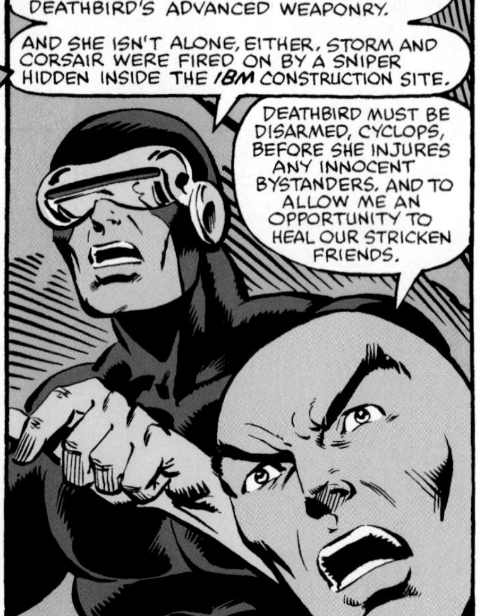
THE POLICE WON'T BE ABLE TO COPE WITH DEATHBIRD'S ADVANCED WEAPONRY.
AND SHE ISN'T ALONE, EITHER. STORM AND CORSAIR WERE FIRED ON BY A SNIPER HIDDEN INSIDE THE IBM CONSTRUCTION SITE.
DEATHBIRD MUST BE DISARMED, CYCLOPS, BEFORE SHE INJURES ANY INNOCENT BYSTANDERS. AND TO ALLOW ME AN OPPORTUNITY TO HEAL OUR STRICKEN FRIENDS.

NO PROBLEM, PROFESSOR.
I'M TRYING TO KAYO HER AS WELL...
... BUT SHE'S AS TOUGH AS WOLVERINE. I'VE HIT HER TWICE, HARD, AND ONLY STUNNED HER.
I DAREN'T USE ANY MORE POWER. MY OPTIC BLASTS AT ANYWHERE NEAR FULL STRENGTH WOULD PROBABLY KILL HER.

THE GRUBBERS FORCE BEAMS HURT ME. I NEED TIME TO RECOVER MY WITS-- AND A BATTLEGROUND WHERE MY FOES ARE AT A DISADVANTAGE.
MISSED!
SHE'S DUCKING INTO THE BUILDING. FLUSH HER OUT, WOLVERINE. BUT WATCH YOURSELF. SHE ISN'T ALONE.
THE MORE, THE MERRIER, PAL.
HEY, TIGRA, YOU WANT TO LEARN HOW TO LIVE DANGEROUSLY, TAG ALONG.

MEANWHILE, OBLIVIOUS TO THE CONFLICT RAGING ABOUT THEM, STORM AND CORSAIR ARE ENGAGED IN A PRIVATE WAR OF THEIR OWN, WAGED WITH ALL THE RUTHLESS FEROCITY THE HUMAN HEART AND SOUL ARE CAPABLE OF.
LEFT UNCHECKED, THEIR FIGHT WOULD NOT END UNTIL ONE OR BOTH OF THEM LAY DEAD.

THE X-MEN, HOWEVER, DON'T INTEND TO LET THINGS COME TO THAT.
STORM, DO NOT FIGHT ME! I AM YOUR FRIEND!
HOLD HER, COLOSSUS! I HAVE CORSAIR!

YOU!
I'VE WAITED--PRAYED--FOR THIS MOMENT, D'KEN! AS YOU KILLED MY WIFE, YEARS AGO--
--NOW I'LL KILL YOU!!
CORSAIR-- NO!
HE THINKS I'M THE SHI'AR EMPEROR!

I COULD HURL HIM OFF WITH AN OPTIC BLAST, BUT I DON'T WANT TO HURT HIM. I...
...I-- CAN'T.

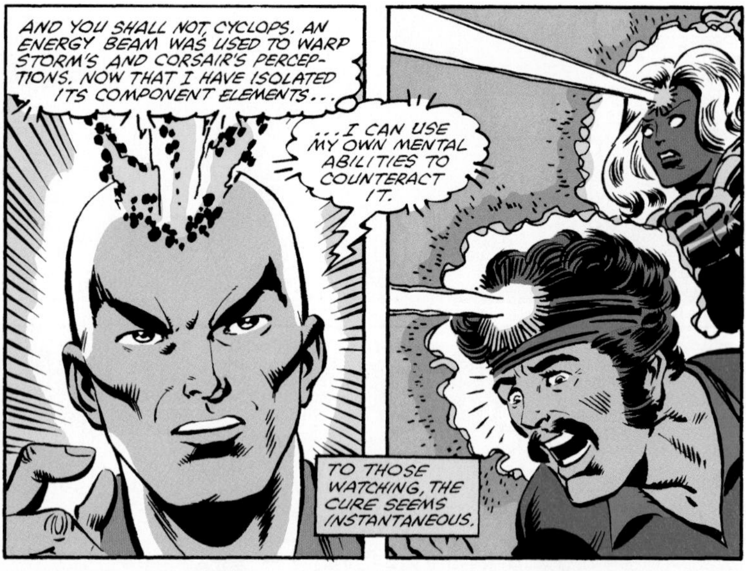
AND YOU SHALL NOT, CYCLOPS. AN ENERGY BEAM WAS USED TO WARP STORM'S AND CORSAIR'S PERCEPTIONS. NOW THAT I HAVE ISOLATED ITS COMPONENT ELEMENTS...
...I CAN USE MY OWN MENTAL ABILITIES TO COUNTERACT IT.
TO THOSE WATCHING, THE CURE SEEMS INSTANTANEOUS.

ONLY XAVIER--AND THE TWO HE SAVED--KNOW HOW FIERCE HIS STRUGGLE WAS, HOW SLIM HIS MARGIN OF VICTORY.
WHAT...? WHO...? SCOTT!
KOFF! KOFF!
REMIND ME... NEVER TO MAKE YOU MAD, CORSAIR. YOU... PLAY FOR KEEPS.

I... I ALMOST--OH, NO. OH, SCOTT, I'M SO SORRY. PERHAPS YOUR FEELINGS ABOUT ME ARE JUSTIFIED.
AND PERHAPS... I PASSED JUDGEMENT BEFORE ALL THE EVIDENCE WAS IN.
THIS WASN'T YOUR FAULT. ONE OF DEATHBIRD'S FLUNKIES FIRED A RAY THAT MADE YOU AND STORM CRAZY.

DEATHBIRD?!
SHE'S PART OF THE REASON I CAME TO EARTH. THE STARJAMMERS LEARNED THAT SHE'S A GUIDING FORCE BEHIND THE REBELLION AGAINST LILANDRA.
IF SHE'S HERE, LILANDRA CAN'T BE FAR AWAY.
WHOEVER THIS "DEATHBIRD" IS--

--SHE HAS MUCH TO ANSWER FOR!
I HAVE A PLAN!
STORM, CORSAIR-- WAIT!

AT THAT MOMENT, HIGH ABOVE THE STREET...
THE CRIPPLED MAMMAL IS A TELEPATH! AND THE LEADER OF DEATHBIRD'S FOES, JUDGING FROM THEIR TREATMENT OF HIM.
IT WILL BE FASCINATING TO OBSERVE THE EFFECT MY PSI-SCREAM WILL HAVE ON SUCH A FINELY-TUNED, AWARE MIND--EH?!!
SNIKT!
THE NAME'S WOLVERINE, SUCKER.
YOU WANT CHARLIE, YOU'LL HAVETA TAKE ME FIRST.
WHO--?!
WITH A CONTEMPTUOUS SNARL, SKÜR'KLL--WARRIOR-PRIME OF THE BROOD--ATTACKS.

THE FIGHT IS AS ONE-SIDED...
...AS IT IS BRIEF.

UNFORTUNATELY, SKÜR'KLL DOES NOT ACT ALONE.
FZAK

STORM HAS NO CHANCE TO EVADE THE TANGLE-WEB AS IT EXPLODES AROUND HER, ENVELOPING HER IN ITS CLINGING, CONSTRICTING STRANDS.
THOUGH SNARED, SHE DOES NOT FALL--FOR HER MIND CONTROLS THE WINDS THAT KEEP HER ALOFT, AND IT IS UNIMPARED--
--BUT THEN, THE WEB BEGINS TO TIGHTEN.

NEARBY, ANOTHER SNIPER ENTERS THE FRAY.
HIS TARGET IS XAVIER.

ONCE MORE, COLOSSUS SHIELDS THE PROFESSOR WITH HIS NIGH-INVULNERABLE ARMORED BODY. IT'S AN INSTINCTIVE REACTION...
...AND A COSTLY ONE.
I'VE BEEN HIT BY SOME FORM OF BOMB!

PROFESSOR, MY CLOTHES-- MY BODY-- I AM BURNING!
CYCLOPS, THAT SHELL WAS FILLED WITH ACID!
TWO SHOTS. TWO X-MEN. DEATHBIRD'S GOONS ARE GOOD.
TIGRA! DIVE FOR STORM! SWING HER TOWARDS WOLVERINE!
I CANNOT HALT THE ACID'S PROGRESS, BUT MY PSI-POWERS CAN AT LEAST NEUTRALIZE THE PAIN IT CAUSES.

AS GOOD AS DONE, CYKE.
THAT SAVES HER. WHO'S GONNA SAVE ME?
STICK AROUND, HOTSHOT. YOU'LL FIND OUT.

STORM DARLIN', DON'T YOU MOVE A FLAMIN' MUSCLE!
I'M-- FREE!!
NOT TOO SHABBY, IF I DO SAY SO MYSELF.
SNAG THE LADYCAT, BABE. I'LL HANDLE THE SNIPERS.

WHEW!
FOR A MOMENT THERE, I WAS BEGINNING TO GET WORRIED.
AS WAS I, TIGRA, A FEW MOMENTS AGO.
THANK YOU FOR MY LIFE.

COLOSSUS!
IT'S ACID. I THOUGHT NOTHING COULD PENETRATE COLOSSUS' ARMOR, BUT THAT STUFF'S EATING STRAIGHT THROUGH HIM.
THAT SMOKE-- IS HE ON FIRE?!
I FEAR MY GOOD FORTUNE... IS AT AN... END, WIND-RIDER.

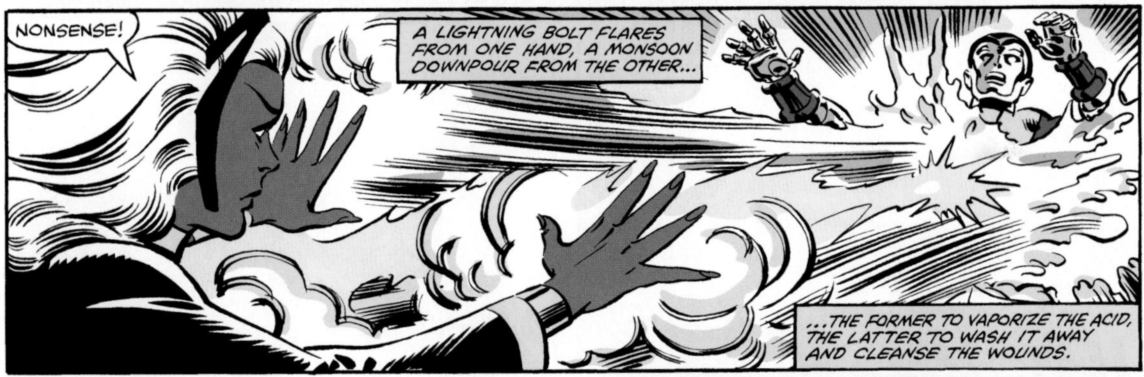
NONSENSE!
A LIGHTNING BOLT FLARES FROM ONE HAND, A MONSOON DOWNPOUR FROM THE OTHER...
...THE FORMER TO VAPORIZE THE ACID, THE LATTER TO WASH IT AWAY AND CLEANSE THE WOUNDS.

I AM A GODDESS OF LIFE, LITTLE BROTHER, AS WELL AS OF STORMS, REMEMBER? IF IT IS WITHIN MY POWER TO SAVE YOU --
--I SHALL.
I... SHOULD NOT HAVE... DOUBTED YOU.
EASY, FELLA. YOU'VE BEEN THROUGH A LOT.

AND HAVE ENDURED, TOVARISCH. AS SOON AS I RECOVER MY STRENGTH, WE SHALL...
NOTHING DOING, COLOSSUS. THIS SCRAP'S OVER FOR YOU. STAY WITH THE PROFESSOR AND TAKE CARE OF HIM.

THE REST OF US WILL CLEAN OUT DEATHBIRD'S NEST.

MEANWHILE...
I'M IMPRESSED, BUB.
YOU ARE NOT ONLY THE UGLIEST SUCKERS I'VE EVER LAID EYES ON, BUT YOU FIGHT BETTER'N ANYONE-- ANYTHING-- I'VE EVER MET.

AN' I'M A MAN WHO VALUES A GOOD ROUGHHOUSE.
FOOL! DEFEAT ONE OF US, DEFEAT ONE THOUSAND-- THE BROOD WILL STILL TRIUMPH!
WANNA BET?

BLESSED GODDESS, WHAT IS *THAT*?
BEATS ME, DARLIN', BUT IT AIN'T HUMAN AN' IT AIN'T NICE. IT CLAIMS TO BELONG TO SOME OUTFIT CALLED THE "***BROOD***," AN' IT'S HOOKED UP WITH DEATHBIRD.
WOLVERINE, IT'S DISINTEGRATING.
YEAH. THEY DO THAT... TIDY BUGGERS, AREN'T THEY?

"THIS WAS THE LAST O' THE SNIPERS, CYKE. THEIR SCENT'S STRONGEST TOWARDS THE BASEMENT. I'LL LAY ODDS THAT'S THEIR HIDEOUT. JUST BEFORE STORM GOT ZAPPED, I SPOTTED CORSAIR HEADIN' THAT WAY."
WHO ***ARE*** THESE SCALEY HORRORS?!
THEY'RE NOT FROM ANY PART OF THE SHI'AR EMPIRE--OR ANY PART OF KNOWN SPACE. HOW DID DEATHBIRD COME TO ALLY HERSELF WITH THEM? WHAT DO THEY WANT?
THAT HATCHWAY MAKES A SUPERB DEFENSIVE POSITION. THERE'S NO WAY I CAN BREACH IT WITHOUT REINFORCE-MENTS.

AND, VIRTUALLY ON CUE...
HAVING A GOOD TIME, POP?
NO COMPLAINTS. WHAT KEPT YOU?
TRAFFIC, WHAT ELSE?
SCOTT, WHEN YOU CALLED ME "POP"...
...IT DIDN'T SOUND LIKE A JOKE, OR AN INSULT.

IT WASN'T.
I DON'T KNOW YOU WELL ENOUGH TO HATE YOU, OR LOVE YOU. I DON'T KNOW YOU AT ALL. BUT I'D LIKE TO LEARN.
FAIR ENOUGH.
C'MON, SONNY...
...LET'S RESCUE THE EMPRESS!

NEITHER DEFENDERS NOR HATCH LAST FOR VERY LONG. BUT WHEN THE DUST SETTLES...

...AND OUR HEROES CHARGE FORWARD...
STAND YOUR GROUND, GRUBBERS, OR THE OLD MAN DIES!
DEATHBIRD-- WITH THE PROFESSOR!
WE LEFT COLOSSUS TO PROTECT HIM! WHAT COULD HAVE HAPPENED?!

SHE MUST BE INHIBTING HIS PSI-POWERS, OR HE'D HAVE USED THEM BY NOW. HER TALONS ARE AT HIS THROAT-- I DARE NOT TRY AN OPTIC BLAST.
WE'VE DONE AS YOU ASKED, DEATH-BIRD. LET HIM GO.
YOUR LOYALTY IS AS COMMEND-ABLE AS YOUR COURAGE, CYCLOPS.

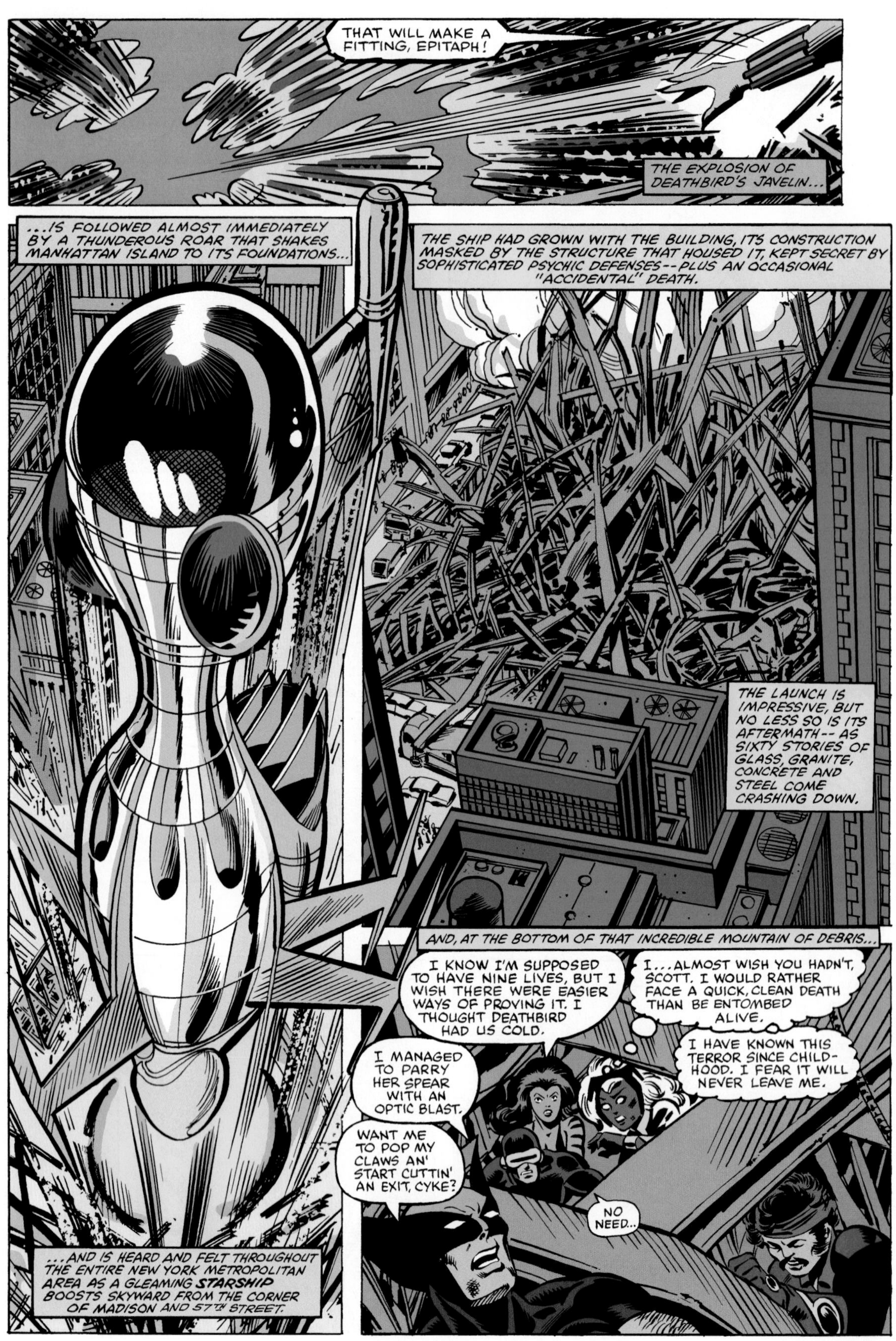
THAT WILL MAKE A FITTING, EPITAPH!
THE EXPLOSION OF DEATHBIRD'S JAVELIN...
...IS FOLLOWED ALMOST IMMEDIATELY BY A THUNDEROUS ROAR THAT SHAKES MANHATTAN ISLAND TO ITS FOUNDATIONS...
THE SHIP HAD GROWN WITH THE BUILDING, ITS CONSTRUCTION MASKED BY THE STRUCTURE THAT HOUSED IT, KEPT SECRET BY SOPHISTICATED PSYCHIC DEFENSES--PLUS AN OCCASIONAL "ACCIDENTAL" DEATH.
THE LAUNCH IS IMPRESSIVE, BUT NO LESS SO IS ITS AFTERMATH-- AS SIXTY STORIES OF GLASS, GRANITE, CONCRETE AND STEEL COME CRASHING DOWN.
...AND IS HEARD AND FELT THROUGHOUT THE ENTIRE NEW YORK METROPOLITAN AREA AS A GLEAMING STARSHIP BOOSTS SKYWARD FROM THE CORNER OF MADISON AND 57TH STREET.
AND, AT THE BOTTOM OF THAT INCREDIBLE MOUNTAIN OF DEBRIS...
I KNOW I'M SUPPOSED TO HAVE NINE LIVES, BUT I WISH THERE WERE EASIER WAYS OF PROVING IT. I THOUGHT DEATHBIRD HAD US COLD.
I...ALMOST WISH YOU HADN'T, SCOTT. I WOULD RATHER FACE A QUICK, CLEAN DEATH THAN BE ENTOMBED ALIVE.
I HAVE KNOWN THIS TERROR SINCE CHILDHOOD. I FEAR IT WILL NEVER LEAVE ME.
I MANAGED TO PARRY HER SPEAR WITH AN OPTIC BLAST.
WANT ME TO POP MY CLAWS AN' START CUTTIN' AN EXIT, CYKE?
NO NEED...

COLOSSUS?
PETER?
SOMEONE CALL AN AMBULANCE!
IF ONE WAS ALREADY HERE, CYKE, IT WOULDN'T MAKE A DIFFERENCE. IF HE WAS IN THE BEST HOSPITAL IN THE WORLD--WITH THE BEST DOCTORS--
--IT WOULDN'T DO ANY GOOD.

YOU'LL BE MISSED, PETEY--
--AND YOU'LL BE AVENGED!
SHOOT. I HATE TO MAKE MATTERS WORSE, BOSS, BUT WE GOT COMPANY.
NO FALSE MOVES, LADIES AND GENTLEMEN--
--YOU'RE UNDER ARREST!
NYPD

NEXT ISSUE: STAR-CHASE!

THE X-MEN THE X-MEN 154

UNCANNY X-MEN #154, PAGE 13 ART BY **DAVE COCKRUM, BOB WIACEK & JOSEF RUBINSTEIN**

60¢
156
APR
02461
CC
© 1982 MARVEL COMICS GROUP
MARVEL® COMICS GROUP
APPROVED BY THE COMICS CODE AUTHORITY
THE UNCANNY
X-MEN™
TM
ENTER--
THE
STARJAMMERS!

Stan Lee PRESENTS: THE X-MEN!

PURSUIT!

I CAN FEEL A PULSE! HE'S STILL ALIVE! ISN'T THERE ANYTHING WE CAN DO?
BELIEVE ME, CYKE. IF THERE WAS, IF IT'D DO ANY GOOD, I'D BE DOIN' IT.
NO FALSE MOVES, LADIES AND GENTS-- YOU'RE UNDER ARREST!
UH-OH. NEW YORK'S FINEST--SCADS OF 'EM, LOADED FOR BEAR AND LOOKING FOR TROUBLE. I'D BETTER HANDLE THINGS. THE X-MEN ARE IN NO SHAPE TO COPE EVEN IF THEY WANTED TO.

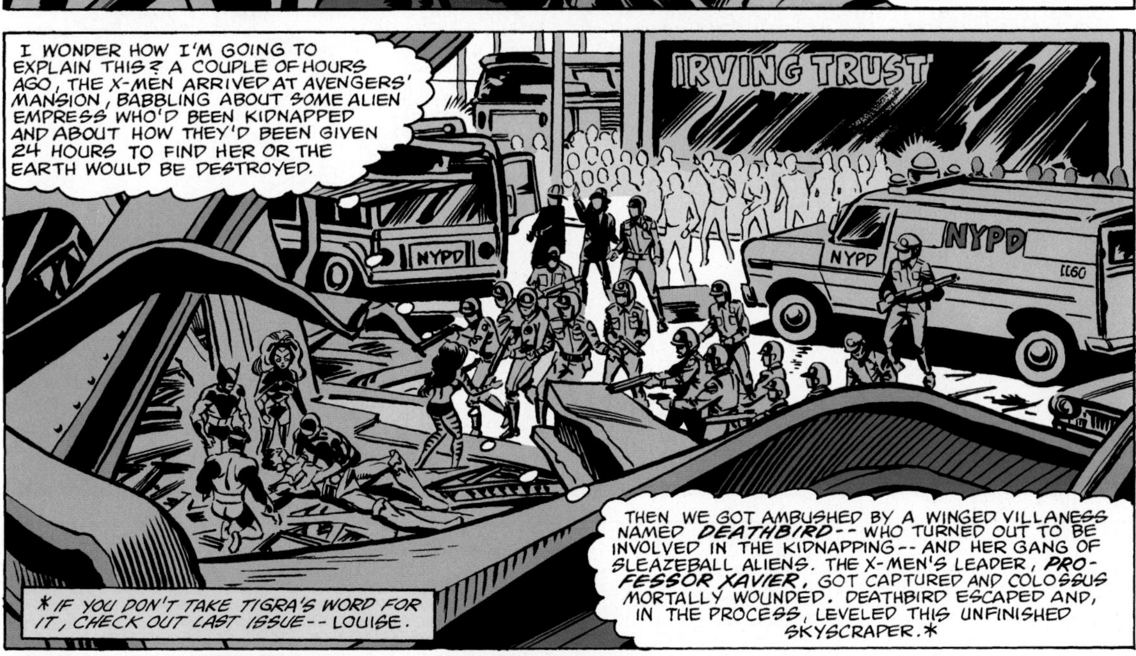
I WONDER HOW I'M GOING TO EXPLAIN THIS? A COUPLE OF HOURS AGO, THE X-MEN ARRIVED AT AVENGERS' MANSION, BABBLING ABOUT SOME ALIEN EMPRESS WHO'D BEEN KIDNAPPED AND ABOUT HOW THEY'D BEEN GIVEN 24 HOURS TO FIND HER OR THE EARTH WOULD BE DESTROYED.
IRVING TRUST
NYPD
NYPD
NYPD
THEN WE GOT AMBUSHED BY A WINGED VILLANESS NAMED DEATHBIRD-- WHO TURNED OUT TO BE INVOLVED IN THE KIDNAPPING-- AND HER GANG OF SLEAZEBALL ALIENS. THE X-MEN'S LEADER, PROFESSOR XAVIER, GOT CAPTURED AND COLOSSUS MORTALLY WOUNDED. DEATHBIRD ESCAPED AND, IN THE PROCESS, LEVELED THIS UNFINISHED SKYSCRAPER.*
*IF YOU DON'T TAKE TIGRA'S WORD FOR IT, CHECK OUT LAST ISSUE-- LOUISE.

WHEW!
I WAS THERE AND EVEN I HAVE TROUBLE BELIEVING MY STORY.
I CAN EXPLAIN OFFICERS, IF YOU'LL LET ME.

I'M TIGRA, ONE OF THE AVENGERS.*
SO WHAT?
YOU CAN'T ARREST US. MY... ASSOCIATES AND I WERE DOING OUR JOB, BATTLING A NOTORIOUS SUPER-VILLAIN.
*THIS STORY TAKES PLACE BEFORE AVENGERS #216, IN WHICH TIGRA QUIT THE GROUP--L.

GIMME A BREAK, WILLYA, LADY? YOU CLOWNS JUST TRASHED A TWO HUNDRED MILLION DOLLAR PROJECT. IT'S A MIRACLE NO ONE WAS KILLED.
LOOK AGAIN, FELLA. SOMEONE WAS.
OH. I'M SORRY. TRULY. BUT SOMEONE HAS TO BE HELD ACCOUNTABLE FOR THIS MESS--AND YOU PEOPLE ARE IT!

AT ROUGHLY THE SAME MOMENT, IN THE F.A.A'S REGIONAL AIR TRAFFIC CONTROL CENTER ON NEARBY LONG ISLAND...
MORNING, ROY. HOW'S LIFE ON THE GRAVEYARD SHIFT?
PRETTY DULL, TONIGHT, PHIL!
YEAH, NO COMPARISON TO THE OTHER DAY WHEN YOU SPOTTED THAT UFO.* PRETTY HAIRY, OL' BUDDY.
*X-MEN #154--L.

YOU'RE TELLING ME. I'VE BEEN A CONTROLLER FOR TWENTY YEARS, MARTY. I'VE NEVER HAD A MOMENT LIKE THAT AND I NEVER WANT TO...
...AGAIN.

PHIL!
ROY, HE TOOK ONE LOOK AT HIS SCREEN AN' KEELED OVER-- GOOD LORD! TH-THAT BLIP! IS IT A MALFUNCTION?
I WISH IT WAS. I'LL TAKE CARE OF PHIL, MARTY.
YOU GET BACK TO YOUR CONSOLE.

"I WANT EVERY AIRCRAFT VECTORED OUT OF THE NEW YORK AREA--FAST!

"WHATEVER THAT THING IS, IT'S HUGE, AND IT'S HEADING DIRECTLY FOR MANHATTAN!

DESPITE THE LATE HOUR, A CONSIDERABLE CROWD HAS GATHERED AT THE CORNER OF 57TH AND MADISON, IN THE AFTERMATH OF THE X-MEN'S BATTLE. NOW, AS THE MOON AND STARS ARE BLOTTED OUT AND THE AIR GROWS SUDDENLY, STRANGELY STILL, ALL EYES TURN UPWARDS...

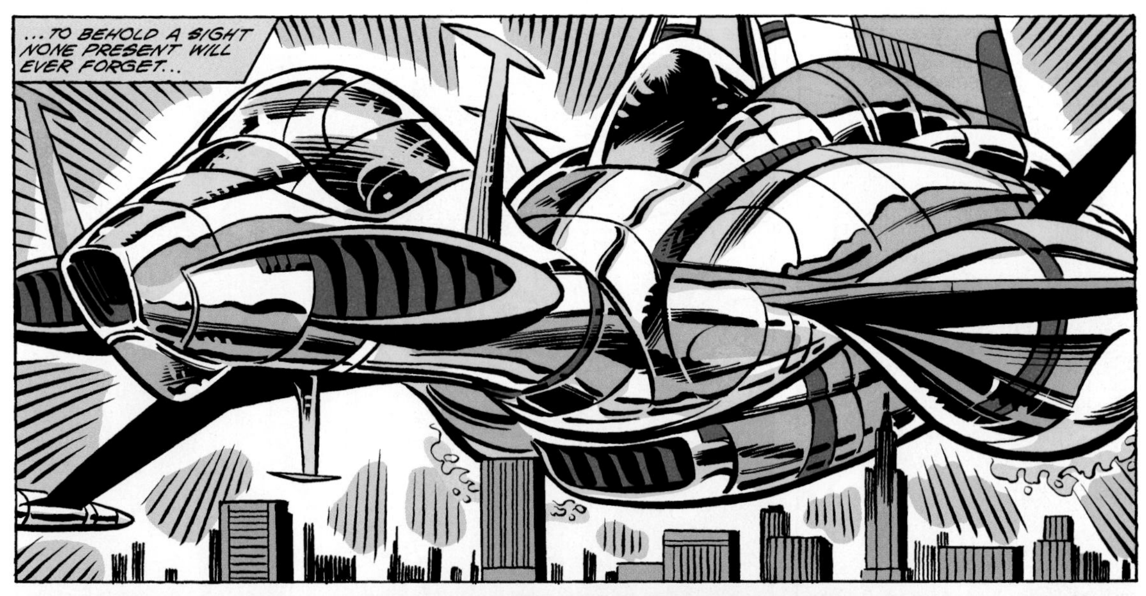
...TO BEHOLD A SIGHT NONE PRESENT WILL EVER FORGET...

AS THE GREAT, GLEAMING STARSHIP HOVERS ABOVE THE CITY--SEEMINGLY CLOSE ENOUGH TO TOUCH--A BEAM OF ENERGY FLASHES FROM ITS BELLY TO THE STREET BELOW. SOME PEOPLE PANIC, BELIEVING IT TO BE A DEATH RAY.
OTHERS STAND THEIR GROUND IN AWE AND WONDERMENT.

THE BEAM ENVELOPES CORSAIR AND THE FOUR X-MEN. THEY DISAPPEAR.
STOP'EM, ARNIE!
I'M GAME, LOU. HOW?!?

AND THEN, AS QUICKLY AS IT HAD ARRIVED...
...THE SPACE-CRAFT DISAPPEARS AS WELL.

ARNIE, HOW WE GONNA REPORT THIS?
PARTNER, I AIN'T EVEN GONNA TRY.
GOOD LUCK, X-MEN. I'VE A FEELING YOU'LL NEED IT.
I...I WISH I COULD HAVE GONE WITH YOU.

ALL THINGS CONSIDERED, TROOPS, WE'VE EITHER JUST BEEN TELEPORTED OUTTA THE FRYIN' PAN AN' INTO THE PROVERBIAL FIRE...
...OR WE'VE JUST BEEN SAVED.

IT IS MOST ASSUREDLY THE LATTER, MY SMALL TERRAN FRIEND!
THE STARJAMMERS!
WELCOME HOME, CORSAIR! IT GLADDENS MY HEART TO SEE YOU!
CHOD! BUT YOU WERE SURROUNDED-- TRAPPED--BY IMPERIAL MARINES! HOW DID YOU ESCAPE?
MIRACULOUSLY, OF COURSE.
CORSAIR, COLOSSUS IS DYING! CAN YOUR CREW HELP HIM?

WE CAN TRY, SON.
THIS LIFE SUPPORT MODULE WILL STABILIZE HIS BODY FUNCTIONS, GIVE HIM AT LEAST A FIGHTING CHANCE. BEYOND THAT, IT'S UP TO OUR MEDIC, SIKORSKY.
THANKS. BOYTHING'S WOUNDS SEVERE, IS LIKEWISE CONDITION.
LOSS PREPARED FOR BE. TERMINATION POSSIBLE.

HE CAN'T DIE! I WON'T LET HIM DIE!
ARE YOU GOD, THEN, THAT YOU CAN PREVENT IT?
I KNOW HOW YOU FEEL, SCOTT. I'VE STOOD HELPLESS OVER THE BODIES OF FRIENDS--AND LOVED ONES-- WISHING, BEGGING, DEMANDING THE POWER TO SAVE THEM.

IT'S OUT OF OUR HANDS. ALL WE CAN DO IS WATCH AND WAIT.
AND PRAY.

MEANWHILE, IN EARTH ORBIT, NIGHTCRAWLER AND KITTY PRYDE REMAIN AS HOSTAGES OF THE SHI'AR TASK FORCE SENT TO RESCUE EMPRESS LILANDRA, OR AVENGE HER.
HOW'S THIS, KURT?
KATZCHEN, YOU'VE BEEN PLAYING WITH THAT CLOTHES-MAKIN' "GIZMO" FOR HOURS. WILL YOU NEVER TIRE OF IT?

ARE YOU KIDDING? I'VE BARELY BEGUN TO EXPLORE ITS POSSIBILITIES. I MEAN, IS THIS OUTFIT SNAZZY OR WHAT? THINK IT'LL TURN A FEW HEADS?
I CAN THINK OF A FEW PLACES WHERE IT WILL GET YOU ARRESTED.
NO FOOLIN'?! WOW!

I ALSO THINK PETER WILL LOVE IT.
THAT'S THE IDEA.
I'M HERE TO RELIEVE YOU, SAPT. ANY PROBLEMS?
NONE. THEY ARE MODEL PRISONERS--THOUGH THE CHILD'S NON-STOP PRATTLE WILL PROBABLY EITHER BORE YOU TO DEATH...
...OR DRIVE YOU MAD. OR BOTH.

WITHIN THE CELL, A THREE-DIMENSIONAL HOLOGRAM FIELD SUDDENLY POPS TO LIFE...
GREETINGS, X-MEN. I TRUST YOUR ACCOMODATIONS ARE SATISFACTORY.
TO WHAT DO WE OWE THE HONOR OF YOUR CALL?
THEY'RE SPLENDID, ADMIRAL LORD SAMEDAR--FOR CELLS.

I THOUGHT YOU WOULD APPRECIATE AN UPDATE ON YOUR COMRADES' PROGRESS. THEIR FOE IS THE SHI'AR RENEGADE DEATHBIRD.
CORSAIR AND STORM WOULD MOST SURELY HAVE BEEN SLAIN HAD IT NOT BEEN FOR THE X-MEN'S TIMELY ARRIVAL.
I'LL BET YOU WERE HEART-BROKEN TO SEE THAT, YOU CREEP.
THEY QUICKLY--PAINFULLY--LEARNED THAT DEATHBIRD WAS NOT ALONE.
COLOSSUS HAS BEEN HIT!
KURT--THAT'S ACID! IT'S EATING RIGHT THROUGH HIS ARMORED BODY!

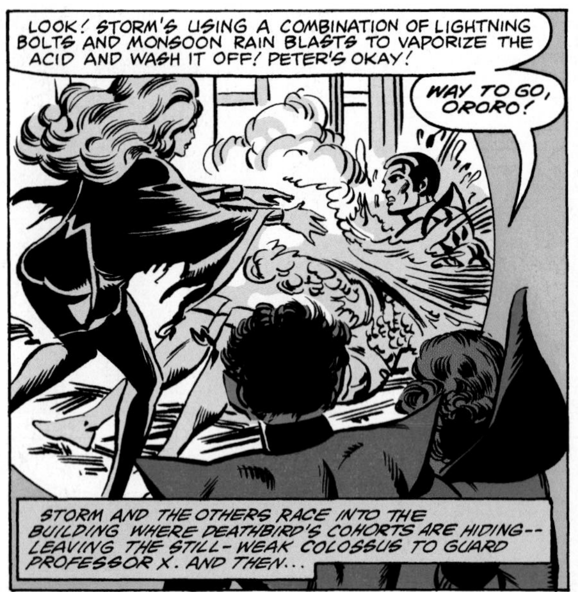
LOOK! STORM'S USING A COMBINATION OF LIGHTNING BOLTS AND MONSOON RAIN BLASTS TO VAPORIZE THE ACID AND WASH IT OFF! PETER'S OKAY!
WAY TO GO, ORORO!
STORM AND THE OTHERS RACE INTO THE BUILDING WHERE DEATHBIRD'S COHORTS ARE HIDING-- LEAVING THE STILL-WEAK COLOSSUS TO GUARD PROFESSOR X. AND THEN...

AARRRGH!!
PETER!

WHY DID YOU STOP THE TAPE?! WHAT HAPPENS NEXT?!?
REGRETTABLY, I DO NOT KNOW. A MALFUNCTION PREVENTED OUR RECORDING OF ANY SUBSEQUENT EVENTS.
IS COLOSSUS DEAD OR ALIVE? YOU MUST KNOW THAT!
THE ADMIRAL'S ONLY ANSWER IS A SLIGHT SMILE, AND A SHAKE OF THE HEAD, BEFORE THE HOLOFIELD GOES BLANK.

OH, PETER. I WANT TO CRY, TO SCREAM. MY HEART--HURTS SO. BUT I WON'T GIVE SAMÉDAR THAT SATISFACTION.
HE SET THIS UP FOR HIS OWN PERSONAL ENJOYMENT--A DOUBLE-FEATURE TREAT--NOT ONLY COLOSSUS BEING KILLED, BUT US WATCHING IT HAPPEN. ALL RIGHT, CREEP, YOU GOT YOUR GIGGLES. ENJOY 'EM WHILE YOU CAN.
THEN IT'LL BE MY TURN.

REPORT YOUR STATUS, LORD SAMÉDAR.
EVERYTHING IS IN READINESS, MILADY. THE EARTH WILL BE DESTROYED AS SCHEDULED. SHOULD CHANCELLOR ARAKI--OR ANY OF THE IMPERIAL GUARD WHO ACCOMPANY HIM--OBJECT, THEY WILL BE DEALT WITH.
I CONGRATULATE YOU ON YOUR PARTIAL TRIUMPH OVER THE X-MEN. BUT I FEAR YOU ARE NOT YET FINISHED WITH THEIR INTERFERANCE. THEY HAVE JOINED FORCES WITH THE STARJAMMERS AND EVEN NOW PURSUE YOUR VESSEL. I, ER, WAS... UNABLE TO STOP THEM.
DID YOU EVEN TRY, SAMÉDAR? NO MATTER, LEAVE THE STARJAMMERS AND THEIR FATE--TO ME. THE EARTH IS YOUR RESPONSIBILITY. YOU HAVE BEEN WELL PAID, ADMIRAL. I EXPECT VALUE FOR MY MONEY--AND ONE WAY OR THE OTHER, I SHALL HAVE IT.

SINCE DEPARTING EARTH ORBIT, DEATH-BIRD'S SHIP HAS BEEN BOOSTING OUT OF THE SOLAR SYSTEM AT ITS MAXIMUM SUB-LIGHT ACCELERATION.
THOUGH IT HAS LONG-SINCE PASSED THE ASTEROID BELT, IT IS STILL TOO DEEP WITHIN THE SUN'S GRAVITY WELL TO RISK SHIFTING INTO WARP SPACE. UNTIL THEN, IT IS VULNER ABLE TO ATTACK.
CHARLES XAVIER KNOWS NOTHING OF THIS, HOWEVER, HIS MIND SHROUDED IN OBLIVION FROM THE MOMENT DEATHBIRD HAULED HIM ABOARD.

BUT AS THE DRUGS BEGIN TO WEAR OFF, AS HIS SYSTEM INSTINCTIVELY FIGHTS THEIR EFFECTS...

...IMAGES SKITTER ACROSS HIS CONSCIOUSNESS.

HE IS A TELEPATH AND AS SUCH, IT IS NATURAL FOR HIS MIND-- AND ITS PSI-SENSES--TO WAKE BEFORE HIS BODY. HIS QUEST-ING THOUGHTS REACH OUT TO A FRIEND...

HE CRIES OUT, HIS SCREAM CHOKING IN HIS THROAT AS HIS EYES FLY OPEN--

...AND EMBRACE A NIGHTMARE, A FIEND FROM THE ABYSS.

--TO BEHOLD THE FACE OF THE WOMAN HE LOVES.

LIL... LILANDRA... IS IT... YOU?

IN MY MIND, I SAW... HORRIBLE--ALIEN--SO... *EVIL*. I SENSED SUCH HATRED, SUCH INSATI-ABLE HUNGER...

IT WAS A DREAM, BELOVED, A SIDE-EFFECT OF THE DRUGS YOU WERE GIVEN. I AM HERE. I AM REAL.

FROM ME, CHARLES, YOU HAVE NOTHING TO FEAR.

LATER...
I'VE PSI-SCANNED LILANDRA COMPLETELY AND FOUND NO PSYCHIC ANOMALIES. IT *IS* HER. THE MENTAL IMAGES I SAW MUST HAVE BEEN HALLU-CINATIONS-- YET I AM STILL UNEASY. WHY?!?
I WAS AFRAID YOU HAD BEEN TORTURED-- OR WORSE.
THAT MAY YET HAPPEN. DEATHBIRD IS NOT FOND OF ME, AND HER CRUELTY KNOWS NO BOUNDS.

SHE BOASTED OF SLAYING COLOSSUS. I WOULD GIVE ANYTHING TO CHANGE THAT.
AH, CHARLES, I HAVE BROUGHT YOU NOTHING BUT MISERY. BECAUSE OF ME, JEAN GREY-- AND NOW COLOSSUS-- HAVE PERISHED. AND I FEAR MORE OF YOUR STUDENTS MAY JOIN THEM BEFORE THIS FIGHT IS DONE.
THERE ARE TIMES I WISH WE HAD NEVER MET, NEVER LOVED.
AS THERE ARE TIMES I MARVEL AT THE GOOD FORTUNE WHICH BROUGHT US TOGETHER. I, TOO, MOURN FOR THOSE WE HAVE LOST. BUT FOR ALL THE GRIEF THAT HAS FOLLOWED US--THAT MAY YET FOLLOW US--I WOULD NOT EXCHANGE OUR LOVE FOR ANYTHING.

NOR WOULD I.
TRULY, LITTLE SISTER? THEN CEDE ME YOUR THRONE AND I WILL GRANT YOU A LIFETIME OF PEACE AND LOVE.
IT IS SUCH A SIMPLE BARGAIN. I CARE FOR POWER, NOT LOVE--YOU FOR LOVE, NOT POWER. THIS GIVES US BOTH OUR HEARTS' DESIRE.

MATRICIDE!
THE ONLY THING I'LL GIVE YOU IS A SPEEDY JOURNEY THROUGH THE GATES OF DEATH!
LILANDRA-- DON'T!
HEED YOUR CRIPPLED PARAMOUR, HATCHLING.

ON THE BEST DAY OF YOUR PATHETIC LIFE, YOU WERE NEVER A MATCH FOR ME.
GNNNGNH!
NO!

DON'T BE ALARMED, XAVIER. HER WOULDS ARE SUPERFICIAL--THOUGH, HAD I WISHED, MY PINION SPURS COULD HAVE CUT HER TO THE BONE.
I WAS FIRST-BORN OF THE AERIE. IT IS I WHO SHOULD WEAR THE CROWN, AND I WHO WILL!

SO DEATHBIRD IS SHI'AR?
AYE. FOR HER UNFORGIVEABLE CRIME, SHE WAS STRIPPED OF RANK AND NAME, CAST OUT OF AERIE FOREVER. AS A HATCHLING I WORSHIPPED HER.
I AM MAJESTRIX SHI'AR. AS LONG AS I LIVE, SHE CANNOT BECOME EMPRESS.

STARJAMMER:
MAGNIFICENT.
THAT IT IS. THIS IS MY FAVORITE SPOT ON THE SHIP.
I LIKE TO SIT UP HERE, BY MYSELF AND WATCH THE STARS FLOW BY. I'VE NEVER TIRED OF THE VIEW. I DOUBT I EVER WILL.
IS THERE ANY WORD ON COLOSSUS OR DEATHBIRD?
IT'S STILL TOUCH AND GO FOR THE LAD, I'M AFRAID, BUT SIKORSKY SOUNDS HOPEFUL. DEATHBIRD'S VESSEL IS SUB-LIGHT-- WE'VE STRONGER ENGINES, BETTER COMPUTERS, WE'RE IN WARP SPACE. IT'S MERELY A MATTER OF TIME BEFORE WE OVERHAUL HER.
ORORO TOLD ME ABOUT JEAN, SON. I DIDN'T KNOW. I'M SORRY.
WHEN SHE DIED, I FELT SO... LOST, SO ALONE--LIKE MY HEART AND SOUL HAD BEEN RIPPED OUT OF ME.
ALL THINGS PASS IN TIME, SCOTT EVEN GRIEF.
DAD... WHAT HAPPENED TO YOU AND MOM? WHAT SPLIT US UP?
"I WAS AN AIR FORCE TEST PILOT, RETURNING FROM LEAVE, IN ALASKA--A CAMPING TRIP WITH YOUR GRAND-PARENTS--TO JOIN PROJECT MERCURY AS AN ASTRONAUT.
NC1101
"YOUR MOTHER--KATHERINE ANN--YOU, YOUR BROTHER ALEX, AND MYSELF WERE FLYING AN OLD DEHAVILAND MOSQUITO I'D REBUILT...
"WE WERE FOLLOWING THE COAST, SOUTH OF CAPE YAKATAGA, WHEN WE GOT A PANIC CALL FROM ANCHORAGE ABOUT AN UNIDENTIFIED CONTACT, HEADING OUR WAY.
"THE NEXT THING WE KNEW, IT WAS RIGHT ON TOP OF US. I TRIED TO REPORT THE SIGHTING...
"...AND THE SHIP OPENED FIRE. I WAS THE BEST PILOT ALIVE, FLYING ONE OF THE FINEST BIRDS EVER BUILT.
"THAT COMBINATION--PLUS A LOT OF LUCK--SAVED US DURING THE INITIAL SALVOS.

"UNFORTUNATELY, THE MOSQUITO IS A WOODEN AIRCRAFT. THAT PROVED OUR UNDOING. A NEAR MISS TORCHED THE FUSELAGE AND THE DOGFIGHT WAS AS GOOD AS OVER.
"WE WERE OVER LAND ANN STRAPPED YOU INTO THE LONE PARACHUTE SHE COULD FIND, WRAPPED YOU AROUND YOUR LITTLE BROTHER...

"...AND SHOVED YOU BOTH OUT THE HATCH.
NC11

"BUT THE SKY WAS FULL OF BLASTER FIRE. A BOLT CLIPPED YOUR 'CHUTE AND THE CANOPY STARTED TO BURN.
"HELPLESS, WE WATCHED YOU FALL, IMAGINING WE COULD HEAR YOUR SCREAMS.
"WE THOUGHT WE WOULD DIE, TOO...
"... UNTIL A TELEPORT BEAM YANKED US ABOARD THE STARSHIP.

"IT WAS A SHI'AR SCOUTING MISSION. TO THEM, ANNE AND I WERE ZOOLOGICAL SPECIMENS, REPRESENTING THE HIGHER ORDERS OF LIFE ON EARTH. WE WERE SEPARATED.
"ON THE IMPERIAL THRONEWORLD, I ESCAPED THE SLAVE PENS AND SET OUT TO FIND HER.

"SHE WAS WITH THE EMPEROR. MY MISTAKE THEN WAS IN TRYING TO KILL HIM WITH MY BARE HANDS INSTEAD OF SHOOTING HIM DOWN WHERE HE STOOD.
"GUARDS CAME TO HIS RESCUE. THEY WANTED TO EXECUTE ME ON THE SPOT...

"...BUT D'KEN HAD OTHER IDEAS.
THIS FEMALE IS IMPORTANT TO YOU, BARBARIAN?
YES!
WOULD YOU... DIE FOR HER?
YES.

SUCH NOBLE SENTIMENTS. THE PENALTY FOR YOUR CRIMES IS DEATH BY SLOW TORTURE--BUT THAT IS TOO QUICK. I WANT YOU TO SUFFER, BARBARIAN.

AND SUFFER YOU SHALL--BY REMEMBERING THIS MOMENT FOR THE REST OF YOUR DAYS!
KATE!!

TWENTY YEARS AGO, SCOTT--YET THE MEMORY IS SO FRESH, SO VIVID, THAT SOMETIMES I FEEL LIKE IT'S JUST ONLY HAPPENED.
I WAS SENTENCED TO THE STAR PITS. THERE, I MET CH'OD, RAZA AND HEPZIBAH. WE BECAME COMRADES, THEN FRIENDS. EVENTUALLY, WE STOLE THE *STARJAMMER* AND ESCAPED. WE'VE BEEN FIGHTING THE EMPIRE EVER SINCE.
FIGHTING. I USED TO HATE IT. THAT'S WHY I BECAME A TEST PILOT, THEN JOINED NASA. I LOVED FLYING, LEARNING--NOT KILLING. I YEARNED TO BE A SCIENTIST, NOT A WARRIOR. LOOK AT ME NOW.

YOU WERE RIGHT, SCOTT, I'M NOT THE SAME MAN I WAS. PERHAPS I'M NOT VERY ADMIRABLE, EITHER. BUT I'M NOT ASHAMED OF WHAT I AM, OR WHAT I'VE DONE.
I UNDERSTAND, DAD--AT LEAST, I THINK I'M BEGINNING TO.
THANKS FOR TELLING ME.

TENDER SCENE. PITY TO BREAK IT UP. DUTY CALLS.
DEATHBIRD'S SHIP ON SHORT-RANGE SCANNERS. INTERCEPT IMMINENT. INTERESTED?
VERY!

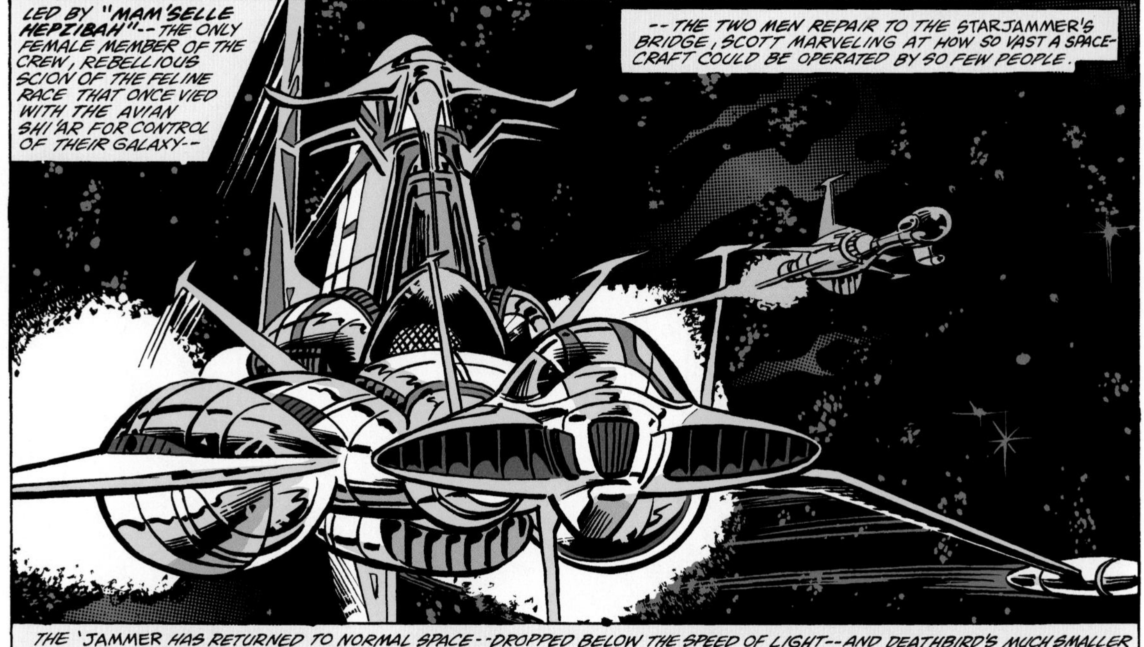
LED BY "MAM'SELLE HEPZIBAH"--THE ONLY FEMALE MEMBER OF THE CREW, REBELLIOUS SCION OF THE FELINE RACE THAT ONCE VIED WITH THE AVIAN SHI'AR FOR CONTROL OF THEIR GALAXY--
--THE TWO MEN REPAIR TO THE STARJAMMER'S BRIDGE, SCOTT MARVELING AT HOW SO VAST A SPACECRAFT COULD BE OPERATED BY SO FEW PEOPLE.
THE 'JAMMER HAS RETURNED TO NORMAL SPACE--DROPPED BELOW THE SPEED OF LIGHT--AND DEATHBIRD'S MUCH SMALLER VESSEL IS IN SIGHT, GETTING CLOSER BY THE SECOND. STRANGELY, IT DOES NOT TRY TO ESCAPE ITS PURSUER--THOUGH IT MUST BE AWARE OF THE STARJAMMER'S APPROACH--NOR DOES IT TRY TO DEFEND ITSELF.

I DON'T LIKE IT, CYKE. THIS CAPER'S GOIN' DOWN WAY TOO EASY--
HUNH?!
WHAT'S THAT ALARM?!
LOOK YOU, K'RIS! THE SCANNERS!
HOW COULD WE HAVE MISSED SUCH A THING?
A CLOAKING DEVICE, PROBABLY. BY THE STARS, I'VE HEARD THE LEGENDS OF SUCH A CRAFT, BUT I NEVER BELIEVED--!

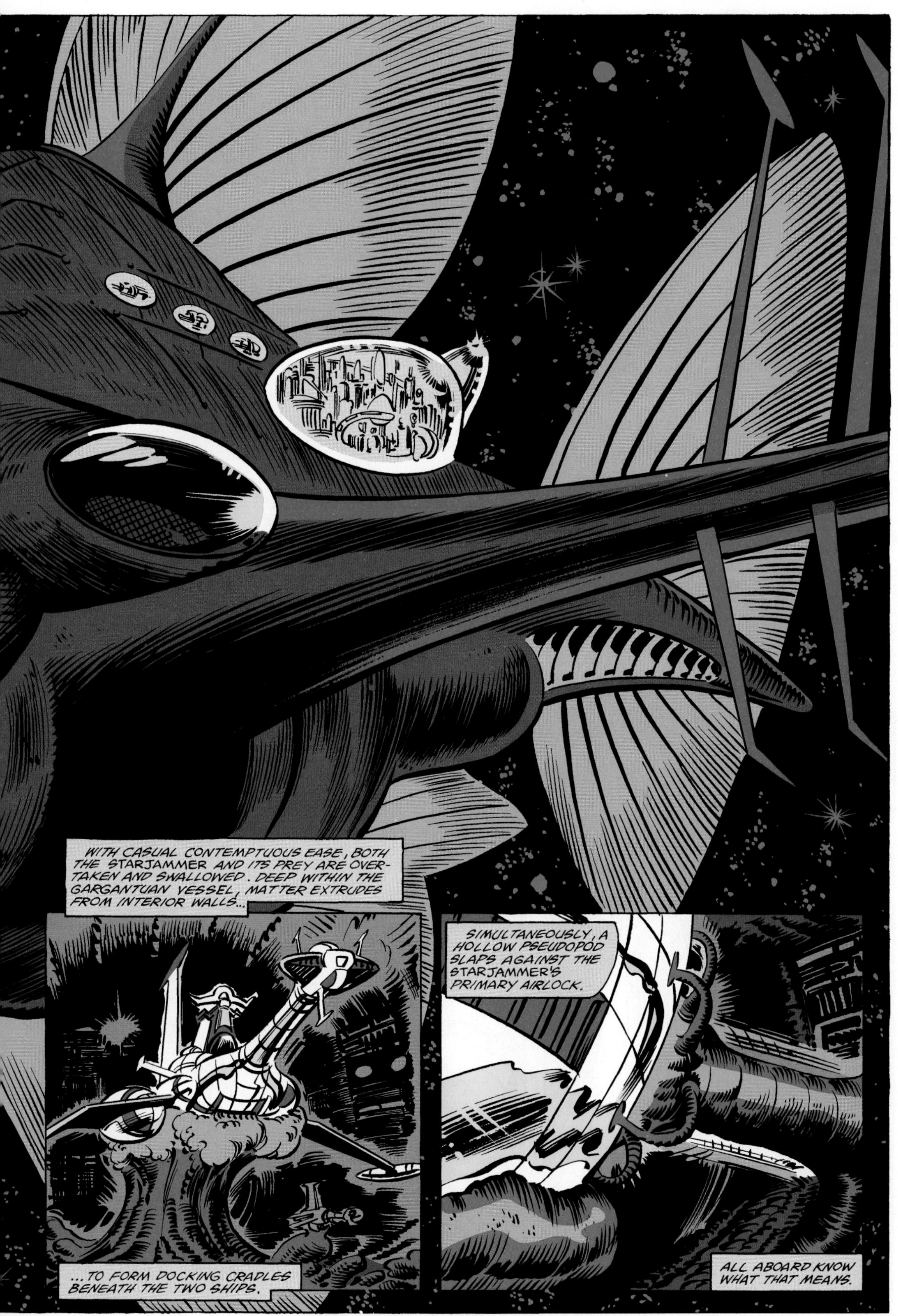
WITH CASUAL CONTEMPTUOUS EASE, BOTH THE STARJAMMER AND ITS PREY ARE OVER-TAKEN AND SWALLOWED. DEEP WITHIN THE GARGANTUAN VESSEL, MATTER EXTRUDES FROM INTERIOR WALLS...
...TO FORM DOCKING CRADLES BENEATH THE TWO SHIPS.
SIMULTANEOUSLY, A HOLLOW PSEUDOPOD SLAPS AGAINST THE STARJAMMER'S PRIMARY AIRLOCK.
ALL ABOARD KNOW WHAT THAT MEANS.

WITHIN THE TUNNEL, A CADRE OF SHOCK TROOPS GATHERS FOR THE ASSAULT, EAGER TO AVENGE THE DEFEAT THEIR BRETHREN SUFFERED AT THE X-MEN'S HANDS, ON EARTH. THEN, WITHOUT WARNING...
BUHWHOOM!
...THE AIRLOCK BLOWS OFF.

DEATHBIRD!
YOU THOUGHT ME SLAIN, BUT COLOSSUS DOES NOT DIE EASILY.
FACE ME, MURDERESS-- IF YOU DARE!

FLANKED BY WOLVERINE AND THE TACITURN, BIONIC WARRIOR, RAZA, THE YOUNG RUSSIAN CHARGES...

...AND MAYHEM ERUPTS WITHIN THE VAST DOCKING BAY.

FOLLOWING IN THEIR WAKE IS A SECOND WAVE COMPRISED OF STORM, HEPZIBAH AND CH'OD.
CHEER UP MY FRIENDS. THE ODDS ARE ONLY A MILLION TO ONE AGAINST US. THAT MAKES IT A FAIR FIGHT!

THESE CREATURES--THEIR VESSEL--REEK OF... EVIL! I'VE NEVER FELT SUCH INSTINCTIVE, NATURAL, ALL-ENCOMPASSING REPULSION. EVERY FIBRE OF MY BEING CRIES OUT FOR ME TO DESTROY THEM UTTERLY.
BUT I SHALL NOT! THEY ARE LIVING, SENTIENT BEINGS--NO MATTER HOW REPULSIVE--AND I AM PLEDGED NEVER TO TAKE A LIFE.
YOU HOLD BACK, WIND-RIDER. A NOBLE GESTURE. ALSO A MISTAKE. SHOW THE "BROOD" THE SAME MERCY THEY WOULD ACCORD YOU.

THERE IS A GENTLER WAY, CH'OD.
AGAINST SUCH AS THESE? WHY BOTHER?
WE ARE WARRIORS, SKY-CHILD. OUR DUTY IS TO SLAY OUR ENEMIES. IF THOU CANST NOT ABIDE THAT, STAND ASIDE!

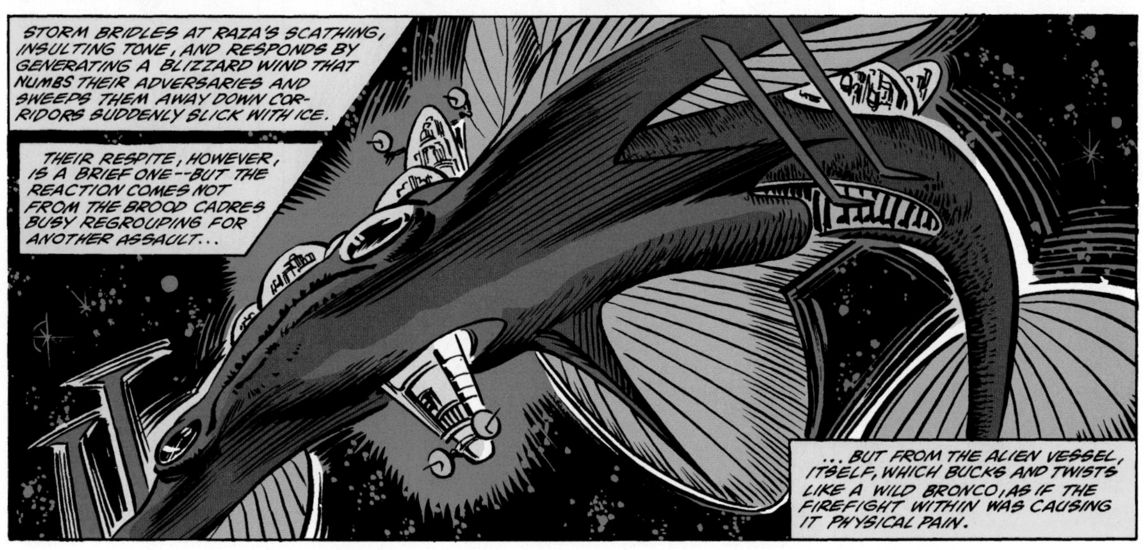
STORM BRIDLES AT RAZA'S SCATHING, INSULTING TONE, AND RESPONDS BY GENERATING A BLIZZARD WIND THAT NUMBS THEIR ADVERSARIES AND SWEEPS THEM AWAY DOWN CORRIDORS SUDDENLY SLICK WITH ICE.
THEIR RESPITE, HOWEVER, IS A BRIEF ONE--BUT THE REACTION COMES NOT FROM THE BROOD CADRES BUSY REGROUPING FOR ANOTHER ASSAULT...
...BUT FROM THE ALIEN VESSEL, ITSELF, WHICH BUCKS AND TWISTS LIKE A WILD BRONCO, AS IF THE FIREFIGHT WITHIN WAS CAUSING IT PHYSICAL PAIN.

FAR FROM THE BATTLE, IN ONE OF THE DOMED CITIES THAT DOT THE VESSEL'S HULL...

CLAN-MASTER, SHIP-SYSTEM CONTROL ELEMENTS APPROACH CRITICAL LEVELS. IT CANNOT WITHSTAND SUCH PUNISHMENT.

WHAT MANNER OF BEINGS DO WE FACE, HAEG'RILL, WHO ARE ABLE TO CAUSE SUCH DAMAGE?! I WANT THEM TAKEN ALIVE. SUCH FORMIDABLE ADVERSARIES MAY PROVE TO BE SPLENDID HOSTS FOR THE MOTHER-QUEEN.

ESTABLISH A ***ZERO-GRAVITY*** ENVIRONMENT IN THE COMBAT ZONE. THAT SHOULD HAMPER THE MAMMALS' EFFECTIVENESS.

AT THAT MOMENT, ABOARD DEATHBIRD'S SHIP...
YOUR FELLOW BEINGS ARE FIGHTING FIERCELY TO LIBERATE YOU, MAJESTRIX. IT IS A SHAME THAT MAGNIFICIENT EFFORT WILL BE IN VAIN.
WHEN THEY REACH THIS COMPARTMENT-- IF THEY REACH IT--THEY WILL FIND...

...NAUGHT BUT YOUR CINDERED CORPSES!
AN INHIBITOR FIELD WITHIN THIS CELL...
CHARLES-- I LOVE YOU.
...NEUTRALIZES MY MENTAL POWERS. WE ARE HELPLESS.
ALIEN "FINGERS" TIGHTEN ON A HALF-DOZEN TRIGGERS...

...BUT THE WEAPONS ARE NEVER FIRED.
ZRAK!
AAIIIII!!

PROFESSOR, ARE YOU--?!
CYCLOPS! THANK HEAVEN!
I'M GLAD TO SEE YOU, LAD, THOUGH I SUSPECT YOUR TIMING COULD HAVE BEEN A BIT IMPROVED.
CORSAIR!
AT YOUR SERVICE, MAJESTRIX, FOR THE PRESENT.

HEY!
GET DOWN--ALL OF YOU!
PROFESSOR?!

MORE ALIENS, CYCLOPS, SNEAKING UP BEHIND YOU!

A WARNING WOULD HAVE SUFFICED, PROFESSOR.
OUTSIDE THE CELL, I'M FREE OF THE INHIBITOR FIELD. MY POWERS HAVE RETURNED!
I CAN STUN MY FOES WITH A PSI-BOLT. AND IN ZERO-GRAVITY, I CAN MANEUVER AS WELL AS ANYONE. MY CRUSHED LEGS ARE NO LONGER A SERIOUS HANDICAP.

WHAT DO YOU THINK YOU'RE DOING, ATTACKING THOSE HORRORS WITH YOUR BARE HANDS?! THEY COULD HAVE RIPPED YOU TO SHREDS. YOU AREN'T TRAINED FOR THIS LINE OF WORK, CHARLES. WE ARE. LEAVE THE ROUGH STUFF TO US.
PERHAPS I ACTED HASTILY AND CARELESSLY, CYCLOPS, AND FOR THAT I APOLOGIZE. BUT THE CREATURES THREATENED ME...
...THREATENED THE WOMAN I LOVE.

I COULD NO LONGER SIT IDLY BY AND DO NOTHING. WHATEVER THE CONSEQUENCES, I HAD TO ACT.
IT WAS A SPLENDID--FOOLISH--GESTURE, MY LOVE.
AND I SHALL TREASURE IT FOREVER.
I CAN'T BLAME HIM, REALLY. IN HIS SHOES, I'D HAVE PROBABLY DONE THE SAME.

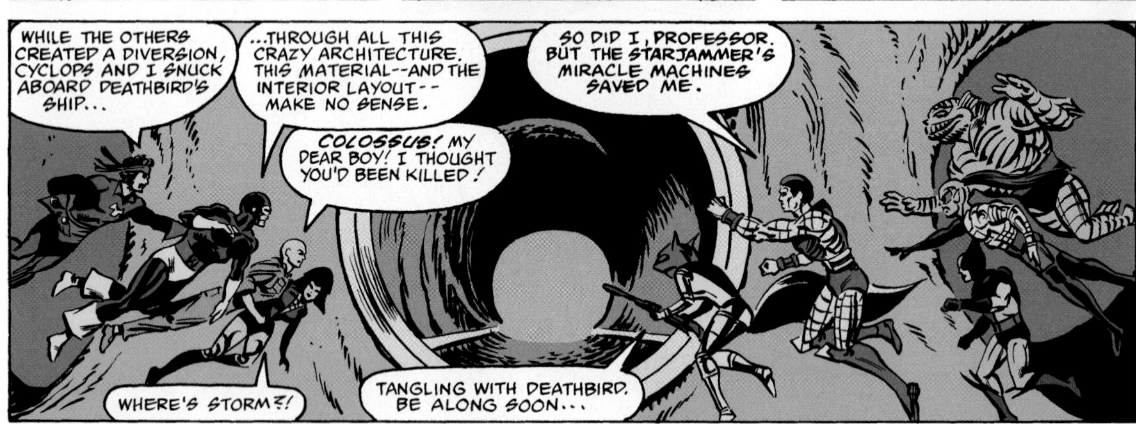
WHILE THE OTHERS CREATED A DIVERSION, CYCLOPS AND I SNUCK ABOARD DEATHBIRD'S SHIP...
...THROUGH ALL THIS CRAZY ARCHITECTURE. THIS MATERIAL--AND THE INTERIOR LAYOUT--MAKE NO SENSE.
COLOSSUS! MY DEAR BOY! I THOUGHT YOU'D BEEN KILLED!
SO DID I, PROFESSOR. BUT THE STARJAMMER'S MIRACLE MACHINES SAVED ME.
WHERE'S STORM?!
TANGLING WITH DEATHBIRD. BE ALONG SOON...

"...IF SHE'S ABLE."
I'VE NEVER FACED ANYONE WITH SUCH SPEED AND AGILITY. SHE'S MANAGED TO ELUDE ALL MY ELEMENTAL ATTACKS.
WHY DO YOU DEFEND LILANDRA? WAS SHE NOT RESPONSIBLE FOR THE EXECUTION OF YOUR FRIEND AND COMRADE, JEAN GREY?!

BY RIGHTS, WE SHOULD BE ALLIES AGAINST THE EMPIRE. WE ARE KINDRED SOULS, WIND-RIDER. JOIN ME!
OR DIE!
IN NO WAY ARE WE ALIKE, DEATHBIRD. AND WHATEVER LILANDRA IS--GOOD OR BAD--

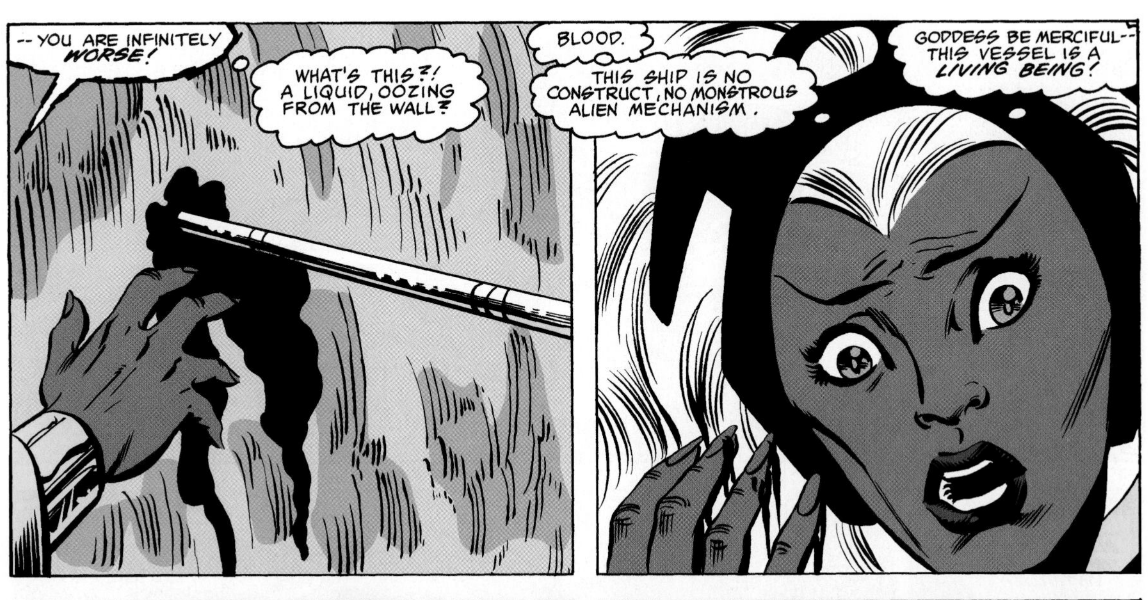
--YOU ARE INFINITELY WORSE!
WHAT'S THIS?! A LIQUID, OOZING FROM THE WALL?
BLOOD.
THIS SHIP IS NO CONSTRUCT, NO MONSTROUS ALIEN MECHANISM.
GODDESS BE MERCIFUL-- THIS VESSEL IS A LIVING BEING!

WHUNFF!
YOU ARE TOO EASILY DISTRACTED, TERRAN. THIS MISTAKE WILL BE YOUR LAST.
HAEG'RILL, OPEN THE PORTAL!
AT DEATHBIRD'S SHOUTED COMMAND, A PORTION OF THE WALL IRISES OPEN, CREATING A MOMENTARY, NIGH-IRRESISTABLE WHIRLPOOL OF AIR...
...THAT SWEEPS THE SEMI-CONSCIOUS STORM OUT OF THE DOCKING BAY...

...AND INTO SPACE.

FORTUNATELY, HER EXIT DOES NOT GO UNNOTICED.
THERE SHE IS!
SHE'LL DIE UNLESS WE REACH HER. CAN WE DO IT?! IS THERE TIME?
ANALYSIS, WALDO.
ALLOWING FOR STORM'S MUTANT PHYSIOLOGY AND THE ENVIRONMENT PARAMETERS-- TO AVOID TERMINATION OF HER LIFE FUNCTIONS, RESCUE MUST BE EFFECTED WITHIN THIRTY SECONDS.
30...

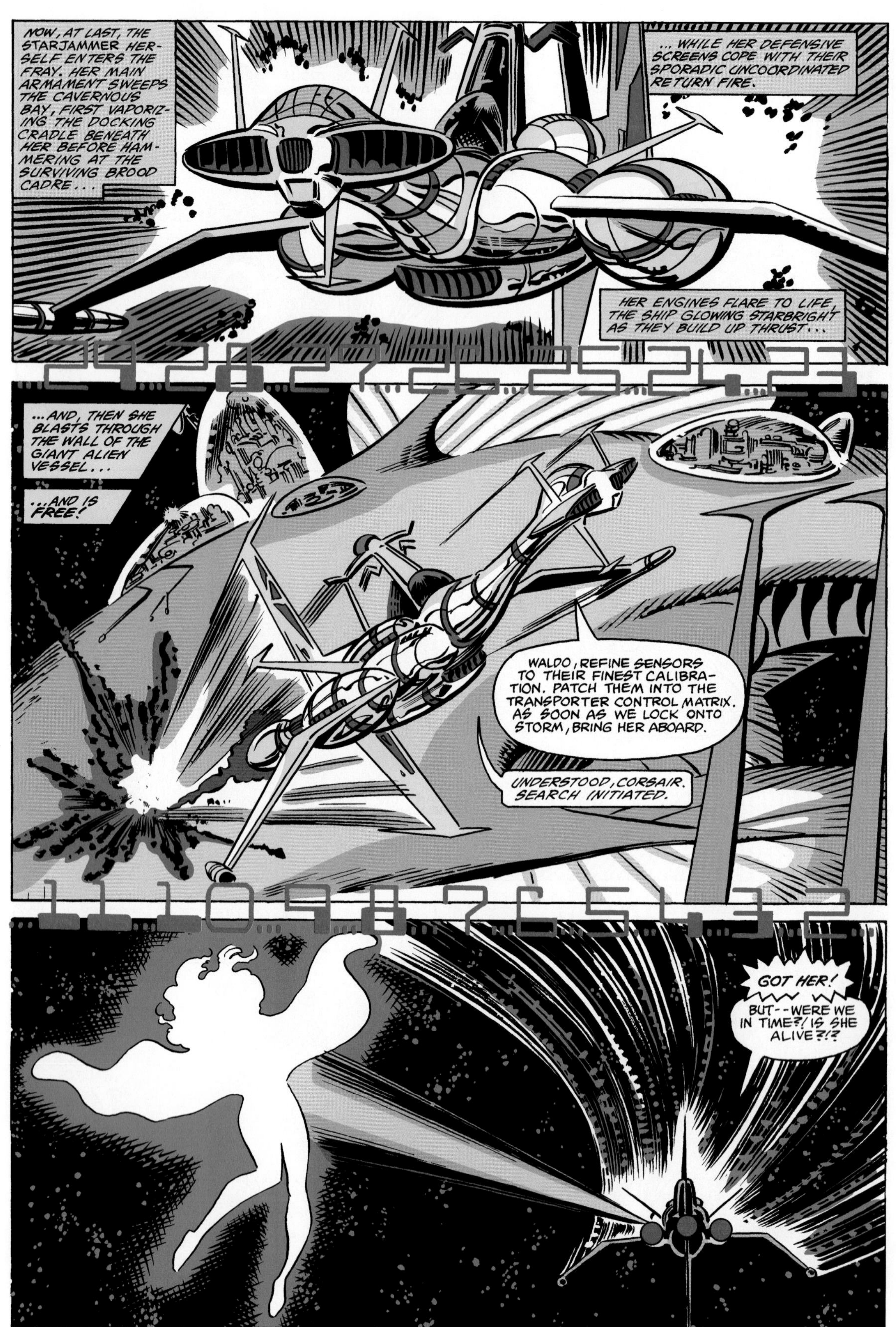
NOW, AT LAST, THE STARJAMMER HERSELF ENTERS THE FRAY. HER MAIN ARMAMENT SWEEPS THE CAVERNOUS BAY, FIRST VAPORIZING THE DOCKING CRADLE BENEATH HER BEFORE HAMMERING AT THE SURVIVING BROOD CADRE...
... WHILE HER DEFENSIVE SCREENS COPE WITH THEIR SPORADIC UNCOORDINATED RETURN FIRE.
HER ENGINES FLARE TO LIFE, THE SHIP GLOWING STARBRIGHT AS THEY BUILD UP THRUST...
29...28...27...26...25...24...23
...AND, THEN SHE BLASTS THROUGH THE WALL OF THE GIANT ALIEN VESSEL...
...AND IS FREE!
WALDO, REFINE SENSORS TO THEIR FINEST CALIBRATION. PATCH THEM INTO THE TRANSPORTER CONTROL MATRIX. AS SOON AS WE LOCK ONTO STORM, BRING HER ABOARD.
UNDERSTOOD, CORSAIR. SEARCH INITIATED.
11...10...9...8...7...6...5...4...3...2
GOT HER!
BUT--WERE WE IN TIME?! IS SHE ALIVE?!?

MUCH LATER AND FAR AWAY...
HOW DO YOU FEEL, ORORO? YOU HAD US PRETTY WORRIED FOR AWHILE.
FROZEN.
BUT GRATEFUL TO BE FEELING ANYTHING AT ALL.
PROFESSOR! THEN SCOTT'S PLAN WORKED!

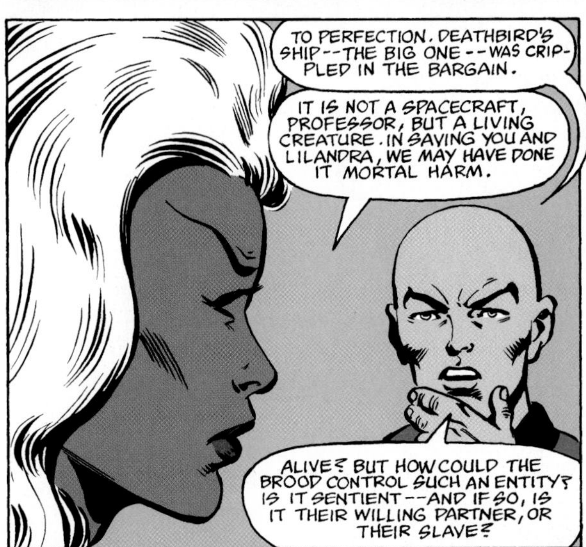
TO PERFECTION. DEATHBIRD'S SHIP--THE BIG ONE--WAS CRIPPLED IN THE BARGAIN.
IT IS NOT A SPACECRAFT, PROFESSOR, BUT A LIVING CREATURE. IN SAVING YOU AND LILANDRA, WE MAY HAVE DONE IT MORTAL HARM.
ALIVE? BUT HOW COULD THE BROOD CONTROL SUCH AN ENTITY? IS IT SENTIENT--AND IF SO, IS IT THEIR WILLING PARTNER, OR THEIR SLAVE?

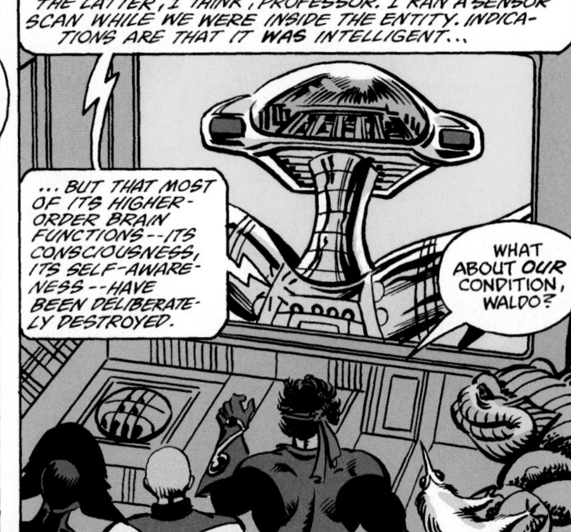
THE LATTER, I THINK, PROFESSOR. I RAN A SENSOR SCAN WHILE WE WERE INSIDE THE ENTITY. INDICATIONS ARE THAT IT WAS INTELLIGENT...
...BUT THAT MOST OF ITS HIGHER-ORDER BRAIN FUNCTIONS--ITS CONSCIOUSNESS, ITS SELF-AWARENESS--HAVE BEEN DELIBERATELY DESTROYED.
WHAT ABOUT OUR CONDITION, WALDO?

IT COULD BE WORSE. WE SUFFERED SOME DAMAGE. I ESTIMATE IT'LL TAKE US 24 HOURS TO EFFECT REPAIRS AND RETURN TO EARTH.
NO! IN LESS THAN SIX HOURS, CHANCELLOR ARAKI'S DEADLINE, I WILL EXPIRE. IF WE CANNOT CONTACT HIM AND ASSURE HIM THAT I AM SAFE, HE WILL DESTROY THE EARTH!
I'M SORRY, MAJESTRIX, BUT THERE IS NO WAY THE STARJAMMER CAN REACH THERE IN TIME. IF WE ARE TERRA'S ONLY HOPE, THEN I'M AFRAID THAT PLANET MAY WELL BE DOOMED!
NEXT:
HIDE-'N-SEEK!
A MATTER OF LIFE AND DEATH!

60¢
157
MAY
02461
© 1982 MARVEL COMICS GROUP
MARVEL® COMICS GROUP
APPROVED BY THE COMICS CODE AUTHORITY
THE UNCANNY
X-MEN™
TM
IT'S PHOENIX! BUT SHE'S DEAD!
SURELY YOU KNOW THAT A PHOENIX DIES--
--ONLY TO BE REBORN AGAIN!
COCKRUM/WIACEK

Stan Lee PRESENTS: THE UNCANNY X-MEN!™
CHRIS CLAREMONT writer * DAVE COCKRUM & BOB WIACEK artists * JANICE CHIANG letterer * DON WARFIELD colorist * LOUISE JONES editor * JIM SHOOTER editor-in-chief
HIDE-'N'-SEEK!
JUST INSIDE THE ORBIT OF PLUTO--OVER TEN BILLION KILOMETERS FROM EARTH--AND FAR BELOW THE PLANE OF THE ECLIPTIC, THE STARJAMMER FLOATS MOTIONLESS IN DEEP SPACE. DAMAGED DURING HER RECENT ESCAPE FROM A FORCE OF UNKNOWN ALIENS*, SHE IS UNDERGOING NECESSARY REPAIRS AT THE HANDS OF HER CREW, LIKEWISE CALLED STAR-JAMMERS, AND THEIR PASSENGERS, THE UNCANNY X-MEN.
BOTH TEAMS ARE HEROES IN THE TRUEST SENSE OF THE WORD, YET, IRONICALLY, TO THEIR RESPECTIVE CULTURES, BOTH ARE OUTLAWS. AS A RESULT, THEIRS HAVE BEEN HARD, DANGEROUS LIVES.
HOW MUCH LONGER, CORSAIR?! EACH SECOND WE DELAY BRINGS THE EARTH CLOSER TO ITS DESTRUCTION!
THE JOB HAS TO BE DONE RIGHT, CYCLOPS, YOU KNOW THAT. IN SPACE--ESPECIALLY IN OUR LINE OF WORK--THERE'S NO MARGIN FOR ERROR.
WE'RE MOVING AS FAST AS WE CAN, AND DOING THE BEST WE CAN. WE'LL HAVE TO BE CONTENT WITH THAT.
*LAST ISH--LOUISE.

NORMALLY, THIS OPERATION WOULD BE CARRIED OUT BY THE SHIP'S ROBOTS, UNDER THE DIRECTION OF THE PRIME COMPUTER, WALDO...
...BUT TO SAVE TIME, THE X-MEN ARE LENDING A HAND. COLOSSUS, IN HIS SUPER-STRONG ARMORED FORM, PEELS BACK HUNKS OF HULL PLATING...

...WHILE WOLVERINE-- EXTRUDING ADAMANTIUM CLAWS FROM THEIR HOUSINGS IN HIS FOREARMS THROUGH APERTURES IN THE BACKS OF HIS HANDS AND, FINALLY, THROUGH SPECIAL GASKETS IN HIS PRESSURE SUIT--
--CUTS THE WRECKAGE FREE.

THEN RAZA--ONE OF THE STARJAMMERS-- USES A MAGNABEAM TO SHUNT THE DEBRIS...

...THROUGH AN ACCESS HATCH TO THE SHIP'S CONVERTORS...
...WHERE IT WILL BE RECYCLED FOR FUTURE USE.

AHHH, WOLVERINE, MY FRIEND, I HAVE NEVER SEEN SO MANY STARS. IT IS A GLORIOUS SIGHT.
ENJOY IT, BUB. YOU'RE PROBABLY ONE OF THE FIRST PEOPLE--CERTAINLY THE FIRST RUSSIAN-- TOO SEE THE MILKY WAY FROM THIS ANGLE.
AND TO THINK--TO KNOW-- THAT THERE IS LIFE OUT THERE. THAT HUMANITY IS NOT ALONE IN THE UNIVERSE.
IF WE AREN'T LUCKY, PETEY, HUMANITY MAY SOON BE DEAD.
I HAVE NOT FORGOTTEN.

NOR HAVE I FORGOTTEN HOW CLOSE I CAME TO MY OWN DEATH.*
THAT HAS PERHAPS MADE ME APPRECIATE THE ENDLESS WONDER OF LIFE ALL THE MORE.
AS THEY MOVE ALONG THE HULL, COLOSSUS WINCES WITH UNACCUSTOMED PAIN AND ABSENTLY RUBS HIS CHEST.
A MIRACLE--THE STARJAMMERS' ADVANCED MEDICAL TECHNOLOGY--HEALED HIS MORTAL WOUNDS ONLY HOURS AGO. SINCE THEN, HE HAS FOUGHT AND WORKED AS IF HE WAS IN PERFECT HEALTH.
YOU'RE A POET, COLOSSUS.
TOVARISCH, WOLVERINE--I WISH I WAS.
*SEE X-MEN'S #'S 155 & 156--L.

AS HE STRAINS TO SHIFT ANOTHER SECTION, HE WONDERS BELATEDLY IF THAT WAS A MISTAKE. THEN WITHOUT WARNING...
AN EXPLOSION--WOLVERINE!

RELAX, PETEY, I'M OKAY. MY SUIT'S INTACT. I'M NOT LOSING ATMOSPHERE, OR--WAITAMINNIT!
MY BACKPACK THRUSTERS HAVE IGNITED!
I CAN'T SHUT 'EM DOWN. THEY'RE SHOOTIN' ME AWAY FROM THE SHIP!

NO FEAR, APELING. RESCUE IMMINANT.
TOO MUCH CLUTTER AROUND THE SHIP. TINY TARGET LIKE WOLVIE HARD TO SCAN.
IF VISUAL CONTACT LOST, TAKE FOREVER TO FIND HIM AGAIN. TIME WE CANNOT SPARE.
BEHIND MAM'SELLE HEPZIBAH, COLOSSUS STRUGGLES TO RISE...
...ONLY TO FIND HE CANNOT.
MY CHEST... I CANNOT FEEL--SO EMPTY, HOLLOW--IT IS SO HARD TO THINK...
NO! NOT AGAIN. THIS CANNOT BE HAPPENING TO ME...
...AGAINNNNN...

WOLVIE--RELAX BODY!
HUH?!?
WHAT'RE YOU DOIN', LADY? WHY DIDN'T YOU JUST SEND A TUG OR SHUTTLE TO PICK ME UP?
MECHANISMS NEEDED ELSEWHERE. EASIER--QUICKER--MORE CERTAIN--TO DO JOB MYSELF.

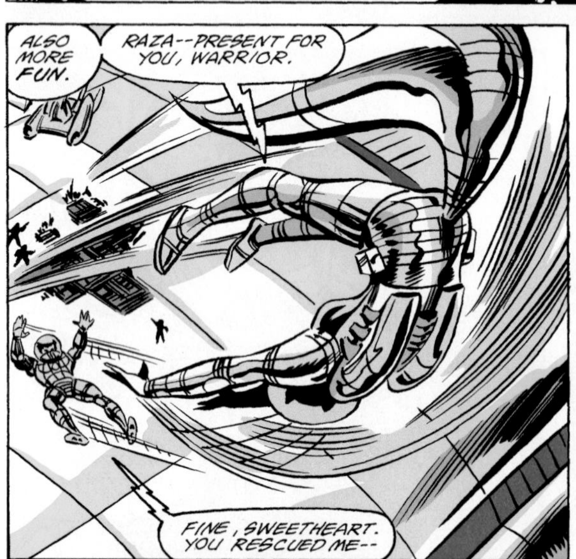
ALSO MORE FUN.
RAZA--PRESENT FOR YOU, WARRIOR.
FINE, SWEETHEART. YOU RESCUED ME--

--WHO'S GONNA SAVE YOU?!
LEAVE THAT TO ME, BUDDY.

WATCH.
SCARLET BEAMS OF FORCE FLASH FROM CYCLOPS' EYES--FOCUSED AND CONTROLLED BY HIS RUBY QUARTZ CRYSTAL VISOR AND HELMET--TO GENTLY NUDGE HEPZIBAH BACK TO THE STARJAMMER.
VERY NICE, SON. I AM IMPRESSED.
THANKS, DAD. PRACTICE MAKES PERFECT.

SENTIMENTS ECHOED BY SELF. GOOD WORK.
MY PLEASURE.
HAH! BOY IS SWASHBUCKLER AND GALLANT, CORSAIR--LIKE FATHER LIKE SON!

CORSAIR, CYCLOPS--TO MY SIDE AT ONCE!
WHAT'S THE MATTER, CH'OD?
COLOSSUS!

MINUTES LATER, IN THE STARJAMMER'S INFIRMARY...
WHEN HE LOST CONSCIOUSNESS, HE AUTOMATICALLY REVERTED TO HUMAN FORM. HIS CONDITION IS SERIOUS, SIKORSKY.
SEE THAT MYSELF, I CAN.
CRIPES, HE'S BLEEDIN' AGAIN.

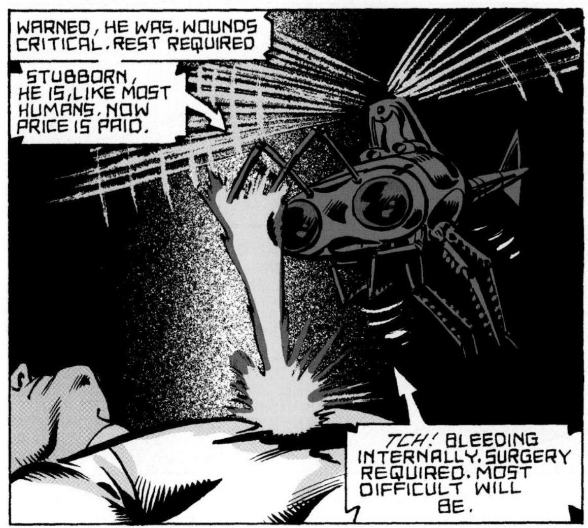
WARNED, HE WAS. WOUNDS CRITICAL. REST REQUIRED
STUBBORN, HE IS, LIKE MOST HUMANS. NOW PRICE IS PAID.
TCH! BLEEDING INTERNALLY. SURGERY REQUIRED. MOST DIFFICULT WILL BE.

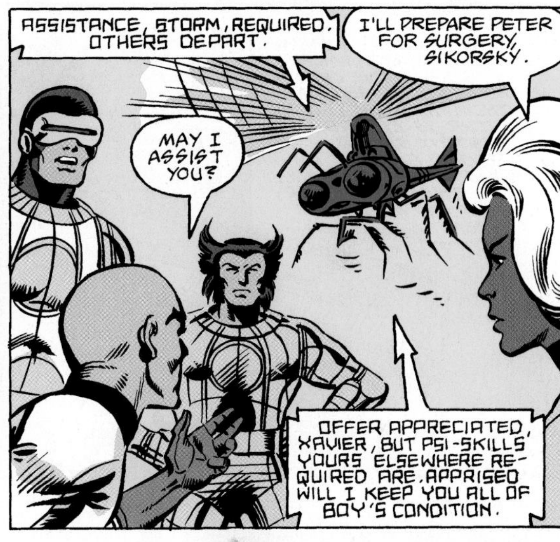
ASSISTANCE, STORM, REQUIRED. OTHERS DEPART.
I'LL PREPARE PETER FOR SURGERY, SIKORSKY.
MAY I ASSIST YOU?
OFFER APPRECIATED, XAVIER, BUT PSI-SKILLS YOURS ELSEWHERE REQUIRED ARE. APPRISED WILL I KEEP YOU ALL OF BOY'S CONDITION.

LET'S GO, PEOPLE. THERE'S NO MORE WE CAN DO HERE.
BULL!
PETEY'S A FRIEND, BUG, AN' I AIN'T LEAVIN' HIM!

SENTIMENT ADMIRABLE. REGRETTABLE MISPLACED. PHYSICIAN, I AM. BEST FOR PATIENT, I KNOW WHAT.
ASKING AM NOT. TELLING-- FOR LAST TIME--

--SCOOT!
HEY!!
SLAM

WOLVERINE, I KNOW HOW YOU FEEL.
THEN HELP ME TRASH THIS DOOR, SCOTTY! THE RUSSKIE NEEDS US!
SIKORSKY SAVED HIM ONCE, WOLVERINE. WE MUST TRUST HIM TO DO SO AGAIN.

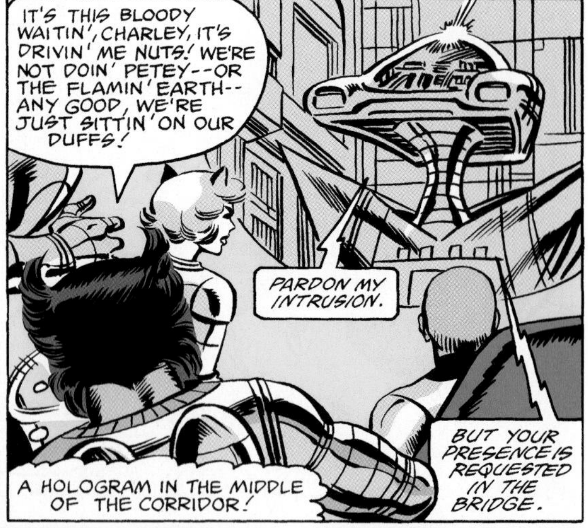
IT'S THIS BLOODY WAITIN', CHARLEY, IT'S DRIVIN' ME NUTS! WE'RE NOT DOIN' PETEY--OR THE FLAMIN' EARTH--ANY GOOD, WE'RE JUST SITTIN' ON OUR DUFFS!
PARDON MY INTRUSION.
A HOLOGRAM IN THE MIDDLE OF THE CORRIDOR!
BUT YOUR PRESENCE IS REQUESTED IN THE BRIDGE.

HEEDING WALDO'S SUMMONS, X-MEN AND STARJAMMERS RUSH TO THE NERVE CENTER OF THE GIANT VESSEL. AWAITING THEM, WITH THE PRIME COMPUTER, IS LILANDRA, MAJESTRIX SHI'AR--RULER OF A GALACTIC EMPIRE AND, IN ADDITION, TRUE LOVE OF CHARLES XAVIER, FOUNDER AND MENTOR OF THE X-MEN.
I USED THE IMPERIAL COMLINK--AND MY PRIVATE CODE--TO REACH CHANCELLOR ARAKI. ONCE I ASSURE HIM THAT I'M FREE AND UNHARMED, HE'LL CALL OFF THE PUNITIVE STRIKE AGAINST EARTH.
CONTACT WAS ESTABLISHED. HE ACKNOWLEDGED MY INITIAL TRANSMISSION. BUT NOW HE WON'T ANSWER. I'VE BEEN CALLING FOR MINUTES WITHOUT REPLY. I FEAR SOMETHING MAY HAVE HAPPENED.

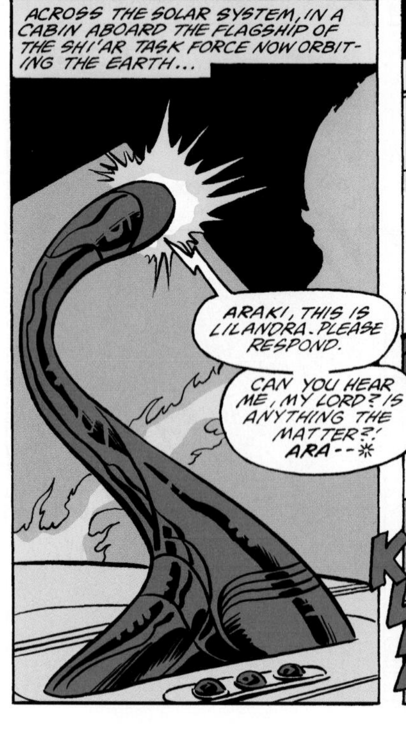
ACROSS THE SOLAR SYSTEM, IN A CABIN ABOARD THE FLAGSHIP OF THE SHI'AR TASK FORCE NOW ORBITING THE EARTH...
ARAKI, THIS IS LILANDRA. PLEASE RESPOND.
CAN YOU HEAR ME, MY LORD? IS ANYTHING THE MATTER?! ARA--*

I FEAR, MAJESTRIX, THAT YOU HAVE HAD YOUR LAST CONVERSATION WITH YOUR BELOVED CHANCELLOR.
KLIK!

A PITY HE DID NOT LISTEN TO REASON. WE WERE FRIENDS AND SLAYING A FRIEND IS ALWAYS...DISTASTEFUL.
COMMAND DECK, THIS IS ADMIRAL LORD SAMEDAR. SUMMON THE BATTLE STAFF AS SOON AS THE STATED DEADLINE HAS EXPIRED, WE WILL EXECUTE CHANCELLOR ARAKI'S ORDERS--
--AND OBLITERATE THE EARTH!!

CONTACT HAS BEEN BROKEN. AND NOW, THE IMPERIAL SUBSPACE FREQUENCIES ARE BEING JAMMED. I CANNOT REACH ANY SHIP IN THE TASK FORCE.
SOUNDS GRIM.
CORSAIR...

...ISN'T THERE ANYTHING WE CAN DO?
ONCE WE'RE FINISHED, WE CAN REACH LOCAL EARTH SPACE IN SECONDS. BUT UNTIL THEN, SON...
...WE'RE IMMOBILIZED. I'M SORRY, SCOTT.

PROFESSOR, WHAT ABOUT A TELEPATHIC MINDLINK WITH NIGHTCRAWLER AND KITTY?
MAGNETO--OUR ARCH-FOE'S--ALTERATION OF THE TERRESTRIAL MAGNETIC FIELD PREVENTED ME FROM EMPLOYING LONG-RANGE PSIONIC COMMUNICATION...
...WITH YOU X-MEN ON EARTH. BUT HERE, THAT OBSTACLE DOES NOT EXIST. IT'S CERTAINLY WORTH A TRY.

XAVIER HAS BEEN CALLED THE STRONGEST MUTANT MIND ON EARTH--

--ONE OF THE MOST POWERFUL EVER BORN--

--AND, TODAY, HE PROVES THAT STATEMENT IS NO BOAST AS HE REACHES ACROSS HALF A STAR SYSTEM...

...TO TWO X-MEN BEING HELD HOSTAGE ABOARD THE SHI'AR FLAGSHIP.

THE EFFORT IS CONSIDERABLE, REQUIRING HIS TOTAL CONCENTRATION. IN THE PROCESS, XAVIER SENSES AN ANOMALY WITHIN HIMSELF--

--SOMETHING ALIEN, UNKNOWN AND SO PROFOUNDLY DISTURBING THAT HE INTERRUPTS THE MINDLINK TO PROBE IT.

THAT PROVES TO BE A MISTAKE.

CHARLES!

AARRRGH!

THAT SCREAM--WHAT HAPPENED?!

I--I DO NOT KNOW, CYCLOPS. HE LIES SO STILL, IS HE--?

HE'S BREATHING, BUT THAT'S ABOUT IT. LET'S GET HIM TO SICK BAY--FAST--LOOKS LIKE SIKORSKY'S GOT HIMSELF ANOTHER PATIENT.

MEANWHILE, IN INTERSTELLAR SPACE-- LIES A CLANSHIP OF THE BROOD, BADLY WOUNDED DURING CORSAIR'S ESCAPE.
IRRIDESCENT FLUID-- THE GREAT CREATURE'S BLOOD-- BOILS FROM A CRUEL GASH IN HIS FLANK, AND HE KEENS HIS PAIN SOFTLY, MINDLESSLY, TO HIMSELF.
THE INJURY WILL HEAL EVENTUALLY, BUT THE PAIN WILL NEVER LEAVE-- FOR THAT IS HOW THE BROOD CONTROLS THEIR LIVING STARSHIP.
AND AS FOR THE SHIP, HE ENDURES BECAUSE HE HAS NO CHOICE, NO BRAIN WITH WHICH TO EVEN DREAM OF FREEDOM. THE BROOD DESTROYED THAT PART OF HIM AGES AGO, WHEN THEY CAPTURED HIM, AND MADE HIM THEIR SLAVE.

THE BROOD ARE NOT A FORGIVING RACE.
NOR DO THEY LIKE LOSING--
--AS THEIR ERSTWHILE ALLY DEATHBIRD, IS DISCOVERING.

BY THE SAME TOKEN, HOWEVER, NEITHER DOES SHE.
I AM OF THE AERIE, THE ROYAL NEST OF SHI'AR! I WAS FIRSTBORN, WINGLEADER OF THE DAWN FLIGHT!
YOU HOLD ME-- YOU DEFY ME--AT YOUR PERIL!
HAEG'RILL, SURELY A CADRE OF WARRIORS-PRIME CAN COPE WITH A SINGLE MAMMAL.

YOUR SECOND-IN-COMMAND CANNOT ANSWER YOU, CLAN-MASTER, NOR CAN HIS CADRE.
YOU CANNOT SLAY US ALL, DEATHBIRD.
PERHAPS. BUT YOU WILL NOT LIVE TO SEE ME FALL.
POINT... WELL TAKEN. I PROPOSE A TRUCE.

A SENSIBLE DECISION.
WHY DID YOUR WARRIORS ATTACK ME?! WE ARE SWORN ALLIES!
WITH ALL RESPECT, RENEGADE...
...YOU COULD NOT HAVE DONE US MORE HARM HAD YOU BEEN OUR DEADLIEST FOE.

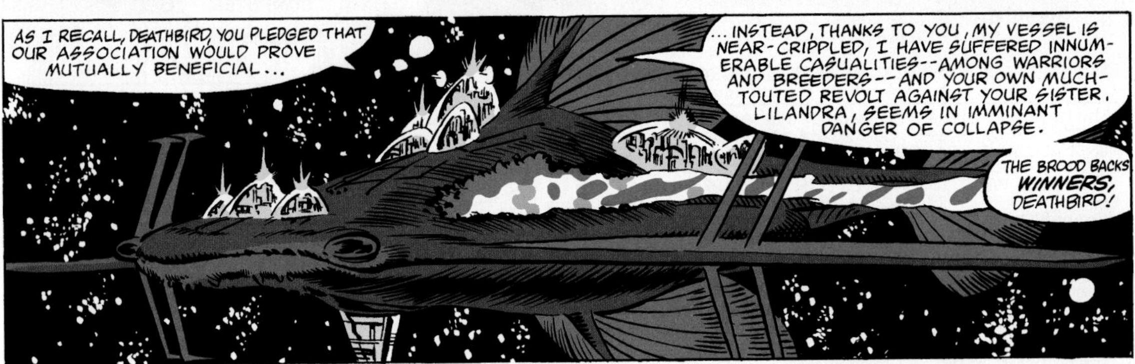
AS I RECALL, DEATHBIRD, YOU PLEDGED THAT OUR ASSOCIATION WOULD PROVE MUTUALLY BENEFICIAL...
...INSTEAD, THANKS TO YOU, MY VESSEL IS NEAR-CRIPPLED, I HAVE SUFFERED INNUMERABLE CASUALITIES--AMONG WARRIORS AND BREEDERS--AND YOUR OWN MUCH-TOUTED REVOLT AGAINST YOUR SISTER, LILANDRA, SEEMS IN IMMINANT DANGER OF COLLAPSE.
THE BROOD BACKS WINNERS, DEATHBIRD!

THEN, KAM'N'EHAR I HAVE NOTHING TO FEAR.
THIS COMPUTER MODULE CONTAINS GENETIC SCANS OF LILANDRA'S CONSORT, XAVIER, AND HIS PUPILS, TAKEN DURING OUR FIGHT ON EARTH AND ABOARD YOUR CLANSHIP.
THEY ARE MUTANTS--

--EACH GIFTED WITH UNIQUE ABILITIES THAT SET THEM APART FROM THE REST OF THEIR RACE.
SPAWN OF THE BLOODMOON! NEVER HAVE I SEEN SUCH READINGS! AS BREEDERS, THEY WOULD SERVE THE "MOTHER OF US ALL" HERSELF!
WE MUST HAVE THEM, DEATHBIRD. AT ANY COST.
LEAVE THAT TO ME.

VERY WELL, RENEGADE. IT SEEMS YOU HAVE NOT YET OUTLIVED YOUR USEFULNESS TO OUR CAUSE. SUCCEED IN THIS, AND NO REWARD WILL BE DENIED YOU. FAIL, HOWEVER...
EITHER WAY, ALIEN, YOU WILL SLAY ME. OR WORSE. I KNEW THAT FROM THE MOMENT WE MET. BUT I AM A SURVIVOR, CLAN-MASTER. BEFORE I AM THROUGH...
...IT IS YOU WHO WILL BEG ME FOR MERCY.
A MERCY THAT WILL BE DENIED!

FIFTY THOUSAND KILOMETERS ABOVE THE PACIFIC--
--HIDDEN FROM DETECTION BY A VAST SOPHISTICATED ARRAY OF CLOAKING DEVICES--THE SHI'AR BATTLE FLEET ORBITS THE EARTH.

AND, ABOARD THE FLAGSHIP...
ANOTHER COSTUME, KATZCHEN? AT THE RATE YOU'RE USING THE SHI'AR CLOTHES-MAKING GIZMO, YOU'LL SOON WEAR THE POOR MACHINE OUT.
I HAVEN'T BEEN PLAYING, KURT, YOU KNOW THAT!
I'VE BEEN USING THE COSTUMER TO TAP INTO THIS SHIP'S PRIME COMPUTER.

HOW CAN YOU SIT SO CALMLY?! WE SAW A VIDEOTAPE OF COLOSSUS BEING KILLED!* THE PROFESSOR'S MINDCALL WAS BROKEN OFF IN MID-SENTENCE! AND NOW, WE'RE UNABLE TO CONTACT CHANCELLOR ARARI, TO TELL HIM WHAT THE PROFESSOR TOLD US--THAT LILANDRA IS OKAY!
WE'VE GOT TO DO SOMETHING!
I AM DOING SOMETHING, KITTY
*LAST ISH--L.

WITH THE DATA YOU SWIPED FROM THE SHIP'S COMPUTERS, I'VE BEEN ABLE TO RIG A PORTABLE COSTUMER, AND--EH? WHAT'S THAT?!
THE SHIP'S BEING CALLED TO BATTLE STATIONS!
NIGHTCRAWLER, THE DEADLINE MUST BE UP! THEY'RE GOING TO DESTROY EARTH!

NOT IF WE CAN HELP IT, RIGHT, KATZCHEN?
QUICKLY, SHE PROGRAMS THE COSTUMER TO CREATE A NEW OUTFIT, AND WHEN IT'S FINISHED...
YEAH.

YOU SURE YOU'LL BE ALL RIGHT?
NO--BUT THAT WON'T STOP ME.
I'M AN X-MAN. YOU GUYS ARE DEPENDING ON ME. I WON'T LET YOU DOWN.
GOOD LUCK, KITTY.

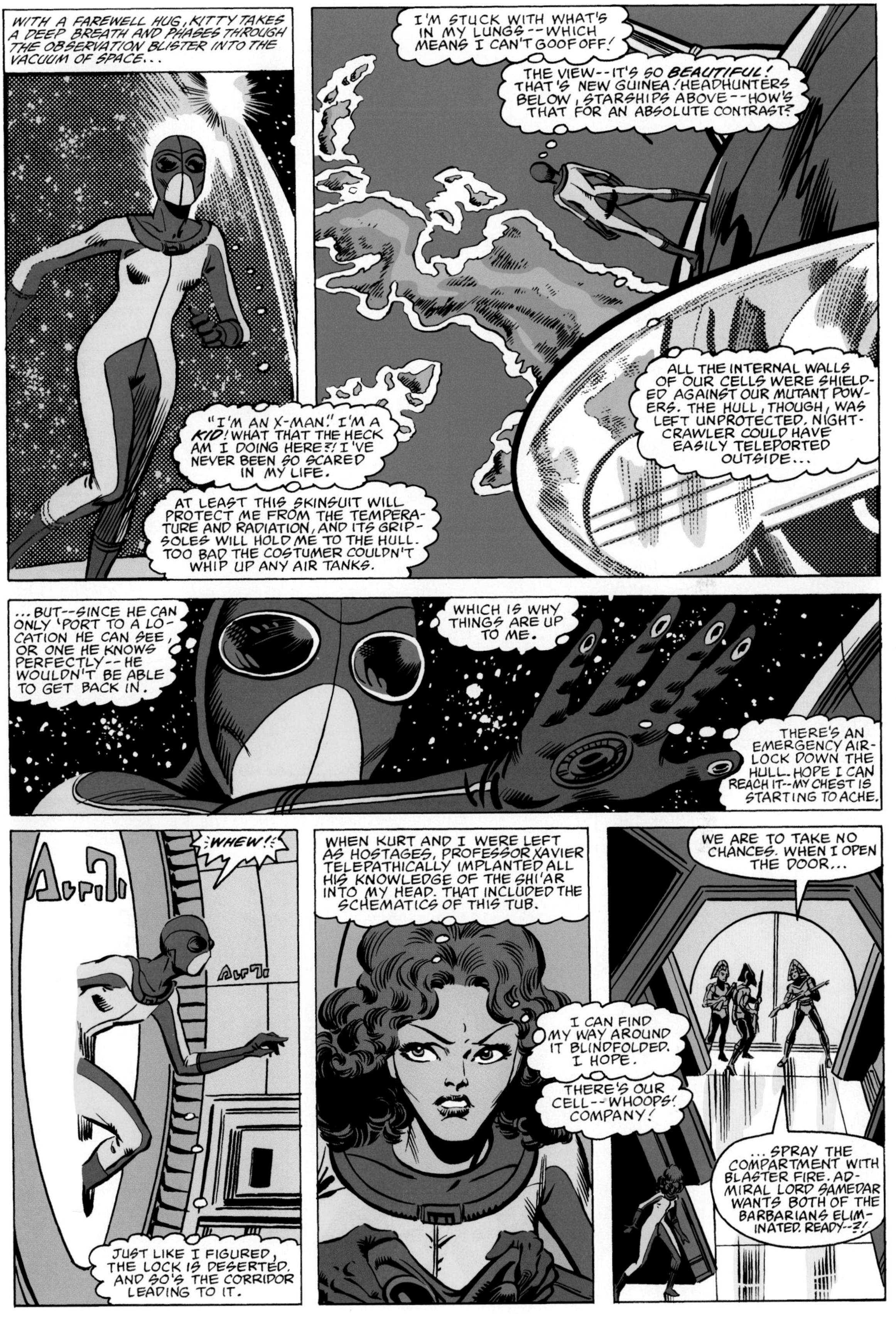

WITH A FAREWELL HUG, KITTY TAKES A DEEP BREATH AND PHASES THROUGH THE OBSERVATION BLISTER INTO THE VACUUM OF SPACE...

"I'M AN X-MAN." I'M A *KID*! WHAT THAT THE HECK AM I DOING HERE?! I'VE NEVER BEEN SO SCARED IN MY LIFE.

AT LEAST THIS SKINSUIT WILL PROTECT ME FROM THE TEMPERATURE AND RADIATION, AND ITS GRIP-SOLES WILL HOLD ME TO THE HULL. TOO BAD THE COSTUMER COULDN'T WHIP UP ANY AIR TANKS.

I'M STUCK WITH WHAT'S IN MY LUNGS--WHICH MEANS I CAN'T GOOF OFF!

THE VIEW--IT'S SO *BEAUTIFUL*! THAT'S NEW GUINEA! HEADHUNTERS BELOW, STARSHIPS ABOVE--HOW'S THAT FOR AN ABSOLUTE CONTRAST?

ALL THE INTERNAL WALLS OF OUR CELLS WERE SHIELDED AGAINST OUR MUTANT POWERS. THE HULL, THOUGH, WAS LEFT UNPROTECTED. NIGHTCRAWLER COULD HAVE EASILY TELEPORTED OUTSIDE...

...BUT--SINCE HE CAN ONLY 'PORT TO A LOCATION HE CAN SEE, OR ONE HE KNOWS PERFECTLY--HE WOULDN'T BE ABLE TO GET BACK IN.
WHICH IS WHY THINGS ARE UP TO ME.
THERE'S AN EMERGENCY AIR-LOCK DOWN THE HULL. HOPE I CAN REACH IT--MY CHEST IS STARTING TO ACHE.

WHEW!
JUST LIKE I FIGURED, THE LOCK IS DESERTED. AND SO'S THE CORRIDOR LEADING TO IT.
WHEN KURT AND I WERE LEFT AS HOSTAGES, PROFESSOR XAVIER TELEPATHICALLY IMPLANTED ALL HIS KNOWLEDGE OF THE SHI'AR INTO MY HEAD. THAT INCLUDED THE SCHEMATICS OF THIS TUB.
I CAN FIND MY WAY AROUND IT BLINDFOLDED. I HOPE.
THERE'S OUR CELL--WHOOPS! COMPANY!
WE ARE TO TAKE NO CHANCES. WHEN I OPEN THE DOOR...
...SPRAY THE COMPARTMENT WITH BLASTER FIRE. ADMIRAL LORD SAMEDAR WANTS BOTH OF THE BARBARIANS ELIMINATED. READY--?!

NOW!
BY THE BLACK NEBULA!
KITTY--?!
NIGHTCRAWLER, LOOK OUT!
THEY'RE HERE TO KILL US!
ONE FACET OF KITTY'S ABILITY TO PHASE THROUGH SOLID OBJECTS IS THAT, WHENEVER SHE DOES SO, SHE DISRUPTS ANY ELECTRONICS SYSTEMS IN HER PATH...

...AS THE THREE IMPERIAL ASSASSINS IMMEDIATELY DISCOVER.
MY COMBAT ARMOR-- SHORT-CIRCUITING!
BAMF
THE OTHER ONE--I MISSED HIM!
WHERE'D HE GO?

THE ANSWER IS AS QUICK...
BAMF
BAMF
BAMF
BAMF
BAMF
...AS IT IS PAINFUL.

MEN OF STEEL, JAWS OF GLASS-- MY KIND OF FOE.
AT LEAST NOW WE KNOW THE ADMIRAL'S IN-TENTIONS. YOU OKAY, KITTY?
UH-HUH.

WE'LL LEAVE THE RIFLES THEY'RE TOO BIG AND CUMBERSOME. HERE'S A HAND-BLASTER AND THE MINI-VERSION OF THE COSTUMER I WAS BUILDING, PROGRAMMED WITH THE DESIGNS WE AGREED ON.
THIS IS A CRAZY PLAN, KURT. D'YOU THINK IT'LL WORK?

WE'LL NEVER KNOW 'TIL WE TRY.
LET'S FIND ARAKI--AND PRAY HE BELIEVES US.

CHANCELLOR--?
MEIN GOTT!
¡GASP!¡
K-KURT--IS... IS HE...?

JA, KATZCHEN. I AM AFRAID SO.
COME AWAY, CHILD. HE IS BEYOND HELP.

HE WAS MURDERED--AND I HAVE A NASTY FEELING ABOUT WHO'S RESPONSIBLE.
THE ADMIRAL. I NEVER LIKED THAT CREEP ANYWAY.
BUT HE COMMANDS THE FLEET. HOW CAN WE STOP HIM?

THE IMPERIAL GUARD! THEY'RE LOYAL TO LILANDRA. AND CONVINCING THEM SHOULD BE SIMPLE. WE'LL JUST LET THEIR TELEPATH, ORACLE, READ XAVIER'S MESSAGE IN OUR MINDS.
KURT, HOW DO WE KNOW THEY'RE LOYAL?
IN TRUTH, KITTY, WE DON'T.
BUT WE HAVE NO ONE ELSE TO TURN TO.

AT THAT MOMENT, ON THE BRIDGE...
TARGET OUR MISSILES AGAINST THE MAJOR POPULATION CENTERS.
ADMIRAL, IT IS MY UNDERSTANDING THAT WE WERE TO LOCATE THE EMPRESS, THEN EFFECT HER RELEASE WITH THE IMPERIAL GUARD, NOT ENGAGE IN A PUNITIVE STRIKE.
THAT "UNDERSTANDING" IS INCORRECT, CAPTAIN.
MAIN BATTERIES LOCKED ON TARGETS. READY TO FIRE.
SHOULD NOT CHANCELLOR ARAKI BE PRESENT?
HE IS... INDISPOSED. I COMMAND THIS OPERATION. YOU HAVE YOUR ORDERS, CAPTAIN--OBEY THEM!

BUT BEFORE THE FATEFUL COMMAND CAN BE GIVEN...
BAMF
BAMF
BAMF
BAMF
BAMF
EXPLOSIONS! I SEE FLAMES--AND THE BRIDGE IS FILLING WITH SMOKE.
SCIENCE OFFICER, ARE WE ON FIRE?! IS THIS AN ATTACK?!
WHAT--???

BAMF
SHARRA AND KYTHRI PRESERVE US!

YOU DO WELL TO CALL UPON YOUR GODS, LORD SAMÉDAR.
FOR ONLY THEY CAN SAVE YOU FROM MY WRATH!
PHOENIX!
THE EVIL ONE--?! BUT THAT'S IMPOSSIBLE--SHE'S DEAD!

SURELY, ADMIRAL, YOU KNOW THAT A PHOENIX DIES ONLY TO BE REBORN.
TERRA IS MY HOME, SHI'AR. YOU THREATEN IT AT YOUR OWN PERIL. YOU SHALL NOT BE WARNED AGAIN.

WITH THAT, SHE DISAPPEARS--IN A BLINDING FLASH OF LIGHT AND SMOKE--
BAMF
--GIGGLING AS SHE SLIPS GHOST-LIKE THROUGH A HALF-DOZEN DECKS.

IN HER WAKE, SHE LEAVES A CREW OF STUNNED, DISBELIEVING--AND IN MANY CASES, TERRIFIED--IMPERIALS.
MINDSCAN THE SHIP, ORACLE--AND SPACE AROUND US! WHOEVER--WHATEVER--THAT ENTITY WAS, FIND IT!
GLADIATOR, IF IT WAS TRULY PHOENIX...
...WHAT WILL WE DO? WHAT CAN WE DO?!

I DON'T KNOW. WHEN LAST WE FOUGHT, IT TOOK THE ENTIRE IMPERIAL GUARD TO BRING HER DOWN--AND EVEN THEN ONLY BECAUSE SHE ALLOWED IT.*
BAMF
MERCIFUL GODS, IF SHE IS REBORN, WE MAY ALL BE AS GOOD AS DEAD.
HURRY UP WITH THAT SCAN, ORACLE. ORACLE? ORACLE!
*X-MEN #137--LOUISE.

ELSEWHERE...
I... KNEW THIS 'PORT WOULD BE ROUGH--IT ALWAYS IS WHEN I CARRY A PASSENGER. I WAS PREPARED--AND EVEN THEN, THE TRANSITION NEARLY TORE ME APART. I FEEL AWFUL.
THE TRIP WAS AS HARD ON ORACLE, TOO.
WHO--?! WHERE--?! WHAT--?!

DON'T BE AFRAID, FRAULEIN. WE MEAN NO HARM.
HI, KURT! DIDJA SEE MY PERFORMANCE? IT WAS FANTASTIC! THINGS WENT BETTER THAN WE HOPED! THEY BELIEVED ME! THEY THOUGHT I WAS REALLY PHOENIX!
NO!

HEY, WAIT! DON'T RUN!
SHE... STILL BELIEVES YOU. STOP HER KITTY!
GROGGY AND WEAK FROM HER TELEPORTATIONS, ORACLE FINDS HERSELF UNABLE TO TELEPATHICALLY SUMMON ASSISTANCE, AND BARELY ABLE TO STAND, LET ALONE RUN.

BUT SHE TRIES, NONETHELESS.
EVEN THOUGH SHE DOESN'T GET VERY FAR.

STOP FIGHTING, ORACLE! I'M NOT PHOENIX, I'M KITTY!
PLEASE LISTEN TO US--HELP US! BEFORE IT'S TOO LATE FOR YOUR PEOPLE, AS WELL AS OURS!
EMPRESS LILANDRA IS ALIVE AND WELL!
WHAT?! AM I TO TAKE THE WORD OF A CHILD DESPERATE TO SAVE HER WORLD?!

YOU'RE A TELEPATH--READ MY THOUGHTS! PROBE AS DEEP AS YOU LIKE, I'VE NOTHING TO HIDE!
AFTER A MOMENT'S WARY HESITATION--STILL SUSPECTING A TRAP--

--ORACLE DOES AS SHE AS BID...
AND A MOMENT AFTER THAT...

GLADIATOR, STARBOLT--TO ME, AT ONCE!
ORACLE!

SOON...
I AM NOT CONVINCED.
STILL, THIS WOULD EXPLAIN THE ADMIRAL'S RECENT UNUSUAL BEHAVIOR.
THEIR STORY IS EASILY CONFIRMED. WE SIMPLY POSTPONE THE BOMBARDMENT OF EARTH LONG ENOUGH TO ESTABLISH CONTACT WITH THE STARJAMMER AND THE MAJESTRIX.
WHATEVER WE DECIDE, WE'D BEST DO IT QUICKLY. I'M PSI-SCANNING THE COMMAND DECK. THEY'RE PREPARING ONCE MORE TO ATTACK!
I CAN SHOW YOU CHANCELLOR ARAKI'S BODY.
THAT PROVES NOTHING YOU COULD HAVE SLAIN HIM YOURSELF.

SAMÉDÀR A TRAITOR? HE'S AN AMBITIOUS MAN. I SUPPOSE FOR THE RIGHT PRICE--AND THE RIGHT ODDS--EVEN HE MIGHT BE TEMPTED.
IF SO, WE HAVE A PROBLEM.
HE'S ACCOMPANIED BY A CONTINGENT OF IMPERIAL GUARD--BORDERERS WHOSE LOYALTY MAY BE TO HIM RATHER THAN THE EMPIRE.
THERE IS NO "MAY" ABOUT IT, GLADIATOR!
SAMÉDÀR-LORD!
A HOLOFIELD! BUT HOW DID HE FIND US?! HOW COULD HE HAVE KNOWN--?!
I AM A CAREFUL MAN. THAT IS HOW THE AMBITIOUS SURVIVE. WHEN YOU SLIPPED AWAY JUST NOW, I HAD A "SPY-EYE" FOLLOW YOU.

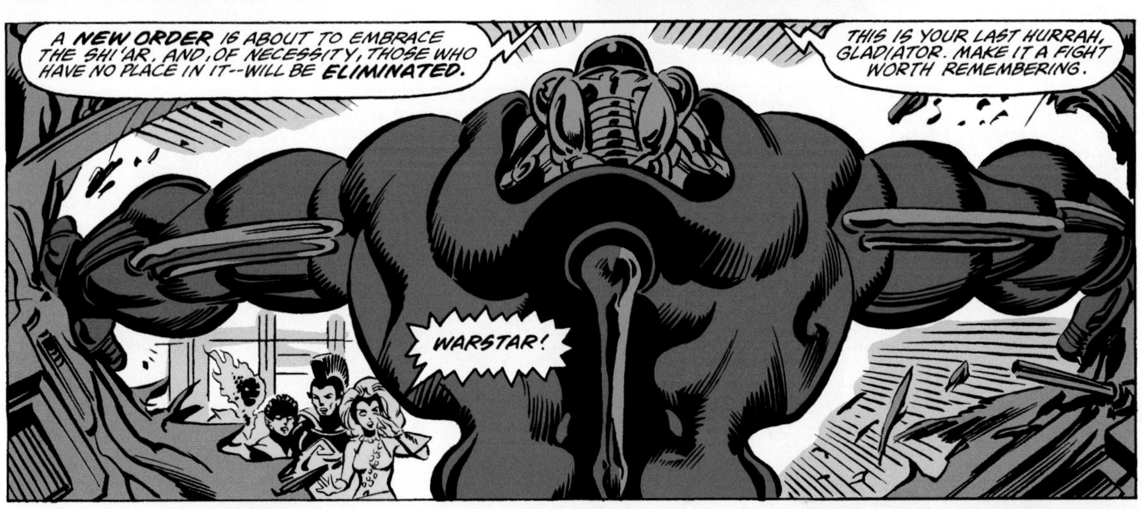
A NEW ORDER IS ABOUT TO EMBRACE THE SHI'AR, AND, OF NECESSITY, THOSE WHO HAVE NO PLACE IN IT--WILL BE ELIMINATED.
THIS IS YOUR LAST HURRAH, GLADIATOR. MAKE IT A FIGHT WORTH REMEMBERING.
WARSTAR!

THAT MECHANOID SYMBIOTE HAS NOT COME ALONE. BUT NO MATTER THE ODDS--
--WE SHALL PREVAIL!
A PROUD BOAST, N'RILL'IRÉE.
BUT A HOLLOW ONE!

THAT HUSSAR, REMAINS TO BE SEEN!
A SINGLE PUNCH CRIPPLES WARSTAR, WHILE--BY GLADIATOR'S SIDE--STARBOLT RAKES THE CHAMBER WITH THE ULTRA-ENERGY BEAMS THAT ARE HIS NAMESAKE.

IN THE LITERAL BLINK OF AN EYE, THE ROOM DISSOLVES INTO ABSOLUTE CHAOS.
AND, AS USUAL, OUR HEROES FIND THEMSELVES IN THE THICK OF IT.
KITTY! WHAT ARE YOU DOING?
I WANT TO HELP! I CAN FIGHT, TOO!
WHOOPS!

NOT HERE, AND NOT THIS WAY!
WHAT HAPPENS TO US ISN'T IMPORTANT, KATZCHEN. WHAT GOOD WILL IT DO TO WIN THIS BATTLE IF, IN THE MEANTIME, THE EARTH IS DESTROYED?!
COMPUTERS ARE THE HEART OF ANY SPACECRAFT. WITHOUT THEM, THIS SHIP--AND SAMEDAR--ARE HELPLESS!
FIND THE CENTRAL CORE, KITTY. PUT IT OUT OF ACTION! MOVE!

GIRL--!
LOOK OUT-- ABOVE YOU-- WEBWING!
EH--?!
YIKES!

SHLUP!

FLOOP
EAT YOUR HEART OUT, DOUG HENNING!
LOOKING AT SOME OF THOSE SLIMEOIDS IS BAD ENOUGH, BUT HAVING THEM GRAB ME-- YUCK!

THIS DREADNOUGHT'S HUGE-- IF I FOLLOW THE CORRIDORS, I'LL NEVER REACH THE CENTRAL CORE IN TIME.
BUT I'VE GOT TO TRY. I WON'T LET MOM 'N' DAD--ALL THE PEOPLE I KNOW AND LOVE--DIE.
EVEN BY PHASING STRAIGHT THROUGH THE SHIP, IT'LL TAKE NEARLY FOREVER.
I'VE GOT TO SUCCEED!

BEHIND KITTY, THE BATTLE RAGES ON.
AND DESPITE THE CONSIDERABLE ODDS AGAINST THEM, NIGHTCRAWLER AND HIS ALLIES NOT ONLY HOLD THEIR OWN, THEY BEGIN TO TURN THE TIDE.

A STATE OF AFFAIRS WHICH DOES NOT SIT WELL WITH A CERTAIN RENEGADE ADMIRAL...
BAMF
INCOMPETENT DOLTS!
MUST I DO EVERYTHING MYSELF?!

THE COMBATANTS FEEL A MOMENT OF EXQUISITE UNENDURABLE AGONY AS THE BROOD WEAPON--MATED SECRETLY TO B'NEE, THE SMALLER PART OF THE WARSTAR SYMBIOTE--DETONATES.
THEN, OF COURSE, THEY FEEL NOTHING.

MEANWHILE, UNAWARE OF WHAT HAS BEFALLEN THE OTHERS...
THIS MUST BE CAUSING FITS UP ON THE BRIDGE.

ONCE I'VE SCRAMBLED THESE PRIMARY COMPUTERS, I'VE GOT TO GO AFTER THE SECONDARY CORE.
I HAVE TO BE CAREFUL, THOUGH. I WANT TO DISABLE THEIR BIG GUNS...

...WITHOUT DAMAGING ANY LIFE SUPPORT SYSTEMS. I DON'T WANT TO HURT ANYONE.
THOUGH, FOR WHAT SHE DID TO PETER, I THINK I'D CHEERFULLY WRING DEATHBIRD'S NECK.
SO INTENT IS KITTY ON HER WORK THAT SHE FAILS TO NOTICE A HIDDEN DEFENSIVE WEAPON SWING HER WAY.

SHE'S IN PHASING MODE--VIRTUALLY INTANGIBLE--CONFIDENT THAT WILL PROTECT HER FROM HARM.
SHE'S WRONG.

I COULD HAVE HAD YOU ALL SLAIN, GLADIATOR, BUT I THOUGHT IT ONLY FITTING THAT YOU BE PRESENT TO WITNESS MY MOMENT OF TRIUMPH.
THEN YOU--AND CAPTAIN K'RK, WHO ALSO FOOLISHLY OPPOSED ME--WILL BE SENT TO A REWARD YOU MOST RICHLY DESERVE.
NO MATTER WHAT YOU DO TO US, YOU'LL FIND THIS A FLEETING, HOLLOW VICTORY, TRAITOR!

ONE REGIME'S TRAITOR IS OFTEN ANOTHER'S HERO, GLADIATOR. IT ALL DEPENDS ON WHO WINS.
BUT WHATEVER MY FINAL FATE, NEITHER YOU, YOUR COMPANIONS--NOR THAT PATHETIC LITTLE PLANET--WILL BE ABLE TO SEE IT.
WEAPONEERS--MAIN BATTERIES--FIRE!

AT THE SPEED OF LIGHT, A BOLT OF ANTI-MATTER PLASMA ERUPTS TOWARDS NORTH AMERICA, TARGETTED ON SAN FRANCISCO.

IT WILL STRIKE WITH THE FORCE OF A GIGATON H-BOMB, VAPORIZING EVERYTHING WITHIN A 100-MILE RADIUS OF GROUND ZERO, AND SPLITTING THE PLANETARY CRUST ALONG THE MAJOR FAULT LINES THAT RIM THE PACIFIC OCEAN.

BUT, AT FAR FASTER THAN THE SPEED OF LIGHT, SKIDDING OUT OF WARP SPACE AT THE LAST INSTANT IN AN AWESOME DISPLAY OF ENGINE POWER AND ASTROGATIONAL SKILL (THE SLIGHTEST ERROR WOULD HAVE RESULTED IN THE DESTRUCTION OF BOTH THE SHIP AND MUCH OF A TERRESTRIAL HEMISPHERE, THEREBY DOING SAMEDAR'S WORK **FOR** HIM)...

...THE **STARJAMMER** INTERCEPTS THE BEAM.

SIMULTANEOUSLY, LILANDRA'S HOLOGRAPHIC IMAGE APPEARS ON THE COMMAND DECK OF EVERY SHIP IN THE FLEET...
HEAR ME, SHI'AR!
I AM ALIVE AND WELL. NO HOSTILE ACTION IS TO BE TAKEN AGAINST THE EARTH.

GLADIATOR, WHY WAS THIS ATTACK BEGUN? WHY ARE YOU UNDER RESTRAINT?! WHERE IS MY CHANCELLOR?!
DEAD, MAJESTRIX--
--SLAIN BY LORD SAMEDAR, WHO IS IN LEAGUE WITH DEATHBIRD.

PLACE HIM UNDER ARREST.
OFFICERS, RELEASE THE X-MEN AND THE LOYAL GUARD. K'RK, ASSUME COMMAND AND WITHRAW THE FLEET BEYOND EARTH'S MOON.

I SHALL BEAM ABOARD DIRECTLY. END TRANSMISSION.
POOR ARAKI. I FEARED THIS WHEN WE COULDN'T CONTACT HIM. I SHALL MISS HIM.
THINGS LOOKED AND SOUNDED PRETTY GRIM OVER THERE. I'M GLAD KURT AND KITTY ARE OKAY.
YES. IT SEEMS DEATHBIRD'S CONSPIRACY IS FAR BROADER AND DEEPER THAN I SUSPECTED.
AND, WORSE, SHE HAS OUTSIDE HELP-- THE "BROOD!" WE HAVE NO IDEA WHERE THEY COME FROM, WHAT THEY WANT, HOW TO DEAL WITH THEM.
I'VE A NASTY FEELING THAT, COMPARED TO THEM, DEATHBIRD'S THREAT IS NEGLIGIBLE!

AT LEAST WE SAVED THE EARTH. THAT'S SOMETHING.
WELL, LOOK WHO'S HERE! HOW DO YOU FEEL, PETER?
BETTER HE IS. BETTER HE WILL GET-- ASSUMING PHYSICIAN'S ORDERS HE FOLLOWS.
I WISH, CYCLOPS, THE SAME COULD BE SAID FOR PROFESSOR XAVIER.
"ACCORDING TO SIKORSKY," STORM SAYS QUIETLY, "WHILE THE PROFESSOR'S BODY IS SUBSTANTIALLY UNHARMED...
"...HIS BRAIN MAY HAVE BEEN COMPLETELY, IRREVOCABLY DESTROYED. HE WILL NOT DIE-- BUT HE MAY WELL LIVE OUT THE REST OF HIS DAYS AS A MINDLESS VEGETABLE."

NEXT ISSUE: JUST WHEN THE X-MEN THOUGHT THEY HAD ENOUGH PROBLEMS... ENTER THE BROTHERHOOD OF EVIL MUTANTS!

60¢
158
JUNE
02461
CC
© 1982 MARVEL COMICS GROUP
MARVEL® COMICS GROUP
APPROVED BY THE COMICS CODE AUTHORITY
THE UNCANNY
X-MEN™
TM
COCKRUM

Stan Lee PRESENTS: THE UNCANNY X-MEN!™

CHRIS CLAREMONT, WRITER * DAVE COCKRUM & BOB WIACEK, ARTISTS * JOE ROSEN, LETTERER * GLYNIS WEIN, COLORIST * LOUISE JONES, EDITOR * JIM SHOOTER, EDITOR-IN-CHIEF

THE LIFE THAT LATE I LED...
IN THE HEART OF THE BERMUDA TRIANGLE, FAR OFF THE BEATEN TRACK, IS AN ISLAND THAT SERVES AS THE TEMPORARY HEADQUARTERS OF THE UNCANNY X-MEN, THE OUTLAW TEAM OF MUTANT SUPER HEROES.
THIS QUARTET DUELING IN A COURTYARD, HOWEVER, ARE NOT THE X-MEN. INDEED, THREE OF THEM AREN'T EVEN HUMAN, THOUGH ALL ARE FRIENDS AND ALLIES OF OUR HEROES. THE BLONDE IS CAROL DANVERS, WHO USED TO BE A SUPER-HERO UNTIL SHE WAS STRIPPED OF HER POWERS MONTHS AGO. THE OTHERS--RAZA, CH'OD (TOGETHER WITH HIS PET COMPANION, CR'REEE) AND MAM'SELLE HEPZIBAH--ARE STARJAMMERS, INTERSTELLAR SWASHBUCKLERS. THEY EXPECTED AN EASY VICTORY OVER CAROL.
I'D HOPED FOR A PLEASANT--ALBEIT MINOR--MORNING'S DIVERSION...
BY THE BLACK NEBULA!
ALLEZ--OOP!
SURPRISINGLY, THINGS HAVEN'T WORKED OUT THAT WAY.

...BUT THIS DUEL IS TURNING OUT SPLENDIDLY!
EASY FOR THOU TO SAY, LUMMOX. SHE HASN'T THROWN THEE YET. THAT HURT!
MISSED!
MONITORING THE BOUT IS N.A.S.A. PHYSICIST PETER CORBEAU, ANOTHER OF THE X-MEN'S TRUSTED ASSOCIATES.
HOW 'BOUT THAT. LOSING YOUR TOUCH, HEPZIBAH?

NO.
FASCINATING. THAT WAS A HEAVY HIT--CAROL HAD NO OPPORTUNITY TO ROLL WITH IT--YET HER BODY HANDLED IT JUST FINE.
CAROL'S BIO-READINGS ARE INCREDIBLE AND HER PERFORMANCE, SUPERB. SHE SHOULD HAVE BEEN SLAUGHTERED LONG AGO, YET SHE ACTUALLY HAS A CHANCE OF WINNING!

PLAYTIME IS OVER, LITTLE BEAUTY.
CH'OD!
THE GIANT ALIEN LUNGES WITH A SPEED THAT BELIES HIS MASSIVE BULK-- ALMOST FASTER THAN THE EYE CAN FOLLOW--

--AND MISSES!
YEEEK!
HOLD HER, RAZA!
YOU WERE SAYING--
MY LEG!
THY FANCY TRICKS WILL AVAIL THEE NAUGHT, LASS. NONE CAN BREAK MY GRIP OF STEEL.
SUPERB EFFORT, SUNHAIR. IMPRESSED EVEN ME.
AYE. DOST THOU YIELD?
DO I HAVE A CHOICE?
NOT IF YOU WANT TO GET UP.
FINKS!

IN ANOTHER PART OF THE ISLAND, PETER RASPUTIN -- WHO, AS COLOSSUS, IS ONE OF THE X-MEN'S MAINSTAYS -- RECUPERATES FROM WOUNDS SUFFERED IN A RECENT BATTLE,* UNDER THE WATCHFUL EYES OF HIS LITTLE SISTER, ILLYANA, AND TEAM-MATE KITTY PRYDE.
<THOSE ARE MARTIANS, LITTLE SNOWFLAKE.>
<ICK!>
PETER'S DOING REAL WELL. HE SHOULD BE HIS OLD SELF IN NO TIME.
I GUESS I SHOULDN'T BE SURPRISED. WE MUTANTS SEEM TO BE A PRETTY TOUGH BREED. CONSIDERING THE X-MEN'S LINE OF WORK, WE HAVE TO BE.
*X-MEN #'S 155-157; **TRANSLATED FROM THE RUSSIAN-- L.

IT SEEMS LIKE I JOINED THE TEAM ONLY YESTERDAY, YET I'VE FOUGHT DEMONS, SUPER-VILLAINS, ALIENS. I'VE SEEN PEOPLE DIE-- VIOLENTLY, HORRIBLY. I'VE ALMOST DIED MYSELF-- MORE THAN ONCE.
IF I HAD ANY SMARTS, I'D CHUCK THIS AND GO BACK TO LIVING A NORMAL LIFE. BUT I'M NOT NORMAL-- NONE OF US ARE. AND OUR POWERS GIVE US SPECIAL RESPONSIBILITIES.
I WONDER NOW... IF THEY GIVE US SPECIAL FEELINGS, TOO?

"WHEN I SAW COLOSSUS KILLED,* I THOUGHT I'D DIE MYSELF. I'D NEVER FELT SO HOLLOW AND EMPTY-- LIKE SOMEBODY HAD RIPPED OUT MY HEART.
"THEN, LATER, WHEN I DISCOVERED HE WAS STILL ALIVE, I KIND OF FELT... WORSE.
*X-MEN #156-- L.

"AT FIRST, I COULDN'T MOVE. HE LOOKED SO BEAUTIFUL, I WAS AFRAID TO DO ANYTHING, SAY ANYTHING-- FOR FEAR THIS WOULD TURN OUT TO BE A DREAM AND HE'D DISAPPEAR IN MY ARMS.
"SUDDENLY, I HATED BEING FOURTEEN-- A KID.
THAT... SCARED ME.

"BUT THEN I HUGGED AND KISSED HIM--TAKING REFUGE FROM EMOTIONS, SENSATIONS--
"--I'D NEVER EXPERIENCED AND DIDN'T UNDERSTAND--
"--IN ACTING LIKE A KID. AND EVERYTHING WAS FINE.
BUT EVERYTHING ISN'T FINE. THE FEELINGS WON'T GO AWAY. THEY WON'T EVEN SETTLE DOWN. I WISH I COULD TALK TO SOMEONE ABOUT THIS--BUT THE PROFESSOR'S SICK AND IT'S NONE OF THE GUYS' BUSINESS.
THAT LEAVES ORORO, BUT... SUPPOSE SHE DOESN'T UNDERSTAND?

WHILE KITTY WRESTLES WITH THE REALITIES OF GROWING UP...
HAST THOU COMPLETED THY EVALUATION OF OUR SPARRING PARTNER, SCHOLAR CORBEAU?
YEAH, PETER. THE SUSPENSE IS MURDER. WHAT'S THE VERDICT?
EXTRAORDINARY! YEARS AGO, WHEN YOU WERE TRANSFORMED INTO MS. MARVEL, YOUR GENETIC STRUCTURE WAS IRREVOCABLY ALTERED. IN ADDITION TO GAINING SUPER-POWERS, YOU WERE EVOLVED INTO A PERFECT PHYSICAL SPECIMEN OF HUMANITY.
YOU MAY HAVE BEEN STRIPPED OF THOSE POWERS, BUT THE BASIC GENETIC MATERIAL AND MODIFICATIONS REMAIN INTACT.

THAT EXPLAINS YOUR SUPERB PERFORMANCE IN OUR DUEL. YOU MAY NOT BE WHAT YOU WERE, BUT YOU ARE FAR SUPERIOR TO AN ORDINARY HUMAN.
I DON'T FEEL SUPERIOR, CH'OD.
I COULD HANDLE LOSING MY POWERS. IT'S THE WAY I LOST THEM THAT HURTS, EVEN AFTER ALL THESE MONTHS.

WHEN YOU LOSE SOMETHING--SOMEONE--THAT FUNDAMENTAL, LASS, ANY WAY HURTS.
MOIRA!
I WAS OBSERVING YOUR WORKOUT ON THE MONITORS. WE'LL REVIEW THE BIO-TELEMETRY THIS EVENING.
FINE. HOW'S THE PROFESSOR?

NO BETTER, NO WORSE. HE BREATHES. HIS HEART BEATS. HIS BODY FUNCTIONS. BEYOND THAT...
DR. MacTAGGERT, LILANDRA SENT ME FOR YOU.
THANK YOU, NIGHTCRAWLER. I'LL BE IN DIRECTLY.

THE GERMAN X-MAN DEPARTS AS HE ARRIVED, TELEPORTING BACK TO THE IMPROVISED MEDICAL CENTRE WITH MOIRA'S MESSAGE. LYING COMATOSE ON A BED IS CHARLES XAVIER, FOUNDER AND MENTOR OF THE X-MEN. BY HIS SIDE, TWO MORE MEMBERS OF THE TEAM--STORM, ITS LEADER, AND WOLVERINE.
NEAR MOIRA STAND LILANDRA, MAJESTRIX SHI'AR, RULER OF A GALACTIC EMPIRE, THE WOMAN XAVIER LOVES, AND ORACLE, OF LILANDRA'S IMPERIAL GUARD, A TELEPATH, PERHAPS THE ONLY PERSON WHO CAN SAVE HIM.
WE'RE AS READY AS WE'LL EVER BE, ORACLE. HE'S ALL YOURS.

SHE HAS SPENT A FULL DAY IN MEDITATION, PREPARING FOR THIS ORDEAL. HER BEING FOCUSED, YET TOTALLY RELAXED, SHE LETS HER THOUGHTS FLY FREE.
SHE WILL FORGE A PSIONIC RAPPORT WITH CHARLES, AND THEN EXAMINE HIM TO DETERMINE WHAT FORCE STRUCK HIM DOWN AND WHETHER OR NOT THE DAMAGE CAN BE REPAIRED.
IT WILL NOT BE AN EASY TASK, MY FRIENDS. BUT ORACLE IS MY EMPIRE'S PREMIER TELEPATH. IF ANYONE CAN SUCCEED...
...IT IS SHE.
FOR A TIME, TO THOSE WATCHING, NOTHING MUCH HAPPENS...
...AS ORACLE PICKS HER WAY--CAUTIOUSLY, CAREFULLY, NOT WANTING TO HARM HER PATIENT OR HERSELF--INTO XAVIER'S MIND.
AND THEN WITHOUT WARNING...
...SHE'S CAUGHT IN A PSYCHIC RIPTIDE AND TUMBLED HEADLONG INTO CHAOS.
IN AN INSTANT, SHE DIES A THOUSAND GRUESOME DEATHS, VICTIM OF A SAVAGE CONFLICT BEING WAGED WITHIN XAVIER'S BRAIN. SHE'S ASSAULTED BY MYRIAD IMAGES, REAL AND IMAGINED. UNABLE TO TELL WHICH IS WHICH, SHE DROWNS IN A MAELSTROM OF AGONY.
SHE SCREAMS, A SHRIEK OF PAIN AND TERROR THAT ECHOES XAVIER'S OWN...
...AND SENSES A CURIOUS DUALITY TO THE MAN'S PSYCHIC AURA, A SENSE OF HUNGER--INSATIABLE, PREDATORY, ALIEN--COUPLED TO SO FOUL AND EVIL A PRESENCE THAT, THE MOMENT SHE PERCEIVES IT, SHE DENIES IT, FORGETS IT.
XAVIER, AWARE OF THIS, SOBS IN FRUSTRATION AND DESPAIR...
...WHILE, AT THE CORE OF HIS BEING, IN HIS VERY SOUL, SOMETHING GRINS IN TRIUMPH.

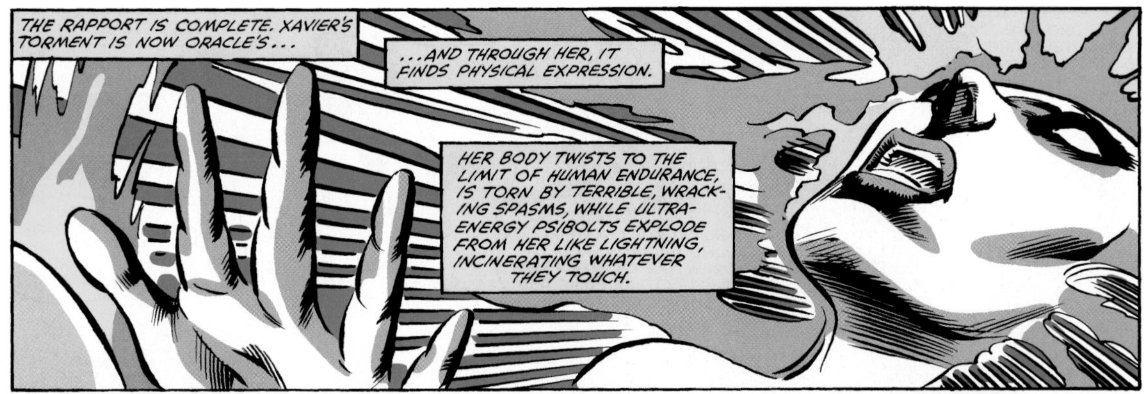
THE RAPPORT IS COMPLETE. XAVIER'S TORMENT IS NOW ORACLE'S...
...AND THROUGH HER, IT FINDS PHYSICAL EXPRESSION.
HER BODY TWISTS TO THE LIMIT OF HUMAN ENDURANCE, IS TORN BY TERRIBLE, WRACKING SPASMS, WHILE ULTRA-ENERGY PSIBOLTS EXPLODE FROM HER LIKE LIGHTNING, INCINERATING WHATEVER THEY TOUCH.

KILL!!
TO LIVE...MUST KILL-- I!!

SHE'S UNDER HIS CONTROL! HE'S ADDING HIS POWER TO HERS, USING THE PSIBOLTS TO ATTACK THE MEDICAL UNIT-- AND HIMSELF!
SUICIDE, CHARLES?! I'D NOT HAVE BELIEVED IT POSSIBLE OF YOU. ARE THINGS SO...HOPELESS?
WOLVERINE, USE YOUR CLAWS TO SEVER THE ENERGY LINK BETWEEN THEM! HURRY, MAN, OR IT'LL BE TOO LATE!

HOW'M I S'POSED TO--
--HEY!
I SHALL GET YOU THERE, WOLVERINE. YOU MUST DO THE REST.

AS STORM'S ELEMENTAL POWERS GENERATE A GALE-FORCE GUST OF WIND TO HURL WOLVERINE ACROSS THE ROOM, THE FEISTY CANADIAN EXTRUDES ADAMANTIUM CLAWS FROM THE BACKS OF HIS HANDS...
...AND SLASHES THEM THROUGH THE POWER FIELD BINDING ORACLE TO XAVIER. AS MOIRA HOPED, THE SUPER-DENSE, UNBREAKABLE METAL DISRUPTS THE DELICATE MATRIX.

...WITH SPECTACULAR RESULTS.
BLAM-MO!

ORORO, THE COMPUTERS ARE BURNING! I HAVE AN EXTINGUISHER ON THIS ONE!
GOOD, KURT. A WHIRLWIND VACUUM SHOULD DRAW THE OXYGEN FROM THESE OTHER FIRES AND SUFFOCATE THEM.
WHEW!
I'M OKAY, STORM.
AS AM I. AND, I THINK, MOIRA.
BUT WHAT OF ORACLE-- AND CHARLES?!

NO CHANGE.
I THOUGHT I HAD KNOWN TRUE LOVE BEFORE I MET YOU. I KNEW NOTHING. WE ARE SIDES OF THE SAME PLANE, HALVES OF A GREATER-- FRIGHTENINGLY WONDERFUL-- WHOLE. WITH YOU, I AM COMPLETE-- AS I KNOW YOU ARE WITH ME.
WITHOUT YOU, I AM A SHADOW. I LIVE, BUT DO NOT PROSPER. AND THOUGH MY DAYS MAY BE LONG AND FRUITFUL, THEY WILL FOREVER LACK... JOY.
EASY, LASS, YOU'VE HAD A NASTY SHOCK.
YOUR CONCERN IS APPRECIATED, BUT UNNECESSARY. I AM WELL. I WISH THE SAME COULD BE SAID FOR XAVIER.
I HAVE NEVER INTERFACED WITH A MIND OF SUCH DEPTH AND COMPLEXITY-- SUCH SUBTLETY! HIS MENTAL DEFENSES ARE PHENOMENAL. HE HAS WITHDRAWN DEEP WITHIN HIMSELF. MOIRA, HE IS AT WAR WITH HIMSELF!
I HAVE DONE MY BEST, BUT NO OUTSIDE FORCE CAN AID HIM. HIS RECOVERY IS COMPLETELY UP TO HIM.

I HEARD AN EXPLOSION, NIGHTCRAWLER. PROBLEMS?
BE CAREFUL WHERE YOU PHASE, KATZCHEN. FIRES ARE STILL BURNING AND MANY OF THESE ELECTRICAL SYSTEMS ARE STILL ACTIVE.
SO I SEE. WHAT HAPPENED?
ORACLE TRIED TO PULL HERR PROFESSOR XAVIER OUT OF HIS COMA.

THINGS DIDN'T WORK OUT, HUH?
YOU MIGHT SAY THAT, KITTEN.
UNDER THE CIRCUMSTANCES, I'M NOT SURE IF YOU GUYS'LL BE INTERESTED...
...BUT THEY'RE TALKING ABOUT THE X-MEN ON TV!

WHAT'S THIS?! SCENES OF OUR BATTLE IN WASHINGTON, D.C. WITH THE BROTHERHOOD OF EVIL MUTANTS?! WHO'S BROADCASTING THEM?
IT IS A SATELLITE TRANSMISSION OF A BRITISH NEWS PROGRAM, "PANORAMA."
THERE ARE A NUMBER OF SO-CALLED "SUPER HERO" TEAMS EXTANT IN THE WORLD TODAY, MOST OF THEM AMERICAN AND CHIEF AMONG THOSE, THE AVENGERS AND THE FANTASTIC FOUR.
"ONE OF THE MOST MYSTERIOUS OF THESE GROUPS IS THE X-MEN, HERE SEEN IN ACTION IN WASHINGTON...
"...AND ONLY DAYS AGO, IN NEW YORK.
"WHAT MAKES THEM UNIQUE IS THE FACT THAT ITS MEMBERS ARE MUTANTS...
"...HUMANS GIFTED--OR CURSED--AT BIRTH WITH EXTRAORDINARY PHYSICAL AND/OR MENTAL ABILITIES.
WITH US TONIGHT TO DISCUSS BOTH MUTANTS AND THE X-MEN IS U.S. SENATOR ROBERT KELLY, CHAIRMAN OF AN AD HOC CONGRESSIONAL COMMITTEE ON MUTANT AFFAIRS. WELCOME, SENATOR.
THANK YOU, MR. CHEEVER. HOWEVER, I'M AFRAID I MUST TAKE ISSUE WITH YOUR CHARACTERIZATION OF THE X-MEN AS "HEROES."
THAT FIGHT IN NEW YORK DESTROYED A 200-MILLION DOLLAR BUILDING--HARDLY THE ACT OF HEROES.
THEY'RE OUTLAWS, PURE AND SIMPLE.
ACH, I DO NOT BELIEVE THIS! WE WERE DEFENDING OURSELVES IN BOTH INSTANCES! SHOULD WE HAVE DONE NOTHING, AND LET OURSELVES-- AND INNOCENT BYSTANDERS-- BE SLAUGHTERED?!
YOU'RE WASTIN' YER BREATH, ELF. THE BEST ARGUMENTS ON EARTH WON'T CONVINCE THAT CREEP. HIS MIND'S MADE UP.
DO THE FACTS SUPPORT SUCH A CONTENTION, SENATOR?
IN EACH CASE THE X-MEN FOUGHT RECOGNIZED CRIMINALS...

...AND, IN WASHINGTON, THEY SAVED YOU FROM CERTAIN ASSASSI-NATION.
THAT REALLY ISN'T THE POINT. WHO ARE THESE X-MEN?! WHAT GIVES THEM THE RIGHT TO TAKE THE LAW INTO THEIR OWN HANDS?!
THINGS ARE OUT OF CONTROL, JOHN. THERE ARE TOO MANY SUPER-BEINGS, TOO MANY MUTANTS, WITH MORE APPEARING VIRTUALLY EVERY DAY--
--NOT MERELY IN THE UNITED STATES, BUT THROUGHOUT THE GLOBE. YET LITTLE IS KNOWN ABOUT THE FORCES-- NATURAL AND ARTIFICIAL --WHICH CREATE THEM, OR OF THE EFFECT THEIR PRESENCE WILL HAVE ON THE REST OF HUMANITY.

YOU SEEM TO BE SAYING THAT MUTANTS ARE DANGEROUS SIMPLY BECAUSE THEY EXIST. THAT'S AN...ODD POSITION FOR AN AVOWED CIVIL LIBERTARIAN LIKE YOURSELF.
I CAN'T DENY IT. BUT THERE ARE CERTAIN EXTRAORDINARY CASES...
...THAT TRANS-CEND MORALITY.

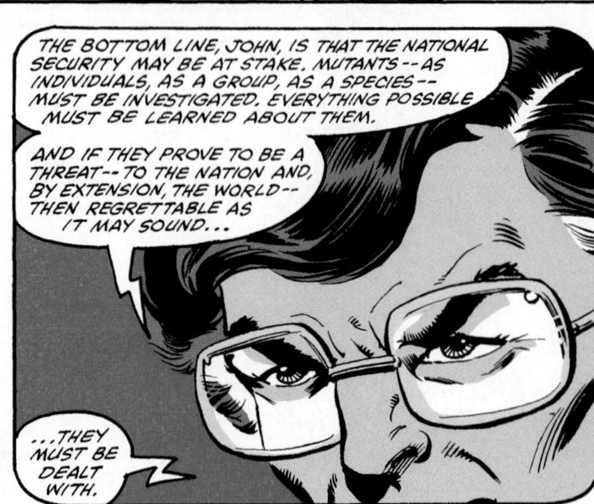
THE BOTTOM LINE, JOHN, IS THAT THE NATIONAL SECURITY MAY BE AT STAKE. MUTANTS--AS INDIVIDUALS, AS A GROUP, AS A SPECIES-- MUST BE INVESTIGATED. EVERYTHING POSSIBLE MUST BE LEARNED ABOUT THEM.
AND IF THEY PROVE TO BE A THREAT--TO THE NATION AND, BY EXTENSION, THE WORLD-- THEN REGRETTABLE AS IT MAY SOUND...
...THEY MUST BE DEALT WITH.

THAT MISERABLE, SANCTI-MONIOUS SOD!
I DON'T UNDERSTAND, MOIRA. MY FOLKS THINK HE'S A GOOD, DECENT MAN --WHY DOES HE HATE US SO?
THE NATURE OF THE BEAST, KIDDO--
--TO FEAR THAT WHICH IS DIFFERENT.

THIS IS TROUBLE. WHEN HE FORMED THE X-MEN, CHARLES WORKED WITH THE GOVERNMENT. THERE ARE COMPU-TER FILES ON THE ORIGINAL TEAM, AND PROBABLY ON YOU LOT, TOO. WE'VE BEEN LUCKY--AND SAFE-- SO FAR, BUT THAT WON'T LAST.
THE FILES HAVE TO BE DESTROYED BEFORE THE X-MEN'S SECURITY IS IRREVOCABLY COMPROMISED.

NO PROBLEM. WE SIMPLY DESIGN AN OPEN-ENDED VIRUS PROGRAM TO ERASE ANY AND ALL REFERENCES TO THE X-MEN AND PLUG IT INTO A CENTRAL FEDERAL DATA BANK. FROM THERE, IT'LL INFECT THE ENTIRE SYSTEM IN NO TIME.
CAN YOU DO THAT, KITTEN?
THE STAR-JAMMERS CAN.

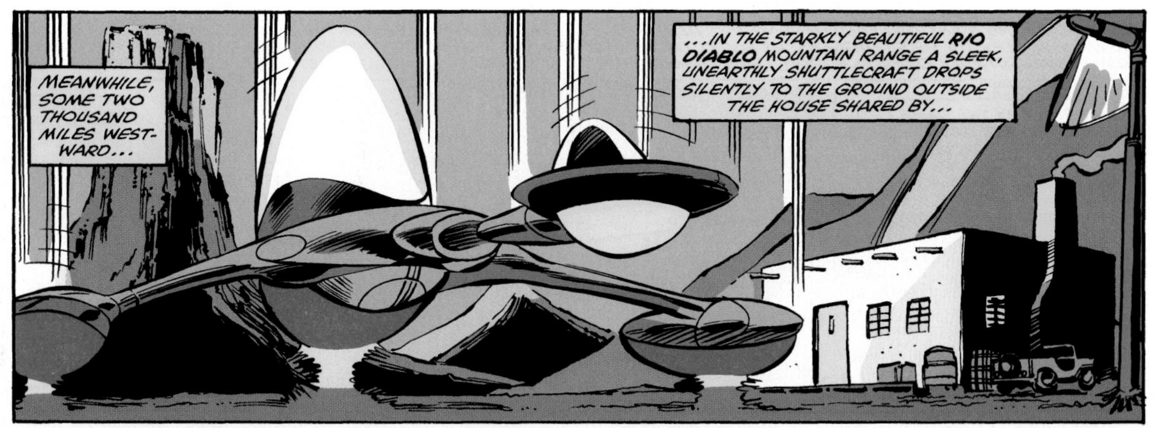
MEANWHILE, SOME TWO THOUSAND MILES WESTWARD...
...IN THE STARKLY BEAUTIFUL RIO DIABLO MOUNTAIN RANGE A SLEEK, UNEARTHLY SHUTTLECRAFT DROPS SILENTLY TO THE GROUND OUTSIDE THE HOUSE SHARED BY...

...FORMER X-MEN LORNA DANE (POLARIS) AND ALEX SUMMERS (HAVOK).
HOW'S DINNER? I'M STARVED!
BE PATIENT, M'LOVE-- OWW!
WHAT'S WRONG?!
Chef

BURNED M'TONGUE. THE CHILI IS SUPERB, BUT HOT! POUR ME A GLASS OF ICE WATER, WILLYA?
I'VE A BETTER IDEA.
MMMMMMMMMM --A WOMAN AFTER MY OWN HEART.
AMONG OTHER THINGS.

NOK NOK NOK
SIGH
MURPHY'S LAW-- IT NEVER FAILS, JUST WHEN THINGS GET INTERESTING.
HOLD THOSE THOUGHTS, SWEETHEART, WHILE I SEE WHO THE HECK IT IS.

H'LO, ALEX.
SCOTT!
LORNA, LOOK WHO'S HERE! WHAT BRINGS YOU TO THIS NECK OF THE WOODS, BIG BROTHER? YOU TIRED OF RAMRODDING THE X-MEN?!
YOU LOOK GREAT! C'MON IN!
ALEX, I'M NOT ALONE.
SO I SEE.

THERE'S NO EASY WAY TO SAY THIS: ALEX, MEET CHRISTOPHER SUMMERS --CORSAIR, LEADER OF THE STARJAMMERS--
--OUR FATHER.

REACTIONS ARE MANY AND VARIED-- AND NOT ALL OF THEM PLEASANT-- BEWILDERMENT AND DISBELIEF VYING WITH ELATION IN ALEX AS HE STRUGGLES, AS SCOTT DID A WEEK AGO, TO ASSIMILATE THIS STUNNING REVELATION. A FOUR-WAY CONVERSATION / REUNION BEGINS OVER DINNER AND IT'S STILL GOING ON WITHOUT LET-UP LATE THE FOLLOWING DAY.
AT ROUGHLY THE SAME TIME, ON THE EAST COAST, AN OFFICIAL-LOOKING CAR APPROACHES THE MAIN ENTRANCE...
...OF A BUILDING KNOWN THROUGHOUT THE WORLD...

...AND THREE PASSENGERS ALIGHT, ONE WEARING THE UNIFORM OF A CAPTAIN IN THE CANADIAN ARMED FORCES, ONE THAT OF A U.S. AIR FORCE COLONEL.
YOU SURE THIS CRAZY STUNT'LL WORK, CAROL?
TRUST ME, WOLVERINE.
NIGHTCRAWLER, YOU WAIT HERE. IF WE HIT TROUBLE, STORM WILL CALL YOU ON HER MICRO-TRANSCEIVER.
JAWOHL, CAROL. TAKE CARE, MEIN FREUNDE, AND GOOD LUCK.

HOWEVER, AS THEY ENTER THE PENTAGON...
EXCUSE ME, CAPTAIN. WE'RE GETTING EXCEPTIONALLY STRONG READINGS FROM OUR METAL DETECTORS.
NO! WOLVERINE, I BEG YOU...
...DO NOTHING RASH.
LIEUTENANT, I HAVEN'T TIME FOR THIS. WE'RE DUE TO BRIEF THE JOINT CHIEFS...

I'LL CLEAR THIS UP, COLONEL.
MY MEDIC CARD, MISTER. A GOOD CHUNK O' MY SKELETON IS METAL. PROSTHETICS. WAR WOUNDS. THAT'S WHAT TRIGGERED YOUR SNOOPER.
MP

FOR A MOMENT, I THOUGHT WE WERE LOST.
NAH. CAROL'N'ME HAD THAT KID PRETTY WELL BUFFALO'D. I WAS WONDERIN', THOUGH, CAROL, ABOUT THE COMMAND PILOT WINGS AN' "FRUIT SALAD" YOU'RE WEARIN'-- ARE THEY LEGIT?
AS MUCH AS YOURS, LOGAN. THE WINGS AND MEDALS WERE EARNED. SO WAS THE RANK. I WAS ALLOWED TO TEMPORARILY UPGRADE FROM MAJOR TO COLONEL ON MISSIONS. THE CLOUT CAME IN USEFUL.
WE'LL NEED IT, TO REACH THE PRIME DATA BANK, IN THE S.I.S.O.--SPECIAL INTELLIGENCE SERVICE OPERATION--VAULT. IT'S THE MOST HEAVILY GUARDED AREA OF THE ENTIRE PENTAGON.

THE PENTAGON WAS ORIGINALLY DESIGNED AS A MILITARY HOSPITAL IN WORLD WAR II; THAT'S WHY THE CORRIDORS ARE SO WIDE--TO ACCOMMODATE DOUBLE AND TRIPLE-PARKED GURNIES.
BECAUSE OF ITS SIZE--AND CONFUSING LAYOUT--PEOPLE ARE ALWAYS GETTING LOST, AND SOME, NATURALLY, ARE RUMORED NEVER TO BE SEEN AGAIN.
THINK THAT'LL HAPPEN TO US, COLONEL?

ANYTHING'S POSSIBLE--OH! I BEG YOUR PARDON.
MA FAULT, COLONEL, AH SHOULD HAVE LOOKED--YOU!
DANVERS!

ROGUE!!
THAT SINGLE WORD IS THICK WITH AGONY AND HATRED, AS THE SAME THOUGHTS RIP LIKE WILDFIRE THROUGH THE MINDS OF BOTH WOMEN...

...TWISTING THE CLOCK BACK ONLY A FEW SHORT MONTHS...
...TO A CALM, FOGGY, SUMMER NIGHT IN SAN FRANCIS-CO...
CAROL WAS STILL MS. MARVEL THEN, A FORM-ER AVENGER, BUILDING A NEW LIFE FOR HERSELF IN THE CITY BY THE BAY.

ROGUE WAS THERE TO AM-BUSH HER, AND ABSORB HER SUPER-POWERS, TO BE USED LATER IN A PLANNED ATTEMPT TO FREE HER CAPTURED BRETHREN IN THE BROTHERHOOD OF EVIL MUTANTS.
BUT SOMETHING WENT WRONG. CAROL FOUGHT TOO LONG, TOO FIERCELY.

AND INSTEAD OF TEMPO-RARILY "STEALING" CAROL'S ABILITIES AND MEMORIES...
...ROGUE'S TRANSFER BECAME PERMANENT.

IT WAS A PHYSICAL AND PSYCHIC TRAUMA THAT SCARRED BOTH WOMEN.*
GET AWAY FROM ME!
UNNNGNH!
*FOR DETAILS, SEE AVENGERS ANNUAL #10--L.

NOT DEAD?! IMPOSSIBLE! THAT BLOW SHOULD HAVE SMASHED YOU TO A PULP!
"ROGUE?!" SHE'S PART O'MYSTIQUE'S BROTHERHOOD OF EVIL MUTANTS!
STOP HER, WOLVERINE!
NO! LEAVE HER TO ME! SHE'S MINE!

SORRY, DARLIN'. I KNOW HOW YOU FEEL, BUT STORM'S THE BOSS.
YOU GOT A LOT TO ANSWER FOR, RED. I SUGGEST YOU STAY REAL COOL--AN', IF YOU'RE LUCKY, YOU WON'T GET HURT.
LAH-DE-DAH, LI'L MAN, Y'ALL GOT ME SHAKIN' IN MY BOOTS.
ONLY PROBLEM IS, THAT IF ANYONE HERE IS GONNA GET HURT--

WHAM!
--IT'S YOU!

NICE TRY. BUT MY BONES ARE LACED WITH ADAMANTIUM. THEY'RE VIRTUALLY UNBREAKABLE.
I HAVE CLAWS, TOO, MADE OUTTA THE SAME STUFF, AN' HONED RAZOR-SHARP. I'D USE 'EM ON YOU...

...BUT YOU AIN'T WORTH THE EFFORT.
BAD MOVE, SHRIMP.

CRIPES! MY ARM-- PINNED!
DIDN'T DANVERS TELL Y'ALL ABOUT ME?
AH ABSORB THE MINDS AN' ABILITIES OF WHOEVER AH TOUCH. THE MEREST FLESH-TO-FLESH CONTACT'LL DO THE TRICK.
BUT AH SEE NO HARM IN HAVIN' A LITTLE FUN IN THE PROCESS, DO YOU, WOLVERINE-HONEY, HMNH?
AH DIDN'T THINK SO.
HE MAKES A CONVULSIVE, DESPERATE EFFORT TO BREAK FREE-- CLAWS EXTENDING FROM HOUSINGS BUILT INTO HIS HANDS AND FOREARMS-- BUT EVEN AS HE DOES SO, HIS MIND GOES BLANK, HIS BODY LIMP...

NO MORE, ROGUE!
AAIII--!

THAT WAS A WARNING SHOT, VILLAIN. I SUGGEST YOU TAKE THE HINT AND DEPART-- WHILE YOU ARE STILL ABLE.
NOT A CHANCE, WITCH. AH'VE BEEN LOOKIN' FOR-WARD TO MEETIN' YOU X-MEN--
--AN' TEARIN' YOU APART!

COLONEL, WHAT'S GOING ON?! ARE YOU OKAY?!
D'YOU NEED HELP, MA'AM-- HEY!!
ALL I NEED, GENTLEMEN, IS THIS!

FIRE AWAY, SUGAR.
WON'T DO YOU NO GOOD.
SHE'S RIGHT, DEVIL TAKE HER SOUL. ALL MS. MARVEL WAS-- ALL I WAS-- SHE IS.
AND WILL BE-- FOREVER.
BLAM BLAM BLAM

WE CANNOT FIGHT HERE. I HAVE NO ROOM TO MANEUVER.
AND WOLVERINE IS IN A COMA. I HAVE NO IDEA HOW BADLY HE WAS AFFECTED. I MUST GET HIM TO SAFETY-- AND DRAW ROGUE AWAY FROM THESE INNOCENT BY-STANDERS.
A HURRICANE GUST OF ARCTIC AIR CREATES A SHEET OF ICE ON THE FLOOR AND SENDS THE STARTLED ROGUE SKIDDING AWAY.

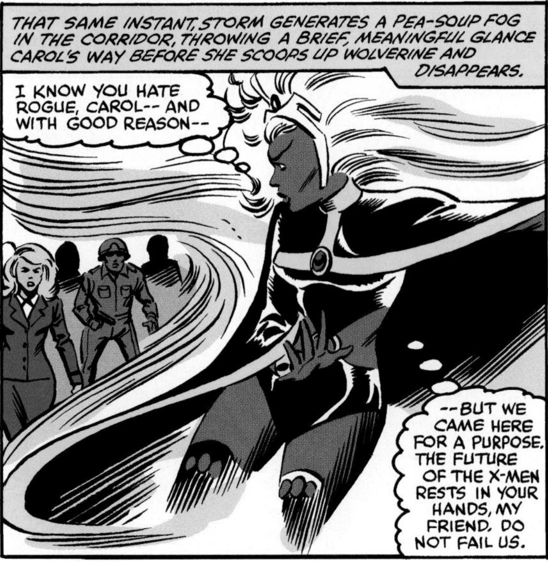
THAT SAME INSTANT, STORM GENERATES A PEA-SOUP FOG IN THE CORRIDOR, THROWING A BRIEF, MEANINGFUL GLANCE CAROL'S WAY BEFORE SHE SCOOPS UP WOLVERINE AND DISAPPEARS.
I KNOW YOU HATE ROGUE, CAROL-- AND WITH GOOD REASON--
--BUT WE CAME HERE FOR A PURPOSE. THE FUTURE OF THE X-MEN RESTS IN YOUR HANDS, MY FRIEND. DO NOT FAIL US.

MOMENTS LATER...
THE FOG'S--GONE! AND SO'RE THOSE WEIRD WOMEN!
I HEARD ONE CALL THE OTHER AN "X-MAN." SOUND A FULL ALERT, CAPTAIN. I WANT THOSE BLASTED MUTIES FOUND--ON THE DOUBLE!
YESSIR!
THE X-MEN ARE IN REAL TROUBLE NOW. AND IT'S MOSTLY MY FAULT.

BUT WHEN I SAW ROGUE, I...COULDN'T HELP MYSELF. SHE TOOK FROM ME EVERYTHING THAT GAVE MY LIFE MEANING.
I DON'T KNOW WHAT HURTS MORE: THAT--OR THE FACT THAT I'LL NEVER BE ABLE TO MAKE HER PAY FOR IT.
DANVERS!

SHE HASN'T SEEN ME.
EVEN IF SHE HAD, IT WOULDN'T MATTER.

NEITHER SHE--NOR ANYONE ELSE--CONNECTS RAVEN DARKHÖLME, CIVIL SERVANT, DEPUTY DIRECTOR OF THE DEFENSE ADVANCED RESEARCH PROJECTS AGENCY...
...WITH MYSTIQUE.
THAT IGNORANCE WILL--VERY SOON NOW--PROVE FATAL.

ELSEWHERE...
WHAT A MESS.
WAS ROGUE ALONE? HAVE WE WALKED INTO THE MIDDLE OF A BROTHERHOOD OPERATION-- AN ASSAULT ON THE PENTAGON? I...DOUBT IT. HER DEMEANOR WAS FAR TOO CASUAL.
WHICH RAISES AN EVEN MORE DISTURBING QUESTION: IF SHE BELONGS HERE, COULD THE BROTHERHOOD BE WORKING IN CONCERT WITH THE AMERICAN GOVERNMENT? THAT SOUNDS BEYOND BELIEF, BUT...

SURPRISE Y'ALL!
THAT RUNT WOLVERINE'S ENHANCED SENSES ARE PRETTY NIFTY, ONCE AH GOT THE HANG OF 'EM...
...TRACKIN' Y'ALL DOWN BECAME A PIECE O' CAKE!
NIGHTCRAWLER! I NEED YOU!

HE CAN'T SAVE YOU, SUGAH.
WANNA BET?
HUH?!?
I HEARD YOUR CALL OVER OUR MICRO-TRANSCEIVER COMLINK, STORM. I TELEPORTED HERE AS QUICKLY AS I COULD. SORRY IT TOOK SO LONG.
I HAVE NO COMPLAINTS, NIGHTCRAWLER. BUT--BE CAREFUL WITH HER! SHE'S DANGEROUS.

SO AM I.
WHERE IS MYSTIQUE, LEIBLING?! SHE AND I HAVE MUCH TO TALK ABOUT. TALK, CHILD--BEFORE THINGS GET ROUGH!
YYIII!

BUB, AH WOULDN'T WORRY ABOUT THOSE QUESTIONS, IF AH WERE YOU.

BAMF
CRUMMP
THEY'RE ACADEMIC TO A CORPSE!

YOU'LL HAVE TO DO BETTER THAN THAT, ROGUE, TO HIT A FOE WHO CAN TELEPORT OUT OF YOUR WAY.
OOOHHHH...
MY SKULL... POUNDIN' FIT TA BUST. FEEL SO FLAMIN' WEAK-- BUT GETTIN' STRONGER EV'RY SECOND! THE EFFECT O' ROGUE'S POWER MUST BE TEMPORARY. THE ABILITIES SHE STOLE FROM ME-- ARE COMIN' BACK!

AH KNOW WHAT'S HAPPENED, RUNT. BUT WHAT AH DID ONCE, AH CAN DO AGAIN.
YOU CAN TRY, BABE. BUT THIS TIME--

--I'M READY FOR YOU!!
BOOM!

MEANWHILE...
RETINAL SCAN, VOICEPRINT AND IDENTICARD CHECK CONFIRMED, COLONEL. ADMITTANCE TO SISO VAULT AUTHORIZED.
THANK YOU.
IT'S NICE TO SEE THAT, WHATEVER ELSE I'VE LOST, I'M STILL AS GOOD A SPY AS EVER.

THE PRIME COMPUTER CENTER--WHAT DOES SHE WANT IN THERE?
FROM THE SOUND OF THINGS, ROGUE AND THE X-MEN ARE KEEPING EACH OTHER BUSY. THAT LEAVES DANVERS AND ME ON OUR OWN.

GOOD. HER DEATH WILL BE A PERSONAL PLEASURE TOO LONG DENIED.
I CAN'T FOLLOW AS MYSELF. MY "RAVEN" IDENTITY IS TOO VALUABLE TO COMPROMISE.
I'LL SIMPLY SHAPE-CHANGE INTO THE FORM OF SOMEONE CAROL TRUSTS: NICHOLAS FURY, DIRECTOR OF SHIELD.* SHE WON'T SUSPECT A THING--UNTIL I STRIKE!
*SHIELD: SUPREME HEADQUARTERS INTERNATIONAL ESPIONAGE LAW-ENFORCEMENT DIVISION--L.

ELSEWHERE...
A FULL-POWER BOLT--AND ROGUE SHRUGS IT OFF WITH A LAUGH.
Y'ALL GET AN "A" FOR EFFORT, STORM.

YOU TRIED. YOU LOST. THERE ARE WORSE EPITAPHS.
NO!!
AT ROGUE'S TOUCH, ORORO FEELS A SUDDEN, TERRIBLE, WRENCHING DISSOLUTION OF SELF AND THEN HER AWARENESS--INDEED, FOR ALL PRACTICAL PURPOSES, HER VERY EXISTENCE AS A SENTIENT BEING--CEASES.

BUT THIS TIME, ROGUE DISCOVERS, SHE MAY HAVE ABSORBED MORE THAN SHE BARGAINED FOR.
STORM'S CONTROL OVER THE WEATHER HAS BEEN HONED AND PERFECTED BY HALF-A-LIFETIME OF PRACTICE AND EXPERIENCE. ROGUE LACKS THOSE CRITICAL ASSETS.

THAT COSTS HER DEARLY.
HAH! THE WEATHER IS EXPLODING OUT OF CONTROL. TOO MUCH IS HAPPENING TOO FAST-- ROGUE CAN'T CONTROL IT. SERVES HER RIGHT.
I'D BEST HAUL STORM OUT OF HARM'S WAY WHILE I HAVE THE CHANCE.

SO MUCH FOR THAT IDEA-- ROGUE'S GENERATED A FLASH FLOOD!
THIS IS NOT GOING WELL!
COULD BE... WORSE, MY FRIEND. MORE ENERGY ROGUE... EXPENDS... FASTER SHE USES UP STOLEN POWERS-- SOONER THEY REVERT TO ORIGINAL OWNERS. I... CAN THINK. SOON, I'LL BE ABLE... TO ACT.
WHAT THEN, STORM?! SHE'S TRASHIN' US BUT GOOD-- HOW DO WE BEAT HER?!

MEANWHILE...
HELLO, CAROL. I'VE BEEN LOOKING FORWARD TO THIS MOMENT.
WHO--?! FURY!
BUT-- WHY THE GUN?!

TO KILL YOU, OF COURSE.
BLAM!

THAT WAS ALMOST TOO QUICK, TOO EASY, CAROL.
I SOMEHOW EXPECTED... BETTER OF YOU.

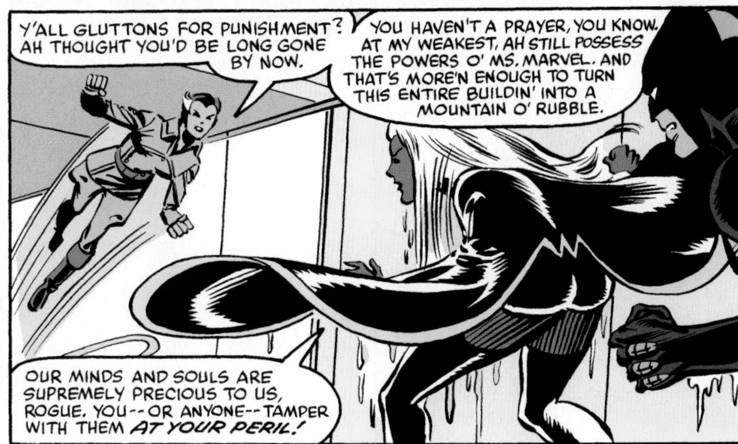
Y'ALL GLUTTONS FOR PUNISHMENT? AH THOUGHT YOU'D BE LONG GONE BY NOW.
YOU HAVEN'T A PRAYER, YOU KNOW. AT MY WEAKEST, AH STILL POSSESS THE POWERS O' MS. MARVEL. AND THAT'S MORE'N ENOUGH TO TURN THIS ENTIRE BUILDIN' INTO A MOUNTAIN O' RUBBLE.
OUR MINDS AND SOULS ARE SUPREMELY PRECIOUS TO US, ROGUE. YOU--OR ANYONE--TAMPER WITH THEM AT YOUR PERIL!

WE ALSO DO NOT LIKE LOSING!
I'VE SNARED HER! SHE'S *YOURS*, WOLVERINE-- BUT DON'T LET HER TOUCH YOU!
I'VE LEARNED MY LESSON, STORM. YOU KEEP HER COVERED, AN' I'LL PUT HER DOWN FOR THE COUNT.

THAT THE BEST YOU CAN DO, SUGAH?
YOU'RE A TOUGH LITTLE COOKIE, AIN'T'CHA, ROGUE? WELL, IF A RIGHT CROSS TO THE JAW WON'T DO THE TRICK...
...LET'S SEE WHAT HAPPENS WHEN I HIT SOME CRITICAL NEURAL PRESSURE POINTS.

SORRY, RUNT. WITH ME--
--ONE SHOT IS *ALL YOU GET!*

DANVERS WAS WORKING WITH THE X-MEN. I WONDER WHAT THEY WANTED FROM THE LIBRARY BANKS?
GUARDS WILL BE HERE ANY SECOND. DANVERS LOOKS DEAD.

BUT I'LL ADMINISTER A *COUP DE GRACE*, JUST TO MAKE SURE--
--UNNNFF!
LOOKS ARE DECEIVING, BUSTER!

THANK HEAVEN FOR MY EXTRAORDINARY REFLEXES. I DODGED QUICKLY ENOUGH SO THAT BULLET ONLY GRAZED ME. MY HEAD HURTS LIKE BLAZES--BUT I'M ALIVE!
OBVIOUSLY, THIS ISN'T NICK FURY, BUT WHO-- I DON'T BELIEVE IT!
HIS FEATURES-- CHANGING BEFORE MY EYES--

--INTO STORM!
NICE PLOY. THE SHOCK OF THAT TRANSFORMATION THREW ME OFF-BALANCE, ALLOWED MY FOE--HE, SHE, IT???--TO SEIZE THE INITIATIVE.
SHE MAY HAVE ORORO'S LOOKS, BUT EVIDENTLY NOT HER POWERS. SHE'S FIGHTING LIKE A NORMAL PERSON.

BIG MISTAKE.
I WAS TRAINED BY THE BEST TO BE THE BEST.
I'VE FIGURED OUT WHO YOU ARE, LADY. AND BECAUSE OF THAT, YOU HAVEN'T A CHANCE.

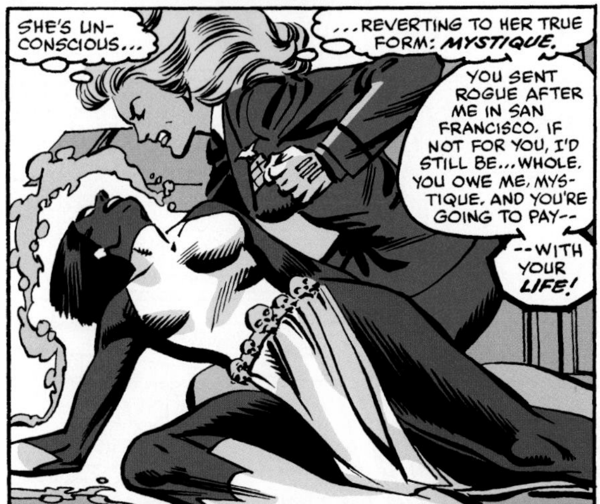
SHE'S UNCONSCIOUS...
...REVERTING TO HER TRUE FORM: MYSTIQUE.
YOU SENT ROGUE AFTER ME IN SAN FRANCISCO. IF NOT FOR YOU, I'D STILL BE... WHOLE. YOU OWE ME, MYSTIQUE. AND YOU'RE GOING TO PAY--
--WITH YOUR LIFE!

HAD ENOUGH, DAHLIN'S? Y'ALL LOOK SO TIRED, WHILE AH FEEL FRESH AS A DAISY.
SHE'S RIGHT, CURSE HER. WE'VE TRIED EVERYTHING, TO NO AVAIL--EH?!
WHAT'S STORM DOING?
YOUR TRIUMPH IS PREMATURE, ROGUE.

A TORNADO!
BEFORE THE YOUNG WOMAN IS FULLY AWARE OF WHAT'S HAPPENING...
...STORM'S CYCLONE SCOOPS HER UP...

...AND CARRIES HER AWAY.

MY WHIRLWIND WON'T HOLD HER LONG. I SUGGEST WE NOT BE HERE WHEN SHE RETURNS.
WHAT ABOUT CAROL AN' THE MISSION?
THIS PLACE IS CRAWLING WITH SECURITY FORCES. BATTERED AND OUTNUMBERED AS WE ARE, WE DARE NOT RISK A BATTLE--WITH THEM OR ROGUE. I AM SORRY, WOLVERINE. ALL WE CAN DO... IS FLEE.

HOWEVER, UNBEKNOWNST TO THEM...
YOU SHOULD HAVE SLAIN ME, DANVERS. WHEN NEXT WE MEET-- AND WE WILL MEET, COUNT ON THAT-- I WILL NOT BE SO MERCIFUL
THERE IS DEATH BETWEEN US!
TAKE HER AWAY. I'LL SECURE THE S.I.S.O. VAULT 'TIL THE DUTY STAFF ARRIVE.

I SHOULD HAVE PULLED THE TRIGGER-- BUT... I COULDN'T. I'M NOT AS RUTHLESS AS I ONCE WAS.
MY "WEAKNESS" WILL COST ME, I'M AFRAID. WITH HER SHAPE-CHANGING ABILITY, MYSTIQUE IS CERTAIN TO ESCAPE -- AND SOON. I MAY HAVE TO SPEND THE REST OF MY LIFE LOOKING OVER MY SHOULDER, WONDERING WHEN SHE'LL STRIKE.
AND THE IRONY IS, I CAN'T EVEN REMEMBER WHY SHE HATES ME SO.* THAT PART OF MY MEMORIES WAS IRREVOCABLY LOST WHEN ROGUE STOLE MY POWERS.
*FOR THAT STORY, SEE FUTURE ISSUES OF MARVEL FANFARE--L.

BUT I'M A SURVIVOR. I'LL HANDLE IT.
THERE--THE VIRUS PROGRAM IS PRIMED AND READY TO GO. ONCE I'VE PUNCHED UP THE X-MEN DATA FILE...
HER FINGERS FLASH OVER THE CONTROL CONSOLE, BUT WHAT APPEARS ON THE SCANSCREENS...

...IS NOT AT ALL WHAT SHE EXPECTS...
WELL! MY SUBCONSCIOUS MUST BE WORKING OVERTIME. I USED THE WRONG ACCESS CODE.
U.S. AIR FORCE, INACTIVE
DANVERS, CAROL S.J
MAJ. 699004 08170
RESIGNED
AVENGERS PERSONNEL FILE # 14
MS. MARVEL
STATUS: INACTIVE
THERE ARE MY PERSONNEL FILES-- AS CAROL DANVERS AND MS. MARVEL.

MY HISTORY--MY LIFE--COMPRESSED ONTO A FRACTION OF MICROCHIP. THE FACES ARE FAMILIAR...
...BUT THE WOMEN THEY REPRESENT ...ARE STRANGERS.
THEY WERE WOMEN OF GREAT PROMISE-- WITH HOPES AND DREAMS. BUT THEIR LIVES ENDED. THEY..."DIED."

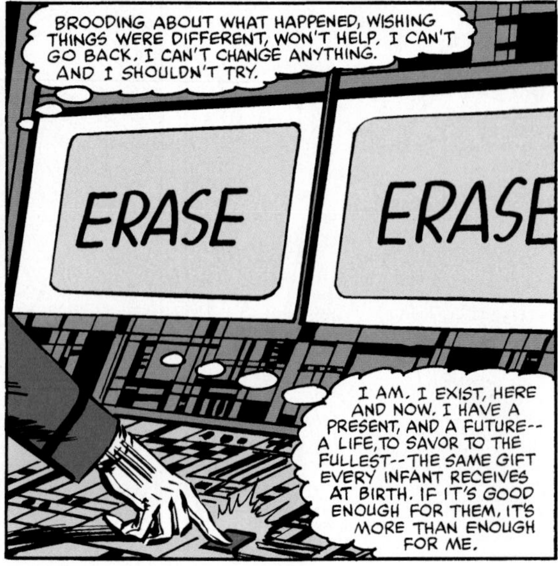
BROODING ABOUT WHAT HAPPENED, WISHING THINGS WERE DIFFERENT, WON'T HELP. I CAN'T GO BACK. I CAN'T CHANGE ANYTHING. AND I SHOULDN'T TRY.
ERASE
ERASE
I AM. I EXIST, HERE AND NOW. I HAVE A PRESENT, AND A FUTURE-- A LIFE, TO SAVOR TO THE FULLEST--THE SAME GIFT EVERY INFANT RECEIVES AT BIRTH. IF IT'S GOOD ENOUGH FOR THEM, IT'S MORE THAN ENOUGH FOR ME.

SOON, OUTSIDE...
NO SIGN OF THE X-MEN OR ROGUE. BUT SECURITY'S PULLING OUT ALL THE STOPS IN THEIR SEARCH FOR THEM. THEY'VE EVEN BROUGHT UP THE ARMY'S FAST REACTION SWAT BATTALION FROM FORT MYERS.
I WONDER HOW THEY'LL EXPLAIN THIS TO THE PRESS.
U.S. ARMY

THE X-MEN WILL PROBABLY END UP PORTRAYED AS THE VILLAINS OF THE PIECE. IF SENATOR KELLY IS ANY INDICATION, THE GOVERNMENT IS ALREADY PARANOID ABOUT MUTANTS. THIS WILL ONLY MAKE MATTERS WORSE.
AND SINCE THE X-MEN HAVE NO OFFICIAL SANCTION, LIKE THE AVENGERS, THEY'VE NO WAY OF TELLING THEIR SIDE OF THINGS.
CAROL-- OVER HERE!
KURT!

IT'S GOOD TO SEE THAT YOU'RE ALL RIGHT. I...KNOW ROGUE'S CAPABILITIES. I FIGURED YOU'D HAVE A FIGHT ON YOUR HANDS.
NO SWEAT, CAROL. WE SHOWED THE KID A SURPRISE OR TWO.
WHAT ABOUT YOU --AND THE MISSION?
EVERYTHING'S TAKEN CARE OF. OFFICIALLY, AS FAR AS THE FEDERAL COMPUTER NETWORK IS CONCERNED, THE X-MEN HAVE CEASED TO EXIST.
WUNDERBAR!

MY SENTIMENTS EXACTLY.
BUT I'LL LAY ODDS IT'LL BE AN INTERESTING TRIP.
AND THEY ARE TOO, IN A WAY. TODAY, I FINALLY LAID MY GHOSTS TO REST. I'M FREE, TO BEGIN MY LIFE ANEW.
I DON'T KNOW WHERE I'LL END UP,

NEXT ISSUE: DRACULA!

UNCANNY X-MEN #156 COVER ART BY **DAVE COCKRUM** & **BOB WIACEK**

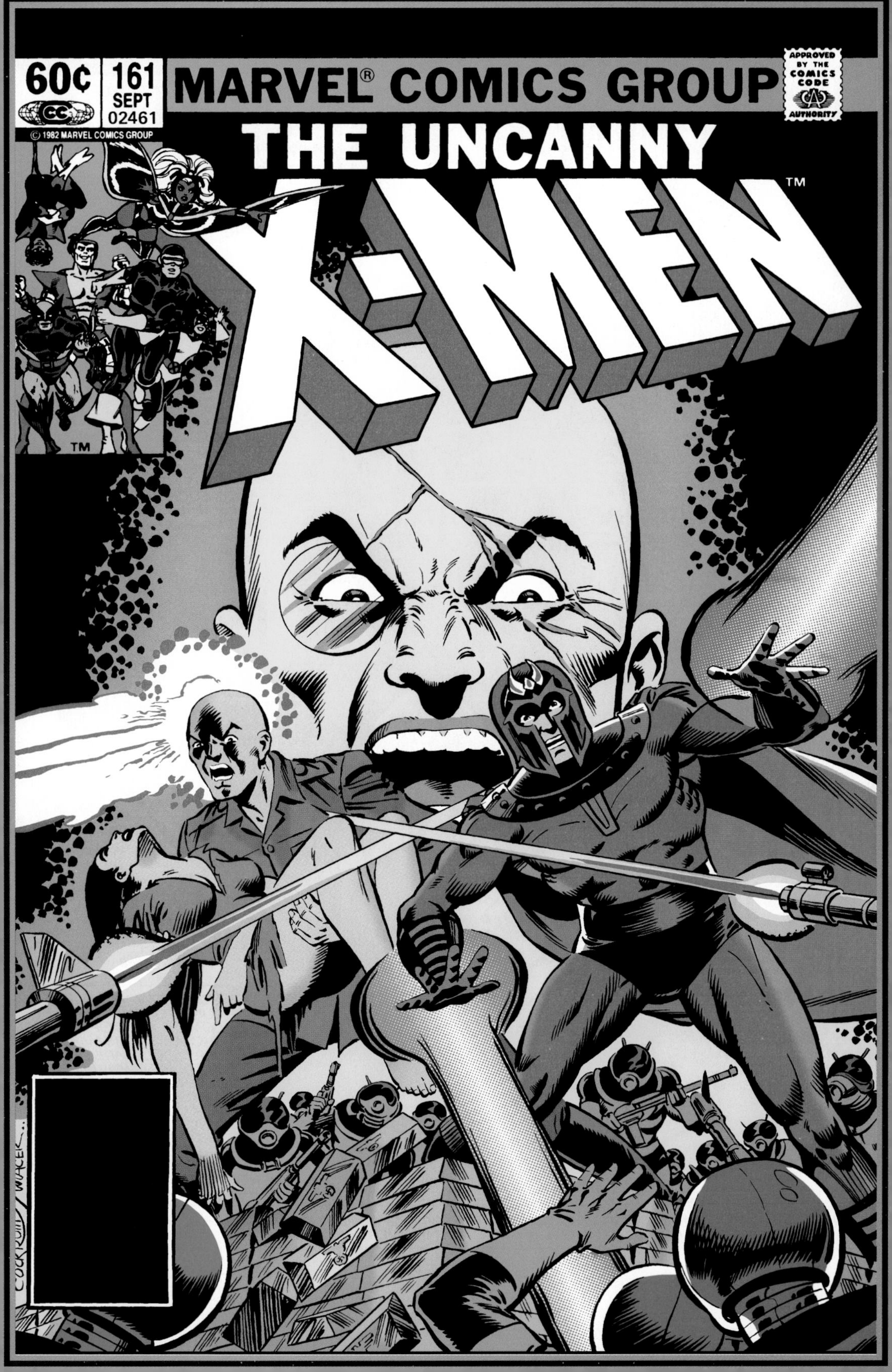

60¢
161
SEPT
02461
MARVEL® COMICS GROUP
APPROVED BY THE COMICS CODE AUTHORITY
© 1982 MARVEL COMICS GROUP
THE UNCANNY
X-MEN™
TM

Stan Lee PRESENTS: THE UNCANNY X-MEN!™

GOLD RUSH!

HIS FACE IS PLACID, ALMOST SERENE, BUT IN THE DEEPEST RECESSES OF HIS BRAIN, CHARLES XAVIER **SCREAMS**-- A NEVER-ENDING SHRIEK THAT MINGLES RAGE AND PAIN, AND A PRIMAL **TERROR** SUCH AS HE HAS NEVER KNOWN.

HE HAS FACED DEATH OFTEN IN HIS LIFE WITHOUT SUCH FEAR--BUT THIS IS WORSE.

SOMEHOW, AN ALIEN CONSCIOUSNESS HAS BECOME A PART OF HIM. HIS THOUGHTS, HIS MIND--HIS VERY SOUL-- ARE NO LONGER QUITE HIS OWN. BIT BY BIT, SECOND BY SECOND, THIS OTHER SELF IS STRIPPING HIM OF HIS HUMANITY AND, TRY AS HE MIGHT, WITH ALL HIS MIGHT...

...HE SEEMS UNABLE TO **STOP** IT.

CHRIS CLAREMONT writer | DAVE COCKRUM penciler & BOB WIACEK inker | TOM ORZECHOWSKI, letterer GLYNIS WEIN, colorist | LOUISE JONES editor | JIM SHOOTER editor-in-chief

Ach, MY FRIENDS, IS THERE NOTHING WE CAN DO?!
IF THERE WAS, ELF...
...DON'T'CHA THINK WE'D BE DOIN' IT?
THERE'S NO CHANGE, SIKORSKY.
IS TO BE EXPECTED, MOIRA-COLLEAGUE. DATA INDICATES--XAVIER'S PSYCHE, MOST FUNDAMENTAL LEVEL ON--A GREAT CONFLICT, RAGING IS. PRIZE IS HIS SANITY, LIFE ITSELF PERHAPS.
BUT XAVIER WARRIOR-LIKE FIGHTS. SURRENDER, REFUSES TO. BATTLE TOO LONG HAS LASTED, TOO MUCH OF BODY'S RESOURCES HAS DRAINED. IF RESOLVED IT IS NOT--AND SOON IT IS NOT--

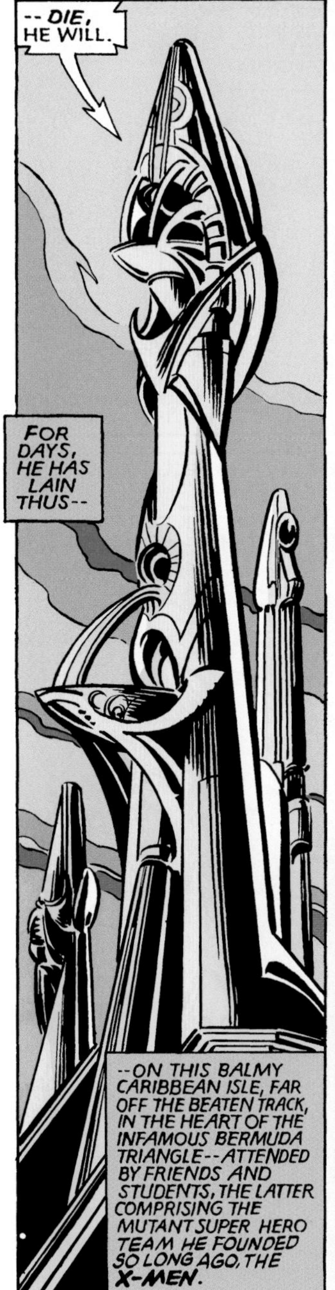
--DIE, HE WILL.
FOR DAYS, HE HAS LAIN THUS--
--ON THIS BALMY CARIBBEAN ISLE, FAR OFF THE BEATEN TRACK, IN THE HEART OF THE INFAMOUS BERMUDA TRIANGLE--ATTENDED BY FRIENDS AND STUDENTS, THE LATTER COMPRISING THE MUTANT SUPER HERO TEAM HE FOUNDED SO LONG AGO, THE X-MEN.

WE'VE TRIED EVERY MEANS POSSIBLE TO BRING HIM AROUND, SCOTT--INCLUDING A MINDPROBE BY ANOTHER TELEPATH. BUT THAT ATTEMPT NEARLY KILLED US ALL. CHARLES' PSIONIC DEFENSES WERE TOO STRONG.
HE SEIZED CONTROL OF THE LASS--
--AND USED HER TO TRY TO DESTROY HIMSELF.

SUICIDE? HIM?! WHAT ARE YOU SAYING, MOIRA--THAT THERE'S NO HOPE?!
THERE'S ALWAYS HOPE.
SPARE ME THE HOMILIES, DOCTOR. UNDER THE CIRCUMSTANCES, THEY RING A LITTLE HOLLOW.

THIS IS AWFUL, LOGAN. I FEEL SO SAD.
HE'S BEEN THROUGH THIS BEFORE, KITTY--WITH JEAN GREY. IT'S A HARD THING FOR A MAN TO FACE--WATCHIN', WAITIN' HELPLESSLY WHILE SOMEONE YOU CARE FOR FIGHTS FOR THEIR LIFE--
BUT SCOTT SOUNDS FURIOUS--WHY?
--ESPECIALLY WHEN YOU FEEL AS DEEPLY AS SCOTTY DOES AN' TRY AS HARD TO HIDE THOSE FEELIN'S. IN THAT WAY, I GUESS HE'N I ARE A LOT ALIKE.

SCOTT...?
CORSAIR, LET ME BE THE ONE TO SPEAK WITH HIM.
HE'S MY SON, ORORO.
AND MY FRIEND. I DO NOT ASK THIS LIGHTLY.
ALL RIGHT, THEN. IF YOU THINK IT BEST.

THAT'S A MAGNIFICENT SUNSET, STORM. DID YOU USE YOUR WEATHER POWERS TO ARRANGE IT?
I AM FLATTERED THAT YOU THINK ME CAPABLE OF SUCH BEAUTY, CYCLOPS-- BUT ALAS, I HAD NO PART IN IT. THIS IS ENTIRELY NATURE'S HANDIWORK.
I MUST CONFESS THAT, IN SOME WAYS, I PREFER THIS ISLE TO OUR OLD HEAD-QUARTERS BACK IN NEW YORK.

WELL, THANKS TO YOU, WE MAY BE HERE QUITE A WHILE.
I BEG YOUR PARDON?
ON MY WAY OUT HERE, I PICKED UP THIS PAPER. THE HEADLINE SPEAKS FOR ITSELF.

THIS KIND OF PUBLICITY IS SOME-THING THE X-MEN CAN ILL AFFORD RIGHT NOW. FOR PITY'S SAKE, WOMAN, WE'RE SUPPOSED TO BE *HEROES!*
THE SITUATION IS INDEED REGRETTABLE, BUT IT COULD NOT BE AVOIDED.
DAILY BUGLE
MUTANTS WRECK PENTAGON
X-MEN IMPLICATED
SENATOR KELLY URGES INVESTIGATION
X-MEN MENACE
NEWS ANALYSIS BY J. JONAH JAMESON
OUR SECURITY WAS IN JEOPARDY. THE THREAT HAD TO BE DEALT WITH. QUICKLY. PERMANENTLY. THE NEED JUSTIFIED THE RISK.

THE X-MEN'S SECRET MAY BE SAFE, ORORO, BUT OUR REP COULDN'T BE WORSE. THE GOVERNMENT WAS ALREADY PARANOID ABOUT MUTANTS. THIS FIASCO'S MADE MATTERS INFINITELY WORSE.
ARE YOU SUGGESTING WE SHOULD HAVE DONE NOTHING?
A BETTER WAY SHOULD HAVE BEEN FOUND TO ACCOMPLISH THE MISSION. I SHOULD'VE BEEN CONSULTED.

I AM TEAM LEADER, SCOTT, NOT YOU.
THEN PERHAPS IT'S TIME I TOOK MY OLD JOB BACK.

IF YOU WISH TO RECLAIM THAT POSITION, CYCLOPS, ALL YOU NEED DO--
IS ASK FOR IT!
ORORO, WAIT!
WHY?
DON'T GO! PLEASE!
YOU HAVE SOMETHING TO SAY?

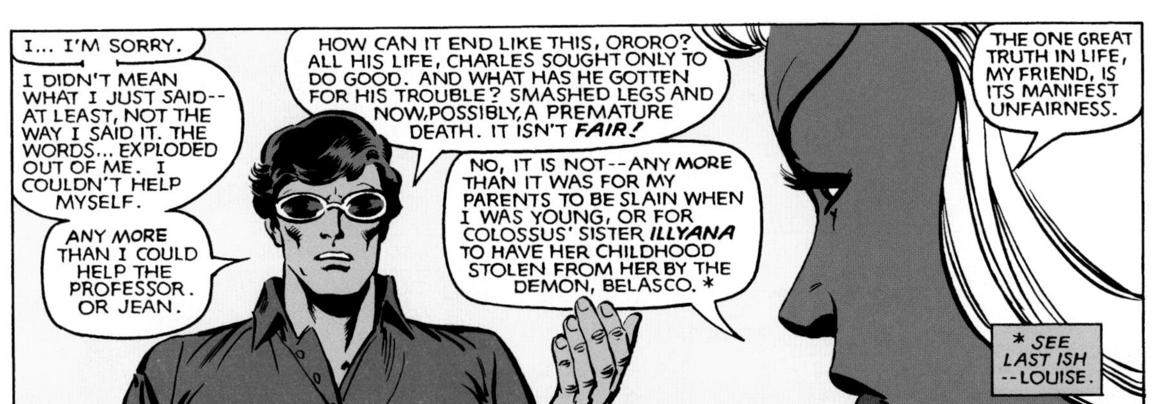
I... I'M SORRY.
I DIDN'T MEAN WHAT I JUST SAID-- AT LEAST, NOT THE WAY I SAID IT. THE WORDS... EXPLODED OUT OF ME. I COULDN'T HELP MYSELF.
ANY MORE THAN I COULD HELP THE PROFESSOR. OR JEAN.
HOW CAN IT END LIKE THIS, ORORO? ALL HIS LIFE, CHARLES SOUGHT ONLY TO DO GOOD. AND WHAT HAS HE GOTTEN FOR HIS TROUBLE? SMASHED LEGS AND NOW, POSSIBLY, A PREMATURE DEATH. IT ISN'T FAIR!
NO, IT IS NOT--ANY MORE THAN IT WAS FOR MY PARENTS TO BE SLAIN WHEN I WAS YOUNG, OR FOR COLOSSUS' SISTER ILLYANA TO HAVE HER CHILDHOOD STOLEN FROM HER BY THE DEMON, BELASCO. *
THE ONE GREAT TRUTH IN LIFE, MY FRIEND, IS ITS MANIFEST UNFAIRNESS.
* SEE LAST ISH --LOUISE.

YOU DON'T UNDERSTAND. WHATEVER I AM-- AS AN X-MAN, AS A MAN-- IS LARGELY DUE TO HIM. HE'S AS MUCH MY FATHER AS CORSAIR.
I... I... LOVE HIM, ORORO.
AND I CAN'T BEAR SEEING HIM LIKE THIS.

IT'S JEAN-- IT'S THE ORPHANAGE, WHERE I GREW UP-- ALL OVER AGAIN. I REACH OUT TO SOMEONE, I CARE, I MAKE MYSELF VULNERABLE AND--WHAM!-- THEY'RE GONE. AND I'M ALONE.
HECKUVA NOTE, ISN'T IT? XAVIER'S DYING, AND I'M FEELING SORRY FOR MYSELF.
SCOTT, BECAUSE OF WHO AND WHAT WE ARE, WE ALL WALK IN THE SHADOW OF THE REAPER.

BUT, BY THE SAME TOKEN, WE ARE NEVER ALONE! THE LOVE YOU BORE JEAN--AND BEAR CHARLES--IS FELT BY US FOR YOU. AND FROM THAT LOVE COMES STRENGTH THAT WILL SUSTAIN US THROUGH ANY TRIAL.
IF HE DIES...
WE WILL GO ON.
I... NEED YOU, ORORO. HELP ME.
FOOLISH MAN, YOU HAD BUT TO ASK.

INSIDE...
...LILANDRA, MAJESTRIX SHI'AR, RULER OF A GALAXY-SPANNING EMPIRE...
...GIVES XAVIER WHAT SHE FEARS IS A LAST EMBRACE, A FAREWELL KISS.
WE HAD SUCH DREAMS, BELOVED.

I WILL NOT SEE THEM TURNED TO DUST BEFORE THEIR TIME.
MY THOUGHTS ONCE REACHED YOU ACROSS A UNIVERSE. HEAR THEM NOW! FIGHT, MY LOVE-- LIVE! IF YOU NEED MY STRENGTH, I GIVE IT GLADLY. BUT FIGHT, CHARLES, FIGHT!
BUT CHARLES REACTS NEITHER TO LILANDRA'S IMPASSIONED PLEA, NOR TO THE TEAR THAT STRIKES HIS CHEEK.
TO HIM, IT IS SPRING, 20 YEARS AGO, IN THE ISRAELI SEAPORT CITY OF HAIFA.
CHARLES!
DANIEL! DANIEL SHOMRON!
IT'S GOOD TO SEE YOU, OLD FRIEND.
I'M GLAD MY MESSAGES FINALLY CAUGHT UP WITH YOU.
YOU'RE LOOKING WELL. YOU HAVE A NICE TIME IN CAIRO?
MY VISIT HAD ITS... MEMORABLE MOMENTS.*
*AS CHRONICLED IN X-MEN #117 -- L.
STILL AS GARRULOUS AS EVER, I SEE. I HEARD YOU AND MOIRA HAD BROKEN UP. I'M SORRY. I THOUGHT YOU WERE VERY HAPPY TOGETHER.
SO DID I.
AND WHAT OF YOU, DANIEL?
I'M STILL A PSYCHIATRIST, BUT MY PATIENTS ARE NOW SURVIVORS OF THE HOLOCAUST-- THE NAZI CONCENTRATION CAMPS--INSTEAD OF BATTLEFIELD CASUALTIES IN A M.A.S.H. UNIT. I REMEMBER HOW WELL YOU WORKED WITH SOME OF THE MOST SEVERE MENTAL CASES. YOU WERE THE BEST INSTINCTIVE PSYCHOLOGIST I'D EVER SEEN.
WELL, OL' BUDDY, I HAVE NEED OF YOUR UNIQUE TALENTS.
THIS IS MY HOSPITAL. VERY SNAZZY. BEFORE INDEPENDENCE IT USED TO BE A POSH RESORT. MY STAFF IS A MIXTURE OF PROFESSIONALS AND VOLUNTEERS LIKE MAGNUS.
WELCOME, DOCTOR. Dr. SHOMRON HAS SPOKEN OFTEN OF YOU.
THE PLEASURE IS MINE.

ACCORDING TO Dr. SHOMRON, YOU'RE A MIRACLE WORKER.
HARDLY. I'VE MERELY BEEN LUCKIER THAN MOST.
FASCINATING! MAGNUS' MIND IS CLOSED TO ME!
HE'S NO TELEPATH, BUT HIS NATURAL PSYCHIC DEFENSES ARE AS FORMIDABLE AS MY OWN. COULD HE BE ANOTHER LIKE ME-- A MUTANT?

THAT TATOO, MAGNUS. WERE YOU--?
AUSCHWITZ. I GREW UP THERE.
AND YOUR FAMILY?
214782
I HAVE NO FAMILY, Dr. XAVIER. ANYMORE.

MOST OF OUR VOLUNTEERS WERE IN CAMPS, CHARLES. THEY BRING A DEGREE OF EMPATHY TO THEIR WORK THAT THE REST OF US CAN'T MATCH. BUT, OCCASIONALLY, THERE COMES A CASE THAT STIMIES OUR BEST EFFORTS.
THIS IS GABRIELLE HALLER. HER EXPERIENCES IN DACHAU SO TRAUMATIZED HER THAT SHE WITHDREW INTO CATATONIC SCHIZOPHRENIA, A TOTAL RETREAT FROM REALITY.
SHE WAS LIKE THIS WHEN SHE ARRIVED HERE. SHE HASN'T IMPROVED YET.

WE'VE TRIED EVERY MEANS HUMANLY POSSIBLE TO BRING HER OUT OF HER TRANCE-- SAVE THOSE INVOLVING PHYSICAL PAIN. SHE'S SUFFERED ENOUGH OF THAT ALREADY.
I CAN'T PROMISE ANYTHING, DAN...
I TURN TO YOU AS A LAST RESORT, CHARLES.

...BUT I'LL GIVE IT MY BEST SHOT.
TO THOSE WATCHING, NOTHING HAPPENS, AS XAVIER SITS FACING THE YOUNG WOMAN.
SIMULTANEOUSLY, THOUGH, UNKNOWN TO THE OTHERS, HE REACHES OUT WITH HIS MIND...

...AND SLIPS GENTLY INTO HERS.
AT FIRST, HE MEETS NO RESISTANCE. HE IS ENVELOPED IN DARKNESS, SILENCE. ALL AROUND HIM IS BARREN, DESOLATE. ALL AWARENESS HAS FLED. HE PRESSES ON, MOVING EVER DEEPER, UNTIL...
A WALL?!?

EMERGING FROM THE WALL-- MONSTERS!
THIS BARRIER MUST BE TO PROTECT GABRIELLE FROM A WORLD TOO HORRIBLE TO ENDURE...
...AND THESE CREATURES, DEFENDERS, TO KEEP HER SELF-IMPOSED SANCTUARY FOREVER INVIOLATE.

SHE EVIDENTLY SENSES MY PRESENCE AND, IN FEAR, LASHES OUT AT ME. SPLENDID!

THAT MEANS HER MIND STILL FUNCTIONS! SHE CAN BE RESTORED TO CONSCIOUSNESS!
HOWEVER, WHILE THESE MAY BE LITERAL FIGMENTS OF HER IMAGINATION, THAT MAKES THEM NO LESS DEADLY. THEY CAN KILL ME -- IF I LET THEM.
HER WILL IS STRONG. SHE'S PUTTING UP A GOOD FIGHT.

I WONDER, THOUGH, IF SHE HAS FOUND PEACE WITHIN HERSELF, HAVE I THE RIGHT TO FORCE HER TO CONFRONT HER PAST, HER PRESENT?
YES!
LIFE IS THE GREATEST OF GIFTS, THE ULTIMATE WONDER. IT SHOULD NEITHER BE TAKEN, NOR WASTED. GABRIELLE MUST BE ALLOWED HER FULL CHANCE TO LIVE, TO GROW, TO BE ALL THAT SHE CAN POSSIBLY BE!

ENERGY FLOWS IN THE SHADOW-LAND AS A HORDE OF DEMONS EMERGE TO CHALLENGE XAVIER. HE IGNORES THEM, CONCENTRATING THE FULL FORCE OF HIS TELEPATHIC MIGHT AGAINST THE WALL.
WITH SURPRISING SUDDENNESS, IT FIRST CRACKS -- LIGHT GLOWING BRIGHT AS A SUPER-NOVA IN THE MULTIPLE FISSURES--AND THEN SHATTERS!

THE LIGHT IS PURE, UNBEARABLE -- THE FACE OF THE GORGON, OR PERHAPS OF THE LORD, OR BOTH -- YET HE DOES NOT LOOK AWAY. HE CANNOT.
HE REMEMBERS A LINE FROM THE BHAGAVAD-GITA -- "I AM BECOME DEATH, THE SHATTERER OF WORLDS."
THEN, THE MAJESTIC RADIANCE FADES, IMAGES FORM, A VOICE IS HEARD. IT IS GABRIELLE, AGE 10.
THROUGH HER YOUNG, INNOCENT EYES, HE RELIVES THE WAR. HE/SHE STANDS PACKED SO TIGHTLY IN A CATTLE CAR THAT THE DEAD CANNOT FALL, BUT REMAIN ON THEIR FEET, SUPPORTED BY THOSE AROUND THEM 'TIL THE CARS ARE UNLOADED
HER GRAND-MOTHER DIES THAT WAY, BY GABY'S SIDE.
THE LUCKY ONES ARE GASSED, THEIR BODIES CREMATED. BUT GABY IS BEAUTIFUL. THE GUARDS LIKE HER.
SO, SHE SURVIVES, YOUNG IN YEARS, ANCIENT IN SPIRIT, INNOCENT NO LONGER.
WAS SHE WICKED, EVIL, THE CHILD WONDERS, THAT SHE SHOULD BE PUNISHED SO? SHE THINKS OF SUICIDE, BUT LACKS THE COURAGE. SHE PRAYS THE GUARDS WILL TIRE OF HER AND SEND HER TO THE GAS CHAMBER. BUT THEY NEVER DO.
INSTEAD, IN THE LAST DAYS OF THE WAR...
...SHE IS DRAGGED BEFORE THE COMMANDANT, WHO POINTS A MAGIC WAND AT HER, CHANTS AN OBSCENE SPELL...
...AND TRANSFORMS HER INTO SOLID GOLD.

MOMMA!
POPPA!!

I DON'T BELIEVE IT!
I PRAYED FOR A MIRACLE, CHARLES, BUT THIS--?! WHAT DID YOU DO?!
WHAT COMES NATURALLY, DANIEL. THAT'S IT, GABY, HAVE A GOOD CRY, THAT'S A DARLING. YOU'RE ALL RIGHT NOW. YOU'RE AMONG FRIENDS. YOU'RE SAFE.
HELP ME PUT HER TO BED, WILL YOU? I'M AFRAID THIS HAS BEEN AN ORDEAL FOR BOTH OF US.

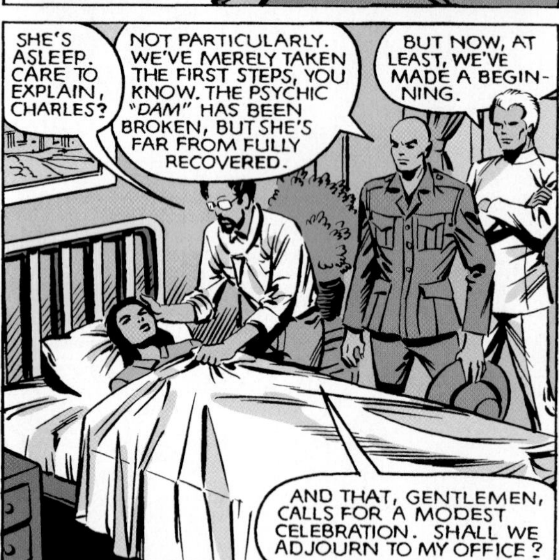
SHE'S ASLEEP. CARE TO EXPLAIN, CHARLES?
NOT PARTICULARLY. WE'VE MERELY TAKEN THE FIRST STEPS, YOU KNOW. THE PSYCHIC "DAM" HAS BEEN BROKEN, BUT SHE'S FAR FROM FULLY RECOVERED.
BUT NOW, AT LEAST, WE'VE MADE A BEGINNING.
AND THAT, GENTLEMEN, CALLS FOR A MODEST CELEBRATION. SHALL WE ADJOURN TO MY OFFICE?

MY FAVORITE "MOUNTAIN SPRING WATER." I'VE BEEN SAVING IT FOR A SPECIAL OCCASION.
I MUST SAY, CHARLES--DURING THAT SESSION, GABY EXPRESSED SOME REMARKABLE VERBAL IMAGES. S.S. GUARDS AS DEMONS AND OGRES, THE CREMATORIUMS AS THE GATES OF HELL. BUT HOW DO YOU ACCOUNT FOR THE LAST ONE, HER TRANSFORMATION INTO A GOLDEN STATUE?
ALL HER OTHER IMAGES WERE GROUNDED IN REALITY. LOGICALLY, THEN, SO MUST THIS ONE.
IT WAS ASSOCIATED WITH EXTRAORDINARY PAIN AND FEAR.

BEYOND THAT, YOUR GUESS IS AS GOOD AS MINE.
WE'LL SORT IT OUT SOONER OR LATER.
THE IMPORTANT THING IS THAT GABY'S FINALLY FULLY CONSCIOUS!
MY FRIENDS, AN IMMODEST TOAST: TO CHARLES, FOR DOING THE DIRTY WORK, AND TO ME, FOR BRINGING HIM HERE!
THE HALLER GIRL--CONSCIOUS?!

THE LEADER MUST BE INFORMED, AT ONCE!
OUR YEARS OF PATIENCE ARE AT LAST ABOUT TO BE REWARDED. THE PRIZE WE HAVE SOUGHT FOR SO LONG IS FINALLY WITHIN OUR GRASP!
SEIG HEIL!

OVER THE WEEKS THAT FOLLOW--AND WITH THE AID OF HER CONSTANT COMPANIONS, XAVIER AND MAGNUS-- GABY BRIDGES THE GULF BETWEEN CHILD- AND ADULTHOOD, HER OLD LIFE IN HOLLAND AND HER NEW ONE IN ISRAEL, WITH REMARKABLE EASE.

... FROM THE GALILEE TO DIVIDED JERUSALEM TO THE NEGEV DESERT. DURING THEIR TRAVELS, XAVIER DISCOVERS IN MAGNUS A FASCINATING, KINDRED SPIRIT-- AND WHEN HE OUTLINES HIS NASCENT THEORIES ON HUMAN EVOLUTIONARY MUTATION, XAVIER IS DELIGHTED TO SEE THAT MAGNUS TAKES HIM SERIOUSLY.

TOGETHER, THE THREE FRIENDS RANGE THROUGHOUT THIS ANCIENT LAND, VIEWING ALL ITS MYRIAD WONDERS...

HOWEVER, HE ALSO COMES TO REALIZE THAT, IN MANY WAYS, MAGNUS HAS BEEN AS DEEPLY SCARRED BY HIS EXPERIENCES AS GABY.

CHARLES, YOU ARE AN IDEALISTIC FOOL.

IF MUTANTS EXIST, HUMANITY WILL **FEAR** THEM AND OUT OF THAT FEAR, TRY TO **DESTROY** THEM.

THERE IS ONLY **ONE** WAY TO GUARANTEE THE SURVIVAL OF *HOMO SUPERIOR*, AND THAT IS FOR **THEM** TO HOLD THE REINS OF POWER.

MAGNUS IS WRONG. SUCH SECURITY CANNOT BE IMPOSED BY FEAR FROM ABOVE. IT MUST GROW FROM UNDERSTANDING...
Ahem!
Hmnh? OH, I'M SORRY, GABY. MY MIND WAS WANDERING.

THEN I'LL HAVE TO USE ALL MY FEMININE WILES...
... TO ATTRACT ITS ATTENTION.
Ahhh, GABY, YOU BELIEVE YOU'RE IN LOVE WITH ME.

BUT YOU AREN'T. NOT REALLY. AND YET, YOUR NEED TO LOVE AND BE LOVED,.. IS AS GENUINE, AS GREAT, AS MY OWN.
I OWE YOU EVERYTHING, DEAR CHARLES. BUT I HAVE NO MEANS OF RE-PAYING YOU...

... SAVE THIS.
I SHOULD NOT DO THIS. BUT IF IT MAKES US BOTH HAPPY AND BRINGS US THE SOLACE WE SEEK...
...WHAT THEN IS THE HARM?

SUDDENLY...
GRENADE!
THE HOSPITAL'S UNDER ATTACK!
OHH!!

FIRST SQUAD, SECURE THE PERIMETER AND NEUTRALIZE ALL DEFENSES!
SECOND SQUAD, OUR OBJECTIVE-- THE HALLER WOMAN-- IS IN THE COURTYARD! SEIZE HER! AND REMEMBER YOUR ORDERS--
--SHE IS TO BE TAKEN ALIVE AND UNHARMED!

WHO ARE THEY, CAPTAIN?! ARAB COMMANDOS? TERRORISTS?!
CONSIDERING THEIR ADVANCED WEAPONRY AND EQUIPMENT, I HOPE NOT.
LISTEN TO THEM! THEY'RE SPEAKING GERMAN!
THE ISRAELI TROOPS MAKE A VALIANT EFFORT...

... BUT THEY'RE OUTNUMBERED AND OUTGUNNED AND THE OUTCOME IS CLEAR FROM THE START.
DOWN, GABY! USE THIS JEEP FOR COVER!
CHARLES, IS IT ANOTHER WAR?!

I DON'T KNOW
I'M RECEIVING STRAY THOUGHTS. THESE MERCENARIES ARE AFTER GABY AND THEY'LL STOP AT NOTHING TO GET HER. BUT WHY?!
THE ISRAELIS HAVEN'T A CHANCE-- UNLESS I USE MY PSI-POWERS TO EVEN THE ODDS--
ARRRGH!
CHARLES!!

FORGET THE MAN. HE'S TODT--DEAD.
NO! CHARLES--NO!
STOP STRUGGLING, JEWESS! ACH, SHE FIGHTS LIKE A SHE-WOLF!
A PITY ABOUT THE ORDERS. A BROKEN JAW WOULD QUICKLY TEACH HER TO RESPECT HER BETTERS.

HER CAPTORS HUSTLE GABY ABOARD ONE OF THE TILT-WING ASSAULT CRAFT, WHILE THE REST OF THE COMMANDO GROUP HEAD FOR THE OTHER--BUT AS ITS ENGINES REV UP TO FULL POWER FOR TAKE-OFF...

...THE TRANSPORT LITERALLY COMES APART AT THE SEAMS...
...METAL SHRAPNEL SPRAYING THE COURTYARD, SLAYING THE STRIKE FORCE ALMOST TO A MAN WHILE MIRACULOUSLY LEAVING THE ISRAELI GUARDS AND PATIENTS UNTOUCHED, THE HOSPITAL UNDAMAGED.

THOSE MEN--CUT TO PIECES, WITHOUT MERCY... A FATE THEY NO DOUBT RICHLY DESERVED.
BUT... I CAN STILL HEAR THEIR DEATH-SCREAMS IN MY MIND, STILL FEEL THEIR SHOCK AND PAIN--AND FEAR--AS THEIR LIVES WERE ABRUPTLY SNUFFED OUT.
ON THE ROOF--MAGNUS!

THAT SAME NIMBUS OF LIGHT SURROUNDED THE PLANE AS IT EXPLODED. WAS MAGNUS RESPONSIBLE?
AAAGKH!
CHARLES, YOU'RE HURT!
NOT SERIOUSLY, MY FRIEND, THOUGH MY HEAD HURTS LIKE THE DEVIL.

MAGNUS, WHAT DID YOU DO TO THAT AIRCRAFT?!
WHAT HAD TO BE DONE. MY ONLY REGRET WAS THAT I WAS UNABLE TO ACT SOONER.
WAS IT NECESSARY TO SLAUGHTER THEM?

THEY WOULD HAVE DONE NO LESS TO US. YOU AMAZE ME, CHARLES. WHEN YOU WERE A SOLDIER, IN KOREA, DID YOU NOT KILL -- WITHOUT HESITATION OR MERCY?
I KILLED TO SURVIVE -- AND THE MEMORY STILL SICKENS ME.
CHARLES, MAGNUS-- WE HAVE A **PRISONER!**
BUT HE WILL NOT IDENTIFY OUR ATTACKERS... OR SAY WHERE THEY TOOK GABRIELLE.
TWO DAYS LATER, 3500 KILOMETERS DUE SOUTH, AT THE FOOT OF A MAJESTIC ESCARPMENT NEAR KENYA'S LAKE RUDOLF...
HE CLAIMS HE DOESN'T SPEAK ENGLISH.
DON'T WORRY, SERGEANT. *ICH SPRECHEN DEUTSCH.*
‹JEWISH SWINE, YOU'LL GET NOTHING FROM ME.›
‹RUDOLF KRANZ, MAJOR, WAFFEN SS -- NOW A SQUAD LEADER FOR SOMETHING CALLED THE **HYDRA BRUDERSCHAFT.**›
‹UN-- UNMÖGLICH! H-HOW COULD YOU HAVE KNOWN--?!›
...A CONVOY OF MILITARY VEHICLES STANDS IN A DEFENSIVE LAAGER, AN ENCAMPMENT. NONE KNOW THEY ARE HERE AND ANYONE UNLUCKY ENOUGH TO FIND OUT WILL BE EXECUTED ON THE SPOT. THE MEN ARE MOSTLY GERMAN -- THE CREAM OF HITLER'S SS, THE DREADED SCHUTZ-STAFFEL -- AND AT THIS POINT IN TIME, THE INSIGNIA THEY WEAR, THE CAUSE THEY FOLLOW, ARE LARGELY UNFAMILIAR TO THE WORLD.
‹THAT'S EASY, HERR KRANZ. I READ MINDS.›
THAT WILL SOON CHANGE -- AS THEY EMERGE ONTO THE INTERNATIONAL STAGE AS THE CRUELIST, DEADLIEST, MOST RUTHLESS AND VICIOUS CRIMINAL/TERRORIST CARTEL IN HISTORY: **HYDRA!**

IT IS DUSK WHEN A TROOPER COMES SKIDDING DOWN THE STEEP, ROCK-STREWN SLOPE, YELLING AT THE TOP OF HIS LUNGS, VOICE CRACKING WITH EXCITEMENT.
WE FOUND IT!
WE FOUND THE CAVE!

HERR BARON, THE WOMAN'S DIRECTIONS WERE PERFECT!
I HEAR, LEUTNANT. IN TRUTH, I DOUBT THERE IS A LIVING BEING BETWEEN HERE AND NAIROBI WHO HAS NOT HEARD YOUR ANNOUNCEMENT.

BECAUSE IT IS GOOD NEWS, AND BECAUSE OF YOUR YOUTH, I SHALL OVERLOOK YOUR DISGRACEFUL LACK OF DISCIPLINE. THIS TIME.
REPEAT THIS TRANSGRESSION, HOWEVER, AND I SHALL NOT BE SO FORGIVING.
I... I AM SORRY, MEIN HERR...
NEVER APOLOGIZE, BOY. IT IS A SIGN OF WEAKNESS.

SO, MY PRETTY BIRD, YOUR SONG HAS LED US TO THE PRIZE WE HAVE SO LONG SOUGHT.
I SHOULD HAVE D-DIED BEFORE I TOLD YOU ANYTHING.
JA, BUT YOU ARE WEAK, GABRIELLE, LIKE ALL YOUR MONGREL RACE.

BRING HER. IT IS ONLY FITTING THAT SHE WITNESS OUR MOMENT OF TRIUMPH...
...SINCE SHE ALONE MADE IT POSSIBLE.

STRUCKER! THAT'S BARON STRUCKER! ONE OF THE MOST WANTED NAZI WAR CRIMINALS!
THE... THINGS HE DID TO GABY-- I SEE THEM, FEEL THEM, IN HER MIND. MAGNUS, HE TORTURED HER!
CALM YOURSELF, CHARLES, OR WE ARE LOST!
WE CANNOT AID GABY-- OR BRING STRUCKER TO JUSTICE-- IF YOU CONTINUE ACTING LIKE A LOVESICK SCHOOLBOY!

CLAD IN UNIFORMS "BORROWED" FROM TWO OF STRUCKER'S MEN--LYING BOUND AND UNCONSCIOUS IN A SUPPLY TRUCK--XAVIER AND MAGNUS FOLLOW THE MAIN PARTY INTO THE CAVE.
IT WAS A BRILLIANT PLOY. IN THE FINAL DAYS OF THE WAR, THE DECISION WAS MADE TO SPIRIT THE FÜHRER'S PERSONAL GOLD RESERVES OUT OF GERMANY...
...IN HOPES THAT IT WOULD SOMEDAY FINANCE A RESURGENCE OF NATIONAL SOCIALISM--OF THE NAZI PARTY--AND EVENTUALLY, A FOURTH REICH!

WHERE BETTER TO HIDE THE GOLD THAN BLACK AFRICA, AMONG SAVAGES. AND WHO BETTER TO TURN INTO A LIVING MAP TO THIS VAULT THAN A JEWESS CHILD. BUT AN ERROR WAS MADE. THE CONDITIONING PROCESS DROVE GABRIELLE INSANE AND THE SECRET WAS LOST--UNTIL TODAY.
BEHIND THAT WALL IS WEALTH BEYOND OUR WILDEST DREAMS--AND SOON IT WILL BE OURS!

WAIT 'TIL THEY BREACH THE WALL. THEN, WITH LUCK, THEY'LL BE SO ENTRANCED BY THE TREASURE THAT WE'LL BE ABLE TO GRAB GABY AND GET AWAY BEFORE ANYONE'S THE WISER.
A SENSIBLE PLAN. BUT HUSH, CHARLES. THEY'RE COMING THIS WAY!

SOON, OUTSIDE...
KLIK
BOOM!

BEHOLD, KAMRADEN! THIS FORTUNE WILL PROVIDE THE FOUNDATION FOR OUR NEW ORDER, A BROTHERHOOD OF TERROR THAT WILL BRING THE DEMOCRACIES, THE COMMUNISTS, EVERY COUNTRY ON EARTH, TO THEIR COLLECTIVE KNEES!
WHERE OUR BELOVED FÜHRER, ADOLF HITLER, FAILED--HYDRA SHALL SUCCEED!
HAIL HYDRA!

GABY, IT'S MAGNUS AND CHARLES. WE'VE COME TO TAKE YOU HOME.
NO! THIS IS A TRICK! YOU'RE GOING TO HURT ME! LET ME GO!
CHARLES, SHUT HER UP! USE YOUR PSI-POWERS, BEFORE SHE'S HEARD!
MY--?! THEN YOU KNOW ABOUT THEM?!
HERR BARON-- WITH THE JEWESS --INTRUDERS!

KILL THEM!
TAKE GABY, CHARLES! GET OUT OF HERE! I'LL COVER YOU!
YOU'LL NEED MY HELP, MAGNUS--!

AGAINST BULLETS, MY FRIEND, I NEED NO HELP.
SURELY BY NOW YOU'VE REALIZED THAT WE ARE TWO OF A KIND.
HE'S A MUTANT, LIKE MYSELF--WITH THE ABILITY TO MANIPULATE METAL OBJECTS. THIS IS FANTASTIC!

GABY'S MIND IS IN TURMOIL-- TOO MANY SHOCKS COMING TOO SOON AFTER HER RECOVERY. IT'S MORE THAN SHE CAN HANDLE-- BLAST!
THERE THEY ARE-- eh?!?
WHERE, FRITZ?! I SEE NO ONE!
I'M MENTALLY AFFECTING THEIR VISUAL PERCEPTIONS, SO THAT THEIR MINDS REFUSE TO ACCEPT WHAT THEIR EYES SEE.

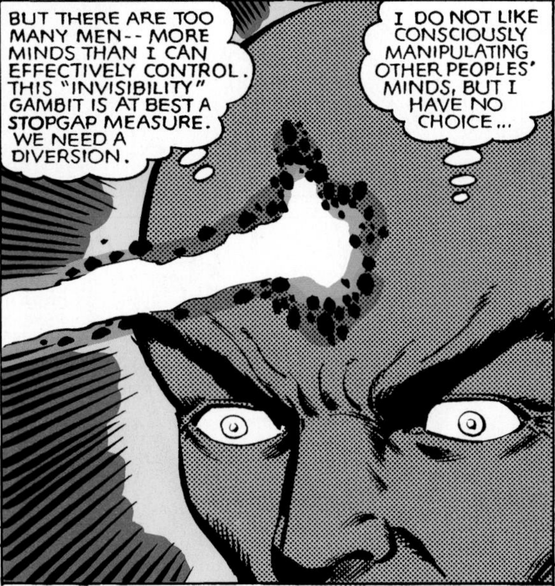
BUT THERE ARE TOO MANY MEN-- MORE MINDS THAN I CAN EFFECTIVELY CONTROL. THIS "INVISIBILITY" GAMBIT IS AT BEST A STOPGAP MEASURE. WE NEED A DIVERSION.
I DO NOT LIKE CONSCIOUSLY MANIPULATING OTHER PEOPLES' MINDS, BUT I HAVE NO CHOICE...

"THIS MAN RESENTS HIS BROTHER OFFICER. ALL I NEED DO IS FAN AND FOCUS THAT RESENTMENT...
ARE YOU TRYING TO MAKE ME LOOK THE FOOL, ROLF?! OPEN YOUR EYES! THEN PERHAPS YOU'LL SEE WHAT I SHOW YOU!

"... UNTIL IT EXPLODES INTO VIOLENCE!"

HE SHIFTS QUICKLY FROM MIND TO MIND, TWISTING EMOTIONS AND PERCEPTIONS...
STOP THIS, YOU MEN! HAVE YOU GONE MAD? STOP, I SAY!
...WITH AN EASE THAT DISTURBS HIM. WITHIN MINUTES, STRUCKER'S ENTIRE FORCE IS HARD AT WORK BATTERING EACH OTHER SENSELESS.

A BRILLIANT STRATEGEM, CHARLES.
IT WAS NECESSARY, BUT I TAKE NO SATISFACTION IN IT.
ONE DAY, MY FRIEND, THAT SQUEAMISHNESS WILL COST YOU. WHAT AILS GABY?
SHE'S GONE INTO SHOCK, REVERTING TO HER PREVIOUS CATATONIC STATE.
I HAVE TO BRING HER OUT OF IT BEFORE SHE WITHDRAWS SO DEEPLY THAT WE'LL NEVER BE ABLE TO REACH HER.

USE YOUR PSI-POWERS. THEY WORKED BEFORE, NO? AND HURRY UP. THE SOONER WE'RE ON OUR WAY, THE BETTER.
I DARE NOT MIND-PROBE HER. SHE'LL BECOME DEPENDANT ON MY ABILITY. THE SLIGHTEST SHOCK WILL BE CAPABLE OF SHATTERING HER PSYCHE, BECAUSE SHE'LL BELIEVE THAT I'LL BE THERE TO PUT THINGS RIGHT AGAIN.
BUT I WON'T BE. SHE MUST DEVELOP A PSYCHIC RESILIENCE TO ENABLE HER TO COPE WITH THE EVERYDAY--AND THE EXTRAORDINARY--STRESSES OF LIFE. AND TO DO THAT, SHE MUST PULL OUT OF THIS HERSELF. SHE MUST WANT TO LIVE!
D'YOU HEAR ME, GABY?! COME BACK! FIGHT!

WORRY NOT ABOUT THE GIRL, GENTLEMEN. FOR HER-- AND FOR YOU-- LIFE WILL SOON HAVE **NO MEANING WHATSOEVER!**
STRUCKER!

I DO NOT KNOW HOW YOU AFFECTED MY MEN, BUT YOU'LL NOT FIND ME SO EASY TO DEFEAT.
HIS RESISTANCE IS STRONGER THAN THE OTHERS-- I CAN'T CONTROL HIS MIND!
THAT GAUNTLET SHATTERED THE BOULDER! I MUST PROTECT GABY FROM THE SHARDS OF FLYING ROCK--!

CHARLES IS INJURED! I MUST KEEP STRUCKER'S ATTENTION AWAY FROM HIM AND GABY-- AND FOCUSED ON ME!
A MOST IMPRESSIVE WEAPON, *HERR BARON*.
IT IS NOTHING. A LESSER FRUIT OF TEUTONIC GENIUS. WE HAVE CHRISTENED IT THE ***SATAN CLAW***.

AND TO YOU GOES THE HONOR OF BEING THE FIRST--
SHKOW!
--TO FALL BENEATH ITS IRRESISTIBLE POWER!

NO, BARON. YOU WILL FIND ME CONSIDERABLY HARDER TO SLAY THAN YOUR COUNTRYMEN DID MY FAMILY AT AUSCHWITZ.
M- MY HAND--! WHAT ARE YOU DOING--?!

MERELY DEMONSTRATING **MY** IRRESISTIBLE POWER--THE ABILITY TO MANIPULATE MAGNETIC FIELDS.
YOUR PRECIOUS CLAW IS MADE PRIMARILY OF FERROUS METALS. THAT MAKES IT PARTICULARLY ***VULNERABLE***.
ARRGH!

HOWEVER, MY INFLUENCE IS NOT LIMITED TO METALS. BY SHAPING NATURAL FORCES, I CAN HURL YOU AWAY WITH BUT A THOUGHT!
UNFORTUNATELY, MY POWER DID NOT MANIFEST ITSELF 'TIL I REACHED ADULTHOOD. BY THEN, THE WAR WAS OVER.

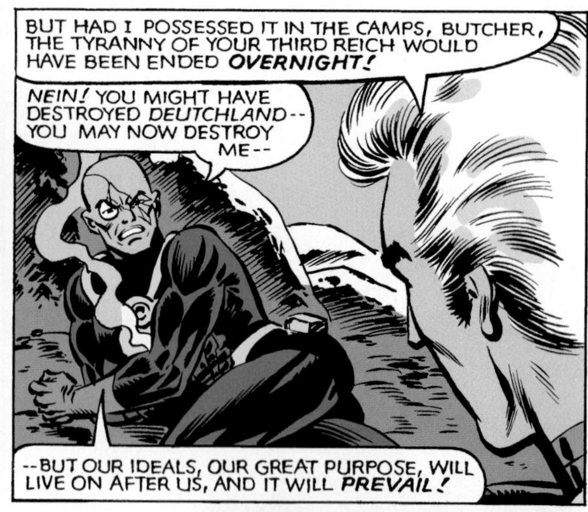
BUT HAD I POSSESSED IT IN THE CAMPS, BUTCHER, THE TYRANNY OF YOUR THIRD REICH WOULD HAVE BEEN ENDED OVERNIGHT!
NEIN! YOU MIGHT HAVE DESTROYED DEUTCHLAND-- YOU MAY NOW DESTROY ME--
--BUT OUR IDEALS, OUR GREAT PURPOSE, WILL LIVE ON AFTER US, AND IT WILL PREVAIL!

ALL THINGS ARE POSSIBLE, NAZI. HATE IS MORE POPULAR THAN LOVE, FEAR MORE PREVALENT THAN TRUST.
IF HUMANITY WISHES TO FOLLOW YOU TO ITS DAMNATION, SO BE IT.
I CARE NOTHING FOR YOU, OR THEM. AND WHEN HOMO SAPIENS ARE NO MORE, HOMO SUPERIOR WILL CLAIM THEIR RIGHTFUL PLACE...

...AS LORDS OF THE EARTH!

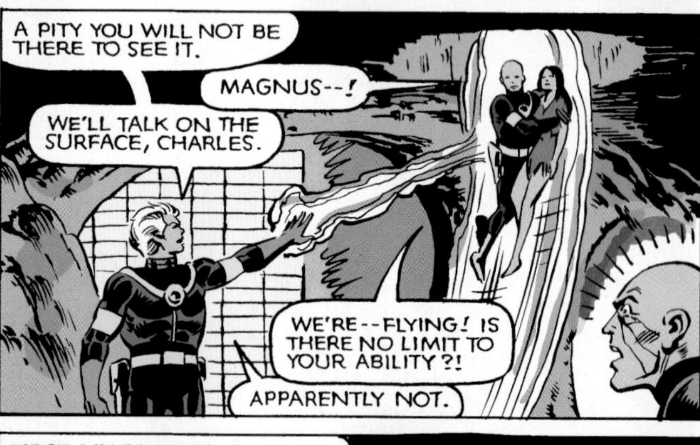
A PITY YOU WILL NOT BE THERE TO SEE IT.
MAGNUS--!
WE'LL TALK ON THE SURFACE, CHARLES.
WE'RE--FLYING! IS THERE NO LIMIT TO YOUR ABILITY?!
APPARENTLY NOT.

FIRST MY FRIENDS, AND NOW THE GOLD. HAVE NO FEAR, BARON, I SHALL PUT YOUR FÜHRER'S FORTUNE TO GOOD USE.
YOU WILL PAY FOR THIS, MAGNUS! WE WILL HUNT YOU DOWN!

TO BE PERFECTLY HONEST, BARON, I DOUBT I WILL HAVE MUCH TO FEAR...
...FROM A GHOST.
THE CAVE-- COLLAPSING!
NO!!

AN IMPRESSIVE SIGHT, IS IT NOT? HOW IS GABY?
I'M NOT CERTAIN. I THINK I REACHED HER. BUT WHAT OF STRUCKER AND HIS MEN, MAGNUS?! WHAT DO YOU MEAN TO DO WITH THAT GOLD?!
DO YOU REALLY NEED TO ASK, MY FRIEND?
YOU ARE FAR TOO TRUSTING, CHARLES, TOO NAIVE. YOU HAVE FAITH IN THE ESSENTIAL GOODNESS OF MAN. IN TIME, YOU WILL LEARN WHAT I HAVE LEARNED--THAT EVEN THOSE YOU LOVE WILL TURN FROM YOU IN HORROR WHEN THEY DISCOVER WHAT YOU TRULY ARE.
MUTANTS WILL NOT GO MEEKLY TO THE GAS CHAMBERS. WE WILL FIGHT...
...AND WE WILL WIN! FAREWELL.
MAGNUS --NO!
Eh?! GABY!
uhhnnn...
MUST THE FUTURE OF HOMO SUPERIOR BE WRITTEN IN BLOOD AND FIRE?! THE WORLD HAS SEEN TOO MUCH OF THAT, MAGNUS-- THERE HAS TO BE A BETTER WAY. AND I INTEND TO FIND IT.
HOW DO YOU FEEL?
S-STRANGE. I... REMEMBER EVERYTHING, YET IT FEELS LIKE SOME FANTASTIC DREAM. I WAS HUDDLED BEHIND A WALL-- IN MY MIND--ALONE, TERRIFIED.
I KNEW NOTHING COULD HURT ME THERE. I'D BE SAFE, PROTECTED, FOREVER. THEN I HEARD YOUR VOICE. I WAS NO LONGER ALONE. IF I LEFT MY HIDING PLACE, I'D RISK BEING HURT, BUT I KNEW THAT IF I STAYED, I'D BE CONDEMNING MYSELF ONCE AGAIN TO A LIVING DEATH. I COULDN'T BEAR THAT.
SCARED OF ONE CHOICE, MORE SCARED OF THE OTHER, I... FOLLOWED YOUR CALL. Oh, CHARLES-- IT'S SO WONDERFUL TO BE ALIVE!
GABY?! GABRIELLE?! OH!?!
PROFESSOR, YOU'RE AWAKE! YOU'RE ALL RIGHT!
I BELIEVE... I AM, STORM. THANKS TO YOU ALL AND MOST ESPECIALLY TO YOU, LILANDRA.
I WAS IN A PSYCHIC VOID, WHERE HIDEOUS MONSTERS TRIED TO DEVOUR ME. I KEPT RUNNING DEEPER INTO MY-SELF TO ESCAPE THEM, BUT I COULDN'T. THEN, I HEARD YOUR VOICE, CALLING ME BACK, GIVING ME HOPE. AND FROM THAT HOPE, I DREW THE STRENGTH TO SURVIVE--AND TRIUMPH.
Ah, MY DEAR CHARLES, I DID WHAT ANY OTHER WOULD FOR THE ONE THEY LOVED.

THE X-MEN'S JOY IS UNBOUNDED-- TEMPERED ONLY BY THEIR CONTINUED CONCERN FOR COLOSSUS' SISTER, ILLYANA.* NOW THAT PROFESSOR XAVIER HAS RECOVERED, HOWEVER, MUCH AS LILANDRA WOULD PREFER TO STAY ON EARTH, DUTY CALLS HER HOME.
A FAREWELL BANQUET IS PLANNED ABOARD HER NEWLY-ARRIVED YACHT, Z'REEE SHAR. ALL ARE INVITED, BUT MOIRA DECIDES THAT XAVIER IS STILL TOO WEAK TO TRAVEL... AND THAT THE EXPERIENCE WOULD PROVE TOO UNSETTLING FOR ILLYANA.
AND AS FOR THE STAR-JAMMERS...
AREN'T YOU COMING, DAD?
*FOR DETAILS, SEE LAST ISSUE -- L.

I RESPECT LILANDRA, SCOTT. BUT I HAVE NO LOVE-- AND LESS TRUST-- FOR THE SHI'AR. ENJOY YOURSELVES, X-MEN. I'LL SEE YOU LATER.
YOU LOOK EXQUISITE, KATYA.
DO I, PETER? YOU LOOK WONDERFUL, TOO.
JA. ALMOST AS GOOD AS ME.
Oh, POOH!

WE'RE AMONG FRIENDS-- SO WHY AM I ON EDGE?! I KEEP SPOTTIN' TRACES OF FAMILIAR SCENTS, BUT I CAN'T PLACE 'EM.
WHAT'S TO WORRY? IF TROUBLE COMES, WE'LL HANDLE IT.
I SALUTE YOU, X-MEN, AS WARRIORS AND FRIENDS.
THE SHI'AR OWE YOU A DEBT...

...THAT CAN NEVER...
...CAN NEVER...
...CAN NEVER...
LILANDRA?!
YOUR MAJESTY, WHAT'S THE MATTER?!

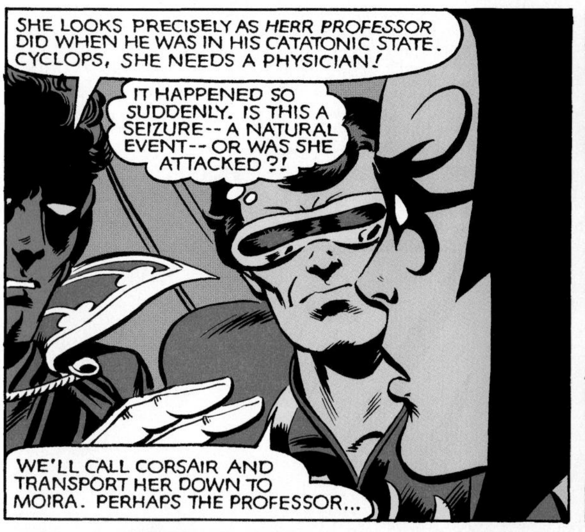

AN INSTANT LATER, A STASIS BOMB HIDDEN BENEATH THE TABLE DETONATES, SMASHING OUR HEROES INTO INSTANT OBLIVION.

A JOURNEY OF A MILLION LIGHT-YEARS BEGINS WITH AN... ESCAPE!

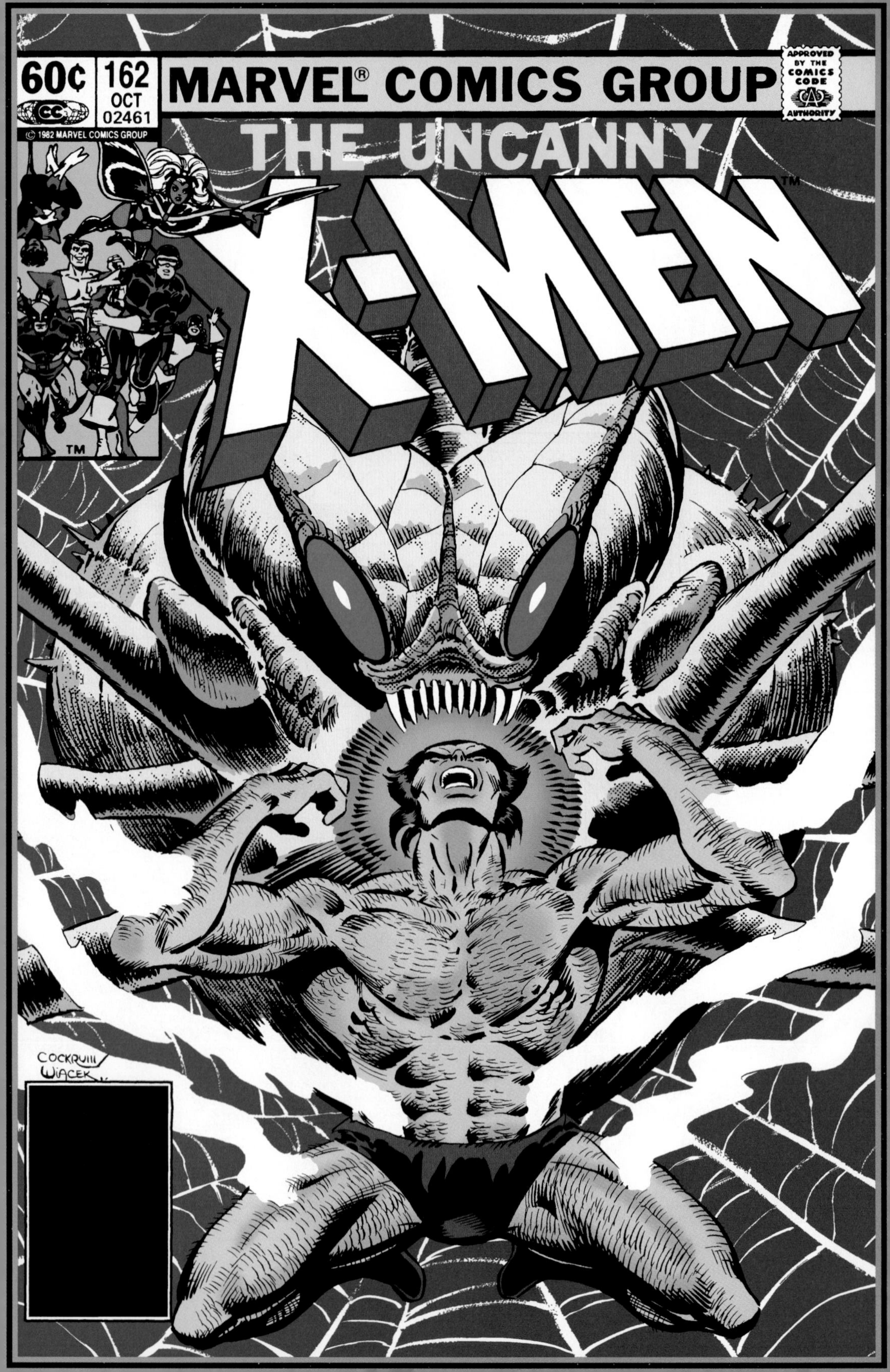
60¢
162
OCT
02461
© 1982 MARVEL COMICS GROUP
MARVEL® COMICS GROUP
APPROVED BY THE COMICS CODE AUTHORITY
THE UNCANNY
X-MEN™
TM
COCKRUM
WIACEK

Stan Lee PRESENTS: THE UNCANNY X-MEN!™

CHRIS CLAREMONT WRITER | DAVE COCKRUM PENCILS & BOB WIACEK INKS | GLYNIS WEIN, COLORIST TOM ORZECHOWSKI, LETTERER | LOUISE JONES EDITOR | JIM SHOOTER ED.-IN-CHIEF

AHHRRR!
PAIN... AGAIN-- GETTIN' WORSE EACH TIME-- FEELS LIKE I'M BEIN' GUTTED BY... A WHITE HOT BLADE.

CRIPES!
SUCKER GASSES ME...
...THEN TRIES TO CRUSH ME. MISTAKE. MY SKELETON'S LACED WITH ADAMANTIUM, THE STRONGEST METAL KNOWN. MY BONES DON'T BREAK.

I HAVE CLAWS, TOO-- RETRACTABLE, HOUSED IN MY FOREARMS, EXTENDED THROUGH APERTURES IN MY HANDS-- FORGED OUT OF THE SAME STUFF.
AN' I KNOW HOW TO USE 'EM.

I WIN.
BIG DEAL.
WHA'S HAPP'NIN'A ME...? COLORS... SO BRIGHT...
POLLEN... A HALLUCINOGEN-- CAN'T RESIST... ITS EFFECTS...
A SHAKE O' THE HEAD AN' I'M BACK IN JAPAN-- MY SECOND HOME-- WONDERIN' WHAT'S REAL, WHAT'S FANTASY. I CAN'T TELL ANYMORE. I'M DROWNIN'-- AN' I DON'T CARE.
BY MY SIDE IS MARIKO YASHIDA. I LOVE HER.
SHE LOVES ME. LIFE'S FULL OF SURPRISES.
< YOU SMILE, LOGAN-SAN.* >
*TRANSLATED FROM THE JAPANESE --LINGUIST LOUISE.
< MERELY THINKING HOW INCONGRUOUS WE LOOK. YOU MUST ADMIT, WE'RE A MISMATCHED PAIR. >
< I ADMIT NOTHING OF THE SORT. YOU ARE AN HONORABLE MAN, LOGAN, WITH THE SOUL AND INNER GRACE OF A TRUE SAMURAI. >
< NO WOMAN COULD ASK FOR MORE. >

< THAT'S A RARE, FINE COMPLIMENT, MARIKO. I THANK YOU. >
< IT IS THE TRUTH. IF ANYONE IS UNWORTHY, IT IS I -- WHO LACK YOUR STRENGTH AND COURAGE. >

<NOW WHO'S BLOWIN' SMOKE? >
< YOU'RE THE BRAVEST WOMAN I KNOW. >

< IT'S GETTING LATE, MARIKO. WE'D BETTER HEAD BACK-- EH?! >
< LOOK. EAGLES-- HEADING OUR WAY. >
AWFUL BIG SUCKERS. SOMETHIN' ABOUT 'EM DOESN'T FEEL QUITE KOSHER.

THERE'S NO COVER ON THIS RIDGE--WE'RE PERFECT TARGETS.
< LOGAN-- WHAT--?! >
< HEAD FOR THE TREE LINE! I'LL EXPLAIN LATER. >
< RIDE, MARIKO! >

YOU HAVE PROVIDED US WITH A SPLENDID HUNT, TERRAN...
... BUT, ALAS, ALL GOOD THINGS MUST EVENTUALLY COME TO AN END.

YEARRRGH!
MARIKO!!

DREAM... THAT WAS A DREAM-- PLEASE... LET IT BE A DREAM...
BROOD HUNTERS-- THEY'VE FOUND ME!
FOOL, DID YOU REALLY THINK THAT WE WOULD NOT?!
YOU ARE ONE OF US, WOLVERINE. NO ONE CAN HELP YOU...

... AND NOTHING SAVE YOU!
THEIR BLASTERS ARE SET FOR STUN. I CAUGHT A SHOT NOT LONG AGO.
I'D RATHER BE DEAD.

THE UNDERGROWTH WORKS IN MY FAVOR. IT SLOWS THE HUNTERS DOWN, CRIPPLES THEIR MANEUVERABILITY.
BUT THIS IS THEIR TURF.
THEY KNOW IT-- I DON'T.

TO ME, MY BROTHERS! I HAVE HIM!
HATE TO TELL YA, BUB, BUT THOSE COME UNDER THE HEADING--

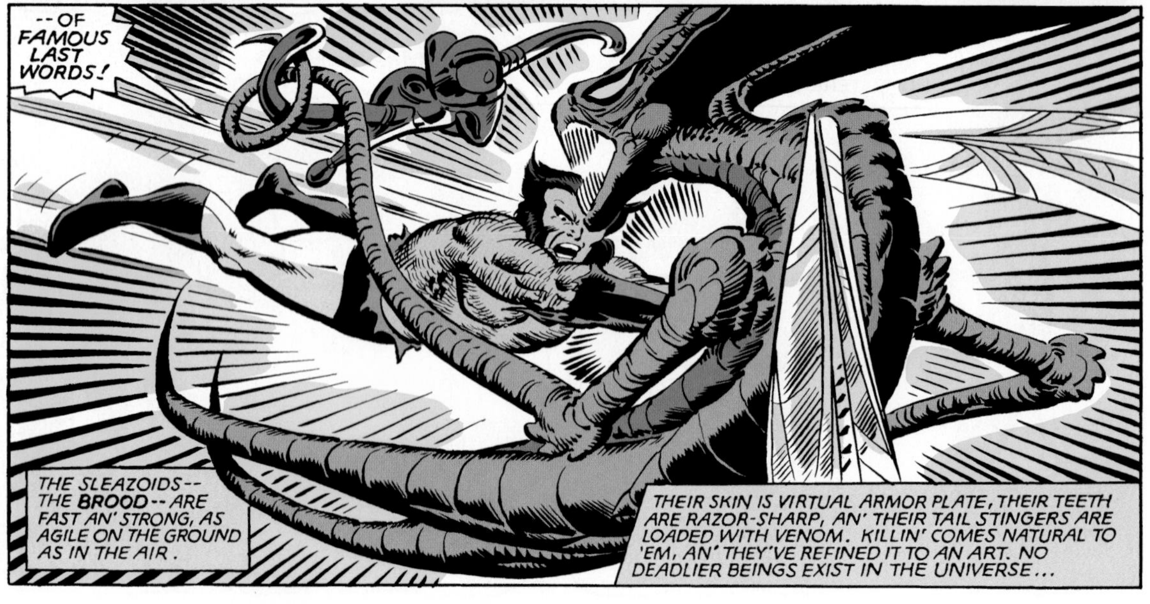
--OF FAMOUS LAST WORDS!
THE SLEAZOIDS-- THE BROOD-- ARE FAST AN' STRONG, AS AGILE ON THE GROUND AS IN THE AIR.
THEIR SKIN IS VIRTUAL ARMOR PLATE, THEIR TEETH ARE RAZOR-SHARP, AN' THEIR TAIL STINGERS ARE LOADED WITH VENOM. KILLIN' COMES NATURAL TO 'EM, AN' THEY'VE REFINED IT TO AN ART. NO DEADLIER BEINGS EXIST IN THE UNIVERSE...

...'CEPT MAYBE ME.
THE HUNTER'S CALL BRINGS HIS BUDDIES, ON THE DOUBLE.

AFTER THAT, THINGS GET INTERESTIN'.

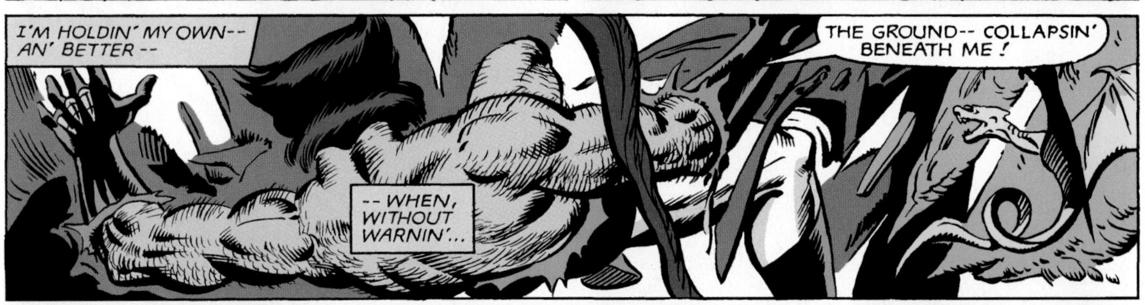
I'M HOLDIN' MY OWN-- AN' BETTER--
--WHEN, WITHOUT WARNIN'...
THE GROUND-- COLLAPSIN' BENEATH ME!

I'M FALLIN'!
A STUN BOLT CLIPS ME ON THE WAY DOWN. BY THE TIME I RECOVER, I'M MOVIN' TOO FAST TO STOP MYSELF-- BUT I TRY, ALL THE SAME.

Y'NEVER KNOW-- A BODY MIGHT GET LUCKY, SOMETHIN' MIGHT WORK.
WRONG.

LIKE I SAID, I'M A MUTANT. MY BODY HAS THE ABILITY TO HEAL ITSELF, FAST. I CAN SURVIVE ALMOST ANY PHYSICAL TRAUMA. BUT A TUMBLE FROM THIS HEIGHT MAY BE A BIT MUCH, EVEN FOR ME.
WHAT THE FLAMIN'--?!

I HIT HARD.
THERE'S A SPLIT-SECOND OF INCREDIBLE PAIN...
...THEN OBLIVION.

LATER...
I'M ALIVE. I'VE DITCHED THE HUNTERS.
THINGS COULD BE WORSE.
IT'S A FEEBLE JOKE. I DON'T LAUGH.
WHEN YOU'RE CONDEMNED TO HELL, DOES IT REALLY MATTER WHETHER THE FLAMES THAT BURN YOU ARE A MILLION DEGREES HOT OR A BILLION? EITHER WAY, IT HURTS.
OKAY, I SURVIVED. HOORAY FOR ME.

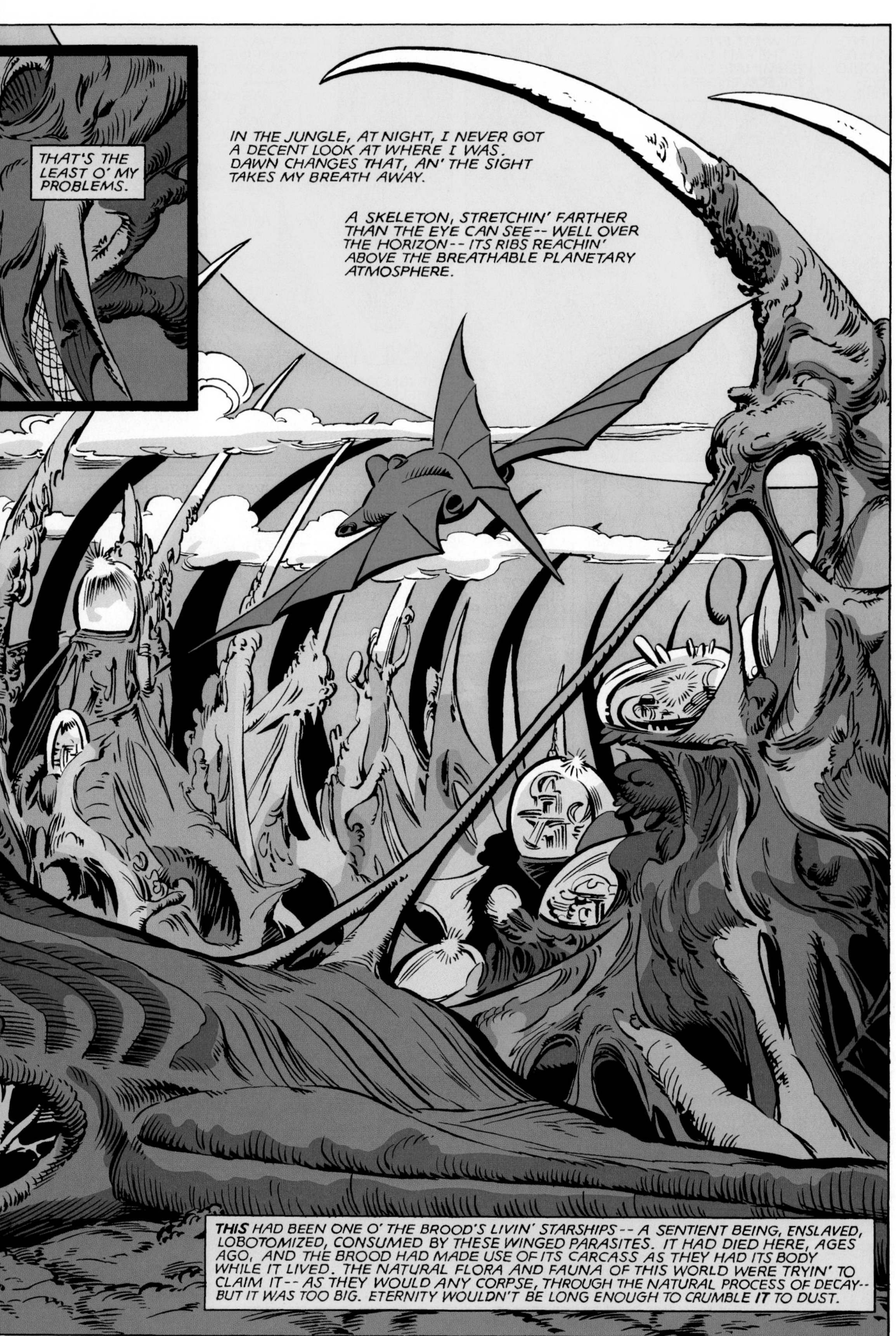
THAT'S THE LEAST O' MY PROBLEMS.
IN THE JUNGLE, AT NIGHT, I NEVER GOT A DECENT LOOK AT WHERE I WAS. DAWN CHANGES THAT, AN' THE SIGHT TAKES MY BREATH AWAY.
A SKELETON, STRETCHIN' FARTHER THAN THE EYE CAN SEE-- WELL OVER THE HORIZON-- ITS RIBS REACHIN' ABOVE THE BREATHABLE PLANETARY ATMOSPHERE.
THIS HAD BEEN ONE O' THE BROOD'S LIVIN' STARSHIPS -- A SENTIENT BEING, ENSLAVED, LOBOTOMIZED, CONSUMED BY THESE WINGED PARASITES. IT HAD DIED HERE, AGES AGO, AND THE BROOD HAD MADE USE OF ITS CARCASS AS THEY HAD ITS BODY WHILE IT LIVED. THE NATURAL FLORA AND FAUNA OF THIS WORLD WERE TRYIN' TO CLAIM IT-- AS THEY WOULD ANY CORPSE, THROUGH THE NATURAL PROCESS OF DECAY-- BUT IT WAS TOO BIG. ETERNITY WOULDN'T BE LONG ENOUGH TO CRUMBLE IT TO DUST.

HUNT-MASTER, SHOULD WE PURSUE?
TO WHAT END, NOVICE? IF THE FALL DID NOT TERMINATE OUR PREY, THE SCAVENGERS WILL.
BUT HE HOSTS A QUEEN! THE GREAT MOTHER WILL SURELY DESIRE CONFIRMATION OF HIS DEATH.

THE WAY IS OPEN, NOVICE, WOLVERINE'S TRAIL EASY TO FOLLOW. YOU MAY DO SO IF YOU WISH.
WE WILL CONVEY OUR CONDOLENCES TO YOUR PROGENY.
I AM NOT AFRAID, HUNT-MASTER!
THE IGNORANT RARELY ARE. SACRIFICE YOUR LIFE, IF YOU WISH. WE WILL RETURN TO BASE.

I HEAR MOVEMENT, FEEL VIBRATIONS IN THE WEB.
I CAN GUESS WHAT THAT MEANS--

--THE WEB-SPINNERS ARE COMIN' TO INVESTIGATE THEIR CATCH.
I'M GLUED IN PLACE. SHOULDN'T BE TOO MUCH TO HANDLE, THOUGH. I'VE GOT SOME FREEDOM OF MOVEMENT.
I'LL POP MY CLAWS AN' CUT MYSELF LOOSE.

WISH MY HEAD WOULD CLEAR. IT'S MUZZY-- IT'S AN EFFORT TO THINK-- AN' NOW IT'S POUNDIN' FIT TO BUST
NO! NOT AGAIN, NOT HERE -- I --
AARRRGH!

I BLINK...
...AND THE WEB BECOMES THE STARSHIP Z'REEE SHAR-- PERSONAL YACHT OF LILANDRA, EMPRESS OF THE SHI'AR.
THE X-MEN HAD RESCUED HER FROM THE BROOD, FOILED A COUP D'ÉTAT AGAINST HER LED BY HER RENEGADE SISTER, DEATHBIRD -- AN' IN THE PROCESS, SAVED THE EARTH FROM DESTRUCTION.

TO SHOW HER APPRECIATION, LIL INVITED US ABOARD HER YACHT FOR A BANQUET -- PART CELEBRATION, PART FAREWELL. SHE WAS RETURNIN' HOME AN' WANTED TO THANK US --
--ME, CAROL DANVERS, CYCLOPS, STORM, COLOSSUS, NIGHTCRAWLER, AN' KITTY PRYDE.

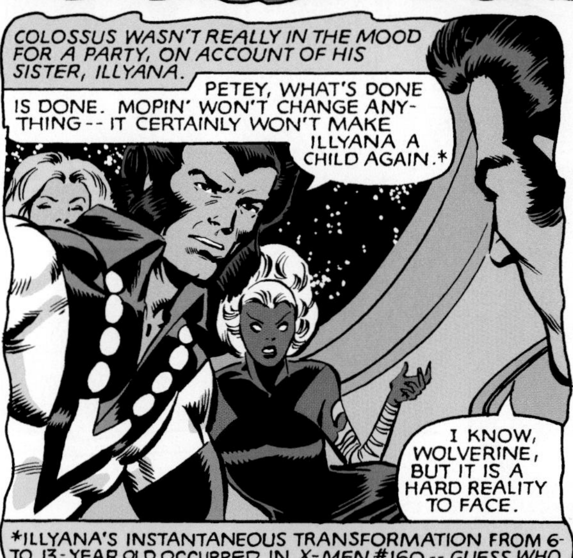
COLOSSUS WASN'T REALLY IN THE MOOD FOR A PARTY, ON ACCOUNT OF HIS SISTER, ILLYANA.
PETEY, WHAT'S DONE IS DONE. MOPIN' WON'T CHANGE ANYTHING -- IT CERTAINLY WON'T MAKE ILLYANA A CHILD AGAIN.*
I KNOW, WOLVERINE, BUT IT IS A HARD REALITY TO FACE.
*ILLYANA'S INSTANTANEOUS TRANSFORMATION FROM 6- TO 13-YEAR OLD OCCURRED IN X-MEN #160 -- GUESS WHO.

MUCH ABOUT OUR BATTLE WITH THE DEMON-LORD BELASCO IS DIFFICULT TO COPE WITH -- NOT THE LEAST OF WHICH WAS MY CONFRONTATION WITH MY OLDER SELF.
THAT STORM WAS A SORCERESS. SHE SAID HALF MY HERITAGE WAS BOUND TO THE ARTS ARCANE. BUT HOW?! I AM A MUTANT, NOT A MAGICIAN.
COULD I TRULY POSSESS SUCH TALENTS?

SUDDENLY...
BEHOLD, FOOLS! LILANDRA, MAJESTRIX SHI'AR, IS NO MORE! LONG LIVE THE NEW EMPRESS! ME!
DEATH-BIRD!

A TRAP. WE TRIED TO REACT...
... BUT A STASIS BOMB ENDED THE FIGHT AS SOON AS IT HAD BEGUN.*
*SEE LAST ISH -- L.

I CAME AWAKE IN PIECES. A... SENSE OF SELF-AWARENESS-- SCRAMBLED, CONFUSED--
--FOLLOWED BY A JUMBLE OF GOBBLEDY-GOOP SOUNDS.
I WAS FLOODED BY A MULTITUDE OF SCENTS.
THEY MADE ME SICK.
LAST CAME SIGHT-- BLURRED, BIZARRE IMAGES SHOT THROUGH WITH BLINDING FLASHES OF COLOR. NOTHIN' MADE SENSE. THEN, AS I STRUGGLED TO RE-GAIN MY PSYCHIC BALANCE...
...EVERYTHING CLICKED INTO FOCUS.
SLEAZOIDS!
THE BROOD-- WE'RE THEIR PRISONERS!
THE OTHERS DIDN'T SEEM TO MIND.
THEY WERE... ENJOYING THEMSELVES!
AN INSTANT LATER, I SAW WHY.
WELCOME, HONORED HEROES, TO THE THRONEWORLD OF THE SHI'AR.
THIS AFFAIR IS BUT A SMALL TOKEN OF OUR GRATITUDE.
MY INTELLECT ACCEPTED THIS AS REALITY, MY SENSES SCREAMED FANTASY. NORMALLY, I'D TRUST MY INSTINCTS EVERY TIME-- BUT I COULDN'T KEEP MY BEARINGS. ONE THOUGHT CONTRADICTED ANOTHER, AND THE HARDER I TRIED TO SORT THINGS OUT...
...THE MORE DISORIENTED I BECAME.
CARE TO DANCE, LOGAN? HEY-- ARE YOU ALL RIGHT?
CAROL, SOMETHIN'S... SCREWY.
THIS -- THIS ISN'T WHAT IT SEEMS. WE'RE BEIN' CONNED-- SET-UP!
SURE WE ARE. WOLVIE, I THINK YOU'RE GETTING PARANOID IN YOUR OLD AGE. RELAX. HAVE FUN. ENJOY THE PARTY.

PARDON OUR INTRUSION, WARRIORS-- BUT WE UNDERSTAND THAT YOUR PHYSIOLOGY, CAROL DANVERS, IS DISSIMILAR TO THAT OF YOUR COMRADES.
I'M NOT A MUTANT, IF THAT'S WHAT YOU MEAN.
PRECISELY. OUR PRELIMINARY DATASCANS ON YOU ARE MOST... INTRIGUING. MY COLLEAGUE AND I WOULD LIKE TO EXAMINE YOU FURTHER.
NOW? OKAY.
CAROL--!
CAROL!!
THIS IS CRAZY! THOSE WINGED CLOWNS ARE SLEAZOIDS!
FIGHT 'EM, CAROL! IT'S A TRICK!
NO GOOD. SHE'S ACTIN' LIKE EV'RYTHING'S...
...NORMAL.
WHAT'S... HAPPENIN' TO ME?! HAVE I FINALLY FLIPPED OUT?!
WOLVERINE, WHAT IS WRONG? WHY DID YOU CALL OUT LIKE THAT TO CAROL?
STORM-- GUYS--DIDN'T YOU SEE? NO, I GUESS NOT.
I GUESS... IT'S ALL IN MY MIND.
THE OTHERS WERE VERY NICE, CONSIDERATE, CONCERNED. I BRUSHED 'EM AWAY. I WAS SO SCARED I COULD BARELY KEEP FROM SHAKIN'. I THOUGHT I'D PUT THE DARK TIMES BEHIND ME.
WE WERE TAKEN BEFORE LIL, FOR OUR AWARDS.
BESIDE HER ON THE DIAS WAS A TALL, WEIRD-LOOKIN' DOLL. AT FIRST SIGHT, I WENT ICE-COLD, SUPERNALLY CALM--
--MY AUTOMATIC REACTION TO A COMBAT SITUATION.
WE WERE IN DANGER--WHY WAS I THE ONLY ONE WHO NOTICED?!

SHE GREETED EACH OF US IN TURN WITH A FOND EMBRACE. THE CEREMONY WENT WITHOUT A HITCH...
NO.
...UNTIL IT WAS KITTY'S TURN.
COME UNTO ME, CHILD. THERE IS NAUGHT TO FEAR.
NO! YOU'RE NOT REAL-- THIS ISN'T POSSIBLE! X-MEN, HELP ME-- I CAN'T PHASE--DON'T LET HER GET ME!
LOGAN!!
THE KID STRUGGLED, TO NO AVAIL. I HEARD HER SCREAMS, WANTED TO ACT--
...BUT I COULDN'T. SOME POWER HELD ME FAST.
HUSH, SMALL ONE.
LOOK INTO MY EYES, HEAR MY VOICE--AM I TRULY SO TERRIBLE TO BEHOLD?
N-NO, PLEASE. DON'T.
DAUGHTER, IT IS DONE.
IT WAS MY TURN.
I WAS THE BIRD...
...SHE, THE COBRA. I KNEW SHE WAS DEATH--AN' WORSE. I KNEW I HAD TO ESCAPE, STOP HER, SOMEHOW. I WAS CLOSE, WE WERE ALONE ON THE DIAS. I COULD USE MY CLAWS. BUT I DID NOTHING...
...AND THEN IT WAS TOO LATE.
ARRRRGH!

MY SCREAM WAKES ME, MEMORIES WASHIN' THROUGH ME LIKE A SCUMMY TIDE.
SHAME TRIGGERS RAGE.
I NEED AN OUTLET FOR THAT RAGE.
I GET ONE. SCAVENGERS, LOOKIN' FOR LUNCH.
THEY FIND A BIT MORE THAN THEY BARGAINED FOR.

I LET MY BERSERKER MOOD SWEEP ME ALONG.
THE X-MEN HAVE NEVER SEEN ME LIKE THIS. PART O' ME HOPES THEY NEVER WILL. I'M THE BEST THERE IS AT WHAT I DO.
BUT WHAT I DO BEST ISN'T VERY NICE.

SOON, THOUGH, MY RAGE -- AND ITS ADRENALIN HIGH -- BEGIN TO FADE. MY CUE TO MAKE MY EXIT.
THE SCAVS HAVE LOST INTEREST IN ME.

AS A MEAL, I'M NOT WORTH THE EFFORT-- ESPECIALLY WHEN THEY CAN TURN ON THEIR OWN WOUNDED AND DEAD.
CUTE.

WHICH WAY, NOW? UP, I THINK. THE SLEAZOIDS PREFER THE HEIGHTS, AS FAR FROM THE PLANETARY SURFACE-- AN' THIS JUNGLE-- AS THEY CAN GET. INTERESTIN'-- THE HUNTERS DIDN'T FOLLOW ME WHEN I FELL. THEY MUST BE PRETTY WARY OF THE JUNGLE AND ITS PREDATORS.
IF WE CAN TURN THAT FEAR TO OUR ADVANTAGE...

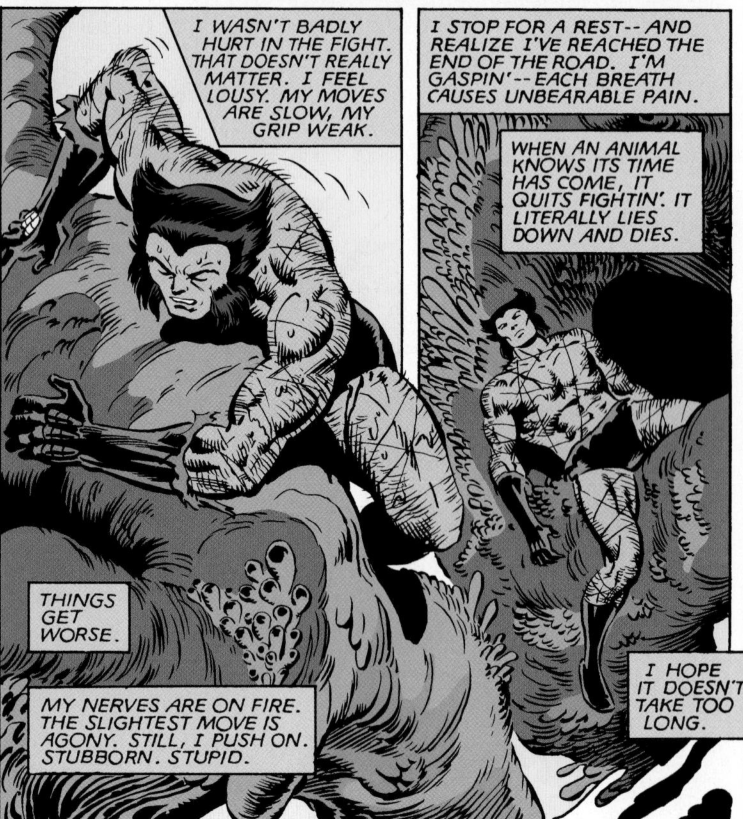
I WASN'T BADLY HURT IN THE FIGHT. THAT DOESN'T REALLY MATTER. I FEEL LOUSY. MY MOVES ARE SLOW, MY GRIP WEAK.
THINGS GET WORSE.
MY NERVES ARE ON FIRE. THE SLIGHTEST MOVE IS AGONY. STILL, I PUSH ON. STUBBORN. STUPID.
I STOP FOR A REST-- AND REALIZE I'VE REACHED THE END OF THE ROAD. I'M GASPIN'-- EACH BREATH CAUSES UNBEARABLE PAIN.
WHEN AN ANIMAL KNOWS ITS TIME HAS COME, IT QUITS FIGHTIN'. IT LITERALLY LIES DOWN AND DIES.
I HOPE IT DOESN'T TAKE TOO LONG.

LAST NIGHT, I WOKE. THAT WAS THE FIRST ATTACK AN' IT WAS A BEAUT, LEAVIN' ME BREATHLESS, SOAKED WITH SWEAT, SHAKIN', SCARED.
BUT MY MIND WAS CLEAR, THE MUZZINESS GONE.
MEMORY TOLD ME I WAS IN MY ROOM IN LILANDRA'S PALACE ON THE SHI'AR THRONEWORLD.
A GLANCE THROUGH THE WINDOW SHOT THAT BELIEF TO BLAZES.
STORM, WAKE UP-- WE GOT TROUBLE!
LOGAN--WHAT IS IT?
DARLIN', YOU WON'T BELIEVE IT.
SHE DIDN'T.
YOU'VE BEEN BEHAVING STRANGELY EVER SINCE OUR ARRIVAL. YOU'RE IN OBVIOUS PAIN NOW. YOU'RE ILL, WOLVERINE, THAT'S ALL.
LET ME SUMMON A PHYSICIAN...
A NERVE PINCH STOPPED HER, KAYO'D HER. I COULDN'T AFFORD DISCOVERY, NOT 'TIL I'D FIGURED OUT WHAT WAS GOIN' ON.
SHE DISMISSED MY STORY OUT OF HAND. THAT'S WAY OUT OF CHARACTER. THE SLEAZOIDS MUST BE AFFECTIN' OUR PERCEPTIONS, TO KEEP US IN LINE.
LOOKS LIKE, FOR THIS CAPER, I'M ON MY OWN.

I MADE ONE STOP BEFORE I LEFT-- KITTY'S ROOM.

KID SHE MAY BE, BUT SHE'S PROVED-- TIME AN' AGAIN-- THAT SHE'S GOT MORE GUTS AN' SMARTS THAN MOST ADULTS. THAN MOST HEROES.

I REMEMBERED HER STRUGGLIN' IN THE THRONE ROOM-- AN' HOW ALL I DID WAS WATCH. WHAT HAD BEEN DONE TO US? WHY WAS **I** SO SICK, AN' NONE OF THE OTHERS?

I WANTED TO TAKE THE KID WITH ME. BUT I'D BE MOVIN' HARD AN' FAST-- AN' PLAYIN' ROUGH-- AN' I COULDN'T GUARANTEE HER SURVIVAL.

FOR NOW, SHE WAS BETTER OFF WHERE SHE WAS.

I'M SORRY, KIDDO.

BUT DON'T FRET. I'LL BE BACK. WE'LL GET OUT OF THIS MESS, AN' COME HOME SAFE AN' SOUND, YOU GOT MY WORD.

THE PROMISE SOUNDED HOLLOW.

SUDDENLY, AN IMAGE FLASHED THROUGH MY MIND-- KITTY CRADLED IN MY ARMS, MY RIGHT HAND LYIN' BELOW HER BREASTBONE, THE STACCATTO CLICK OF CLAWS EXTENDING, RETRACTING, THE LIGHT FADIN' FROM HER EYES...

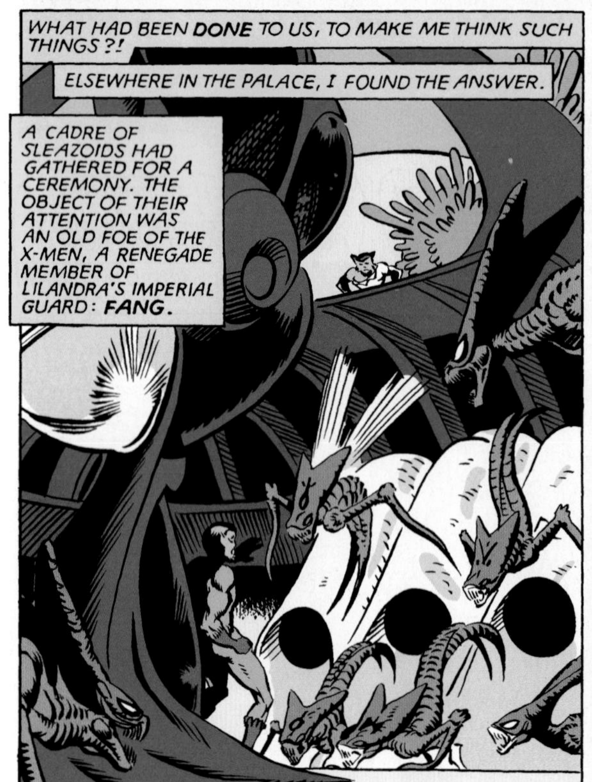

WHAT HAD BEEN **DONE** TO US, TO MAKE ME THINK SUCH THINGS?!
ELSEWHERE IN THE PALACE, I FOUND THE ANSWER.
A CADRE OF SLEAZOIDS HAD GATHERED FOR A CEREMONY. THE OBJECT OF THEIR ATTENTION WAS AN OLD FOE OF THE X-MEN, A RENEGADE MEMBER OF LILANDRA'S IMPERIAL GUARD: **FANG**.

I GRINNED. SERVED THE SUCKER RIGHT IF THE BROOD-- FOR WHOM HE'D WORKED TO OVERTHROW LIL-- WERE GONNA REWARD HIS TREACHERY WITH TORTURE OR EXECUTION.
HE WAS PLEADIN'. THEY WERE LAUGHIN'. SURPRISINGLY, I UNDERSTOOD THEIR LANGUAGE.
FANG'S BODY BEGAN TO SMOKE. HE SHRIEKED. I STOPPED GRINNIN'.

WHY... ARE YOU DOING... THIS?! MY MISTRESS, DEATHBIRD, IS YOUR ALLY!
THE BROOD NEEDS NO ALLIES, OUTWORLDER. THERE ARE ONLY ENEMIES--AND SLAVES! WE USED DEATHBIRD...
...AS WE NOW USE YOU!
"THE EMBRYO OF A WARRIOR-PRIME WAS IMPLANTED WITHIN YOU. THAT EGG HAS NOW REACHED MATURITY. IT IS 'HATCHING.'
"IT WILL CONSUME YOU, FANG, TRANSFORM YOU.
"AND, IN THE PROCESS, ABSORB THE TOTALITY...
"... OF YOUR MEMORIES, YOUR ABILITIES, YOUR GENETIC POTENTIAL.
"FAREWELL, 'ALLY.' YOU GAVE YOUR LIFE FOR THE NOBLEST OF REASONS--
"... THAT ONE OF THE BROOD MIGHT BE BORN!"
THE PIECES FELL INTO PLACE. THE CEREMONY IN THE THRONE ROOM FINALLY MADE SENSE.
WE'D BEEN INFECTED, TOO-- MADE HOSTS FOR THEIR QUEEN'S EGGS. WHAT HAPPENED TO FANG--WOULD HAPPEN TO US.
NO!!
AN INTRUDER!
ONE OF THE X-MEN!
SEIZE HIM!
THE CHASE WAS ON.

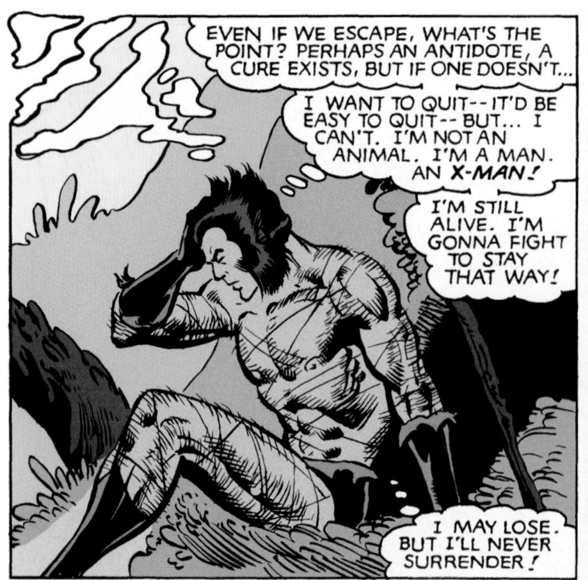
EVEN IF WE ESCAPE, WHAT'S THE POINT? PERHAPS AN ANTIDOTE, A CURE EXISTS, BUT IF ONE DOESN'T...
I WANT TO QUIT-- IT'D BE EASY TO QUIT-- BUT... I CAN'T. I'M NOT AN ANIMAL. I'M A MAN. AN X-MAN!
I'M STILL ALIVE. I'M GONNA FIGHT TO STAY THAT WAY!
I MAY LOSE. BUT I'LL NEVER SURRENDER!

THAT NOISE -- A SLEAZOID!
I RECOGNIZE THE MARKINGS-- IT'S THE WARRIOR FANG HOSTED. I LIKE THE IRONY.

HE'S MY TICKET BACK INTO THE PALACE. BY SKY-DIVING, I CAN REACH HIM.
IT'S RISKY-- IF HE HEARS ME AND DODGES, THERE'S NOTHIN' BUT MILES OF OPEN AIR BETWEEN ME AND THE GROUND.

MY KIND OF GAMBLE. I PLAY IT PERFECTLY.
THE SLEAZOID IS ON HIS FIRST FLIGHT, TESTING HIS WINGS.
INEXPERIENCED, A LITTLE OVERCONFIDENT AND CARELESS, HIS MIND ON OTHER THINGS...

...HE NEVER KNOWS WHAT HITS HIM.
SNIKT!

HE TRIES TO IMPALE ME ON HIS STINGERS. I MAKE SURE HE CAN'T.

THAT'S ALL SHE WROTE, BUB. COOPERATE, OR I'LL GUT YOU.
I'M NOT BLUFFING.
HE KNOWS IT.

HE DOES AS HE'S TOLD, CONFIDENT-- HE TELLS ME-- THAT HE'S CARRYIN' ME TO CERTAIN DEATH.
YOUR FATE IS SEALED, HUMAN.
SO'S YOURS, IF YOU DON'T SHUT UP.

THEN...
...ANOTHER ATTACK, THE WORST YET, SO MUCH PAIN, HITTIN' SO FAST, THAT I CAN'T EVEN SCREAM.
FOR MY PRISONER, IT'S A GOLDEN OPPORTUNITY.

HE MAKES THE MOST OF IT.
BROTHERS-- A PRESENT FOR YOU!

WOLVERINE, HOW NICE OF YOU TO DROP IN.
TAKE HIM, HUNTERS. BUT IF HE RESISTS--
--KILL HIM!

THEY DO THEIR BEST.

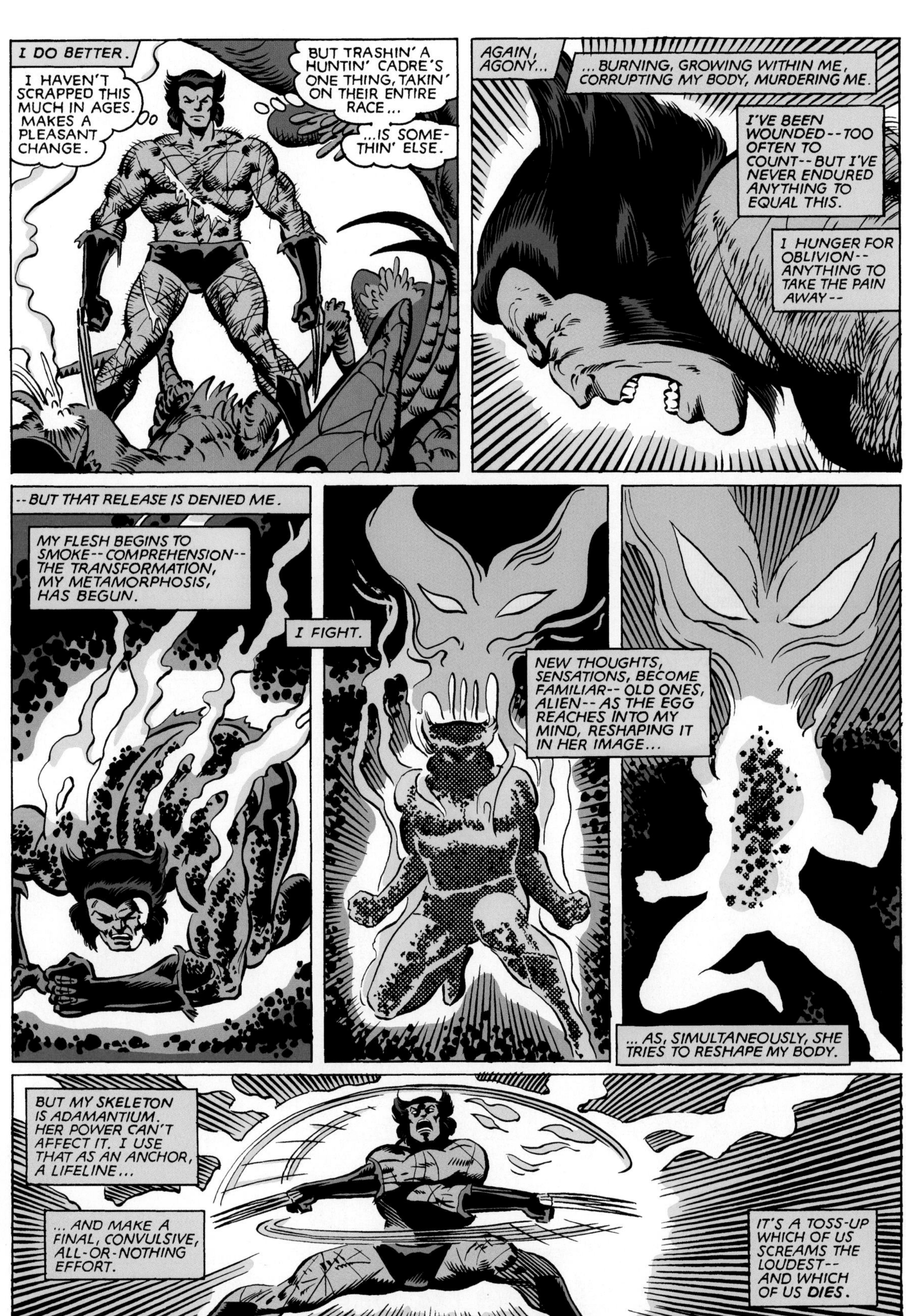
I DO BETTER.
I HAVEN'T SCRAPPED THIS MUCH IN AGES. MAKES A PLEASANT CHANGE.
BUT TRASHIN' A HUNTIN' CADRE'S ONE THING, TAKIN' ON THEIR ENTIRE RACE...
...IS SOMETHIN' ELSE.
AGAIN, AGONY...
...BURNING, GROWING WITHIN ME, CORRUPTING MY BODY, MURDERING ME.
I'VE BEEN WOUNDED--TOO OFTEN TO COUNT--BUT I'VE NEVER ENDURED ANYTHING TO EQUAL THIS.
I HUNGER FOR OBLIVION--ANYTHING TO TAKE THE PAIN AWAY--
--BUT THAT RELEASE IS DENIED ME.
MY FLESH BEGINS TO SMOKE--COMPREHENSION--THE TRANSFORMATION, MY METAMORPHOSIS, HAS BEGUN.
I FIGHT.
NEW THOUGHTS, SENSATIONS, BECOME FAMILIAR--OLD ONES, ALIEN--AS THE EGG REACHES INTO MY MIND, RESHAPING IT IN HER IMAGE...
...AS, SIMULTANEOUSLY, SHE TRIES TO RESHAPE MY BODY.
BUT MY SKELETON IS ADAMANTIUM. HER POWER CAN'T AFFECT IT. I USE THAT AS AN ANCHOR, A LIFELINE...
...AND MAKE A FINAL, CONVULSIVE, ALL-OR-NOTHING EFFORT.
IT'S A TOSS-UP WHICH OF US SCREAMS THE LOUDEST--AND WHICH OF US DIES.

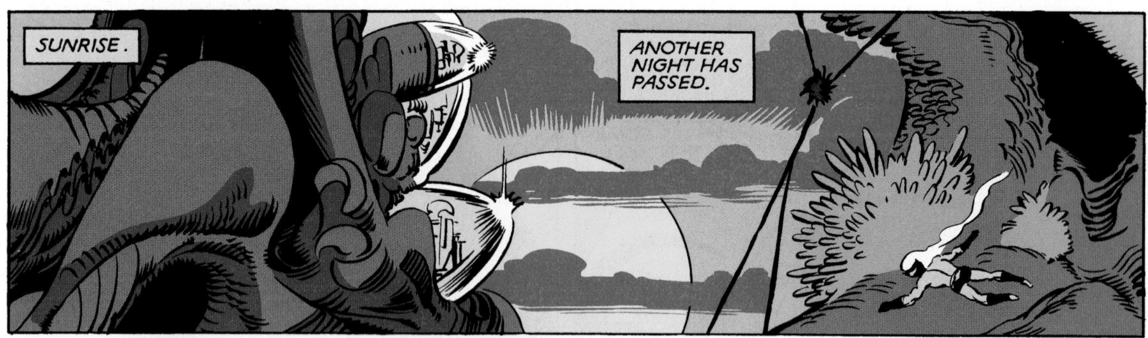

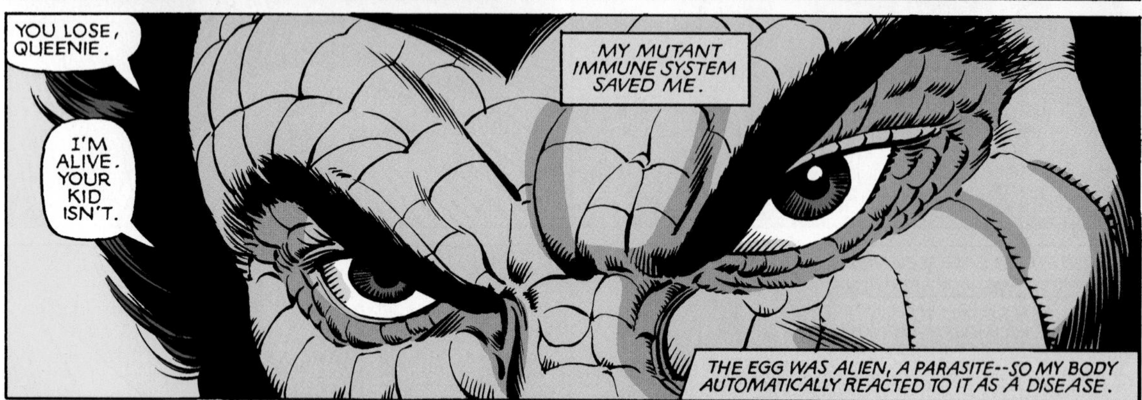

YOU LOSE, QUEENIE.
I'M ALIVE. YOUR KID ISN'T.
MY MUTANT IMMUNE SYSTEM SAVED ME.
THE EGG WAS ALIEN, A PARASITE--SO MY BODY AUTOMATICALLY REACTED TO IT AS A DISEASE.

THAT WAS WHY I WAS SO SICK...SIDE-EFFECTS OF MY BODY'S STRUGGLE TO EXPUNGE THE INVADER, AND ITS TO SURVIVE. BUT ALTHOUGH IT NEVER GAINED MORE THAN A TOEHOLD, THE EGG STILL PUT UP A HELLUVA FIGHT.
I ALMOST LOST. AN' THE STRAIN FLAMIN' NEAR KILLED ME.

I CAN SEE THE PALACE, IMAGINE THE X-MEN HYPNOTISED-'N'-HAPPY WITHIN.
THEY'RE INFECTED, TOO. ONLY I CAN'T SAVE 'EM THE WAY I DID MYSELF. FOR ALL I KNOW, I MAY ALREADY BE TOO LATE. THEIR METAMOR-PHOSES MAY ALREADY HAVE TAKEN PLACE.

I REMEMBER MY HALLUCINATION ABOUT KILLING KITTY. IF I HAVE TO-- IF SHE CAN'T BE CURED-- I'LL DO IT.
I'LL... KILL THEM ALL. MY FRIENDS.
THEN, IT'LL BE THE SLEAZOIDS' TURN.

NEXT RESCUE MISSION!

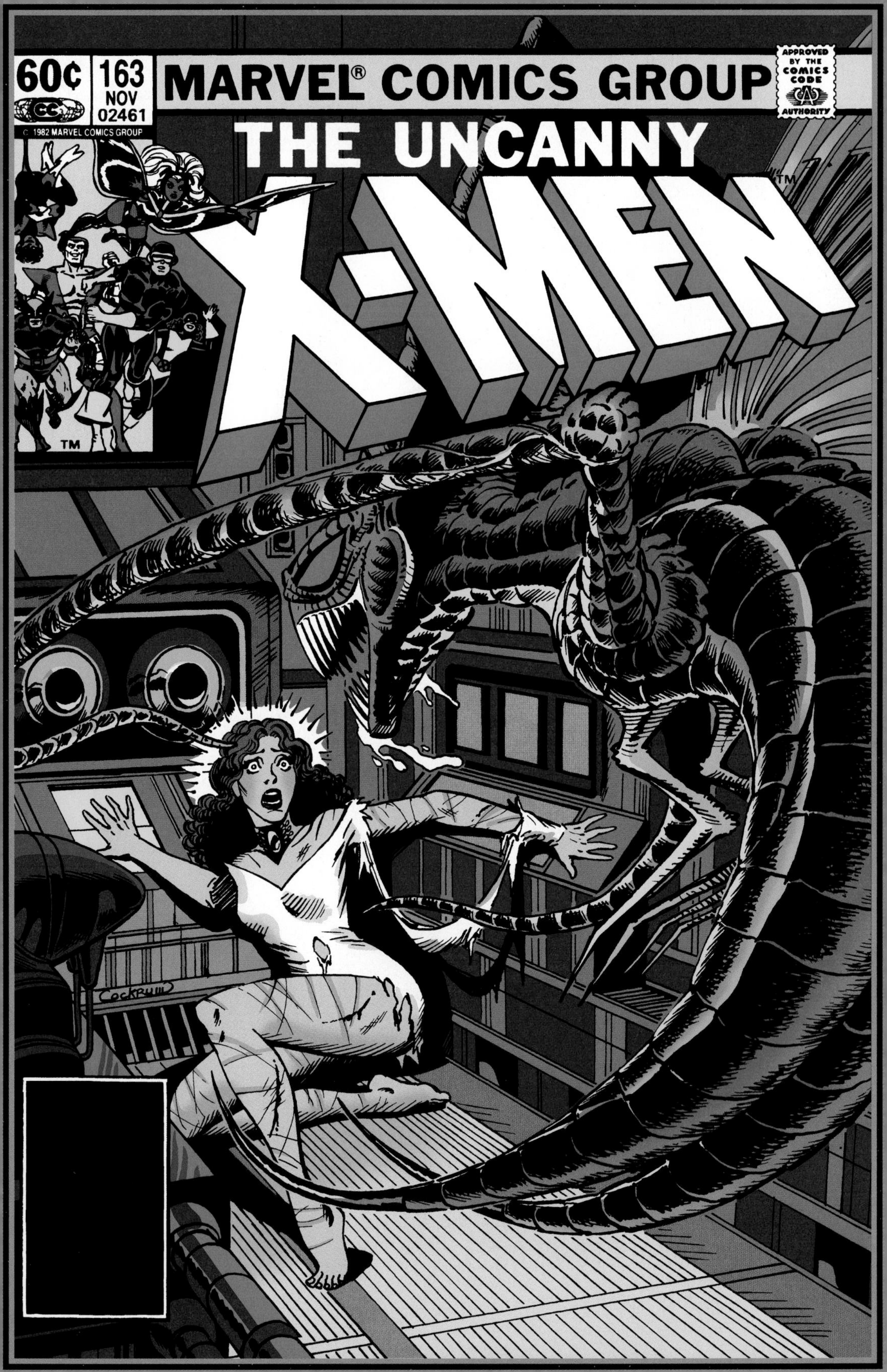
60¢
163
NOV
02461
MARVEL® COMICS GROUP
APPROVED BY THE COMICS CODE AUTHORITY
© 1982 MARVEL COMICS GROUP
THE UNCANNY
X-MEN
TM
TM
COCKRUM

RESCUE MISSION

A STAN LEE PRESENTATION-- STARRING THE UNCANNY X-MEN!
SHE SHRIEKS. SHE HOWLS. SHE SOBS. BUT THE TORMENT NEVER ENDS.
OUR SUBJECT--WHOSE PERSONAL IDENTIFICATION IS CAROL DANVERS--IS A BIPEDAL HOMONID, FEMALE, LEVEL TWO ON THE STANDARD EVOLUTIONARY SCALE. HER COMPANIONS, THE X-MEN, ARE MUTANTS--GENETIC DEVIANTS FROM THEIR RACIAL NORM, ENDOWED WITH EXTRAORDINARY PHYSICAL AND MENTAL ABILITIES.
THAT IS WHY WE OF THE BROOD ACQUIRED THEM AS HOST FORMS FOR THE PROGENY OF OUR GREAT MOTHER. DURING THE FINAL METAMORPHOSIS, EACH HATCHLING WILL ABSORB THE POWERS AND GENETIC POTENTIAL OF ITS HOST.
HOWEVER, THIS CREATURE IS AN ANOMALY. NEITHER MUTANT NOR BASELINE HUMAN, HER DNA MATRIX IS UNIQUE.
CHRIS CLAREMONT SCRIPTER
DAVE COCKRUM & BOB WIACEK ARTISTS
JOE ROSEN LETTERER
BOB SHAREN COLORIST
LOUISE JONES EDITOR
JIM SHOOTER EDITOR-IN-CHIEF

AT THE MOMENT, TO HELP DETERMINE THE FULL RAMIFICATIONS OF OUR FINDINGS...
...WE ARE SUBJECTING HER TO EVOLUTIONARY MODIFICATION.

HER PHYSICAL FORM WE CAN ALTER AT WILL. WHAT HAS PROVEN MOST FASCINATING IS HER PSYCHIC RESISTANCE.
THOUGH SHE IS EXPERIENCING SUPPOSEDLY UNENDURABLE PAIN, SHE REMAINS AWARE OF ALL THAT TRANSPIRES."

SHE REMAINS SANE. AND DEFIANT, TO AN EXTENT I WOULD NOT HAVE BELIEVED POSSIBLE.
DZÍLÒS, PROVIDE SOME REFRESHMENT FOR OUR GUESTS.
AT ONCE, SCHOLAR.

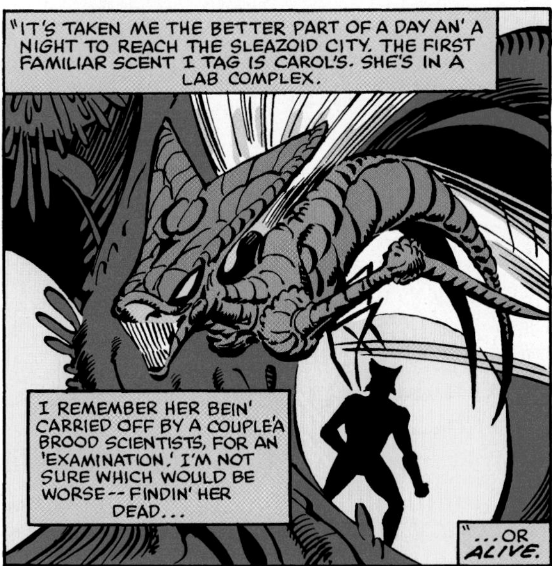
"IT'S TAKEN ME THE BETTER PART OF A DAY AN' A NIGHT TO REACH THE SLEAZOID CITY. THE FIRST FAMILIAR SCENT I TAG IS CAROL'S. SHE'S IN A LAB COMPLEX.
I REMEMBER HER BEIN' CARRIED OFF BY A COUPLE'A BROOD SCIENTISTS, FOR AN 'EXAMINATION.' I'M NOT SURE WHICH WOULD BE WORSE -- FINDIN' HER DEAD...
"...OR *ALIVE*.

"I FOLLOW THE TECHNO.
"I FIGURE HE'LL BE MY TICKET INTO THE LAB

THE LUMINATORS-- THEY'VE GONE OUT!
WHAT IS HAPPENING?! WHO IS THERE?!

FOR WHAT IT'S WORTH, BUB--
--THE NAME IS *WOLVERINE!*
SNIKT!

"THE SUCKER FIGHTS--
"--FOR ALL THE GOOD THAT DOES HIM.

EVENIN', GENTS.
THE X-MAN-- WOLVERINE!
HE IS A RENEGADE-- SLAY HIM!

BUB--
--I WAS HOPIN' YOU'D SAY THAT.

"MY CLAWS ARE PURE ADAMANTIUM-- THE STRONGEST METAL KNOWN-- RAZOR-KEEN, RETRACTABLE INTO MY FOREARMS. MY SKELETON'S LACED WITH THE SAME STUFF, MAKIN' MY BONES VIRTUALLY UNBREAKABLE.
"WHAT CLASSES ME AS A MUTANT, THOUGH, IS MY BODY'S NATURAL ABILITY TO HEAL ANY WOUND, CURE ANY DISEASE. EXTENSIONS O' THAT BASIC TALENT GIVE ME FANTASTICALLY KEEN SENSES AN' ABILITIES. I'M FAST, STRONG, AGILE--HELL ON WHEELS.
"DEFINITE ASSETS IN MY LINE O' WORK.

"TECHNICALLY, I'M A SUPER HERO, ONE O' THE GOOD GUYS.
"BEFORE THAT, I WAS AN AGENT, CANADIAN SECRET SERVICE.
"BEFORE THAT, A COMMANDO.

"BY BIRTH, TRAININ', CHOICE, I'M A WARRIOR--
"--THE BEST THERE IS--
"--AS THIS CROWD QUICKLY LEARNS.

"I HEAR A MOAN...
"CAROL.
"WE GO BACK A WAYS, SHE AN' I-- WE WORKED TOGETHER A LOT WHEN SHE WAS A PART OF U.S. AIR FORCE INTELLIGENCE-- SHE'S A FRIEND.
"WHEN THE RUSSIAN KGB CAPTURED HER, I WAS ONE O' THE TEAM THAT DISOBEYED ORDERS AN' PULLED HER OUT.

"SHE WAS A LOVELY LADY--SKIN AN' SOUL.
"NOW SHE'S BARELY RECOGNIZABLE AS A HUMAN BEING.

"HER FEATURES FLOW LIKE HOT WAX SHAPED BY SOME SICKO SCULPTOR'S HANDS, SHIFTING WITHOUT RHYME OR REASON. OBVIOUSLY, THE SLEAZOID GIZMO IS RESPONSIBLE.
"PROBLEM IS, HOW TO SHUT THE SUCKER DOWN.
SHOULD I EVEN TRY? THERE'S NO GUARANTEE SHE'LL REVERT TO HUMAN. MAYBE IT'D BE BETTER TO PUT HER OUT OF HER MISERY. FIRST, CAROL...
...THEN THE X-MEN.

"I CAN'T MAKE HEAD NOR TAIL OUT OF THE CONTROLS, SO I DECIDE TO LEAVE WELL ENOUGH ALONE--FIDDLIN'LL ONLY MAKE THINGS WORSE.
"INSTEAD, I CROSS MY FINGERS...
"...AN' WRECK EVERYTHING IN SIGHT. SIMPLE. EFFECTIVE. LIKE ME.

"I'M LUCKIER THAN I DESERVE.
"I HOPE CAROL FEELS THE SAME.

EASY, DARLIN'. YOU'VE HAD A ROUGH RIDE, BUT I THINK YOU'RE GONNA BE OKAY.
FIRE... BURNING WITHIN ME-- SO BRIGHT, SO... BEAUTIFUL. LOGAN-- HELP ME!
"I DON'T KNOW HOW.

"I'VE BEEN LYIN', O' COURSE. CAROL ISN'T ALL RIGHT.
"SHE KNOWS IT.
"SHE LOOKS NORMAL, BUT APPEARANCE DON'T MATTER BEANS.
"HER SCENT'S NO LONGER HUMAN. THAT SCARES US BOTH.

"BUT WE'RE PROFESSIONALS WITH A JOB TO DO. SO WE COPE AS BEST WE CAN.
THAT'S TWICE I OWE YOU MY LIFE, LOGAN.
WHO'S COUNTIN'?
WE GOTTA ROLL, CAROL, BEFORE SOMEONE NOTICES OUR LITTLE FRACAS.

FINE WITH ME.
STRANGE. AFTER ALL THE SLEAZOIDS PUT ME THROUGH, YOU'D THINK I'D BE WEAK, PHYSICALLY SHOT TO PIECES. BUT I FEEL BETTER THAN I HAVE IN AGES, LITERALLY BURSTING WITH ENERGY.
LET'S HOPE IT LASTS, DARLIN', 'CAUSE WE'LL SURE NEED IT BEFORE WE'RE THROUGH.
LOGAN, DO YOU THINK WE HAVE A CHANCE?
DOES IT MATTER?
NO, I SUPPOSE NOT.

MEANWHILE--
--BACK ON EARTH, ON A SPRAWLING ESTATE SOME FORTY MILES FROM NEW YORK CITY, A MANSION IS BEING REBUILT. UNTIL RECENTLY, IT HOUSED PROFESSOR CHARLES XAVIER'S SCHOOL FOR GIFTED YOUNGSTERS, AND SERVED AS HOME AND SECRET HEADQUARTERS OF THE X-MEN.
THE SILENT SPARKLE OF A TRANSPORTER HERALDS THE ARRIVAL OF TWO FIGURES ON THE LAWN. THEY'RE EXPECTED.
ALEX! CORSAIR!
HI, LORNA.

THE YOUNG WOMAN IS LORNA DANE; THE YOUNG MAN, ALEX SUMMERS--MUTANTS, LOVERS, PART-TIME X-MEN. THE OTHER MAN IS ALEX'S FATHER-- CHRISTOPHER SUMMERS, FORMER MAJOR, USAF. NOW, AS CORSAIR, HE LEADS A BAND OF INTER-STELLAR FREE-BOOTERS, THE STARJAMMERS.
WHAT'S THE NEWS?
LOUSY.

THE X-MEN AND EMPRESS LILANDRA HAVE BEEN KIDNAPPED.

LILANDRA'S SISTER, DEATHBIRD, IS MAKING A BID TO SEIZE THE SHI'AR THRONE. THAT WHOLE GALACTIC EMPIRE IS COMING APART AT THE SEAMS, AS EVERYONE CHOOSES SIDES. EVIDENTLY, DEATHBIRD ALLIED HERSELF WITH A RACE OF ALIENS FROM BEYOND KNOWN SPACE, THE BROOD.

THE PRICE OF THEIR AID WAS THE X-MEN'S LIVES.
DEATHBIRD DELIVERED, AND THE BROOD IMMEDIATELY TOOK THEM TO THEIR HOMEWORLD, WHEREVER THE BLAZES THAT IS. HEAVEN ONLY KNOWS THEIR FATE.

MY BROTHER, MY FRIENDS--THEY COULD BE DEAD, OR WORSE--
--AND THERE'S 'NOT A BLASTED THING I CAN DO TO HELP THEM!!

AN ENERGY BOLT--ARE WE UNDER ATTACK?!
CORSAIR REACTS AUTOMATICALLY, WITH THE SPEED OF THOUGHT, USING THE PHASING JEWELS ON HIS GLOVES TO SUMMON HIS HAND WEAPONS. IN A SPLIT-SECOND, HE'S READY FOR ACTION.
SORRY, DAD. MY FAULT. FALSE ALARM.
I UNDERSTAND, SON. WE ALL NEED TO BLOW OFF SOME STEAM.

YOU SEEM T' BE A MITE NERVOUS, MAJOR.
BETTER NERVOUS THAN DEAD, DR. MACTAGGERT.
GOOD POINT. MIGHT I ASK YUIR PLANS?
MY SON HAS BEEN KIDNAPPED. I INTEND TO RESCUE HIM. OR AVENGE HIM.

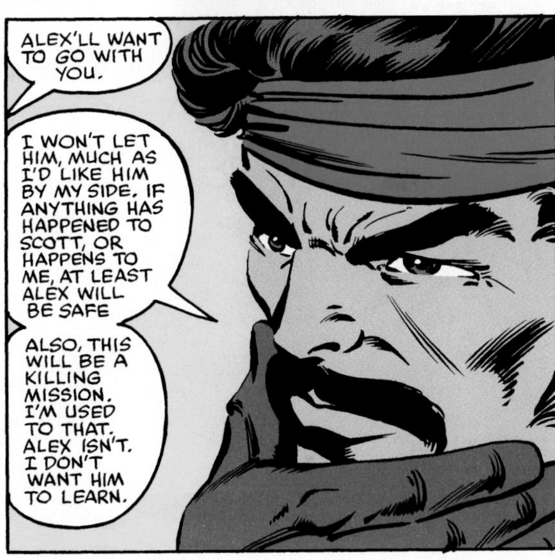
ALEX'LL WANT TO GO WITH YOU.
I WON'T LET HIM, MUCH AS I'D LIKE HIM BY MY SIDE. IF ANYTHING HAS HAPPENED TO SCOTT, OR HAPPENS TO ME, AT LEAST ALEX WILL BE SAFE
ALSO, THIS WILL BE A KILLING MISSION. I'M USED TO THAT. ALEX ISN'T. I DON'T WANT HIM TO LEARN.

WE'LL BE WARPING OUT OF ORBIT AS SOON AS I BEAM UP. I WANTED TO SAY GOOD-BYE TO YOU AND PROFESSOR XAVIER.
CHARLES ISN'T HERE. HE'S TAKING THIS VERY HARD, CHRIS--NOT SO MUCH THAT THE X-MEN ARE IN DANGER, BUT THAT, FOR ALL HIS POWER, HE WAS AND IS UNABLE TO DO ANYTHING ABOUT IT.
HE'S A STRONG MAN, MOIRA. HE'LL RECOVER.

HE'S LOST THE WOMAN HE LOVES AND HIS BELOVED X-MEN, HIS FAMILY. HE'S ALONE, CHRIS. AYE, HE'S STRONG, BUT EVEN THE STRONGEST BACK HAS ITS BREAKING POINT.
I FEAR, FOR CHARLEY, THIS MAY BE IT.
FAREWELL, CORSAIR. GOOD LUCK.

A GALAXY AWAY, SCOTT SUMMERS-- ALEX' OLDER BROTHER--RUNS FOR HIS LIFE.
A BROOD HUNTING CADRE--BUT THAT'S IMPOSSIBLE!
ISN'T IT? WHAT IS THIS PLACE--NOT THE EARTH, THAT'S FOR SURE--WHERE THE DEVIL AM I?
SO HARD TO REMEMBER... AND NONE OF THOSE MEMORIES MAKE ANY SENSE. THE BROOD ISN'T GIVING ME A CHANCE TO SORT THINGS OUT, EITHER.
EACH TIME MY OPTIC BLASTS KAYO ONE OF THEM, ANOTHER HUNTER POPS UP TO TAKE HIS PLACE.
I HOPE THE REST OF THE X-MEN ARE ALL RIGHT--IF THEY'RE IN THE SAME FIX, WE-- EH?!!
SCOTT-- CYCLOPS-- OVER HERE!
IN A MINUTE, STORM--
--AS SOON AS I'VE TAKEN CARE OF BUSINESS!
WELCOME, SISTER. WE HAVE BEEN EAGERLY AWAITING YOU.
NO!
HE TURNS TOWARDS HIS FRIENDS AND TEAM-MATES...
...ONLY TO HAVE HIS GREETING BECOME A STRANGLED CRY OF HORROR AND DENIAL.
WHAT HAVE YOU DONE WITH THE X-MEN?!
MY DEAR CYCLOPS, WE ARE THE X-MEN.

NO!!
SCREAM DENIALS 'TIL YOUR LUNGS BURST AND YOUR HEART CRACKS, CYCLOPS, THEY WILL CHANGE NOTHING.
YOUR FATE IS SEALED, YOUR METAMORPHOSIS INEVITABLE. LOOK!
THAT REFLECTION --IT'S ONE OF THE BROOD-- IT'S... ME!
NOT AS YOU ARE, HUMAN-- BUT AS YOU WILL SOON BECOME.
OUR GREAT MOTHER IMPLANTED AN EGG WITHIN YOU.
EVEN NOW, IT GROWS, IT THRIVES.
NO POWER IN THE UNIVERSE CAN SAVE YOU.
FANGS AND CLAWS TEAR AT HIM, STRIPPING AWAY HIS HUMANITY...
...REVEALING THE YOUNG QUEEN NESTLING IN HIS SOUL.
DESPAIR SWEEPS THROUGH HIM AND WHEN SHE DRAWS HIM CLOSE, TO HIS DOOM, HE DOES NOT RESIST. BUT THEN, SUDDENLY...
HANDS-- BRUSHING THE OTHERS ASIDE--!
P-PROFESSOR XAVIER--?!?
AM I LOSING MY MIND?! AM I ALREADY INSANE?!
HELP ME!
SUCH AID WAS GIVEN WHEN I FIRST TRAINED YOU, CYCLOPS. THEREIN LIES YOUR SALVATION.
THE IMAGE IS A PHANTOM, HE REALIZES.

ALL THE IMAGES ARE PHANTOMS, REAL--AND THREATENING--ONLY SO LONG AS HE ALLOWS THEM TO BE SO.
XAVIER IS THE MOST POWERFUL TELEPATH ON EARTH. FROM THE BEGINNING, HE TRAINED THE X-MEN TO RESIST PSIONIC ATTACKS.
CYCLOPS DRAWS ON ALL HE'S LEARNED, ON COURAGE PROVEN ON SCORES OF BATTLEFIELDS, ON STRENGTH HE NEVER KNEW HE POSSESSED...

...AND WAKES.
OH!!
OH.
A DREAM --IT WAS A DREAM. THANK... HEAVEN.
IMAGES...FADING SO FAST --CAN'T HOLD ONTO THEM. I DON'T REALLY WANT TO.

THE SKY--SO MANY MOONS. WE'RE A LONG WAY FROM HOME.
MEMORY TELLS ME WE'RE SUPPOSED TO BE ON LILANDRA'S THRONEWORLD, BUT THIS LOOKS NOTHING LIKE THE PROFESSOR'S DESCRIPTIONS.
STORM...?

SHE'S IN A TRANCE.
I DON'T WANT TO DISTURB HER--THAT COULD PROVE DANGEROUS FOR BOTH OF US-- BUT I THINK I'D BETTER.
I REMEMBER OUR BEING HONORED FOR RESCUING LILANDRA--YET OUR CLOTHES ARE IN TATTERS. AND MY NIGHTMARE INDICATES SOME SORT OF PSYCHIC CONFLICT. IF SOMEONE IS MANIPULATING OUR MINDS...
HE STEPS FORWARD, THEN FREEZES AS BEFORE HIS DISBELIEVING EYES...

...ENERGY COALESCES AROUND ORORO INTO THE FORM OF ONE OF THE CREATURES FROM HIS NIGHTMARE. THE YOUNG QUEEN SMILES AT HIM...

...AND A BOLT OF LIGHTNING SPLITS THE SKY.
THE ASTRAL IMAGE FADES.

THAT... WAS STORM'S DOING. IS SHE DREAMING, TOO, LIKE I WAS?
WHAT DOES ALL THIS MEAN?! WHAT'S BEEN DONE TO US?!
I HAVE TO WAKE HER!

ORORO...?
SCOTT?
WHY...WHY AM I WEEPING?

I AM LOST-- BEREFT OF MY SELF--AND... AT WAR WITH MYSELF, WITHOUT KNOWING WHY.
I WISH I HAD MORE THAN WORDS TO OFFER, ORORO.
ESPECIALLY WHEN THOSE WORDS SOUND HOLLOW AND MEANINGLESS.

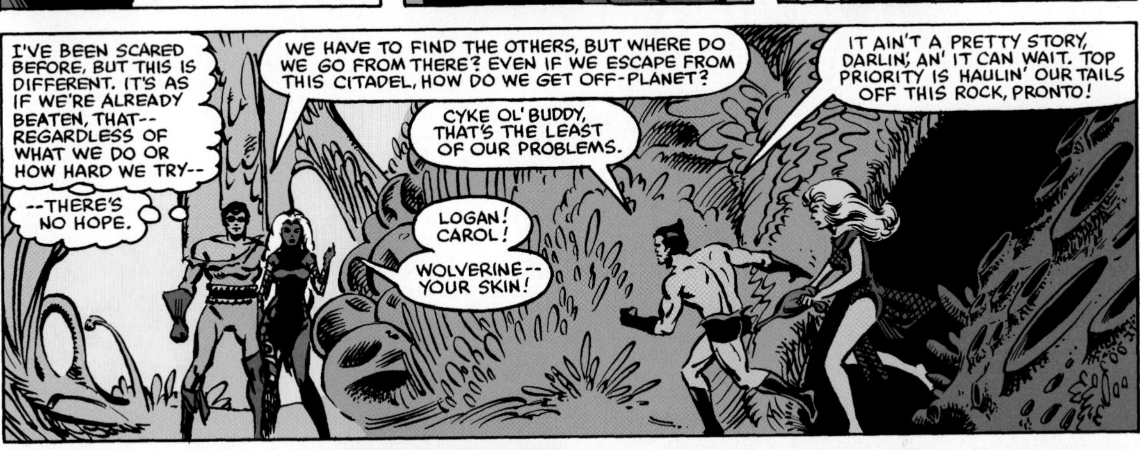
I'VE BEEN SCARED BEFORE, BUT THIS IS DIFFERENT. IT'S AS IF WE'RE ALREADY BEATEN, THAT-- REGARDLESS OF WHAT WE DO OR HOW HARD WE TRY--
--THERE'S NO HOPE.
WE HAVE TO FIND THE OTHERS, BUT WHERE DO WE GO FROM THERE? EVEN IF WE ESCAPE FROM THIS CITADEL, HOW DO WE GET OFF-PLANET?
CYKE OL' BUDDY, THAT'S THE LEAST OF OUR PROBLEMS.
IT AIN'T A PRETTY STORY, DARLIN', AN' IT CAN WAIT. TOP PRIORITY IS HAULIN' OUR TAILS OFF THIS ROCK, PRONTO!
LOGAN! CAROL!
WOLVERINE-- YOUR SKIN!

I'M OPEN TO SUGGESTIONS.
SIMPLE-- WE SWIPE LILANDRA'S YACHT.
IT'S HERE?!
NOT QUITE.

"THE SLEAZOID CITY IS BUILT INTO THE CARCASS O' ONE O' THEIR LIVIN' STARSHIPS. THE SKELETON'S SO FLAMIN' BIG, ITS BONES REACH ABOVE THE BREATHEABLE ATMOSPHERE. LIL'S YACHT IS MOORED TO THE TOP O' ONE OF THE MAIN RIBS.
"WE REACH IT, WE TAKE IT, WE GONE."
THE QUARTET GOES TO SUMMON THE TEAM'S OTHER MEMBERS AND...

...SOON...
CYCLOPS, I AM CONFUSED. DESPITE ALL YOU HAVE TOLD ME, I STILL PERCEIVE THIS AS LILANDRA'S PALACE. IT MAKES ME UNCOMFORTABLE TO SNEAK ABOUT, AS IF WE WERE IN SOME ENEMY'S CAMP.
WE *ARE* IN THE ENEMY'S CAMP, PETER, TRUST ME.
COLOSSUS, KITTY AND NIGHTCRAWLER STILL PERCEIVE ILLUSION, NOT REALITY. THAT COULD CAUSE PROBLEMS IF WE HAVE TO FIGHT.
THIS WAY, CYKE. LIL'S SCENT'S STILL STRONG.
THANK GOODNESS FOR WOLVERINE'S TRACKING ABILITIES. WITHOUT THEM, WE'D BE LOST FOREVER IN THIS MAZE.
I HATED SPLITTING THE TEAM, BUT I HAD NO ALTERNATIVE. WHILE WE FIND LILANDRA, IT'S UP TO STORM'S GROUP TO STEAL THE YACHT.
I WISH I KNEW WHAT WAS BOTHERING WOLVERINE. IT HAS SOMETHING TO DO WITH HIS WEIRD SKIN PATTERNING, BUT HE WON'T TALK ABOUT IT.
FASCINATING. THESE CORRIDORS DON'T APPEAR TO BE CONSTRUCTED, BUT THE RESULT OF SOME NATURAL, ORGANIC PROCESS.
TO ME, THEY FEEL LIKE NORMAL HALLWAYS.
AND WHEN I TOUCH THE WALLS, I FEEL METAL.
I SHOULD TELL CYKE ABOUT THE EGGS THE X-MEN ARE HOSTING, BUT I CAN'T. NOT YET. AN' HOW DO I TELL HIM THE REST--
--THAT MY BODY'S HEALING FACTOR DESTROYED THE EGG IMPLANTED IN ME, THAT *I'M* FINE.
SUPPOSE THERE'S NO CURE FOR THE OTHERS--WHAT THEN? DO I WATCH MY FRIENDS TRANSFORM INTO SLEAZOIDS?
OR DO I KILL THEM?
TUNNEL BRANCHES, CYKE. LEFT ONE LEADS TO LIL. RIGHT ONE--CRIPES, WE HIT THE JACKPOT!
THE QUEEN'S DOWN THERE--THE BROOD'S *GREAT MOTHER!* WE NAIL HER, WE'LL CRIPPLE THE WHOLE OUTFIT!

LEAVE HER BE, WOLVERINE. THAT ISN'T WHY WE'RE HERE.
THIS IS NO TIME FOR YOUR FLAMIN' NAMBY-PAMBY RULES, SUMMERS! THIS IS *WAR!*
THE X-MEN DON'T KILL, LOGAN.
GENTLEMEN, I SUGGEST YOU POST-PONE YOUR DISCUSSION.

WE HAVE *COMPANY!*
COLOSSUS, *ARMOR UP!*
THE HUMANS ARE TO BE TAKEN ALIVE--AND HARMED AS LITTLE AS POSSIBLE!
I'LL HAVE THE HEARTS OF WHOEVER DISOBEYS!
WITH A THOUGHT, THE YOUNG RUSSIAN TRANSFORMS HIS BODY FROM FLESH AND BLOOD...
...TO ORGANIC STEEL--SUPER-STRONG, WELL-NIGH INVULNERABLE--

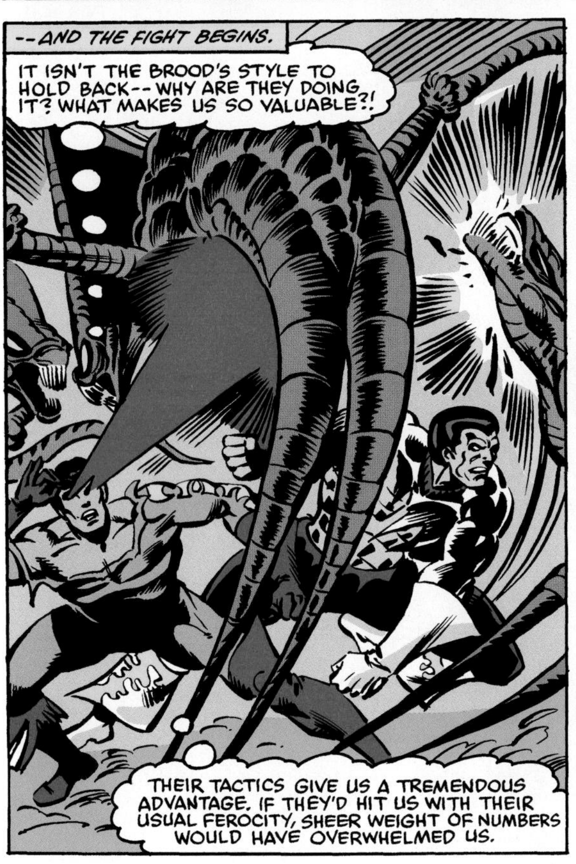
--AND THE FIGHT BEGINS.
IT ISN'T THE BROOD'S STYLE TO HOLD BACK--WHY ARE THEY DOING IT? WHAT MAKES US SO VALUABLE?!
THEIR TACTICS GIVE US A TREMENDOUS ADVANTAGE. IF THEY'D HIT US WITH THEIR USUAL FEROCITY, SHEER WEIGHT OF NUMBERS WOULD HAVE OVERWHELMED US.

MY BLASTER WON'T DO MUCH GOOD HERE. YOU GUYS HOLD THE FORT--
--I'LL SPRING LILANDRA!

CYKE, BACK ME UP! THE THREE OF US CAN PUNCH OUR WAY THROUGH TO THE QUEEN'S CHAMBER!
I TOLD YOU FORGET ABOUT HER!
NOT HARDLY, BUB.
WOLVERINE, WE HAVE TO STAY TOGETHER!

YOU WANT ME, PAL, YOU FOLLOW ME!

G'DAY, MAMA-- REMEMBER ME?
BUTCHER! I SENSE NO LIFE WITHIN YOU! THE IMPLANT IS NO MORE!
YUP, CRYIN' SHAME, AIN'T IT.

HOLD THAT POSE, SLEAZY.
I'LL DO THE SAME FOR YOU.

WOLVERINE-- STOP!
BY THE WHITE WOLF!
SAVE YOUR BREATH, PETEY.
I'M NOT LIS'NIN.

THESE... CREATURES-- THEY ARE NOT LILANDRA'S RACE! MY VISION--MY MIND--ARE CLEARING...
...IN TIME TO SEE HOW CRITICAL OUR SITUATION TRULY IS. I AM GLAD KITTY IS NOT HERE. I FEAR THIS MAY PROVE TO BE THE X-MEN'S LAST STAND.
CYCLOPS--HERE COME REINFORCEMENTS!

LEAVE THEM TO US, *TOVARISCH.*
NICE SHOOTING, MAJESTY.
THE SHI'AR ARE WARRIORS, TOO, CAROL--AND OUR PROWESS CONQUERED A GALAXY.
THE BROOD WILL RUE THE DAY THEY CHOSE ME FOR A FOE--AS WILL MY RENEGADE SISTER.

WE HAVE WHAT WE CAME FOR, CYCLOPS.
I SUGGEST A STRATEGIC WITHDRAWAL.
YOU HEARD THE LADY, TROOPS.

NO WAY, BUSTER!
I DON'T LEAVE A JOB BEFORE IT'S FINISHED.

HOW 'BOUT I CARRY YOU OUT, MISTER.
YOU'RE WELCOME TO TRY.
STAYING HERE COULD FINISH US ALL!
WE'RE AS GOOD AS DEAD ALREADY, THANKS TO THE QUEEN. AT LEAST KILLING HER BALANCES THE SCALES!
DO WHAT YOU LIKE, CYKE-- I'M *STAYIN'!*

ELSEWHERE...
IT IS GOOD TO FLY ONCE MORE, BUT THERE ARE ROUGH EDGES TO MY POWERS THAT DISTURB ME. I AM NO LONGER IN HARMONY WITH MYSELF OR THIS WORLD.
I AM AS HIGH AS I CAN GO, MY FRIENDS. THE REST IS UP TO YOU.
TAKE A DEEP BREATH, KATZCHEN.
I APOLOGIZE IN ADVANCE FOR THE ROUGH RIDE.

WE ARE STILL MILES BELOW THE YACHT. TELEPORTING THAT DISTANCE BY HIMSELF COULD BE A STRAIN FOR NIGHTCRAWLER.
CARRYING KITTY-- SMALL THOUGH SHE IS--MAY PROVE MORE THAN EITHER OF THEM CAN BEAR.
IF SO, WE ARE DOOMED.
BAMF
WITH HIS CHARACTERISTIC BURST OF SMOKE AND FLAME, NIGHTCRAWLER DISAPPEARS.

A MOMENT LATER...
ZZZAP
GODDESS!

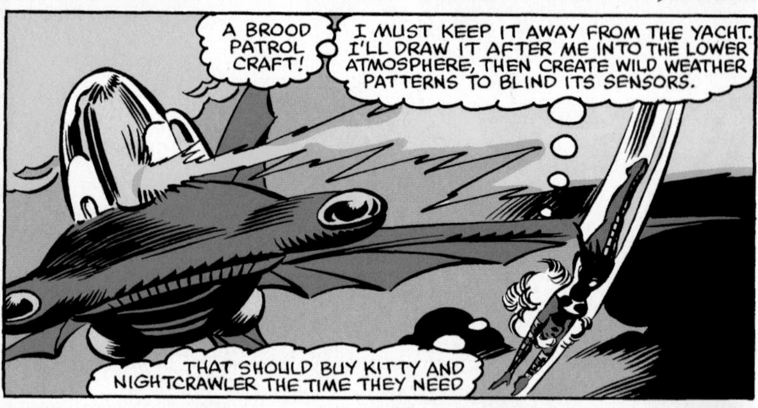
A BROOD PATROL CRAFT!
I MUST KEEP IT AWAY FROM THE YACHT. I'LL DRAW IT AFTER ME INTO THE LOWER ATMOSPHERE, THEN CREATE WILD WEATHER PATTERNS TO BLIND ITS SENSORS.
THAT SHOULD BUY KITTY AND NIGHTCRAWLER THE TIME THEY NEED

MADE IT-- BARELY. DON'T UNDERSTAND--I WAS GETTING MORE USED TO CARRYING PASSENGERS. I COULDN'T MAINTAIN CONCENTRATION. WE WERE ...NEARLY TRAPPED IN TRANSITION.
I HAVE A FIRM GRIP ON THE HULL. NOW SCOOT INSIDE, MY GIRL--AND FOR PITY'S SAKE, HURRY!

SHE HAS ONLY MINUTES TO REACH THE AIRLOCK AND PULL ME INSIDE...
...BEFORE I FREEZE TO DEATH--OR SUFFOCATE!

BRRRRR!
IT WAS FRIGID OUT THERE. POOR NIGHT-CRAWLER-- EVEN WITH HIS FURRY SKIN, THAT COLD MUST BE BRUTAL. IF ONLY HE COULD HAVE TELEPORTED ABOARD.
BUT HE CAN ONLY 'PORT TO PLACES HE CAN SEE, OR THOSE HE KNOWS INTIMATELY. DARN, I WISH I COULD PHASE MORE THAN JUST MYSELF. I COULD HAVE BROUGHT HIM IN WITH ME.
THERE'S THE AIR-LOCK.

HALT, HUMAN!!
YYIIII!

YIELD, OR SUFFER THE CONSEQUENCES!
A SLEAZOID!
ORORO AND WOLVERINE TOLD ME ABOUT THEM, BUT I NEVER IMAGINED THEY'D BE SO HORRIBLE!
WATCH IT! HE'S GOOD WITH THOSE STINGERS!
MY ORDERS ARE TO TAKE YOU ALIVE, X-MAN.

THEREFORE, MY VENOM WILL MERELY STUN YOU. BUT THE EFFECT, THOUGH TRANSITORY, IS MOST UNPLEASANT.
I CAN'T WASTE TIME SPARRING WITH THIS CREEP. NIGHTCRAWLER NEEDS ME!

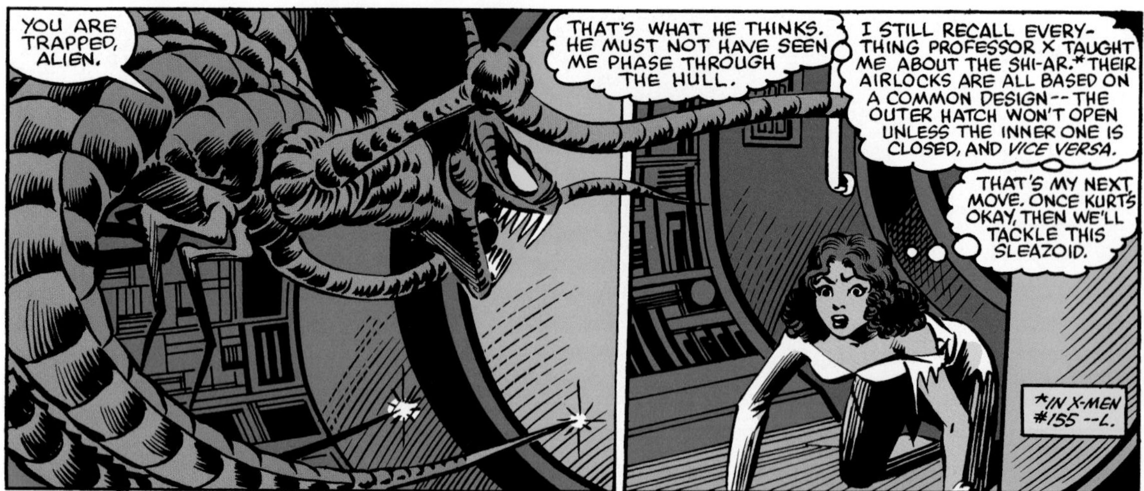
YOU ARE TRAPPED, ALIEN.
THAT'S WHAT HE THINKS. HE MUST NOT HAVE SEEN ME PHASE THROUGH THE HULL.
I STILL RECALL EVERYTHING PROFESSOR X TAUGHT ME ABOUT THE SHI-AR.* THEIR AIRLOCKS ARE ALL BASED ON A COMMON DESIGN-- THE OUTER HATCH WON'T OPEN UNLESS THE INNER ONE IS CLOSED, AND VICE VERSA.
THAT'S MY NEXT MOVE. ONCE KURT'S OKAY, THEN WE'LL TACKLE THIS SLEAZOID.
*IN X-MEN #155 --L.

THE CONTROLS ARE BEHIND ME-- SHOOT, THE INNER HATCH IS LOCKED LIKE WE FIGURED. IT CAN'T BE OPENED FROM THE OUTSIDE.
OH, NO-- I WASN'T FAST ENOUGH FREEING THE LOCK! THE SLEAZOID'S COMING AFTER ME!
PLEASE, DOOR. CLOSE IN TIME-- PLEASE!

YOUR GAME IS AMUSING, CHILD, BUT I WEARY OF IT.
NOW WHAT? EVERYTHING'S SET. IF I CYCLE THE AIRLOCK --AND PHASE-- I SHOULD BE ABLE TO HOLD ON WHILE THE EXPLOSIVE DECOMPRESSION VOIDS THE SLEAZOID FROM THE SHIP.
BUT-- THAT'D BE MURDER.
I-- I CAN'T!

STAND AWAY FROM THE CONTROLS.
UH-UH. YOU GO BACK THE WAY WE CAME OR WE'RE BOTH DEAD.
YOU'RE BLUFFING.
CALL ME.

WITH PLEASURE-- BY THE VOID!
YOU'VE BECOME *INTANGIBLE!*
SURPRISE!
I'LL DUCK OUT TO THE CORRIDOR, THEN BACK IN HERE AFTER HE FOLLOWS ME. BUT THIS IS TAKING SO MUCH TIME-- NIGHTCRAWLER'S DYING!
KITTY LUNGES FOR THE INNER HATCH, PHASING RIGHT THROUGH THE GUARD. ENRAGED, HE TWISTS FRANTICALLY IN MID-AIR, IN A DESPERATE, FUTILE ATTEMPT TO GRAB HER.

IN THE PROCESS, ONE OF HIS FLAILING TENTACLES...
...SLAPS THE CONTROL PANEL.
THE 'LOCK CYCLES.

AND HE IS GONE.
I... I DIDN'T WANT THIS. I DIDN'T MEAN IT. I KNOW HE PROBABLY DESERVED HIS FATE-- THAT HE'D HAVE KILLED ME WITHOUT HESITATION-- THAT WOLVERINE WOULD SAY I DID RIGHT.
BUT I'M NOT WOLVERINE. AND... I DON'T WANT TO BECOME LIKE HIM.
UNNNFF!
WAS IT ALL FOR NOTHING?! KURT'S LIKE A BLOCK OF ICE, FROZEN TO THE MARROW! OH, LORD, HEAR MY PRAYER--
--LET MY FRIEND LIVE!

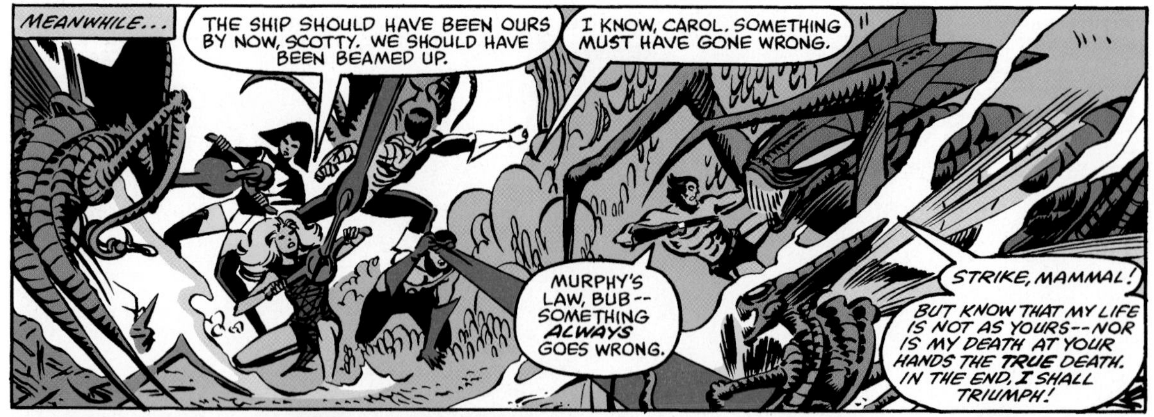
MEANWHILE...
THE SHIP SHOULD HAVE BEEN OURS BY NOW, SCOTTY. WE SHOULD HAVE BEEN BEAMED UP.
I KNOW, CAROL. SOMETHING MUST HAVE GONE WRONG.
MURPHY'S LAW, BUB-- SOMETHING ALWAYS GOES WRONG.
STRIKE, MAMMAL!
BUT KNOW THAT MY LIFE IS NOT AS YOURS--NOR IS MY DEATH AT YOUR HANDS THE TRUE DEATH. IN THE END, I SHALL TRIUMPH!

WOLVERINE'S REACHED THE QUEEN!
LOGAN--NO!!
YOU ARE A FOOL, CYCLOPS. THIS TIME, WOLVERINE IS IN THE RIGHT. WE FIGHT A WAR, AGAINST THE DEADLIEST OF ENEMIES. THERE IS NO PLACE HERE FOR CHIVALRY OR HONOR. ONLY DEATH, LIFE, DEFEAT, VICTORY.

MY SENTIMENTS EXACTLY, LIL.
'BYE, BABE.

WHAT THE FLAMIN'--!?!
THE ALIENS ARE DIS-APPEARING!
A TRANS-PORTER!

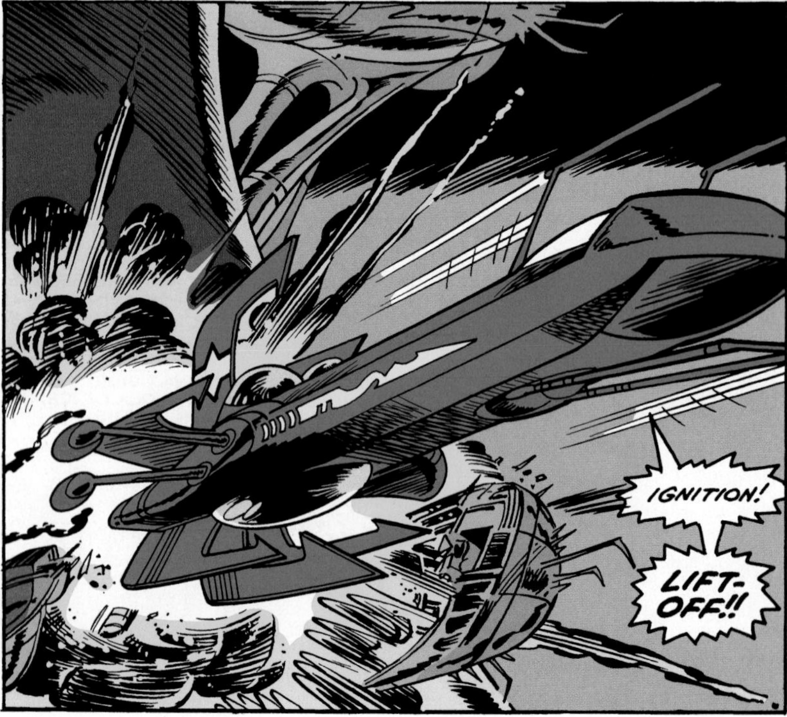
IGNITION!
LIFT-OFF!!

NEXT ISSUE: BINARY STAR!

60¢
164
DEC
02461
© 1982 MARVEL COMICS GROUP
MARVEL® COMICS GROUP
APPROVED BY THE COMICS CODE AUTHORITY
THE UNCANNY
X-MEN
TM

STAN LEE INTRODUCES
BINARY STAR!
STARRING THE UNCANNY X-MEN!
CHRIS CLAREMONT WRITER
DAVE COCKRUM PENCILER
BOB WIACEK FINISHER
JOE ROSEN LETTERER
JANINE CASEY COLORIST
LOUISE JONES EDITOR
JIM SHOOTER EDITOR-IN-CHIEF
STORM
COLOSSUS
NIGHTCRAWLER
LILANDRA
CYCLOPS
WOLVERINE
CAROL DANVERS
KITTY PRYDE
X-MEN--WE'RE UNDER ATTACK!

HUNT-MASTER T'CRILĒĒ REPORTING CONTACT WITH ALIEN VESSEL-- IMPERIAL SHI'AR YACHT Z'REEE SHAR.
VELOCITY: POINT FOUR LIGHT AND INCREASING. COURSE: OUT OF THIS SYSTEM, AT MAXIMUM ACCELERATION.

BIO-SCANS INDICATE MULTIPLE LIFEFORMS ABOARD, ALSO ALIEN, PROBABLY THE SHI'AR EMPRESS, LILANDRA, AND THE TERRANS CAPTURED WITH HER, THE X-MEN.
WE HAVE FIRED WARNING SHOTS, BUT THE TARGET HAS NOT RESPONDED.
TACTICAL PROJECTION IS THAT THE TARGET WILL SHIFT INTO WARP AS SOON AS IT IS ABLE. MY CADRE LACKS FASTER-THAN-LIGHT CAPABILITY.

REQUEST INSTRUCTIONS.
T'CRILĒĒ, HEED THE WORDS OF YOUR GREAT MOTHER. THE X-MEN AND LILANDRA HAVE INDEED ESCAPED-- WRECKING THE INNER HIVE AND NEARLY SLAYING ME IN THE PROCESS.
THEIR STARSHIP IS TO BE DISABLED, AND ALL ABOARD TAKEN ALIVE AND UNHARMED --WITH ONE EXCEPTION.

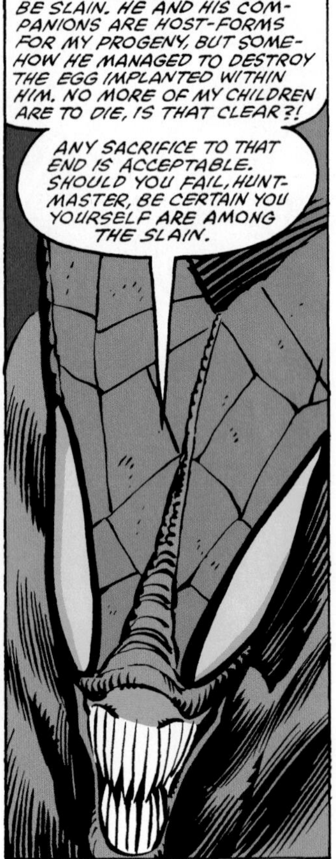
THE X-MAN, WOLVERINE, MAY BE SLAIN. HE AND HIS COMPANIONS ARE HOST-FORMS FOR MY PROGENY, BUT SOMEHOW HE MANAGED TO DESTROY THE EGG IMPLANTED WITHIN HIM. NO MORE OF MY CHILDREN ARE TO DIE, IS THAT CLEAR?!
ANY SACRIFICE TO THAT END IS ACCEPTABLE. SHOULD YOU FAIL, HUNT-MASTER, BE CERTAIN YOU YOURSELF ARE AMONG THE SLAIN.

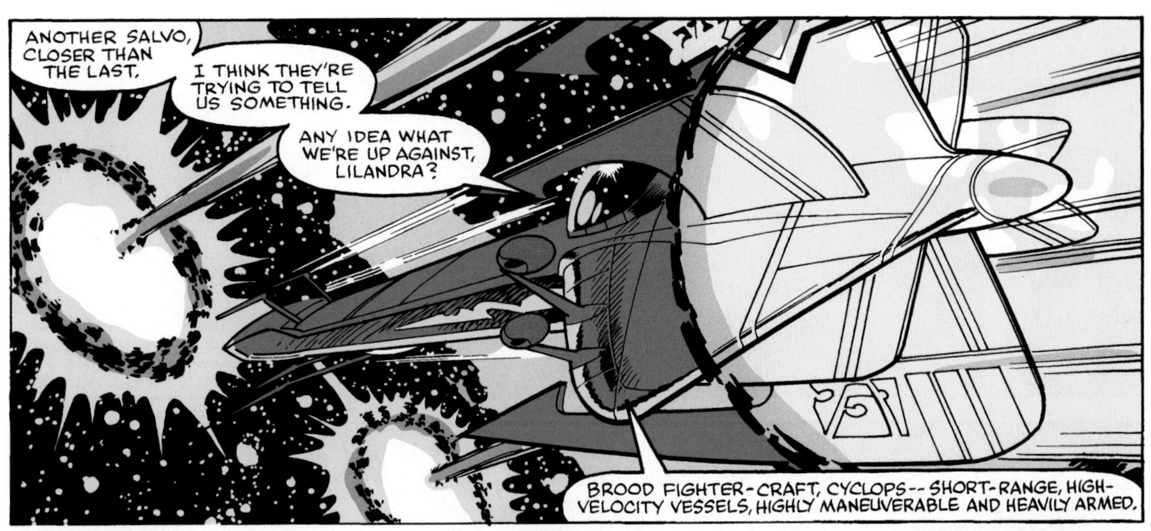
ANOTHER SALVO, CLOSER THAN THE LAST.
I THINK THEY'RE TRYING TO TELL US SOMETHING.
ANY IDEA WHAT WE'RE UP AGAINST, LILANDRA?
BROOD FIGHTER-CRAFT, CYCLOPS-- SHORT-RANGE, HIGH-VELOCITY VESSELS, HIGHLY MANEUVERABLE AND HEAVILY ARMED.

CAN WE OUTRUN THEM?
SO LONG AS WE REMAIN SUB-LIGHT, NO. AND WE ARE STILL TOO DEEP WITHIN THIS STAR'S GRAVITY WELL TO SHIFT INTO WARP SPACE.
CAN WE FIGHT?
Z'REEE SHAR IS A PLEASURE CRAFT, NOT A WARSHIP.

THEY KEEP MISSING, CAROL. THEY MUST BE VERY POOR SHOTS.
FAR FROM IT, COLOSSUS. THEY'RE SHOOTING WIDE DELIBERATELY, TO GET US TO SURRENDER. I WONDER WHY?

SO DO I. THE BROOD'S BEEN HANDLING US WITH KID GLOVES EVER SINCE THEY KIDNAPPED US.
I CANNOT DIVERT ANY MORE POWER TO THE SHIELDS. I NEED IT FOR THE ENGINES.
WE HAVE WEAPONS, CYCLOPS, MINIMAL THOUGH THEY ARE.

"USE THEM--AND YOUR OWN MUTANT POWERS--TO KEEP THE BROOD AT BAY."
LEAVING KITTY PRYDE TO CARE FOR NIGHTCRAWLER--INJURED DURING THE ESCAPE--
--CAROL DANVERS, COLOSSUS AND WOLVERINE RACE FOR THE WEAPONS CONTROL CENTER.

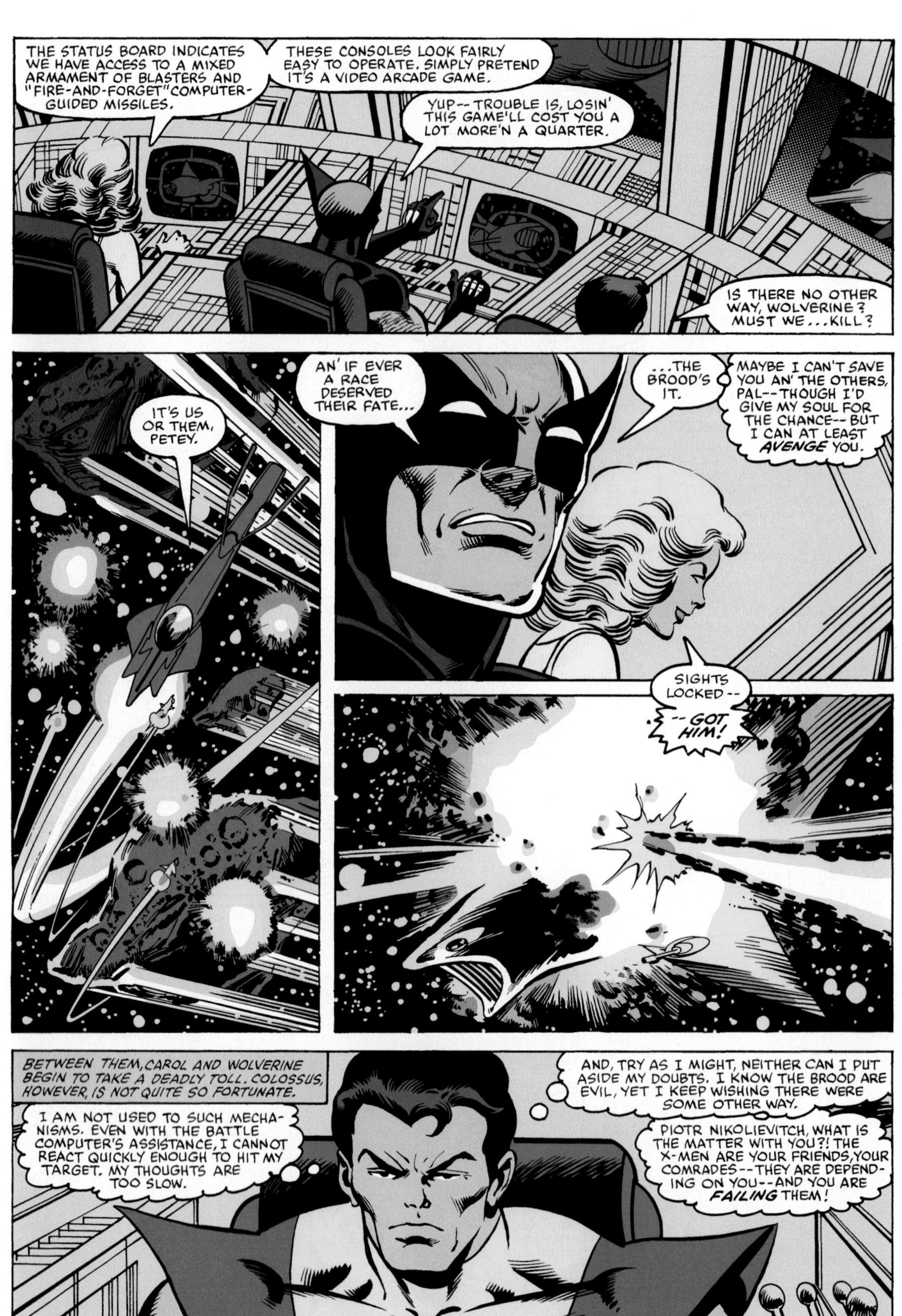
THE STATUS BOARD INDICATES WE HAVE ACCESS TO A MIXED ARMAMENT OF BLASTERS AND "FIRE-AND-FORGET" COMPUTER-GUIDED MISSILES.
THESE CONSOLES LOOK FAIRLY EASY TO OPERATE. SIMPLY PRETEND IT'S A VIDEO ARCADE GAME.
YUP-- TROUBLE IS, LOSIN' THIS GAME'LL COST YOU A LOT MORE'N A QUARTER.
IS THERE NO OTHER WAY, WOLVERINE? MUST WE...KILL?
IT'S US OR THEM, PETEY.
AN' IF EVER A RACE DESERVED THEIR FATE...
...THE BROOD'S IT.
MAYBE I CAN'T SAVE YOU AN' THE OTHERS, PAL--THOUGH I'D GIVE MY SOUL FOR THE CHANCE--BUT I CAN AT LEAST AVENGE YOU.
SIGHTS LOCKED--
--GOT HIM!
BETWEEN THEM, CAROL AND WOLVERINE BEGIN TO TAKE A DEADLY TOLL. COLOSSUS, HOWEVER, IS NOT QUITE SO FORTUNATE.
I AM NOT USED TO SUCH MECHANISMS. EVEN WITH THE BATTLE COMPUTER'S ASSISTANCE, I CANNOT REACT QUICKLY ENOUGH TO HIT MY TARGET. MY THOUGHTS ARE TOO SLOW.
AND, TRY AS I MIGHT, NEITHER CAN I PUT ASIDE MY DOUBTS. I KNOW THE BROOD ARE EVIL, YET I KEEP WISHING THERE WERE SOME OTHER WAY.
PIOTR NIKOLIEVITCH, WHAT IS THE MATTER WITH YOU?! THE X-MEN ARE YOUR FRIENDS, YOUR COMRADES--THEY ARE DEPENDING ON YOU--AND YOU ARE FAILING THEM!

ELSEWHERE...
INCREDIBLE! THE YACHT'S EXTRUDED A TEMPORARY BLISTER OF RUBY QUARTZ--JUST LIKE MY VISOR--SO THAT I CAN FIRE MY OPTIC BLASTS WITHOUT DAMAGING THE SHIP.
WOLVERINE KNOWS SOMETHING HE ISN'T TELLING ABOUT US AND THE BROOD.

HE'S NEVER BEEN SHY ABOUT SPEAKING HIS MIND BEFORE, SO IT MUST BE AS UNPLEASANT AS IT IS IMPORTANT.
WHEN WE GET OUT OF THIS--IF WE DO--I'LL HAVE TO MAKE HIM TALK. THAT SHOULD BE FUN.
WHY ARE WE HERE?! WHAT DOES THE BROOD WANT WITH US?!
HERE COME THE FIGHTERS. THESE SEEM TO BE LIVING CREATURES, AS ARE THE BROOD STARSHIPS.
I'LL HAVE TO BE CAREFUL--SO MY SHOTS FORCE THEM TO DISENGAGE WITHOUT SERIOUSLY HURTING THEM.

MEANWHILE, ON THE OPPOSITE SIDE OF THE HULL...
MY WEATHER POWERS HAVE LIMITED EFFECTIVENESS IN SPACE.
WE ARE TOO FAR FROM THE SUN--
--AND IT WOULD REQUIRE TOO MUCH CONCENTRATION--FOR ME TO MANIPULATE THE SOLAR WIND. I AM FORCED TO CALL UPON MY LIGHTNING.

I HAVE SWORN NEVER TO TAKE A LIFE, YET WHERE THE BROOD ARE CONCERNED, I AM SORELY TEMPTED TO BREAK THAT VOW.
HOWEVER, WHILE THEY ARE CONSUMMATE EVIL, THEIR VESSELS ARE NOT. I CANNOT DO THEM HARM.
I WILL USE THE LIGHTNING TO STUN--BLESSED GODDESS, NO!
THE BOLTS ARE OUT OF CONTROL! THE SHIPS--I'VE KILLED THEM!!

ALL HUNTERS FROM T'CRILĒE-- IGNORE OUR CASUALTIES, MAINTAIN THE ATTACK! CONCENTRATE ON THE ENGINEERING SECTION!
THEIR SHIELDS ARE BUCKLING!

WE'VE BEEN HIT!
IS IT SERIOUS?!
THE CONTROL ELEMENTS OF THE WARP DRIVE ARE INOPERATIVE. WE CAN'T EFFECT REPAIRS FROM INSIDE THE SHIP. SOMEONE HAS TO GO ON E.V.A.*
I'LL DO IT.
* EXTRA-VEHICULAR ACTIVITY-- "ROCKY" JONES, SPACE RANGER.

NO YOU WON'T! YOU'RE BARELY ABLE TO STAND.
AND BESIDES, WHAT'LL YOU DO OUT THERE...
...WHEN THE SLEAZOIDS SHOOT AT YOU-- DUCK?!

KITTY, WE HEARD WHAT YOU INTEND. I WON'T ALLOW IT!
IT'S TOO DANGEROUS!
THAT'S CRAZY, SCOTT. I'M THE ONLY ONE FOR WHOM IT ISN'T DANGEROUS.

IF ANY BEAMS COME MY WAY, I'LL PHASE THROUGH 'EM AS EASILY AS I PHASE INTO THIS PRESSURE SUIT.
AND USING THE SUIT'S VIDEO CAMERA AND RADIO, LILANDRA CAN MONITOR MY PROGRESS...
...AND TELL ME WHAT TO DO.
I'LL BE CAREFUL, SCOTT. I PROMISE. AND I'LL BE ALL RIGHT.

AFTER MAKING CERTAIN SHE HAS THE NECESSARY EQUIPMENT AND THAT IT'S FUNCTIONING PROPERLY...
...KITTY PHASES THROUGH THE PRIMARY HULL.
WOW!
"STAR WARS" WAS NEVER LIKE THIS!

THE BUSTED MODULE IS AFT, BENEATH THE SOLAR FINS.
I WANT TO RUN, BUT I CAN'T. I'M NOT USING A SAFETY LINE. ONE MISSTEP'LL THROW ME OFF INTO SPACE...
...AND THE OTHERS WON'T BE ABLE TO STOP AND COME BACK FOR ME.

AT THAT MOMENT, IN WEAPONS CONTROL...
WHAT THE--?!?
MY VISION SUDDENLY WENT BLURRY-- I SAW COLORS, IMAGES I NEVER DREAMED POSSIBLE.
BUT EVERYTHING'S NORMAL NOW. PROBABLY STRESS-- A DELAYED REACTION TO THE TREATMENT I RECEIVED FROM THE BROOD.

ON THE YACHT'S HULL-- AN X-MAN-- THE YOUNGLING!
USE STUN AND 'PRESSOR BEAMS ON HER! TRY TO KNOCK HER LOOSE. ONCE SHE'S IN FREE SPACE, WE CAN EASILY TAKE HER PRISONER.

SPAWN OF THE BLOODMOON--MY BOLTS HAVE NO EFFECT!
WHEW!
I KNOW I'VE BEEN THROUGH MOMENTS LIKE THIS BEFORE...

...BUT THEY DON'T GET ANY EASIER. I CAN'T HELP WONDERING WHAT'LL HAPPEN THE ONE TIME MY POWER DOESN'T WORK.
WHY'D I OPEN MY BIG MOUTH ANYWAY?! WHAT AM I DOING HERE?! I'M JUST A KID.
NO. NOT ANYMORE. I'M AN X-MAN. I EARNED MY PLACE ON THE TEAM-- AND HERE'S WHERE I PROVE IT!

THEY'RE HITTING US FROM ALL SIDES--MORE THAN WE CAN HANDLE!

AND OUR RETURN FIRE'S SLACKENING OFF! STORM, ARE YOU OKAY?!

THEY'RE CLOBBERING US, ORORO. WHY AREN'T YOU USING YOUR LIGHTNING AGAINST THE FIGHTERS?!

I...CANNOT.

MY POWERS NO LONGER YIELD TO MY WILL. IF I USE THEM, I WILL KILL. AND THAT I CANNOT DO--

--FOR YOU, FOR...KITTY. FOR ANYONE.

SO FAR, SO GOOD, LILANDRA. I REPLACED THE PRIMARY--**OWW!**

*KITTY, WHAT'S THE MATTER?! WHY DID YOU SCREAM?! **KITTY!?!***

N-NO PROBLEM, REALLY.

SHRAPNEL FROM A NEAR MISS. DIDN'T SEE IT COMING, DIDN'T... PHASE. MY SUIT AUTOMATICALLY SEALED ITSELF, SO I HAVEN'T LOST MUCH AIR.

WEAPONS CONTROL...

ANOTHER SPELL OF WEIRDNESS--WORSE THAN BEFORE. THE SENSATIONS AREN'T UNPLEASANT, JUST TOTALLY STRANGE.

THE BROOD SUBJECTED ME TO EVOLUTIONARY MODIFICATION. I GUESS THEY MUST HAVE TRIGGERED SOMETHING INSIDE ME--BUT WHAT?!

I'M BLEEDING, BUT I DON'T THINK IT'S SERIOUS. HURTS LIKE BLAZES, THOUGH.

INSIDE IMMEDIATELY! YOUR MISSION'S CANCELLED!

NO, I'M STAYING! I'M ALMOST FINISHED, LILANDRA! A FEW MORE MINUTES AND WE'LL BE SAFE!

SO LITTLE TIME, YET FOR KITTY...

...IT MAY WELL BE THE REST OF HER LIFE.

THE SAME, IN A WAY, HOLDS TRUE FOR CAROL.
YEARS AGO, A FREAK ACCIDENT COMBINED THE BEST GENETIC ELEMENTS OF HUMAN AND THE ANCIENT, STAR-FARING KREE TO TRANSFORM HER INTO MS. MARVEL.
AND WHILE SHE LATER LOST HER SUPER-POWERS TO THE MUTANT ROGUE, THOSE HYBRID GENES REMAINED. NOW, THANKS TO THE BROOD'S MEDDLING, THEIR UNTAPPED POTENTIAL IS BEING REALIZED. WITH A VENGEANCE.

SHE CRIES OUT--IN WONDER MORE THAN FEAR, FOR THE PROCESS SEEMS SURPRISINGLY NATURAL...

...RATHER LIKE A BUTTERFLY EMERGING FROM ITS CHRYSALIS.

A BLINDING LIGHT FLARES WITHIN HER SOUL, A THING APART FROM HER THAT INSTANTLY BECOMES A PART OF HER TO FORM A UNION THAT WILL LAST 'TIL DEATH.

THE LIGHT IS POWER...

...AND CAROL USES IT, WITHOUT HESITATION.

EVERYTHING'S FIXED! THROW THE SWITCH, LILANDRA!
THROW US INTO WARP!

BLESS YOU, CHILD! WE'RE ON OUR WAY!
KITTY, ARE YOU THERE?!
KITTY!!!

PROFESSOR XAVIER'S SCHOOL FOR GIFTED YOUNGSTERS--SALEM CENTER, NEW YORK.
THE TITLE IS SOMETHING OF A MISNOMER THESE DAYS. THOUGH THE MANSION HAS BEEN REBUILT-- BETTER THAN BEFORE, COURTESY OF CONSTRUCTION ROBOTS PROVIDED BY LILANDRA--
--THE SCHOOL IS, IN TRUTH, NO MORE.

AS A YOUNG MAN, CHARLES XAVIER HAD A DREAM, OF AN EARTH WHERE HUMANITY AND MUTANTKIND LIVED TOGETHER IN PEACE. TO FULFILL THAT DREAM--
--AND TO PROTECT THE WORLD FROM THE DEPREDATIONS OF EVIL MUTANTS--HE FORMED THIS SCHOOL, WHOSE STUDENTS BECAME THE UNCANNY X-MEN. UNSUNG HEROES, FEARED, OFTEN HATED, BY THE VERY PEOPLE THEY WERE SWORN TO SAVE.

THEY BECAME HIS SURROGATE CHILDREN-- WHOM HE LOVED WITH ALL HIS HEART.
AND, SINCE THEIR ABDUCTION, HIS NIGHTS HAVE BECOME HAUNTED, HIS HANDS, HE BELIEVES, COVERED WITH BLOOD.
THE DREAM MAY STILL BE GOOD...

...BUT THIS DREAMER IS DONE.
YOU CALL ME, PROFESSOR?
DINNER'S READY, ILLYANA.
GREAT! I'M STARVED!

THE GIRL IS ILLYANA RASPUTIN, COLOSSUS' SISTER.
I'VE BEEN EXPLORING THE HOUSE. IT'S ALMOST EXACTLY AS I REMEMBER IT...
...THOUGH IT'S A BIT SPOOKY WITH JUST THE TWO OF US HERE.

MOIRA WILL BE BACK ON MONDAY.
THAT'S WONDERFUL! I LIKE DR. MacTAGGERT A LOT.
I'M SURE SHE'LL BE PLEASED TO HEAR THAT.
I LIKE YOU, TOO, PROFESSOR. HONEST.

PROFESSOR, SOMETIMES I HEAR YOUR VOICE PERFECTLY CLEARLY, BUT YOU'RE NOWHERE AROUND.
AND I DON'T ACTUALLY HEAR ANYTHING--THAT IS, WITH MY EARS--THE WORDS SEEM TO POP INTO MY HEAD. HOW IS THAT?

AND HOW COME, BEFORE I RETURNED HERE WITH YOU AND DR. MacTAGGERT, I COULD ONLY SPEAK RUSSIAN? I REMEMBER YOU TOUCHING MY FOREHEAD ONE NIGHT AS I FELL ASLEEP AND THE NEXT MORNING, WHEN I WOKE UP, I SPOKE PERFECT ENGLISH!
I TAUGHT YOU, WHILE YOU SLEPT.
I FIGURED THAT--BUT HOW?!
WITH MY THOUGHTS.
OH!

I AM A MUTANT, LIKE YOUR BROTHER PETER. BUT WHERE HE TRANSFORMS HIS BODY INTO ORGANIC STEEL, I READ MINDS. DIFFERENT PEOPLE, DIFFERENT ABILITIES.
DO... DO YOU KNOW WHAT I'M THINKING?
A TELEPATH SHOULD NEVER INDISCRIMINATELY MINDSCAN PEOPLE, ESPECIALLY THOSE IN HIS CARE. YOUR SECRETS ARE SAFE FROM ME, CHILD.
PROFESSOR, AM I A MUTANT?
PERHAPS. I'M NOT SURE.

I CAN DO NEAT THINGS, TOO, JUST LIKE PIOTR!
SUCH AS WHAT?
OH... THINGS.
ILLYANA'S THOUGHTS ARE PROTECTED BY AN EXTRA-ORDINARILY POWERFUL AND SOPHISTICATED PSIONIC SHIELD.
IT COULD BE NATURAL--BUT I DOUBT IT. ACCORDING TO MOIRA, SHE WAS ABDUCTED BY A DEMON-LORD NAMED BELASCO, AND HELD FOR SEVEN YEARS IN HIS MYSTIC DOMAIN--THOUGH ONLY MOMENTS PASSED HERE ON EARTH.*
WHAT SHE EXPERIENCED THERE--FOR GOOD OR ILL--NO ONE KNOWS.
I OUGHT TO INVESTI-GATE--FIND A WAY TO PIERCE THAT BARRIER--BUT... I NO LONGER CARE ENOUGH TO MAKE THE ATTEMPT. LET MOIRA DEAL WITH HER. ALL I WANT...
...IS TO BE LEFT ALONE.
*X-MEN #160--L.

UUUHHHNNNNNNN
I MUST BE ALIVE. I HURT... TOO MUCH TO BE... ANYTHING ELSE.
SO HARD... TO MOVE... FEEL SO TIRED... WEAK...
HELLO! IS ANYONE THERE?! CAN ANYONE HEAR ME?!
KITTY?
CAROL! THANK HEAVEN! IS THAT...
...YOU?!?

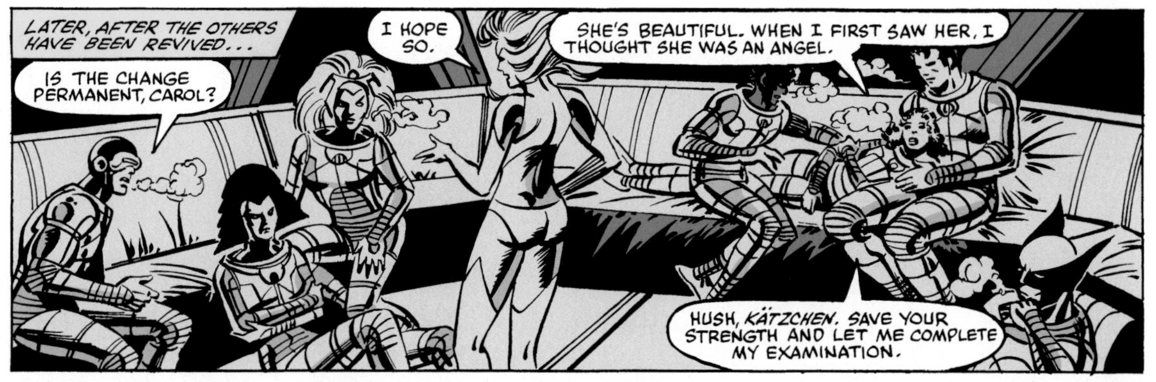

...WHAT'S NEEDED IS THE FUNCTIONAL EQUIVALENT OF A STAR.

SHE KNOWS INSTINCTIVELY WHAT MUST BE DONE.

ONCE MORE, SHE REACHES WITHIN HERSELF--TO THE LIGHT IN HER SOUL THAT FEELS NEW-BORN, YET AS OLD AS TIME...

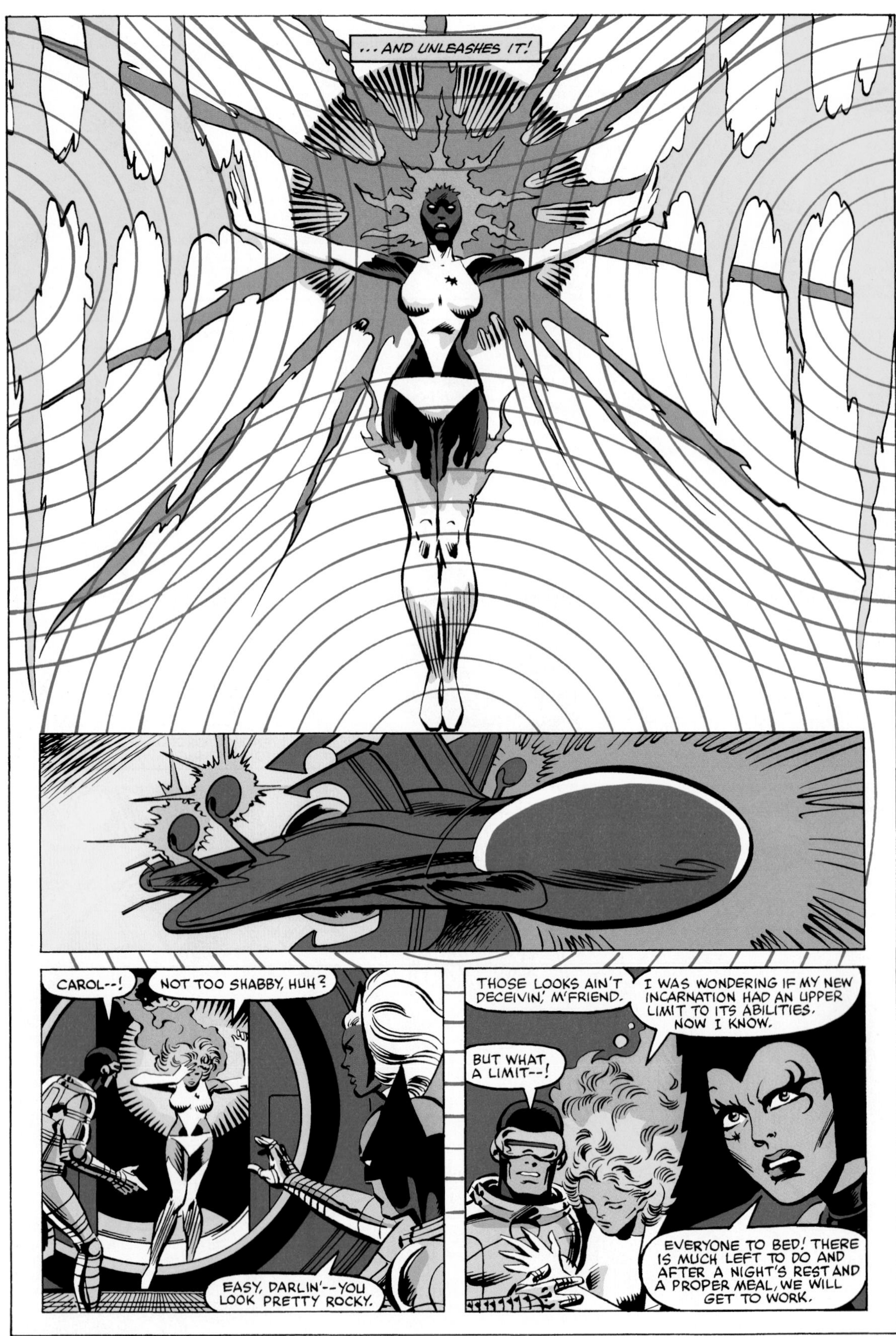

...AND UNLEASHES IT!
CAROL--!
NOT TOO SHABBY, HUH?
EASY, DARLIN'--YOU LOOK PRETTY ROCKY.
THOSE LOOKS AIN'T DECEIVIN,' M'FRIEND.
I WAS WONDERING IF MY NEW INCARNATION HAD AN UPPER LIMIT TO ITS ABILITIES. NOW I KNOW.
BUT WHAT A LIMIT--!
EVERYONE TO BED! THERE IS MUCH LEFT TO DO AND AFTER A NIGHT'S REST AND A PROPER MEAL, WE WILL GET TO WORK.

AND SO...
MY OLD FRIEND, **CAPTAIN MARVEL** WAS GIFTED WITH **COSMIC AWARENESS**-- AN ABILITY TO BECOME ONE WITH THE UNIVERSE. I THINK I'VE GONE BEYOND THAT.
HIS WAS A SPIRITUAL MERGER, MINE IS PHYSICAL. SOMEHOW, WHEN I USE MY POWER, I TAP INTO A WHITE HOLE--MY ENERGY SOURCE IS THE PRIMAL FABRIC OF A UNIVERSE!

LIKE A STAR, I CAN GENERATE HEAT, LIGHT--RADIATION ACROSS THE SPECTRUM-- GRAVITY. AND MY PERCEPTIONS --COLOSSUS, YOU CAN'T IMAGINE WHAT I SEE, HOW WONDROUS IT IS.
YOU SOUND VERY HAPPY.
DON'T I THOUGH!

SUCH ABILITIES WOULD BE INVALUABLE TO THE X-MEN.
YOU INVITING ME TO JOIN, *TOVARISCH*?
YOU ARE NOW A MUTANT, AND YOU HAVE ALWAYS BEEN A FRIEND.
BEST OFFER I'VE HAD ALL DAY, BIG FELLA.
BUT IT'D MEAN LIVING AND WORKING ON EARTH.
WHAT IS WRONG WITH THAT?
NOTHING. EVERYTHING.

WHEN I WAS A TEENAGER, I HITCHHIKED TO CAPE CANAVERAL TO WATCH AN APOLLO LAUNCH. MY DAD WHALED THE TAR OUTTA ME, BUT IT WAS WORTH IT. I WANTED SO BADLY TO BE AN ASTRONAUT-- TO EXPLORE SPACE, DISCOVER NEW WORLDS, ALIEN CIVILIZATIONS.
AS MS. MARVEL, I ALMOST MADE IT.
NOW, SUDDENLY, MY DREAM'S COME TRUE-- BEYOND MY WILDEST EXPECTATIONS!

BUT THERE'S A PRICE. RETURNING WITH YOU MEANS REJECTING MY HEART'S DESIRE-- BUT FULFILLING THAT DESIRE MEANS LEAVING EVERYONE, EVERYTHING I LOVE.
EARTH WAS **CAROL DANVERS'** HOME, COLOSSUS. BUT I FEAR IT HAS NO PLACE FOR--
--**BINARY.**

STOP FIDGETING. I'M NEARLY FINISHED.
DEEP BREATH. AGAIN. COUGH.
KOFF!
WHAT'S THE VERDICT, DOC? WILL I LIVE?
UMMM...
GREAT ANSWER. ARE YOU SURE YOU KNOW WHAT YOU'RE DOING?

LET'S HOPE SO, FOR YOUR SAKE.
YOU'RE BETTER, BUT NOT YET BEST.
I FEEL FINE, KURT.

EXCEPT I FEEL ROTTEN GOOFING OFF IN BED WHILE THE REST OF YOU ARE WORKING SO HARD.
HOW NOBLE. YOU'RE ENTITLED TO GOOF OFF, KIDDO. YOU'RE SICK.
STAY IN BED, TRY TO SLEEP, DRINK MORE HOT LEMON-HONEY TEA AND CHICKEN BROTH. I'LL CHECK ON YOU IN A FEW HOURS. *VERSTEHEN? SEHR GUT. AUF WEIDERSEHEN, KÄTZCHEN.*

WITH THAT, NIGHTCRAWLER TELEPORTS TO THE COMMAND DECK, HIS SMILE TURNING INTO A TROUBLED FROWN.

CYCLOPS, WHAT'S THE STATUS OF THE COMPUTERS-- SPECIFICALLY, THE MEDISCAN SYSTEMS?

THE WHOLE NETWORK HAS TO BE PURGED AND RECYCLED, KURT. NOTHING'LL BE ON-LINE ANY SOON. WHY? PROBLEMS?

PERHAPS. I'VE JUST EXAMINED KITTY. SHE'S FULLY RECOVERED.

THAT'S A PROBLEM?

BARELY A DAY AGO, SHE WAS DYING.

THE SHRAPNEL TORE A NASTY HOLE IN HER SIDE, INTRODUCING RADIOACTIVE ELEMENTS INTO HER BLOOD-STREAM. FROM THAT, AND THE WARP TRANSITION, SHE ABSORBED ENOUGH HARD RADIATION TO KILL A SCORE OF PEOPLE. SHE SHOULDN'T HAVE SURVIVED THE NIGHT, YET AT THIS MOMENT SHE'S IN PERFECT HEALTH.

NOTHING I DID HEALED HER, BUT I'D VERY MUCH LIKE TO LEARN WHAT DID...

SOME QUESTIONS ARE BETTER LEFT UNANSWERED, ELF.
WHAT THE BLAZES IS THAT SUPPOSED TO MEAN?
THE KID'S FINE-- WHAT MORE D'YOU WANT?
THE REASON WHY MEIN FREUND.

YOU'VE BEEN LURKING ABOUT LIKE A BLASTED SPECTRE EVER SINCE WE ESCAPED FROM THE BROOD. MAYBE IT'S TIME YOU EXPLAINED YOURSELF.
WHY DIDN'T YOU HELP ME NAIL THEIR QUEEN WHEN WE HAD THE CHANCE, CYKE?! THAT WOULD HAVE DONE SOME REAL DAMAGE-- POSSIBLY CRIPPLED THEIR ENTIRE RACE!
I TOLD YOU, WOLVERINE: X-MEN DON'T KILL.

SNIKT
WANNA BET?

SORRY. I... DIDN'T MEAN T' DO THAT. I GUESS ALL THAT'S HAPPENED HAS DRIVEN ME KIND'A BUGGY.
YOU'RE RIGHT, WHAT'S THERE TO GET UPSET ABOUT? WE ESCAPED, WITH OUR SKINS INTACT. EV'RYTHIN'S HUNKY-FLAMIN'-DORY.

MEIN GOTT.
WE ARE, FRIENDS, HE AND I, SCOTT. PERHAPS HE WILL TALK TO ME.
STAY WITH LILANDRA, KURT. GIVE HER A HAND.
THERE'S A PATTERN FORMING--KITTY'S ONE PIECE, LOGAN'S ANOTHER--AND I MEAN TO FIND OUT WHAT IT IS.

THE SHUTTLE BAY...
THIS IS THE ONLY SPACE LARGE ENOUGH FOR ME TO CREATE ANY TRUE WEATHER. HERE, AT LAST, I CAN FLY.
WHEN I TRIED TO ATTUNE MY SPIRIT TO THAT OF THE BROOD'S WORLD--THE BETTER TO UTILIZE MY POWERS THERE--AND FAILED, I BELIEVED IT WAS BECAUSE THE BROOD HAD SO TOTALLY CORRUPTED THE PLANET'S LIFE-FORCE.
BUT I FEAR THE FAULT WAS MINE.
I AM LOSING TOUCH WITH MY ESSENTIAL SELF.

SOME ELEMENT IS DISRUPTING THE CRITICAL HARMONY OF MIND, BODY AND SOUL. I MUST FIND IT...
...AND PUT THINGS RIGHT...

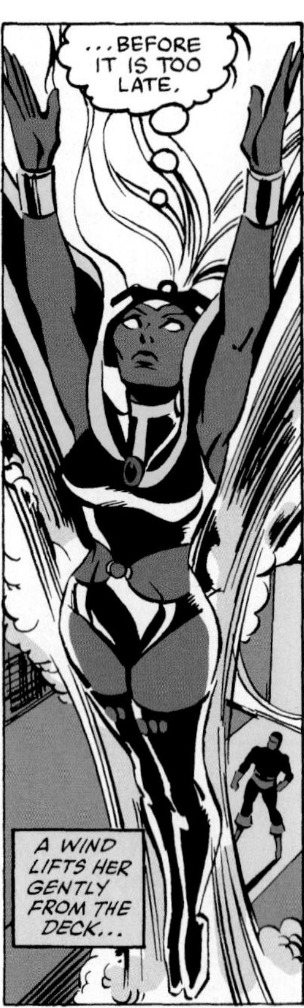
...BEFORE IT IS TOO LATE.
A WIND LIFTS HER GENTLY FROM THE DECK...

...BUT THEN, WITHOUT WARNING...
AAHHHRRR!!

STORM!
ORORO!!

LEAVE ME BE, SCOTT, I BEG YOU. I AM UNINJURED AND I WOULD REALLY RATHER BE LEFT ALONE.
NO DICE, THAT'S MY RIFF.
SOMETHING'S TEARING US APART, ORORO. IF WE DENY ITS EXISTENCE, IF WE TURN AWAY FROM THOSE WHO WANT TO HELP US, WE'RE AS GOOD AS DEAD.

I FEAR I AM BEYOND YOUR HELP. I AM CONSECRATED TO LIFE. MY MUTANT POWERS--AND MORE IMPORTANTLY, MY VERY SOUL--ARE BOUND TO THE PRIMAL FORCE OF A LIVING WORLD, OUR EARTH.
REMOVED FROM THAT ENVIRONMENT, MY ABILITIES--IN AND OF THEMSELVES--REMAIN UNIMPAIRED. I AM AS STRONG, IN PURELY PHYSICAL TERMS, AS I EVER WAS.

BUT MY SOUL IS STRICKEN. MY SPIRIT IS WASTING AWAY, AND THE LONGER I AM SEPARATED FROM MY HOME, THE MORE I WILL LOSE.
HOW WILL I EVER REGAIN THOSE MISSING, RAVAGED PIECES OF MYSELF, SCOTT? AND WHEN THERE'S NOTHING LEFT, WHAT WILL BECOME OF ME?! CAN A BODY LIVE WITHOUT ITS SOUL?!

BEING ABOARD THIS VESSEL ONLY MAKES MATTERS WORSE. LOOK ABOUT YOU--NOTHING BUT STEEL. COLD METAL, UNLIVING PLASTICS, SYNTHETICS.
I HATE IT!
I NEED LIFE TO SUSTAIN ME. THERE IS NONE HERE. NOT EVEN THE JOY AND LOVE I FELT FOR THE X-MEN.
I DON'T UNDERSTAND. WE HAVEN'T CHANGED. WE STILL FEEL THE SAME.
BUT I AM CHANGING--I HAVE BEEN EVER SINCE OUR ESCAPE--DEEP DOWN IN THE CORE OF MY BEING! AND I KNOW NEITHER THE CAUSE NOR THE FINAL EFFECT.

OHHH--!?!
THAT DOES IT, I'M CALLING NIGHTCRAWLER. YOU'RE SICK, ORORO, YOU SHOULD BE IN BED.

IS THIS NOT IRONIC? KITTY MIRACULOUSLY RECOVERS FROM SEEMINGLY MORTAL WOUNDS WHILE I--WHO'VE NEVER BEEN ILL A DAY IN MY LIFE--FALL PREY TO SOME MYSTERIOUS MALADY.
IT IS AS IF I HAVE BECOME A STRANGER TO MYSELF, INHABITING A BODY NO LONGER...
...MY OWN--BRIGHT LADY, COULD THAT BE THE ANSWER?!

IT IS SO OBVIOUS, SO UNTHINKABLE, I NEVER CONSIDERED IT.
SCOTT, I SENSE... LIFE WITHIN ME!
A... CHILD!

BUT HOW CAN THIS BE?!
I MUST PROBE DEEPER-- WHERE DO YOU COME FROM, MY LITTLE ONE? WHO--?
NO.
OH, NO!

GODDESS!

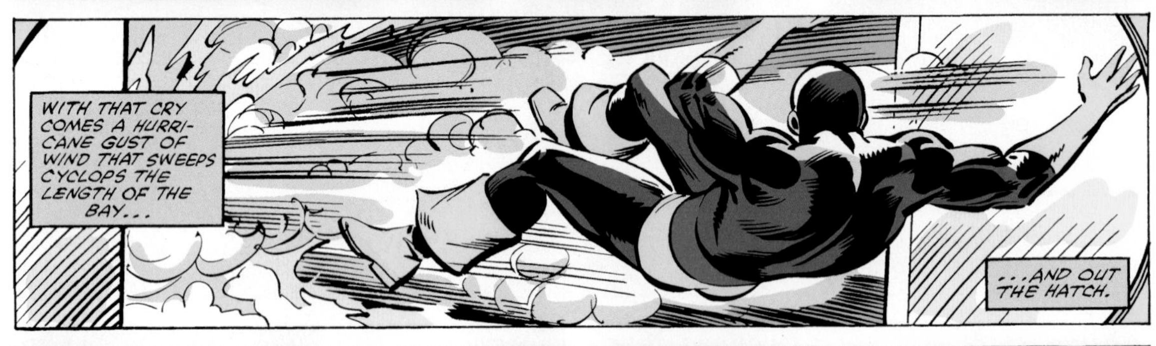
WITH THAT CRY COMES A HURRI-CANE GUST OF WIND THAT SWEEPS CYCLOPS THE LENGTH OF THE BAY...
...AND OUT THE HATCH.

SLAM!
ORORO?!?

STORM!?!

SHE WENT BERSERK, TOOK A SCOUTSHIP, BLASTED OFF. BUT WHY LEAVE HER COSTUME BEHIND?
CAROL, BRING HER BACK. WE HAVE NO OPERATIONAL SENSORS. ONCE SHE'S OUT OF SIGHT IN THIS CLOUD, WE'LL NEVER FIND HER.
YOU EVER FIGURE THAT MIGHT BE WHAT SHE WANTS.

SHE'S IRRATIONAL.
WITH GOOD REASON, BUB.
LIKE WHAT?! I'M IN NO MOOD FOR GAMES, PAL. YOUR EXPLANATION'S LONG OVERDUE!

YEAH, I GUESS IT IS.
I SHOULD'A TOLD YOU ON SLEAZEWORLD, OR AFTER WE CUT LOOSE INTO SPACE.
I TRIED A FEW TIMES--BUT I COULDN'T. IT HURT TOO MUCH.

I THOUGHT O' KILLIN' YOU--COULDN'T DO THAT, EITHER. I FIGURED THERE WAS HOPE, THERE'S ALWAYS HOPE, WE'D SOMEHOW GET LUCKY, RUN INTO A MIRACLE.
WHO KNOWS, I COULD BE RIGHT.
BUT I WOULDN'T COUNT ON IT.

WHEN THE SLEAZOIDS CAPTURED US, WE WERE TAKEN BEFORE THEIR QUEEN--THEY CALL HER THE "GREAT MOTHER"--AN' SHE IMPLANTED AN EGG IN EACH OF US.

EACH EGG CONTAINS AN EMBRYONIC QUEEN. IT BONDED ITSELF TO OUR NERVOUS SYSTEMS, SO IT CAN'T BE SURGICALLY REMOVED. WHEN IT HATCHES, A PHYSICAL METAMORPHOSIS OCCURS.

THE HOST-BODY IS RESHAPED INTO THE BIRTH-FORM OF THE YOUNG SLEAZOID. IN THE PROCESS, IT ABSORBS THE GENETIC POTENTIAL AND ABILITIES OF THE HOST, TO PASS ON TO ITS PROGENY.

NEXT ISSUE: TRANSFIGURATIONS!

60¢
165
JAN
02461
© 1982 MARVEL COMICS GROUP
MARVEL® COMICS GROUP
APPROVED BY THE COMICS CODE AUTHORITY
THE UNCANNY
X-MEN™
TM
DMS 8 82

Stan Lee PRESENTS...
TRANSFIGURATIONS!
POSSIBLY THE LAST STAND OF THE UNCANNY X-MEN!
EXPLOSIVE DECOMPRESSION!
WE'RE BEING SUCKED OUT INTO SPACE!!
CHRIS CLAREMONT WRITER
PAUL SMITH PENCILER
BOB WIACEK INKER
L. VARLEY, COLORIST
TOM ORZECHOWSKI, LETTERER
LOUISE JONES, EDITOR
JIM SHOOTER, Ed.-IN-CHIEF

THE INTERNAL HATCHES HAVE ALREADY SEALED TO PROTECT THE REST OF THE SHIP-- WE'RE TRAPPED IN HERE! LUCKILY, THE HANGAR BAY IS SO LARGE, IT'LL BE A WHILE BEFORE ITS ATMOSPHERE FULLY VOIDS. WE'LL HAVE TIME TO ACT.
THE WIND IS TERRIFIC-- LIKE BEING CAUGHT IN A TWISTER!
COLOSSUS-- SHIFT TO ARMOR! BLOCK THE HOLE WITH YOUR BODY! DON'T LET ANYONE BE SWEPT PAST!

I WILL DO MY BEST, CYCLOPS.
AS HE RELEASES HIS HANDHOLD, PETER RASPUTIN TRIGGERS HIS BODY'S LIGHTNING TRANS-FORMATION FROM FLESH AND BLOOD...

...TO ORGANIC STEEL, BECOMING IN THE PROCESS LARGER, STRONGER, MORE MASSIVE.
I MUST GAUGE MY MOVE PERFECTLY.
DESPITE THAT, HE IS CARRIED ALOFT AS EASILY AS A SCRAP OF PAPER.

THE SLIGHTEST MISTAKE WILL SEND ME HURTLING INTO SPACE, WHERE EVEN MY ARMORED FORM CANNOT LONG SURVIVE.
WHUNFFF!
I AM HERE, TOVARISCH!
BUT I DO NOT KNOW HOW LONG I CAN STAY!

NIGHTCRAWLER, TELEPORT WITH LILANDRA TO THE BRIDGE!
ACTIVATE THE DAMAGE CONTROL SYSTEMS!
BAMF
WITH A BURST OF SMOKE AND FLAME, AND THE "BAMF" OF IMPLODING AIR-- UNHEARD IN THE DIN-- THE GERMAN-BORN X-MAN VANISHES...

...TO INSTANTLY REAPPEAR ON THE VESSEL'S COMMAND DECK.
THIS STUNT FELT AWFUL THE FIRST TIME WE TRIED IT, NIGHTCRAWLER.
IT HASN'T IMPROVED WITH AGE.
MY APOLOGIES, EMPRESS. I'M NOT MYSELF THESE DAYS.
BUT THEN, WHO AMONG US IS?
THE WORDS ARE JAUNTY, BUT THERE'S AN UNDERTONE OF BITTERNESS AND DESPAIR THAT LILANDRA UNDERSTANDS ONLY TOO WELL.
SCREEEEEEEE!
THE REPAIR SYSTEMS HAVE FAILED.
WE'LL HAVE TO KEY IN EACH FUNCTION MANUALLY.
I'LL DIVERT MORE AIR TO THE HANGAR. THAT SHOULD BUY US THE TIME WE NEED.
WHY BOTHER? WE'RE ONLY POSTPONING THE INEVITABLE. WE ARE DOOMED, LILANDRA.
PERHAPS, MY FRIEND. BUT WOLVERINE COULD BE WRONG.
WE HAVE TO PLUG THAT BREACH!
WOLVERINE, CUT LOOSE A CHUNK OF THE DECK!
--THEY MOVE THROUGH STEEL AS EASILY AS AIR.
THE BLADES ARE ADAMANTIUM--UNBREAKABLE, RAZOR-KEEN, RETRACTABLE INTO BIONIC HOUSINGS IN HIS FOREARMS--
BUT AS LILANDRA TRIES TO MAINTAIN PRESSURE IN THE BAY--SO THE X-MEN WILL HAVE AIR TO BREATHE--THE WIND SUDDENLY INTENSIFIES...
...YANKING WOLVERINE FREE.
BRACE YOURSELF, COMRADE. THIS WILL HURT.
SAME GOES FOR YOU, BUDDY.
MY SKELETON'S LACED WITH ADAMANTIUM, REMEMBER. IT DON'T BREAK.

WHOULLF!
I AM SORRY, MY FRIEND. I WARNED YOU.
THANKS A HEAP.
COLOSSUS, GET OUT OF THE WAY!
OPTIC BLASTS OF NIGH-IRRESISTIBLE FORCE...
...FIRE FROM CYCLOPS' EYES TO FINISH THE JOB WOLVERINE BEGAN.
HERE IT COMES, PETEY!
I AM MOVING AS FAST AS I CAN!
KANG!
WHEW!
THAT WAS TOO FLAMIN' CLOSE FOR-- CRIPES!
WE'RE FALLIN'!
WITH HULL INTEGRITY RESTORED BY THE X-MEN'S IMPROVISED PATCH...
...THE DECOMPRESSION ENDS, ITS WIND DISAPPEARS...
...AND THE SHIP'S GRAVITY--ARTIFICIAL THOUGH IT MAY BE--ONCE MORE REASSERTS ITSELF.
COLOSSUS!
KRASH!
HE'S FINE, KITTY. I'M FINE.
EV'RYTHING'S HUNKY-DORY.
THAT IS, IF YOU IGNORE THE FACT THAT THE X-MEN ARE AS GOOD AS DEAD.

MEANWHILE, BACK ON EARTH...
...AT THE MANSION WHICH ONCE HOUSED **PROFESSOR XAVIER'S SCHOOL FOR GIFTED YOUNGSTERS**--AND SERVED AS SECRET HEADQUARTERS FOR THE X-MEN, THE TEAM OF MUTANT HEROES FOUNDED BY XAVIER--
--A LOVELY SUMMER AFTERNOON IS PASSED BY **STEVIE HUNTER, MOIRA MacTAGGERT** AND **ILLYANA RASPUTIN,** COLOSSUS' YOUNGER SISTER.
ANY WORD?
NONE.

I FEEL A BIT GHOULISH ENJOYING MYSELF-- KNOWING THAT THE X-MEN COULD BE DEAD, OR WORSE.
SO DO I. BUT IT'S BEEN WEEKS SINCE THEY WERE KIDNAPPED. AN' HARSH AS IT SOUNDS, LIFE MUST GO ON.
I'M GLAD O' YUIR COMPANY, STEVIE. THIS PLACE WAS TURNIN' INTO A MAUSOLEUM-- AN' BIDDIN' FAIR T' DRIVE ME AN' THE CHILD DAFT.

HOW'S CHARLES TAKING THINGS?
NOT WELL. OCH, LASS, YOU SHOULD'A SEEN HIM WHEN WE FIRST MET. WHAT A MAN!
I FEAR HE'S NEVER REALLY RECOVERED FROM THE LOSS O' HIS LEGS.

HE'D GIVE HIS MUTANT POWERS-- HIS VERY SOUL-- T' BE WI' THE X-MEN RIGHT NOW, T' LEAD THEM. HE WAS BORN T' BE A HERO. BUT INSTEAD HE MUST STAY BEHIND WHILE OTHERS BATTLE IN HIS STEAD.

HE CHAFES AT THA' RESTRICTION.

I FEEL SOMETHING OF THE SAME SENSE OF LOSS WHENEVER I GO TO THE BALLET...

...AND THAT SAME DESPERATE WILLINGNESS TO PAY ANY PRICE TO RETURN TO WHAT I WAS. IT'S NOT AN EASY THING TO COPE WITH.

AYE. IN CHARLEY'S CASE, THINGS ARE MADE WORSE BY HIS BELIEF THA' HE'S FAILED THE X-MEN AS HE DID JEAN GREY...

...AND THA' THEY'LL SUFFER THE SAME FATE.

KEEP AN EYE ON ILLYANA, WILL YOU, WHILE I'M INSIDE TALKIN' T' CHARLES?

SURE-- AHHRRR!

STEVIE!

'M'OKAY. JUST A SPASM. IT'LL PASS.
I WAS IN AN ACCIDENT, YEARS AGO. SHATTERED MY KNEE. DOCS FIXED IT VIRTUALLY GOOD AS NEW. I CAN WALK. I CAN EVEN DANCE, A LITTLE, IN CLASS.

THE ONLY THING I CAN'T DO IS PERFORM.
NO GREAT LOSS, I S'POSE. NO WORSE THAN LOSING YOUR SOUL.

CHARLES...

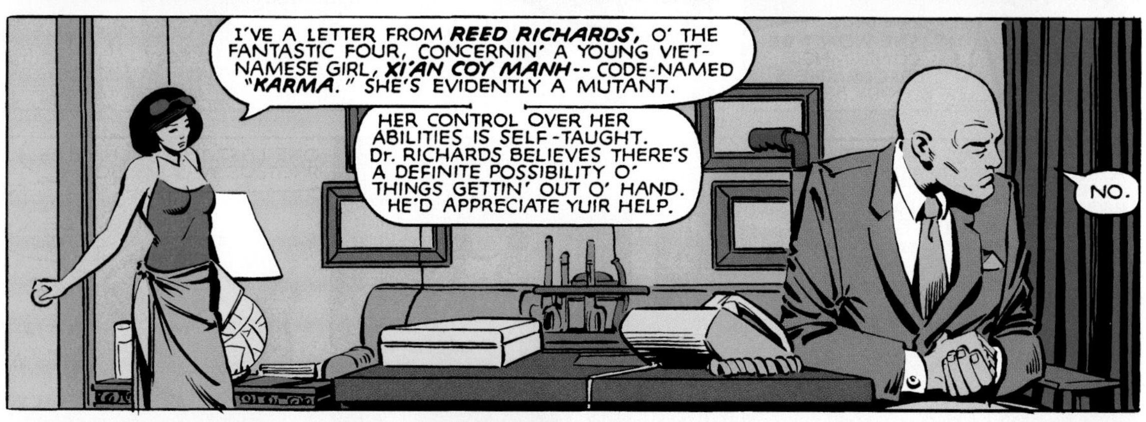
I'VE A LETTER FROM REED RICHARDS, O' THE FANTASTIC FOUR, CONCERNIN' A YOUNG VIET-NAMESE GIRL, XI'AN COY MANH-- CODE-NAMED "KARMA." SHE'S EVIDENTLY A MUTANT.
HER CONTROL OVER HER ABILITIES IS SELF-TAUGHT. Dr. RICHARDS BELIEVES THERE'S A DEFINITE POSSIBILITY O' THINGS GETTIN' OUT O' HAND. HE'D APPRECIATE YUIR HELP.
NO.

AS YOU WISH.
NO ARGUMENT, MOIRA? I'M SURPRISED.

WE'VE FOUGHT ENOUGH THESE PAST WEEKS, CHARLES. I'M DONE WI' SCREAMIN', AN' BREAKIN' MY HEART TRYIN' T' BUDGE AN IMMOVABLE OBJECT.
IT'S YOUR LIFE. YOU MAY LIVE IT AS Y' PLEASE.
FORTUNATELY FOR THE GIRL, THERE ARE OTHER OPTIONS.
YOU?
PERHAPS. WE'VE BEEN ASSOCIATES IN MUTANT RESEARCH SINCE BEFORE YOU FOUNDED THE X-MEN. I DARESAY I COULD DO A FAIR JOB.
BUT I WAS THINKIN' MORE ALONG THE LINES O' MAGNETO-- IF WE CAN FIND HIM--OR EMMA FROST'S "MASSACHUSETTS ACADEMY."
ARE YOU INSANE, WOMAN?! MAGNETO IS THE X-MEN'S GREATEST FOE AND Ms. FROST'S COHORTS IN THE HELLFIRE CLUB ARE ALMOST AS BAD!
YOU'D TURN THAT CHILD OVER TO VILLAINS--EVIL MUTANTS?!

AYE! BECAUSE WI' THEM, SHE'LL HAVE THE BEST POSSIBLE OPPORTUNITY T' LEARN HOW TO COPE WI' HER ABILITIES!
SHE WON'T BE CONDEMNED BEFORE SHE'S BLOODY BEGUN!

IS THAT THE ONLY CHOICE: THEM OR ME?
MOIRA, YOU AREN'T BEING FAIR. I CANNOT BRING ANOTHER CHILD INTO THIS PLACE, ONLY TO SEE HER DESTROYED. THE X-MEN ARE MY FAMILY-- I LOVE THEM AS I WOULD MY CHILDREN--YOU'VE NO CONCEPTION OF HOW MUCH IT HURTS TO LOSE THEM...

OH NO?
FORGIVE ME, MOIRA. I DIDN'T MEAN... I DIDN'T THINK...

ABOUT PROTEUS, CHARLES. MY SON. A ROGUE MUTANT, AS WICKED AS THEY COME. HE MURDERED A HALF-DOZEN PEOPLE AN', IN THE END, THE X-MEN AN' I HAD NO ALTERNATIVE BUT TO KILL HIM.
IF I'D SWALLOWED MY PRIDE-- AN' MY SHAME-- AN' TURNED TO YOU FOR HELP...
...THINGS MIGHT HA' TURNED OUT DIFFERENTLY.
DON'T SENTENCE KARMA TO A SIMILAR FATE.
ONE LAST THING, CHARLES. PROTEUS WAS MY BOY.
HE COULD HA' BEEN OURS.

HE SITS IN SILENT DARKNESS AFTER SHE LEAVES, WATCHING THE SUNSET, EMOTIONS AND MEMORIES RUNNING RIOT WITHIN HIM AS HIS MIND LOOKS BACK ON YOUNGER, HAPPIER DAYS--WHEN HE AND MOIRA WERE IN LOVE--TO CONSIDER WHAT WAS, AND WHAT MIGHT HAVE BEEN.
HE THINKS OF HIS OATHS, AS TEACHER AND PHYSICIAN...
...AND OF A GIRL HE'S NEVER MET...

...WHOSE LIFE IS IN HIS HANDS.
THEN, AT LAST, A DECISION IS MADE-- A RUBICON CROSSED-- AND HE REACHES OUT FOR REED RICHARDS' LETTER, AND THE TELEPHONE.

A SHI'AR SHUTTLE...
...DRIFTING AIMLESSLY THROUGH THE SAME NEBULA THAT EN-SHROUDS LILANDRA'S IMPERIAL YACHT, Z'REEE SHAR.

ABOARD, ORORO-- WHO, AS STORM, IS LEADER OF THE X-MEN-- SICK AT HEART BECAUSE SHE HAS BETRAYED HER TRUST BY DESERTING HER FRIENDS...
...STRICKEN TO HER SOUL BY THE REASON FOR THAT BETRAYAL.
WHAT AM I TO DO?!

A LIFE GROWS WITHIN ME, AN EGG IM-PLANTED BY THE MOTHER QUEEN OF THE BROOD. IT HAS JOINED ITS ESSENCE TO MINE. IT SPREADS THROUGH ME BODY AND SOUL, LIKE SOME LOATHSOME DISEASE, CORRUPTING EVERYTHING IT TOUCHES, RESHAPING ME IN ITS OWN IMAGE.
IF UNCHECKED, IT WILL CONSUME ME. I WILL DIE. IT WILL LIVE IN MY PLACE.

BUT IT IS NOT A DISEASE, IT IS A SENTIENT BEING.
AND AS THE X-MAN, STORM-- AS THE "GODDESS," ORORO-- I AM CONSECRATED TO LIFE, SWORN TO PRESERVE IT AT ALL COSTS.

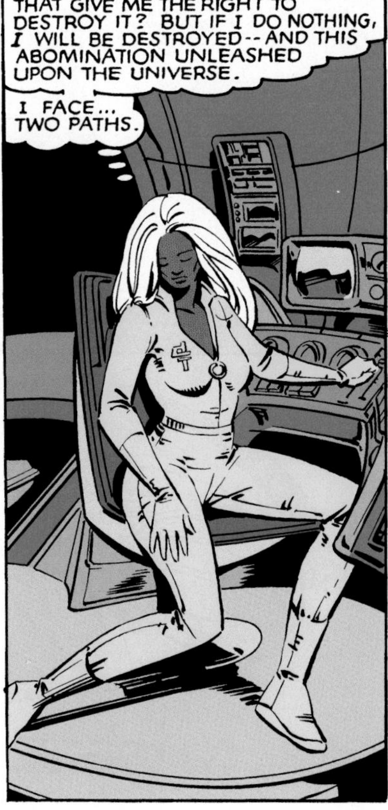
THIS CREATURE IS EVIL-- BUT DOES THAT GIVE ME THE RIGHT TO DESTROY IT? BUT IF I DO NOTHING, I WILL BE DESTROYED-- AND THIS ABOMINATION UNLEASHED UPON THE UNIVERSE.
I FACE... TWO PATHS.

ONE PRESERVES MY BELIEFS-- THOUGH IT MEANS MY DEATH AND PROBABLY THAT OF COUNTLESS OTHERS BESIDES. THE ALTERNA-TIVE MAY SAVE ME-- BUT WHAT THEN OF MY SOUL, OF THE BELIEFS THAT GIVE EXISTENCE MEANING?
GODDESS, I AM SO FAR FROM HOME. I FEEL SO LOST, SO ALONE. BLESSED LADY, HEAR MY PLEA! I BEG YOU--
--HELP ME!!

Eh--?!
MY HANDS--?!?

WHAT!?!

NNOOOOOOOooo

THE METAMORPHOSIS IS NEARLY COMPLETE...
...WHEN THE SHUTTLE EMERGES FROM THE NEBULA...
THE LIGHT-- SO BRILLIANT, SO BLINDING-- WHAT CAN IT BE?
STARS!
FILLING THE SKY--NOTHING BUT STARS!
I... I'M MYSELF AGAIN!
THIS MUST BE THE GALACTIC CORE. MILLIONS OF SUNS, CRAMMED INTO A RELATIVELY TINY VOLUME OF SPACE-- LIVING STARS, LIVING WORLDS, AND FROM EACH I DRAW BOTH SPIRITUAL AND MATERIAL SUSTENANCE.
THAT SUDDEN INFLUX OF POWER CAUGHT THE EMBRYO OFF-GUARD AND ENABLED ME ME TO REVERSE THE TRANSFORMATION. I DOUBT I WILL BE SO FORTUNATE A SECOND TIME. THE EMBRYO'S INFLUENCE GROWS WITH EACH PASSING SECOND. EVEN HERE I CANNOT WITHSTAND IT FOR MUCH LONGER. IF I AM TO ACT...
... I MUST DO SO NOW!

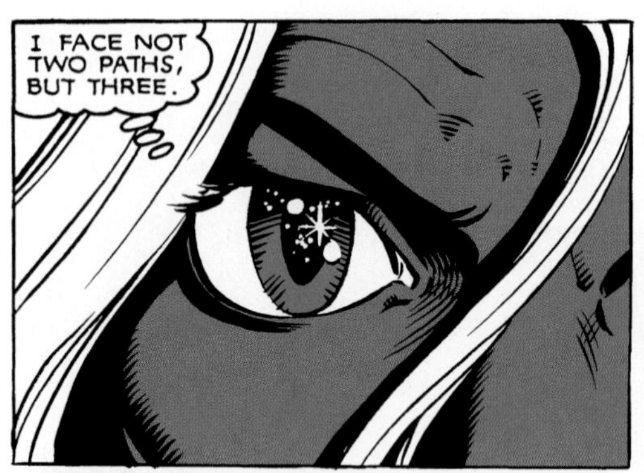
I FACE NOT TWO PATHS, BUT THREE.

OUT OF FEAR, I DENIED THE ONE I KNEW IN MY HEART THAT I WOULD TAKE.
I COULD NOT FACE THE X-MEN, TAINTED AS I WAS BY THE MONSTER WITHIN ME, AND SO I FLED. I WISH I COULD SEE THEM NOW, TO TELL THEM HOW MUCH I LOVE THEM ALL...
...TO BID THEM FAREWELL.
WITH A LAST LINGERING LOOK AT THE CELESTIAL GLORY ABOUT HER...

...STORM SUMMONS THE POWER OF THE ENTIRE CORE.
AND, FOR THE BRIEFEST OF MOMENTS, A NEW STAR SHINES IN THE FIRMAMENT.
THE PROCESS IS SURPRISINGLY SIMPLE, NO MORE ACTUALLY THAN SHE DOES WHEN SHE DRAWS ENERGY FROM THE EARTH TO MANIPULATE THE WEATHER-- BUT, IN THIS CASE, THINGS ARE MAGNIFIED TO AN UNIMAGINABLE DEGREE.
AS STORM HOPES, THE EMBRYO DOES NOT SURVIVE THE ORDEAL.

NEITHER DOES SHE.

ELSEWHERE...
ANOTHER DAY'S WORK, LILANDRA, AND WE SHOULD BE READY TO ROLL.

THE QUESTION IS, WHERE DO WE GO?

HOW 'BOUT BACK THE WAY WE CAME, TA FINISH WHAT WE STARTED.

TO SLEAZEWORLD? TO TAKE ON THE BROOD? SIX PEOPLE IN AN ARMED YACHT VERSUS AN ENTIRE RACE?! YOU'RE TALKING SUICIDE, LOGAN.

WHAT'VE WE GOT TO LOSE? THE X-MEN ARE LIVIN' ON BORROWED TIME, ANYWAY. THE MOTHER QUEEN IMPLANTED AN EGG IN EACH O' US. BECAUSE O' MY MUTANT POWER-- MY BODY'S ABILITY TA HEAL ANY WOUND OR ILLNESS--THE ONE I GOT WAS ZAPPED.

BUT YOURS'RE HEALTHY, GROWIN'. SOONER OR LATER, THEY'LL MATURE. D'YOU WANT TO SIT AROUND AN' WAIT FOR THAT TA HAPPEN...

... OR PAY THE BROOD BACK FOR WHAT THEY'VE DONE?

I AM *MAJESTRIX SHI'AR*-- EMPRESS OF A WARRIOR RACE! I WILL SHOW THE BROOD THE IDENTICAL MERCY THEY HAVE GRANTED US.
FROM THIS MOMENT ON, WHEREVER, WHENEVER I FIND THEM-- BE THEY HIGH-BORN OR LOW, ADULT OR CHILD--

--THEIR LIVES ARE *MINE!*

SOUNDS GOOD TA ME, DARLIN'.

AND... TO ME.
GOD HELP US ALL.

LATER...
IT TOOK A LOT FOR SCOTTY TO ADMIT THOSE KIND'A FEELINGS--THEY GO AGAINST EV'RYTHIN' HE BELIEVES IN, EV'RYTHIN' XAVIER TAUGHT HIM. IT'S A HARD THING TA TOSS AWAY YER IDEALS.
ME, I COULD NEVER AFFORD 'EM.

WHAT'S THIS--?! ELF--PRAYIN'???
...IN NOMINE PATRI, ET FILII, ET SPIRITU SANCTI--AMEN.
WHAT'S DOIN', BUB?

WHAT DOES IT LOOK LIKE?

INCONGRUOUS. I GUESS I NEVER FIGURED YOU FOR THE RELIGIOUS TYPE.
WHY, DON'T I LOOK THE PART?
I ADMIT I'M RARELY SEEN IN A CHURCH--BUT I DRAW COMFORT FROM MY BELIEFS AND FROM PRAYER. SUCH COMFORT IS DEARLY NEEDED NOW--BY US ALL.
YOU SHOULD TRY IT, LOGAN. WHO KNOWS, YOU MIGHT LIKE IT.
I DID, IN THE ARMY. A MISTAKE.

I BELIEVE IN NOTHIN'--NEVER HAVE, NEVER WILL.
WHAT MATTERS IS WHAT I CAN SEE, HEAR, SMELL, TASTE, TOUCH--
--TANGIBLE THINGS, PHYSICAL THINGS. REALITY. THE REST IS IMAGINATION.

AND YOU HAVE NO USE FOR THAT?
NOPE.
I AM SORRY, MY FRIEND.

I NEVER REALIZED HOW UTTERLY, INESCAPABLY ALONE YOU MUST BE--WITH NOTHING TO HOLD ONTO BUT YOURSELF. MORE ALONE THAN I--DESPITE MY OUTRE APPEARANCE--COULD EVER BE.
I AIN'T ALONE, BUB--I GOT YOU.
C'MON, LESSEE IF THEY GOT ANY BREW ON THIS BUCKET.

LATER STILL, IN KITTY'S CABIN...
SHE'S THE YOUNGEST X-MAN, 14 YEARS OLD--
--A BIRTHDAY HAVING PASSED WHILE SHE WAS IN SPACE, WITHOUT HER KNOWING--

--AND SHE'S COME A LONG WAY FROM HER HOMETOWN OF DEERFIELD, ILLINOIS.
SHE WONDERS IF SHE'LL EVER SEE IT AGAIN.

IN FRONT OF THE OTHERS, SHE TRIED TO LOOK AS BRAVE AS SHE COULD. BUT IN THIS CABIN, BY HERSELF, THE TEARS CAME AND WOULDN'T STOP UNTIL, AT LAST, EXHAUSTED EMOTIONALLY AND PHYSICALLY...
...SHE FINALLY FELL ASLEEP...

...ONLY TO FIND HERSELF STANDING IN A CEMETARY, IN CHICAGO. AT FIRST, SHE'S ECSTATIC TO BE HOME AND WITH HER PARENTS, BUT THEN THEY SHUSH HER STERNLY, TELLING HER THIS IS NO OCCASION FOR SUCH JOY AND HIGH SPIRITS.
CHASTENED, KITTY COMPOSES HERSELF. THE X-MEN ARE HERE TOO, EVEN ORORO. BUT THEIR EXPRESSIONS MATCH HER PARENTS', THEIR GAZE FOCUSED ON AN OPEN COFFIN.
BELATEDLY, KITTY REALIZES IT'S A FUNERAL AND HER CHEEKS FLUSH WITH EMBARRASMENT. HOW COULD SHE HAVE BEHAVED SO BADLY?

BUT WHO'S DEAD, SHE WONDERS, AS SHE'S LED TO THE GRAVE TO PAY HER LAST RESPECTS.
ONE LOOK GIVES HER THE ANSWER.

THE CORPSE OPENS ITS EYES AND SMILES...
...AND THEN IT ISN'T HUMAN ANYMORE, IT'S A SLEAZOID -- LIKE THE MOTHER QUEEN, ONLY SMALLER, AND YET THERE'S SOMETHING IN THE WAY IT MOVES AND ACTS THAT REMINDS KITTY OF HERSELF.
IT GRABS HER. SHE TRIES TO PHASE THROUGH ITS TENTACLES, BUT HER POWER NO LONGER WORKS. SHE CLAWS AT THE GROUND WITH ALL HER MIGHT, BUT HER MUSCLES ARE NO MATCH FOR THE YOUNG QUEEN'S. SHE SCREAMS FOR HELP, BUT HER FRIENDS, HER PARENTS, DO NOTHING...
...AS SHE'S DRAGGED INTO THE COFFIN, INTO THE GRAVE.
THE SLEAZOID HOLDS HER TIGHT, GATHERS HER CLOSE, A LOVING EMBRACE. FLESH DISSOLVES, REALITIES BLUR-- AND WHERE THERE WERE TWO BEINGS, ONLY ONE REMAINS. IT IS A YOUNG QUEEN OF THE BROOD.
IT IS KITTY PRYDE.
NO!!
KATYA, KATYA, KATYA, DO NOT FEAR, IT IS ALL RIGHT...
...I AM HERE, I WILL PROTECT YOU...
...shhhhh, THERE'S A GIRL...
P-PETER...?

A BAD DREAM, KITTY?
A DOOZY.
THEY HAVE BEEN MAKING THE ROUNDS LATELY. NONE OF US ARE SLEEPING WELL, IF AT ALL.
YEAH. EXCEPT THE REALITY WHEN WE WAKE IS JUST AS BAD AS THE NIGHTMARES. MAYBE WORSE.

WOULD YOU CARE TO TALK ABOUT IT? YOU MIGHT FEEL BETTER.
NO!

KATYA, IT IS NO CRIME TO BE AFRAID.
I'M NOT AFRAID!

OF COURSE YOU AREN'T. MY ERROR.
PETER, I... I DON'T WANT TO DIE!

WHO DOES?

PETER NIKOLIEVITCH RASPUTIN, DON'T YOU *DARE* LAUGH AT ME!
THIS ISN'T FUNNY! THIS ISN'T A JOKE!

IT IS EITHER LAUGH OR CRY, LITTLE ONE, AND I REFUSE TO DO THOSE MONSTERS -- THE BROOD -- THE HONOR OF TEARS.

PETER, DON'T YOU UNDERSTAND -- ARE YOU TOO STUPID OR JUST TOO SCARED TO ACCEPT THE TRUTH?
WE'RE GOING TO DIE!

DA.
YES, KITTY, WE ARE.
WHAT YOU DO NOT COMPREHEND IS THAT WE ARE DYING FROM THE MOMENT OF BIRTH, INDEED FROM THE INSTANT OF CONCEPTION. CREATION BEARS WITHIN ITSELF THE SEEDS OF ITS OWN DESTRUCTION.
OUR LIVES ARE FINITE THINGS. WE LIVE OUR ALLOTED SPAN AND ARE NO MORE. REGARDLESS OF WHAT WE MAY DO, HOW HARD WE TRY, THE BEST WE CAN HOPE FOR IS A BRIEF DELAY OF THE INEVITABLE.

IT IS SAD, EVEN CRUEL. BUT IT IS ALSO OUR MOST FUNDAMENTAL REALITY, TO BE FACED AND ACCEPTED.
DYING AFTER A LONG, FULL LIFE, OKAY, I GUESS. DYING IN BATTLE, OKAY. I CAN HANDLE THEM.

BUT TO END LIKE THIS... TO HAVE THIS ALIEN... THING INSIDE ME, GROWING LIKE A CANCER...
... KNOWING THAT I COULD TURN INTO A SLEAZOID AT ANY MOMENT--
-- PETER, IT'S MORE THAN I CAN BEAR!

I KEEP WONDERING, SUPPOSE WE DON'T REALLY DIE WHEN THE METAMORPHOSIS OCCURS, SUPPOSE SOME PART OF OUR AWARENESS SURVIVES IN THE SLEAZOID INCARNATION?
TO BECOME SO HORRIBLE A CREATURE IS AWFUL ENOUGH, BUT TO REMEMBER AT THE SAME TIME WHAT I WAS...
AGAIN, THERE ARE TEARS.

AGAIN, PETER COMFORTS HER UNTIL THE EMOTIONAL STORM PASSES.
THANKS, PETER. I REALLY NEEDED THIS.
ANY TIME.
GEE, I WISH I WAS OLDER.
SO DO I.

YOU'RE FOOLING, RIGHT? HUMORING THE KID, TO PERK UP HER SPIRITS?
I KNEW PRECISELY WHAT YOU MEANT, KATYA.

I HAVE NEVER BEEN MORE SERIOUS.

HOWEVER, LITTLE ONE, YOU ARE NOT OLDER.
IT... IT DOESN'T MATTER.
YES, IT DOES.

WHY?! WHEN YOU'RE DOOMED, WHAT'S THE POINT OF PLAYING BY SOCIETY'S STUPID RULES?!
THIS IS NOT THE PROPER TIME OR PLACE.
WE MAY NEVER GET ANOTHER CHANCE!

YOU NEVER KNOW. THE UNIVERSE IS FULL OF SURPRISES.
MOST OF 'EM NASTY--
--PETER!

LOOK!!
BY THE WHITE WOLF!

ORORO?!!
KITTEN...
...LITTLE BROTHER...
...HOW GOOD IT IS TO SEE YOU.

YOUR TEETH, YOUR EYES-- THE MARKS OF A VAMPIRE!
THAT'S NOT RIGHT.

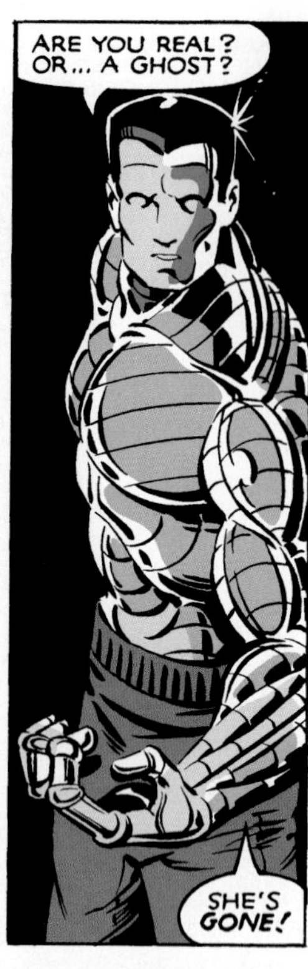
ARE YOU REAL? OR... A GHOST?
SHE'S GONE!

Phaugggh!
A BREWMEISTER, YOU AIN'T, BUB.
IT'S AN ALIEN FOOD SYNTHESIZER, WHAT DID YOU EXPECT?
THE MACHINE -- AND THE BEER-- SHOULD IMPROVE WITH PRACTICE.

I HOPE SO.
LOGAN... KURT...
HIYA, 'RORO.
'CAUSE THIS STUFF DOESN'T EVEN RATE AS ROTGUT.
Huh?!?

STORM!!
NIGHTCRAWLER--?!
I SAW, I HEARD-- BUT I DID NOT BELIEVE!

NOTHIN'. ROOM'S EMPTY.
WAS SHE EVER HERE? COULD BE YOUR CONCOCTION'S MORE POTENT THAN WE FIGURED.
COULD BE WE'RE CRACKIN' UP.

BUT I FEEL FINE.
SOBER. SANE.
THERE, MY FRIEND! SHE'S BACK!

NOT QUITE. THE ONE I SAW WAS TALLER.
A CHILD?
EVERYTHING IS SO BIG! NO--IT IS I WHO AM SMALL.

Sigh.
THIS ISN'T RIGHT, EITHER.
WHAT IS WRONG, LIEBCHEN? CAN WE HELP?
ACH!
SHE'S DISAPPEARING.

AN ILLUSION-- A 3-D IMAGE--YET, WHEN YOU PASSED THROUGH HER, SHE LOOKED AS SURPRISED AS YOU DID.
WE MUST ALERT THE OTHERS!

CAN WE GET OUT OF HERE, LILANDRA?
I HAVE A CONTACT-- VERY LARGE, VERY CLOSE-- BUT THE NEBULA SCRAMBLES OUR SENSORS, PREVENTING ANY ACCURATE SCANS.
BAMF
CYCLOPS, WOLVERINE AND I HAVE HAD THE MOST AMAZING EXPERIENCE.
WAS IT STORM? WE SAW HER, TOO!

'RORO? RELAX, BABE, YOU'RE AMONG FRIENDS.
NO NEED TA BE SCARED.

WOLVERINE, IT'S A HOLOGRAPHIC PROJECTION, IT ISN'T REAL.
WRONG, BUB.
I THOUGHT SO TOO BUT MY SENSES TELL ME IT'S STORM. I'M FOLLOWIN' THEIR LEAD.

CRIPES, HER FEATURES ARE CHANGIN'-- GETTIN' OLDER!
MY BELOVED FRIENDS, FORGIVE THESE CLUMSY ATTEMPTS TO CONTACT YOU. I AM IMPROVING MY CONTROL WITH EXPERIENCE...
...BUT IT IS PROVING FAR MORE DIFFICULT THAN I IMAGINED.

VISUAL CONTACT!
CYCLOPS, IT'S ONE OF THE BROOD'S LIVING STAR-SHIPS!

WE'RE BEING SWALLOWED WHOLE!

FULL POWER TO THE ENGINES! THE REST OF YOU, ACTIVATE THE SHIP'S COMBAT SYSTEMS!
LET'S PUNCH OUR WAY OUT OF HERE, PRONTO!

IN 30 DAYS, THE X-MEN'S FINAL CONFRONTATION WITH THE BROOD, WHEREIN THEY'LL EITHER ...

LIVE FREE, OR DIE!

MARVEL® COMICS GROUP
DOUBLE-SIZED ISSUE!
APPROVED BY THE COMICS CODE AUTHORITY
$1.00
166 FEB 02461
© 1982 MARVEL COMICS GROUP
X-MEN™
TM

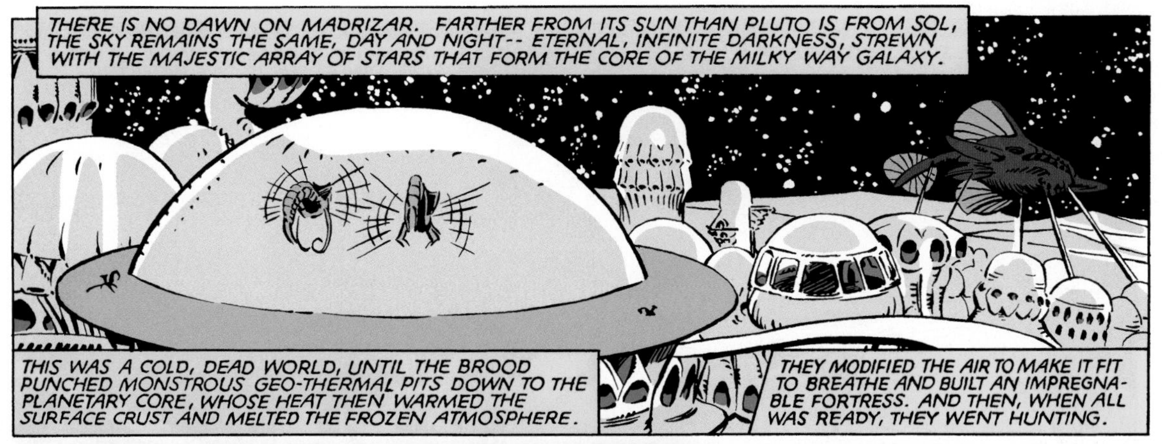
THERE IS NO DAWN ON MADRIZAR. FARTHER FROM ITS SUN THAN PLUTO IS FROM SOL, THE SKY REMAINS THE SAME, DAY AND NIGHT-- ETERNAL, INFINITE DARKNESS, STREWN WITH THE MAJESTIC ARRAY OF STARS THAT FORM THE CORE OF THE MILKY WAY GALAXY.
THIS WAS A COLD, DEAD WORLD, UNTIL THE BROOD PUNCHED MONSTROUS GEO-THERMAL PITS DOWN TO THE PLANETARY CORE, WHOSE HEAT THEN WARMED THE SURFACE CRUST AND MELTED THE FROZEN ATMOSPHERE.
THEY MODIFIED THE AIR TO MAKE IT FIT TO BREATHE AND BUILT AN IMPREGNABLE FORTRESS. AND THEN, WHEN ALL WAS READY, THEY WENT HUNTING.

THEIR PREY: THE ACANTI--
--GREAT, GENTLE, SENTIENT BEINGS WHO LEGEND SAYS HAVE ROAMED THE SPACEWAYS SINCE CREATION.

A PRIME SPECIMEN, HUNT-MASTER--SEE HOW IT STRUGGLES. THE BEAST WILL SERVE US LONG AND WELL.
WE INFECTED IT WITH THE SLAVER VIRUS WHEN WE MADE INITIAL CONTACT. ALREADY, MOST OF ITS HIGHER REASONING CENTERS --ITS CONSCIOUS MIND AND SELF-AWARENESS--HAVE BEEN DESTROYED.
SOON NOW, THE BEAST WILL BE COMPLETELY TRACTABLE.

SLAVE-MASTER, HAS THERE BEEN ANY FURTHER WORD ON THOSE ACCURSED TERRANS--THE X-MEN?
NOTHING SINCE THEIR ESCAPE. BUT THEIR FATE IS AS CERTAIN AS THAT OF YOUR ACANTI CAPTIVE-- eh?!
HUNT-MASTER-- LOOK!
THAT LIGHT-- WHAT DOES IT MEAN?! WHAT IS HAPPENING?!?

THE ANSWER IS AS SPECTACULAR AS IT IS FINAL.
HER NAME IS **BINARY.** AND IN A VERY REAL SENSE, SHE IS ONE WITH THE UNIVERSE-- LINKED BODY AND SOUL TO A WHITE HOLE, WITH ACCESS TO ITS VIRTUALLY LIMITLESS POWER. LIKE A STAR, SHE CAN GENERATE HEAT, LIGHT, GRAVITY-- ENERGY IN ALL ITS MYRIAD FORMS.

SHE IS A FRIEND OF THOSE SELFSAME X-MEN. SHE IS HERE TO AVENGE THEM.
STAN LEE PRESENTS THE UNCANNY X-MEN-- WHO THIS DAY WILL EITHER...
LIVE FREE OR DIE!
CHRIS CLAREMONT SCRIPTER
PAUL SMITH PENCILER
BOB WIACEK INKER
TOM ORZECHOWSKI LETTERER
GLYNIS WEIN COLORIST
LOUISE JONES EDITOR
JIM SHOOTER EDITOR-IN-CHIEF

THE BROOD RESISTS...
...FOR ALL THE GOOD IT DOES THEM.

HER WORK IS QUICKLY DONE--THE CARNAGE SHE HAS WROUGHT, ABSOLUTE--WITH ONE EXCEPTION, THE ACANTI.
BE PATIENT, OLD DUFFER. I'LL HAVE YOU OFF THOSE BARBS AND ON YOUR WAY IN A JIFFY.

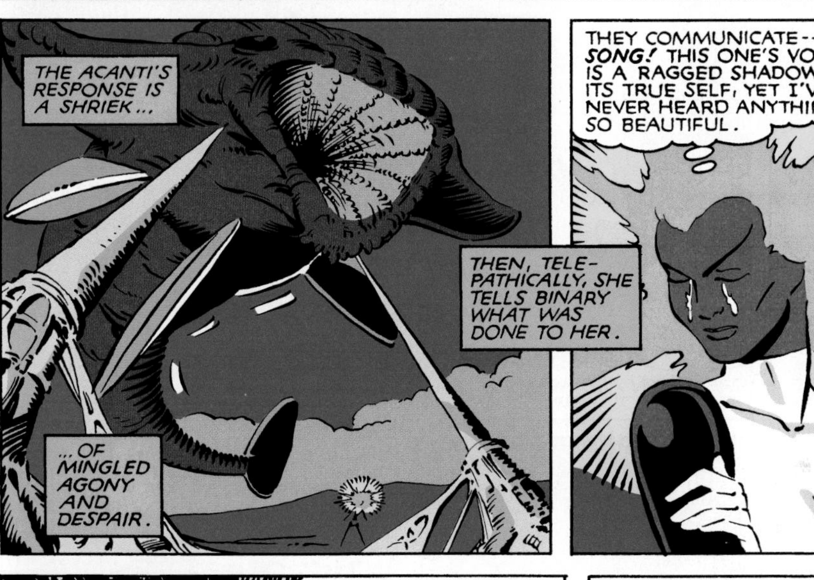
THE ACANTI'S RESPONSE IS A SHRIEK...
...OF MINGLED AGONY AND DESPAIR.
THEY COMMUNICATE--IN SONG! THIS ONE'S VOICE IS A RAGGED SHADOW OF ITS TRUE SELF, YET I'VE NEVER HEARD ANYTHING SO BEAUTIFUL.
THEN, TELEPATHICALLY, SHE TELLS BINARY WHAT WAS DONE TO HER.

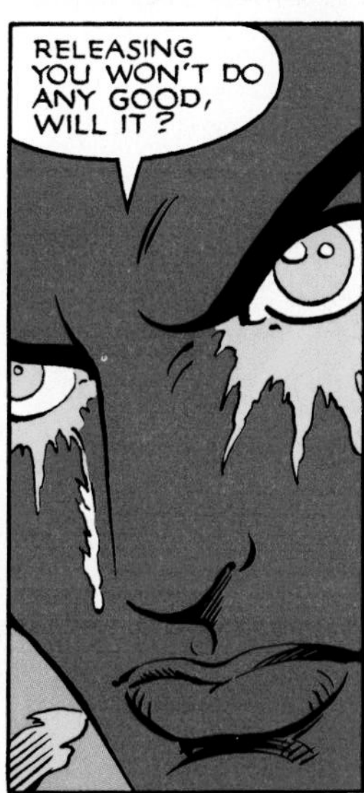
RELEASING YOU WON'T DO ANY GOOD, WILL IT?

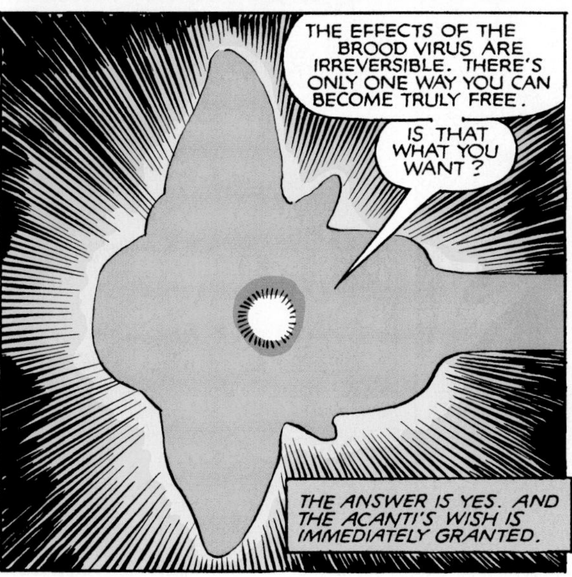
THE EFFECTS OF THE BROOD VIRUS ARE IRREVERSIBLE. THERE'S ONLY ONE WAY YOU CAN BECOME TRULY FREE.
IS THAT WHAT YOU WANT?
THE ANSWER IS YES. AND THE ACANTI'S WISH IS IMMEDIATELY GRANTED.

THAT'S ANOTHER LIFE THE BROOD OWES ME, ONE I WAS HELPLESS TO SAVE--AS I WAS WITH THE X-MEN AND... MYSELF.
AT FIRST, AFTER MY METAMORPHOSIS INTO BINARY, I WAS ECSTATIC. I THOUGHT THAT AT LAST I'D FOUND MY HEART'S DESIRE.
BUT ALL I'VE DONE SINCE IS WHAT I DID BEFORE--AS CAROL DANVERS--FIGHT, KILL, SURVIVE. THERE'S NO JOY IN ME ANYMORE, ONLY GRIEF. AND HATE.
THE BROOD HELPED MAKE ME WHAT I AM. IT'S A MISTAKE THEY'LL LIVE TO REGRET.

GOING MY WAY?
HUH?!? STORM!?!
THIS IS WONDERFUL! IT'S CRAZY! IT'S IMPOSSIBLE!
I THOUGHT I'D NEVER SEE YOU AGAIN-- THAT YOU'D EITHER BE DEAD OR TRANSFORMED INTO A YOUNG QUEEN OF THE BROOD.
IN A SENSE, CAROL, I SUFFERED BOTH FATES. AND NEITHER.

EXPLAIN YOURSELF. YOU'RE NO TELEPATH, YET I HEAR YOUR PROJECTED THOUGHTS. AND HOW CAN YOU SURVIVE, UNPROTECTED, WITHOUT A PRESSURE SUIT, IN DEEP SPACE?

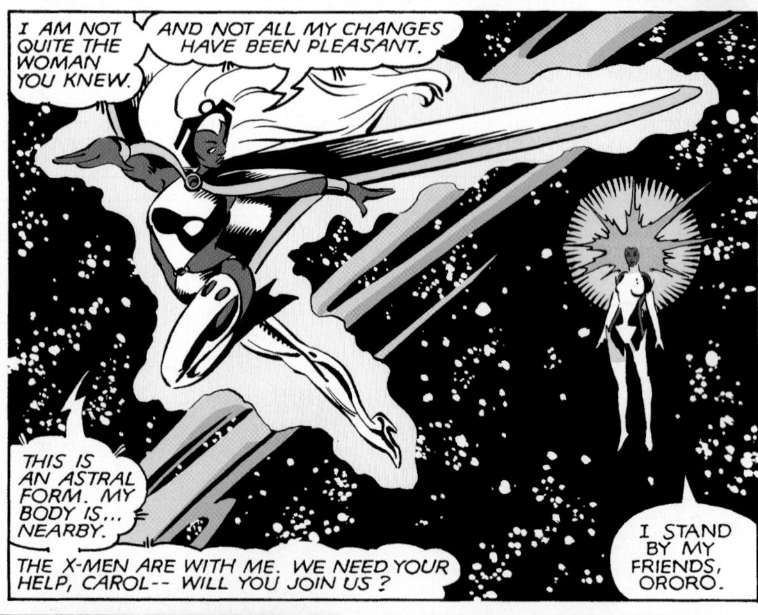
I AM NOT QUITE THE WOMAN YOU KNEW.
AND NOT ALL MY CHANGES HAVE BEEN PLEASANT.
THIS IS AN ASTRAL FORM. MY BODY IS... NEARBY.
THE X-MEN ARE WITH ME. WE NEED YOUR HELP, CAROL-- WILL YOU JOIN US?
I STAND BY MY FRIENDS, ORORO.

I HOPED YOU WOULD.
BEHOLD OUR DESTINATION! IS HE NOT MAGNIFICENT? YET DESPITE HIS VAST SIZE AND POWER, HE IS STILL NO MORE THAN AN INFANT, AS VULNERABLE AND FRAGILE AS ANY NEWBORN HUMAN CHILD.
I JUST MET AN ADULT OF THE SPECIES ON MADRIZAR. I... KILLED HER, ORORO.

I HEARD HER DEATHSONG. HAD YOU NOT, CAROL, I WOULD HAVE--TO SPARE HER FROM BECOMING ONE OF THE BROOD'S LIVING STARSHIPS.
Uh, STORM-- IS THIS PART OF THE TRIP REALLY NECESSARY?
TRUST ME, CAROL. I WON'T BITE.

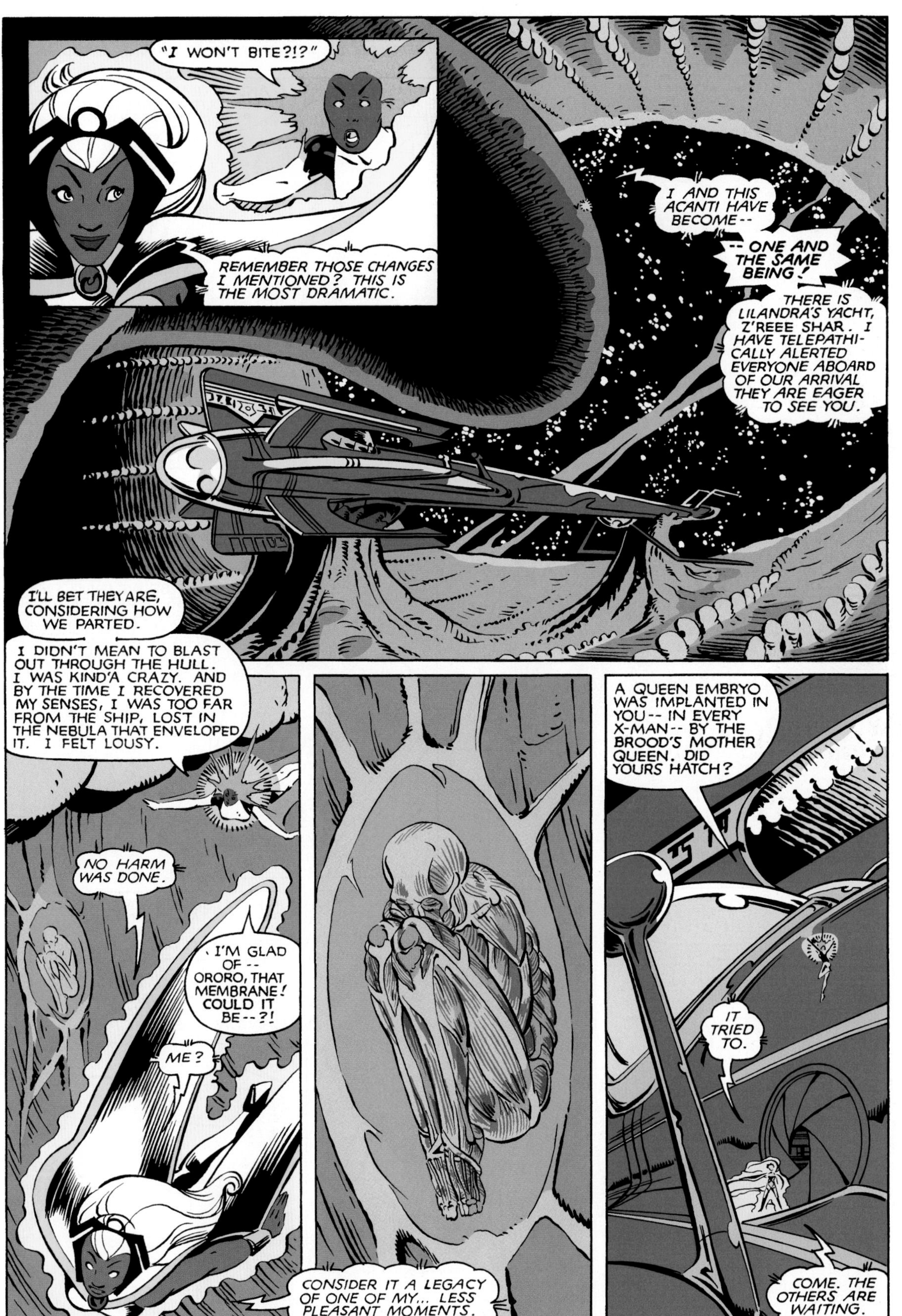
"I WON'T BITE?!?"
REMEMBER THOSE CHANGES I MENTIONED? THIS IS THE MOST DRAMATIC.
I AND THIS ACANTI HAVE BECOME--
-- ONE AND THE SAME BEING!
THERE IS LILANDRA'S YACHT, Z'REEE SHAR. I HAVE TELEPATHICALLY ALERTED EVERYONE ABOARD OF OUR ARRIVAL THEY ARE EAGER TO SEE YOU.
I'LL BET THEY ARE, CONSIDERING HOW WE PARTED.
I DIDN'T MEAN TO BLAST OUT THROUGH THE HULL. I WAS KIND'A CRAZY. AND BY THE TIME I RECOVERED MY SENSES, I WAS TOO FAR FROM THE SHIP, LOST IN THE NEBULA THAT ENVELOPED IT. I FELT LOUSY.
NO HARM WAS DONE.
I'M GLAD OF -- ORORO, THAT MEMBRANE! COULD IT BE--?!
ME?
CONSIDER IT A LEGACY OF ONE OF MY... LESS PLEASANT MOMENTS.
A QUEEN EMBRYO WAS IMPLANTED IN YOU-- IN EVERY X-MAN-- BY THE BROOD'S MOTHER QUEEN. DID YOURS HATCH?
IT TRIED TO.
COME. THE OTHERS ARE WAITING.

SIX LOST SOULS: ONE ALIEN, **LILANDRA,** EXPATRIATE RULER OF THE GALAXY-SPANNING SHI'AR EMPIRE, AND FIVE HUMAN-- **CYCLOPS, COLOSSUS, KITTY PRYDE, WOLVERINE** AND **NIGHTCRAWLER**-- MUTANTS, GIFTED WITH ABILITIES THAT SET THEM APART FROM THE REST OF THEIR SPECIES, FORGED INTO A TEAM OF UNSUNG, OCCASIONALLY OUTLAW, HEROES KNOWN AS THE **X-MEN**.

WE HAD SOME PRETTY HAIRY MOMENTS, THANKS TO YOU, CAROL.*
YEAH. NOTHIN' LIKE AN EXPLOSIVE DECOMPRESSION T' REALLY LIVEN UP A DAY.
NEXT TIME, I'LL BE MORE CAREFUL.
AND TAKE THE SUSPENSE AND FUN OUT OF OUR LIVES? PERISH THE THOUGHT.
*SEE OUR LAST TWO ISSUES -- L.

I DON'T UNDERSTAND-- WHY IS EVERYONE CRACKING JOKES, ACTING LIKE NOTHING'S WRONG?!
KATYA...
WE'VE BEEN MURDERED! WE ALL CARRY QUEEN EMBRYOS INSIDE US! WHEN THEY HATCH, WE'LL TURN INTO SLEAZOIDS!
AND THERE'S NOTHING WE CAN DO TO PREVENT IT!

SHE IS RIGHT, MY FRIENDS.
PARTLY, COLOSSUS. BUT Y'KNOW, KITTEN, WHEN THINGS ARE UNBEARABLE-- AS THEY ARE NOW-- SOMETIMES THE ONLY WAY T'COPE IS BY LAUGHIN'.
MAYBE WE CAN'T STOP THESE TRANSFORMATIONS --'CEPT BY DYIN'-- BUT WE CAN MAKE SURE THE SLEAZOIDS NEVER PULL THIS STUNT WITH ANYONE ELSE.

YOU MENTIONED THIS BEFORE, WOLVERINE-- A SUICIDE ATTACK ON THE BROOD HOMEWORLD?
WHY NOT, CYCLOPS? SINCE WE ARE ALREADY DOOMED, WE HAVE NOTHING TO LOSE. IF WE KILL THEIR MOTHER QUEEN...

YOU WOULD ACCOMPLISH NOTHING.
THE STAKES HERE ARE FAR HIGHER THAN MERE VENGEANCE.

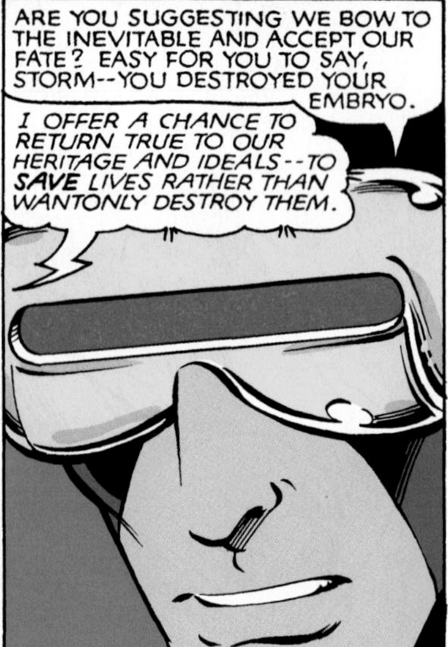

ARE YOU SUGGESTING WE BOW TO THE INEVITABLE AND ACCEPT OUR FATE? EASY FOR YOU TO SAY, STORM--YOU DESTROYED YOUR EMBRYO.
I OFFER A CHANCE TO RETURN TRUE TO OUR HERITAGE AND IDEALS--TO SAVE LIVES RATHER THAN WANTONLY DESTROY THEM.

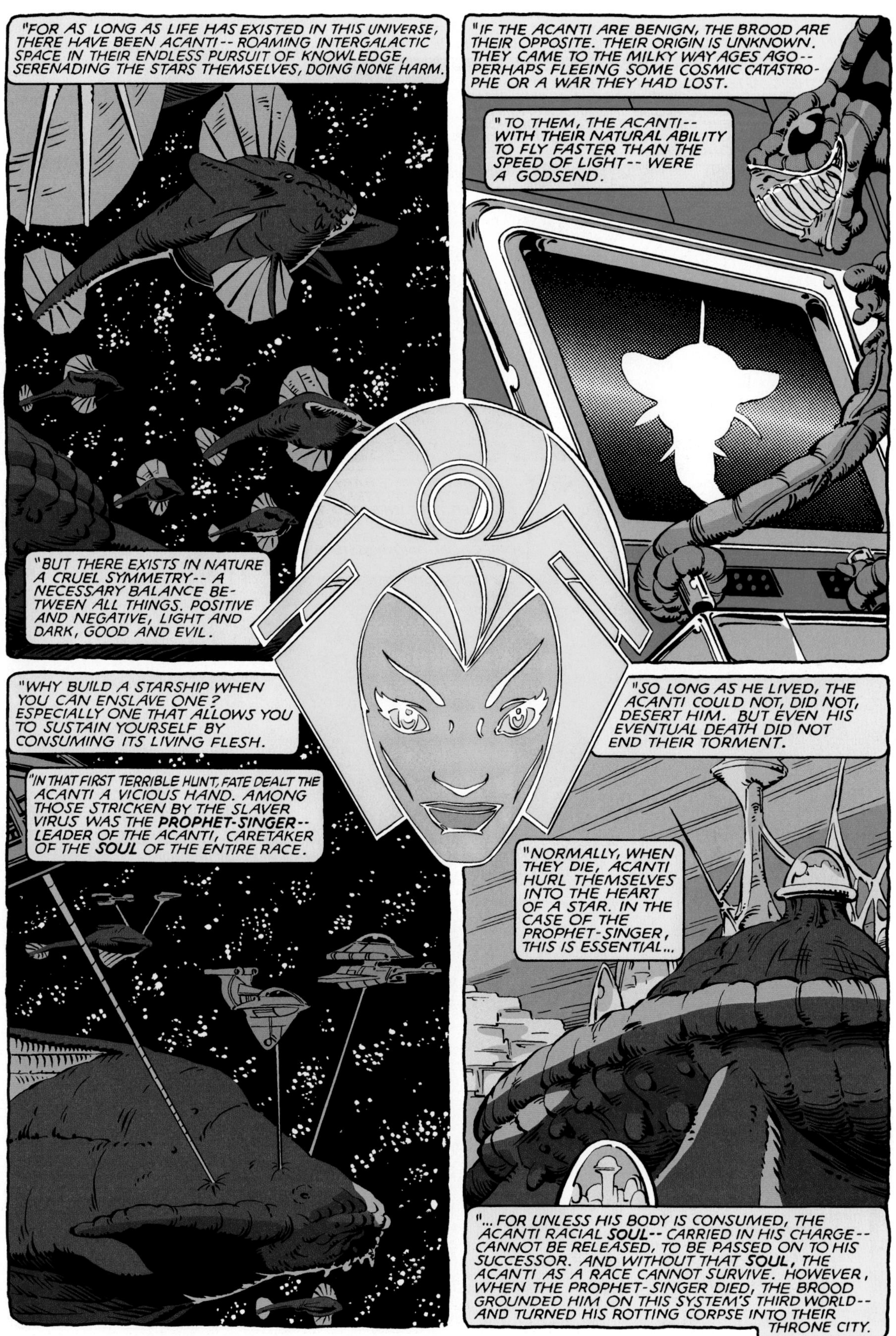
"FOR AS LONG AS LIFE HAS EXISTED IN THIS UNIVERSE, THERE HAVE BEEN ACANTI -- ROAMING INTERGALACTIC SPACE IN THEIR ENDLESS PURSUIT OF KNOWLEDGE, SERENADING THE STARS THEMSELVES, DOING NONE HARM.
"BUT THERE EXISTS IN NATURE A CRUEL SYMMETRY-- A NECESSARY BALANCE BETWEEN ALL THINGS. POSITIVE AND NEGATIVE, LIGHT AND DARK, GOOD AND EVIL.
"IF THE ACANTI ARE BENIGN, THE BROOD ARE THEIR OPPOSITE. THEIR ORIGIN IS UNKNOWN. THEY CAME TO THE MILKY WAY AGES AGO-- PERHAPS FLEEING SOME COSMIC CATASTROPHE OR A WAR THEY HAD LOST.
"TO THEM, THE ACANTI-- WITH THEIR NATURAL ABILITY TO FLY FASTER THAN THE SPEED OF LIGHT-- WERE A GODSEND.
"WHY BUILD A STARSHIP WHEN YOU CAN ENSLAVE ONE? ESPECIALLY ONE THAT ALLOWS YOU TO SUSTAIN YOURSELF BY CONSUMING ITS LIVING FLESH.
"IN THAT FIRST TERRIBLE HUNT, FATE DEALT THE ACANTI A VICIOUS HAND. AMONG THOSE STRICKEN BY THE SLAVER VIRUS WAS THE PROPHET-SINGER-- LEADER OF THE ACANTI, CARETAKER OF THE SOUL OF THE ENTIRE RACE.
"SO LONG AS HE LIVED, THE ACANTI COULD NOT, DID NOT, DESERT HIM. BUT EVEN HIS EVENTUAL DEATH DID NOT END THEIR TORMENT.
"NORMALLY, WHEN THEY DIE, ACANTI HURL THEMSELVES INTO THE HEART OF A STAR. IN THE CASE OF THE PROPHET-SINGER, THIS IS ESSENTIAL...
"... FOR UNLESS HIS BODY IS CONSUMED, THE ACANTI RACIAL SOUL-- CARRIED IN HIS CHARGE-- CANNOT BE RELEASED, TO BE PASSED ON TO HIS SUCCESSOR. AND WITHOUT THAT SOUL, THE ACANTI AS A RACE CANNOT SURVIVE. HOWEVER, WHEN THE PROPHET-SINGER DIED, THE BROOD GROUNDED HIM ON THIS SYSTEM'S THIRD WORLD-- AND TURNED HIS ROTTING CORPSE INTO THEIR THRONE CITY.

"THE SOUL REMAINS TRAPPED WITHIN THE CARCASS -- AND THE ACANTI REMAIN BOUND TO IT. DOOMED IF THEY LEAVE, DOOMED IF THEY REMAIN.
"THEN, AFTER AEONS IN BONDAGE, THE SURVIVORS -- THE PITIFULLY FEW ACANTI WHO HAD MANAGED TO ELUDE THE BROOD HUNTING CADRES -- WERE SWEPT BY A BURST OF HOPE. A PROPHET-SINGER, THE FIRST IN GENERATIONS, HAD BEEN CONCEIVED.
"BUT BEFORE THE BABY COULD COME TO TERM, HIS MOTHER WAS INFECTED WITH THE SLAVER VIRUS. RATHER THAN RISK HER SON'S INFECTION AND POSSIBLE ENSLAVEMENT...
"...SHE GAVE PREMATURE BIRTH.
"IT WAS SHE WHOM YOU FOUND ON MADRIZAR, CAROL, HER LIFE YOU BROUGHT TO A MERCIFUL END.
"BUT THE BABY HAD BEEN BORN TOO SOON. IT WAS TOO FRAGILE TO SURVIVE -- ITS MIND UNABLE YET TO COPE WITH THE DEMANDS PLACED UPON IT -- EVEN WITH THE AID OF ITS ADULT BRETHREN. THAT WAS WHEN THE ACANTI FOUND ME, FLOATING THROUGH SPACE, IN THE LAST MOMENTS OF MY OWN LIFE.
"THEY BONDED ME INTO A PHYSICAL AND PSYCHIC RAPPORT WITH THE INFANT. I PROVIDE THE AWARENESS, THE CONSCIOUS DIRECTION -- THE... WILL -- NECESSARY TO SUSTAIN HIM, UNTIL HIS OWN MIND DEVELOPS SUFFICIENTLY TO HANDLE THAT RESPONSIBILITY.
"IN RETURN, HIS BODY'S NATURAL HEALING ABILITIES RESTORE MY BODY TO HEALTH.

THUS IS A CRITICAL PERSONAL BALANCE RESTORED. AS "GODDESS" AND WOMAN, I AM CONSECRATED TO LIFE, SWORN TO PRESERVE IT. YET I DESTROYED THE QUEEN EMBRYO IMPLANTED WITHIN ME.
NOW, HOWEVER, I HAVE AN OPPORTUNITY TO SAVE AN EQUALLY HELPLESS LIFE. TO GIVE INSTEAD OF TAKE.

AND WHAT I DO FOR ONE, THE X-MEN MIGHT DO FOR AN ENTIRE RACE.
IF WE CAN RELEASE THE SOUL, SO THAT IT CAN BE PASSED ON TO THIS CHILD, HE CAN THEN LEAD THE ACANTI TO SAFETY.
WHERE DO WE FIND THIS SOUL, 'RORO?

IN THE HEAD OF THE SKELETON, AT ITS BASE.
FIGURES. I BEEN THERE, DARLIN'-- SOME VERY NASTY CRITTERS CLAIM THAT TURF, BEINGS EVEN THE BROOD ARE SCARED OF.
IN THAT CASE, LOGAN, WE OUGHT TO FIT RIGHT IN.

MY FRIENDS, I AM TIRED OF RUNNING, AND OF BEING A VICTIM. IF I AM TO DIE, I WOULD PREFER TO DO IT FIGHTING FOR SOMETHING, RATHER THAN AGAINST.
LET US SAVE THE ACANTI, IF WE CAN.
CAN WE, GUYS? PLEASE?

I THINK WE'RE AGREED ON THIS. BUT HOW TO BEST ACCOMPLISH THAT OBJECTIVE?
SUPPOSE STORM AND BINARY CREATE A DIVERSION, TO DRAW AS MUCH OF THE BROOD'S ATTENTION, AND THE BATTLE FLEET, AS POSSIBLE, AWAY FROM THE PLANET. SIMULTANEOUSLY, THE REST OF US BEAM DOWN TO THE SKELETON TO MAKE A RUN FOR THE SOUL.
IF WE KEEP LILANDRA'S YACHT HERE INSIDE THE BABY, THE SHIP'S SHIELDS MASKING IT FROM BROOD SENSORS, THEY'LL HAVE NO IDEA THE X-MEN ARE INVOLVED. WE COULD FINISH THE JOB BEFORE THEY'RE EVEN AWARE OF US.

SOUNDS FEASIBLE. BUT I'D PREFER IT IF CAROL'N' I DID THE DIRTSIDE WORK, WHILE YOU AN' THE OTHERS STAY UP HERE WITH STORM.
WHY?
BECAUSE WE'RE FREE OF THE IMPLANTS, CYKE. WE THREE ARE THE ONLY PEOPLE WE CAN TRUST.
YOU ALL SEEM NORMAL--BUT THAT COULD CHANGE. ANYTIME. ANYWHERE. IF IT'S IN THE MIDDLE OF THIS CAPER, IN A FIREFIGHT, IT COULD MAKE ALL THE DIFFER-ENCE.
SO WHY NOT COVER YOURSELF BEFORE YOU EVEN BEGIN? YOU'VE GOT CLAWS, WOLVERINE. USE 'EM! IF THAT'S HOW YOU FEEL--
--KILL US NOW!
THAT WAY, NEITHER YOU NOR WE WILL HAVE ANYTHING MORE TO FEAR!
THIS IS THE MOMENT I'VE BEEN WAITIN' FOR-- AN' DREADIN'. I CAN'T SAVE 'EM. I SWORE I'D SEE 'EM DEAD BEFORE I'D ALLOW THEIR METAMORPHOSIS INTO SLEAZ-OIDS. EACH SECOND I DELAY INCREASES THE RISK THAT I'LL FAIL. SO WHY DO I HESITATE?
THEY'RE MY FRIENDS!
WELL, MISTER, WHAT'LL IT BE?
"AN' BECAUSE THEY ARE MY FRIENDS, I OWE 'EM LIFE...
"... OR A QUICK, CLEAN DEATH."
NO!!
SNIKT!

STOP IT, BOTH OF YOU-- STOP IT!
STAND ASIDE, KITTY. LET THE LITTLE MAN DO WHAT HE DOES BEST. IT IS THE SENSIBLE, REASONABLE THING TO DO, RIGHT, WOLVERINE?
SHUT UP, SCOTT! THAT'S CRAZY!

LOGAN, I KNOW WHAT'S HAPPENING INSIDE ME. I'VE NEVER BEEN SO SCARED. BUT I'M NOT GONNA GIVE UP. MAYBE THIS IS A HOPELESS FIGHT, BUT I WON'T QUIT.
AND PART OF NOT QUITTING MEANS STANDING BESIDE MY FELLOW X-MEN, ALL OF US, TOGETHER TO THE END-- AS A TEAM, LOGAN! A FAMILY!
IF WE MEAN ANYTHING TO EACH OTHER-- IF BEING AN X-MAN MEANS ANYTHING-- THIS IS WHERE AND HOW WE PROVE IT!
I'M NOT ARGUIN', KID--THIS WAS CYKE'S CHALLENGE.

OBJECTION NOTED--AND OVERRULED, WOLVERINE. WE'LL USE MY PLAN.
MY APOLOGIES, ORORO, FOR USURPING YOUR ROLE AS TEAM LEADER.
YOU WERE MY PREDECESSOR, SCOTT, AND, AT THE MOMENT, I AM IN NO POSITION TO LEAD.
TELL ME, CAN YOU UTILIZE YOUR WEATHER POWERS IN THIS ACANTI FORM?

I BELIEVE SO, BUT THERE IS CONSIDERABLE RISK. MY HUMAN BODY IS STILL IN CRITICAL CONDITION. IT MIGHT NOT SURVIVE THE STRAIN.
IF IT DOES NOT, MY CONSCIOUSNESS WILL REMAIN TRAPPED IN THIS FORM.

I HATE TO ASK THIS OF YOU, BUT SHOULD IT BECOME NECESSARY FOR US TO CALL ON THOSE ABILITIES...
I CANNOT PLACE THIS CHILD IN DANGER, SCOTT-- BUT, ASIDE FROM THAT...

...I WILL DO WHAT MUST BE DONE...
...WHATEVER THE COST.

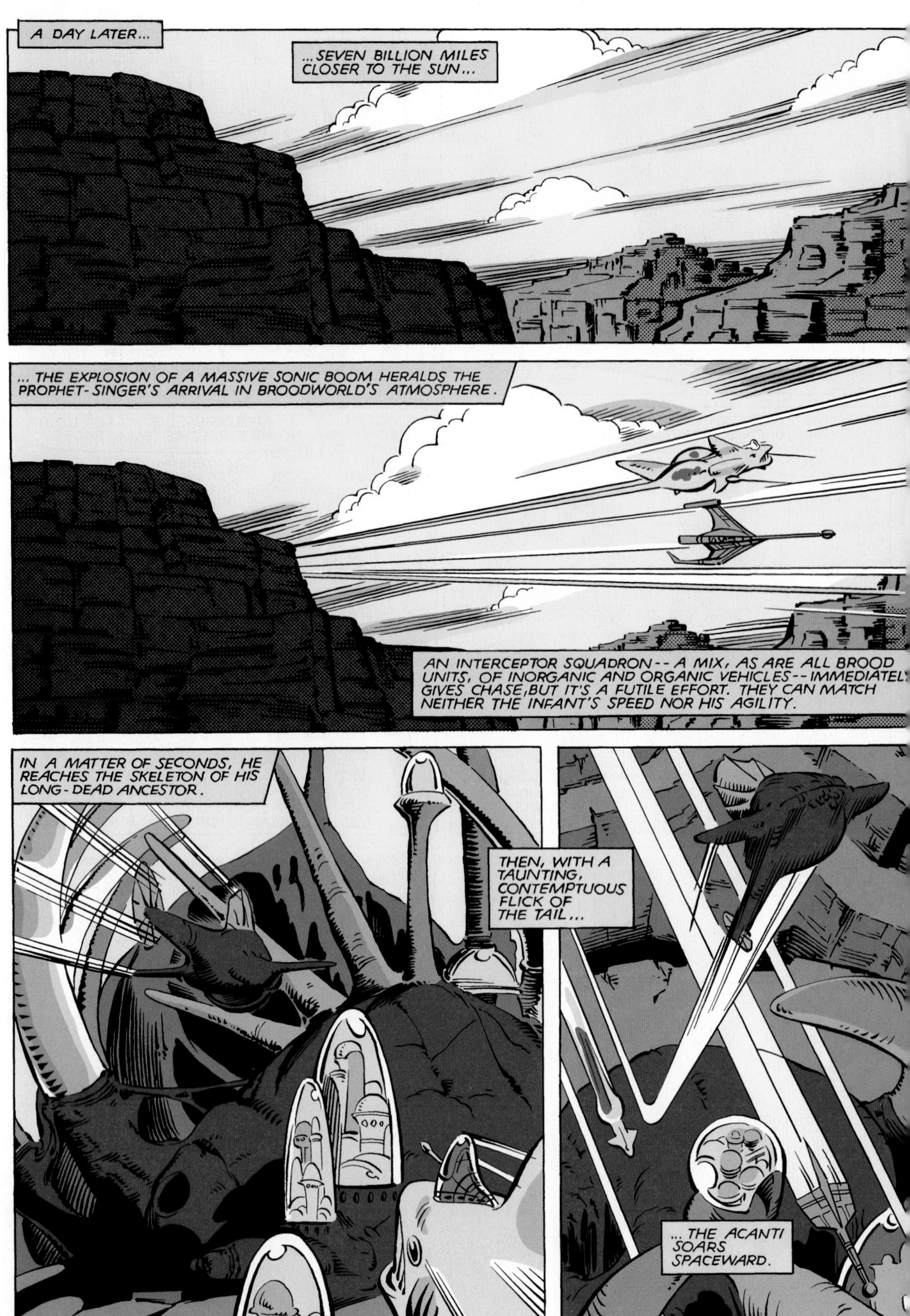
A DAY LATER...
...SEVEN BILLION MILES CLOSER TO THE SUN...
...THE EXPLOSION OF A MASSIVE SONIC BOOM HERALDS THE PROPHET-SINGER'S ARRIVAL IN BROODWORLD'S ATMOSPHERE.
AN INTERCEPTOR SQUADRON--A MIX, AS ARE ALL BROOD UNITS, OF INORGANIC AND ORGANIC VEHICLES--IMMEDIATELY GIVES CHASE, BUT IT'S A FUTILE EFFORT. THEY CAN MATCH NEITHER THE INFANT'S SPEED NOR HIS AGILITY.
IN A MATTER OF SECONDS, HE REACHES THE SKELETON OF HIS LONG-DEAD ANCESTOR.
THEN, WITH A TAUNTING, CONTEMPTUOUS FLICK OF THE TAIL...
...THE ACANTI SOARS SPACEWARD.

WHILE, WITHIN HIM...
I RECEIVED THE APPROVAL OF THE ACANTI ELDERS BEFORE AGREEING TO SCOTT'S PLAN--BUT SUPPOSE SOMETHING GOES WRONG? IF WE--IF... I--FAIL, IT WILL MEAN THE DESTRUCTION NOT ONLY OF THIS INNOCENT CHILD BUT OF ALL THE ACANTI'S HOPES AND DREAMS.
AND YET, WHAT REAL ALTERNATIVE HAVE WE?
NICE RIDE, DARLIN'
REMIND ME TO PICK UP MY STOMACH ON THE WAY BACK.
REPORT TO THE TRANSPORTER ROOM, X-MEN.
IT'S TIME TO GO.
YOU HEARD THE EMPRESS, PEOPLE--
--MOVE OUT!
RELAX, BUB. WE KNOW WHAT TO DO.

HAVE YOU CHECKED YOUR CALCULATIONS, LILANDRA? ACCURACY IS ESSENTIAL. THE SLIGHTEST ERROR COULD MATERIALIZE US INSIDE THE PLANET OR HUNDREDS OF FEET UP IN THE AIR.
CYCLOPS! LILANDRA'S AN EMPRESS! YOU SHOULDN'T TALK TO HER LIKE THAT!
HMNH! I THOUGHT, WOLVERINE, MEIN FREUND, THAT YOU WERE OUR MASTER OF TACT AND DIPLOMACY.
CYCLOPS DOES SEEM TO BE TAKING HIS RESPONSIBILITIES RATHER SERIOUSLY.
SURE DOES, ELF.
I KNOW THE DANGERS, CYCLOPS, AND HAVE COMPENSATED FOR THEM.

IF YOU ARE AFRAID, STAY ABOARD.
I'M A CAREFUL MAN, MAJESTRIX.
I DON'T WANT ANY OF US HURT.

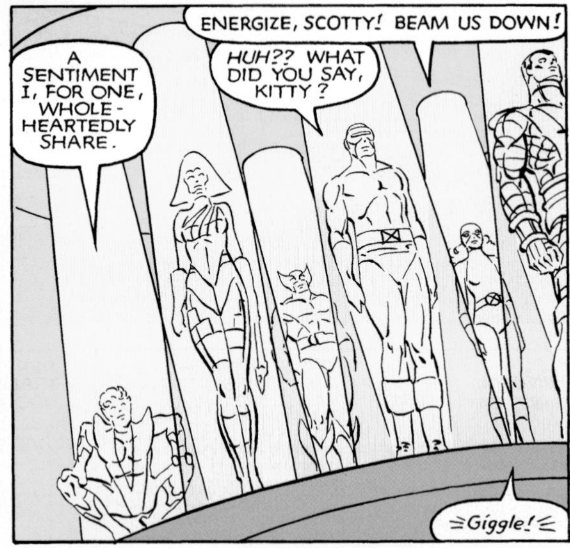
A SENTIMENT I, FOR ONE, WHOLE-HEARTEDLY SHARE.
ENERGIZE, SCOTTY! BEAM US DOWN!
HUH?? WHAT DID YOU SAY, KITTY?
Giggle!

BEFORE THE SOUND OF KITTY'S LAUGHTER FADES, THE ACANTI IS BEYOND THE ORBITS OF BROODWORLD'S INNER MOONS...
... AND DESPITE HERSELF, ORORO LUXURIATES IN THE SENSUAL JOY OF FLIGHT-- A TREAT DENIED FOR FAR TOO LONG-- FEELING THE GENTLE CARESS OF THE SOLAR WIND, THE FLUX AND FLOW OF MYRIAD ENERGY FIELDS AS THEY COURSE AROUND AND THROUGH HER.

A DISTURBANCE IN THOSE FIELDS DRAWS HER ATTENTION AFT-- AND SHE SMILES IN GRIM SATISFACTION.
THE BROOD HAVE TAKEN THE BAIT.

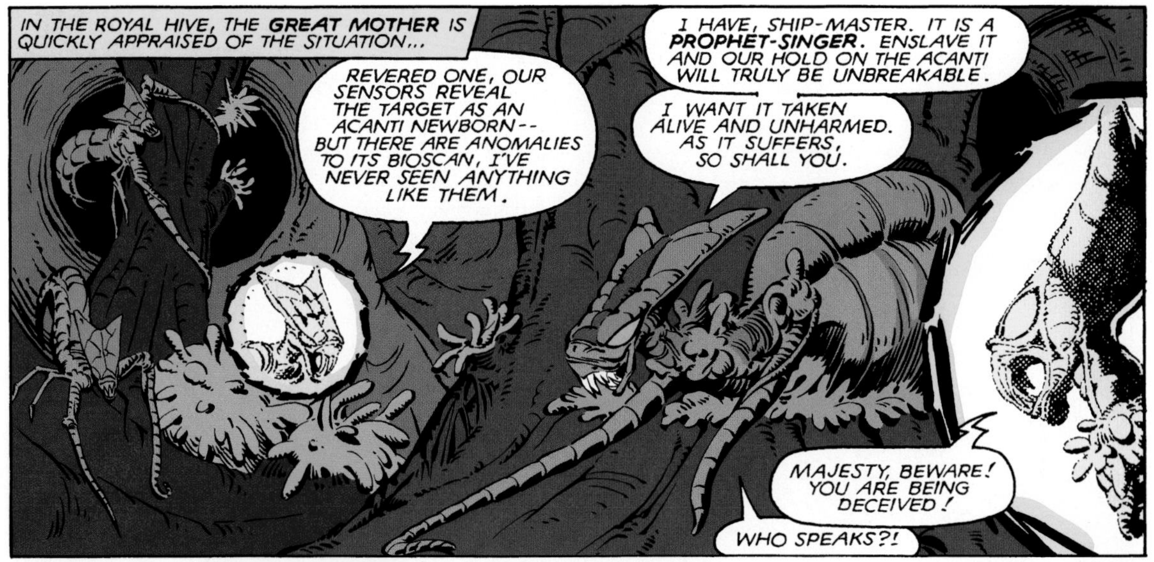
IN THE ROYAL HIVE, THE GREAT MOTHER IS QUICKLY APPRAISED OF THE SITUATION...
REVERED ONE, OUR SENSORS REVEAL THE TARGET AS AN ACANTI NEWBORN-- BUT THERE ARE ANOMALIES TO ITS BIOSCAN, I'VE NEVER SEEN ANYTHING LIKE THEM.
I HAVE, SHIP-MASTER. IT IS A PROPHET-SINGER. ENSLAVE IT AND OUR HOLD ON THE ACANTI WILL TRULY BE UNBREAKABLE.
I WANT IT TAKEN ALIVE AND UNHARMED. AS IT SUFFERS, SO SHALL YOU.
MAJESTY, BEWARE! YOU ARE BEING DECEIVED!
WHO SPEAKS?!

DO YOU NOT RECOGNIZE ONE OF YOUR OWN PROGENY?
WHILE YOUR FLEET CHASES THE ACANTI WHELP...

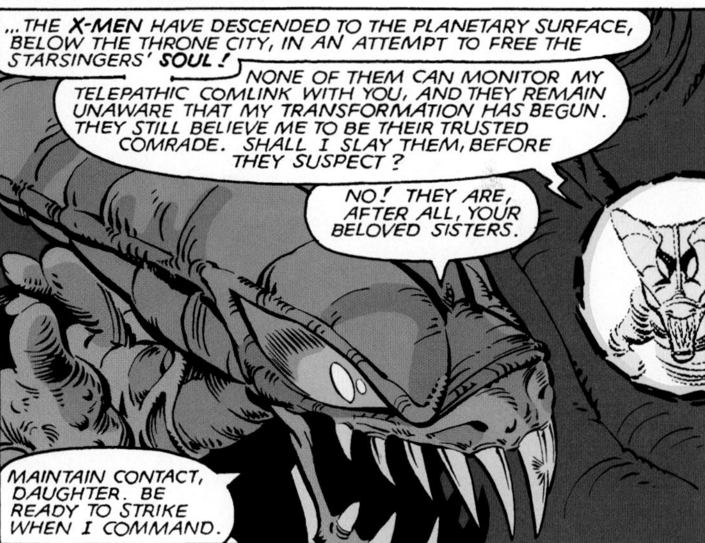
...THE X-MEN HAVE DESCENDED TO THE PLANETARY SURFACE, BELOW THE THRONE CITY, IN AN ATTEMPT TO FREE THE STARSINGERS' SOUL!
NONE OF THEM CAN MONITOR MY TELEPATHIC COMLINK WITH YOU, AND THEY REMAIN UNAWARE THAT MY TRANSFORMATION HAS BEGUN. THEY STILL BELIEVE ME TO BE THEIR TRUSTED COMRADE. SHALL I SLAY THEM, BEFORE THEY SUSPECT?
NO! THEY ARE, AFTER ALL, YOUR BELOVED SISTERS.
MAINTAIN CONTACT, DAUGHTER. BE READY TO STRIKE WHEN I COMMAND.

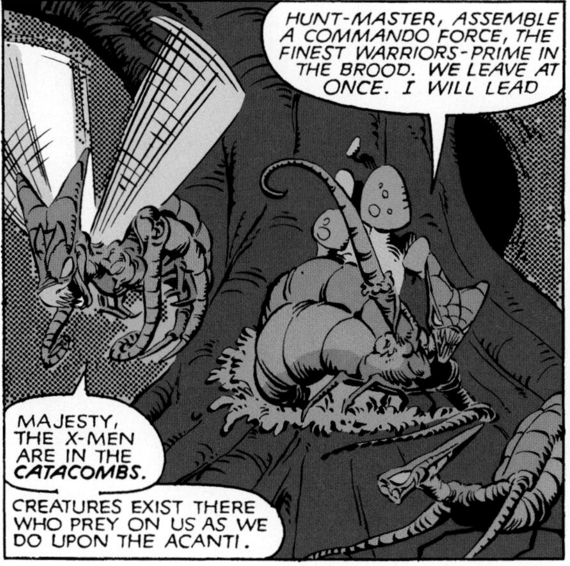
HUNT-MASTER, ASSEMBLE A COMMANDO FORCE, THE FINEST WARRIORS-PRIME IN THE BROOD. WE LEAVE AT ONCE. I WILL LEAD
MAJESTY, THE X-MEN ARE IN THE CATACOMBS.
CREATURES EXIST THERE WHO PREY ON US AS WE DO UPON THE ACANTI.

I OFFER A CHOICE, HUNT-MASTER: FACE THEIR WRATH--
--OR MINE.

MEANWHILE...
YUCK!
UNGLAUBLICH! THIS PLACE SMELLS WORSE THAN IT LOOKS, AND IT LOOKS AWFUL.

I WANT TO GO HOME.
SMART KID.
COLD FEET, WOLVERINE? I DIDN'T THINK ANYTHING COULD SPOOK YOU.
YOU WANT TO MAKE SMART REMARKS, BUB, WAIT'LL WE'VE MET THE OPPOSITION.
WHERE DO WE GO FROM HERE?

DOWN.
STORM TELEPATHICALLY KEYED ME INTO THE SOUL'S "SCENT." MY ENHANCED SENSES ARE ALREADY LOCKING IN ON IT.
STAY CLOSE AN' STAY READY. THE PLANTS ARE JUST AS DANGEROUS AS THE ANIMALS, AN' THE TWILIGHT DARKNESS O' THESE TUNNELS WORKS IN THEIR FAVOR.
I WONDER HOW ORORO'S DOING?
I HOPE SHE AND BINARY ARE OKAY.
THEY CAN TAKE CARE O' THEMSELVES, PUN'KIN. YOU MAKE SURE YOU DO THE SAME.

AT THAT MOMENT, OUT IN SPACE...
WE ARE GAINING ON THE INFANT, SHIP-MASTER!

EXCELLENT. FOR ALL ITS ABILITIES, THE CHILD LACKS THE ENDURANCE OF OUR ADULT VESSELS.
WEAPONEER, AS SOON AS WE ARE WITHIN RANGE, OPEN FIRE.
NEW CONTACT, SIR!...

...MOVING BETWEEN US AND THE ACANTI!
IDENTIFY!
UNKNOWN, SIR! BUT ITS ENERGY READINGS ARE OFF MY SCALE!

WHATEVER THAT THING IS, IT GLOWS-- LIKE A STAR!
BATTLE SCREENS TO MAXIMUM STRENGTH! WEAPONEER, BLAST IT OUT OF SPACE!

THE ORDERS COME TOO LATE...
... AS DOES THE REALIZATION THAT, THIS TIME, THE BROOD ARE NOT HUNTERS, BUT PREY.

BINARY DRAWS FIRST-BLOOD.

CAROL WAS TRAINED AS A WARRIOR-- AS WERE WOLVERINE AND LILANDRA.
KILLING IS A FACT OF THEIR LIVES, A NECESSARY REALITY.
TO ME, THOUGH, IT IS ANATHEMA.

I HATE THE BROOD WITH EVERY FIBRE OF MY BEING...
...YET STILL I MUST FIND ANOTHER WAY.
ORORO'S PERCEPTIONS SUBTLY ALTER THE UNIVERSE WE SEE...

...EMPTY SPACE, BRIGHT STARS, SOLID PLANETS--
--BECOME A MULTI-COLORED PANORAMA FILLED WITH CONSTANTLY-SHIFTING PATTERNS OF ENERGY...

...PRIMAL NATURAL FORCES WHICH STORM SHAPES AS A SCULPTRESS DOES HER CLAY. IT ISN'T EASY. IN SPACE, THE ELEMENTS ARE MUCH MORE POWERFUL THAN IN A PLANETARY ATMOSPHERE, THE STRENGTH REQUIRED TO MANIPULATE THEM CORRESPONDINGLY GREATER.
AT HER COMMAND, LIGHTNING FLARES STAR-BRIGHT IN THE DARKNESS, TO STUN A BROODSHIP AND ALL ABOARD.
SHE GOES BLIND WITH PAIN-- SENSES AN AWFUL TEARING DEEP WITHIN AS HER STILL-HEALING HUMAN BODY IS PUSHED FAR BEYOND ITS LIMITS-- YET SHE DOES NOT RELENT.

WHILE, IN THE CATACOMBS...
...NIGHTCRAWLER SKITTERS ALONG THE WALLS, TELEPORTING IN AND OUT OF HARM'S WAY, USING HIS ACROBAT'S AGILITY TO HANDLE AS MANY FOES AS POSSIBLE.
COLOSSUS, HIS ARMORED FORM COMPOSED OF SUPER-STRONG, NIGH-INVULNERABLE ORGANIC STEEL, RESORTS TO BRUTE FORCE.
WOLVERINE USES HIS CLAWS.

KITTY TRIES TO HELP, THEN SUDDENLY DISCOVERS SHE HAS TROUBLES OF HER OWN.
YI'LLLP!
FOR AN INSTANT, SHE'S TOO SCARED TO REACT.

THEN, HER TRAINING TAKES OVER...
... AND SHE PHASES THROUGH THE WALL, OUT OF THE CREATURE'S GRASP.

IN THE GENERAL MELÉE, HER ABRUPT DEPARTURE GOES UNNOTICED.
THIS IS ONLY THE BEGINNIN', CYKE. THINGS GET HAIRIER, THE DEEPER WE GO.
YOU WANT TO QUIT, LITTLE MAN -- BE MY GUEST.
WHAT GIVES?! HE AN' I'RE SNIPIN' LIKE WE DID IN THE OLD DAYS, WHEN WE HATED EACH OTHER'S GUTS.
AN' TALK ABOUT ROLE-REVERSAL-- I'M S'POSED T' BE THE PSYCHO-KILLER AN' HIM THE BOSS. BUT HE'S SCRAPPIN' LIKE A BERSERKER AN' LEAVIN' ME T' CALL THE SHOTS.

ELSEWHERE ...
OWW!
NEXT TIME, I REALLY MUST WATCH WHERE I'M PHASING.
I SLIPPED NOT ONLY THROUGH THAT CREEPY-CRAWLY-- UGH!-- BUT THROUGH THE WALL IT WAS BASHING ME AGAINST. I MAY FLY THROUGH THE AIR WITH THE GREATEST OF EASE --

-- BUT MY LANDINGS LEAVE A BIT TO BE DESIRED.
WHERE AM I?
NOW THAT'S AN ORIGINAL LINE.

OH!
MY GOSH!
SLEAZOID SKELETONS -- SCATTERED ALL OVER THE PLACE. PICKED CLEAN, TOO. Uh-oh -- SOME OF THE BONES ARE SHINY. THEY MUST HAVE BEEN PRETTY RECENT KILLS.

THIS IS A NEST. WITH EGGS IN IT. AND ONE OF 'EM'S CRACKED OPEN.
GREAT.
THOSE SLEAZOIDS LOOK RIPPED TO SHREDS. IF WHATEVER LIVES HERE CAN DO THAT TO THEM, I SHUDDER TO THINK OF WHAT IT COULD DO TO ME.

SO WHY STICK AROUND TO FIND OUT?
USING HER PHASING POWER TO LITERALLY WALK ON AIR, KITTY HEADS FOR THE NEAREST EXIT...

...BLISSFULLY UNAWARE THAT SHE'S BEING WATCHED...
...AND FOLLOWED.

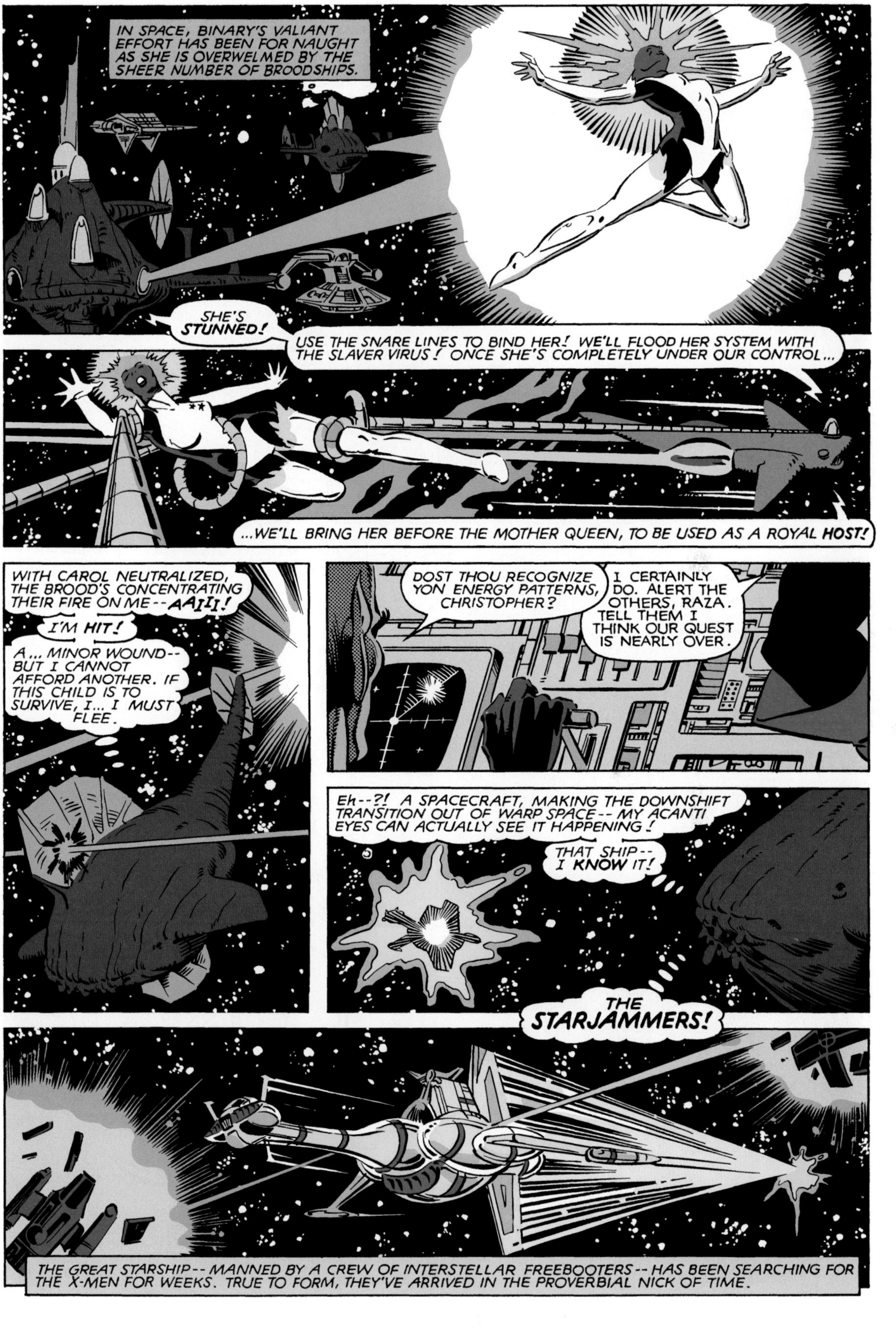

IN SPACE, BINARY'S VALIANT EFFORT HAS BEEN FOR NAUGHT AS SHE IS OVERWELMED BY THE SHEER NUMBER OF BROODSHIPS.

SHE'S **STUNNED!**

USE THE SNARE LINES TO BIND HER! WE'LL FLOOD HER SYSTEM WITH THE SLAVER VIRUS! ONCE SHE'S COMPLETELY UNDER OUR CONTROL...

...WE'LL BRING HER BEFORE THE MOTHER QUEEN, TO BE USED AS A ROYAL **HOST!**

WITH CAROL NEUTRALIZED, THE BROOD'S CONCENTRATING THEIR FIRE ON ME--**AAIII!**
I'M **HIT!**
A... MINOR WOUND--BUT I CANNOT AFFORD ANOTHER. IF THIS CHILD IS TO SURVIVE, I... I MUST FLEE.

DOST THOU RECOGNIZE YON ENERGY PATTERNS, CHRISTOPHER?
I CERTAINLY DO. ALERT THE OTHERS, RAZA. TELL THEM I THINK OUR QUEST IS NEARLY OVER.

Eh--?! A SPACECRAFT, MAKING THE DOWNSHIFT TRANSITION OUT OF WARP SPACE-- MY ACANTI EYES CAN ACTUALLY SEE IT HAPPENING!
THAT SHIP-- I **KNOW** IT!
THE **STARJAMMERS!**

THE GREAT STARSHIP-- MANNED BY A CREW OF INTERSTELLAR FREEBOOTERS-- HAS BEEN SEARCHING FOR THE X-MEN FOR WEEKS. TRUE TO FORM, THEY'VE ARRIVED IN THE PROVERBIAL NICK OF TIME.

THAT IS, TO SAVE STORM.
CYKE, WHERE'S KITTY?! I HAVEN'T SEEN HER IN A WHILE!
SHE KNEW THE RISKS, AND ACCEPTED THEM.
BUT IF YOU'RE SO CONCERNED, WOLVERINE, WHY DON'T YOU GO LOOK FOR HER.

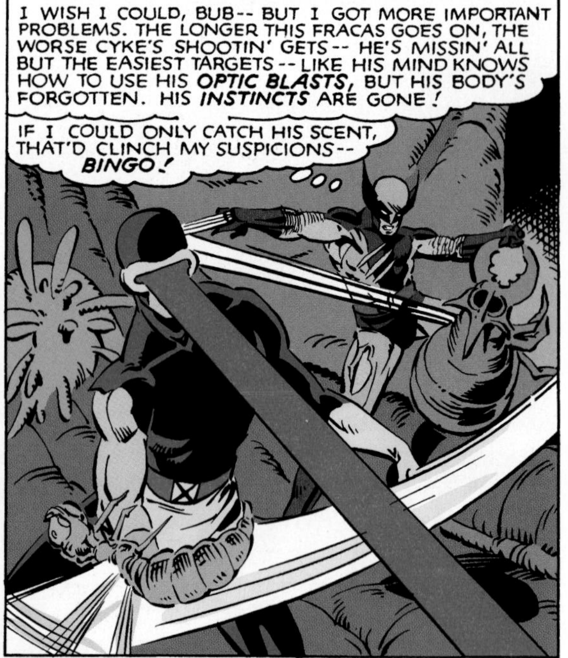
I WISH I COULD, BUB-- BUT I GOT MORE IMPORTANT PROBLEMS. THE LONGER THIS FRACAS GOES ON, THE WORSE CYKE'S SHOOTIN' GETS-- HE'S MISSIN' ALL BUT THE EASIEST TARGETS--LIKE HIS MIND KNOWS HOW TO USE HIS OPTIC BLASTS, BUT HIS BODY'S FORGOTTEN. HIS INSTINCTS ARE GONE!
IF I COULD ONLY CATCH HIS SCENT, THAT'D CLINCH MY SUSPICIONS-- BINGO!

WOLVERINE! WHAT ARE YOU DOING?!
YOU MADMAN-- I'M NOT THE ENEMY!
WRONG, BUB. I'VE BEEN WORRYIN' SINCE WE STARTED ABOUT A TRAITOR IN THE GROUP--
--AN' I THINK I JUST FOUND ONE!

YOUR DISCOVERY WILL NOT SAVE YOU, HUMAN.
THE SAME TRANSFORMATION WHICH CLAIMS ME --
--WILL SOON CLAIM YOU ALL!
UNNNGNH!
WHUNNFFF!

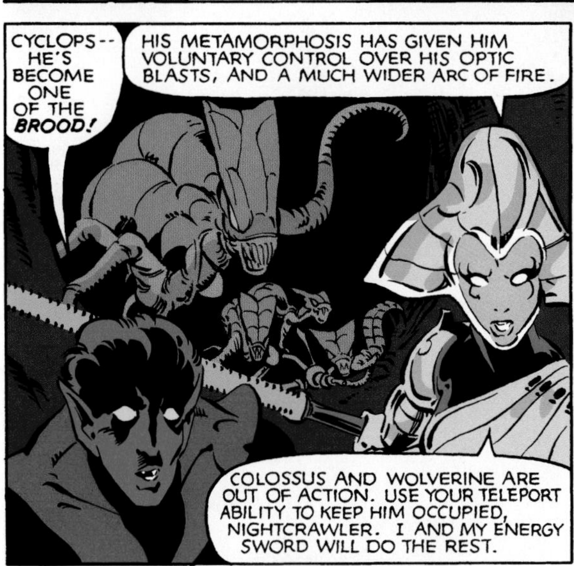
CYCLOPS-- HE'S BECOME ONE OF THE ***BROOD!***
HIS METAMORPHOSIS HAS GIVEN HIM VOLUNTARY CONTROL OVER HIS OPTIC BLASTS, AND A MUCH WIDER ARC OF FIRE.
COLOSSUS AND WOLVERINE ARE OUT OF ACTION. USE YOUR TELEPORT ABILITY TO KEEP HIM OCCUPIED, NIGHTCRAWLER. I AND MY ENERGY SWORD WILL DO THE REST.

NO, MAJESTRIX, I'M AFRAID YOU WON'T.

ZAP!

THE HOSTS ARE UNHARMED, REVERED MOTHER, AND BIOSCANS INDICATE THAT THE EMBRYOS ARE IN PERFECT CONDITION.
SPLENDID. SO NEAR THEIR GOAL--AND SUCCESS--AND YET SO FAR. SUCH A PITY.
I MUST CONFESS, DAUGHTER, THAT I AM IMPRESSED BY THE PROWESS OF YOUR COMPEERS. YOU MANAGED TO FRIGHTEN OFF THE PREDATORS THAT HAUNT THESE LOWER DEPTHS, A FEAT EVEN MY FINEST WARRIORS HAVE NEVER ACCOMPLISHED.
THEY'LL BE BACK.
BY WHICH TIME WE'LL BE LONG GONE.
WOLVERINE'S IMPLANT WAS DESTROYED. WILL YOU TRY AGAIN, OR SHALL I SLAY HIM?

NO, TO BOTH. HIS BODY'S MUTANT IMMUNE SYSTEM WILL AUTOMATICALLY ATTACK THAT EGG AS IT DID THE FIRST. AND I WANT THE PLEASURE OF KILLING HIM MYSELF. I SHALL EAT HIM ALIVE--HE WILL WATCH AS I CONSUME EACH SUCCULENT MORSEL.
FOR THE SERVICE YOU HAVE DONE ME, DAUGHTER, YOU MAY SHARE IN THE FEAST.
HUNT-MASTER, PREPARE THE PRISONERS FOR TRANSPORT. AS SOON AS WE RECAPTURE THE YOUNGLING, KITTY--
--WE WILL ASCEND TO THE ROYAL HIVE.

SPEAKING OF KITTY...
...SHE'S WONDERING IF LEAVING THE NEST WAS SUCH A GOOD IDEA.

THERE ARE SLEAZOIDS EVERY-WHERE! THESE TUNNELS ARE FULL OF 'EM!
I'VE BEEN ON THE RUN SINCE THEY SPOTTED ME. DON'T KNOW HOW MUCH LONGER I CAN KEEP UP THIS PACE.

I THINK I'M LOST, TOO.
WNGNUMFF!

I COULDN'T PHASE!
I MUST BE SO TIRED I CAN'T FOCUS THE PROPER CONCEN-TRATION!
OH, NO! THE SLEAZOIDS--!
HERE, BROTHERS!

IT WAS A MAGNIFICENT HUNT, BUT THE PRIZE IS AT LAST OURS!
AS A TRIBUTE TO YOUR COURAGE, LITTLE ONE, WE WOULD ORDINARILY FEAST ON YOUR LIVING HEART...
...BUT THE GREAT MOTHER WISHES YOU RETURNED TO HER ALIVE AND UNHARMED. PITY.

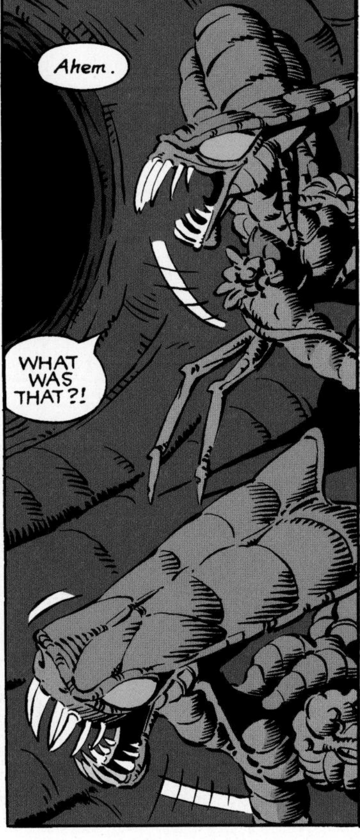
Ahem.
WHAT WAS THAT?!

BY THE BLACK NEBULA!!

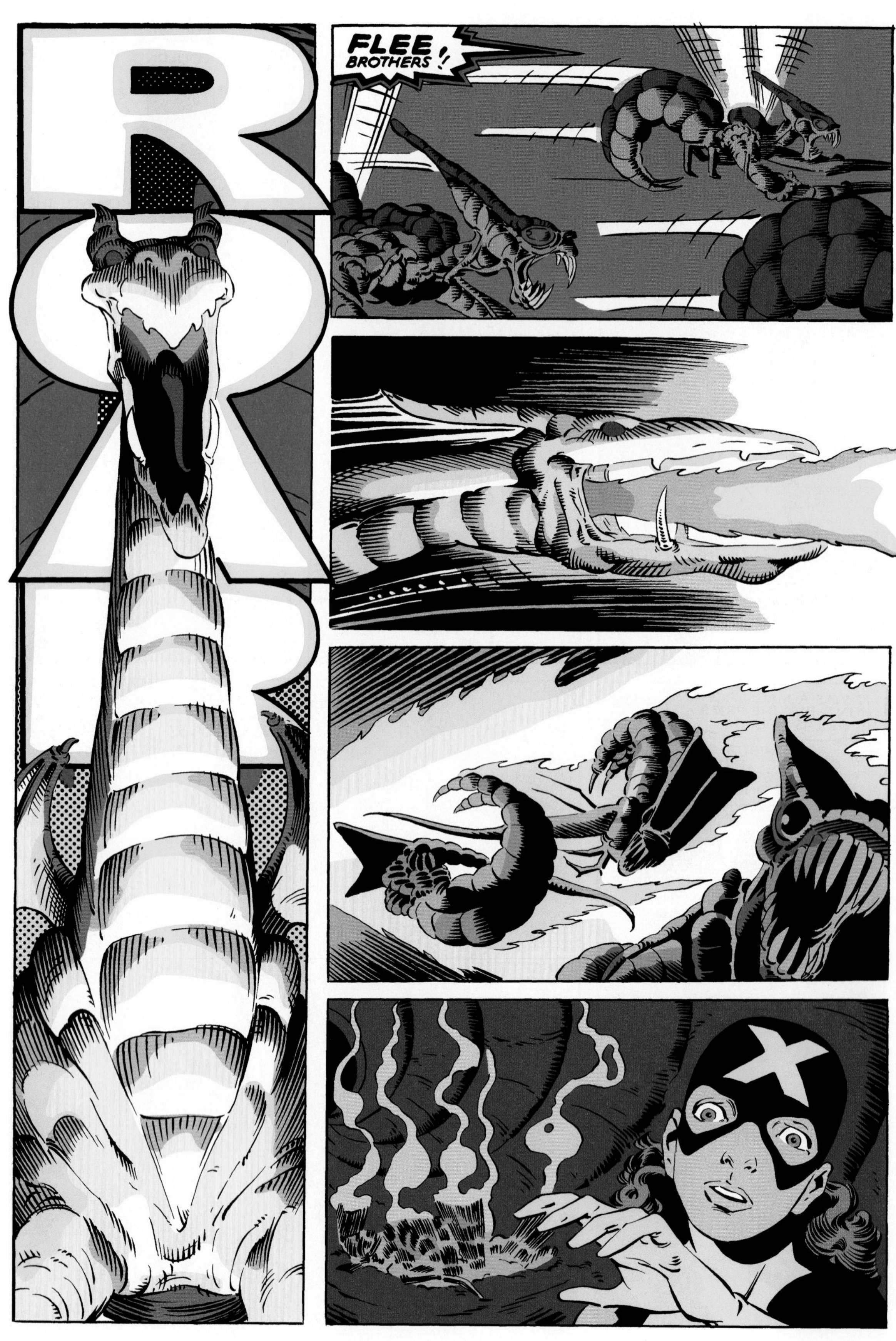
ROAR
FLEE BROTHERS!

FLAPFLAPFLAPFLAPFLAPFLAP
I DON'T BELIEVE THIS. ARE YOU FOR REAL? ARE YOU FRIENDLY?
YOU MUST BE. I'M STILL ALIVE.

YIKES!
LOOK OUT, DRAGON!

HUH--?!?

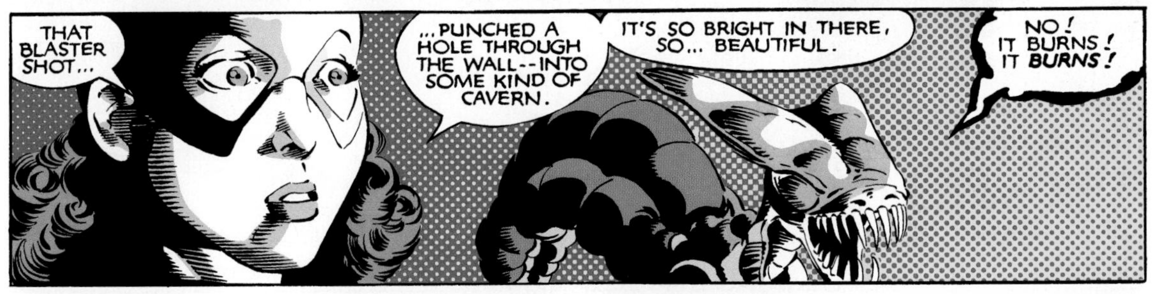
THAT BLASTER SHOT...
...PUNCHED A HOLE THROUGH THE WALL--INTO SOME KIND OF CAVERN.
IT'S SO BRIGHT IN THERE, SO... BEAUTIFUL.
NO! IT BURNS! IT BURNS!

WHAT ARE YOU TALKING ABOUT? THERE'S NO PAIN...
...ONLY MUSIC...
...CALLING TO ME...

THEY DISAPPEAR INTO THE BLINDING RADIANCE...
...AND, SECONDS LATER, THE SILENCE IS BROKEN BY A SCREAM.

NOT FAR AWAY...
REVERED MOTHER, WE HAVE LOST CONTACT WITH THE CADRE PURSUING THE YOUNGLING.
WHAT A SHAME. PERHAPS THEY RAN INTO SOMETHING THAT ATE THEM.
ENJOY YOUR DEFIANCE, MAJESTRIX-- FOR THE LITTLE TIME LEFT TO YOU. SOON, MIND AND BODY WILL CHANGE...
...AND YOUR TRUE SELVES WILL STAND REVEALED FOR ALL THE UNIVERSE TO BEHOLD. AND FEAR.

THAT MOMENT IS NEARER THAN YOU THINK.
AARRRGH!
M-MOTHER--I HURT! MAKE IT STOP, PLEASE!
ENDURE, DAUGHTER. IT IS YOUR HOST BODY...

...RESISTING THE METAMORPHOSIS...
GRAGKGH!
MY OPTIC BLASTS -- THEY'RE OUT OF CONTROL!

SLEAZOIDS DON'T HAVE EYELIDS. SCOTTY CAN'T BLOCK THE BEAMS NOW-- 'CEPT WITH HIS HANDS--
--AN' THE EMBRYO'S TOO INEXPERIENCED AN' PANICKED T' THINK O' THAT.
I GOT A CHANCE T' MAKE A MOVE.

WOLVERINE! I'VE KILLED HIM!

NOT HARDLY, BUB.
I MOVED SO A GLANCING BLOW FROM THOSE BEAMS O' CYKE'S WOULD TRASH MY SHACKLES.

IF I'D CAUGHT A FULL BLAST, I'D O' BEEN NOTHIN' BUT PULP AN' ADAMANTIUM BONES. IT WAS AN ALL-'R-NOTHIN' LONGSHOT-- MY KIND'A GAMBLE--

--AN' IT PAID OFF!
GOTTA MOVE FAST--HE'S GETTIN' THINGS BACK UNDER CONTROL.

BOY'S IN AGONY. I KNOW HOW HE FEELS. *
KRAK
*WOLVERINE UNDERWENT HIS OWN FORTUNATELY UNSUCCESSFUL META-MORPHOSIS IN X-MEN #162 -- L.

WISH I COULD PUT HIM OUTTA HIS MISERY-- BUT, FOR THE MOMENT, HE'S MORE USE T' ME ALIVE.
WARRIORS-- YIELD OR I POP MY CLAWS ON THE QUEEN AN' CYCLOPS BOTH.

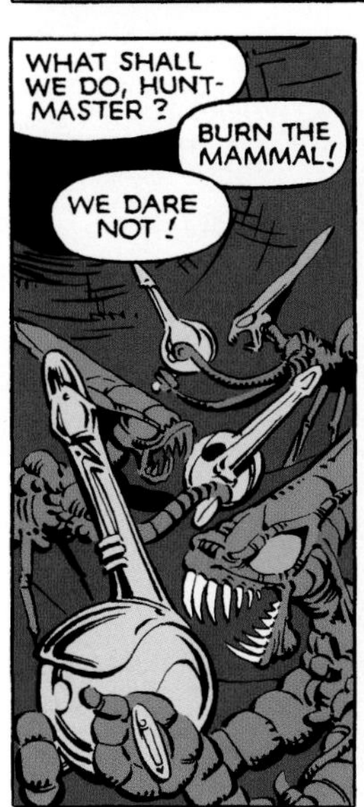
WHAT SHALL WE DO, HUNT-MASTER ?
BURN THE MAMMAL!
WE DARE NOT!

DROP THE WEAPONS, CREEPS--
--OR SHE DIES!

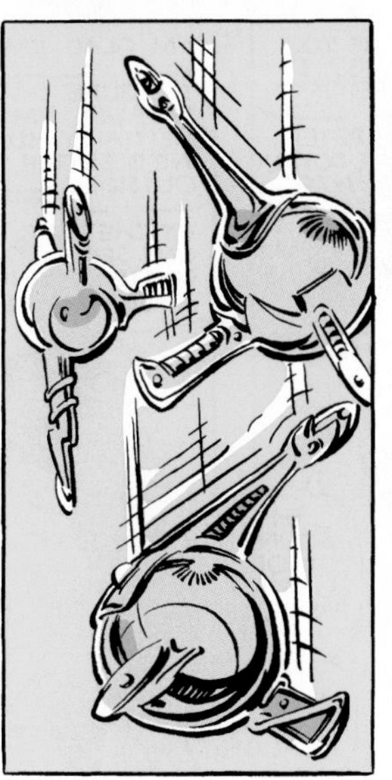

SMART MOVE.
NOW RELEASE THE X-MEN.

THE X-MEN COVER CYCLOPS' EYES WITH HIS VISOR, WHILE THE SHACKLES ARE USED TO BIND THE BROOD WARRIORS, WHO ARE THEN LEFT BEHIND AS OUR HEROES CONTINUE ON THROUGH THE CATACOMBS, UNTIL...
WE'VE ARRIVED, TROOPS.
I MARK KITTY'S SCENT--AN' A SLEAZOID'S--BOTH HEADIN' INTO THAT CAVERN.

YOU NEEDN'T WORRY ABOUT THE WARRIOR, WOLVERINE. THE SOUL JUDGED HIM AS IT DOES ALL WHO BEHOLD IT...
KITTY... ???

...AND FOUND HIM WANTING.
HEY, PUN'KIN, YOU ALL RIGHT?
SURE. IT'S JUST THAT WHAT I... SAW TAKES A LITTLE GETTING USED TO.
THE WARRIOR TURNED TO CRYSTAL, LOGAN, RIGHT BEFORE MY EYES. I FELT SO STRANGE THEN, I THOUGHT THE SAME THING WOULD HAPPEN TO ME, BUT IT DIDN'T.

AND YOU WEREN'T SCARED EVEN A BIT!
KATYA, I AM PROUD OF YOU!

ARE YOU KIDDING? I WAS PETRIFIED.
HEY! PETER, PUT ME DOWN! Giggle!
THAT SOUNDS MORE LIKE MY FAVORITE KITTEN.
IT IS GOOD TO HEAR YOU LAUGH.
I'M GLAD I'M STILL ABLE TO.
I FIGURE I WASN'T AFFECTED BECAUSE I'M STILL FUNDAMENTALLY HUMAN. BUT MAYBE WE'D BETTER LEAVE THE QUEEN OUTSIDE.
BY THE WAY, ANYONE SEE A LITTLE... CRITTER FLYING AROUND HERE?
NOPE. WHY?
Oh... NOTHING IMPORTANT.

X-MEN, YOU ARE FLESH OF MY FLESH. WHERE YOU GO...
...SO SHALL I.

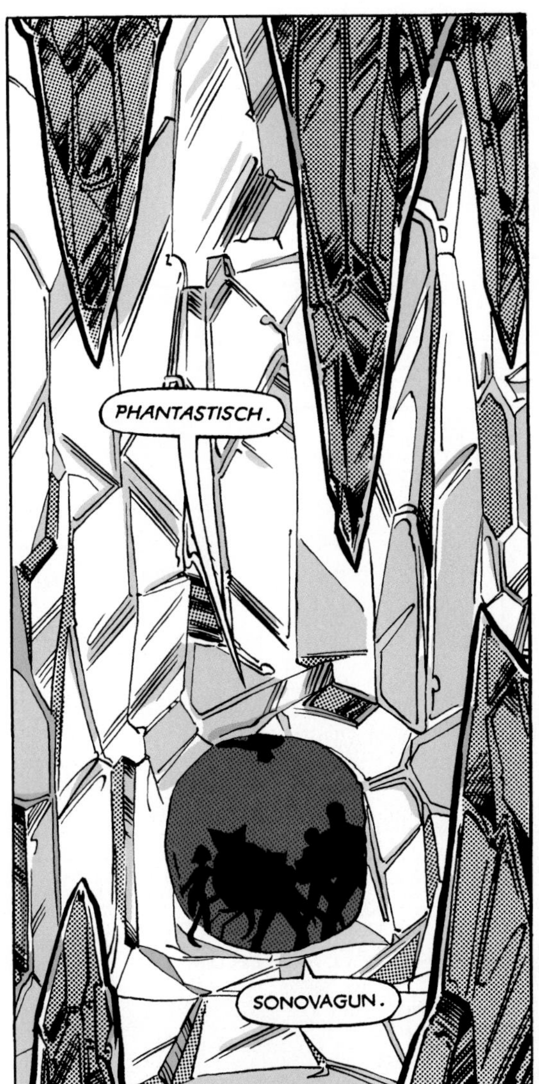
PHANTASTISCH.
SONOVAGUN.

CAN YOU FEEL THE LOVE, GUYS? WE'RE STRANGERS-- ALIENS--YET THE SOUL WELCOMES US.
WELCOMES YOU, PERHAPS, YOUNGLING--

--BUT I SENSE ONLY A HATRED AS DEEP AND ABIDING AS MY OWN.
BY THE WHITE WOLF!
COMRADES, LOOK AT THE CRYSTAL BENEATH THE QUEEN!

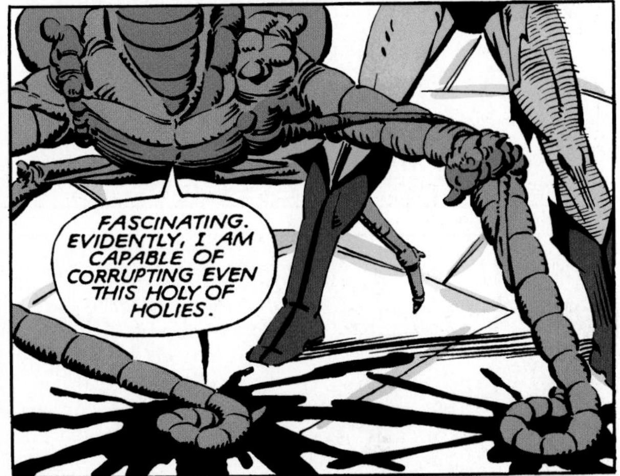
FASCINATING. EVIDENTLY, I AM CAPABLE OF CORRUPTING EVEN THIS HOLY OF HOLIES.

AND SO, IT SEEMS, ARE MY CHILDREN.
NO!
OUTTA HERE, EVERY-BODY-- BEFORE IT'S TOO LATE!

IT IS ALREADY TOO LATE, WOLVERINE, FOR THEM--
--AND YOU!
AAHHRRR!

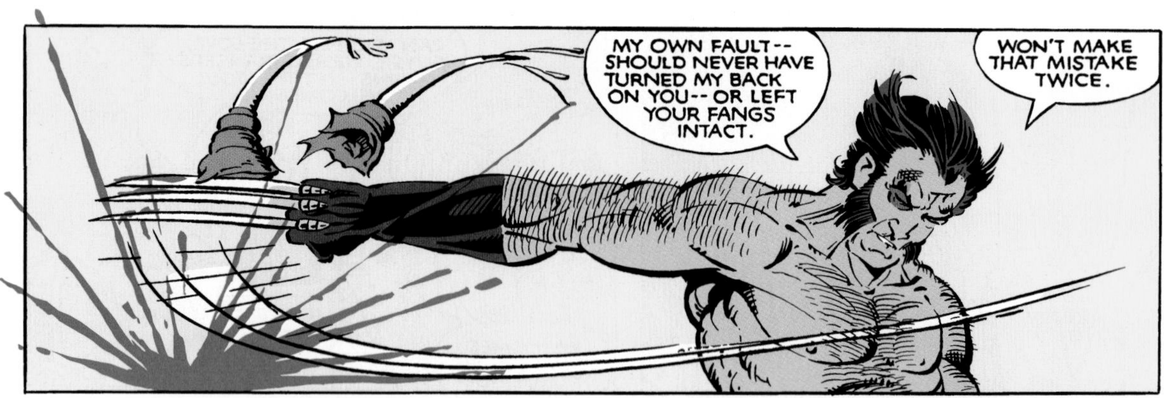
MY OWN FAULT-- SHOULD NEVER HAVE TURNED MY BACK ON YOU-- OR LEFT YOUR FANGS INTACT.
WON'T MAKE THAT MISTAKE TWICE.

TRUE, LITTLE MAN-- FOR YOU ARE ABOUT TO DIE.

NOT... YET, MAMA!
TOOK ONE HECKUVA JOLT-- MAYBE MORE VENOM THAN MY SYSTEM CAN HANDLE.

BUT I AIN'T LETTIN' THAT STOP ME. NOT 'TIL I'VE DONE...

A MAJESTIC SIGHT, IS IT NOT?
THE EMPATHIC RESONANCE OF THEIR METAMORPHOSIS ALREADY SATURATES THIS CHAMBER.
AS THEY ARE CONSUMED, SO SHALL THE ACANTI SOUL BE TRANSFORMED WITH THEM. NO LONGER WILL WE HAVE TO HUNT THE STARSINGERS. THEY WILL SERVE US WILLINGLY-- BECAUSE ACANTI AND BROOD WILL HAVE BECOME ONE!

OUR RULE WILL SPREAD ACROSS THE STARS, OUR MANIFEST DESTINY FULFILLED!
WANNA... BET?

FIRST THEM, QUEENIE.
SNIKT

THEN-- WITH MY LAST BREATH, IF NEED BE--
--YOU!

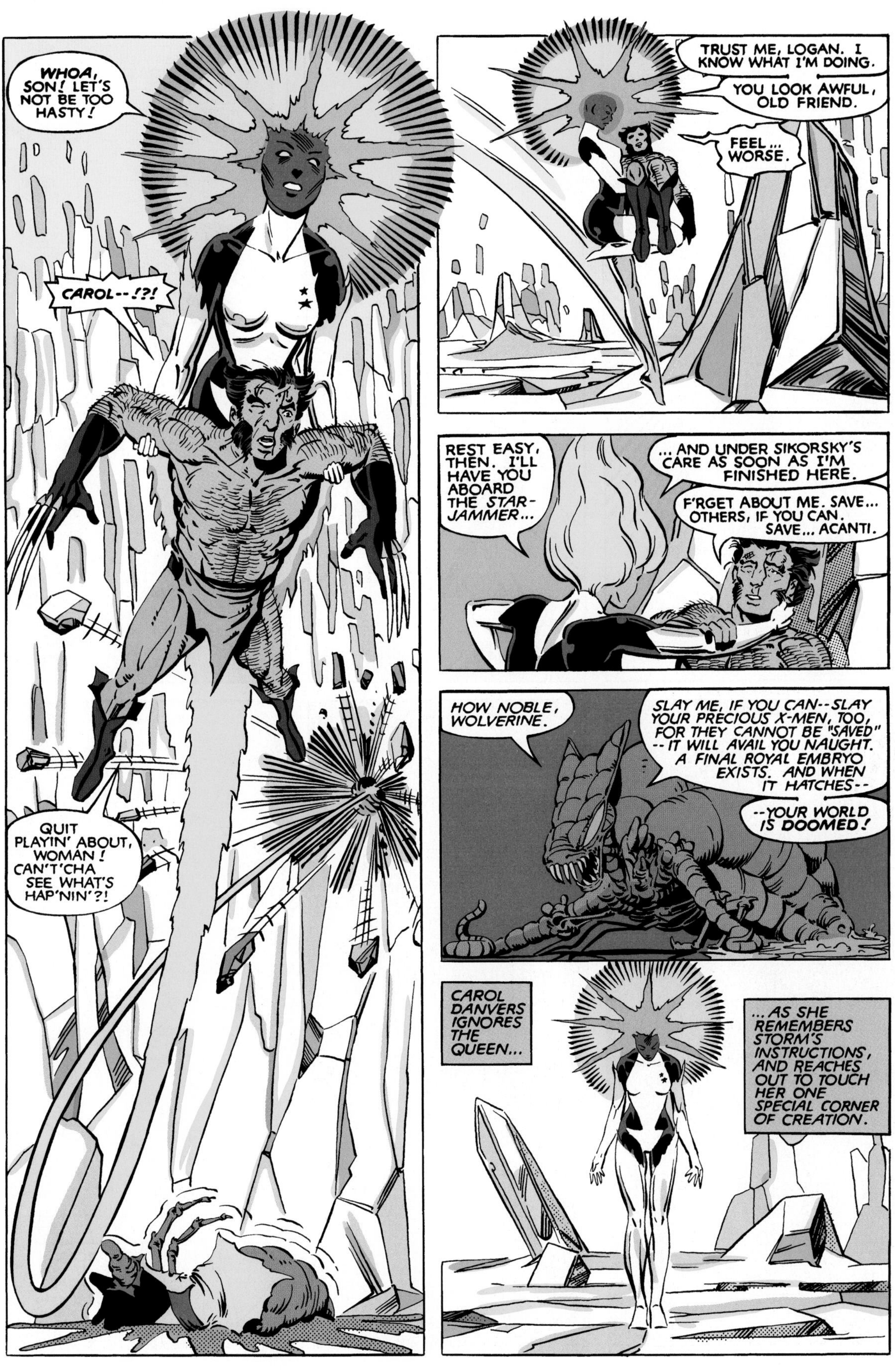
WHOA, SON! LET'S NOT BE TOO HASTY!
CAROL--!?!
QUIT PLAYIN' ABOUT, WOMAN! CAN'T'CHA SEE WHAT'S HAP'NIN'?!
TRUST ME, LOGAN. I KNOW WHAT I'M DOING.
YOU LOOK AWFUL, OLD FRIEND.
FEEL... WORSE.
REST EASY, THEN. I'LL HAVE YOU ABOARD THE STAR-JAMMER...
...AND UNDER SIKORSKY'S CARE AS SOON AS I'M FINISHED HERE.
F'RGET ABOUT ME. SAVE... OTHERS, IF YOU CAN. SAVE... ACANTI.
HOW NOBLE, WOLVERINE.
SLAY ME, IF YOU CAN--SLAY YOUR PRECIOUS X-MEN, TOO, FOR THEY CANNOT BE "SAVED" --IT WILL AVAIL YOU NAUGHT. A FINAL ROYAL EMBRYO EXISTS. AND WHEN IT HATCHES--
--YOUR WORLD IS DOOMED!
CAROL DANVERS IGNORES THE QUEEN...
...AS SHE REMEMBERS STORM'S INSTRUCTIONS, AND REACHES OUT TO TOUCH HER ONE SPECIAL CORNER OF CREATION.

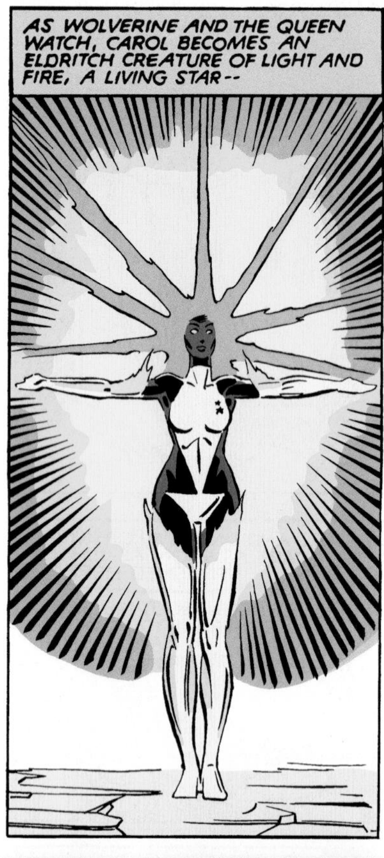
AS WOLVERINE AND THE QUEEN WATCH, CAROL BECOMES AN ELDRITCH CREATURE OF LIGHT AND FIRE, A LIVING STAR--

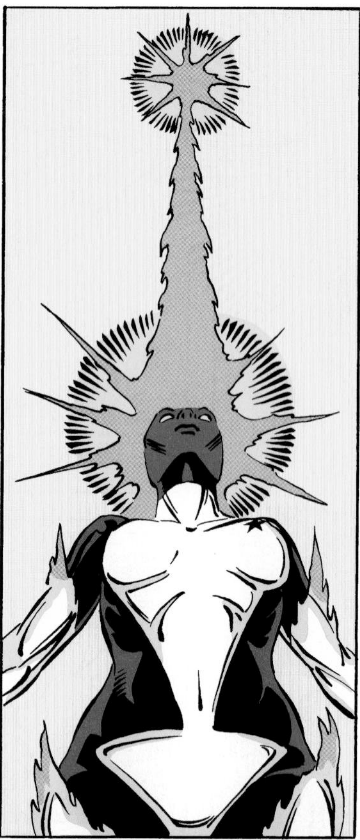

--HER CELESTIAL RADIANCE REFLECTED AND AMPLIFIED BY THE CRYSTAL CAVERN--UNTIL, FINALLY, SHE'S GENERATED ENOUGH POWER TO RELEASE THE ACANTI SOUL.

A BLINDING BOLT OF ENERGY RIPS UPWARD INTO SPACE...
...LEAVING IN ITS WAKE A SONG OF LONGING AND JOY AND ETERNAL LOVE.

AND THUS, AFTER UNTOLD AEONS...
...THE UNION OF SOUL AND LIVING PROPHETSINGER IS ONCE MORE COMPLETE.

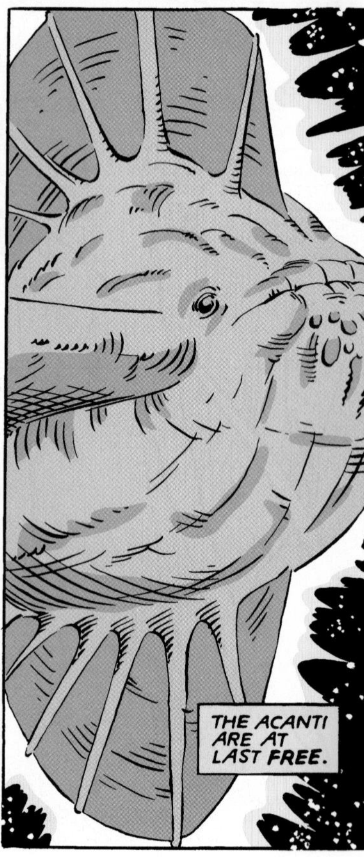
THE ACANTI ARE AT LAST FREE.

Oh...
... MY!
NOT BAD, IF I DO SAY SO MYSELF. BEATS MY LAST BIG STUNT ALL HOLLOW.*
I'VE NEVER FELT SO WRECKED-- I CAN BARELY STAND-- BUT IT WAS WORTH IT.
*SEE X-MEN #164 -- LOUISE.

LOGAN...? HOW'S BY YOU?
DARLIN', WE GOTTA STOP MEETIN' LIKE THIS.
SPOILSPORT.
CAROL -- THE... OTHERS! EVEN WITH THE SOUL FREE...

... WE CAN'T LET THEIR METAMORPHOSES BE COMPLETED.
IT'S A MOOT POINT, PARTNER. TAKE A LOOK.

I THINK THE SOUL TOOK CARE OF THINGS FOR US...
... BY PURGING THE SLEAZOID ELEMENTS FROM THEIR BODIES.
AND INSTEAD OF CORRUPTING THE ACANTI...

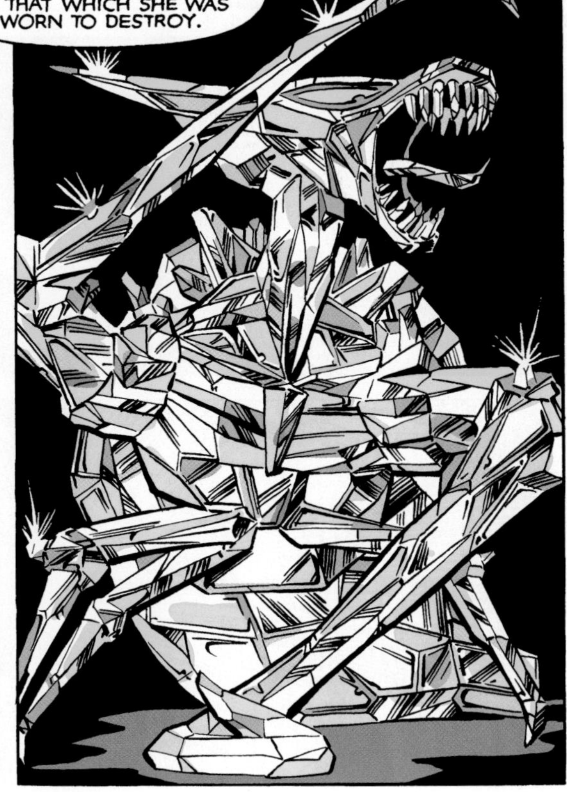
... IT SEEMS THE BROOD QUEEN WAS MADE AS PURE AS THAT WHICH SHE WAS SWORN TO DESTROY.

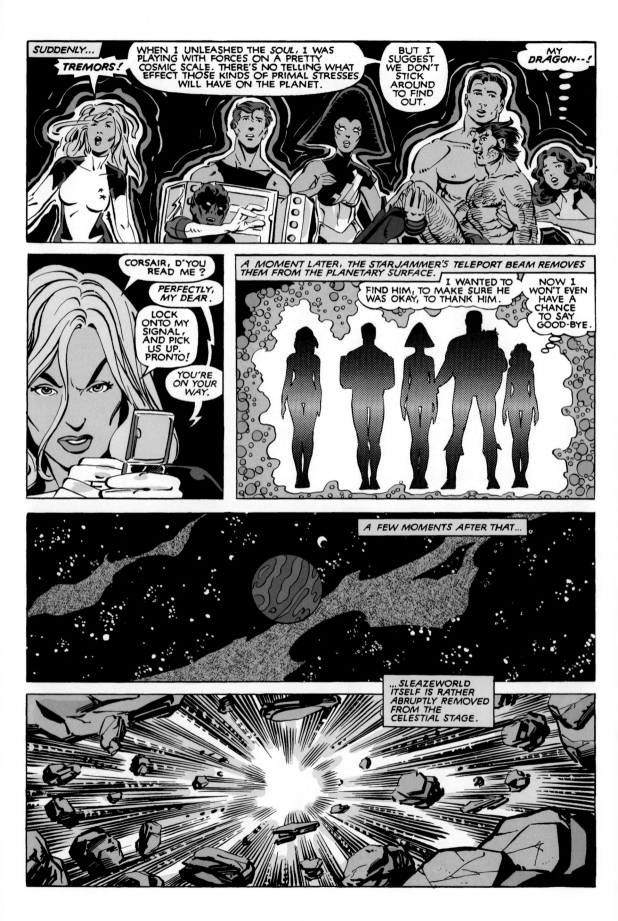

SUDDENLY...
TREMORS!
WHEN I UNLEASHED THE SOUL, I WAS PLAYING WITH FORCES ON A PRETTY COSMIC SCALE. THERE'S NO TELLING WHAT EFFECT THOSE KINDS OF PRIMAL STRESSES WILL HAVE ON THE PLANET.
BUT I SUGGEST WE DON'T STICK AROUND TO FIND OUT.
MY DRAGON--!

CORSAIR, D'YOU READ ME?
PERFECTLY, MY DEAR.
LOCK ONTO MY SIGNAL, AND PICK US UP. PRONTO!
YOU'RE ON YOUR WAY.

A MOMENT LATER, THE STARJAMMER'S TELEPORT BEAM REMOVES THEM FROM THE PLANETARY SURFACE.
I WANTED TO FIND HIM, TO MAKE SURE HE WAS OKAY, TO THANK HIM.
NOW I WON'T EVEN HAVE A CHANCE TO SAY GOOD-BYE.

A FEW MOMENTS AFTER THAT...
...SLEAZEWORLD ITSELF IS RATHER ABRUPTLY REMOVED FROM THE CELESTIAL STAGE.

SOMETIME LATER, IN THE STARJAMMER'S MEDICAL BAY...
WOLVERINE! NUMBSKULL, YOU ARE! UP, SHOULD NOT YOU BE!
GIVE IT A REST, WILLYA, SIKORSKY?
PHYSICIAN, YOURS, AM I CURSED TO BE! IF NOT YOU, MY ORDERS OBEY, THEN RESPONSIBILITY I DENY, YOUR HEALTH, THE STATE OF FOR!
YOU REALLY SHOULD BE IN BED, MEIN FREUND. IT WAS TOUCH AND GO FOR AWHILE-- YOU VERY NEARLY DIDN'T SURVIVE.
I'LL TAKE MY CHANCES, ELF.
WHEN I'M SICK, I HAVE TO DO THINGS I DON'T LIKE, LOGAN --FOR MY OWN GOOD. SO SHOULD YOU.

THAT'S TELLING HIM, KITTY!
BRAVE GIRL. YOU REALLY CARE FOR THE X-MEN, DON'T YOU, SCOTT?
THEY'RE MY FAMILY, DAD. AS MUCH, I SUPPOSE, AS THE STARJAMMERS HAVE BECOME YOURS.
SOMETHING BOTHERING YOU?
SLEAZEWORLD. DESTROYING A PLANET, EVEN UNINTENTIONALLY, IS HARD TO LIVE WITH.
IT OUGHT TO BE-- EVEN WHEN IT'S INTENTIONAL.

YOU BALANCE THE LIVES SACRIFICED WHEN SLEAZEWORLD DIED WITH THOSE THAT WOULD HAVE BEEN LOST HAD WE DONE NOTHING AND ALLOWED THE ACANTI TO CONTINUE TO BE HUNTED, THE BROOD TO EXPAND. AND YOU PRAY YOU DID THE RIGHT THING.
CORSAIR...
YES, HEPZIBAH?
SURPRISE.

HELLO.

ORORO!!
YOU'RE REAL AGAIN! YOU'RE ALIVE! YOU'RE OKAY!!

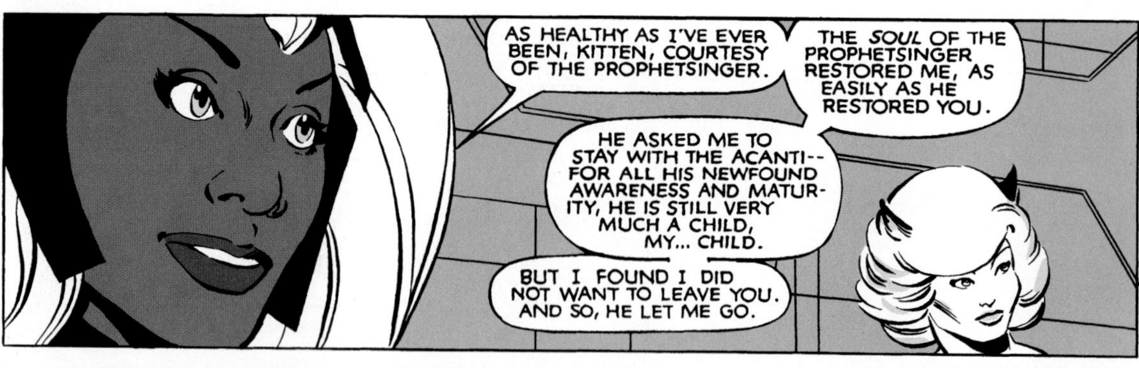

TO BE CONCLUDED IN 30 DAYS -- AS THE X-MEN MEET THE NEW MUTANTS IN...

THE GOLDILOCKS SYNDROME!

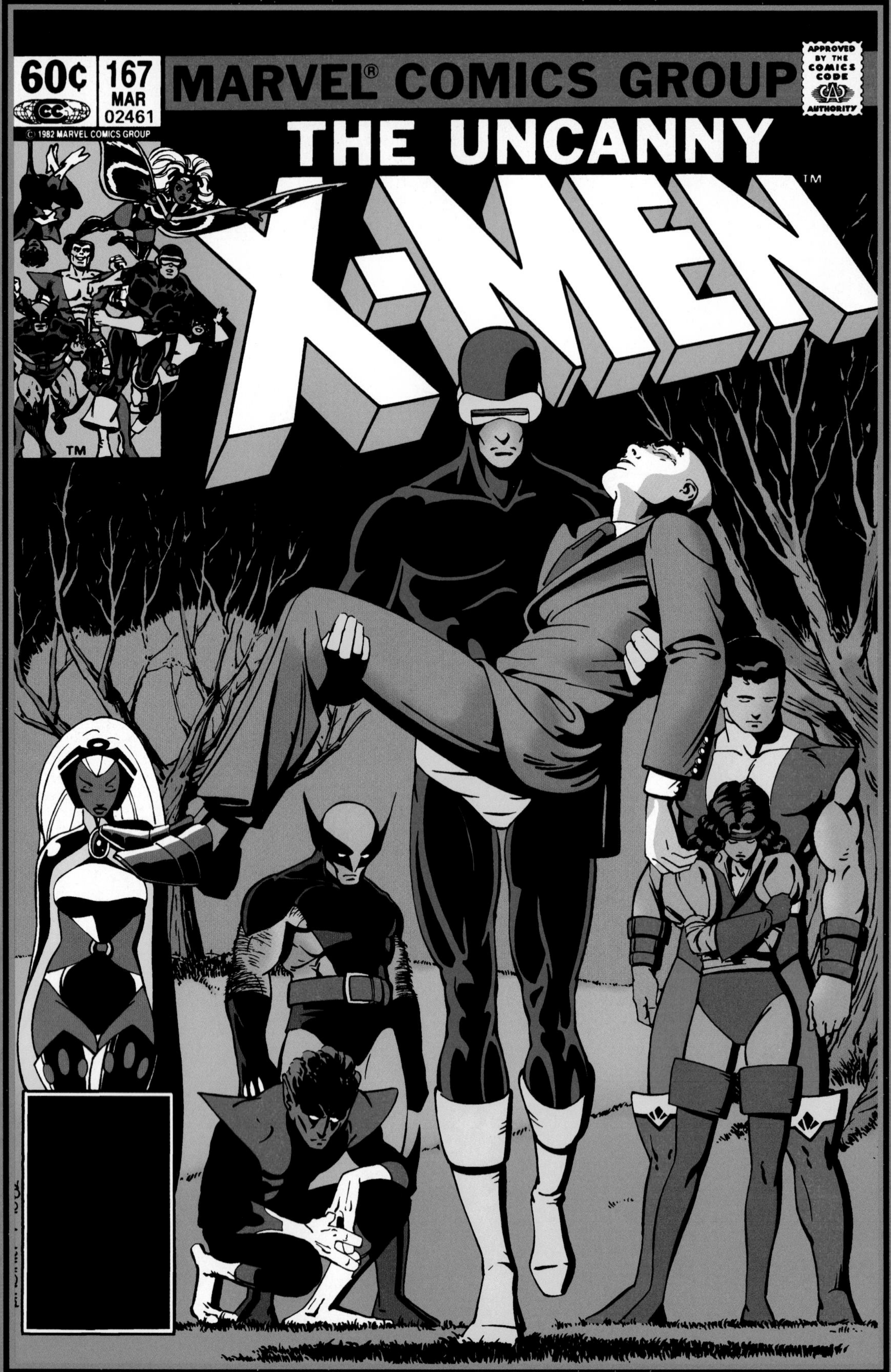
60¢
167
MAR
02461
MARVEL® COMICS GROUP
APPROVED BY THE COMICS CODE AUTHORITY
© 1982 MARVEL COMICS GROUP
THE UNCANNY
X-MEN™
TM

JUST OUTSIDE THE TOWN OF SALEM CENTER-- ROUGHLY AN HOUR'S DRIVE UPSTATE FROM NEW YORK CITY-- LIES PROFESSOR CHARLES XAVIER'S SCHOOL FOR GIFTED YOUNGSTERS...
... A VERY RECLUSIVE, EXCLUSIVE, PRIVATE ACADEMY WHOSE STUDENT BODY CURRENTLY CONSISTS OF FIVE UNIQUE YOUNG INDIVIDUALS.

THEY ARE MUTANTS...
...GIFTED--OR CURSED, DEPENDING ON ONE'S POINT-OF-VIEW--WITH POWERS AND ABILITIES THAT SET THEM APART FROM THE REST OF HUMANITY.

XAVIER ONLY RECENTLY GATHERED THEM TO TEACH THEM HOW TO COPE WITH THEIR NASCENT TALENTS, TO ENABLE THEM TO FUNCTION IN A WORLD THAT DISTRUSTS-- AND OCCASIONALLY HATES-- THEM, SIMPLY BECAUSE THEY EXIST.

SAM GUTHRIE.
WAY T' GO, MAGNUM! LOOK AT THAT MAN MOVE!
HE SURE IS CUTE.
Y' SHOULD NA' THINK SUCH THOUGHTS, DANI. THEY'RE NA' PROPER.
HE IS VERRA HANDSOME, THOUGH.
RAHNE SINCLAIR.
XI'AN COY MANH.
DANIELLE MOONSTAR.
ROBERTO da COSTA.
THEY ARE NOT THE FIRST TO BE TAUGHT BY XAVIER-- HIMSELF A TELEPATH, THE STRONGEST MUTANT MIND ON EARTH --BUT THEY MAY WELL TURN OUT TO BE THE LAST.

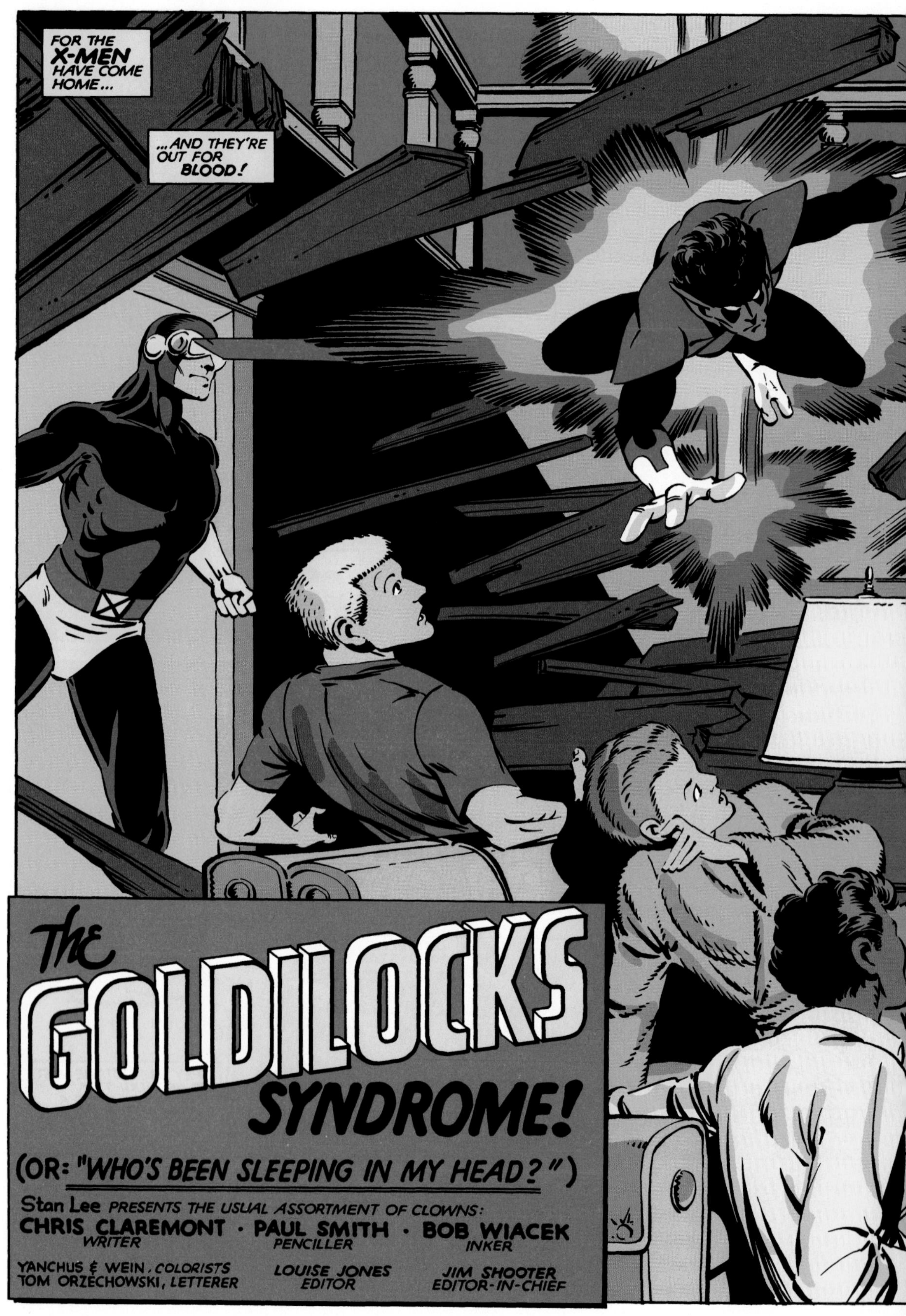
FOR THE X-MEN HAVE COME HOME...
...AND THEY'RE OUT FOR BLOOD!
The GOLDILOCKS SYNDROME!
(OR: "WHO'S BEEN SLEEPING IN MY HEAD?")
Stan Lee PRESENTS THE USUAL ASSORTMENT OF CLOWNS:
CHRIS CLAREMONT · PAUL SMITH · BOB WIACEK
WRITER PENCILLER INKER
YANCHUS & WEIN, COLORISTS
TOM ORZECHOWSKI, LETTERER
LOUISE JONES EDITOR
JIM SHOOTER EDITOR-IN-CHIEF

PICK YOAH TARGETS, PEOPLE!
AH'LL TAKE CARE O' THE BIG FELLA!
COLOSSUS-- LOOK OUT!

CYCLOPS' WARNING COMES TOO LATE AS SAM MENTALLY IGNITES THE THERMO-CHEMICAL REACTION WHICH FORMS THE ESSENCE OF HIS MUTANT POWER-- WITH SPECTACULAR RESULTS.
IT'S A GOOD THING AH'M PRETTY MUCH INVULNERABLE AS CANNONBALL.
AH FEEL LIKE AH JUST SLAMMED FULL-TILT INTO A MOUNTAIN!

THESE KIDS HAVE GUTS. THEY OBVIOUSLY DON'T RECOGNIZE US-- COULD IT BE THAT CHARLES HASN'T TOLD THEM ABOUT THE X-MEN?
I WISH WE HAD TIME TO EXPLAIN-- BUT THE SLIGHTEST DELAY COULD PROVE FATAL!
YOW!
WE MEAN NO HARM! HIT THE FLOOR, STAY OUT OF OUR WAY, AND YOU'LL BE ALL RIGHT!

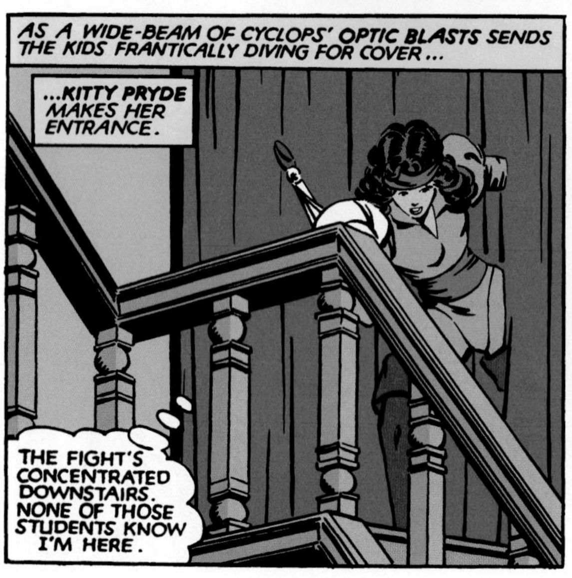
AS A WIDE-BEAM OF CYCLOPS' OPTIC BLASTS SENDS THE KIDS FRANTICALLY DIVING FOR COVER...
...KITTY PRYDE MAKES HER ENTRANCE.
THE FIGHT'S CONCENTRATED DOWNSTAIRS. NONE OF THOSE STUDENTS KNOW I'M HERE.

AND THEY'RE NOT GOING TO FIND OUT. I'LL PHASE THROUGH ALL THE WALLS BETWEEN HERE AND THE PROFESSOR'S STUDY. I HOPE THE OTHERS BEAT ME TO IT. FAT CHANCE.
WHAT IF WE'RE WRONG ABOUT THE PROFESSOR?! WHAT IF WE'RE MAKING A TERRIBLE MISTAKE?!

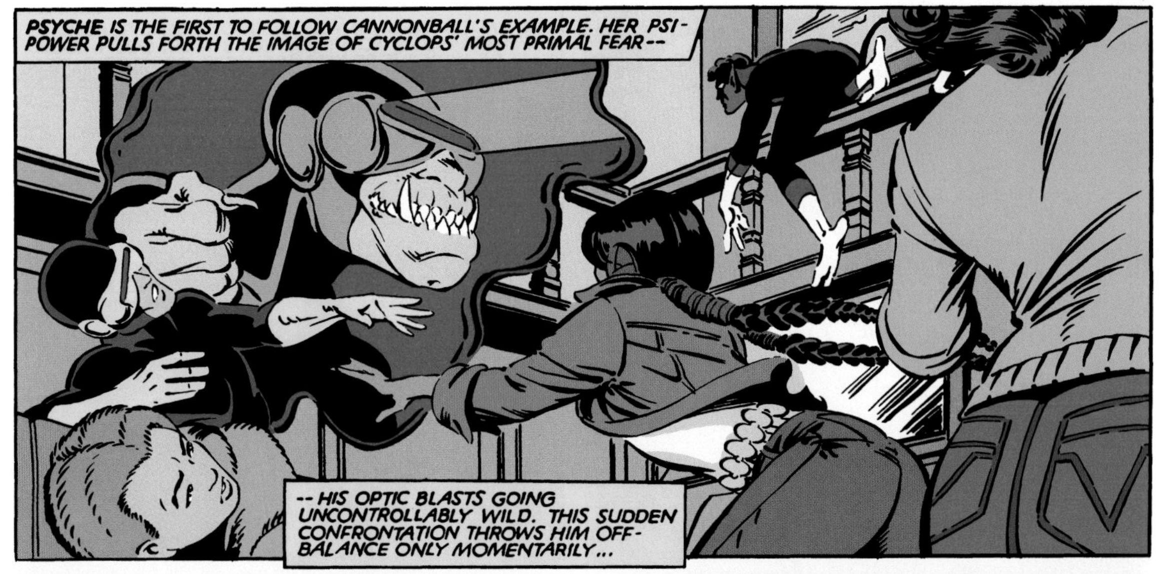
PSYCHE IS THE FIRST TO FOLLOW CANNONBALL'S EXAMPLE. HER PSI-POWER PULLS FORTH THE IMAGE OF CYCLOPS' MOST PRIMAL FEAR--
--HIS OPTIC BLASTS GOING UNCONTROLLABLY WILD. THIS SUDDEN CONFRONTATION THROWS HIM OFF-BALANCE ONLY MOMENTARILY...

...BUT IT ALLOWS HER REMAINING TEAM-MATES TO MAKE MOVES OF THEIR OWN.
RAHNE SHIFTS FROM HUMAN TO WOLF...

...WHILE ROBERTO TRANSMUTES THE KINETIC ENERGY OF THE SUN INTO RAW STRENGTH-- FOR ALL THE GOOD IT DOES HIM...
...AGAINST WOLVERINE'S ENHANCED PHYSICAL ABILITIES AND UNBREAKABLE ADAMANTIUM-LACED SKELETON.

CHARLEY MAY BE ROBBIN' THE CRADLE, BUT HE HASN'T LOST HIS TOUCH.
IF THESE KIDS HAD THE SKILL T' MATCH THEIR SPUNK, THEY'D BE DANGEROUS.

STOP!
KARMA IS THE OLDEST OF THE NEW MUTANTS. SHE POSSESSES PEOPLE.
WHA-- ?!?
LADY--GET OUTTA... MY... HEAD!
HE'S BREAKING MY HOLD ON HIM! C'EST IMPOSSIBLE-- THAT HAS NEVER HAPPENED BEFORE!

SO FAR, SO GOOD.
DARN IT!
DURING OUR FINAL BATTLE WITH THE BROOD, THEIR QUEEN BOASTED THAT ONE OF HER ROYAL EMBRYOS STILL EXISTED. WOLVIE FIGURED IT HAD BEEN IMPLANTED IN PROFESSOR XAVIER.*
IF HE'S RIGHT, WHEN THE THING HATCHES, IT'LL ABSORB THE PROFESSOR'S PSI-POWERS AND BECOME VIRTUALLY UNBEATABLE. IT-- AND ITS CHILDREN-- WILL PREY ON THE HUMAN RACE UNTIL THEY OVERRUN THE PLANET.
*LAST ISH-- LOUISE.

THE BROOD INSTINCTIVELY SEEK OUT GENETICALLY SUPERIOR HOSTS FOR THEIR EGGS-- oh, GOSH, COULD THAT BE WHY THOSE KIDS ARE HERE, TO HOST QUEEN EMBRYOS AS THE X-MEN DID ON SLEAZEWORLD?!
THERE'S THE PROFESSOR-- AND HE'S HUMAN!! THANK HEAVEN, I DON'T HAVE TO SHOOT.
HEY, WAITAMINNIT-- HOW COME HE'S ASLEEP? IF THAT SCRAP IN THE LIVING ROOM WASN'T ENOUGH TO WAKE HIM...

...MY THOUGHTS SHOULD HAVE DONE THE TRICK. I'M TRYING TO SHIELD 'EM, LIKE HE TAUGHT ME, BUT I'M SO EXCITED AN' SCARED, I'M PROBABLY DOING A LOUSY JOB.
PROFESSOR...?

YOU SHOULD HAVE HEEDED WOLVERINE'S INJUNCTION, CHILD, AND FIRED.
YOUR HESITATION WILL COST YOU DEAR.

OH, NO!
ZARK!

THAT SOUND... COMING FROM UPSTAIRS!
A BLASTER--

DON'T WORRY, SHAN-- I'LL HANDLE THIS BRUTE!

KITTY!

HE OWES ME A REMATCH!

NICE TRY, BOY...

...BUT NO CIGAR!
UNNNNGNH!

NICE DOGGY! GOOD DOGGY! MUCH AS I'D REALLY LOVE TO STAY AND PLAY WITH YOU, DUTY CALLS.
AUF WEIDERSEHN!
BAMF

IN A BURST OF FLAME AND BRIMSTONE STENCH THAT LEAVES RAHNE CHOKING AND COUGHING ON THE FLOOR, NIGHTCRAWLER TELEPORTS FROM HER...
...TO HER FRIENDS.
OUCH!

BUT THEN...

KITTY!

--FEAR RATHER FOR YOURSELVES!

THE X-MEN HAVE SEEN THIS BEFORE-- AND UNDERGONE IT, TO AN EXTENT--

--BUT TIME AND EXPERIENCE HAVE NOT DIMINISHED THE HORROR AS THIS MAN THEY KNOW AND LOVE IS TRANSFORMED BEFORE THEIR EYES.

THEY DO NOT ACT-- BUT MERELY STAND, WATCHING IN MUTE DISBELIEF.

IN A TWINKLING, IT IS OVER.

CHARLES XAVIER IS NO MORE.

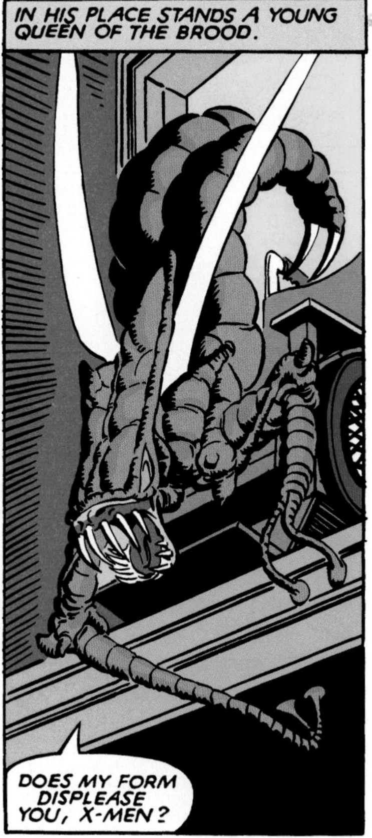

IN HIS PLACE STANDS A YOUNG QUEEN OF THE BROOD.
DOES MY FORM DISPLEASE YOU, X-MEN?

IF SO, THAT CAN BE SPEEDILY REMIDIED BY YOUR OWN METAMORPHOSES--
--OR YOUR DEATHS!

TO COIN A PHRASE:
...WANNA BET?

SPLOW!
LENIN'S GHOST!

A BROOD QUEEN-- WE ARRIVED TOO LATE!
THE BOY WHO ATTACKED ME LOOKED AS YOUNG AS I DID WHEN I JOINED THE X-MEN. I HOPE I DID NOT HURT HIM.

THE CREATURE IS NOT EVEN STUNNED! I MUST NOT LET IT ESCAPE!
AND HOW WILL YOU STOP ME, HUMAN...
...WHEN MY MENTAL POWERS ENABLE ME TO READ YOUR EVERY THOUGHT; TO COUNTER YOUR PLANS THE MOMENT YOU CONCEIVE THEM?!

WERE WE SEEING THINGS?! DID PROFESSOR X TURN INTO SOME KIND'A MONSTER -- THE SAME KIND WE FOUGHT BEFORE?! *
STAY OUTTA THIS, YOU KIDS -- WE'LL HANDLE IT.
FORGET THAT, BUSTER! WHO DO YOU CREEPS THINK YOU ARE, ANYWAY?!
THE X-MEN.
THERE, CYCLOPS -- BY THE TREE LINE!
BUT -- YOU ARE SUPPOSED TO BE DEAD!
*SEE NEW MUTANTS #3 --L.

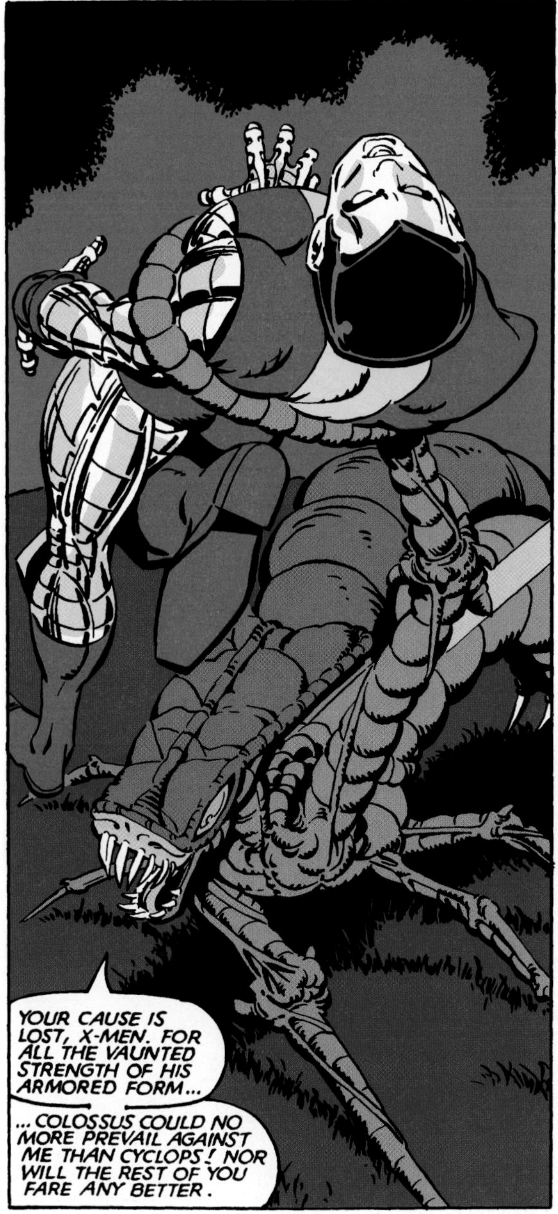
YOUR CAUSE IS LOST, X-MEN. FOR ALL THE VAUNTED STRENGTH OF HIS ARMORED FORM...
... COLOSSUS COULD NO MORE PREVAIL AGAINST ME THAN CYCLOPS! NOR WILL THE REST OF YOU FARE ANY BETTER.

IF YOU WOULD LIVE...
... I SUGGEST YOU FLEE.

SOUNDS LIKE SENSIBLE ADVICE -- THE KIND I BEEN IGNORIN' SINCE I WAS BORN.
WE'VE COME A FAR PIECE FOR THIS SCRAP, SLEAZY...

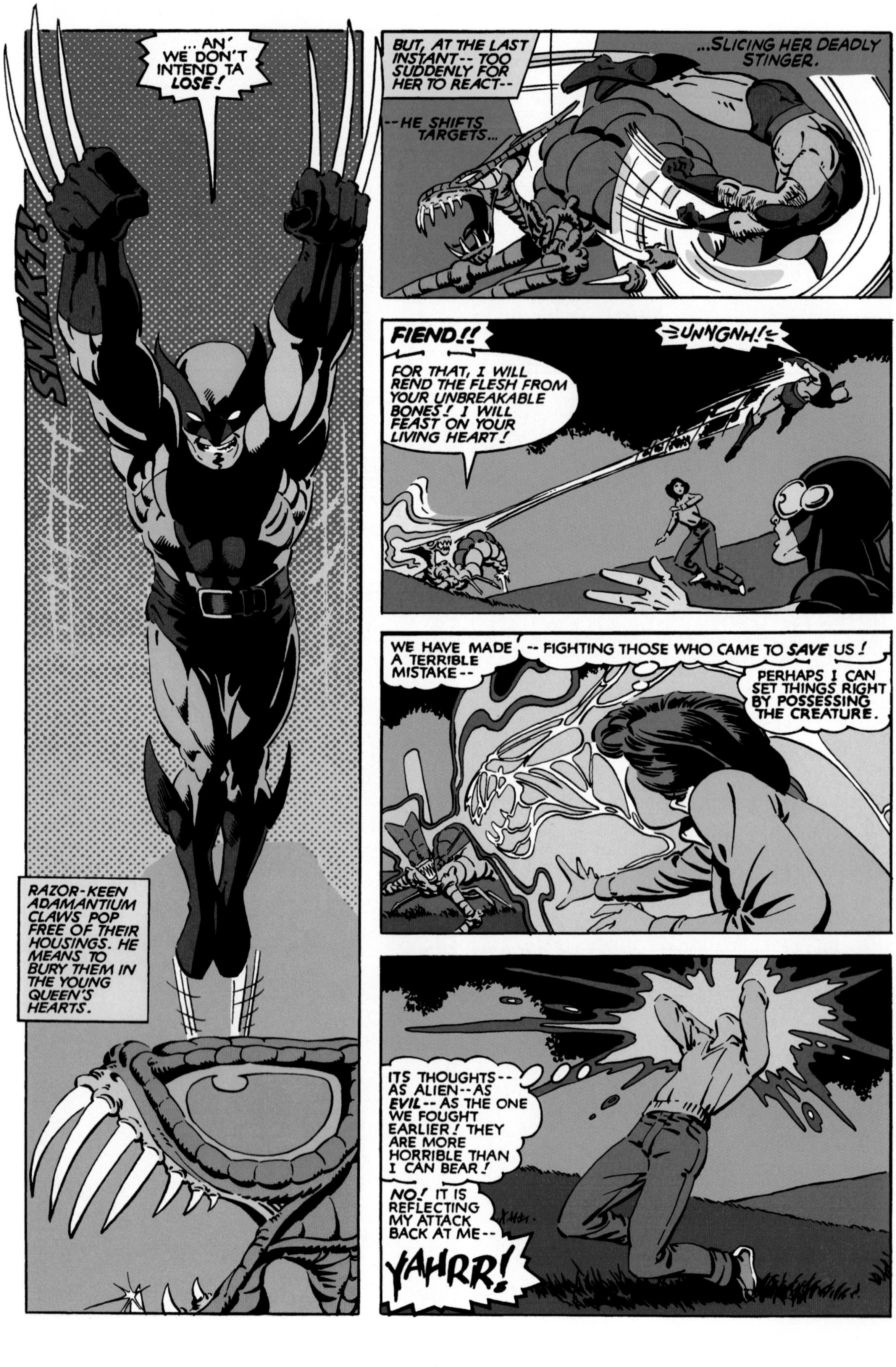

... AN' WE DON'T INTEND TA *LOSE!*

SNIKT!

RAZOR-KEEN ADAMANTIUM CLAWS POP FREE OF THEIR HOUSINGS. HE MEANS TO BURY THEM IN THE YOUNG QUEEN'S HEARTS.

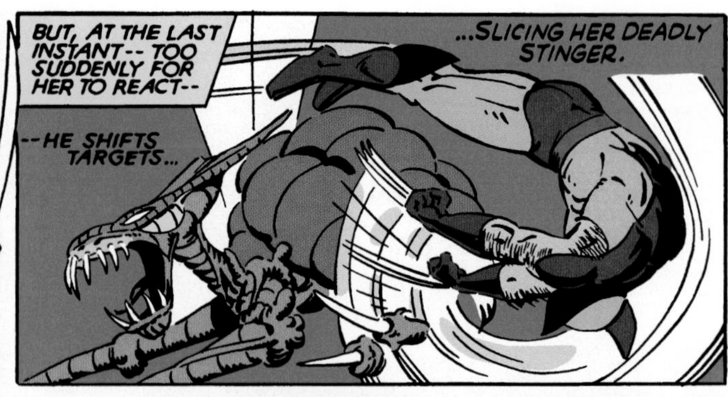

BUT, AT THE LAST INSTANT-- TOO SUDDENLY FOR HER TO REACT--
--HE SHIFTS TARGETS...
...SLICING HER DEADLY STINGER.

FIEND!!
FOR THAT, I WILL REND THE FLESH FROM YOUR UNBREAKABLE BONES! I WILL FEAST ON YOUR LIVING HEART!
UNNGNH!

WE HAVE MADE A TERRIBLE MISTAKE--
-- FIGHTING THOSE WHO CAME TO SAVE US!
PERHAPS I CAN SET THINGS RIGHT BY POSSESSING THE CREATURE.

ITS THOUGHTS-- AS ALIEN--AS EVIL-- AS THE ONE WE FOUGHT EARLIER! THEY ARE MORE HORRIBLE THAN I CAN BEAR!
NO! IT IS REFLECTING MY ATTACK BACK AT ME--
YAHRR!

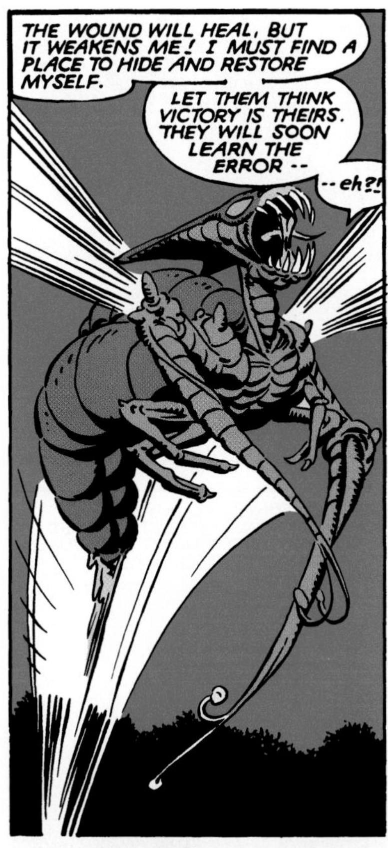
THE WOUND WILL HEAL, BUT IT WEAKENS ME! I MUST FIND A PLACE TO HIDE AND RESTORE MYSELF.
LET THEM THINK VICTORY IS THEIRS. THEY WILL SOON LEARN THE ERROR --
-- eh?!

WHAT IS THAT?!

THE NAME'S BINARY!
I HATE TO DISILLUSION YOU, MONSTER, BUT FROM US--
-- THERE IS NO ESCAPE.

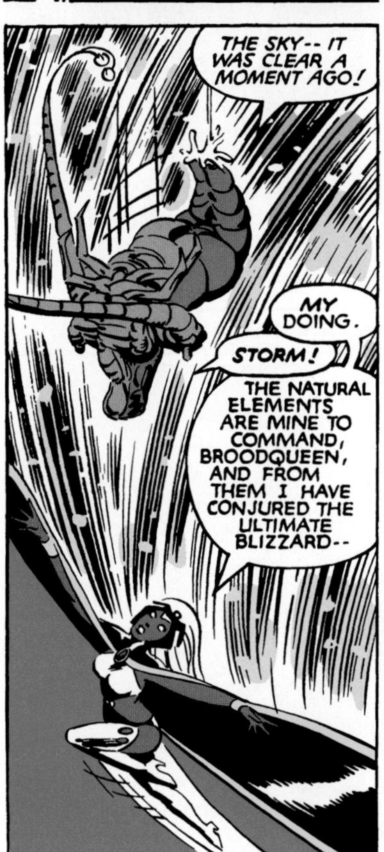
THE SKY-- IT WAS CLEAR A MOMENT AGO!
MY DOING.
STORM!
THE NATURAL ELEMENTS ARE MINE TO COMMAND, BROODQUEEN, AND FROM THEM I HAVE CONJURED THE ULTIMATE BLIZZARD--

-- CLOUD AND FOG TO DISORIENT YOU, WIND TO MOVE YOU WHERE I WISH, SNOW AND ICE AND COLD TO FREEZE YOU TO THE MARROW.
NO!

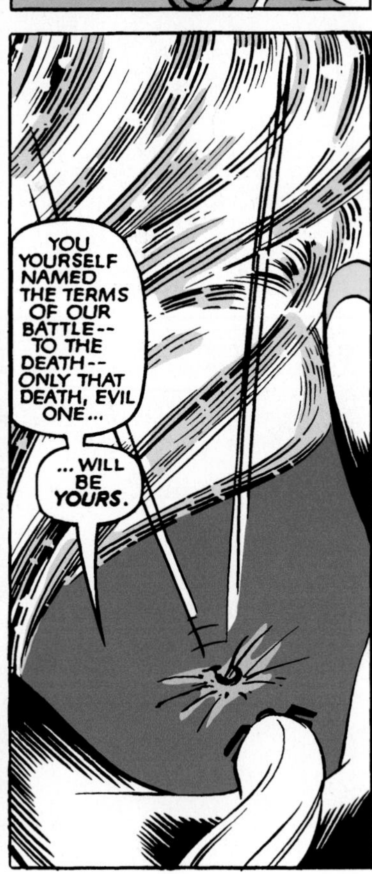
YOU YOURSELF NAMED THE TERMS OF OUR BATTLE-- TO THE DEATH-- ONLY THAT DEATH, EVIL ONE...
... WILL BE YOURS.

NICE WORK, ORORO.
THE QUEEN ISN'T MOVING, IS SHE DEAD?
IF SHE ISN'T KURT, SHE SOON WILL BE.
I COULD HAVE SLAIN HER WITH A LIGHTNING BOLT...
... BUT I COULD NOT BRING MYSELF TO DO IT.
NO SHAME IN BEIN' WHAT YOU ARE, DARLIN'.

I'M THE KILLER ON THIS TEAM, REMEMBER?
NOT THIS TIME, WOLVERINE. I WAS THE FIRST X-MAN. IT'S MY RIGHT -- MY RESPONSIBILITY.

FORGIVE ME, PROFESSOR. IF THERE WAS ANY ALTERNATIVE...
THERE IS... NONE, SCOTT...
PROFESSOR?!?
Y-YES. MENTAL TRANSFOR-MATION... INCOMPLETE...

... BEEN RESISTING... ALL MY MIGHT... SHOCK OF STORM'S ASSAULT ENABLED ME... TO GAIN UPPER HAND. EVENTUALLY, THOUGH, BROOD PERSONA WILL OVERWHELM ME.
THAT MUST NOT COME TO PASS. FOR THE GOOD OF EARTH, OF HUMANITY...
... KILL ME, SCOTT, I BEG YOU!
YOU HEARD THE MAN.

I ALSO HEARD PHOENIX PLAY THIS RIFF BEFORE SHE DIED! I NEVER HAD A CHANCE TO SAVE THE WOMAN I LOVED.
I'M DAMNED IF I'M GOING TO WATCH CHARLES XAVIER GO THE SAME WAY.

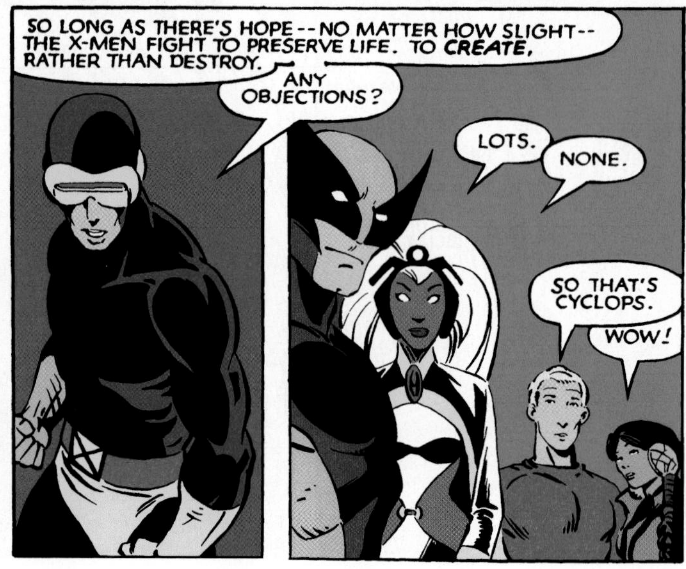
SO LONG AS THERE'S HOPE -- NO MATTER HOW SLIGHT -- THE X-MEN FIGHT TO PRESERVE LIFE. TO CREATE, RATHER THAN DESTROY.
ANY OBJECTIONS?
LOTS.
NONE.
SO THAT'S CYCLOPS.
WOW!

LATER, ABOARD THE STARJAMMER, IN EARTH ORBIT...
THE PROFESSOR'S BEEN UNDER SIKORSKY'S MEDISCANNERS AN AWFULLY LONG TIME. I WISH THERE WAS SOME NEWS.
BE PATIENT, SCOTT. IT'LL COME.
AM I CHASING RAINBOWS, DAD?
DOES THAT MAKE A DIFFERENCE?
NOT REALLY.

SIKORSKY! Dr. MacTAGGERT! IS IT OVER?
OVER--HAH! BEGUN, CYCLOPS, WE BARELY HAVE.
THEY CANNA REVERSE THE METAMORPHOSIS, BUT SIKORSKY THINKS HE CAN TAKE THE TISSUE SAMPLES COLLECTED FROM CHARLES WHEN HE WAS LAST ABOARD, AN' CLONE HIM A NEW BODY. THEN, WE TRANSPLANT HIS MIND FROM ONE TO T' OTHER.
IS SUCH A THING POSSIBLE?
LONGSHOT, IS, CHOICE, THERE IS NONE. PERMISSION GIVEN, PROCEDURE BEGUN HAS.

NEARBY, IN ANOTHER WARD OF THE SHIP'S MEDICAL BAY...
BEHOLD, ILLYANA-- OUR SLEEPING BEAUTY AT LAST AWAKES.
HOW'RE YOU DOING, KITTY? MY BIG BROTHER 'N' I WERE BEGINNING TO WONDER IF YOU WERE GOING TO STAY IN DREAMLAND FOREVER.

PETER!
ILLYANA!!
Oh, GOSH, YOU'RE ALL RIGHT! I'M ALL RIGHT. THIS IS GREAT!

I SHARED THIS VIGIL TOO, KITTEN. YET YOUR THOUGHTS ARE OF YOUR BEST FRIEND AND THE MAN YOU BELIEVE YOU LOVE... WHERE ONCE THEY WOULD HAVE BEEN OF ME.
IT IS ONLY NATURAL. CHANGE IS AN ESSENTIAL PART OF NATURE, AND THIS, ONE I HAVE LONG EXPECTED. BUT NOW THAT IT HAS ACTUALLY HAPPENED...
...WHY DO I FEEL SO ALONE?

AGH, WIND-RIDER, STOP PITYING YOURSELF.
I HAD NO RIGHT TO ASSUME THE ROLE OF PARENT-- THOUGH I DID SO GLADLY. BUT I COPED BEFORE-- ALBEIT IN BLISSFUL IGNORANCE--

--AND WILL DO SO NOW.
KURT?
AM I INTRUDING?

NEVER, DEAR LADY. YOUR PRESENCE IS ALWAYS WELCOME.
FLATTERER.
THAT'S ME--THE SILVER-TONGUED, BLUE-FURRED DEVIL.
WHOSE DELIGHT IS IN MAKING PEOPLE LAUGH.

SOME MORE THAN OTHERS, IT SEEMS.
PROBLEMS?
NO MORE THAN I EXPECTED. NOTHING I HAVEN'T EXPERIENCED BEFORE.
DO Y'ALL BELIEVE THIS VIEW?
I CAN SEE MY MOUNTAINS!

THE JURY IS STILL OUT ON WHETHER OR NOT THEY'LL ACCEPT ME. IT'S ONE THING TO WATCH SOMEONE LIKE ME ON A CINEMA OR TELEVISION SCREEN ...
... QUITE ANOTHER TO SHARE A DINNER TABLE WITH HIM.
KITTY WAS FRIGHTENED OF YOU AT FIRST. SHE GOT OVER IT.

SO WILL THEY.

THIS WAITING IS DRIVING ME CRAZY. IF ONLY THERE WAS SOMETHING I COULD DO.
IN MANY WAYS, DAD, CHARLES XAVIER IS AS MUCH MY FATHER AS YOU.
I KNOW. I ENVY HIM. BUT, FOR THE HAND HE HAD IN SHAPING YOUR CHARACTER, SCOTT-- IN MAKING YOU THE MAN YOU ARE TODAY-- I OWE HIM A DEBT I CAN NEVER REPAY.
WHAT ARE YOUR PLANS? WILL YOU REMAIN ON EARTH?

FOR AWHILE. THERE ARE PEOPLE TO SEE, YEARS TO CATCH UP ON -- BUT THOSE YEARS ARE THE MAIN REASON WHY, IN THE END, I'LL RETURN TO SPACE.
I'VE BEEN AWAY TOO LONG, SCOTT-- THIS ISN'T THE WORLD I REMEMBER-- I'M DECADES BEHIND THE TIMES YET CENTURIES AHEAD OF THEM. CHRISTOPHER SUMMERS-- MAJOR, U.S. AIR FORCE -- IS NO MORE. I'M CORSAIR.
EARTH ISN'T MY HOME ANYMORE, THE STARJAMMER IS.

WHEN YOU LEAVE...
...WILL YOU TAKE ME WITH YOU?
IF THAT'S WHAT YOU WANT, THEN GLADLY.

BUT IN THE MEANTIME, I'VE RUN SOME CHECKS. ANNE'S-- YOUR MOTHER'S-- FOLKS ARE DEAD, BUT MINE ARE GOING STRONG.
INTERESTED IN MEETING YOUR GRANDPARENTS?

I HAVE GRAND-PARENTS?!?
MOST EVERY-ONE DOES.
WHAT ARE THEY LIKE?!
ONLY ONE SURE WAY TO FIND OUT.
YOU BET I'M INTERESTED! JUST TRY TO KEEP ME AWAY!

WOULDN'T THINK OF IT. RIGHT NOW, THOUGH, YOU TOO BIG AND GROWN UP...
...TO GIVE YOUR OLD MAN A HUG?

CORSAIR!
SO MUCH FOR TENDER MOMENTS. WHAT'S UP, RAZA?
WE HAVE A GUEST, CHRISTOPHER.

THAT'S GLADIATOR, HEAD OF LILANDRA'S IMPERIAL GUARD! WHAT'S HE DOING HERE?
GOOD QUESTION, CONSIDERING HE SWORE NEVER TO WALK THESE DECKS UNTIL HE'D SEEN THE STARJAMMERS DEAD OR ENSLAVED. HE ISN'T A MAN TO LIGHTLY BREAK AN OATH.
YOU'RE A LONG WAY FROM HOME. IS THIS A SOCIAL CALL, OR BUSINESS?

PIRATE, I DEMAND TO SEE THE MAJESTRIX-- EMPRESS LILANDRA-- AT ONCE!

ON MY SHIP, LORD PRAETOR, YOU DO NOT "DEMAND" OF ME...
...YOU ASK.

THOU HAST E'ER BEEN ILL-MANNERED, COUSIN.
HAVE A CARE, RENEGADE.
WE LIKE YOU TOO, IMPERIAL. CARE TO ARGUE POINT?

ANOTHER TIME, LADY HEPZIBAH, WITH PLEASURE.
CORSAIR, I CRAVE AN AUDIENCE...
...WITH MY EMPRESS.

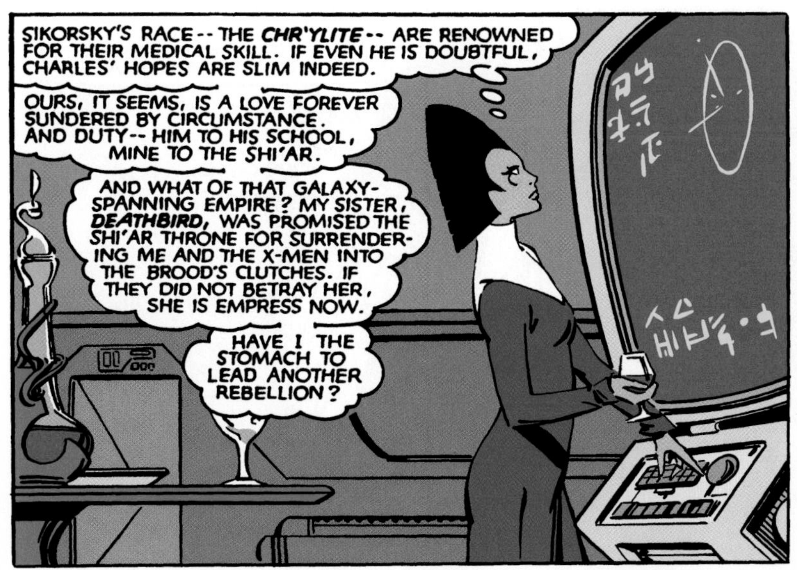
SIKORSKY'S RACE -- THE CHR'YLITE -- ARE RENOWNED FOR THEIR MEDICAL SKILL. IF EVEN HE IS DOUBTFUL, CHARLES' HOPES ARE SLIM INDEED.
OURS, IT SEEMS, IS A LOVE FOREVER SUNDERED BY CIRCUMSTANCE. AND DUTY -- HIM TO HIS SCHOOL, MINE TO THE SHI'AR.
AND WHAT OF THAT GALAXY-SPANNING EMPIRE? MY SISTER, DEATHBIRD, WAS PROMISED THE SHI'AR THRONE FOR SURRENDERING ME AND THE X-MEN INTO THE BROOD'S CLUTCHES. IF THEY DID NOT BETRAY HER, SHE IS EMPRESS NOW.
HAVE I THE STOMACH TO LEAD ANOTHER REBELLION?

MAJESTRIX!
I BRING GRAVE NEWS.

I'VE GUESSED IT, MY FRIEND. MY SISTER AT LAST HAS HER HEART'S DESIRE. PERHAPS WE SHOULD LEAVE HER TO ENJOY IT IN PEACE.
THERE WILL BE NO PEACE, SO LONG AS DEATHBIRD RULES.
SHE IS UNFIT, LILANDRA -- AS MAD, IN HER OWN WAY, AS YOUR BROTHER D'KEN.

WE ARE, I FEAR, A MAD FAMILY. IT SIMPLY HASN'T TOUCHED ME YET.
THERE IS MORE. UPON ARRIVAL HERE, I UNINTENTIONALLY CAME INTO CONFLICT WITH THE FANTASTIC FOUR.* I LATER LEARNED THAT THEY HAD RECENTLY ENCOUNTERED GALACTUS.
*FF #'S 249 & 250 -- L.

MAJESTRIX, THE SHATTERER OF WORLDS HAD RETURNED TO EARTH TO DIE!
THEN HIS THREAT IS FINALLY ENDED?

WOULD THAT IT WERE. WITH THE INTERVENTION OF REED RICHARDS, GALACTUS WAS RESTORED TO HEALTH, GIVEN A NEW HERALD AND SET FREE!
THAT MEDDLING, UNMITIGATED -- FOOL!

NEW YORK CITY -- THE BAXTER BUILDING --
-- HOME OF THE WORLD'S GREATEST SUPER HERO TEAM.

REED RICHARDS -- LEADER OF THE FANTASTIC FOUR -- ARISE TO HEAR OUR WORDS OF ROYAL JUDGMENT!
Hmnh?
GOOD GRIEF!

DON'T BE ALARMED, SUE -- IT'S MERELY A HOLOGRAPHIC PROJECTION, A THREE-DIMENSIONAL IMAGE.
WE ARE LILANDRA, MAJESTRIX SHI'AR. WE HAVE BEEN INFORMED OF YOUR CRIME.
CRIME?! WHAT CRIME?!

KNOW, SUSAN, RICHARDS, THAT GALACTUS IS THE ENEMY OF ALL THAT LIVES -- FOR HE DESTROYS THOSE MOST RARE AND PRECIOUS OF RESOURCES, PLANETS CAPABLE OF SUPPORTING LIFE -- AND THAT BY SAVING HIM, YOU HAVE BRANDED YOURSELVES HIS ALLIES.
SHOULD HE CONSUME ANY SUCH WORLD KNOWN TO US, YOU WILL BE IN PART RESPONSIBLE FOR THAT HOLOCAUST AND WILL BE HELD ACCOUNTABLE FOR IT, TO THE FULLEST EXTENT OF SHI'AR LAW.

REED, WE HEARD SUE CRY OUT -- HOLY CATS!
STAND FAST, JOHN STORM AND BENJAMIN GRIMM.

IT IS PAST TIME THAT THE PEOPLE OF EARTH REALIZED THEY DO NOT STAND ALONE IN THE COSMOS, AND ACKNOWLEDGED THEIR RESPONSIBILITY TO THEIR FELLOW SENTIENT BEINGS.
CONSIDER THIS FAIR WARNING, TERRANS.

SHE'S GONE!
GOOD RIDDANCE.

AS LILANDRA'S IMAGE FADES FROM VIEW ON EARTH, SO TOO DOES THE ARMOR CREATED BY THE STARJAMMER'S HOLO-SYSTEM TO CLOTHE THE IMAGE.

MY THANKS, CORSAIR.
I TRUST Dr. RICHARDS WAS SUITABLY IMPRESSED. NOT THAT I CAN DO ANYTHING AT PRESENT TO MAKE GOOD MY PLEDGE-- ONCE AGAIN, I AM A SHADOW PRINCESS, A WOMAN WITHOUT A WORLD.
THERE ARE WORSE FATES.

HI, GUYS! DIDJA MISS US?!
HAVE WE GOT A SURPRISE FOR YOU!
DO WE DO GOOD WORK, OR WHAT?
GREETINGS, X-MEN AND STARJAMMERS.
HELLO, LILANDRA.

PROFESSOR XAVIER!!
YOU'RE ALL RIGHT!

IN FACT, SCOTT, I AM BETTER THAN EVER.

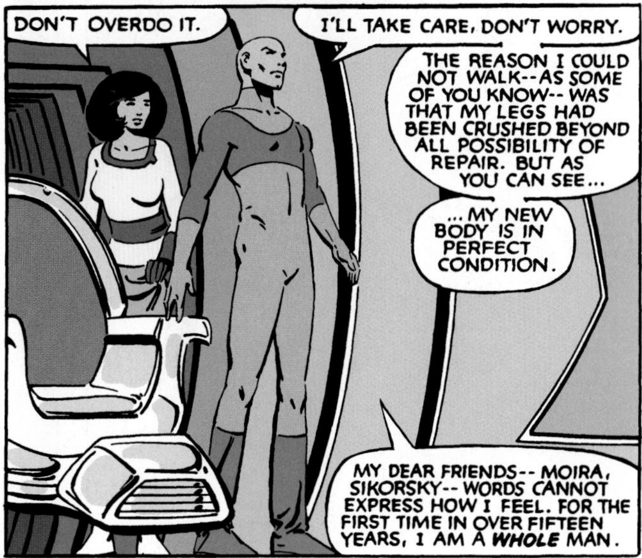

DON'T OVERDO IT.
I'LL TAKE CARE, DON'T WORRY.
THE REASON I COULD NOT WALK--AS SOME OF YOU KNOW-- WAS THAT MY LEGS HAD BEEN CRUSHED BEYOND ALL POSSIBILITY OF REPAIR. BUT AS YOU CAN SEE...
...MY NEW BODY IS IN PERFECT CONDITION.
MY DEAR FRIENDS-- MOIRA, SIKORSKY-- WORDS CANNOT EXPRESS HOW I FEEL. FOR THE FIRST TIME IN OVER FIFTEEN YEARS, I AM A WHOLE MAN.

ARRRGH!
CHARLES!
BLOODY HELL, I WAS AFRAID O' THIS! LILANDRA, GI' ME A HAND WI' HIM, QUICK!
BELOVED!
I THOUGHT THE OPERATION WAS A COMPLETE SUCCESS! WHAT HAS GONE WRONG?
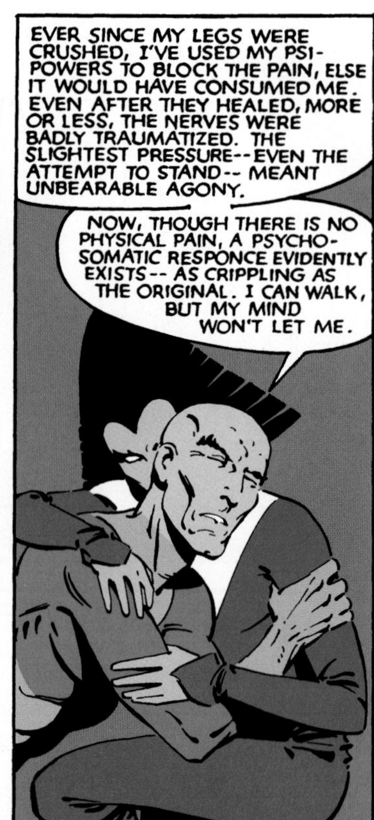
EVER SINCE MY LEGS WERE CRUSHED, I'VE USED MY PSI-POWERS TO BLOCK THE PAIN, ELSE IT WOULD HAVE CONSUMED ME. EVEN AFTER THEY HEALED, MORE OR LESS, THE NERVES WERE BADLY TRAUMATIZED. THE SLIGHTEST PRESSURE--EVEN THE ATTEMPT TO STAND--MEANT UNBEARABLE AGONY.
NOW, THOUGH THERE IS NO PHYSICAL PAIN, A PSYCHO-SOMATIC RESPONCE EVIDENTLY EXISTS--AS CRIPPLING AS THE ORIGINAL. I CAN WALK, BUT MY MIND WON'T LET ME.

THA' CAN CHANGE, CHARLEY, PROVIDED Y' WORK AT IT. HOW-EVER, YOU'RE A STUBBORN MAN, WI' A STUBBORN SUBCONSCIOUS--OVERCOMING SUCH INGRAINED CONDITIONING WON'T BE EASY.
GEE, PROFESSOR, YOU'LL BE ABLE TO TRAIN IN THE DANGER ROOM, JUST LIKE US.

AND SHOULD YOU NEED ENCOURAGEMENT, MY LOVE, I SHALL DO MY BEST TO PROVIDE IT.
AN' IF LIL'S T.L.C. DOES NA' DO THE TRICK...
...I'LL KICK YOU IN THE BUTT.
TRUST US, CHARLEY-LUV. WE'LL HAVE YOU ON YUIR FEET IN NO TIME.

I'LL HOLD YOU TO THAT, MOIRA.
Sigh!
I HAVE RARELY WITNESSED SO HAPPY A DAY. TO SEE THOSE I FEARED LOST FOREVER RETURN HOME ALIVE AND WELL. TO BE ALIVE AND WELL MYSELF. THERE ARE MORE BLESSINGS THAN ANY MAN DESERVES.
AS YOU X-MEN HAVE NO DOUBT NOTICED, I HAVE ADMITTED NEW STUDENTS TO THE SCHOOL. I APOLOGIZE FOR THE CIRCUMSTANCES OF YOUR INITIAL MEETING. I HOPE YOU'LL ALL BECOME FRIENDS.
SOUNDS GREAT TO US.
ONE TUSSLE WITH COLOSSUS WAS MORE'N ENOUGH F'R ME.

THE FEELING, TOVARISCH, IS MUTUAL. HAD YOU STRUCK HARDER ...
THERE IS AN ADDITIONAL BENEFIT TO THE INTRODUCTION OF THE NEW MUTANTS. AT LAST, KITTY WILL BE ABLE TO STUDY WITH CHILDREN HER OWN AGE.
HUH? SAYS WHO?! I'M AN X-MAN!

THAT WAS AN OVERSIGHT-- AND AN ERROR--ON MY PART.
YOU ARE TOO YOUNG, KITTY, AND TOO LITTLE IS KNOWN ABOUT YOUR POWERS. IN THE X-MEN'S PRIMARY ROLE--OF COMBATTING EVIL MUTANTS--THE RISKS ARE TOO GREAT. THAT, I CANNOT ALLOW. AS SOON AS WE RETURN TO EARTH...
...YOU ARE TO LEAVE THE X-MEN--AND JOIN THE NEW MUTANTS.

MY DECISION IS FINAL.
NEXT ISSUE: KITTY'S REACTION, OR --
"PROFESSOR XAVIER IS A JERK!"

In 1983, Marvel published *Special Edition X-Men #1*, a reprint of *Giant-Size X-Men #1* with an all-new backup story. Set shortly after the conclusion of the "Brood Saga" in *Uncanny X-Men #167*, this story featured the X-Men throwing Kitty Pryde a surprise party to make up for the birthday she had missed while stranded in space.

The Starjammers appeared for a single panel in this story; it would be their last appearance illustrated by Dave Cockrum published for seven years.

WRITER **CHRIS CLAREMONT** • PENCILER **DAVE COCKRUM** • INKER **HILARY BARTA** • COLORIST **ANDY YANCHUS**
LETTERER **DAVID CODY WEISS** • ASSISTANT EDITOR **DANNY FINGEROTH** • EDITOR **LOUISE JONES**

Following the X-Men's return to Earth, Kitty Pryde discovered a Sidri infestation in the basement of the rebuilt X-Mansion and defeated them with the help of Lockheed, the alien dragon who had secretly followed her home from Sleazeworld. Impressed, Professor X reinstated Kitty to the ranks of the X-Men. Soon after, Sikorsky fixed the problems with Professor X's cloned body and he fully regained the ability to walk.

Binary and Lilandra joined the Starjammers, and the team returned to Shi'ar space with the goal of overthrowing Deathbird and returning Lilandra to her rightful throne. However, despite many raids and battles, the Starjammers were unable to defeat Deathbird's loyalists and soon found themselves hunted as outlaws across the Shi'ar Empire.

When Professor X was attacked and badly injured by an anti-mutant mob, Lilandra sensed his failing health through her psychic link. Battling through Shi'ar forces, the Starjammers made a dangerous return to Earth, where they beamed Professor X to their ship and fled. Sikorsky cured Professor X once again, but the Starjammers explained that between the Shi'ar patrols and the damage to their ship, they could not return him to Earth any time soon – if at all. Professor X would miss the X-Men, but he took solace in the fact that he was reunited with Lilandra and could finally fight by her side.

Back on Earth, the X-Men expanded into several teams. Cyclops retired from the X-Men, but he was soon overjoyed to learn that Phoenix was not actually Marvel Girl at all, but a cosmic entity called the Phoenix Force that had taken her place – and that the real Marvel Girl was still alive! The original five X-Men reunited, formed a team called X-Factor and eventually took up residence on a sentient Celestial ship.

Elsewhere, Nightcrawler, Kitty Pryde and Lockheed helped found a British-based group called Excalibur. Their new teammates were Captain Britain, Meggan, Widget and Rachel Summers – Cyclops and Marvel Girl's daughter from an alternate future who had traveled back in time to the present and who had become the new human host of the cosmic Phoenix Force.

Now, on an otherwise routine raid in Shi'ar territory, the Starjammers are about to learn of a power that could mean the difference between success and failure for their struggling rebellion...

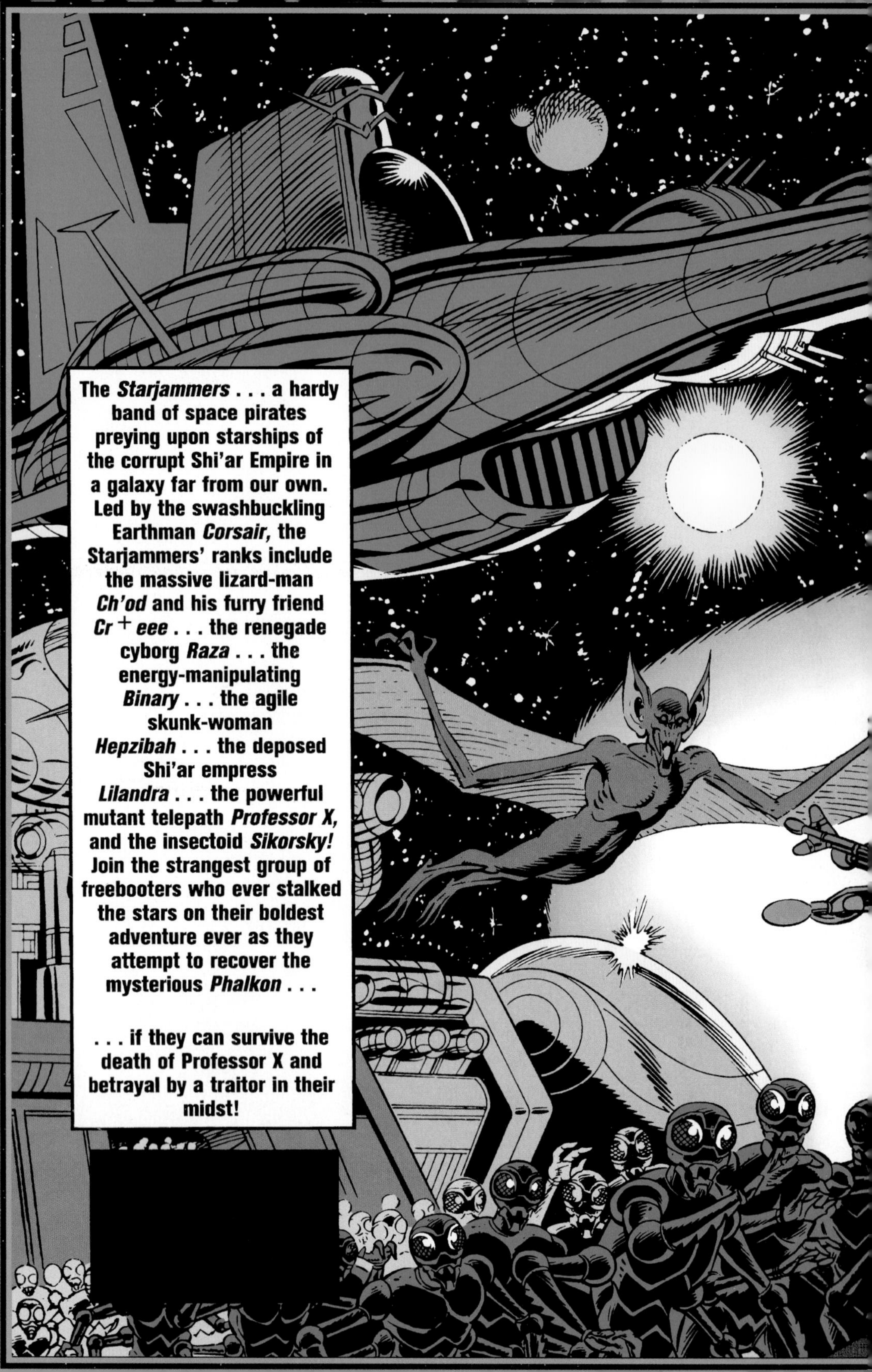
The *Starjammers* . . . a hardy band of space pirates preying upon starships of the corrupt Shi'ar Empire in a galaxy far from our own. Led by the swashbuckling Earthman *Corsair,* the Starjammers' ranks include the massive lizard-man *Ch'od* and his furry friend *Cr + eee* . . . the renegade cyborg *Raza* . . . the energy-manipulating *Binary* . . . the agile skunk-woman *Hepzibah* . . . the deposed Shi'ar empress *Lilandra* . . . the powerful mutant telepath *Professor X,* and the insectoid *Sikorsky!* Join the strangest group of freebooters who ever stalked the stars on their boldest adventure ever as they attempt to recover the mysterious *Phalkon* . . .
. . . if they can survive the death of Professor X and betrayal by a traitor in their midst!

MARVEL COMICS
X-MEN SPOTLIGHT ON . . .
01513
1 of 2
$4.50 US
$5.50 CAN
STARJAMMERS

PHALKON QUEST PART 1

TERRY KAVANAGH
writer

DAVE COCKRUM
penciler

JEFF ALBRECHT
inker

JOHN WILCOX
colorist

AGUSTIN MAS
letterer

JEFF ALBRECHT
logo design

KELLY CORVESE
assistant editor

MARK GRUENWALD
editor

TOM DeFALCO
editor in chief

OKAY, LIL, CHARLEY, DROP THE CLOAKING FIELD AND...
...ATTACK!
<WHA--?! ENEMY FIRE FROM PORT. NOTIFY THE COMMANDER-- IT'S THE STARJAMMERS!
<THOSE REBEL PIRATES ARE FOOLS! THEY'LL NEVER BREACH OUR DEFLECTORS, AND SENSORS SHOW...>
<...THEIR SHIELDS AREN'T EVEN UP!>
CORSAIR, I WOULD REALLY APPRECIATE IT IF YOU WOULD STOP CALLING ME "CHARLEY"...
...AND AS FOR THIS "PLAN" OF YOURS--
--IT STINKS!
<COMMANDER, THEIR SMALLER SHIP IS ABLE TO EXECUTE INTRICATE EVASIVE MANEUVERS THAT OUR FREIGHTER CAN'T MATCH.>
<FIRE PHLAZERS-- QUICKLY!>
NOW, WHAT WERE YOU ALL SO WORRIED ABOUT?
HERE IT COMES!
KONK
SPUTTER
SPUTTER
IT WORKED...

...DIDN'T IT?
WALDO TO STARJAMMERS-- IMPACT IMMINENT!
SOME PLAN, INDEED.
YIIK
ACTIVATE TELEPORTER--
--WE'RE GOING TO PENETRATE THEIR SHIELDS BY GOING RIGHT THROUGH THE PHLAZER BLAST!
CHAPTER I
BOARDING PARTY
COCKRUM - Albrecht

BE CAREFUL, CHARLES. EVEN WITH WALDO'S AID, THE STRAIN OF PSIONICALLY REPLACING OUR SHIELDS--
LILAAAAAAANDRAAAAAAARRGH!
WALDO, IF THE OTHERS ARE OFF-SHIP, BRING THE SHIELDS BACK UP--NOW!

MEANWHILE, IN THE STORAGE HOLDS OF THE FREIGHTER...
FZZZZT
DID ANYONE ELSE HEAR THAT HORRIBLE...SCREAM JUST BEFORE WE TELEPORTED? I THINK IT WAS PROFESSOR XAVIER--!
WE HAD TO DROP OUR SHIELDS TO BE ABLE TO TELEPORT--
DOESN'T MATTER. PLAN OF CAPTAIN CORSAIR...

...WORKED!
IT DID?
WE JUST GOT HERE, CR+EEE.
FLAME ON!

JUST TESTING OUT SOME NEW BATTLE-CRIES, CH'OD.
FAP
EXCUSE ME, BINARY?
PFOW
PFOW
I THINK THAT LAST ONE'S COPYRIGHTED BACK HOME, CAROL.
EARTHERS--!

I COULD'VE GUESSED THESE HOLDS WOULD BE EMPTY--THAT WAS TOO EASY.
WE NEED TO FIND THE COMMANDER OF THIS HEAP.
CAPTAIN, MY CYBERNETIC CIRCUITS HATH GIVEN ME A FAIR TRANSLATION OF THIS SIGNPOST. THE COMMANDER'S QUARTERS SHOULD BE DIRECTLY THROUGH...

...HERE!
FIGURES.
BURN UP?
FIZZLE FORWARD?

FLASH FRY!

FZAP

RIGHT! CH'OD, *YOU* TAKE OUT THE REST OF THE COMMANDER'S GUARDS...

...RAZA, BINARY-- LOOT THE SHIP. HIT THE GALLEYS--TAKE *EVERYTHING*.

YOU'RE COMING WITH ME, *HEPZIBAH!*

AND THIS CREW WILL SURVIVE ON *WHAT,* CAPTAIN CORSAIR?

?!

NOT NOW, CR+EEE.

EEEEE!

OOOOOH!

THIS GEEZER'S OUR LAST CHANCE TO TURN A *PROFIT* ON THIS RAID--

FOR THE *REBELLION.*

OF COURSE, FOR THE REBELLION.

MOVE IT, BALDY, AND DON'T EVEN BOTHER TO TRY THAT "OFFICIAL" GARBAGE WITH *THE STARJAMMERS.* WE'RE *PIRATES*--

MY NAME IS OOOO2O AND I AM SHIP COMMANDER OF THE--

FOR THE REBELLION.

RIGHT--AND WE DON'T HAVE TO PLAY BY THE *RULES*.

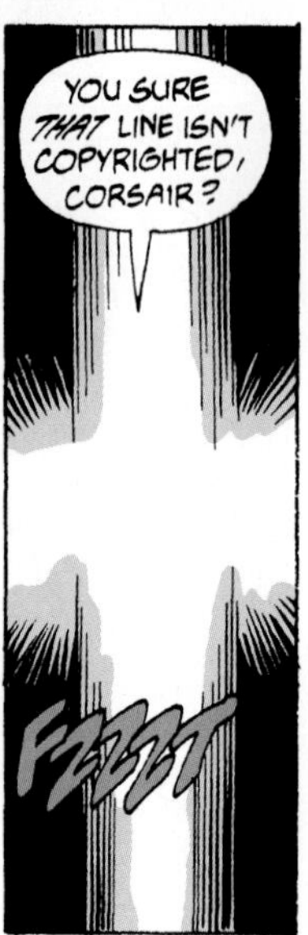

FIELD MISSION ACCOMPLISHED... SORT OF.
OF COURSE YOU CAN GO NOW, CR+REEE.
WHAT DO YOU MEAN "TOO LATE"? NO, NOT ON MY SHOULDER...

SHIP STATUS, LIL?
AHEM I FEEL BETTER QUALIFIED TO ANSWER THAT, SIR. TO PUT IT IN YOUR TERMS--"WE'VE BEEN BETTER".
THANKS, WALDO, BUT I WAS ASKING ABOUT THE CREW.
WELL, EXCUSE ME...!
IT WAS ONLY WITH THE AID OF WALDO THAT I HAVE BEEN ABLE TO KEEP US INTACT FOR THE PAST EIGHT MINUTES...
...AND THE STARJAMMER'S SHIELDS CANNOT TAKE MUCH MORE OF THIS BARRAGE.
REALLY, CORSAIR, ATTACKING A FREIGHTER OMEGA CLASS?! THEIR WEAPONRY ALONE--
AND XAVIER?

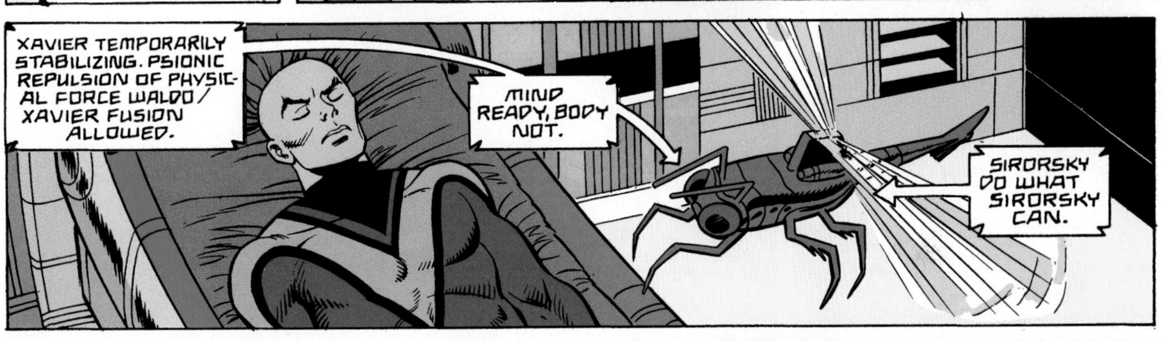
XAVIER TEMPORARILY STABILIZING. PSIONIC REPULSION OF PHYSICAL FORCE WALDO/XAVIER FUSION ALLOWED.
MIND READY, BODY NOT.
SIRORSKY DO WHAT SIRORSKY CAN.

RIGHT NOW, WE'VE GOT TO SAVE THE 'JAMMER...
GOT IT--WE'LL KEELHAUL THE COMMANDER!
I HOPE THIS WORKS. I'VE SEEN IT IN PLENTY OF MOVIES...
...BUT THIS TIME IT'LL HAVE A DIFFERENT PURPOSE.
CH'OD, RAZA--HERE'S THE PLAN...

YOU CAN'T DO THIS! IT'S AGAINST ALL THE RULES OF INTERSTELLAR--
OPEN YON AIRLOCK, CH'OD.
GIVE HIM A PRESSURE SUIT FIRST, RAZA.

WHY?

CORSAIR'S PLAN WILL WORK BETTER IF HE'S ALIVE.

FREIGHTER OMEGA CLASS, CEASE FIRE IMMEDIATELY OR RISK HARMING YOUR COMMANDER. MAINTAIN A DISTANCE OF 50,000 KILOMETERS...
OKAY, LIL, WE'VE GOT THEM BEYOND FIRING RANGE. BRING UP THE CLOAKING SHIELDS.
I'M AFRAID I KNOW WHAT THE NEXT THING I HAVE TO DO IS.

SOON...
OKAY, COMMANDER, SINCE YOUR HOLDS WERE BASICALLY EMPTY, IT FOLLOWS THAT YOUR FREIGHTER WAS ON ITS WAY TO PICKUP SUPPLIES.
WHERE WERE YOU GOING?
W-W-WE--
WE'RE AT THE VERY EDGE OF YOUR SHI'AR EMPIRE. THERE'S NO ONE AROUND TO HELP YOU.
H-H-HELP-P--
THIS ISN'T WORKING. HE'S TOO SCARED.

GREAT. NOW THE WHOLE CREW'S WATCHING. HOW FAR AM I WILLING TO GO FOR THIS REBELLION?
C'MON, COMMANDER. ONE MORE STEP AND YOUR MAGNETIC BOOTS WILL BE USELESS.

DOES CORSAIR REALLY MEAN TO KILL HIM?
I DOUBT THAT HE IS MAN ENOUGH.

I REPEAT--WHERE WERE YOU HEADED?
PH-PH-PHALKON--

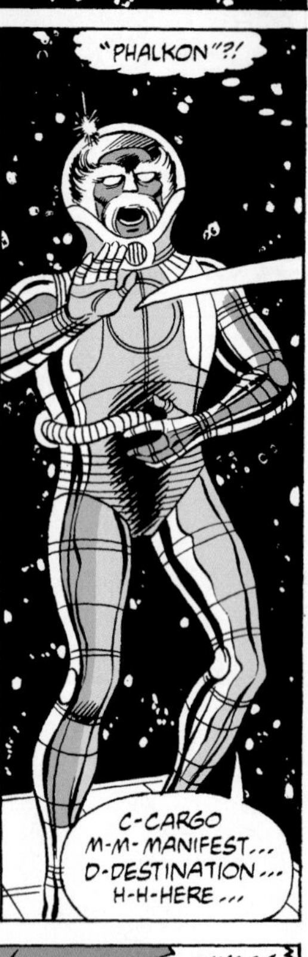
"PHALKON"?!
C-CARGO M-M-MANIFEST... D-DESTINATION... H-H-HERE...

N-NO--THE CODES! I FORGOT THE C--
AAAARRGH!

WHOA!
I'M OFF THE MAGNETIC GANGPLANK...
WHAT HAVE I DONE NOW?

WHAT HATH HE DONE NOW?!
KERASH
THE PORTHOLE--!

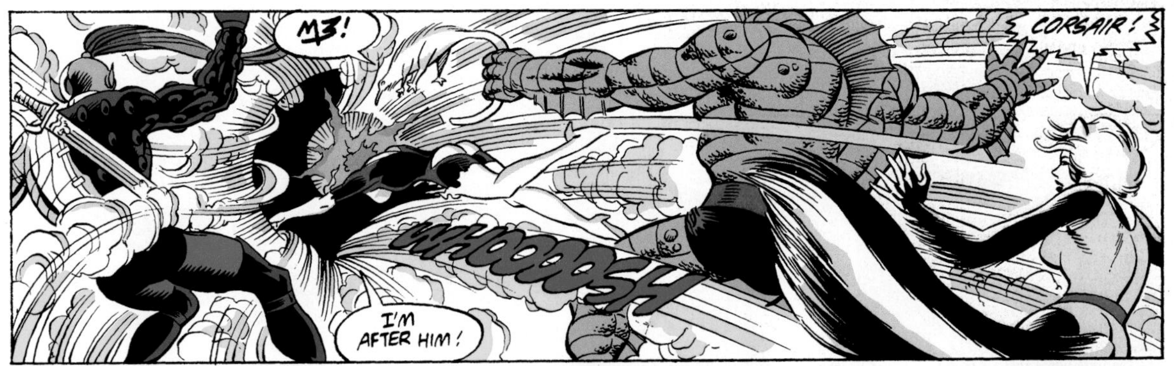
M3!
CORSAIR!
WHOOOOOSH
I'M AFTER HIM!

I DON'T MEAN TO HURRY YOU, FRIEND RAZA, BUT EVEN MY HIDE--

NO FEAR, CH'OD, MY SWORD HATH ALREADY DONE THE DELICATE WORK...
...NOW MY MUSCLES AND GEARS CAN DO THE REST.

AND HEPZIBAH...?
I LAST SAW HER BOUNDING AFTER YON PROJECTILE.
IT WAS ALL WE COULD DO TO STAND OUR GROUND.

"TRUE, CH'OD, BUT HEPZIBAH IS A CAT OF A VERY DIFFERENT BREED."
ATMOSPHERE LEAVING SHIP FASTER THAN IT CAN BE REPLACED.
I AM WARRIOR. WHAT CAN I DO?

GETTING HARD TO BREATHE.
HMMM...
THERE.
PLUNK

CAPTAIN, ARE YOU--
NOT SMART, CORSAIR. THIS SHIP'S ALREADY SUSTAINED ENOUGH DAMAGE AND SIKORSKY INFORMS ME THAT LITTLE EPISODE DID NOT HELP CHARLES'S CONDITION ANY...
WORSE YET, LIL, WE'VE JUST LOST THE "MAP" THAT WOULD'VE GIVEN US THE LOCATION OF "PHALKON"!

PHALKON? I HAD ASSUMED ITS POWER WAS JUST A MYTH.
WELL, THOSE WERE PRETTY SERIOUS SECURITY PROCEDURES FOR A "MYTH." BUT I GUESS WE'LL NEVER KNOW NOW...
MAYBE WE WILL. I MANAGED TO TRACK THE INDIVIDUAL DIRECTIONS OF THOSE FOUR MAP PODS AS THEY ZIPPED AWAY.
AND SOON...
...SORRY, HEPZIBAH, BUT LIL SAYS THAT THE FIFTH POD WAS A HOMING-BEACON HEADED STRAIGHT FOR THE SHI'AR THRONEWORLD.
WE HAVE TO SPLIT UP LIKE THIS IF WE'RE GOING TO BEAT LIL'S SISTER, DEATHBIRD, TO THE "MAP."
BECAUSE IT'S YOUR HOME PLANET, CR+REEE, YOU HAVE NOTHING TO FEAR THERE, DO YOU?
THEN WE'RE READY FOR OUR PHALKON QUEST...
FZZT
FZZT
FZZT
FZZT

SIKORSY TO BRIDGE.
AND XAVIER INTO COMA HAS SLIPPED.
LILANDRA HERE, SIKORSKY. I'M A LITTLE BUSY UP HERE RIGHT NOW. THE SHI'AR FREIGHTER MUST HAVE SEEN THEIR COMMANDER'S EXPLOSION...
...THEY'RE RESUMING THE ATTACK!
TWOOM

ELSEWHERE...
THIS IS NOT MY KIND OF MOVIE...
GRRRRR...

HEAT UP?!

CHAPTER II
CASTAWAY
COCKRUM - Albrecht
FZZZZZZZMMM
A MOON IN THE GROF SYSTEM...
NICE-- THIS SURE LOOKS LIKE IT'S GOING TO BE SOME FUN PLACE.
AT LEAST THE ATMOSPHERE'S BREATHABLE--LIKE OUR SENSORS TOLD US.
NEARBY...
SOMEONE HAS COME... FINALLY!
GGGRRRRR...

HOPEFULLY, LILANDRA 'PORTED ME SOMEWHERE NEAR THE PROBE...
...'CAUSE THIS SHI'AR "COMPASS" CERTAINLY ISN'T GOING TO BE MUCH HELP TO ME IN FINDING IT. THING NEEDS A NAVIGATOR TO INTERPRET IT.
WHERE IS RAZA WHEN I NEED HIM ANYWAY?
"BOOTY"?! HEPZIBAH'S RIGHT--I MAY BE GETTING INTO THIS SPACE PIRATE ROLE TOO MUCH FOR MY OWN GOOD...
THREE SUNS DON'T MAKE IT EASY TO DEDUCE A DIRECTION...
AH... HE AND BINARY ARE PROBABLY HAVING THEIR OWN PROBLEMS RECOVERING THEIR PORTION OF OUR BOOTY.
...BUT, BEST I CAN FIGURE, THIS IS THE WAY TO HEAD.
TOWARDS THAT SPOOKY CASTLE IN THE DISTANCE...
...OF COURSE.
WHO CAN BLAME ME IF I LOSE TRACK OF REALITY NOW AND THEN WHEN I'M WITH THE STARJAMMERS?
AT LEAST THEY'VE TAUGHT ME TO BE PREPARED.
ACTUALLY, THE BOY SCOUTS TAUGHT ME THAT AND ERROL FLYNN MOVIES TAUGHT ME HOW TO FIGHT. BUT EARTH'S A LONG WAY AWAY NOW...
THNNNNNNN
...AND ERROL FLYNN NEVER HAD THE LUXURY OF CARRYING HIS WEAPONS IN AN OTHER-DIMENSIONAL POCKET.
GUESS THERE IS SOMETHING TO BE SAID FOR SHI'AR TECHNOLOGY.
SOON...
BEEN THINKING AN AWFUL LOT ABOUT EARTH LATELY.
IT'S NOT LIKE I LEFT ANYTHING BEHIND WHEN LIL'S CRAZY BROTHER FIRST KIDNAPPED ME INTO SLAVERY AND... KILLED KATHERINE.
MAYBE I NEVER REALLY TRIED TO GET BACK HOME BECAUSE THEY REMINDED ME TOO MUCH OF WHAT I'D LOST.
BUT THEY'RE BOTH GROWN MEN NOW.
EXCEPT, OF COURSE, FOR OUR SONS, ALEX AND SCOTT.
SHHICK
FORGET IT.
I FEEL LIKE I'M NOT GETTING ANYWHERE... FAST. HOW CAN IT BE SO HOT WHEN NO LIGHT IS EVEN PENETRATING THIS FAR INTO THIS FOREST?!
THE INSTINCT THAT AWOKE US AFTER SO LONG WAS CORRECT, MER...
YES, VAM... MEAT APPROACHES!

EVENTUALLY...
GREAT. IF MY CALCULATIONS ARE CORRECT--WHICH I DOUBT--THIS SHOULD BE ABOUT HALFWAY TO THE POD'S LANDING SITE.
NO WATER LEFT... AND THE SUNS HAVEN'T LET UP FOR A MINUTE. OBVIOUSLY, THIS PLACE HAS NO NIGHT.
NO LIFE EITHER--EVEN THE VEGETATION IS DEAD. WONDER WHAT CAUSED ALL THIS...

MAYBE I CAN SCROUNGE UP SOME SUPPLIES IN HERE.
PROBABLY A WASTE OF TIME BUT HERE GOES...

HELLO! ANYBODY HOME?
KNEW IT.
NO DOORS--JUST WINDOWS... ALL OF THE LOWER ONES BOARDED UP.

WELL...MIGHT AS WELL START HEADING--

WAIT--WHAT WAS THAT UP THERE?!
GET BACK, VAM, IT'S SEEN US.

NOTHING--GUESS I'M STARTING TO HALLUCINATE NOW.

THIS WHOLE PLANET IS SORT OF SPOOKY. I HOPE I'M AT LEAST GOING IN THE RIGHT DIRECTION...
...BUT IT WOULDN'T SURPRISE ME IF--

YIIIIKES!
GREETINGS, CORSAIR!

XAVIER ?! OR HIS GHO--
HARDLY, CORSAIR.
EVEN THE SPECIAL PROPERTIES OF YOUR RAPIER WOULD HAVE FOUND IT DIFFICULT TO AFFECT MY ASTRAL FORM.
THEN WHAT THE #@*! ARE YOU TRYING TO DO?! I ALMOST SKEWERED YOU!
MY BODY IS STILL ON THE SHIP AND SHOWS NO SIGNS OF IMPROVEMENT-- IN FACT, MY COMA SEEMS TO HAVE TAKEN A TURN FOR THE WORSE.

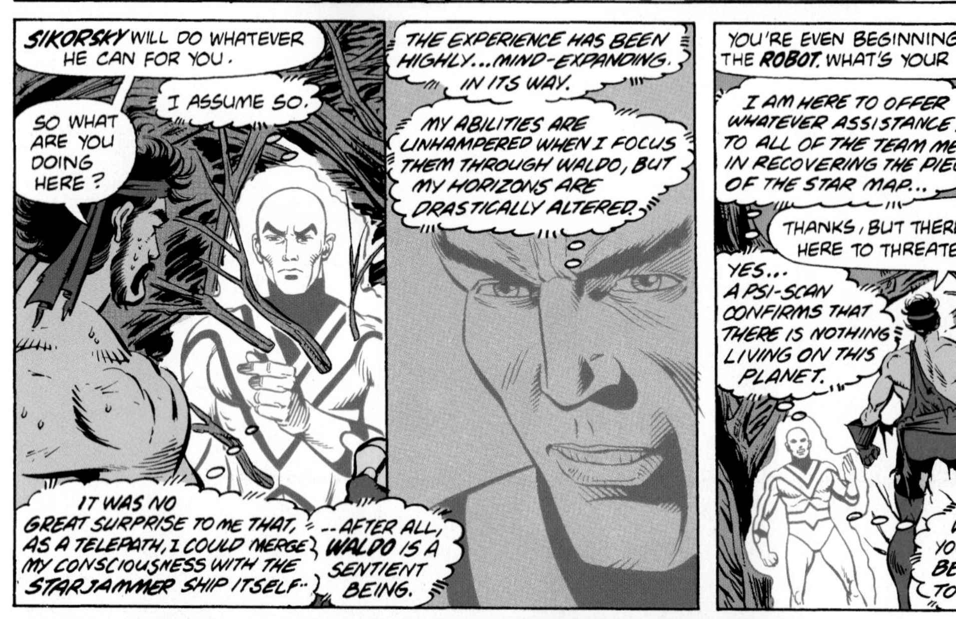
SIKORSKY WILL DO WHATEVER HE CAN FOR YOU.
I ASSUME SO.
SO WHAT ARE YOU DOING HERE?
THE EXPERIENCE HAS BEEN HIGHLY...MIND-EXPANDING. IN ITS WAY.
MY ABILITIES ARE UNHAMPERED WHEN I FOCUS THEM THROUGH WALDO, BUT MY HORIZONS ARE DRASTICALLY ALTERED.
IT WAS NO GREAT SURPRISE TO ME THAT, AS A TELEPATH, I COULD MERGE MY CONSCIOUSNESS WITH THE STARJAMMER SHIP ITSELF--
--AFTER ALL, WALDO IS A SENTIENT BEING.

YOU'RE EVEN BEGINNING TO SOUND LIKE THE ROBOT. WHAT'S YOUR POINT, XAVIER?
I AM HERE TO OFFER WHATEVER ASSISTANCE I CAN TO ALL OF THE TEAM MEMBERS IN RECOVERING THE PIECES OF THE STAR MAP...
THANKS, BUT THERE'S NOTHING HERE TO THREATEN ME.
YES... A PSI-SCAN CONFIRMS THAT THERE IS NOTHING LIVING ON THIS PLANET.
I JUST NEED TO KNOW WHERE--
1500 METERS BACK IN THE DIRECTION YOU CAME FROM.
RETURN HERE WITH THE PROBE AND YOU'LL AUTOMATICALLY BE TELEPORTED BACK TO THE STARJAMMER.

NOW I'M OFF TO SEE TO CH'OD AND HEPZIBAH...
POP
HEPZIBAH--!? IS SHE ALL RIGHT?! XAVIER...?
XAVIER--!
HE'S MORE FRUSTRATING THAN EVER. BUT HE DID MANAGE TO REMIND ME OF THE REAL REASON I CHOSE TO STAY WITH THIS GROUP-- HEPZIBAH.

AS LONG AS MY CAT-LADY'S COMMITTED TO THIS REBELLION... SO AM I.
AND, AS MUCH AS I HATE TO ADMIT IT, I PROBABLY HAVE XAVIER TO THANK FOR HOW WELL MY KIDS TURNED OUT.

SKKRRREEEEEEEEEEEE
WHHOOAAAA!
ROOOOWWR

AAAIIIEEEEEEE
SHASH
BACK OFF, CREEP!

DOWN, GIRL, DOWN!
RROOWWFFF
NO, MER-- THE UNFAMILIAR SUBSTANCE... THE SQUAWKING FEAST WIELDS IS HURTFUL! RETREAT--COME TO ME...

GOT TO GET HIGHER, INTO THE DENSER BRANCHES, WHERE THOSE CREATURES-- WHATEVER THEY ARE-- CAN'T MANEUVER.

YOU MUST RETRIEVE THE TREASURE THE FLICKERING MEAT SPOKE OF AND BRING IT TO OUR KEEP. I WILL REND THIS MEAL.
BE WARY, VAM

AS ALWAYS, MY MATE... FOR YOU.
NOW GO. IT IS CLOSE. AND SOON WE WILL FEED AGAIN... FREELY.

SKRREEEEE
THEY MUST BE USING SOME KIND OF TELEPATHY TO COMMUNICATE--LIKE XAVIER. I CAN UNDERSTAND EVERYTHING THEY'RE SAYING.
AND I DON'T LIKE WHAT I'M HEARING ONE BIT.

SHUCT
I'M OUT OF HERE!

NO--MER! WHY HAVE YOU RETU--
SNAK
URK...

...I... COULD NOT... LEAVE YOU... ALONE... VAMMMM

NOOOOOO!

YOUR HUNGER IS ENDED, MER.
AND, THANKS TO THIS, MINE WILL SOON BE WELL SATISFIED!

MUCH LATER...
OKAY, I'LL TRY ONE MORE TIME...

I JUST WISH I HADN'T HAD TO ABANDON MY GRAPPLING PROJECTOR EARLIER.
THIS IS NEVER GOING T--

WELL, WHAT DO YOU KNOW--?!
CHK

ALL OF A SUDDEN, I'M THANKFUL FOR THE UNEARTHLY TOUGHNESS OF ALL THOSE BRANCHES I HAD TO HACK MY WAY THROUGH.
I JUST HOPE THE "ROPE" I WHITTLED OUT OF THEM HOLDS UP AS WELL.

MADE IT!
KERASH

NOW TO FIGURE OUT WHERE THAT THING WOULD HAVE TAKEN THE POD.
IF IT RETURNS TO THE TELEPORT SITE WITH IT...
...I'D HATE TO THINK ABOUT WHAT MIGHT HAPPEN BACK ON THE SHIP.

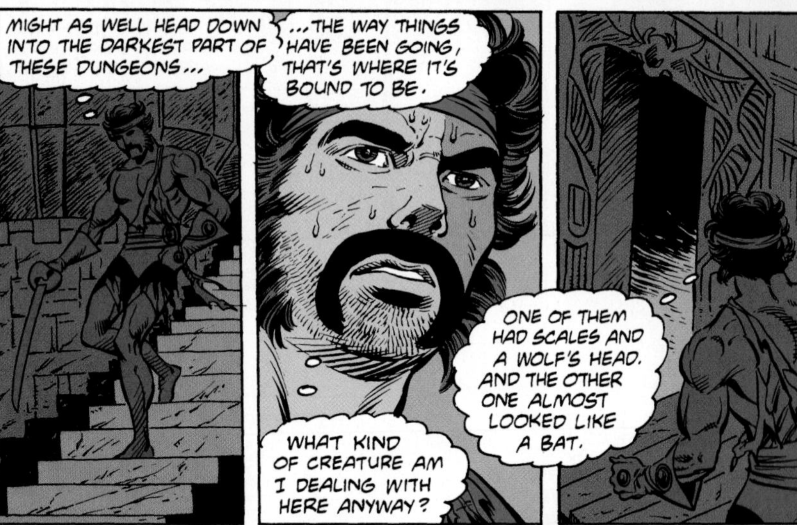
MIGHT AS WELL HEAD DOWN INTO THE DARKEST PART OF THESE DUNGEONS...
...THE WAY THINGS HAVE BEEN GOING, THAT'S WHERE IT'S BOUND TO BE.
ONE OF THEM HAD SCALES AND A WOLF'S HEAD. AND THE OTHER ONE ALMOST LOOKED LIKE A BAT.
WHAT KIND OF CREATURE AM I DEALING WITH HERE ANYWAY?

OF COURSE--A VAMPIRE OF SOME SORT! NO WONDER XAVIER FOUND NOTHING LIVING.
THERE'S THE POD.
I DON'T WANT TO HURT THIS CREATURE--IT'S NOT MY PLANET. HAVE TO GRAB THE PIECE OF THE MAP AND GET OUT OF HERE BEFORE--

KRREEEAAAAAAAAA
THERE GOES THAT IDEA.
HEY, HANG ON A MINUTE--
--WAIT!

OH, GREAT--IT CAN'T UNDERSTAND ME. MUST BE THE PSI-SHIELDS XAVIER PLACED IN ALL OF OUR MINDS.
BLEED, BABBLING MEAT!

AT LEAST MY SWORD HAS SOME EFFECT ON IT.
I'VE SEE NOTHING INORGANIC AT ALL ON THIS PLANET. THE STEEL ALONE MUST BE SO ALIEN TO THE THING.
JUST LIKE CREATURES OF EARTH LEGEND WHO WERE AFFECTED BY SILVER BULLETS AND SUCH!

MY MATE AND I HAD BEEN SO ALONE SINCE OUR DARK HOME GREW SUNS LONG AGO AND OUR PEOPLE FLED IN PAIN. NOW I AM THE LAST...
...AND I TOO WOULD FINALLY ABANDON OUR HOME.
BUT, FIRST, I WILL DEVOUR MER'S DESTROYER!

WONDER IF--ITS SPECIES HAPPENED UPON EARTH!
AS METAMORPHS, THEY COULD HAVE BEEN THE BASIS FOR OUR LEGENDS ABOUT VAMPIRES, WEREWOLVES, OR DRAGONS!

I STILL DON'T WANT TO KILL IT... BUT, IF I HAVE TO, THIS SWORD IS GOING STRAIGHT INTO ITS HEART--

I ALMOST SENSE THOUGHTS FROM THIS MEAT...
NO CONCERN. I DO SENSE A FEAR...

...OF DOING THIS!
SHIKT

PHOK
OH, MY LORD!

SKKRRREEEEE
SH
SLA
IT HAD NO EFFECT. ITS HEART PROBABLY ISN'T EVEN LOCATED THERE.

THERE'S NO WAY THIS BEAST AND I CAN COMMUNICATE. ITS SPECIES AND MINE HAVE NOTHING IN COMMON...
URK
CHOK

...NOTHING AT ALL!
SHWK

I JUST WISH I DIDN'T HAVE TO HEAR HIM DIE IN MY HEAD...
URRGGGLLEE...

IT SEEMS I DON'T HAVE ALL THAT MUCH IN COMMON WITH MY OWN SPECIES ANYMORE EITHER.
EARTH AND ITS MORAL CODE ARE BEHIND ME FOREVER.
THE PHALKON QUEST IS ALL THAT'S IMPORTANT NOW...

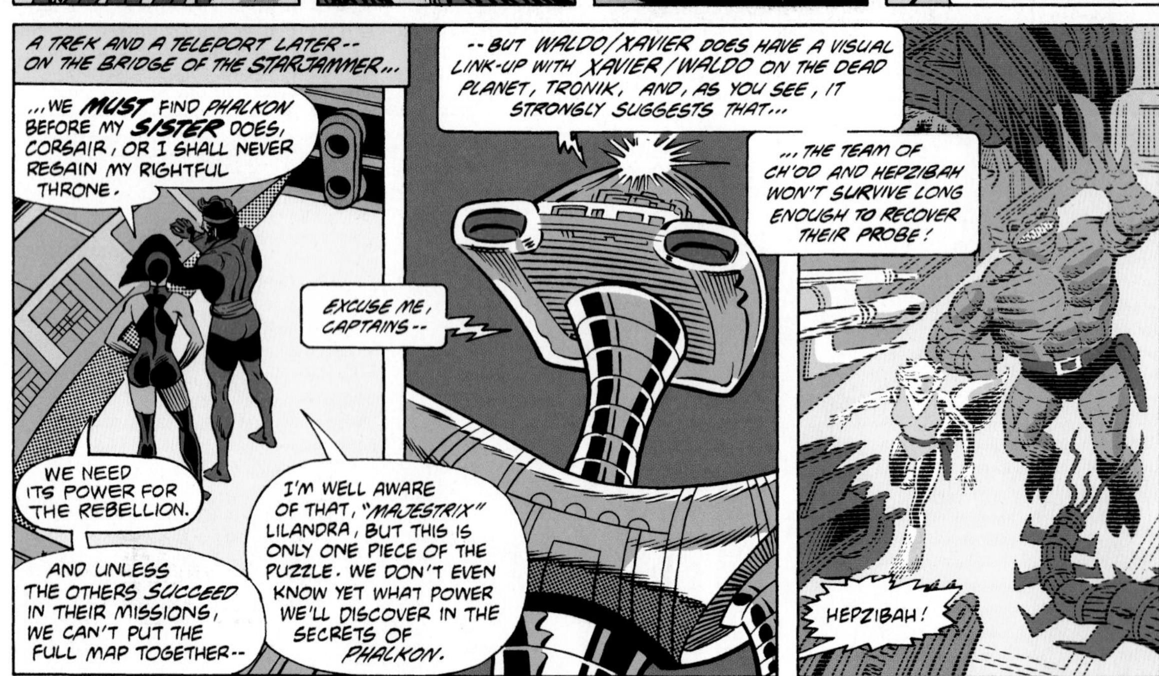
A TREK AND A TELEPORT LATER-- ON THE BRIDGE OF THE STARJAMMER...
...WE MUST FIND PHALKON BEFORE MY SISTER DOES, CORSAIR, OR I SHALL NEVER REGAIN MY RIGHTFUL THRONE.
WE NEED ITS POWER FOR THE REBELLION.
AND UNLESS THE OTHERS SUCCEED IN THEIR MISSIONS, WE CAN'T PUT THE FULL MAP TOGETHER--
I'M WELL AWARE OF THAT, "MAJESTRIX" LILANDRA, BUT THIS IS ONLY ONE PIECE OF THE PUZZLE. WE DON'T EVEN KNOW YET WHAT POWER WE'LL DISCOVER IN THE SECRETS OF PHALKON.
EXCUSE ME, CAPTAINS--
--BUT WALDO/XAVIER DOES HAVE A VISUAL LINK-UP WITH XAVIER/WALDO ON THE DEAD PLANET, TRONIK, AND, AS YOU SEE, IT STRONGLY SUGGESTS THAT...
...THE TEAM OF CH'OD AND HEPZIBAH WON'T SURVIVE LONG ENOUGH TO RECOVER THEIR PROBE!
HEPZIBAH!

CHAPTER III
PLUNDER
THE PLANET TRONIK...
WE ARE AT A DEAD END, FRIEND XAVIER. THIS MYSTERIOUS PLANET WAS SUPPOSED TO HAVE PERISHED LONG AGO WHEN A COMET PASSED TOO CLOSE, DRAWING AWAY ITS ATMOSPHERE.
YET HEPZIBAH AND I HAVE BEEN FIGHTING THIS WORLD'S DEFENSES SINCE WE ARRIVED.
THERE ARE NO LIFE-FORMS TO BE FOUND ANYWHERE... YET THE MAP POD WAS NOT AT ITS LANDING SITE--
-- WHERE IS IT?!
XAVIER/WALDO IS AS BAFFLED AS YOU ARE, CH'OD. THE ALIEN BIO-METALLIC SUBSTANCE THAT SEEMS TO LITERALLY COVER THIS ENTIRE WORLD...
...REFLECTS OUR TELEPATHIC ABILITIES RIGHT BACK AT OUR ASTRAL FORM. ALTHOUGH NO LONGER AFFECTED BY THE PHYSICAL, THIS IS ACTUALLY QUITE PAINFU--
COCKRUM-Albrecht
GGRRRRR
QUIET, BOTH. RISING HAIRS ON HEPZIBAH'S NECK TELL OF--

--DANGER!
THE ENTIRE WALL--!

CH'OD--!?
THOOOM

YOU CALLED, HEPZIBAH?
SKRANCH

THIS WOULD SEEM TO BE THE ONLY WAY TO MAKE PROGRESS--

YAAAAH!
THUMP

WELL, SINCE XAVIER/WALDO APPEARS TO BE OF NO HELP HERE AS IS...
CH'OD, BACK!
ZZZT
ZT
ZT

...WE'LL TAKE OUR LEAVE.
SHOOR
EVERY BLAST, ENTIRE AREA REACTS.

POP
YOU MAY SAY THAT AGAIN...

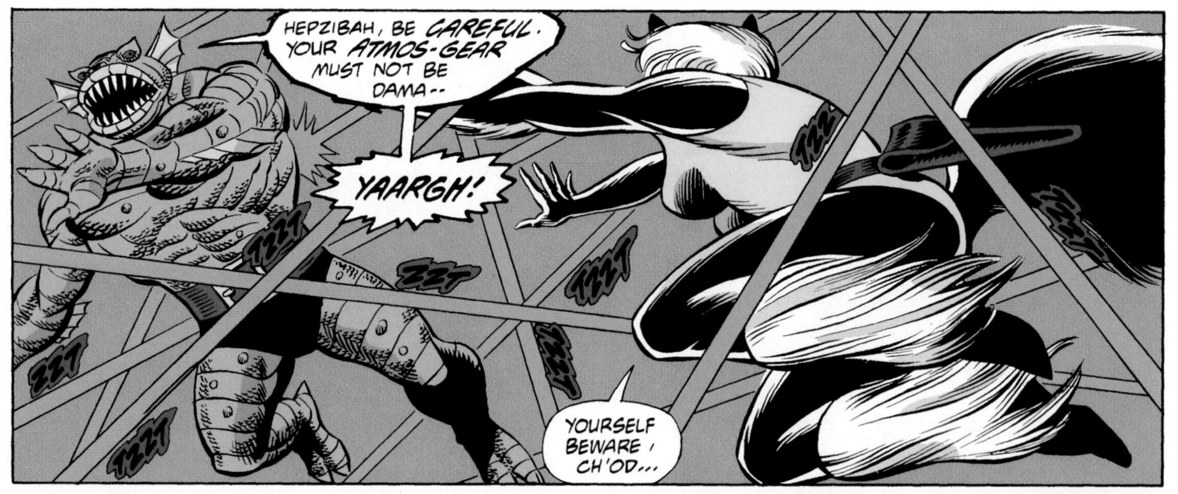

HEPZIBAH, BE CAREFUL. YOUR ATMOS-GEAR MUST NOT BE DAMA--
YAARGH!
YOURSELF BEWARE, CH'OD...

...HEPZIBAH SCARED NOT.
HERE-- HEPZIBAH FEELS... PULSE.

SKHRRT
AND CLAWS SHE HAS.

EEEEEEEEEEEEEEEE
THE LASERS HAVE STOPPED--!

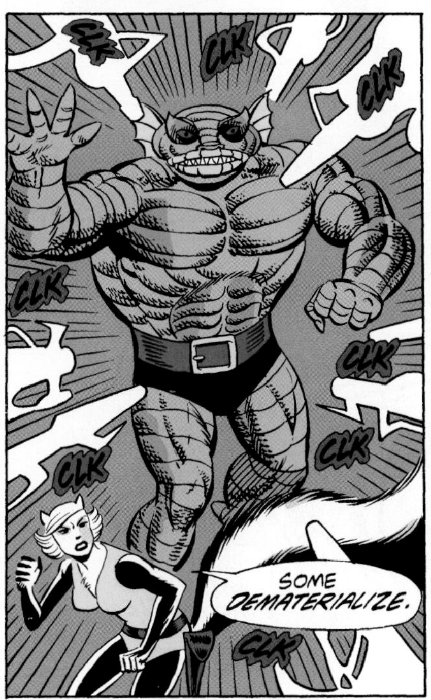

SOME DEMATERIALIZE.

THANK YOU, HEPZIBAH. I AM NOT SURE THAT EVEN MY HIDE COULD HAVE TAKEN MUCH MORE... AND I AM NOWHERE NEAR AS AGILE AS YOU--
DANGER OVER NOT. OTHER WEAPONS-- BETTER, IMPROVED-- PREPARE TO FIRE...

MEANWHILE, BACK ON THE STARJAMMER SHIP...
CORSAIR, WE MUST KNOW WHERE YOUR PORTION OF THE "BOOTY" NOW IS...
I WANT TO HEAR ABOUT HEPZIBAH FIRST. HOW IS SHE? HOW--
CHARLES, YOU NEED REST. YOUR BODY IS STILL IN A COMA--
THANKS TO THE RAID I ARRANGED-- BUT YOU DON'T HAVE TO RUB IT IN, LIL.
PRINCESS LILANDRA CORRECT. BODY WORSE, NEEDS MIND TO HEAL.

AND THE OTHER STARJAMMERS NEED XAVIER/WALDO NOW.
"XAVIER/WALDO"?
I DON'T KNOW, CHARLEY--YOU WEREN'T ALL THAT MUCH HELP TO ME ON MY MISSION...
CORSAIR--I SEEK TO AID HEPZIBAH AND CH'OD.
THE MAP POD IS ON THE BRIDGE WITH WALDO.

BUT TRY AND REMEMBER WHO'S THE CAPTAIN OF THIS CREW, XAVIE-
POP
OH, CHARLES... MERGING YOUR CONSCIOUSNESS WITH WALDO MAY HAVE BEEN A VERY BAD IDEA.

ON THE BRIDGE...
POP
IT IS GOOD TO SEE FELLOW XAVIER/WALDO.
WALDO/XAVIER IS ATTEMPTING TO STABILIZE LINK WITH BINARY AND RAZA'S AWAY TEAM...
...BUT WE HAVE A MORE IMMEDIATE PROBLEM TO RELATE--
NOT RIGHT NOW, WALDO.

WE JUST NEED THE RECOVERED PIECE OF THE PHALKON MAP FOR A MOMENT...
SNFF SNFF
WALDO/XAVIER HAS DISCOVERED EVIDENCE OF SABOTAGE FROM WITHIN
POP
OH, WELL-- WALDO/XAVIER CAN'T REMEMBER WHAT IT WANTED TO SAY ANYWAY...
...OR WAS THAT PART OF THE PROBLEM MAYBE?

WHILE BACK ON TRONIK...
I ASSUME IT IS NOW MY TURN TO COME TO THE RESCUE--
--USING THE RIP BEGUN BY MY TEAMMATE.
ZZZZ
ZZZZ
TZZZT
ZZZZ
ZZZZ
TZZZT
TZZZT
TZZZT
SHRPPPPP

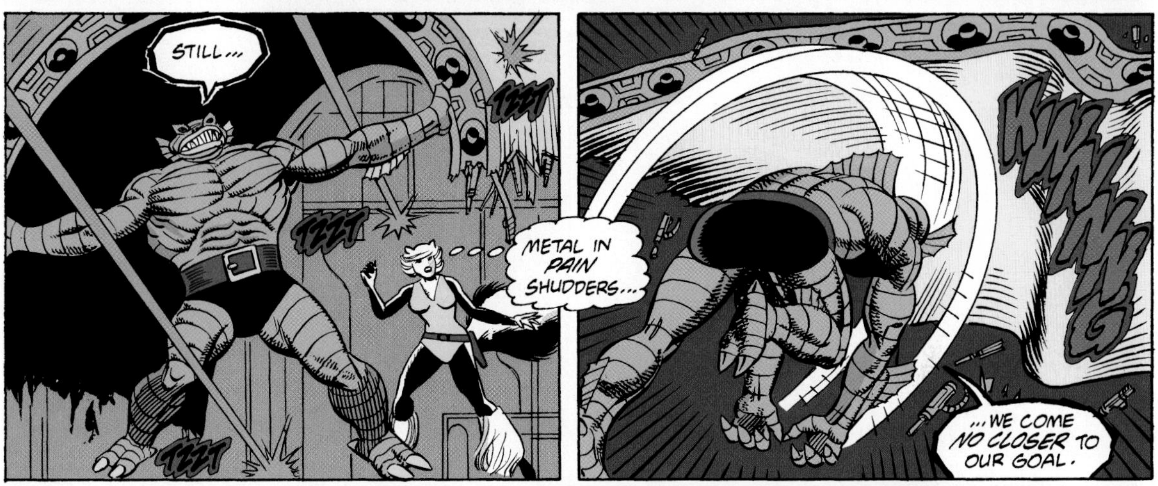
STILL...
TZZZT
TZZZT
METAL IN PAIN SHUDDERS...
TZZZT
KWNNNG
...WE COME NO CLOSER TO OUR GOAL.

POP
NOT TRUE, CH'OD. YOU ARE AS GOOD AS THERE...
...ONCE WE TELEPATHICALLY IMPART THE SCENT OF THE PODS TO HEPZIBAH.
SNFF SNFF
SNFF
NO!

CH'OD MOVE THAT WAY--
POOM
OOF

--HEPZIBAH SCOOT THIS WAY.

INTERESTING. TRUE ACID RAIN. HEPZIBAH IS QUICK...
...BUT NOW THEY ARE BEYOND MY HELP--INSIDE THE BIO-METALLIC STRUCTURES.
HSSSSSSH
TSS
HSSSSSSH
TSS
TSS
TSS
POP

INSIDE...
RAAAARGH
THOOM
ZTTZ
TZZT
TZZT

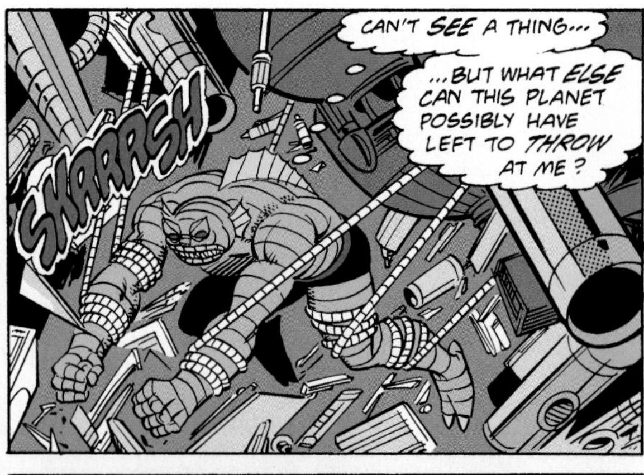
CAN'T SEE A THING...
...BUT WHAT ELSE CAN THIS PLANET POSSIBLY HAVE LEFT TO THROW AT ME?
SHRRSH

RRRRMMMMMBBBLLLL
I HAD TO ASK?!

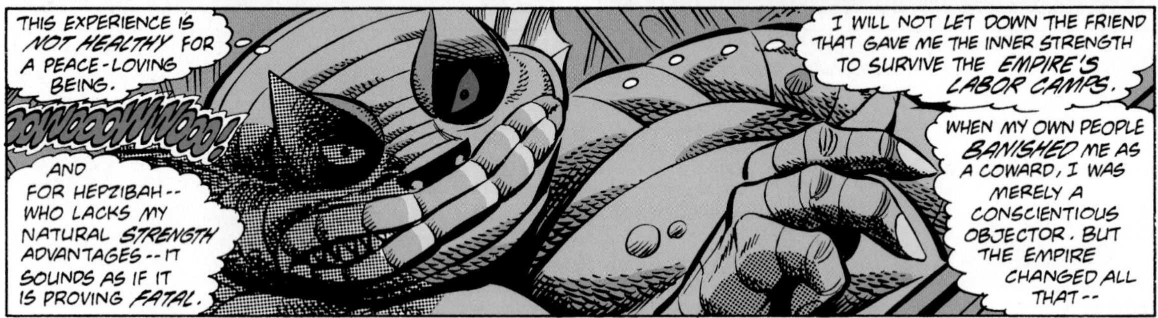
THIS EXPERIENCE IS NOT HEALTHY FOR A PEACE-LOVING BEING.
OOWOOOWWOOO!
AND FOR HEPZIBAH-- WHO LACKS MY NATURAL STRENGTH ADVANTAGES--IT SOUNDS AS IF IT IS PROVING FATAL.
I WILL NOT LET DOWN THE FRIEND THAT GAVE ME THE INNER STRENGTH TO SURVIVE THE EMPIRE'S LABOR CAMPS.
WHEN MY OWN PEOPLE BANISHED ME AS A COWARD, I WAS MERELY A CONSCIENTIOUS OBJECTOR. BUT THE EMPIRE CHANGED ALL THAT--

--I CAN NOW TAKE FORWARD ACTION FREELY...
...TOWARDS THE SOURCE OF THIS NIGHTMARE.
KRR

AND THAT MEANS FOLLOWING THE PATH OF MOST RESISTANCE.
ZZZZZZZZZZZ
ZZZZZZZZZZ
WHO WAS IT THAT SAID I WAS TOO BIG TO HAVE ANY BRAINS?!
AND I THINK HE MIGHT HAVE BEEN CORRECT.
ACTUALLY, I THINK IT WAS CR+EEE.

IN THE MEANTIME...
BIG TROUBLE HEPZIBAH IN.
LUCKY IN DARK CAN SEE...

...AND GEARS CAN HEAR.
WWNGGG
FRAAAZZZZZZZZ
HATE THIS WORLD--NOT LIKE HOME.
BUT HOME FOREVER LOST. ONLY EMPIRE KNOWS WHERE HEPZIBAH TAKEN FROM.

HERE NO PLACE TO CURL UP.
NO CORSAIR TO CURL UP WITH.
SNFF SNFF
FORWARD POD IS--

SWSW

OOOWOOOOOWWOOOOOOOOOOO
NO GOOD. TO POD MUST GET.
WALLS CLOSING IN...
...HERDING WRONG WAY--
--THROUGH HERE MUST SLIP.
POOR CH'OD--POWER VENTS TOO SMALL FOR BULK.

LUCKY HEPZIBAH'S BONES FLEXI--
KLLLNNG
YIIEEEPPP!

KRSHH
HEPZIBAH -- I HEARD YOU HOWL! I THOUGHT YOU HAD--
HEPZIBAH WORRIED ABOUT CH'OD AS WELL...
YIP!
...BUT WORRY NOW ABOUT THAT.
OF COURSE... THE DOMINANT LIFE-FORM ON THIS WORLD WAS--AND IS--PURELY MECHANICAL. IT LAY DORMANT UNTIL A NEW POWER SOURCE CAME ALONG--THE MAP POD.
BUT WE CANNOT JUST--
SHHHRRK
SHHRRRK
HEPZIBAH CAN.
NO-- THE PLANET IS ONLY ACTING IN SELF-DEFENSE.
YIPYIPYIIEEEEEE
ZKRAAKL
THEN BACK ON THE STARJAMMER...
NO, HEPZIBAH-- TO SAVE YOU, YOU FORCED ME TO ACTIVATE OUR TELEPORT-HOME SIGNAL WHILE YOU HELD THE POD. A WHOLE WORLD HAD TO DIE--
A BARREN WORLD THAT UNIVERSE MIGHT LIVE.
BUT BEFORE WE WOULD FREE IT FROM DEATHBIRD'S TYRANNY WITH THE LEGENDARY POWER OF "PHALKON"--
--WHICH WE HAVE ALREADY LEARNED BY ANALYZING CORSAIR'S PIECE OF THE MAP IS NOT EVEN THE TRUE NAME OF THE PLANET WE SEEK--
"--THE OTHER STARJAMMERS MUST FIRST SUCCEED IN RECOVERING THE REMAINING PIECES OF THE MAP BEFORE THE EMPIRE'S REINFORCEMENTS ARRIVE!"

CHAPTER IV
WENCHES
THE PLANET LUPUS...
YIP YIP
BONG BONG BONG
Cockrum • Albrecht

CRREEEEEEEK
BONG BONG

BONG
#@%
*&!!

BONG

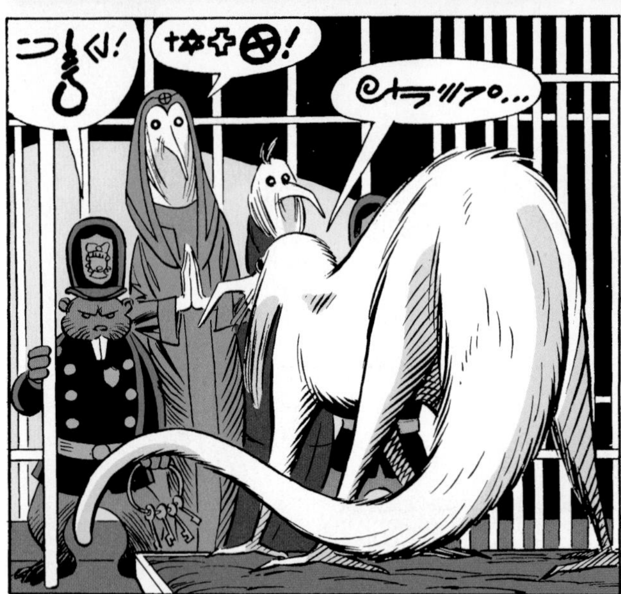

...N!

SWSH

SLSH
AIIEEEE
URK
SLSH

AWOOGA AWOOGA
AWOOGA AWOOGA AWOOGA

PNG

WHOK
ACK

WHUD
WHOK
BWING
BWING
POOM
PNG
BASH

OOOOOOOO
AAAAAA
UUHHHHHHHH

POING

SPEAKING OF THE STARJAMMERS -- BACK ON THEIR SHIP...
SO THIS IS WHAT CR+EEE FEARED SO MUCH ABOUT RETURNING TO HIS HOME PLANET--
--WE MUST HELP HIM!
NO HELP HE NEEDS, CH'OD.
HE WILL NEVER FIND HIS PIECE OF THE MAP TO "PHALKON" THIS WAY, HEPZIBAH.
I'M NOT EVEN SURE I BELIEVE ANY OF THIS. I MEAN, KEYSTONE KOPS--?!
HOW MANY MORE TIMES MUST WE EXPLAIN THIS TO YOU, CORSAIR?

WE ARE NOT SUPPLYING AN EXACT REPRESENTION OF WHAT CR+EEE IS EXPERIENCING--

--MERELY A TELEPATHIC "ANTHROPOMORPHICATION" OF SORTS THAT YOUR LIMITED INTELLIGENCES CAN COMPREHEND.

CR+EEE'S MENTALITY IS FAR TOO ALIEN FOR EVEN XAVIER/WALDO TO BE ABLE TO UNDERSTAND HIS LANGUAGE-- EXCEPT IN SPOTS--

--BUT HE SEEMS TO BE WANTED FOR SOME PREVIOUS SOCIAL CRIME COMPLETELY UNCONNECTED TO HIS SEARCH FOR THE MAP POD.

I'D BEST REMIND HIM OF HIS GOAL.

ALL STARJAMMERS ON RUN FROM SOMETHING...SKWAWK RUNNING ON EMPTY... MY WORLD IS EMPTY WITHOUT YOU, BABE...

IGNORE WALDO/XAVIER, FRIENDS. THE "MERGING" WAS BETTER FOR US THAN IT WAS FOR THEM.

AND WE SHOULD BE WITH CR+EEE...

POP

BREEP SICK BAY TO BRIDGE-- EMERGENCY.

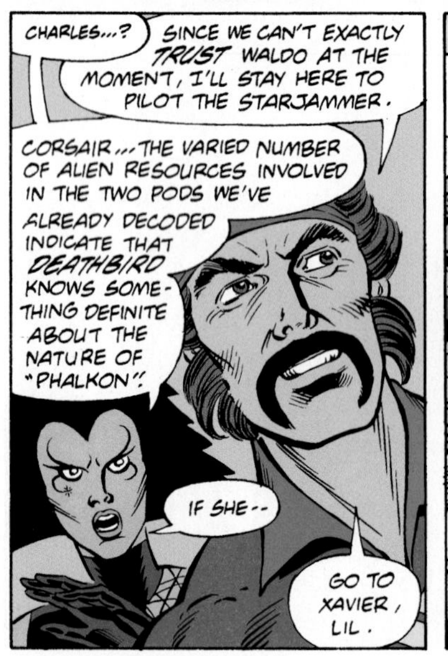

CHARLES...?
SINCE WE CAN'T EXACTLY TRUST WALDO AT THE MOMENT, I'LL STAY HERE TO PILOT THE STARJAMMER.
CORSAIR... THE VARIED NUMBER OF ALIEN RESOURCES INVOLVED IN THE TWO PODS WE'VE ALREADY DECODED INDICATE THAT DEATHBIRD KNOWS SOMETHING DEFINITE ABOUT THE NATURE OF "PHALKON"!
IF SHE--
GO TO XAVIER, LIL.

MOMENTS LATER...
SIKORSKY, WHAT IS IT? HAS CHARLES'S BODY COME OUT OF ITS COMA--?
SIKORSKY SORRY, MAJESTRIX LILANDRA--
--BUT BODY OF XAVIER NOW...

...DEAD.

MEANWHILE, BACK ON THE PLANET LUPUS ...
NAY!
NUTHING!
#?

FLIGHT BALLOONS!

#@%&!!
WOOOOOOOSH

HMMMMMMMMMM

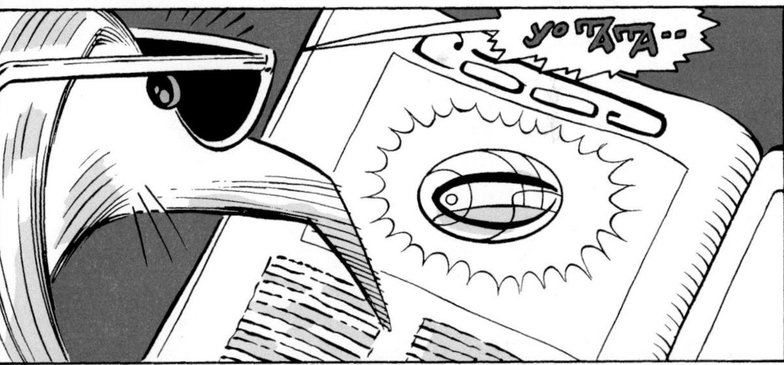

PONG
PING

SOON...
RAP RAP
RAP

#@%
*&!--?

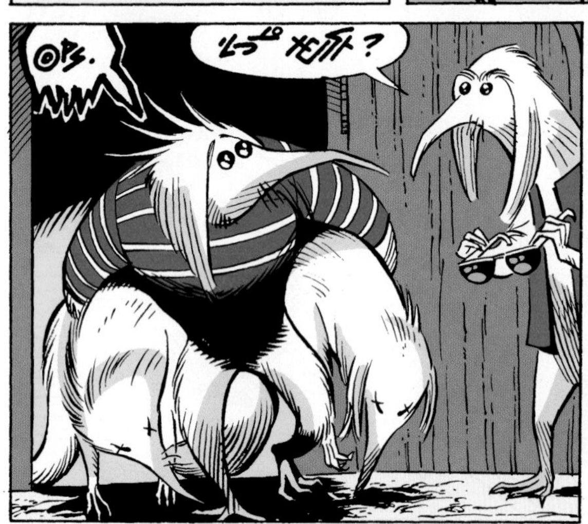

SLAM
YIP

YIP
YIP
YIP
YIP

KRSH
YAIE!

FRK...
YIP YIP
YIP YIP

THAT NIGHT-CYCLE...

CREEEEEK

?

AWOOGA
AWOOGA AWOOGA

SPR
NG

AWOOGA AWOOGA
#@%*&!!
WOK

WAK
WOK
YIP
YIP
YIP
YIP

POP
WE MAY HAVE ARRIVED TOO LATE.
DUCK!
#@%*&!!
SOLP!

#@%*&!!
POING

"THIS IS FASCINATING. THIS FEMALE AND HER... BROOD SEEM TO BE THE VICTIMS OF WHATEVER CRIME CR+EEE WAS CHARGED WITH.
YIP
"BUT SHE APPEARS TO HAVE FORGIVEN HIM COMPLETELY AND DROPPED ALL THE CHARGES -- SHE EVEN RECOVERED THE MAP POD FOR CR+EEE."
YIP

WE MAY NOT UNDERSTAND CR+EEE'S LANGUAGE-- BUT WE DO UNDERSTAND WHAT HIS EYES SAY.
TIME TO TELEPORT HOME, CR+EEE...
POING

FZ
ZT
AND SO, BACK ON THE SHIP...
YIP

OUR NEW FAMILY--!
ALREADY...?
I'M IN THE MOOD FOR... SKWAWK NEW INFORMATION INPUT--LINK WITH RAZA AND BINARY CUT OFF-- FROM WITHIN THE STARJAMMER-- TRAITOR-- SKWAWK...
YIP

CHAPTER V
HOLDING ACTION
THE PLANET CH''RP..
THIS IS REALLY GETTING RIDICULOUS, RAZA!
CHT
CHT
CHT
CHT
CHT
CHT
CHT
CHT
CHT
CHT
CHT
CHT

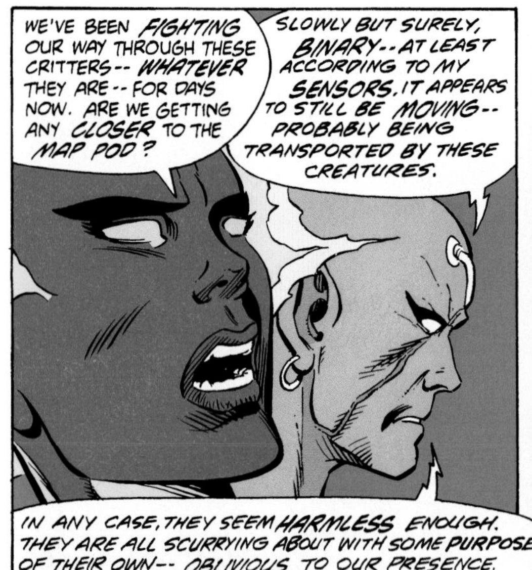
WE'VE BEEN FIGHTING OUR WAY THROUGH THESE CRITTERS-- WHATEVER THEY ARE-- FOR DAYS NOW. ARE WE GETTING ANY CLOSER TO THE MAP POD?
SLOWLY BUT SURELY, BINARY--AT LEAST ACCORDING TO MY SENSORS. IT APPEARS TO STILL BE MOVING-- PROBABLY BEING TRANSPORTED BY THESE CREATURES.
IN ANY CASE, THEY SEEM HARMLESS ENOUGH. THEY ARE ALL SCURRYING ABOUT WITH SOME PURPOSE OF THEIR OWN-- OBLIVIOUS TO OUR PRESENCE.
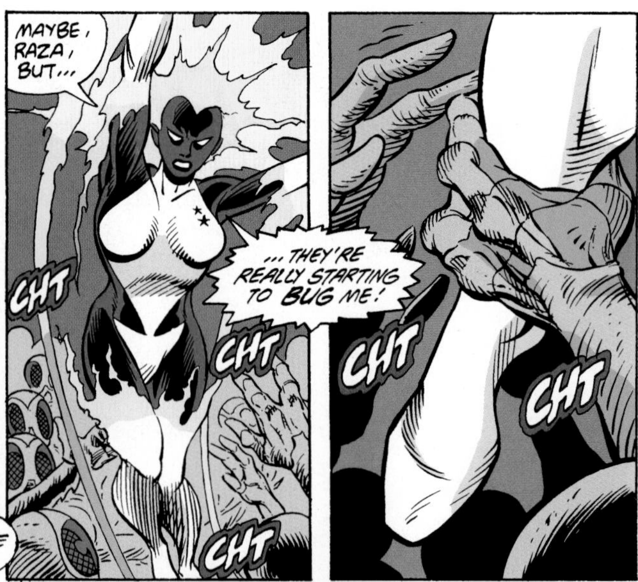
MAYBE, RAZA, BUT...
...THEY'RE REALLY STARTING TO BUG ME!
CHT
CHT
CHT
CHT
CHT

CHT
CHT
CHT
RAZA--!
CHT
CHT
CHT

I AM COMING, FAIR DAMSEL.
PERHAPS THAT IS NOT QUITE THE CORRECT TERM IN THIS CASE.
CHT
CHT
CHT

CHT
THERE SEEM TO BE MORE AND MORE OF THEM.
BUT HOW CAN THAT BE?
CHT

HOW COULD THERE POSSIBLY BE MORE?
CHT
CHT
CHT
CHT

CHT
CHT
CHT
CHT
CHT
CHT
CHT
CHT
CHT
CHT

CHT
CHT
BA-WHOOM!
CHT

AH... FINALLY BOUGHT US SOME BREATHING SPACE.
NOT THAT YOU CAN APPRECIATE IT, RAZA, WHAT WITH YOUR CIRCUITS AND GEARS PROCESSING ALL YOUR ATMOSPHERE FOR YOU.

IT MATTERS LITTLE IN ANY CASE, BINARY. THE INSECTOIDS HAVE RETURNED.
FRZZAT
CHT
CHT

COMING FROM BEHIND HER...
...MUST INTERCE--

BINARY--!
CHT
CHT
CHT

RAZA!
RAZA?

OH MY GOD, HE'S BURIED UNDERNEATH THEM ALREADY!

ALL MY POWER IS TOTALLY USELESS IN THIS SITUATION. THESE THINGS REPLACE THEMSELVES--FROM WHO KNOWS WHERE--AS QUICKLY AS I DISPATCH THEM.
CHT
CHT
CHT
CHT

NO CHOICE--MIGHT AS WELL LET THEM TAKE ME TO WHEREVER THEY'RE TAKING RAZA.
HIS SENSORS ARE OUR ONLY HOPE OF COMPLETING THIS MISSION--FINDING THE LAST PIECE OF THE MAP TO THE LEGENDARY POWER OF "PHALKON."
CHT
CHT
CHT
CHT
CHT
CHT
CHT
CHT
CHT
ASSUMING, OF COURSE, THAT ALL OF THE OTHER STARJAMMERS HAVE SUCCEEDED IN THEIR MISSIONS...!

MEANWHILE, ABOVE THE PLANET...
POP
SINCE WE LOST THE LINK TO RAZA AND BINARY'S AWAY TEAM, XAVIER/WALDO IS THEIR ONLY HOPE.
EVEN IF IT MEANS WE MUST SCAN THE ENTIRE PLANET TELEPATHICALLY.
CHT CHT CHT CHT CHT CHT CHT
SO FAR WE CAN'T LOCK ON TO ANYTHING EXCEPT A STRANGE "BUZZ"...
...THAT GETS MORE AND MORE PAINFUL AS WE NEAR THE ODDLY-SHIFTING LANDSCAPE.
GODS--LITERALLY EVERYTHING ON THE PLANET IS ENTIRELY MADE UP OF THOSE INSECT-LIKE ALIENS. WHERE ARE RAZA AND BINARY? WHERE IS THE MAP POD?
GOOD--WALDO/XAVIER MUST BE MANIFESTING ALL OF THIS BACK ON THE SHIP FOR YOU, LILANDRA. BUT WE'RE GOING IN CLOSER NOW AND PROBABLY WON'T BE ABLE TO...
CHARLES, WAIT--RETURN TO THE STARJAMMER! THERES SOMETHING YOU SHOULD KNOW ABOUT YOUR BODY--!
HE IS GONE...I HAVE LOST CONTACT WITH HIM TOTALLY.
SOON ENOUGH, XAVIER DISCOVER BODY DEAD.
WHTHOOM
WHA-- FROM STARBOARD!?
THE EMPIRE FREIGHTER IS BACK--WITH REINFORCEMENTS... FIVE EMPIRE STAR-RATS.
BUT THEY'RE BASED ON THE SHI'AR THRONEWORLD--AND THE FREIGHTER CREW COULD HARDLY EVEN HAVE FOUND THEIR DEAD CAPTAIN YET...
...HOW COULD THEY HAVE ARRIVED SO--
UNLESS...WALDO HAS BEEN BEHAVING SO ERRATICALLY... HE MUST HAVE CONTACTED DEATHBIRD--BETRAYED US TO MY SISTER!
WE ARE GOING TO NEED ALL THE OTHER STARJAMMERS UP ON THE BRIDGE TO FLY AND DEFEND THIS SHIP MANUALLY--!
SIKORSKY--WHERE ARE YOU GOING?
SICK BAY. XAVIER'S BODY, MUST BE WITH.

BACK ON THE PLANET CH'RP...
WELCOME BACK TO THE LAND OF THE LIVING, RAZA.
THE LITTLE WEIRDOS SEEM TO BE BACKING OFF A LITTLE...
CHT
CHT
CHT
PERHAPS THEY HAVE NOW "GOT US WHERE THEY WANT US," AS YOU EARTHERS ARE SO FOND OF SAYING.

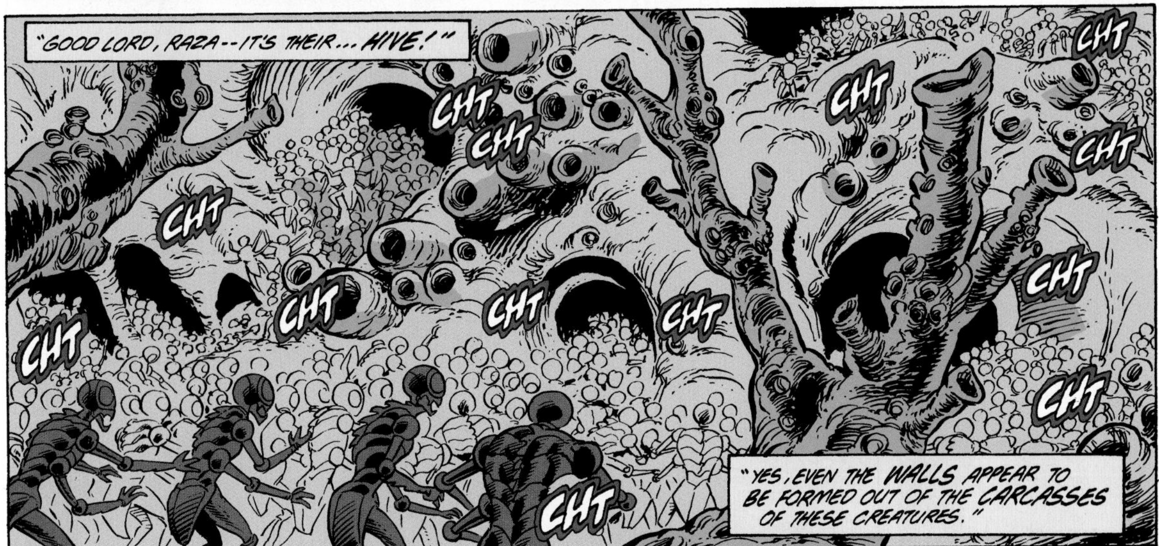
"GOOD LORD, RAZA--IT'S THEIR... HIVE!"
CHT
CHT
CHT
CHT
CHT
CHT
CHT
CHT
CHT
CHT
CHT
CHT
"YES, EVEN THE WALLS APPEAR TO BE FORMED OUT OF THE CARCASSES OF THESE CREATURES."

"AND THAT CAN ONLY BE THEIR...'QUEEN MOTHER.'"
CHT
CHT
CHT
CHT
CHT
CHT
"I QUESTION THE GENDER, BINARY, BUT IT DOES SEEM TO BE... REPRODUCING IN SOME WAY. THE CREATURES ARE SWARMING OUT AROUND IT."

CHT
MNCH
CHT
CHT
"AND IT'S EATING THE DEAD ONES AT THE SAME TIME."

THIS IS DISGUSTING, RAZA, AND I PLAN ON DOING SOMETHING ABOUT IT--RIGHT NOW!
BINARY--WAIT! LOOK IN ITS EYES... THERE'S SOMETHING--

WHO CARES?!
FRZZT
FRAAZZ
CHT
CHT
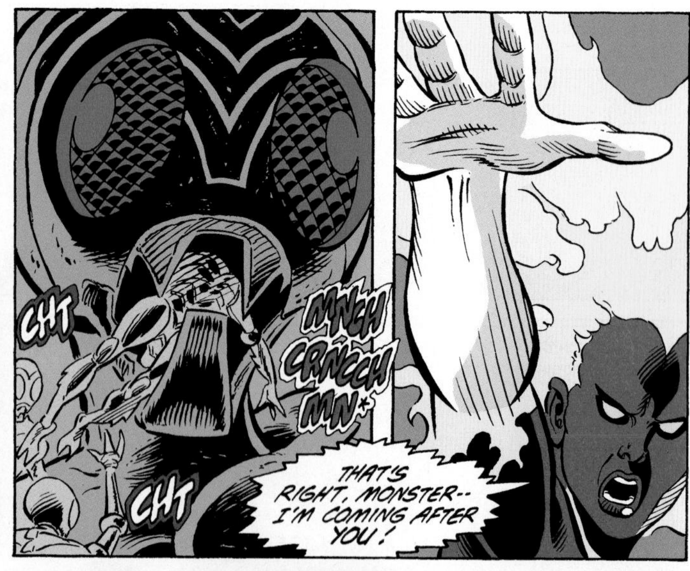
CHT
MNCH CRNCCH MN*
CHT
THAT'S RIGHT, MONSTER-- I'M COMING AFTER YOU!

CHT
CHT
CHT
FRZZT
GET READY TO FR--!
CHT
CHT

AS I SUSPECTED, THERE IS A SENTIENCE--OF SOME FORM--AT WORK HERE.
THE LARGE CREATURE SEEMS TO HAVE RECOGNIZED THE THREAT FROM BINARY--AND ALL THE SMALL ONES ARE REACTING TO IT, PROTECTING THE LARGE ONE.
THEIR LOSS.

CHT
FWHOOM
CHT

THAT'S IT!

I'M TAKING YOU DOWN--
--EVEN IF I HAVE TO GO THROUGH YOUR WHOLE "FAMILY" TO DO IT!
CHT
CHT
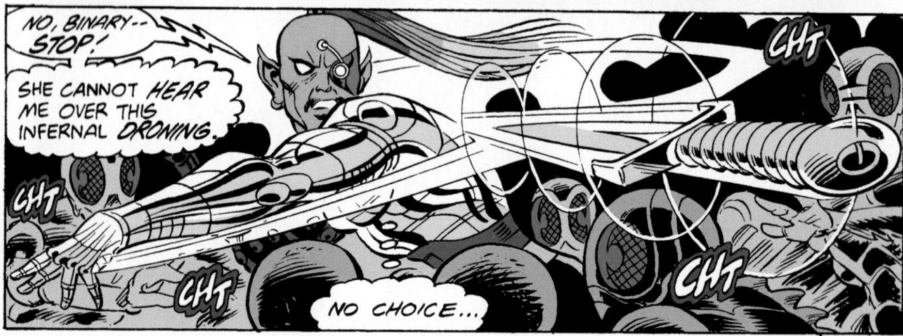
NO, BINARY-- STOP!
SHE CANNOT HEAR ME OVER THIS INFERNAL DRONING.
CHT
CHT
CHT
CHT
CHT
NO CHOICE...

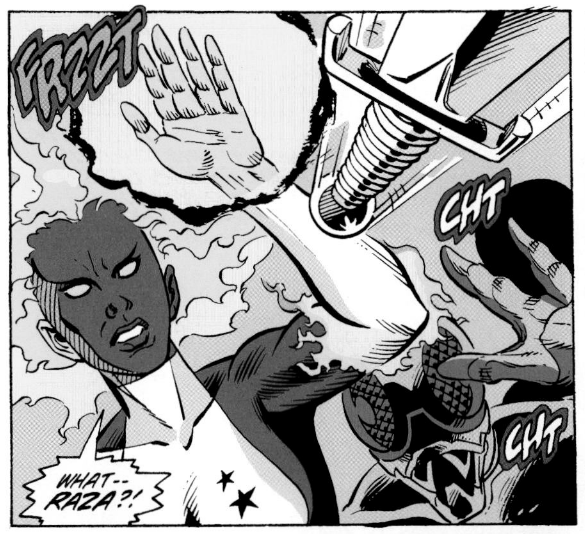
FRZZT
CHT
CHT
WHAT-- RAZA?!

NO!
FRZZ
KONK
ZAP

HER OWN POWER WOULD SEEM TO BE THE ONLY WAY TO STOP SO POWERFUL... AND FIERY A FEMALE.
BUT I STILL HAVE EVERY REASON TO HOPE THAT SHE WILL FORGIVE ME.
MY CIRCUITS--WHICH BINARY RIDICULED EARLIER--HAVE INFORMED ME THAT THE OBJECT OF OUR SEARCH IS RIGHT HERE...

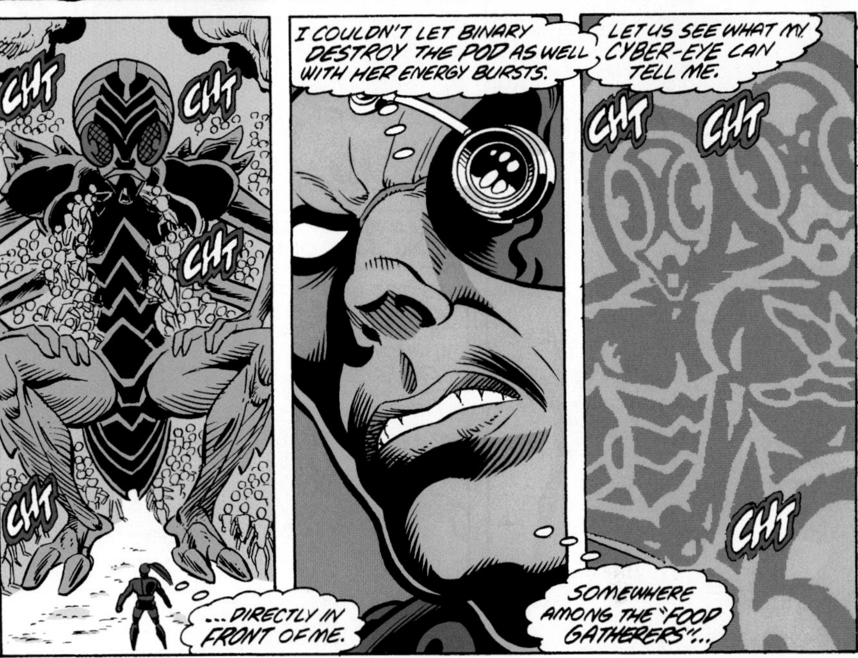
CHT
CHT
CHT
CHT
...DIRECTLY IN FRONT OF ME.
I COULDN'T LET BINARY DESTROY THE POD AS WELL WITH HER ENERGY BURSTS.
LET US SEE WHAT MY CYBER-EYE CAN TELL ME.
CHT
CHT
CHT
SOMEWHERE AMONG THE "FOOD GATHERERS"...

"...RIGHT THERE-- THE MAP POD."

BY THE TRAINING MOON OF SATURN--
--NO!
CHOMP
GREAT, RAZA--YOU PUT ME OUT OF THE BATTLE JUST LONG ENOUGH TO ALLOW THAT YUCHOID TO SWALLOW THE LAST LINK TO "PHALKON"!

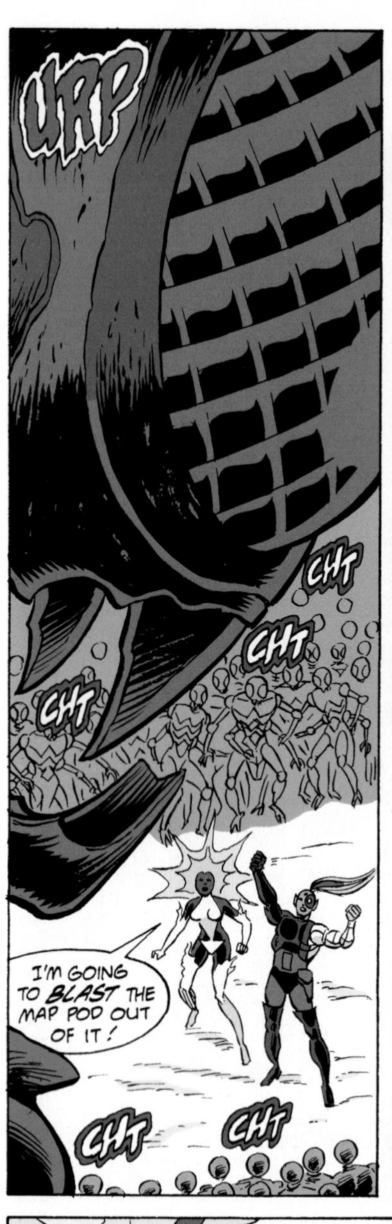
URP
CHT
CHT
CHT
I'M GOING TO BLAST THE MAP POD OUT OF IT!
CHT
CHT

NO, BINARY, THAT SHOULD NOT BE NECESSARY. MY INTERNAL COMPUTERS ARE ALREADY WORKING ON A WAY TO COMMUNICATE WITH THE HIVEHEAD.
WHY BOTHER?!
POP
WE HAVE FINALLY FOUND YOU. YOU MUST TELEPORT BACK TO THE STARJAMMER IMMEDIATELY-- WITH OR WITHOUT YOUR PIECE OF THE "PHALKON" MAP.
OUR "CONNECTION" WITH WALDO/ XAVIER--WHICH WE ARE HAVING INCREASING DIFFICULTY MAINTAINING THROUGH THIS "PSYCHIC WHITE NOISE"--
--TELLS US THAT THEY MAY HAVE TO PUT UP THEIR SHIELDS SOON AND MOVE.
WE SHALL NOT RETURN WITHOUT THE INFORMATION MAJESTRIX LILANDRA REQUIRES.
COULD YOU OF ALL PEOPLE BE GOING SOFT ON US, RAZA?
IT'S TOO LATE FOR "COMMUNICATING"-- THE POD IS PROBABLY ALREADY BEING DIGESTED.
THAT IS EXACTLY WHAT I AM HOPING.
YOU'RE NUTS!
I'M GOING IN AFTER THAT POD...

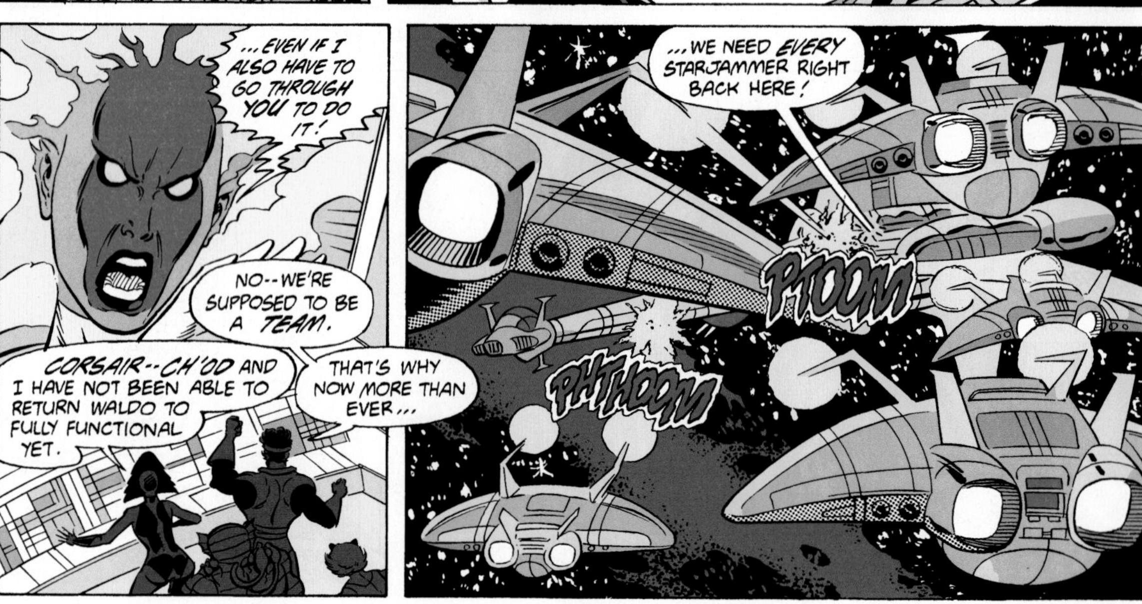
...EVEN IF I ALSO HAVE TO GO THROUGH YOU TO DO IT!
NO--WE'RE SUPPOSED TO BE A TEAM.
CORSAIR--CH'OD AND I HAVE NOT BEEN ABLE TO RETURN WALDO TO FULLY FUNCTIONAL YET.
THAT'S WHY NOW MORE THAN EVER...
...WE NEED EVERY STARJAMMER RIGHT BACK HERE!
PTOOM
PHTHOOM

CHAPTER VI
MUTINY
BUT, BEFORE ANOTHER COMMAND CAN BE ISSUED ON THE BRIDGE OF THE STARJAMMER SPACECRAFT...
YEEP
A DIRECT HIT--!
AARRRGH!
GRRRRR
YIP
PHA
BOOM
YIP
YIP
THE EMPIRE'S STAR-RATS HAVE BREECHED A PORTION OF OUR SHIELDS...!

WHOOSH
WORSE YET, LIL, THEY'VE BREECHED THE SHIP ITSELF--
CORSAIR!
HEPZIBAH--?!

NOTHING BETWEEN US AND THE VACUUM OF SPACE BUT A SMALL HOLE--GETTING BIGGER BY THE SECOND.
SORRY, SHIP... HAVE TO ANCHOR MYSELF.
CHHH
NOW WHERE'S MY CAT LADY?
HEPZIBAH
HEPZIBAH IS ATTEMPTING TO HELP CR'EEE...
...WHILE CH'OD MUST SIMPLY HOLD ON--FOR AS LONG AS I AM ABLE--FOR THE SAKE OF MY LITTLE FRIEND'S NEW FAMILY.
YIP
YIP

"BUT WHY DOES THE SHIP TAKE SO LONG TO REPAIR ITSELF? HAVE WALDO'S RECENT BOUTS OF UNRELIABILITY SOMEHOW SPREAD TO THE STARJAMMER ITSELF?"
YEEP
REACH CR'EEE CANNOT...
SKRRRREEEEE

WHOOOOSH

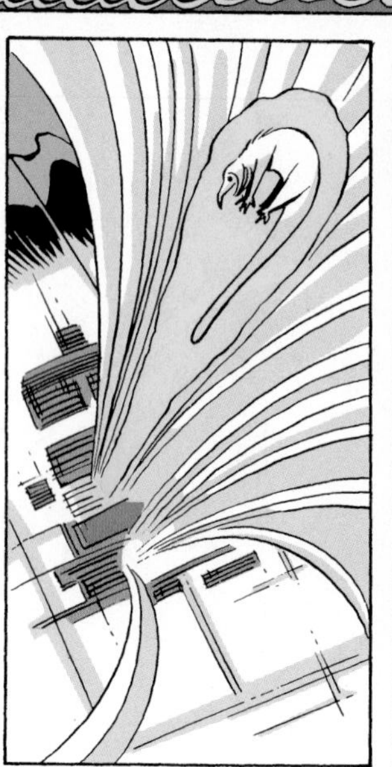

MEANWHILE, ON THE PLANET CH"RP IT'S STARJAMMER VS. STARJAMMER...
GET OUT OF MY WAY, RAZA, OR SO HELP ME--!
CHT
WOULD THAT I COULD, BINARY...
...BUT I CANNOT.
CHT
CHT
CHT

THIS "PHALKON QUEST" IS THE FIRST SERIOUS THING THE STARJAMMERS HAVE TRIED TO DO SINCE WE TOOK ON THE MANTLE OF "REBEL PIRATES"...
...AND YOU PICK NOW TO CRACK YOUR FIRST JOKE?!
I HAVE TO GET THE LAST MAP POD BEFORE THAT CREATURE FULLY DIGESTS IT--
I WILL NOT LET YOU KILL THE MYTH.

XAVIER--!
XAVIER/WALDO NOW.
IF WHAT I SUSPECT IS INDEED TRUE, YOU SHOULD BE ABLE TO ACCESS THE NECESSARY INFORMATION FROM THE HIVE HEAD TELEPATHICALLY.
THAT MONSTER ATE THE POD, IT DIDN'T MEMORIZE IT.

THIS WAS SOMEWHAT PAINFUL THE LAST TIME WE TRIED LINKING UP WITH THESE CREATURES BUT...
AAAAH, THIS IS QUITE... DIFFERENT.
AND...
...WE HAVE THE LAST PIECE OF THE MAP TO PHALKON.
WE CAN ALL RETURN TO THE STARJAMMER NOW.
CHT
FZ
ZT
CHT
HELLO...?
FZ
ZT

QUITE SIMPLE, DEAR LADY--

YOU KNOW, BUSTER, I'VE BEEN MEANING TO MENTION HOW MUCH I HATE IT WHEN YOU CALL ME THOSE SEXIST NICKNAMES.

REALLY, BINARY? I THOUGHT THEM SIMPLY... POETIC.

IN ANY CASE, MY INTERNAL COMPUTERS TOOK SOME TIME TO IDENTIFY THAT PARTICULAR CULTURE.

BUT ONCE I REALIZED THAT-- AMONG MANY OTHER ODDITIES-- THE SPECIES ABSORBED KNOWLEDGE THROUGH INGESTION AND WERE TELEPATHIC ON A VERY PRIMAL LEVEL--

YEAH, YEAH, BUT WE COULD HAVE GOTTEN IT MY WAY, TOO. WHY WOULDN'T YOU LET ME KILL IT, RAZA?

BECAUSE THEIR KIND IS CLOSELY TIED TO YOUR MODERN EARTH... IN MOST INTERESTING WAYS.

YOU'VE CERTAINLY GOT ME INTERESTED BUT...

WHRRRRRR

...DO YOU MIND IF WE CONTINUE THIS DISCUSSION LATER?

SWSH

SWSH

SH

AS YOU WISH, FAIR ONE.

SLAM!
WAS THAT SIKORSKY--
--WITH A BATTALION OF EMPIRE TROOPERS?

CLK

THUD!
TOO WEIRD.

HI, GUYS.
I'M JUST WILD ABOUT HARRY...

BEFORE YOU EVEN ASK... CR+EEE'S FAMILY--AT LILANDRA'S INSTRUCTIONS--ARE RESPONSIBLE FOR SLAMMING THOSE DOORS SHUT IN THE TROOPER'S FACES UP THERE.
YIP
YIP
YIP
YIP

WE'VE BEEN TRYING TO KEEP THEM BUSY SINCE WE... LOST CR+EEE.
WE'VE BEEN FORCED TO GO UNDERGROUND IN THESE SENSOR-PROOF SECRET PASSAGES OF OUR OWN SHIP THANKS TO SIKORSKY--
TRAITOR TELEPORT SOLDIERS TO MEDICAL BAY DIRECTLY.
AND HE'LL PAY FOR IT WHEN I GET MY HANDS ON HIM.

AND HE ARRANGED TO HAVE CHARLES'S MIND ALONG WITH THE LAST PORTION OF THE MAP TO PHALKON--DRAWN DIRECTLY BACK TO HIS COMATOSE BODY THERE.
BUT NOW THAT WE'RE UP TO FULL FIGHTING STRENGTH AGAIN, WE'RE GOING TO GET BOTH OF THEM BACK!

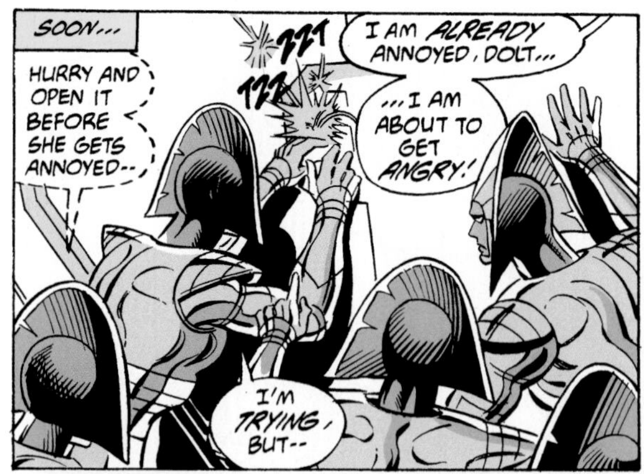
SOON...
HURRY AND OPEN IT BEFORE SHE GETS ANNOYED--
ZZZ
ZZZ
I AM ALREADY ANNOYED, DOLT...
...I AM ABOUT TO GET ANGRY!
I'M TRYING, BUT--

SWSH
SWSH
WHOOOAA!
I DON'T THINK I DID THAT...!

ZAPT
FIRE!
ZAPT
ZAPT
ZAPT
ZAPT
GET THEM BEFORE THEY GET US!

UH... THERE'S NOBODY OUT HERE.
BRILLIANT DEDUCTION, BABOB.
THEN CAN WE GO BACK INSIDE WITH THE REST OF THE BATTALION NOW?

I REALLY HATE THIS.
SLAM
THAT ALIEN HOWL--?!
YEEEEEEEEEEEEEEEEEEP

THE INFERNAL STARJAMMERS MUST HAVE RETURNED.
YOU FOUR COME WITH ME--OUR COMMANDER WILL WANT TO DEFILE THE EX-MAJESTRIX LILANDRA'S HEAD PERSONALLY!
DO WE REALLY HAVE TO?

ATOMIZE IT!
HA--THIS IS WHAT YOU WERE SO AFRAID OF, WIWARTO?!
YEEP
WELL...

ZAPT
ZAPT
ZAPT
ZAPT
PH
BOOM
WEEP WEEP WEEP WEEP

AAARGH!
NOW, SEE... THIS IS WHAT I WAS SO AFRAID OF.
WHA-TOOM

THAT WAS TOO EASY.
LET US HOPE OUR COMRADES FARE AS WELL.

WHILE OUTSIDE THE MEDICAL BAY...
CAN YOU GUYS INSIDE DO ANYTHING TO GET IT OPEN?
WHAT WAS THAT NOISE DOWN THE HALL?
I DON'T KNOW...

...BUT IT CAME FROM THE DIRECTION THE OTHERS W--
BABOB?
THUD THUD THUD
PUPUGLI?! MIMOZA?!

DON'T WORRY ABOUT THEM, TROOPS...
LET US IN... PLEASE.

...WORRY ABOUT US!
HISSSS

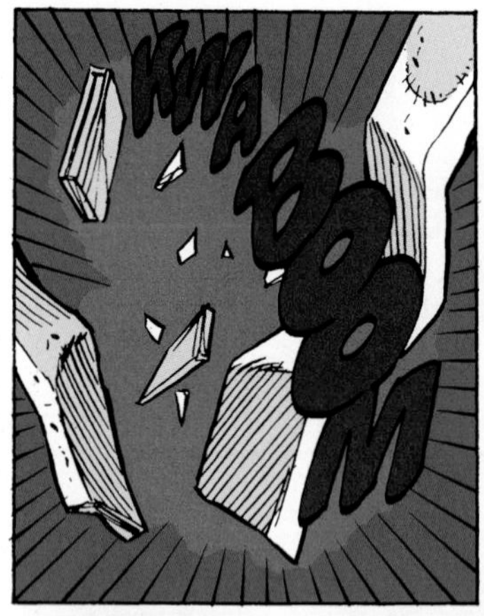
KWABOOOOM

PHZZAT
PHZZAT
PHZZAT
PHZZAT
PHZZAT
PHZZAT
PHZZAT
PHZZAT
FRZZAT
ENTRANCE TO MEDICAL BAY GAINED, CAPTAIN "SIR".
BINARY'S STARTING TO DEVELOP AN "ATTITUDE"... AND THAT COULD BE A PROBLEM.

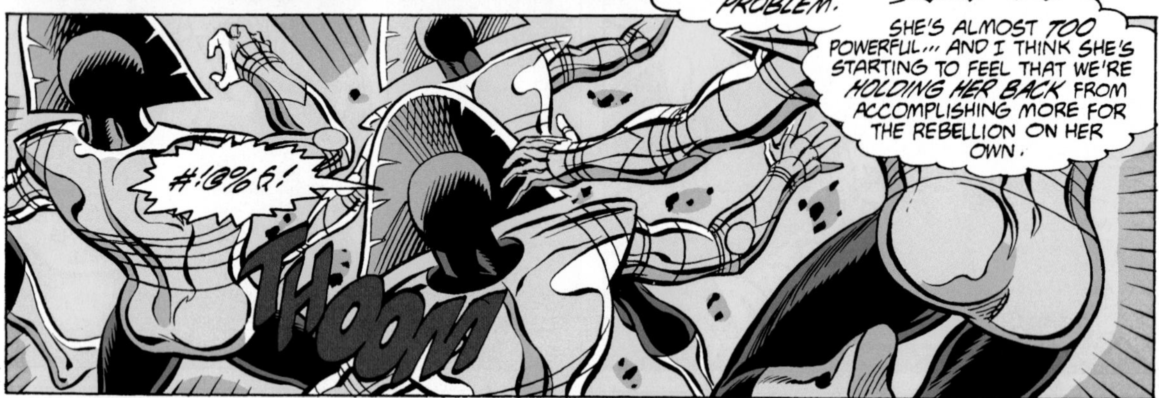
SHE'S ALMOST TOO POWERFUL... AND I THINK SHE'S STARTING TO FEEL THAT WE'RE HOLDING HER BACK FROM ACCOMPLISHING MORE FOR THE REBELLION ON HER OWN.
#!@%&!
THOOM

BUT THERE'S A METHOD TO MY MADNESS. I HAVE A LONGER-RANGE GOAL IN MIND...
AVOIDING THE DOOR AND GOING DIRECTLY THROUGH THE WALL WORKED OUT QUITE WELL, CORSAIR.

YES, NOW WE HAVE CHARLES BACK--AND WE FINALLY HAVE THE COMPLETE MAP TO PHALKON--!
SKREEEE
FROM THE RAFTERS ABOVE--
--DEATHBIRD?!

YES, DEAR SISTER. YOUR MOTLEY CREW MAY HAVE THE MAP FOR THE MOMENT...
...BUT I NOW HAVE YOU--
--RIGHT WHERE I HAVE ALWAYS WANTED YOU!
UNNH
FORGET ABOUT ME, CORSAIR... IF SHE WANTS IT SO MUCH, IT MUST BE REAL... GO AFTER PHALKO--

DEATHBIRD IS GONE... AND THE MAJESTRIX TELEPORTED AWAY WITH HER.
BUT THE POWER OF PHALKON IS ALMOST WITHIN OUR GRASP...
CONCLUDES NEXT ISSUE!

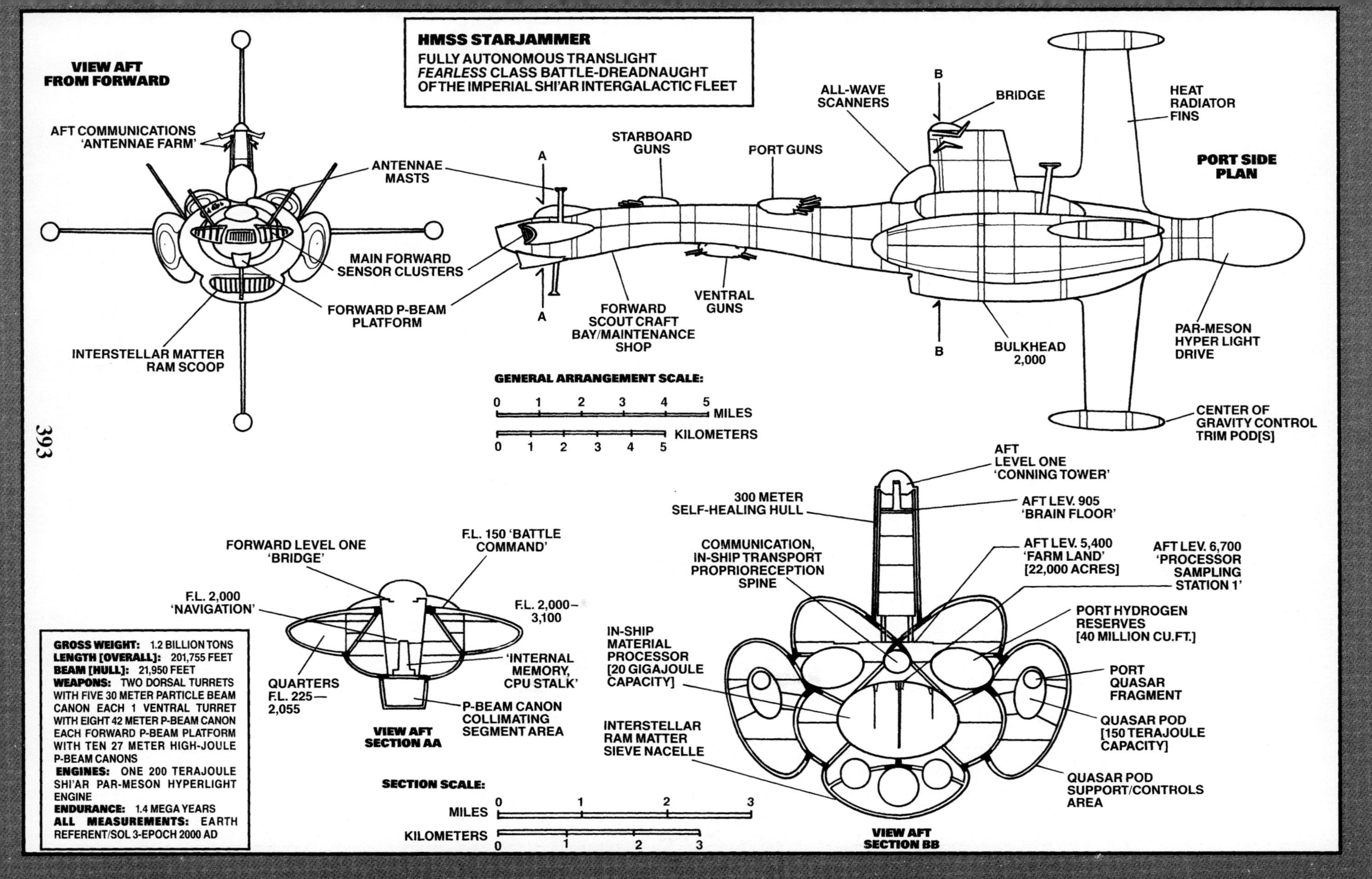
HMSS STARJAMMER
FULLY AUTONOMOUS TRANSLIGHT
FEARLESS CLASS BATTLE-DREADNAUGHT
OF THE IMPERIAL SHI'AR INTERGALACTIC FLEET
VIEW AFT
FROM FORWARD
AFT COMMUNICATIONS
'ANTENNAE FARM'
ANTENNAE
MASTS
MAIN FORWARD
SENSOR CLUSTERS
FORWARD P-BEAM
PLATFORM
INTERSTELLAR MATTER
RAM SCOOP
A
A
STARBOARD
GUNS
PORT GUNS
ALL-WAVE
SCANNERS
B
BRIDGE
HEAT
RADIATOR
FINS
PORT SIDE
PLAN
FORWARD
SCOUT CRAFT
BAY/MAINTENANCE
SHOP
VENTRAL
GUNS
B
BULKHEAD
2,000
PAR-MESON
HYPER LIGHT
DRIVE
CENTER OF
GRAVITY CONTROL
TRIM POD[S]
GENERAL ARRANGEMENT SCALE:
0 1 2 3 4 5 MILES
0 1 2 3 4 5 KILOMETERS
AFT
LEVEL ONE
'CONNING TOWER'
300 METER
SELF-HEALING HULL
AFT LEV. 905
'BRAIN FLOOR'
COMMUNICATION,
IN-SHIP TRANSPORT
PROPRIORECEPTION
SPINE
AFT LEV. 5,400
'FARM LAND'
[22,000 ACRES]
AFT LEV. 6,700
'PROCESSOR
SAMPLING
STATION 1'
PORT HYDROGEN
RESERVES
[40 MILLION CU.FT.]
IN-SHIP
MATERIAL
PROCESSOR
[20 GIGAJOULE
CAPACITY]
PORT
QUASAR
FRAGMENT
QUASAR POD
[150 TERAJOULE
CAPACITY]
INTERSTELLAR
RAM MATTER
SIEVE NACELLE
QUASAR POD
SUPPORT/CONTROLS
AREA
VIEW AFT
SECTION BB
FORWARD LEVEL ONE
'BRIDGE'
F.L. 150 'BATTLE
COMMAND'
F.L. 2,000
'NAVIGATION'
F.L. 2,000–
3,100
'INTERNAL
MEMORY,
CPU STALK'
QUARTERS
F.L. 225—
2,055
P-BEAM CANON
COLLIMATING
SEGMENT AREA
VIEW AFT
SECTION AA
SECTION SCALE:
MILES 0 1 2 3
KILOMETERS 0 1 2 3
GROSS WEIGHT: 1.2 BILLION TONS
LENGTH [OVERALL]: 201,755 FEET
BEAM [HULL]: 21,950 FEET
WEAPONS: TWO DORSAL TURRETS WITH FIVE 30 METER PARTICLE BEAM CANON EACH 1 VENTRAL TURRET WITH EIGHT 42 METER P-BEAM CANON EACH FORWARD P-BEAM PLATFORM WITH TEN 27 METER HIGH-JOULE P-BEAM CANONS
ENGINES: ONE 200 TERAJOULE SHI'AR PAR-MESON HYPERLIGHT ENGINE
ENDURANCE: 1.4 MEGA YEARS
ALL MEASUREMENTS: EARTH REFERENT/SOL 3-EPOCH 2000 AD

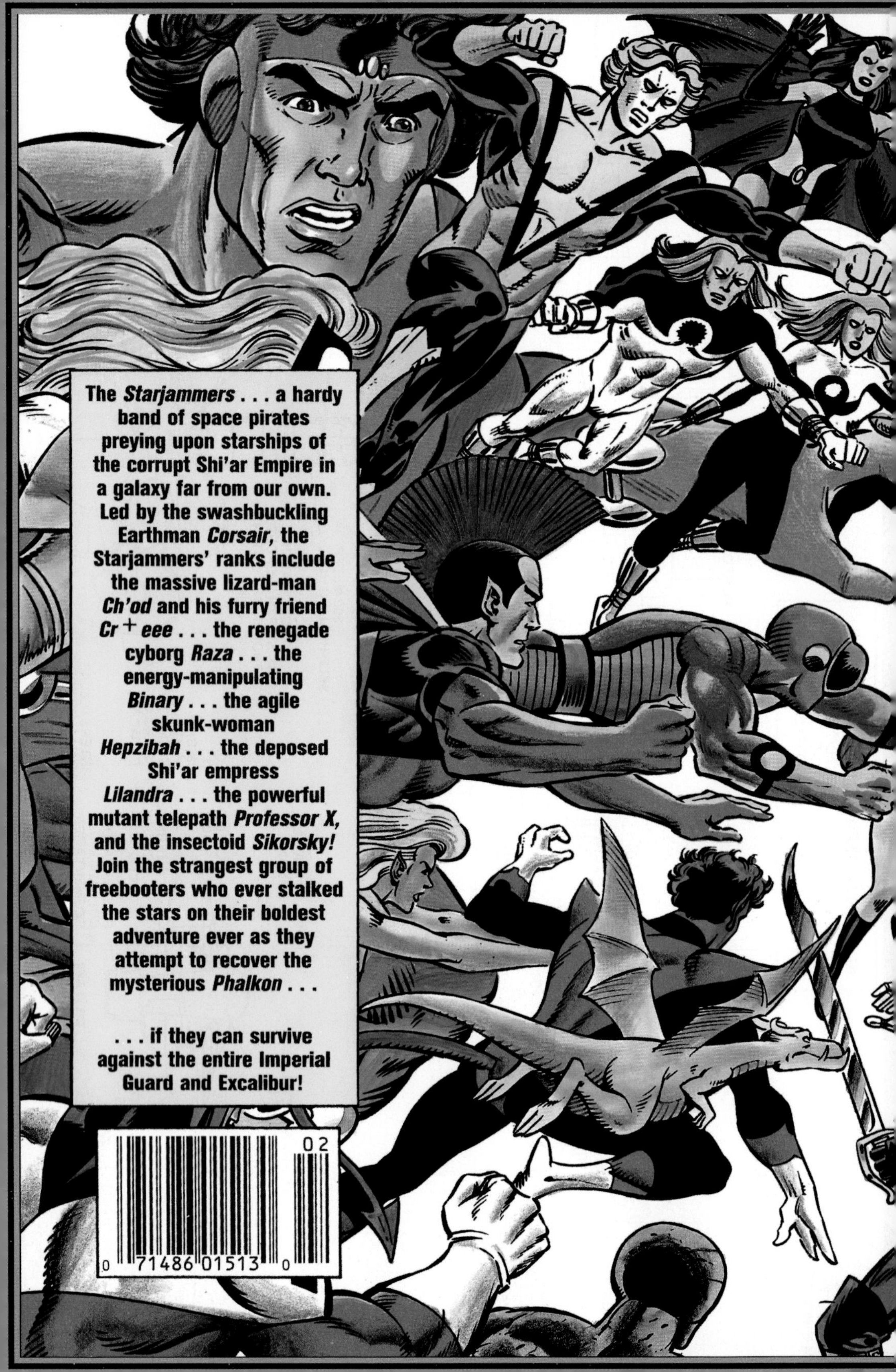
The *Starjammers* . . . a hardy band of space pirates preying upon starships of the corrupt Shi'ar Empire in a galaxy far from our own. Led by the swashbuckling Earthman *Corsair*, the Starjammers' ranks include the massive lizard-man *Ch'od* and his furry friend *Cr + eee* . . . the renegade cyborg *Raza* . . . the energy-manipulating *Binary* . . . the agile skunk-woman *Hepzibah* . . . the deposed Shi'ar empress *Lilandra* . . . the powerful mutant telepath *Professor X*, and the insectoid *Sikorsky!* Join the strangest group of freebooters who ever stalked the stars on their boldest adventure ever as they attempt to recover the mysterious *Phalkon* . . .
. . . if they can survive against the entire Imperial Guard and Excalibur!
02
0 71486 01513 0

MARVEL COMICS
X-MEN
SPOTLIGHT ON . . .
01513
#2 of 2
$4.50 US
$5.50 CAN
STARJAMMERS
TM

THE BRIDGE OF DEATHBIRD'S SHI'AR COMMAND CRAFT...

FIRE ON THE STARJAMMER, DOLTS--DESTROY THE CREW BUT NOT THE SENTIENT SHIP ITSELF... NOT YET.

I WILL SLAUGHTER MY BELOVED SISTER LILANDRA MYSELF NOW--

I WILL NOT BEG, DEATHBIRD.

--AND ENJOY IT!

ALERT THE REST OF THE SURROUNDING SQUADRON--

--BARRAGE THAT SPACECRAFT FROM ALL SIDES!

CHAPTER I

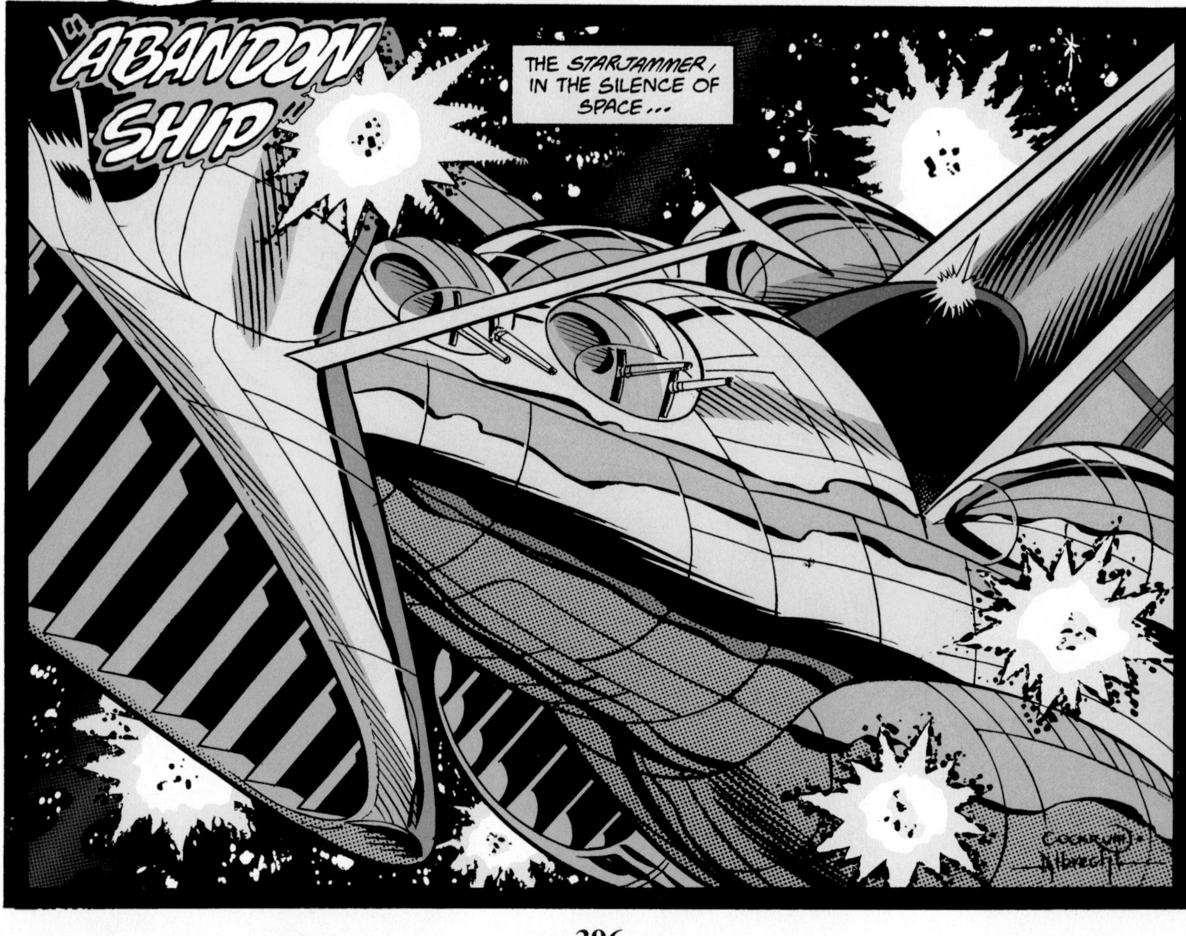

"ABANDON SHIP!"

THE STARJAMMER, IN THE SILENCE OF SPACE...

MAJESTRIX-- THE GUESTS WE'VE BEEN EXPECTING ARE ONLY THREE TELEPORT STATIONS AWAY.
BLIP BLIP BLIP
THEY COME... SOON.
THEN PREPARE FOR THEM, FOOL, AND DON'T DISTRA--
WAK
I WOULD HAVE THOUGHT YOU WOULD HAVE LEARNED FROM THE EXPERIENCES OF OUR SHARED CHILDHOOD, DEATHBIRD...
WHOK
...THAT I AM EVER FASTER THAN YOU.
SKRITTTCH
EVEN IF THAT WERE TRUE, DEAR SISTER...
PHT PHT PHT PHT
...MUCH MORE RECENT RESULTS PROVE THAT I AM THE MOST POWERFUL!

CAN'T LET DEATHBIRD'S SPARKQUILLS CONNECT AT ALL...
VHRRRR*
MAJESTRIX LILANDRA...
SIKORSKY WAS HIT... BY A SHOT MEANT FOR ME!
THIS MAKES NO SENSE--HE BETRAYED US...
...SIKORSKY SORRY.
NOW THAT THIS TRAITOR HAS SERVED HIS ONLY USEFUL PURPOSE BY ALERTING ME TO YOUR "PHALKON QUEST"--
--WE CAN BE RID OF HIM!
NO CHOICE REALLY--NO MATTER HOW UNDIGNIFIED...
...I MUST FOLLOW.
COMMANDER--OUR SENSORS SHOW THAT THE STARJAMMER IS... DYING.
BUT THERE IS AN ANOMALY OF SORTS...

THIS MAY NOT HAVE BEEN A VERY GOOD PLAN AFTER ALL.
NO CHANCE TO GET A GRIP ON THIS THICK... GOOP.

AFTER HER, YOU FOOLS--
WE CAN'T FIT THROUGH THE WASTE DISPOSAL CHUTE--?!

--NOW!

POOM
POOM
COMMANDER, THROUGH THE REAR VIEWPORT, DROPPING THEIR CLOAKING FIELD--
THE STARJAMMERS!

AHHH, CORSAIR, YOUR LITTLE SURPRISE FOR DEATHBIRD APPEARS TO HAVE WORKED.
EVEN THOUGH IT MEANT ABANDONING THE STARJAMMER.
BUT THEY'VE STARTED FIRING ON THE STARSKIMMER NOW, CH'OD--
YIP
YIP
"--IT'S TIME FOR YOU TO JOIN HEPZIBAH AND RAZA IN THE HANGAR."
SKUTTLE-BUG PRIMED.
THEN, HEPZIBAH...
--I'LL TAKE CARE OF CR'EE'S MOURNING FAMILY--
YIP
YIP
HEEP
YIP
YIP
...WE ARE OFF TO BATTLE!
FIVE OF THE EMPIRE'S LARGER STAR-RATS AGAINST THREE OF OUR SMALLER SKUTTLE-BUGS...
SO CHEAT WE WILL, CH'OD.

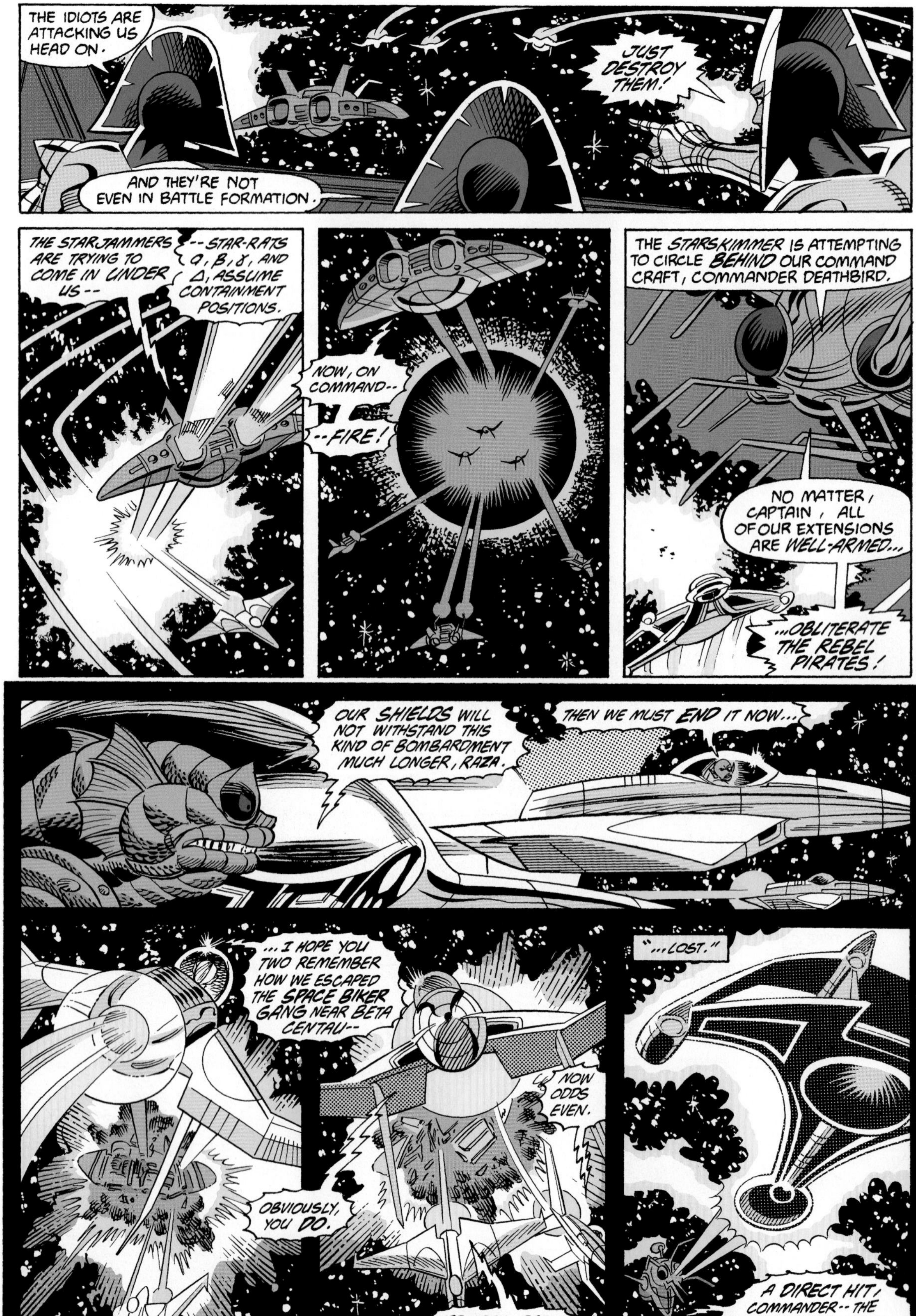

THE IDIOTS ARE ATTACKING US HEAD ON.
AND THEY'RE NOT EVEN IN BATTLE FORMATION.
JUST DESTROY THEM!

THE STARJAMMERS ARE TRYING TO COME IN UNDER US--
--STAR-RATS α, β, γ, AND Δ, ASSUME CONTAINMENT POSITIONS.

NOW, ON COMMAND--
--FIRE!

THE STARSKIMMER IS ATTEMPTING TO CIRCLE BEHIND OUR COMMAND CRAFT, COMMANDER DEATHBIRD.
NO MATTER, CAPTAIN, ALL OF OUR EXTENSIONS ARE WELL-ARMED...
...OBLITERATE THE REBEL PIRATES!

OUR SHIELDS WILL NOT WITHSTAND THIS KIND OF BOMBARDMENT MUCH LONGER, RAZA.
THEN WE MUST END IT NOW...

...I HOPE YOU TWO REMEMBER HOW WE ESCAPED THE SPACE BIKER GANG NEAR BETA CENTAU--
OBVIOUSLY, YOU DO.
NOW ODDS EVEN.
HEPZIBAH, RAZA-- THE COMMUNI-LINK WITH CORSAIR IS...
"...LOST."
A DIRECT HIT, COMMANDER-- THE STARSKIMMER SAILED RIGHT INTO OUR LINE OF FIRE!

YESSSSS!
ALLLLL RIGHT!
FINALLY!
AND SOON MY INSIPID SISTER WILL FOLLOW HER FELLOW STARJAMMERS INTO OBLIVION!

NOW TELL ME WHY I SHOULD NOT DESTROY YOU LIKE THE TRAITOR YOU ARE, SIKORSKY.
SOME OF THIS GARBAGE COULD PROVE USEFUL.
ONE MOMENT PLEASE, MAJESTRIX LILANDRA, WHILE SIKORSKY REPAIRS SELF.
DURING LAST REGULAR LINK-UP TO FREE GALACTIC MEDICAL DATABASE, SIKORSKY INFECTED BY "COMPUTER VIRUS"...
...APPARENTLY PLANTED BY MINION OF PRETENDER DEATHBIRD.
AND WHY SHOULD I BELIEVE YOU?
ONCE PROGRAMMING TO BETRAY STARJAMMERS COMPLETED, SIKORSKY FREE OF VIRUS...
...AND SIKORSKY ONCE MORE WILLING TO DIE FOR TRUE MAJESTRIX LILANDRA.

COMMANDER, THE STARSKIMMER IS... REAPPEARING RIGHT BESIDE US.
NOOOOO! HOW MANY TIMES WILL YOU MORONS FALL FOR THE SAME TRICK?!

HEPZIBAH--CH'OD IS TOO CLOSE TO THAT STAR-RAT. HE MUST USE LONGER-RANGE MISSILES TO DAMAGE THEIR CRAFT...

THE KILLER INSTINCT CH'OD LACKS...

NOR RAZA.

...HEPZIBAH DOES NOT.

THE LAST STAR-RAT FLEES...

...THANK THE PANTHEON.

DROP YOUR SHIELDS AND LET'S TALK, DEATHBIRD.

ARE YOU COMPLETELY MAD, REBEL?

BE SENSIBLE, WOMAN. WE'RE TOO CLOSE TO EACH OTHER FOR EITHER OF US TO RISK FIRING ANYWAY...

...BUT IT'S THE ONLY WAY WE CAN PARLEY COMFORTABLY.

C'MON, DEATHBIRD--YOU DROP YOUR SHIELDS AND I'LL DROP MINE.

YOUR STAR-RATS ARE GONE AND MY STARJAMMERS ARE ON THEIR WAY BACK IN THEIR ARMED SHIPS.
YOU MAY HAVE THE BIGGER SHIP, DEATHBIRD, BUT WE HAVE YOU OUTNUMBERED.
NOW LET'S TALK.
WE HAVE ABSOLUTELY NOTHING TO DISCUSS, CORSAIR.
THE POWER OF PHALKON WILL FOREVER CEMENT MY RULE-- AND I WILL TAKE ITS LOCATION FROM YOUR SHIP'S COMPUTERS BY FORCE!
I'LL SEE YOU IN--
MAJESTRIX--

-- THEY ARE ALMOST HERE...
AND THE SHIELDS MUST BE DOWN SO THEY CAN TELEPORT IN.

I HAVE RECONSIDERED, CORSAIR. WE WILL LOWER OUR SHIELDS AND... TALK.
CAPTAIN-- LOWER SHIELDS.
OKAY, DEATHBIRD, LET'S START WITH LILANDRA...

... WHERE IS SH--
WHA--?!
PH
BOOM
NEVER MIND.

VHRRRRRRRRRR
REMEMBER, SIKORSKY--
--DEATHBIRD IS MINE!

PERFECT. ANOTHER PLAN THAT WORKED. NOW I CAN TELEPORT LIL BACK TO--

PHUUK

NOT YET, CORSAIR.

HUH?!

HOW DID SHE--?!

WHY DOES SHE--?!

I KNOW YOU WELL ENOUGH TO GUESS WHAT YOU HAVE PLANNED, CORSAIR, BUT THIS HAS BECOME PERSONAL...

FWEAT

... REAL PERSONAL!

AGHK!

KR

ZT

UHHHNN...

FINE, SISTER-- I WANTED TO KILL YOU MYSELF ANYWAY!

WE MUST DO SOMETHING.

DON'T YOU DARE, CH'OD.

DEATHBIRD HAS HAD THIS COMING FOR A LONG TIME...
PLOOOP

...AND I CAN HANDLE IT ALL ON MY OWN.

FOR THE SHI'AR PEOPLE... FOR CHARLES...!

FZ ZT

GRRRAR

IMPERIAL GUARD!

TELEPORTING IN BEHIND LILANDRA-- WARSTAR, HUSSAR, QUASAR, MANTA, AND ONE I'VE NEVER SEEN BEFORE...

ZENITH...

...IT IS ZENITH!

HERE COME THE RESERVES!
BINARY--!
WHRRRRR
FWASH
THANK THE GODS...!
NOOOOOO!
FZZT
CHAPTER II
FIRST GUARD

WHRRRRR
KZZZT
NOOOOOOO!
YOU'VE GOT LILANDRA BACK ON THE STARSKIMMER, HEPZIBAH.
NOW GET US OUT OF HERE, RAZA-- FAST.
YIP
YIP
AYE, CAPTAIN.
I HAD DEATHBIRD, CORSAIR. ONE THRUST AND I WOULD HAVE REGAINED MY RIGHTFUL EMPIRE!
WHY COULD YOU NOT HAVE WAITED?!
YOU... IDIOT!
KLANG
BECAUSE THE IMPERIAL GUARDSMEN TELEPORTING IN BEHIND YOU WOULDN'T HAVE WAITED.
LOOK, LADY, WE ABANDONED YOUR SO-CALLED "PHALKON QUEST" AND TOOK A BIG ENOUGH RISK AS IT WAS TRYING TO GET YOU BACK --
--AGAINST MY BETTER INSTINCTS--
--WE WEREN'T ABOUT TO HANG AROUND FOR YOUR PERSONAL VENDETTA.
NOW LET ME AT THAT TRAITOROUS SIKORSKY--
WHRRRRR
URK
NO.
HE HELPED ME. I HAVE REASON TO BELIEVE HE WAS BUT A PAWN OF MY EVIL SISTER
WHRRRRR
BULL.
HE WILL HAVE A CHANCE TO PROVE HIMSELF.
DEATHBIRD IS TOO CLOSE. WE WILL NEED EVERY STARJAMMER TO RETRIEVE THE POWER OF PHALKON.
DID I DO GOOD, CAPTAIN CORSAIR SIR?
PERFECT TIMING, BINARY-- ACROSS THE BOARD.
DESPITE YOUR ATTITUDE.
NOW, TO RECOVER THE COMPLETE MAP TO "PHALKON"...
...ALL WE HAVE TO DO IS RETAKE THE STARJAMMER!
YEEP
YIP
YIP
CR'EEE'S FAMILY, CH'OD WORRIES ABOUT. MOURN TEAMMATE, NO TIME.

A LOWER LOADING DOCK OF THE JUST-MENTIONED DESERTED STARJAMMER SHIP...

MEANWHILE, ON THE SHI'AR COMMAND CRAFT...

NOOO!

I'VE GOT YOU, DEATHBIRD.

QUASAR-- STAY WITH ME.

FWOOOOOOOOOOOOOOOOOOOOOOOOOOO

AS I HAVE GOT YOU, TROOPER.

THERE ARE STILL OTHERS, ZENITH...

...BUT HUSSAR WILL DO WHAT SHE CAN.

WRAK

BACK IN THE STARJAMMER LOADING DOCK...
WHILE ON THE BRIDGE...
ZZ
NOW, GUARDSMEN, YOU SEE WHY IT PAYS TO STICK WITH ME... AND MY PERSONAL TELEPORTER.
BUT THE LIVES LOST--
ARE MEANINGLESS COMPARED TO THE POWER I WILL COMMAND WHEN WE HAVE PHALKON.
I ALONE HAVE DEDUCED EXACTLY WHAT IT IS ALREADY...
ZT
...AND NOW WE NEED ONLY RETRIEVE ITS LOCATION FROM THIS DERELICT'S COMPUTER BANKS.
TO DO THAT SHIP MUST FUNCTION. STARJAMMER, DYSFUNCTIONAL.
WHICH IS WHY I HAD THE FORESIGHT TO RECRUIT ZENITH--A BEING WITH THE POWER TO FEED OFF THE POTENTIAL ENERGY OF OTHER BEINGS.
AFTER ALL, WHAT HAS MORE POTENTIAL THAN A TOTALLY DEAD SENTIENT SPACESHIP?!
AT YOUR COMMAND, MAJESTRIX.
JUMP-START THE SHIP, ZENITH!
KRACKLECHLE
WHILE, OUTSIDE THE STARJAMMER...
THE SHIP IS COMING TO LIFE, CORSAIR.
BUT THAT'S IMPOSSIBLE, UNLESS THERE'S SOMEONE ON BOARD THAT WE DON'T KNOW ABOUT...
DOWN IN THE LOADING DOCK...
WELL... FANCY MEETING YOU HERE.
BEEP

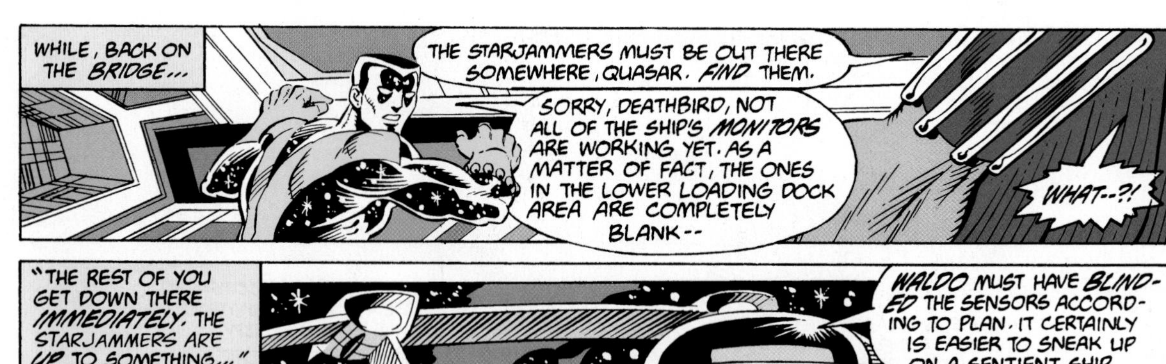
WHILE, BACK ON THE BRIDGE...
THE STARJAMMERS MUST BE OUT THERE SOMEWHERE, QUASAR. FIND THEM.
SORRY, DEATHBIRD, NOT ALL OF THE SHIP'S MONITORS ARE WORKING YET. AS A MATTER OF FACT, THE ONES IN THE LOWER LOADING DOCK AREA ARE COMPLETELY BLANK--
WHAT--?!

"THE REST OF YOU GET DOWN THERE IMMEDIATELY. THE STARJAMMERS ARE UP TO SOMETHING..."
WALDO MUST HAVE BLINDED THE SENSORS ACCORDING TO PLAN. IT CERTAINLY IS EASIER TO SNEAK UP ON A SENTIENT SHIP THAT'S ALREADY ON OUR SIDE.
WHSHHHHH

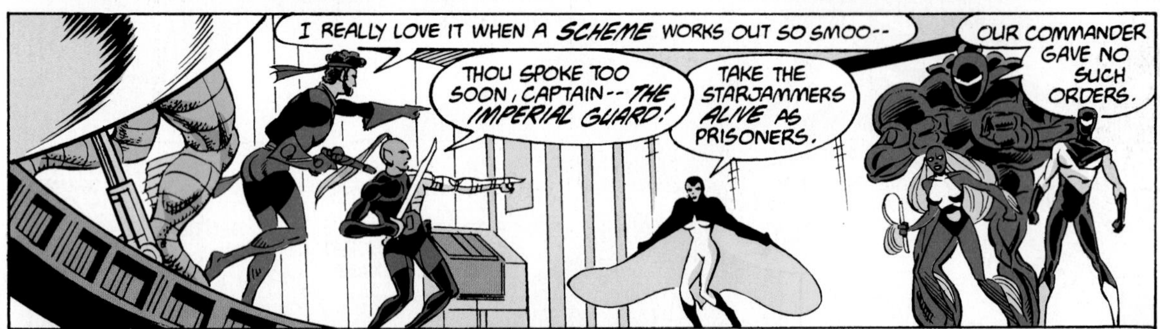
I REALLY LOVE IT WHEN A SCHEME WORKS OUT SO SMOO--
THOU SPOKE TOO SOON, CAPTAIN-- THE IMPERIAL GUARD!
TAKE THE STARJAMMERS ALIVE AS PRISONERS.
OUR COMMANDER GAVE NO SUCH ORDERS.

WELL... PLAN B THEN.
RIGHT-- LET'S KICK SOME SERIOUS BUTT!

I DON'T BELIEVE WE'VE MET BEFORE...
FRZZST
I AM ZENITH. AND, I WILL BE YOUR CONQUEROR FOR DEATHBIRD... AND THE IMPERIAL EMPIRE.

FOOM
I AM SORRY, C'CIL. THIS HURTS ME MORE THAN YOU.
I DOUBT IT.

HHSSSSSS
KRAK
ZZACK
MY ELECTRO-WHIP WILL KEEP YOUR CLAWS FAR AWAY FROM ME, HEPZIBAH.

HUSSAR TOO LATE ALREADY.
COME CLOSER, TRAITOR TO THE TRUE MAJESTRIX LILANDRA...
...AND I SHALL MAKE AN EXCEPTION TO MY CREED AGAINST CARVING A LADY.

MANTA IS NO "LADY", RAZA--
--NOR AM I A TRAITOR...TO MY TRUE CAUSE.
AAARGH!

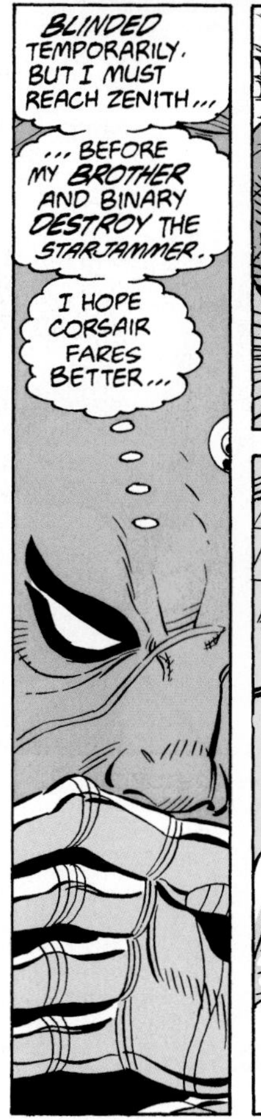
BLINDED TEMPORARILY. BUT I MUST REACH ZENITH...
...BEFORE MY BROTHER AND BINARY DESTROY THE STARJAMMER.
I HOPE CORSAIR FARES BETTER...

FWRZZAT
FWUD
ER... C'CIL... I COULD USE SOME HELP HERE.
YIP
YIP
YIP
YIP
YIP

THIS ZENITH CHARACTER WON'T BACK OFF...
...AND HE CERTAINLY PACKS A MEAN PUNCH!
WE WILL FINISH THIS OUT HERE, WOMAN.

HULL BREACHED.
NOT TO WORRY. WALDO WILL EFFECT IMMEDIATE REPAIRS AND SAVE STARJAMMERS FROM ANOTHER DECOMPRESSION CRISIS.
WHOOOOOSH
THANK THE PANTHEON FOR THAT.

YOU JUST MADE A MAJOR MISTAKE, BUDDY...
...NOW BINARY CAN REALLY CUT LOOSE!
NO MATTER HOW MUCH ENERGY YOU WIELD...
...I CAN ACCESS THE POTENTIAL POWER OF YOUR TOP LIMIT.

EH... NOTHING'S HAPPENING...
Y-YOU HAVE NO LIMIT TO YOUR POWER!

I ALREADY KNEW THAT, PAL.

AND, WITHOUT RAZA AROUND TO STOP ME--
--I CAN PROVE IT!
DID YOU SAY RAZAAAAAAAAARGH!

KRASH
ENOUGH OUT OF YOU ALREADY.

THE METAL OF MY SWORD IS NOT AFFECTED BY THE ENERGIES IN YOUR WHIP, HUSSAR.
IMPERIAL GUARD STARJAMMERS TEAMWORK NOW FACE.
HOLD IT, DEATHBIRD!
CORSAIR!?
HATED LEAVING THE OTHER STARJAMMERS IN THE MIDDLE OF A BATTLE.
BUT LIL STAYED ON THE STARSKIMMER WITH XAVIER'S BODY...
...AND SOMEONE HAS TO STOP THIS MADWOMAN BEFORE SHE--
HOLD, CORSAIR!
I NEED ONLY ANOTHER MINUTE, QUASAR.
USE THE TIME TO KILL HIM!

I DO NOT WISH TO BE DOING THIS, CORSAIR.
POK
UGH!
SKRASH
WELL, YOU CAN'T TELL BY ME, BIG GUY.

I WILL TRY AND MAKE THIS QUICK AND PAI--

WHAT?!
YEEP
YEEP
YEEP

YEEEAAARGH!

CR*EEE!?
YEEP

YOUR FAMILY'S GOING TO BE THRILLED TO SEE YOU, PAL--AND WE'LL ALL WANT TO HEAR HOW YOU SURVIVED YOUR LITTLE "SPACEWALK"...
...BUT FIRST WE'VE GOT TO STOP DEATHBIRD BEFORE SHE GETS THE MAP TO--
TOO LATE, FOOL...
YEEP
YEEP

...THE POWER OF PHALKON IS MINE!
AND THE UNIVERSE WILL SOON BE AS WELL!

--SO THE STARJAMMER ITSELF SAVED YOU BY EXTENDING A POD...
WHAT HAPPENED TO ZENITH?
HE WAS DEFEATED BY HIGHER MATH.
IMPERIAL GUARD, WITH DEATHBIRD, TELEPORT OFF-SHIP.
YEEP YEEP
YIP YIP
THE COMPUTER CONSOLE IS DESTROYED. THE SHIP IS CRIPPLED AND WE NO LONGER HAVE ANY RECORDS OF THE MAP TO PHALKON.
DON'T RUB IT IN, LIL.
THE "SPACE RACE" IS ON...
...AND WE'RE LOSING BADLY!

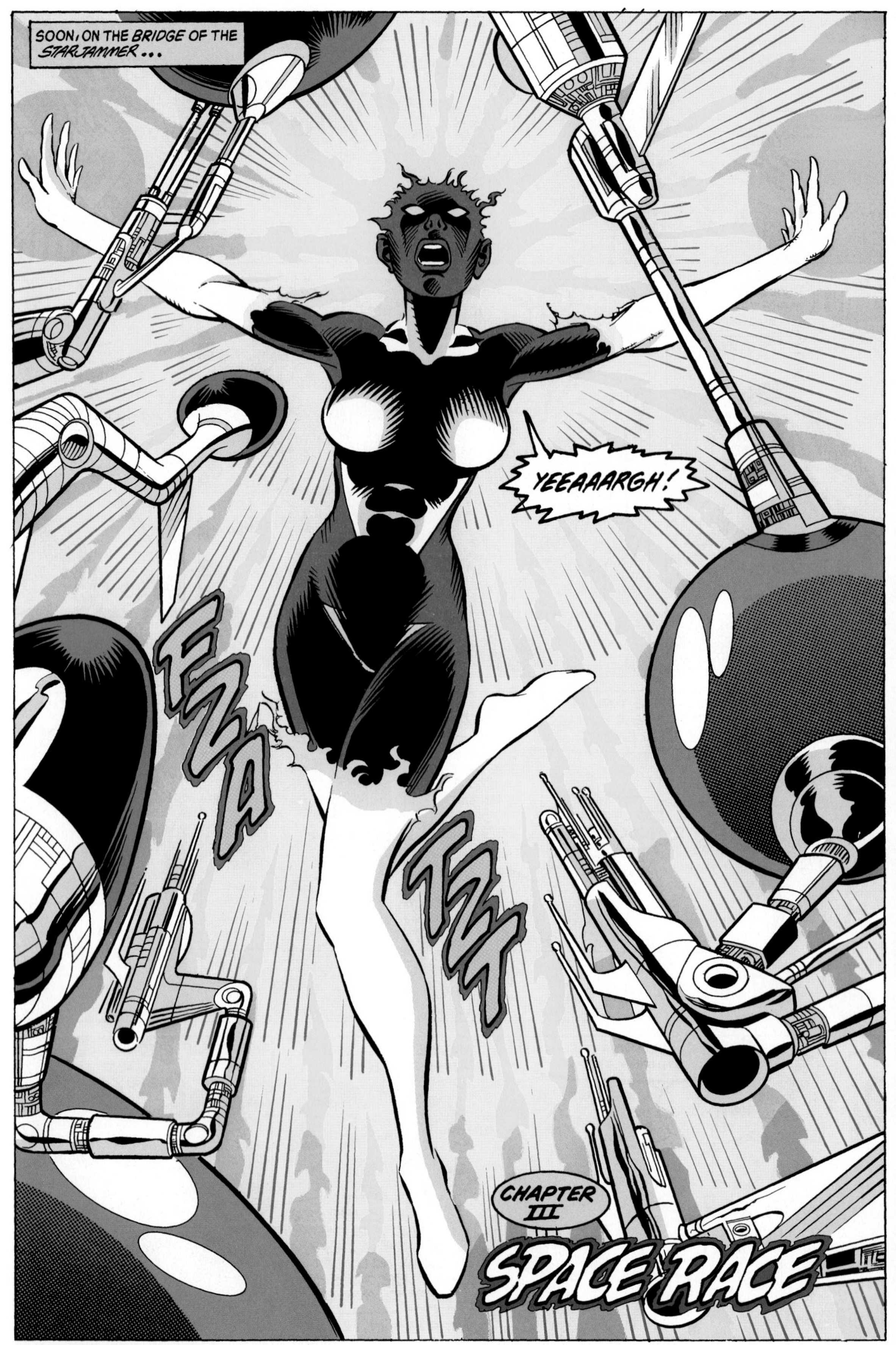
SOON, ON THE BRIDGE OF THE STARJAMMER...
YEEAAARGH!
CHAPTER III
SPACE RACE

TURN OFF THE JUICE, BINARY-- RIGHT NOW!

YES, SIR.
TO CAROL DANVERS, BINARY REVERTED.

NOT FOR LONG, HEPZIBAH!
TOWARDS THE END OF THE TRANSFER, IT ALMOST SEEMED LIKE THE STARJAMMER WAS STEALING THE POWER FROM ME...
...INSTEAD OF WAITING FOR ME TO OFFER IT.
NOW THAT BINARY'S RECHARGED THE SHIP--
BROUGHT THE STARJAMMER BACK TO LIFE, ACTUALLY, CORSAIR. IT IS A SENTIENT CREATURE, AFTER ALL--
IN ANY CASE, CH'OD, WE ARE BACK IN THE RACE TO PHALKON.

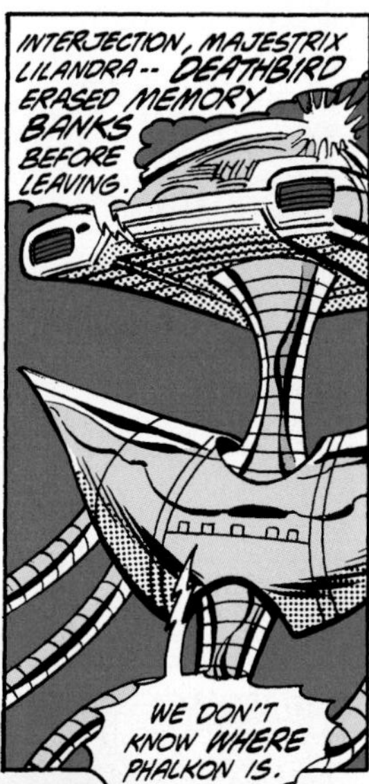
INTERJECTION, MAJESTRIX LILANDRA-- DEATHBIRD ERASED MEMORY BANKS BEFORE LEAVING.
WE DON'T KNOW WHERE PHALKON IS.

I LIKED YOU BETTER WHEN YOU WERE SINGING ELEVATOR MUSIC, WALDO.
HE IS RIGHT, CORSAIR. AND WE CANNOT FOLLOW DEATHBIRD-- WE DO NOT EVEN KNOW WHAT KIND OF SHIP SHE IS USING.

AND THE ONE THING I CAN ASSURE YOU OF ABOUT MY SISTER IS THAT SHE HAS UNDOUBTEDLY SETS TRAPS FOR US ALREA--

THAT'S IT, LIL!
I'VE GOT A BRILLIANT IDEA!
ER... TURN OFF ALL THE SHIELDS AND DEFENSE SYSTEMS.

WHAT--?!
ART THOU MAD?!

ACTUALLY, RAZA, OUR CAPTAIN'S SUGGESTION SEEMS QUITE CANNY.
AND I HAVE ALREADY COMPLIED WITH HIS ORDERS.
I TAKE BACK EVERYTHING I SAID ABOUT YOU, WALDO.

NOW WE JUST HAVE TO FLY THE STARJAMMER IN EVER-WIDENING CIRCLES UNTIL--

WHOOAAA!
HSSS
THOOM

WORKED LIKE A CHARM.
IF YOU ARE TRYING TO GET US KILLED.
THE HULL HAS BEEN BREACHED BY ONE OF DEATH-BIRD'S ASTER-MINES.
THE STARJAMMER WILL REPAIR ITSELF, AND YOU'LL GET US OUT OF THE MINE-FIELD, LIL.
BUT NOW WE KNOW WHICH DIRECTION SHE DIDN'T WANT US TO GO.

IN TANDEM WITH WALDO, OUR COMPUTER SPEED INCREASES GEOMETRICALLY. A QUICK SCAN OF THE STAR-CHARTS...
ONLY ONE DESTINATION POSSIBLE ON THIS ROUTE--
--PLANET EARTH.

AND ANALYSIS OF THE TYPE OF ASTER-MINE EMPLOYED BY DEATHBIRD REVEALS SHE IS TRAVELING IN AN IMPERIAL WARWHIP.
EARTH?!
HEY-- MY NEWS IS SERIOUS, TOO. THE WARWHIP IS STATE-OF-THE-ART... FASTEST SHIP IN THE LINE... LOTS OF WEAPONS...

SOON, ABOARD THE MULTI-SPECIES REC ROOM OF THE STARJAMMER...
STILL NOT QUITE RECOVERED FROM THAT "BOUT" WITH THE SHIP-- IF IT REALLY EVEN HAPPENED.
DOESN'T MATTER. AS LONG AS I'M OUT HERE IN SPACE--CLOSE TO THE STARS-- MY POWERS SHOULD RECHARGE BEFORE WE REACH EARTH.
EARTH--NOW THERE'S SOMETHING I'M NOT REALLY LOOKING FORWARD TO...
IT IS PAINFULLY OBVIOUS THAT SOMETHING IS BOTHERING YOU, RAZA. IS IT ANYTHING THAT I MIGHT BE ABLE TO--
CHOD!
I AM ONLY TOO HAPPY THAT CR'EE HAS DISTRACTED CH'OD.

I AM NOT YET READY TO TELL ANYONE ABOUT MY RELATIONSHIP TO ZENITH... UNTIL I HAVE DECIDED WHAT SHOULD BE DONE.
EXCUSE ME, BINARY-- MIGHT I JOIN YOU?
WHY NOT, RAZA-- IT'S NOT LIKE I'VE GOT ANYTHING BETTER TO DO RIGHT NOW...
AH, MY LITTLE "RESURRECTED" FRIEND AND HIS HAPPY FAMILY...
I MUST REMEMBER TO THANK THE SHIP AGAIN FOR YOUR RESCUE.
YEEP
YIP
YIP
YIP
YIP
YIP
YIP
SHUX!

ACTUALLY...
... IT MIGHT EVEN TAKE MY MIND OFF THE FACT THAT I'M WASTING MY TIME WITH THIS TWO-BIT OUTFIT ANYWAY.

I DON'T GET ENOUGH OPPORTUNITIES TO GO UP AGAINST POWERHOUSES LIKE THAT ZENITH CHARACTER.
... NOT THAT EVEN HE REALLY STOOD A CHANCE--
EXCUSE ME ONCE AGAIN...

...BUT I JUST REMEMBERED A PRIOR ENGAGEMENT.
YEAH, SURE, RAZA... WHAT-EVER.

VERY STRANGE. I TRULY BELIEVED THAT OUR CYBORG COMPATRIOT HAD BEGUN TO DEVELOP A VERY UNCHARACTERISTIC FONDNESS FOR BINARY.
YIP
WHICH MAKES ME WONDER HOW HEPZIBAH IS HAN-DLING THIS... WAITING.

IN CORSAIR'S CABIN...
I'M GLAD WE'VE FINALLY FOUND A CHANCE TO BE ALONE, HEPZIBAH.
NONE OF US SHOULD BE NEEDED ON THE BRIDGE UNTIL THE LAST-- SLIGHTLY MORE DANGEROUS--LEG OF THE ROUTE RAZA AND I CHARTED FOR THE SHIP.
PURRRRRR
BUT EVEN IF WE MANAGE TO BEAT DEATHBIRD TO EARTH... AND WHATEVER THE TREASURE IS AT THE END OF OUR "PHALKON QUEST"... I HAVE A FEELING THINGS ARE GOING TO GET HAIRY--
--ER... MESSY.
HAHAHA HAHAHAHA
SCARE HEPZIBAH, CORSAIR NEED NOT.

SEDUCE HEPZIBAH, CORSAIR NEED NOT.

UHM... CARE FOR A GLASS OF THUPPOXIAN THUNDER-SCREAM?
NO...

CAN'T SEEM TO BE MY USUAL SILVER-TONGUED SELF AROUND--
...HEPZIBATH THIRSTY.
GULPGULP
--THIS INCREDIBLE... WOMAN!

HAHAHA
HAHAHAHAH

AT THE CABIN DOOR...
I HAD THOUGHT TO PASS THE TIME UNTIL WE REACH EARTH WITH HEPZIBAH...
...BUT OBVIOUSLY I WOULD BE OF FAR MORE USE IN THE MEDICAL BAY CHECKING UP ON SIKORSKY.

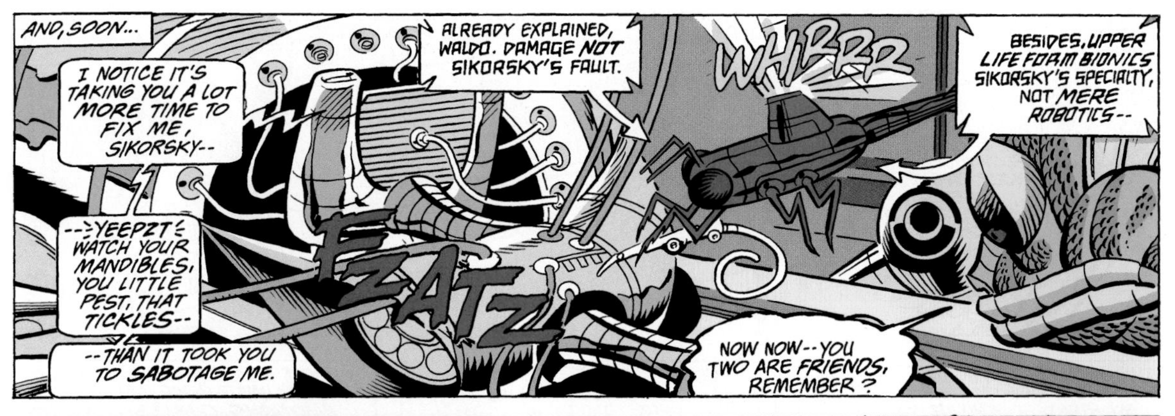
AND, SOON...
I NOTICE IT'S TAKING YOU A LOT MORE TIME TO FIX ME, SIKORSKY--
ALREADY EXPLAINED, WALDO. DAMAGE NOT SIKORSKY'S FAULT.
WHIRRR
BESIDES, UPPER LIFE FORM BIONICS SIKORSKY'S SPECIALTY, NOT MERE ROBOTICS--
--YEEPZT! WATCH YOUR MANDIBLES, YOU LITTLE PEST, THAT TICKLES--
FZATZ
--THAN IT TOOK YOU TO SABOTAGE ME.
NOW NOW--YOU TWO ARE FRIENDS, REMEMBER?

BUT SIKORSKY WAS "BRAINWASHED" BY DEATHBIRD. MAJESTRIX LILANDRA HAS ACCEPTED THAT--
WHIRRR
THEN I HAVE AS WELL.
FZATZ
OW!
--WHY WILL WALDO NOT FORGIVE SIKORSKY?

SINCE YOU APPEAR TO FINALLY BE THROUGH, I'LL JUST TODDLE OFF TO REPAIR THE DAMAGE YOU BEGAN TO DO TO THE STARJAMMER THROUGH ME AS WELL.
WHIRRR
YOU ARE BOTH MORE HUMAN THAN YOU KNOW.
WALDO FEELS BETRAYED BY AN ACT THAT CLEARLY WAS NOT YOUR FAULT...
...AND YOU, SIKORSKY, ARE TOO STUBBORN TO APOLOGIZE FOR IT.

WHIRRR
ZZZZTZZZZ

EXCUSE ME. I'D LIKE TO BE ALONE...
...WITH CHARLES.
OF COURSE, MAJESTRIX LILANDRA.
EVERYONE--CLEAR OUT!
THANKS, WALDO.
ZZZZZTZZZZ

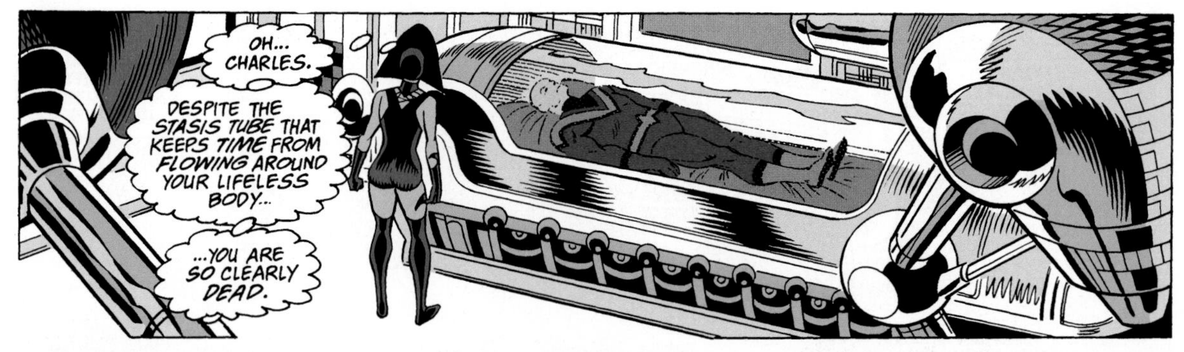
OH... CHARLES.
DESPITE THE STASIS TUBE THAT KEEPS TIME FROM FLOWING AROUND YOUR LIFELESS BODY...
...YOU ARE SO CLEARLY DEAD.

THANKS TO CORSAIR AND HIS HALF-MAD SCHEMES TO HELP ME REGAIN MY RIGHTFUL SHI'AR THRONE...
...NOW YOU HAVE BEEN TAKEN FROM THE REBELLION.
AND FROM ME.
AND DESPITE THE FACT THAT IT IS DEEMED UNSEEMLY FOR ONE OF MY STATION...

...I HAVE COME HERE SIMPLY TO CRY.

WITHOUT EVER TRYING, YOU TAUGHT ME THE IMPORTANCE OF MY EMOTIONS, CHARLES--EVEN THOUGH YOU PREACHED CONTROL.
BUT I STILL WANT TO TOUCH YOU.

AND, ALTHOUGH I HAVE TRIED, TEARS WILL NOT HELP SOOTHE MY HATRED FOR DEATHBIRD AT ALL.
CURSE YOU, SISTER...

...AND CURSE CORSAIR...
...AND CURSE THE USELESS TECHNOLOGY THAT KEEPS CHARLES FROM ME--
SHUMP

NO.
SLAM
WHO DARES--?!

MEANWHILE...

I HOPE RAZA WILL BE MORE WILLING TO OPEN UP TO ME NOW THAT HE HAS HAD SOME TIME TO THINK.

I DO NOT RELISH THE IDEA OF GOING INTO BATTLE WITH A TEAMMATE WHO IS DISTRACTED.

RAP RAP

NOTHING. PERHAPS IF I KNOCK A LITTLE LOUDER...

KWOOOM

I APOLOGIZE FOR THE CONDITION OF YOUR DOOR, RAZA, BUT IF YOU HAD--

RAZA?

I AM VERY PLEASED THOU ART HERE, CH'OD.

I HAVE MUCH TO TELL THEE...

WHILE BACK IN THE MEDICAL BAY...
YOU!
HOW DARE YOU PRESUME TO COME BETWEEN CHARLES AND MYSELF IN ANY WAY?!
THAT THING HAS TO STAY SHUT IF--

WHAT DIFFERENCE COULD IT POSSIBLY MAKE?! THANKS TO YOU, HE IS DEAD, CORSAIR!
BUT IF MY SUSPICIONS ABOUT THE NATURE OF "PHALKON" ARE CORRECT... THE COMMON UNIVERSAL AWE, THE INVOLVEMENT OF EARTH--

PHALKON?!
CHARLES IS DEAD, AND ALL YOU CARE ABOUT IS YOUR MORONIC TREASURE HUNT!
WHOA--HEY!

IT'S A TREASURE HUNT FOR THE SAKE OF YOUR REBELLION, LIL--REMEMBER?
I--

--KNOW. I AM SO SORRY, CORSAIR.
FOR EVERYTHING.

AROOOAROO
NEEDED AT PROPER STATIONS, ALL CREW. DANGER ZONES, APPROACH.
FOR INTERRUPTION, CAPTAINS, HEPZIBAH SORRY...
...VERY SORRY.

TOO SOON...
WHFF
WHFF
WHFF

AS USUAL, YOUR PLAN IS FAR TOO DANGEROUS, CORSAIR.
EVEN THOUGH THE STARJAMMER IS SOMEHOW OPERATING AT 186% EFFICIENCY SINCE BINARY'S BOOST, THE SHIP IS ALREADY FEELING THE STRAIN OF THAT TRIPLE HYPER-SPACE-LEAP.
THIS IS YOUR "PHALKON QUEST", LILANDRA. IF WE'RE GOING TO USE "PHALKON"-- WHATEVER IT IS--TO OVERTHROW YOUR DESPOT SISTER...

...IT'S GOING TO BE THANKS TO YOUR DEFT HANDS AT THE CONTROLS OF THE SHIP.
OF COURSE, WE ARE NOT RUSHING BECAUSE EARTH IS YOUR HOME PLANET, WHERE YOUR FAMILY RESIDES.

ESPECIALLY NOW THAT WE'VE POPPED OUT IN THE MIDDLE OF AN ASTEROID FIELD.

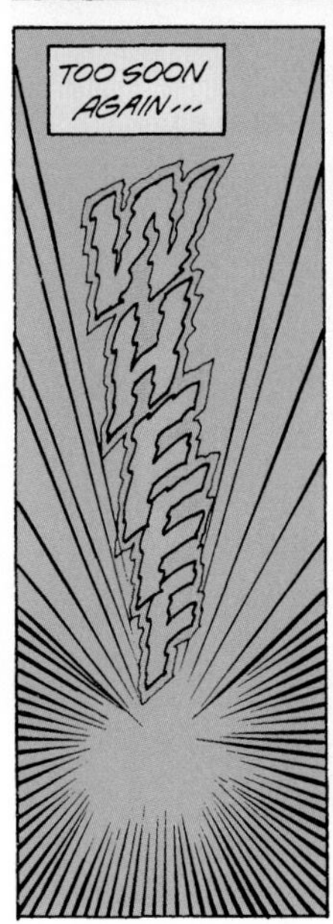
TOO SOON AGAIN...
WHFFF

OOPS.

WE'RE OUT OF HERE!

THE STARJAMMER IS NOT YET READY TO HYPER-LEAP AGAIN, CORSAIR.
SHOOT ONLY SO MANY "SPACE DRAGONS", RAZA AND I CAN.
NOW WE UNDERSTAND WHY THIS PARTICULAR ROUTE IS AVOIDED.

IT GOT US HERE--
--NICE MOVE, LILANDRA--

--IN TIME TO CATCH UP WITH DEATHBIRD'S SHIP, DIDN'T IT?

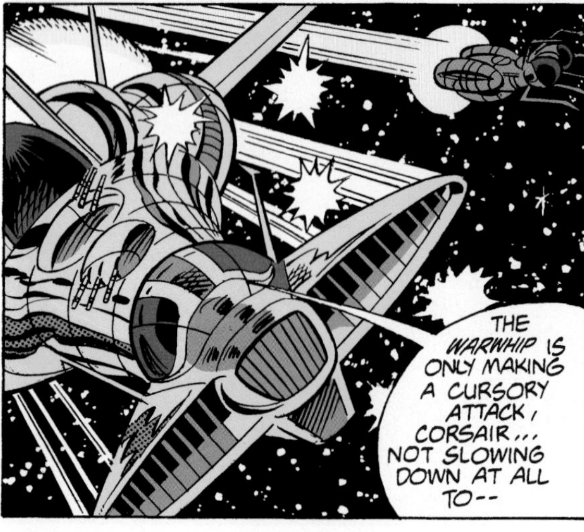
THE WARWHIP IS ONLY MAKING A CURSORY ATTACK, CORSAIR... NOT SLOWING DOWN AT ALL TO--

--STOP US.
AND THAT'S WHY, LIL--

"-- WE'VE ALREADY LOST THE RACE!
"HALF OF THE IMPERIAL ARMADA IS WAITING BETWEEN EARTH AND US...

"...BUT DEATHBIRD ZIPS RIGHT THROUGH."

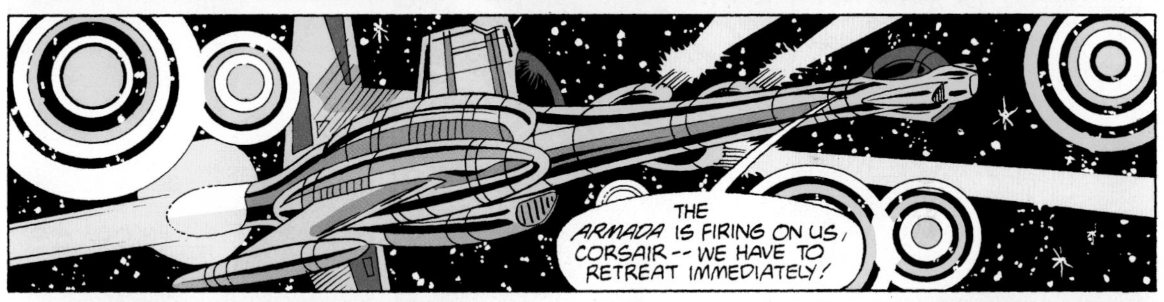
THE ARMADA IS FIRING ON US, CORSAIR -- WE HAVE TO RETREAT IMMEDIATELY!

NO!
WE'VE ALREADY LOST SIGHT OF DEATHBIRD'S SHIP. AND SHE'S THE ONLY ONE WHO KNOWS WHERE--NEVER MIND, WHAT-- "PHALKON" IS.

LOCKED ON STARJAMMER, ENEMY PHLAZERS.
WE'VE ONLY ONE CHOICE...
AS USUAL, CR+EEE.
...WE'RE GOING IN DEEPER.

HIT THE CLOAKING FIELD, LIL... AND REDUCE ALL POWER LEVELS TO MINIMUM.

THAT'S MY PLAN.
OF COURSE. HOW SILLY OF ME TO ASK.
WITH YOUR DEFT HANDS AT THE MANUAL CONTRO--
SPARE US.

THE GOOD NEWS IS THAT I'VE FOUND A POWER SOURCE ON EARTH THAT MATCHES THE TYPE OF ENERGY USED IN THE WARWHIP'S MOTORS.

AS SOON AS WE'RE OUT THE OTHER SIDE OF THE ARMADA...

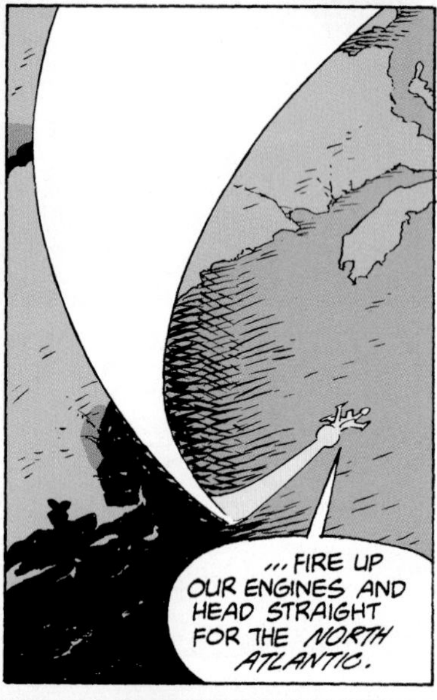

...FIRE UP OUR ENGINES AND HEAD STRAIGHT FOR THE NORTH ATLANTIC.

WE MADE IT, CORSAIR--THERE'S THE WARWHIP.
NOW WHAT IS THE "BAD NEWS"?
THE SENSORS ARE ALSO REGISTERING ANOTHER POWER SOURCE-- OF INCREDIBLE PROPORTIONS-- LITERALLY ON TOP OF THE WITCH'S SHIP.

DEATHBIRD HAS ALREADY RECOVERED THE POWER OF PHALKON!

"HOLD, CORSAIR, THEY ARE ALL UNCONSCIOUS."
"AND WHAT OF THAT STRANGELY-GLOWING 'COCOON'"?
"WE'LL FIND OUT SOON ENOUGH, TEAM..."

FZZ
THERE-- IT IS... PHALKON.
LOOK AT THE RAW ENERGY LEAKING AROUND IT--
NOBODY TAKES A STEP CLOSER UNTIL I CHECK IT OUT.
ZZT
MY CYBERNETIC EYE REVEALS SOMETHING-- OR SOMEONE-- WITHIN.

NONSENSE, CORSAIR. WHATEVER THE POWER OF PHALKON IS, I INTEND TO USE IT TO DESTROY MY SISTER'S FALSE EMPIRE.

IT CAN'T BE!?

JUST AS I WILL NOW DESTROY HER WITH MY BARE HANDS.

LIL'S OFF AFTER DEATHBIRD AND CORSAIR SEEMS TOO STUNNED TO STOP HER.

I WAS AFRAID OF THIS!

TOO TRUE.

YEEP

HHSSSS

NOT RACHEL SUMMERS... PHALKON CAN'T BE--

PHOENIX IS A MEMBER OF EXCALIBUR, BUSTER...

AND WE TAKE CARE OF OUR OWN!

GGRRRR

HHSSSS

EX-WHO?

WHAT?! RISING THROUGH THE HULL--?!

NIGHT-CRAWLER?
URF
BINARY.
?
Uhf!
CORSAIR.
KITTY?
UNDER THE CIRCUMSTANCES, I PREFER SHADOWCAT.
PHOENIX!
PART IV FREE-FOR-ALL

HOLD, CORSAIR.
YEAH, WE JUST FINISHED WITH YOUR MAJESTRIX LILANDRA'S ADVANCE GUARD...
...AFTER THEY SURPRISED RACHEL IN OUR LIGHTHOUSE AND TRAPPED HER IN THIS DEVICE--
DON'T BE RIDICULOUS, SHADOWCAT. THESE TROOPS AREN'T OURS...

...BUT THERE ARE PLENTY MORE WAITING JUST OUTSIDE EARTH'S ATMOSPHERE FOR DEATHBIRD'S SIGNAL. WE CAN'T WASTE ANY TI--
NIGHTCRAWLER TOLD YOU TO STAY PUT.
FRZZT

THE FOOLS DON'T YET REALIZE THAT DEATHBIRD IS ALREADY CONSCIOUS--
--THEY ARE ALL SO INVOLVED IN THEIR OWN CONFRONTATION.

GGRRRR
ER... GGRRRR...
YEEP
SQYKK!
YIP
YIP
YIP
YIP
YIP

WE CAN ONLY ASSUME THAT THIS IS MORE OF THE SHI'AR EMPIRE'S "REVENGE" ON THE ORIGINAL PHOENIX...*
...AND WE WILL NOT ALLOW IT TO BE EXTENDED TOWARDS RACHEL SUMMERS AS WELL.
YOU ARE VERY WRONG, NIGHTCRAWLER. AS YOU WELL KNOW MY SISTER DEATHBIRD HAS USURPED MY THRONE --ALTHOUGH HAD YOU NOT JUST INTERRUPTED MY VENGEANCE...
* AS DEPICTED IN THE ALMOST LEGENDARY X-MEN #137.

LILANDRA'S DISTRACTION, PERFECT CHANCE TO--

MEGGAN WARNED YOU BUT NONE OF YOU WILL LISTEN!
HHSSSS

NO HARM WILL COME TO A MEMBER OF EXCALIBUR WHILE CAPTAIN BRITAIN IS--
PURRFECT. CAPTAIN BRITAIN IS PURRFECT...
HUH?!

RELEASE HEPZIBAH, COWARD, AND FACE A MAN!
AARGH!
SLASH
NO, RAZA-- STOP!

I'D RATHER FACE A MAN ANY DAY, SIR...
...BECAUSE I CAN DO THIS!
THOOM
YOOOW!
ENOUGH OUT OF "EXCALIBUR" ALREADY--
--LET'S TAKE 'EM, STAR-JAMMERS!

"MEGGAN", IS IT? I AM CH'OD AND I DO NOT WISH TO HARM YO--
MEIN GOTT!
AND WHAT MAKES YOU THINK YOU WILL BE ABLE TO...
...ONCE I ASSUME A MORE APPROPRIATE FORM.
FFRR
ZAT
THIS IS TOTALLY OUT OF CONTROL!
I CAN'T HIT A... "WOMAN".
I MUST HIT A WOMAN.
GGGRRRR

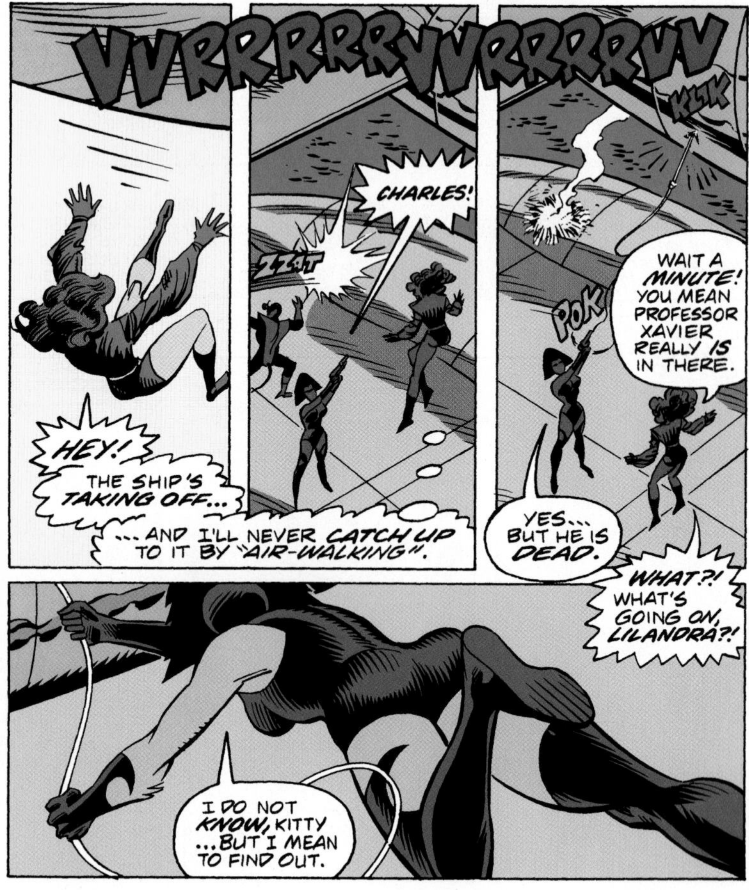

GGRRRRR
FFRRRM
THOOM
HOLD IT, EVERY-BODY!
WHUD
HHSSSSSS

I PREFER NOT TO SLAY AN *UNARMED* FOE, NIGHT-CRAWLER.
I NEEDN'T BE UNARMED FOR LONG, RAZA.
AND THE WAY I REMEMBER OUR *SPARRING SESSIONS*...
...WE WERE QUITE *EVENLY* MATCHED.
KLING
THEN YOU RECALL THEM *INCORRECTLY*. FOR YOU ALWAYS *LACKED* MY--
--*KILLER INSTINCT!*
PERHAPS *YOUR* MEMORY *IS* BETTER--
--FOR I ALSO SEEM TO RECALL THAT WE WERE *FRIENDS*, NOT FOES.
SLISH

--THE IMPERIAL GUARD HAS ARRIVED ?!
YOU KNOW THESE BEINGS, CORSAIR ?
MOST OF THEM. THEY WORK FOR DEATH-BIRD--RELUCTANTLY--BUT THEY HAVE A GRUDGE OR TWO AGAINST US AT THE MOMENT.
FIGURES.

MEANWHILE, FURTHER OUT OVER THE ATLANTIC...

YEAH, BUT ARCHANGEL WAS ONLY THE ANGEL BACK THEN. THIS IS A WHOLE NEW BALL GAME--

CYCLOPS'S POINT PRECISELY, ICEMAN. WITH THE ESTEEMED PROFESSOR TRAVERSING DEEP SPACE, WE MUST LEARN HOW TO LEARN FOR OURSELVES.

COME ON, X-FACTOR, PUT SOME EFFORT INTO THIS TRAINING SESSION!

BOBBY-- PROFESSOR XAVIER RAN YOU THROUGH THIS SCENARIO WITH WARREN HUNDREDS OF TIME IN THE DANGER ROOM.

SHRAKT

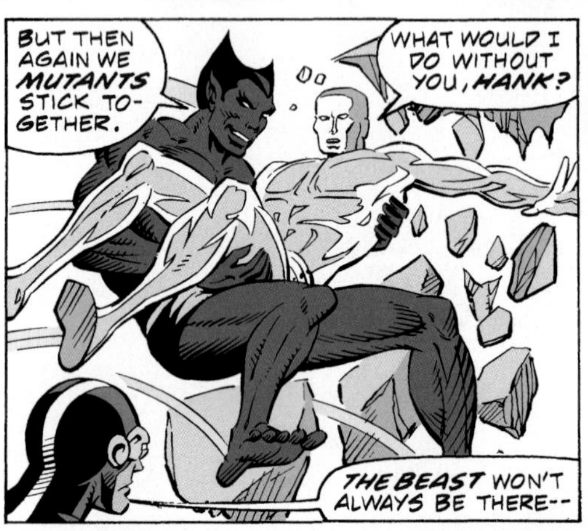

WHILE, BACK WITH THE STARJAMMERS...
I'LL TAKE OUT GLADIATOR-- HE'S THEIR MOST POWERFUL.
YOU'D BETTER BE JOKING, CAP.
THEN HE SHOULD BE MINE, BINARY.
ZZZAT
TOOM

BESIDES, AS SOON AS YOU'RE FINISHED WITH SMASHER...
...THERE'S ALWAYS TITAN.
POOOM

I GUESS WE'RE FIGHTING WITH THE STARJAMMERS NOW...
I HAVE GOT HER, TEMPEST.
NO, ELECTRON, I'VE ALREADY BUILT UP A CHARGE...
OH WELL, SIX OF ONE... TWO DOZEN OF THE OTHER--

TZTZ
ZTZZT
OOOOH... I SORT OF ENJOYED THAT.

SOONER OR LATER, I SHALT FIND A VITAL ORGAN, BLACKTHORN...
DOES PLANT LIFE DEPEND ON VITAL ORGANS, RAZA?
SHKT
MEGGAN, I WANT YOU OUT OF THIS MADHOUSE N--

--OW!
WOK
NOT "MEGGAN," NIGHTCRAWLER -- JUST YOUR OLD PAL, HOBGOBLIN.

THIS IS WHAT I REALLY NEEDED--AN HONEST-TO-GOODNESS BAD GUY TO TAKE MY FRUSTRATIONS OUT ON...
THE IMPERIAL GUARD ARE NOT "BAD GUYS," BINARY--

--WE FIGHT FOR WHOEVER HOLDS THE SHI'AR THRONE ...EVEN IF THAT ONE BE DEATHBIRD.
FFRRZZZZZA ATT

BATOOM
AND GLADIATOR IS NO ONE'S PUNCHING BAG!
Uhhn...

ACCORDING TO OUR FILES, THIS "LOCKHEED" CREATURE IS NOT OF TERRESTRIAL ORIGIN...
...BUT HE STILL SHOULD NOT BE ABLE TO MATCH IMPULSE BLAST FOR BLAST --NOTHING SHOULD!
ROWR

WE ARE NEW TO THE IMPERIAL GUARD--
--SO WE SHOULD INTRODUCE OURSELVES.
SHE IS WHITE NOISE.
AND HE IS BLACK LIGHT.

AND THIS IS WHY.
POOT
EEEEEE
OOOPS. EXCUSE ME, EARTH-QUAKE.
HSSSS
GET BACK, MENTOR, ONLY STARBOLT SHOULD PROTECT THE LADY ORACLE.

YEEAAAGH!
AW, I GUESS OL' EARTHQUAKE FAINTED--

WHA--?!
BUT I'M SUPPOSED TO BE INTANGIBLE...
AND SO YOU ARE, SHADOWCAT. HOWEVER...

POK
...ASTRA IS AS WELL!

Ugh... HAVE TO GET THESE CREATURES OFF ME...
YEEP
YIP
YIP
YIP
YIP
YIP

...CALL UP THE DARKNESS...
NIGHTSIDE-- NO! NOW I CAN'T SEE TO CAST MY SPELLS--

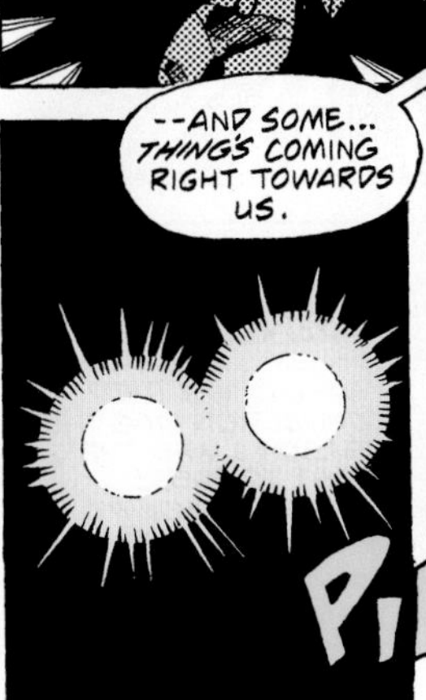
--AND SOME... THING'S COMING RIGHT TOWARDS US.
PING

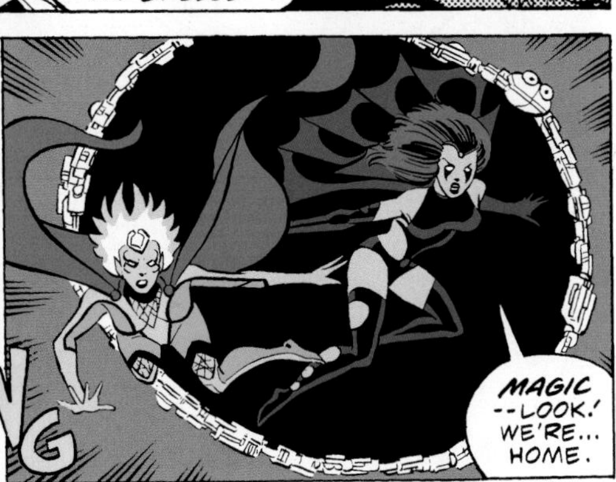
MAGIC --LOOK! WE'RE... HOME.

BUUURP

EEEYARGH!
THNT

TELL ME AGAIN ABOUT HOW YOU HAVE THE POWER TO "SUPER-THINK," MENTOR.
EXTREMELY INTERESTING. AND NOW THE ODDS SEEM TO BE TURNING IN OUR FAVOR...
ZZZAP

JUST OUTSIDE EARTH'S ATMOSPHERE, WHERE DEATHBIRD'S ARMADA WAITS...
SHIP TO THE RESCUE.
1121 222 12.

OUTSIDE--IT'S THE STARJAMMER, WITH A STAR-VESSEL THAT CAN ONLY BELONG TO...
...THE CELESTIALS!
THE MONITORS ARE GOING WILD--ALL OF THE SENTIENT SHIPS IN THE FLEET ARE...

"...DESERTING."

TAKE THAT... AND THAT ...AND THAT...
WHAT TRANSPIRES WITHOUT, SCOTT?
WE NEED TO REACH THE BRIDGE TO ANSWER THAT.
WELL, MY FRIEND, CAN WE CALL IT EVEN NOW?
22!

BUT, BACK DOWN ON EARTH...
I SHOULD HAVE TRUSTED THE STARJAMMER. THE SHIP--AND ITS "FRIEND"--HAVE EVERYTHING UNDER CONTROL UP THERE.
I HAVE FAR MORE PRESSING MATTERS AWAITING ME HERE.

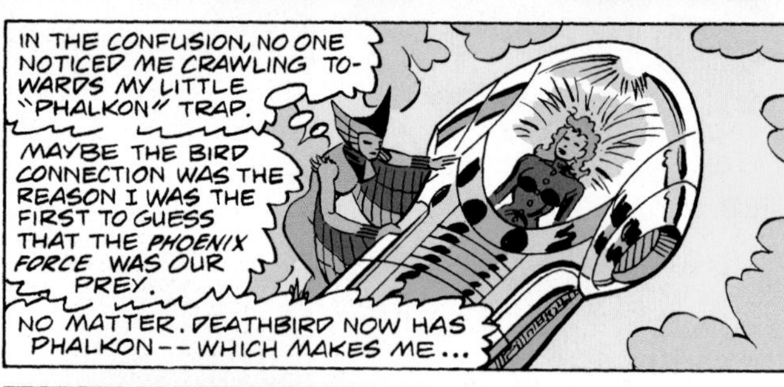
IN THE CONFUSION, NO ONE NOTICED ME CRAWLING TOWARDS MY LITTLE "PHALKON" TRAP.
MAYBE THE BIRD CONNECTION WAS THE REASON I WAS THE FIRST TO GUESS THAT THE PHOENIX FORCE WAS OUR PREY.
NO MATTER. DEATHBIRD NOW HAS PHALKON--WHICH MAKES ME...

...DEATH PHOENIX!
KRZCKLE

OH, MY GOD, DEATHBIRD'S BEGUN SOME KIND OF ENERGY TRANSFER FROM--
RACHEL! I'LL HAVE TO TRY ANOTHER TELEPORT--

PLEASE DO NOT BOTHER, NIGHTCRAWLER...
NO! NOT YET--

NOW, SISTER, THERE SHALL FINALLY BE A RECKONING..

...SHE IS MINE!
KRAK

NO-- MOTHER!
AAARGH!
EEEEEEEEEE

OUR FIRST DUTY IS TO THE MAJESTRIX.
I'VE GOT MY MOTHER.
IMPERIAL GUARD-- GATHER YOUR WOUNDED COMRADES AND FOLLOW BLACK LIGHT THROUGH THAT ABANDONED TELEPORTAL BEFORE IT CLOSES.

YOU OKAY, RAY?
FINE, KITTY --JUST A LITTLE DRAINED...
HEY, THIS THING'S STILL HOT.

NOW IT'S TIME FOR SOMEBODY TO EXPLAIN WHAT'S GOING ON HERE!
MORE TO THE POINT-- WHAT IS THIS ABOUT PROFESSOR XAVIER BEING DEAD?!

BELIEVE IT OR NOT, I HAVE AN IDEA ABOUT THAT...

MONTHS LATER--
--AT THE OUTERMOST EDGE OF DEATHBIRD'S EMPIRE--

--ON THE FARTHEST PLANET UNDER HER SWAY...
--TOO DULL FOR WORDS, PUPUGLI.

DON'T WORRY ABOUT IT. AT THE RATE DEATHBIRD'S RAPING THE RESOURCES OF THIS MUDBALL, IT'LL BE DEAD SOON ENOUGH, MIMOZA...
...AND WE'LL BE WINGING OUR WAY TOWARDS SOME NEW EXOTIC LOCALE.

ANYPLACE WOULD BE BETTER THAN HERE.

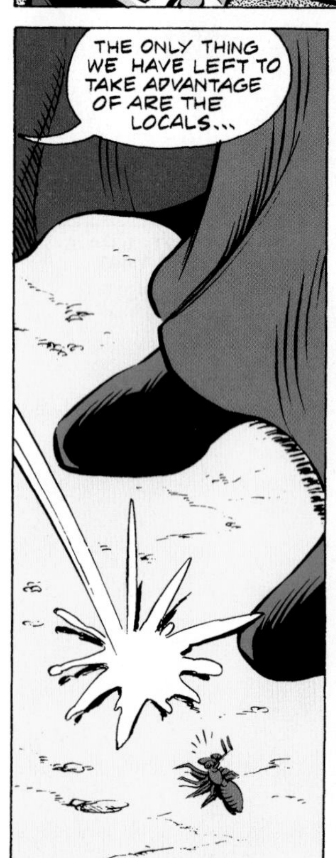
THE ONLY THING WE HAVE LEFT TO TAKE ADVANTAGE OF ARE THE LOCALS...

...AND WHO WANTS 'EM?!
JOIN THE ARMY AND SEE THE UNIVERSE--HAH!
GRRRR

INSIDE.

QUIET, HEPZIBAH. YOU'LL GIVE AWAY THE MUNITIONS WE'RE SMUGGLI--
DON'T CARE, CORSAIR. TROOPER SCU--

WE SECRETED THE STARSKIMMER HERE DISGUISED AS A LOCAL HABITAT AS YOU ORDERED, CAPTAIN.
WHRRRR
YIP
YEEP
SCOUTING MISSION REVEALED LOCATION OF LONE TROOPER GARRISON ON THE PLANET.
AND HERE ARE THE LOCAL REBELLION LEADERS, BUT...
WE HAVE REVIEWED YOUR MAPS AND PLANS CAREFULLY, CORSAIR.
AND WE FIND THEM QUITE FEASIBLE.
HOWEVER, WE ARE NOT SURE OUR PEOPLE ARE READY FOR REVOLUTION YET...

WE THINK THEY WILL BE IF WE GIVE THEM A SYMBOL TO RALLY AROUND.
A SYMBOL REPRESENTING A FORCE THAT IS RECOGNIZED AND FEARED THROUGHOUT THE GALAXIES -- WHETHER IT IS KNOWN AS PHALKON OR WHATEVER.
JUST BACK FROM THE DEAD AS OF THIS MORNING --

-- INTRODUCING BALD PHOENIX!
I DO NOT THINK SO, CORSAIR. I FEEL SILLY ENOUGH IN THIS COSTUME ALREADY.

IF WE ARE TO PUT THE PORTION OF PHOENIX POWER STOLEN BY DEATHBIRD'S APPARATUS TO GOOD USE...
... WE MUST DO SO BEFORE IT WEARS OFF.
OR WORSE.

DEATHBIRD WILL FALL!
SKRSH

AND SOON...
FOR FREEDOM!
TOOM
AAARGH!
DEATH TO DEATHBIRD THE USURPER!
TWOP
TWOP
FRZAP
FOR THE TRUE MAJESTRIX LILANDRA!
TOO MANY OF THEM...

AND THIS PLANET IS JUST THE BEGINNING--
SCHOOT
SCH
URK...
--THE STARJAMMERS ARE RE-TAKING THE SHI'AR EMPIRE!

HAVE NONE OF YOU SENSE ENOUGH TO FLEE?!
BABOOM
FALL BACK!
AND DIE LIKE THE COWARDS THOU ART!

POOM
BY THE EMPIRE, MIMOZA, IT'S--
THE PHOENIX!

BOOM
WHRRR
EVERYONE RALLY AROUND THE PHOENIX--
THIS OUTPOST MAY BE DOOMED, BUT DEATHBIRD'S WILL SHALL STILL BE DONE...
...LILANDRA WILL DIE!

YIKES!
EH... SIKORSKY--?!
WHRRRRR
HE JUST SAVED YOUR LIFE, LIL...

...I GUESS HE IS ONE OF THE GOOD GUYS AGAIN AFTER ALL.
FWHOOM
SCHOOM

AS USUAL OF LATE, CORSAIR HAS LEFT HEPZIBAH FAR TOO VULNERABLE...
WHUD

PERHAPS IF BINARY WERE TO LEARN MORE ABOUT TEAMWORK...
YEEEAAAGH!
KWAKOOM

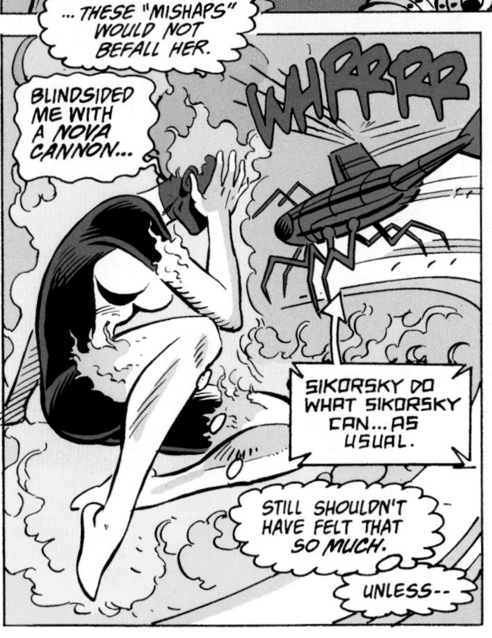
...THESE "MISHAPS" WOULD NOT BEFALL HER.
WHRRRR
BLINDSIDED ME WITH A NOVA CANNON...
SIKORSKY DO WHAT SIKORSKY CAN...AS USUAL.
STILL SHOULDN'T HAVE FELT THAT SO MUCH.
UNLESS--

--THE SHIP TOOK EVEN MORE OUT OF ME THAN I THOUGHT DURING THE POWER DRAIN EARLIER...
...QUITE LITERALLY!

"DOESN'T MATTER RIGHT NOW ANYWAY. THE BATTLE'S AS GOOD AS OVER FOR THE EMPIRE. THIS PLANET IS FREE."
AND, SILENT AND UNSEEN, A SHI'AR SPY-EYE HOVERS NEARBY, MONITORING THE FINAL DEFEAT OF DEATHBIRD'S TROOPS...

FOR THE REBELLION!
FOR LILANDRA!
ERZAT
TOOM
ZAP
ZAZT
TZAM
KBOOM
HSSS
FOR HONOR AND GLORY!

ON THE SHI'AR THRONE-WORLD...

ARRH! LILANDRA AND HER STAR-JAMMERS! THEY ARE TAKING FULL ADVANTAGE OF THEIR SUCCESS IN THE PHALKON QUEST.

THAT PLANET WILL FALL TO THEM IN A MATTER OF DAYS UNLESS WE GET REINFORCE-MENTS THERE IMMEDIATELY

BUT, MAJESTRIX DEATHBIRD, THERE IS INSURGENCE THROUGH-OUT THAT SECTION OF THE EMPIRE INSPIRED BY THE STARJAMMERS AND THEIR ALLIANCE WITH THE PHOENIX FORCE.

WE CAN SPARE NO TROOPS THERE FOR A DRIED-OUT PLANET.

ARE YOU QUESTIONING MY ORDERS, OFFICER TARQ ?!

N-NO, MAJESTRIX...

I JUST THOUGHT TO SUGGEST ANOTHER PLANET AS A SUITABLE REPLACEMENT--A SOURCE OF GREAT POWER AND MANY OF YOUR CURRENT PROBLEMS...

YES--EARTH! EARTH WILL JOIN MY EMPIRE NEXT!

AND SOON, BACK IN HIS PRIVATE QUARTERS--

--STANDING BEFORE HIS MIRROR...
ALL WENT WELL.
DEATH-BIRD HAS SET HER SIGHTS ON PLANET EARTH.

OF COURSE, TARQ. THE CULT OF DEATH COULD EXPECT NO LESS OF THE WELL-LAID PLANS...

...OF THE MAD GOD OF DEATH HIMSELF!
HAIL, THANOS!
HAIL THANOS!
THE BEGINNING OF... THE END!

EARLY STARJAMMERS CHARACTER DESIGNS BY **DAVE COCKRUM**. THOUGH BOTH CHARACTERS WERE ULTIMATELY UNUSED BLOODSTAR'S CHEST EMBLEM AND SWORD WERE CARRIED OVER INTO CORSAIR'S DESIGN. THE NAME "STARJAMMERS" WAS

Dave Cockrum

BRAIN FOR P.C. WAS PROBABLY EITHER CLONED & RAISED FROM INFANCY IN THE P.C.M. IDENTITY OR SUPPLIED--IN AMNESIAC STATE--BY FATALLY-INJURED ADULTS.

P.C.M. MK. 4

Psionic Control Module MK. 4

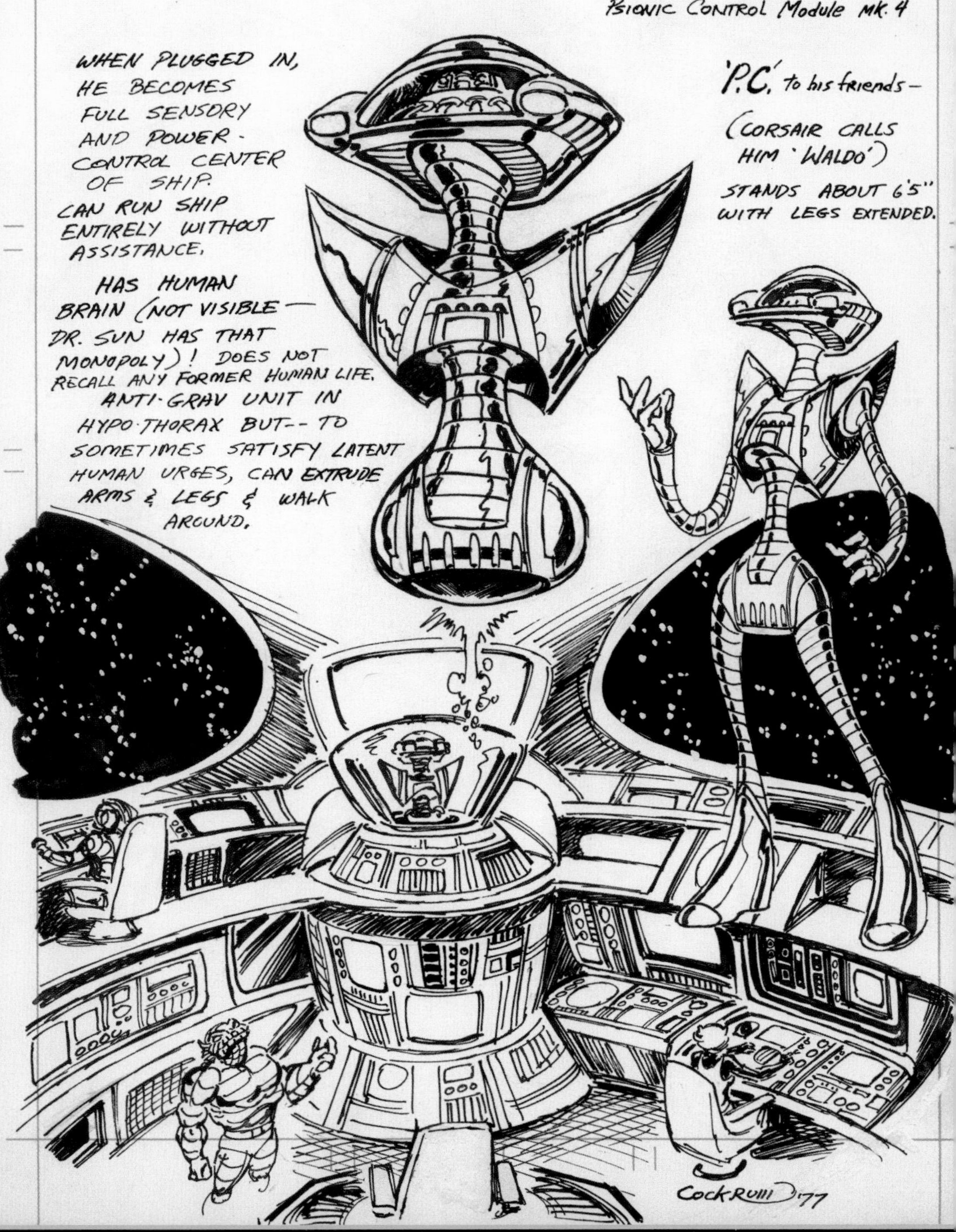

WHEN PLUGGED IN, HE BECOMES FULL SENSORY AND POWER-CONTROL CENTER OF SHIP. CAN RUN SHIP ENTIRELY WITHOUT ASSISTANCE.
HAS HUMAN BRAIN (NOT VISIBLE—DR. SUN HAS THAT MONOPOLY)! DOES NOT RECALL ANY FORMER HUMAN LIFE.
ANTI-GRAV UNIT IN HYPO-THORAX BUT--TO SOMETIMES SATISFY LATENT HUMAN URGES, CAN EXTRUDE ARMS & LEGS & WALK AROUND.
'P.C.' to his friends—
(CORSAIR CALLS HIM 'WALDO')
STANDS ABOUT 6'5" WITH LEGS EXTENDED.
COCKRUM '77

DAVE COCKRUM DREW THIS SKETCH OF CORSAIR ON THE BACK OF THE ORIGINAL ART BOARD FOR ***X-MEN #104***, PAGE 17, CORSAIR AND CH'OD'S FIRST ON-PANEL APPEARANCE. [THE TAPE AND SLIGHT IMAGE MISMATCH AROUND CORSAIR'S ARM WAS CAUSED WHEN A PANEL FROM THAT PAGE WAS CUT OUT AND REPOSITIONED.]

HERE'S THE SOLUTION TO SOMETHING THAT'S BOTHERED ME FOR QUITE SOME TIME: WHERE THE HELL DOES CORSAIR KEEP HIS PISTOLS?

THOSE GIZMOS ON HIS GLOVES MATERIALIZE THE PISTOLS ON A MENTAL COMMAND — MAYBE THE SWORD TOO, THO IN X-MEN #107 I SHOWED THE SWORD HANGING IN A SCABBARD AT HIS SIDE —

EITHER THE PISTOLS ARE KEPT "OUT OF SYNC" WITH THIS SPACE-TIME PLANE UNTIL NEEDED (AND THUS ARE ALWAYS MORE-OR-LESS 'AT HAND'), OR POSSIBLY THEY'RE TELEPORTED BACK TO THE SHIP WHEN NOT IN USE. THE LATTER WOULD SHOOT THE HELL OUT OF HIS USING THEM IN <u>THIS</u> STORY, THO — I THINK THE FIRST METHOD IS BEST. I GUESS THE SWORD MUST BE HANDLED THAT WAY TOO, SINCE I HAVEN'T BEEN DRAWING IT HANGING AT HIS SIDE.

THIS NOTE ABOUT CORSAIR, FROM **DAVE COCKRUM** TO **CHRIS CLAREMONT**, WAS WRITTEN ON THE BACK OF THE ORIGINAL ART BOARD FOR ***UNCANNY X-MEN #154***, PAGE 13. COCKRUM FIRST DREW CORSAIR'S PISTOLS

STARJAMMERS

The Starjammers are a small band of space pirates who cruise the Shi'ar galaxy, plundering starships to exact revenge against the Shi'ar Empire (see *Shi'ar*). Over twenty years ago U.S. Air Force test pilot Major Christopher Summers was flying himself, his wife Katherine Anne, and their sons Scott and Alexander (see *Cyclops, Havok*) in a private plane when it was attacked by a Shi'ar starship on an exploratory mission to Earth. The two boys escaped, but Christopher Summers and his wife were teleported aboard the Shi'ar craft, and taken to the Shi'ar Imperial Throneworld. After arrival, Katherine Anne was murdered before her husband's eyes, and Summers was placed in the slave pits, where political prisoners and criminals were held. There he met Ch'od, Hepzibah, and Raza. The four stole a starship and escaped. They called their ship the *Starjammer* (they have had at least two ships by this name) and themselves the Starjammers. The Starjammers are allies of the deposed Shi'ar Princess Lilandra, but with the ascension of her sister Deathbird to the throne, they are still outlaws.

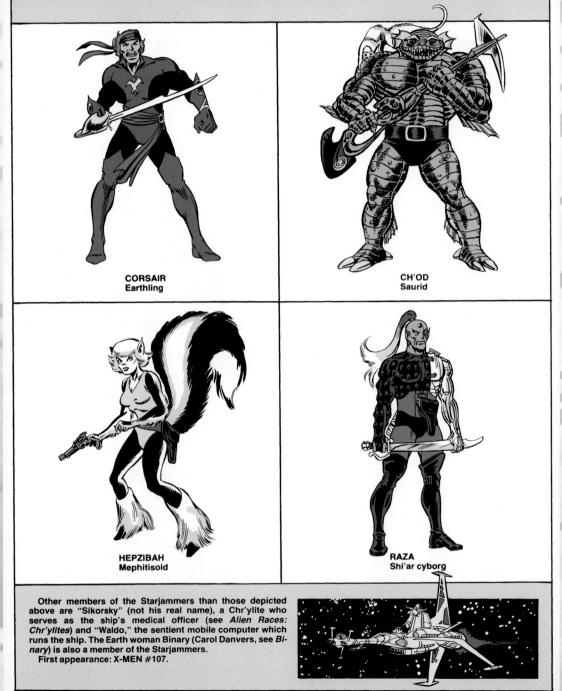

CORSAIR
Earthling

CH'OD
Saurid

HEPZIBAH
Mephitisoid

RAZA
Shi'ar cyborg

Other members of the Starjammers than those depicted above are "Sikorsky" (not his real name), a Chr'ylite who serves as the ship's medical officer (see *Alien Races: Chr'ylites*) and "Waldo," the sentient mobile computer which runs the ship. The Earth woman Binary (Carol Danvers, see *Binary*) is also a member of the Starjammers.

First appearance: X-MEN #107.

OFFICIAL HANDBOOK OF THE MARVEL UNIVERSE PROFILE BY MARK GRUENWALD, DAVE COCKRUM, JOSEF RUBINSTEIN & ANDY YANCHUS

OFFICIAL HANDBOOK OF THE MARVEL UNIVERSE PROFILE ART BY
DAVE COCKRUM, JOSEF RUBINSTEIN & ANDY YANCHUS

THE UNCA X-MEN™ Vol. 1, No. 156, April, 1982. (U.S.P.S. 539-950) Published by MARVEL COMICS GROUP, James E. Galton, President. Stan Lee, Publisher. Michael Hobs ice-President, Publishing. Milton Schiffman, Vice-President, Production. OFFICE OF PUBLICATION: 575 MADISON AVENUE, NEW YORK, N.Y. 10022. Controlled Circulat ostage paid at New York, NY and at additional mailing office. Published monthly. Copyright © 1982 by Marvel Comics Group, a division of Cadence Industries Corporation. All rig eserved. Price 60¢ per copy in the U.S. and Canada. Subscription rate $7.20 for 12 issues. Canada, $8.20. Foreign, $9.20. Printed in the U.S.A. No similarity between any of the mes, characters, persons, and/or institutions in this magazine with those of any living or dead person or institution is intended, and any such similarity which may exist is purely co dental. This periodical may not be sold except by authorized dealers and is sold subject to the conditions that it shall not be sold or distributed with any part of its cover or markings r moved, nor in a mutilated condition. THE UNCANNY X-MEN (including all prominent characters featured in the issue), and the distinctive likenesses thereof, are trademarks of the MARVEL COMICS GROUP. Postmaster: Send address changes to Subscription Dept., Marvel Comics Group, 575 Madison Avenue, New York, N.Y. 10022.

UNCANNY X-MEN #156, PAGE 1 ART BY **DAVE COCKRUM & BOB WIACEK**

COURTESY OF HERITAGEAUCTIONS.COM

***UNCANNY X-MEN* #156**, PAGE 22 ART BY **DAVE COCKRUM** & **BOB WIACEK**

MEANWHILE, SOME TWO THOUSAND MILES WEST-WARD...
...IN THE STARKLY BEAUTIFUL RIO DIABLO MOUNTAIN RANGE A SLEEK, UNEARTHLY SHUTTLECRAFT DROPS SILENTLY TO THE GROUND OUTSIDE THE HOUSE SHARED BY...

...FORMER X-MEN LORNA DANE (POLARIS) AND ALEX SUMMERS (HAVOK).
HOW'S DINNER? I'M STARVED!
BE PATIENT, M'LOVE-- OWW!
WHAT'S WRONG?!

BURNED M'TONGUE. THE CHILI IS SUPERB, BUT HOT! POUR ME A GLASS OF ICE WATER, WILLYA?
I'VE A BETTER IDEA.
MMMMMMMMM --A WOMAN AFTER MY OWN HEART,
AMONG OTHER THINGS.

NOK NOK NOK
SIGH
MURPHY'S LAW-- IT NEVER FAILS, JUST WHEN THINGS GET INTERESTING.
HOLD THOSE THOUGHTS, SWEETHEART, WHILE I SEE WHO THE HECK IT IS.

H'LO, ALEX.
SCOTT!
LORNA, LOOK WHO'S HERE! WHAT BRINGS YOU TO THIS NECK OF THE WOODS, BIG BROTHER?! YOU TIRED OF RAM-RODDING THE X-MEN?!
YOU LOOK GREAT! C'MON IN!
ALEX, I'M NOT ALONE.
SO I SEE.

THERE'S NO EASY WAY TO SAY THIS: ALEX, MEET CHRISTOPHER SUMMERS --CORSAIR, LEADER OF THE STARJAMMERS--
--OUR FATHER.

X-MEN: SPOTLIGHT ON STARJAMMERS #1 PAGE 6 ART BY DAVE COCKRUM & JEFF ALBRECHT

X-MEN SPOTLIGHT ON
MARVEL FORTNIGHTLY
Book STARJAMMERS Issue# 1
MZ!
CORSAIR!
SHHHRRROOOOSH
I'M AFTER HIM!
I DON'T MEAN TO HURRY YOU, FRIEND RAZA, BUT EVEN MY HIDE--
NO FEAR, CH'OD, MY SWORD HATH ALREADY DONE THE DELICATE WORK...
...NOW MY MUSCLES AND GEARS CAN DO THE REST.
AND HEPZIBAH...?
I LAST SAW HER BOUNDING AFTER YON PROJECTILE.
IT WAS ALL WE COULD DO TO STAND OUR GROUND.
"TRUE, CH'OD, BUT HEPZIBAH IS A CAT OF A VERY DIFFERENT BREED."
ATMOSPHERE LEAVING SHIP FASTER THAN IT CAN BE REPLACED.
I AM WARRIOR. WHAT CAN I DO?
GETTING HARD TO BREATHE.
HMMM...
THERE.
PLUNK
CAPTAIN, ARE YOU--
NOT SMART, CORSAIR. THIS SHIP'S ALREADY SUSTAINED ENOUGH DAMAGE AND SIKORSKY INFORMS ME THAT LITTLE EPISODE DID NOT HELP CHARLES'S CONDITION ANY...
WORSE YET, LIL, WE'VE JUST LOST THE "MAP" THAT WOULD'VE GIVEN US THE LOCATION OF "PHALKON"!
7
X-MEN: SPOTLIGHT ON STARJAMMERS #1 PAGE 7 ART BY DAVE COCKRUM & JEFF ALBRECHT

OUR SHIELDS WILL NOT WITHSTAND THIS KIND OF BOMBARDMENT MUCH LONGER, RAZA.

THEN WE MUST END IT NOW...

...I HOPE YOU TWO REMEMBER HOW WE ESCAPED THE SPACE BIKER GANG NEAR BETA CENTAU--

NOW ODDS EVEN.

OBVIOUSLY, YOU DO.

HEPZIBAH, RAZA-- THE COMMUNI-LINK WITH CORSAIR IS...

"...LOST."

A DIRECT HIT, COMMANDER-- THE STARSKIMMER SAILED RIGHT INTO OUR LINE OF FIRE!

X-MEN- SPOTLIGHT ON STARJAMMERS #2 PAGE 22 ART BY DAVE COCKRUM & JEFF ALBRECHT